BROADWAY
THE AMERICAN MUSICAL

LAURENCE MASLON

Based on the documentary film by

MICHAEL KANTOR

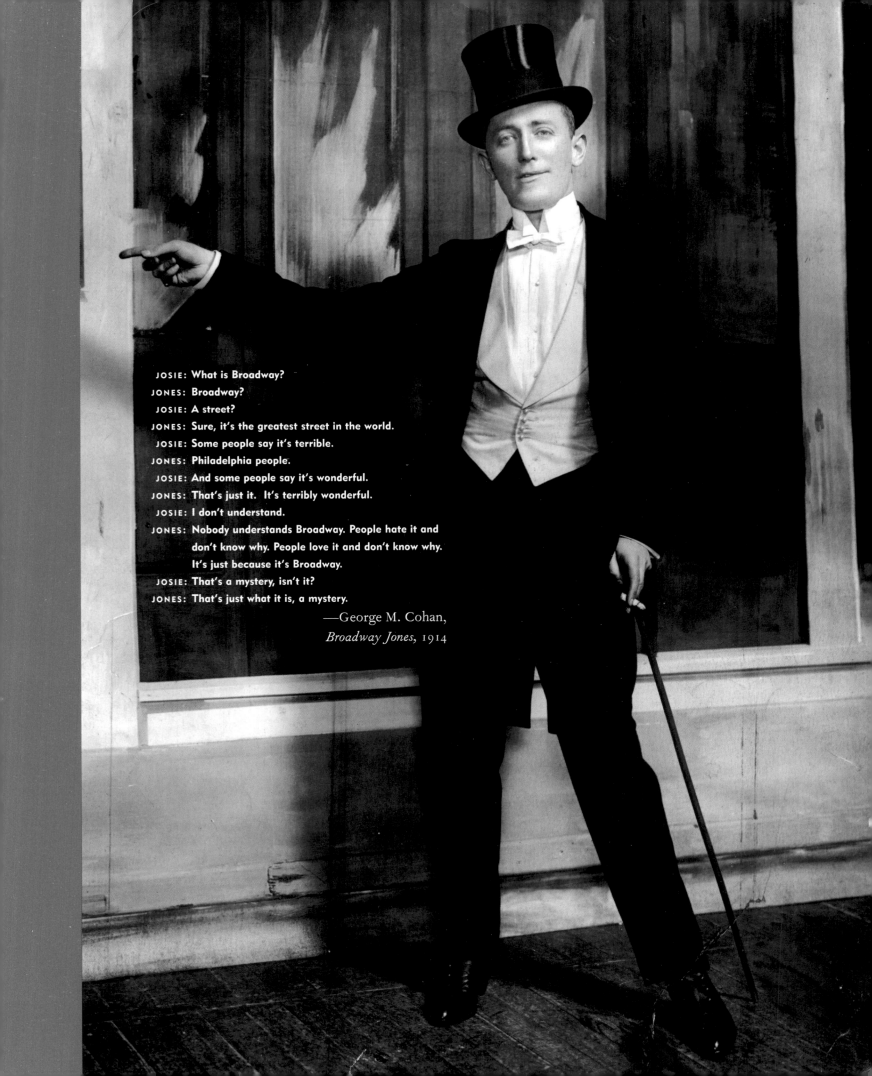

JOSIE: What is Broadway?

JONES: Broadway?

JOSIE: A street?

JONES: Sure, it's the greatest street in the world.

JOSIE: Some people say it's terrible.

JONES: Philadelphia people.

JOSIE: And some people say it's wonderful.

JONES: That's just it. It's terribly wonderful.

JOSIE: I don't understand.

JONES: Nobody understands Broadway. People hate it and
don't know why. People love it and don't know why.
It's just because it's Broadway.

JOSIE: That's a mystery, isn't it?

JONES: That's just what it is, a mystery.

—George M. Cohan,
Broadway Jones, 1914

Every race in every age has picked out some one street, one square, one Acropolis mount or Waterloo Bridge to celebrate. . . . Let it be known to the Americanologist of 3000 A.D. that we idolized a strange, boomerang-shaped, nightly fiery thoroughfare of broken hearts and blessed events, which we called Broadway. That will explain us.

—Gilbert Gabriel, *New York American*, 1929

BROADWAY
THE AMERICAN MUSICAL

LAURENCE MASLON

Based on the documentary film by

MICHAEL KANTOR

A COPRODUCTION OF GHOST LIGHT FILMS AND THIRTEEN/WNET NEW YORK

APPLAUSE
THEATRE & CINEMA BOOKS

AN IMPRINT OF
HAL•LEONARD®

PUBLISHED IN 2010 BY APPLAUSE THEATRE & CINEMA BOOKS

An Imprint of Hal Leonard Corporation

7777 West Bluemound Road

Milwaukee, WI 53213

Trade Book Division Editorial Offices

19 West 21st Street, New York, NY 10010

Hardcover published in 2004 by Bulfinch Press

Printed in China through Colorcraft Ltd.,Hong Kong

BOOK DESIGN BY BTDNYC

Book composition and cover design by Damien Castaneda. Front cover photographs, from left: Fred Astaire, Ethel Merman, and Joel Grey courtesy of Photofest; Raffiki courtesy of Disney; and Elphaba © Joan Marcus. B'WAY logo by B. T. Whitehill. Back cover photograph © Joan Marcus. Author illustration by Laurence Maslon.

THE LIBRARY OF CONGRESS HAS CATALOGUED THE HARDCOVER EDITION AS FOLLOWS:

Kantor, Michael.

      Broadway : the American musical / Michael Kantor ; Laurence Maslon—1st ed.

      p. cm.

      Includes bibliographical references (p.) and index.

      Contents: A real live nephew of my Uncle Sam (1893-1919)—Syncopated city (1920-1929)—

      I got plenty o' nuttin' (1930-1941)—Oh, what a beautiful mornin' (1942-1960)—Tradition (1960-1980)—

      Lullaby of Broadway (1980-present).

      ISBN 0-8212-2905-2 (alk. paper)

      1. Musicals—New York (State)—New York—History and criticism.

      I. Maslon, Laurence.

      II. Title.

ML1711.8.N3K34 2004

782.1'4'097471—dc22

2003069715

ISBN 978-1-4234-9103-3

www.applausepub.com

CAPTIONS FOR PAGES i–xi

  iii.   *George M. Cohan.*

  iv-v.   *Hamming, jamming, and scramming a lot in* Spamalot *(2005).*

  vi.   *Times Square.*

  viii.   *Ziegfeld Girl Margaret Morris.*

  ix.   *Mary Stuart Masterson, Antonio Banderas, and Jane Krakowski in* Nine.

  x-xi.   *counter-clockwise from top left: George M. Cohan in* Little Millionaire; *Eubie Blake (l.) and Noble Sissle;*

      Ethel Merman; Alan Cumming in Cabaret; *Michael Crawford and Sarah Brightman in* The Phantom of the Opera;

      Gwen Verdon (l.) and Chita Rivera in Chicago; *Robert Preston in* The Music Man.

  xiii.   *Julie Andrews.*

  1.   *Nathan Lane as Prologus in* A Funny Thing Happened on the Way to the Forum.

To Emma,

Sacha,

and Twyla—

three singular sensations

—MK

To my father,

my favorite Townsend Harris grad,

And to my dear mother,

who gave this funny world to me

—LM

CONTENTS

FOREWORD

On a steamy early summer day in June 2004, I found myself on the stage of the immaculately restored New Amsterdam Theater, surrounded by the African veldt created out of Julie Taymor's vast imagination for *The Lion King*. I had been asked by producer and director Michael Kantor to introduce the six episodes of the groundbreaking PBS documentary *Broadway: The American Musical*, and we began our first day of filming on the very stage where Florenz Ziegfeld cultivated his immortal *Follies* at the beginning of the twentieth century.

I was so pleased that Michael asked me to participate because the Broadway musical has been a passion of mine for so long. It was about time, truthfully, for this kind of attention to be paid to such an influential art form. I had wanted to be a part of something like this for many, many years, so I was simply delighted to arrive at the New Amsterdam to film our introductory sequence.

During one of the breaks in filming, a very kind representative of the Disney Company asked if we wanted to take the elevator up to the tenth floor of the building to view the nightclub that Ziegfeld has installed in the roof garden for his *Midnight Frolic* in 1915. How could any fan of the musical resist? This is where both Will Rogers and Eddie Cantor made their Broadway debuts. When the rickety elevator gate opened up, we walked into a decrepit hall, with tattered curtains, broken windows, ripped-up seats—perhaps there was even a pigeon or two, I don't recall. It looked for all the world like the perfect set for Stephen Sondheim's *Follies*—you could feel the ghosts of dozens of leggy chorines hovering in the rafters.

But those were not the ghosts that haunted me. For I had been in this room before, on January 3, 1956—on a day as freezing cold as this day was stifling hot: it was the first rehearsal of *My Fair Lady*. This was where we had our first read-through of *My Fair Lady*, with Fritz Loewe playing the piano and Alan Jay Lerner singing all the songs. This was where the gifted director Moss Hart barricaded me over a long weekend, where he essentially "pasted" the part of Eliza Doolittle onto me. This was the room that Rex Harrison stomped out of when he thought he needed more to sing in the song "Without You" (he was right—he was given more lyrics when we got to New Haven). This was where the British cast members broke for tea every day at four in the afternoon, tea that was lovingly brewed by yours truly.

These are just a few of the memories that *Broadway: The American Musical* evoked in me. When I was recording the narration for the series, I literally wept at a couple of things that moved me so much. The overture to *My Fair Lady* was playing underneath some of the narration and my heart melted. I said, "You cannot imagine what that makes me feel. It takes me immediately back to sitting in my dressing room, putting on my makeup, eight performances a week." There is something visceral about the appeal of a great American musical, whether you are starring in one, or seeing one for the first time as a youngster. *It grabs you.*

The thing about musicals is that they are for anybody viewing them—child or adult—larger than life. They're wondrous things to pull off. A great musical is something to be cherished forever. The cast album becomes a friend.

I'll always be grateful to the American musical for taking me in as a friend as well. Like so many others who found their identities on the Broadway stage, I was not born here. I had come from across the ocean, more than a bit nervous, very shy and green, to make my debut in New York in *The Boyfriend*, still in my teens. This fascinating companion volume to the series begins with a quintessential Broadway story, that of a little boy who came from the depths of privation in czarist Russia, across the ocean, and wound up as the very personification of American music: Irving Berlin.

So, let's start at the very beginning, which, we all know, is a very good place to start. . . .

Julie Andrews
Los Angeles

INTRODUCTION

Most of the histories of the American musical have focused, understandably, on the "musical" aspect of the genre; this book puts the "American" center stage. The Broadway musical defines our culture and is, in turn, defined by it. The musical tells its stories in music, in lyrics, in dialogue, in performance, and in dance. Each of these elements is a potent cultural indicator on its own; put together, they provide a frequently brash, occasionally thoughtful, always colorful portrait of our country. Like many of the best Broadway performers, this version of American history demands to be heard.

Once upon a time, when New York theater was the most prestigious performance art form in the country, Broadway musicals were the boldest, bravest expression of the American character. Even though the theater lost its preeminence over the course of the last century, its journey to redefine itself and prove itself relevant again makes for a compelling story, indicative of many trends and tensions in our popular culture. The musical has always reflected different social and political forces—patriotism, skepticism, commercial consumption, escapism, revolt, globalization—and has put those onstage for everyone to see. In one way, the history of the musical can be read as a kind of history of, say, seventeenth-century Europe: a defined territory struggling to survive, constantly under siege by economic forces, sometimes winning, sometimes losing. Its story contains the rise and fall of several dynasties: great leaders emerge, come into their own, pass from the scene, and are replaced by a new generation. Like any national history, the epic of the Broadway musical has its heroes and its villains, and in the end, if the voice of the people is not exactly the voice of God, it is the voice of the bottom line, which in show business might as well be the same thing.

A thousand different factors go into both the performance and the reception of a musical. This book shows how this complicated amalgamation has been put together over the course of a century. Because *Broadway: The American Musical*, as a series and as a book, focuses on a myriad of cultural factors, it must be selective. There are many cherished productions, performances, and personalities that have been cut out of town, as it were. If it is any consolation, many of the authors' favorites didn't make it to "Broadway" either.

In addition to the historical narrative, this book explores several other key aspects of the musical. The lyrics to more than a dozen songs are reprinted in their entirety; these were either seminal in the development of the songwriting craft or are wonderfully indicative of the culture that brought them onto the stage and into the world. Seven productions have been spotlighted; each show is either a brilliant reflection of its time or *sui generis* or both. Performers who have devoted their careers to the Broadway stage—not an easy sacrifice to make—are showcased in each chapter's "Who's Who"; certain major figures are dealt with at greater length in the narrative. One aspect of the book that will appeal to readers interested in cultural history are the six essays about Broadway and its relation to other forces, such as Hollywood, television, and real estate, that have been key allies and adversaries to the industry of Broadway. Archives of newly recovered source material, as well as essays taken from the extensive interviews conducted for the documentary series, allow the great artists of the musical to speak for themselves.

The series *Broadway: The American Musical* is grounded by the nearly sixty interviews with major figures conducted specifically for the program. Most of the direct quotes in the narrative are taken from these precious sources, and a complete list of interviewees is included at the back of the book. The more historical sources quoted in the book are marked by the date of their publication. This paperback edition has been updated to include as much information about the Broadway season as possible, up to the end of 2009; although the last five years were not part of the PBS series, the updated text has been conceived and organized in the spirit of the series and the previous edition.

At the end of every theatrical season, there is a barrage of articles asking, "Whither the Broadway musical?" This book does not presume to foretell where the musical is going; it simply tries to figure out how it got where it is today. In the best of all worlds, the book and the series will excite their audiences enough to make them contribute to the history of the American musical—as creator, performer, or spectator. The best reason to revel in the past is that it gives one the passion to embrace the future.

Curtain up . . .

"Playgoers, I bid you welcome!

The theater is a temple and we shall employ

every device we know in our desire to divert you!"

A REAL LIVE NEPHEW OF MY UNCLE SAM'S

(1 8 9 3 – 1 9 1 9)

Overture

Every nation, it seems,
Sailed across with their dreams
To my New York.
Every color and race
Found a comfortable place
In my New York.
The Dutchmen bought Manhattan Island for a flask of booze,
Then sold controlling interest to the Irish and the Jews—
And what chance has a Jones
With the Cohens and Malones
In my New York?

Irving Berlin, "My New York" (1927)

It's 1893. A five-year-old Russian boy, nauseated from two weeks on a packed ship, crammed into a processing line on Ellis Island, odd and embarrassed in what he'd later call his shabby "Jew clothes"—he must have felt all alone. Once ferried from the tiny island to the larger one called Manhattan, he and his family of ten were thrown into a jabbering, noisy, cacophonous cosmopolis of races from around the world, each with its own clothes, rituals, smells, languages, sounds, tunes. Would he have kept his ears open as they trudged past compacted hutches of humanity to find their new home on the Lower East Side? What would he have heard?

Through open windows and on the city streets, he would have heard the devout hymns of Moody and Sanky; an Italian organ grinder's Neapolitan love song; a piano student practicing a Liszt sonata; a brass band drilling to a thunderous Sousa tattoo; a dry-goods salesman whistling a Gilbert and Sullivan tune; someone's daughter humming a Stephen Foster air; a Jewish peddler singing about going back to his "ol' Virginny" home; his children, in a circle, chanting "Huliet, Huliet, Kinderlach"; a black man—the boy would have never seen a black man before—recalling a spiritual threnody from his Mississippi childhood; an attractive redhead wistfully reminding her beau that "many a heart would be broken, after the ball"; a bricklayer pretending to be Caruso; a wedding accompanied by "Oh, Promise Me" on the spinet; a rare gramophone squawking to the world that someone's sweetheart was "the man in the moon"; a schoolteacher recently moved from Terre Haute, Indiana, teaching her grammar school students the words to a sixty-year-old sentimental ballad, "Woodman, Spare That Tree"; a pianist, transplanted from Kansas City, amusing ladies of dubious virtue with improvised lyrics to a popular tune, lyrics that would have titillated the five-year-old boy, if only he had known New York street slang.

And yet, not one of these songs was a Broadway song, not in the conventional sense. There wasn't even a Broadway yet. There was a street called Broadway, sure, and Israel Baline and his family would have crossed it as they stumbled to their new home—a tenement flat between Chinatown and the Bowery—but this was far downtown. *Broadway*—the lights, the legends, the Times Square theatrical district, the mythical empire of the American musical—simply didn't exist in 1893. As he grew up, young Israel—side by side with dozens of driven, courageous, eccentric artists—would have to create the Broadway musical out of whole cloth, using scraps of borrowed traditions, bringing it to life by flashes of original ingenuity and talent. Along the way, they would push New York's theatre scene from downtown to midtown, and as it moved north along Broadway, the theater—its songs, its style, and its audience—would change completely. Israel Baline would change along with it, reinventing everything about himself—his language, his manners, his name—everything except his innate hunger to succeed in this terrifying, electrifying new country.

Of all the thousands upon thousands of immigrant stories, of all the fables of the American dream, none were as improbable, none were as *satisfying*, as the story of Irving Berlin.

"The tenants in McNally's row of flats"
ETHNIC VARIETY STAGES

The humble origins of the little Russian boy were shared by millions of New Yorkers. The nineteenth century saw an astounding and relentless parade of immigrants flow through the Port of New York to the banks of the Hudson River. In the early part of the century, it was the Irish and then the Germans who emigrated here to escape poverty, but toward the end of the century, the additional burden of political oppression sent the Jews of Eastern Europe and the Italians to America as well. Between 1880 and 1919, 5.5 million immigrants from Europe made their home in New York. More than 1.2 million newcomers arrived in 1907 alone—a million of them Jews, almost half of whom settled in the compact, noisome, teeming confines of the Lower East Side.

In the Balkanized ethnic neighborhoods of the Lower East Side and the Bowery, every racial group had its own social customs and its form of musical entertainment. It was just a short leap from the musician playing in the corner of the local pub or tavern to a more

Orchard Street in New York's Lower East Side, c. 1898. This teeming ethnic enclave was the home to some of the most American of musical artists.

presentational social center: a stage at one end, and seats for tired workingmen to enjoy these local shows with a glass of liquid refreshment in hand. This was the evolution of the variety stage. Initially, no one could care less about the other fellow's variety act across town; but as downtown Manhattan began to shift and blend its ethnic divisions, the many ethnic variety shows began to enlarge and diversify its audiences.

By virtue of their earlier appearance on American shores, the Irish developed their own form of entertainment first. For more than a dozen years, beginning in 1878, Edward "Ned" Harrigan and his partner Tony Hart developed a series of "knockdown and slap-bang" farces about the burgeoning Irish enclave in New York. Playing off gaelic chauvinism, while adding some time-honored comedic buffooneries, the Harrigan & Hart shows were often built around the Mulligan Guards, a fictitious Hibernian legion trying to establish itself in a multiethnic world. The Bowery tenements provided an unending cast of characters:

It's Ireland and Italy, Jerusalem and Germany,
Oh, Chinamen and nagers, and a paradise for cats,
All jumbled up together in the snow or rainy weather,
They represent the tenants in McNally's row of flats.
    —Harrigan (music) and Braham (lyrics), *McSorley's Inflation* (1882)

LEFT: *Ned Harrigan and Tony Hart, c. 1879.*

RIGHT: *Joe Weber (r.) and Lew Fields (center), c. 1910. The team's obstreperous blend of physical slapstick, dialect jokes, puns, and spoofs of current Broadway shows, such as their 1898* Cyranose de Bric-a-Brac, *made them enormously popular.*

Harrigan leavened his parodies with a dose of sympathy for the plight of his Irish immigrants: proud, pompous, yet forever trying to find a place in a society that was spiraling beyond their comprehension. "Harrigan was in the habit of deploring, half-jestingly, the [immigrants] who wouldn't come to his theater because the incidents he showed on stage were indistinguishable from what they experienced at home," wrote the team's biographer, E.J. Kahn.

It wasn't long before the Jewish immigrants got into the act and, in a parallel development to the classical Yiddish Theater on Second Avenue, they created their own vibrant musical traditions. The comic duo Joe Weber and Lew Fields disguised their more obvious Hebraic roots by taking on the "Dutch" characteristics of two immigrants, Mike and Meyer, forever assaulting each other and the English language. After spending fifteen years performing on the Bowery, Weber and Fields opened their own music hall in 1896 at Broadway and 29th Street and the team soon became the undisputed champions of burlesque comedy. The titles of Weber and Fields's nearly dozen shows display some notion of their blissful nonsense: *Hoity-Toity, Fiddle-dee-dee, Whoop-dee-doo, Roly Poly,* and *Hokey Pokey.*

By the time Weber and Fields endured the first of their many breakups in 1904, the ethnic variety stage was beginning—like the well-padded character played by Weber—to burst at the seams. Technological advances in transportation, such as the streetcar and, later, the subway, allowed immigrants to venture from their neighborhoods and seek out the rest of Manhattan and, possibly, their fortune. Soon Irishmen, Jews, Germans, and Italians all learned that show business let them leap the hurdles placed before them in the New World; "Where else," Minnie Marx, the mother of the Marx Brothers, reasoned sensibly, "can people who don't know anything make money?" As the new century progressed, ethnic entertainers took a deep breath and burst from the confines of the Old World and its culture to claim their share of the dollar bills being pushed through the wickets of box offices in theaters north of Houston Street, up along the winding street called Broadway, and beyond.

"*Come on and hear, come on and hear*"
IRVING BERLIN

I would ask him as a little kid, "What was it like being poor, Daddy?" and he would say, "Poor? What is poor? It was what I knew. I always had enough to eat, and I was never cold, only too hot in the summer, and so I slept out on the fire escape." I suppose he must have felt that living [on the Lower East Side] under various hardships and challenges gave him a kind of grip. I mean, it helped form his character and his determination.

—Mary Ellin Barrett, Irving Berlin's Daughter

Berlin in his offices at Waterson, Berlin & Snyder, c. 1916.

When Izzy Baline was about twelve or thirteen, his father, a cantor in a Jewish synagogue, died. Knowing he had to contribute his share to the household income, he took a quick survey of his options—stevedore, peddler, working in a sweatshop—and went, as his daughter put it, "on the lam." He became, essentially, a street person, wandering through the cruel slums of Chinatown and the Bowery, sleeping on park benches or in flophouses. He started singing songs on the street for anyone who'd listen and find enough charity to toss the kid a couple of pennies. His dream was to move indoors, to become a singing waiter in a saloon in Chinatown, and he got his wish at the Pelham Café, under the eye of "Nigger Mike," a Russian Jew with a very dark complexion.

Izzy would toil from dinnertime to closing time, schlepping trays and singing popular songs with his own made-up dirty lyrics. He put his ethnic parody numbers across, while deftly scooping the nickels that customers would throw at him into a little pile with his left foot. The ethnic numbers always went over particularly well. No one took offense because to be singled out as a Jew or an Italian or an Irishman in a comedy song was not to be excluded, but to be included. It meant you were recognized, you were part of the city, you were here to stay. Learning how to

invite the other fellow into your world, by means of a funny song or a senti-mental ballad, was a skill that Baline cultivated during his days at the Pelham and it served him in good stead throughout his career.

When Mike heard that the singing waiters at a rival Bowery saloon had one of their songs published, he ordered his house pianist to compose one for the team. For lyrics, he turned to the kid who excelled at dirty parodies, and since the rival's song used Italian dialect, Izzy Baline did too. When the song, "Marie from Sunny Italy," was published, there was a printer's error and the young man's name was misspelled, right there on the front cover: "I. Berlin." He let it go, thinking it was a good name for a songwriter. The song itself made him 37 cents, but it also made Irving Berlin into an American.

The songwriting industry of the city, Tin Pan Alley, beckoned and Berlin, with no musical training whatsoever save the intuition to pick out the notes on a keyboard, was on his way to becoming the most successful composer of the twentieth century. Being a songwriter early in the century was like being a peddler on the Lower East Side. You had to hawk a vast cartload of all kinds of wares—and you couldn't be shy about it. Berlin sold a song for a vaudeville star here, an interpolation in a Broadway revue there, and his specialty numbers began to sell more than 300,000 copies. He wrote all kinds of ethnic material: songs in Italian dialect, black-dialect "coon songs," and a variety of Yiddish songs with titles such as "Yiddle on Your Fiddle (Play Some Rag Time)."

In 1911, Berlin became a full partner in the music publishing firm of Waterson and Snyder, with his name embossed in gold letters on the office door. That same year, amid a flurry of other writing assignments, Berlin turned his hand to a novelty number about the current craze for ragtime music. Ragtime was considered scandalous back then—the devil's music—because it mixed classes and races, and forced the syncopations of black neighborhoods into the respectable parlors of the white middle class. But Berlin held the door open for ragtime, making it safe for America: "Come on along, come on along, let me take you by the hand." "Alexander's Ragtime Band" became the fastest-selling piece of sheet music of all time—a million copies in just a few months—and that black ragtime leader man, Alexander, was soon smilingly invited into millions of homes across the country.

The tune made Berlin into one of the twentieth century's new sensations: a celebrity songwriter. He sang in a vaudeville revue on Broadway ("He had a voice only a dog could hear, very high-pitched," recalled Kitty Carlisle Hart), wrote the first songs for Bert Williams and Fanny Brice to sing in the *Ziegfeld Follies*, and was inducted into the exclusive show biz clan, the Friars Club.

The real basis of Berlin's success is industry—ceaseless, cruel, torturing industry. There is scarcely a waking minute when he is not engaged either in teaching his songs to a vaudeville player, or composing new ones. His regular hours are from noon to daybreak. All night long he usually keeps himself prisoner in his apartment, bent on evolving a new melody which will set the whole world to beating time.
—Rennold Wolf, Lyricist, 1913

The only thing that seemed to slow Berlin down was the tragic death of his first wife, from typhus, only six months after their wedding in 1912. But, as he would do for millions of listeners over the decades, Berlin spun inspiration out of misery, this time with a wholly unexpected ballad, "When I Lost You." A veritable haiku of grief, it sold more than a million copies.

In 1914, the producer Florenz Ziegfeld took his *Follies* on tour after its initial engagement at the New Amsterdam, leaving his trademark theater temporarily available, and Irving Berlin was poised to clear the final hurdle in his lightning sprint to fame: his own Broadway show. He knew that the Broadway stage had become the premiere bandstand for a composer to get recognized in the United States. It wasn't enough to have your songs stuck in someone else's show—to have a show of your own, control over it, that was the important thing. *Watch Your Step: A Syncopated Show in Three Acts* was an ambitious production for 1914. It had a story. It had a score by only one composer. It even considered itself to be a ragtime opera. As Mary Ellin Barrett described it:

Irving Berlin sheet music.

> [Berlin] was able to give us songs that anyone could relate to, situations that anyone could understand. And he was able to give people like my mother and father, who were lovely middle-class people who were not that sophisticated, a place to go, songs to listen to, songs to cherish for the rest of their lives.
>
> **—Jerry Herman,** Songwriter

It was the first ragtime musical, the first musical to really incorporate the beat of popular music. It had ragtime; it had fox trots; it had a tango; there was dancing in the title. It was written for Vernon and Irene Castle [the dancing duo sensation of their time], and it was as much a dancing as a singing show, and it even "ragged" grand opera. The hit song was "Play a Simple Melody," which was his first double number, a great song, with the old-fashioned melody vying against the "Play me some rag" syncopation. It was a fresh spirit in that show. It was a young man's show on a young Broadway, a young Broadway in terms of what the musical theater was going to be.

By the time *Watch Your Step* opened, the supremacy of the Europe from which Berlin escaped twenty years earlier was about to vanish, and America was poised to be the focus of the world's attention. He recognized what profound changes were about to occur in the musical landscape of his new country in 1914: "All the old rhythm is gone and in its place is heard the hum of an engine, the whirr of wheels, the explosion of an exhaust. The leisurely songs that men hummed to the clatter of horses' hooves do not fit this new rhythm. The new age demands new music for new action."

Berlin not only inherited a modern world; he helped to invent it.

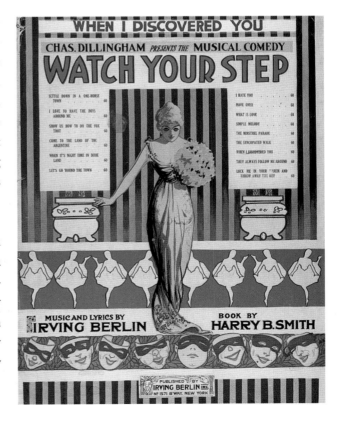

BROADWAY is one of the country's longest boulevards, stretching more than 150 miles from the Battery all the way upstate to Albany. But in the early part of the twentieth century, a half block on West 28th Street, between Broadway and Sixth Avenue, held more power over the young entertainment industry than the entire stretch of Broadway.

The coinage of the name Tin Pan Alley is somewhat shrouded by the mists of history. The most commonly agreed-upon story is that reporter and sometime lyricist Monroe Rosenfeld was interviewing the songwriter Harry Von Tilzer at his offices on West 28th Street. By 1903, most of the song publishing businesses had moved there and all along the street, in the days before air conditioning, pianos could be heard banging away from every open office window. "It sounds like the clanging together of so many tin pans," remarked Rosenfeld, and a legend was born.

The origins of Tin Pan Alley extend back to the gentility of the Victorian age. Following the Civil War, the home became the center of family entertainment. Every middle-class family—and lower-middle-class family with aspirations—had a piano in the parlor. In the days before mechanical reproduction of music, singing around the parlor piano was the only way to hear, and learn about, new music.

Sheet music of traditional songs had always been available to the consumer, but by the 1890s, music publishers had made an interesting discovery: by exploiting various fads and sentiments, they could *make* the public buy sheet music.

The breakthrough was a sentimental ballad, written by a Milwaukee songwriter named Charles K. Harris, whose previous novelty numbers included "Bake That Matzoh Pie." In 1892, Harris composed the ballad "After the Ball," which tells of a misunderstanding at a dance that condemns the narrator to a life of bachelorhood. The song was interpolated into the farce *A Trip to Chinatown*, and became the first song to sell more than one million pieces of sheet music; eventually four million more copies found themselves on the family Steinway. Harris, in a moment of entrepreneurial inspiration, insisted on publishing the song himself and, within a decade, had business offices in Milwaukee, Chicago, and New York.

Music publishers ranged all over the country, but by the turn of the century, they had to be in New York to ensure themselves a place in the market and access to the level of performer and songwriter the city had to offer. M. Witmark and Sons moved to West 28th Street in 1893, and soon such publishers as T.B. Harms, Remick & Co., and the Leo Feist Music Publishing Company—each of whom would provide ground-level jobs for the most famous songwriters of the 1910s and '20s—followed suit. The Theater District in the West 20s provided the publishers with the best outlets to promote their material. Publishers fought the promotional battle on all fronts. The first charge was led by the song plugger, an indomitable chap who would play a song anywhere—at offices, in bars, in theater lobbies, backstage, occasionally from the back of a truck—in hopes of getting a producer to put it in a show, or having a singer make it her own novelty number. Often a youngster was planted in the balcony of the theater as a "stooge" to sing the song in question back to the performer to prove how "catchy" the song was. (An adolescent Irving Berlin was employed as a stooge in the early 1900s by Harry Von Tilzer.) The publishers also employed batteries of house arrangers—musically gifted piano players who could take a promising tune from an untrained composer and supply it with just the right chord structure to set the nation's toes a-tapping.

Vaudeville stars became voracious consumers of novelty song material, which they could take across the country, and the publishers practically stumbled over themselves to get their songs "placed" with a star. (The process also worked the other way, when a struggling act begged the plugger for a sure-fire hit.) Each song told its own story, contained by its own conceit or cliché, and rarely articulated itself in the voice of a perceptible character. Only a fraction of these popular songs were written for a specific stage production, and those that did appear on Broadway were thrown into shows with an indifference that could only be called casual.

Gathering of ASCAP songwriters, 1915. Among the group are Jerome Kern (far left); Oscar Hammerstein, grandfather of the lyricist (seated at the piano); Rudolf Friml (with mustache, above Hammerstein); a gray-bearded John Philip Sousa (middle); and Irving Berlin (far right).

Tin Pan Alley on West 28th Street, c. 1905. In 1913, Remick's hired a teenaged George Gershwin to be one of its song pluggers.

Following the success of "After the Ball," sentimental ballads dominated the sheet music industry. Chaste sweethearts, broken romances, the innocence of youth, and the transcendent wisdom of Mother were some of the more popular tropes, usually written from the point of view of some omniscient narrator with more than a touch of Longfellow or Edgar A. Guest about him. Million-plus sellers such as "In the Baggage Coach Ahead," "The Sidewalks of New York," "The Band Played On," "(She's Only) A Bird in a Gilded Cage," "In the Good Old Summertime," "Down by the Old Mill Stream," and "Sweet Adeline" have been burnished into the American consciousness by an amalgam of school primers, Warner Bros. cartoons, M-G-M musical anthologies, and Marx Brothers movies that defies documentation.

Tin Pan Alley songs were written for no grander purpose than to make money, and by 1910, almost a hundred of them had sold more than a million copies each. That year alone, at least 2 billion copies of sheet music had been purchased by the American populace. As the country diversified, so did the songs of Tin Pan Alley, which never met a novelty or innovation it couldn't sing about. "Meet Me in St. Louis" was dashed off to capitalize on the St. Louis Exposition in 1904 and "Take Me Out to the Ball Game" was written on the heels of the first World Series by Harry Von Tilzer's brother, who had never even been to a baseball game.

Ethnic songs became popular. An embarrassing but successful genre called the "coon song" ridiculed both the rural manners and urban pretensions of African Americans, but its ragtime rhythms gave the world such hits as "Bill Bailey, Won't You Please Come Home?," "Under the Bamboo Tree," and "Alexander's Ragtime Band," as well as many less printable titles. It soon seemed as if every Irish lass was named "Mary," and valentines to sweethearts in the Italian and Yiddish communities were soon joined by love songs to swains living on the Hawaiian islands or on Indian reservations. The romance of technology turned into the technology of romance as the telephone ("Hello, Central, Give Me Heaven"), the bicycle ("Daisy Bell," known as "A Bicycle Built for Two"), and the automobile ("In My Merry Oldsmobile") were all exploited for their novelty. When all else failed, one could always appeal to nostalgia for the hometown left behind; there were songs about not only every neighborhood in the city, but every state in the Union. "If song-writers always wrote about their home state, what a big Jewish population Tennessee must have," observed a character in George S. Kaufman and Ring Lardner's spoof of Tin Pan Alley, *June Moon*.

The enormous income stream of Tin Pan Alley brought along its own consequences: in 1914, a delegation of composers, lyricists, and publishers met to discuss the artists' rights to copyright protection and royalty payments. Led by composer Victor Herbert, the group constituted itself as the American Society of Composers, Authors and Publishers, known to posterity as ASCAP. In 1915, ASCAP brought a suit against a Broadway restaurant whose orchestra was playing Herbert selections without authorization. In a case that was eventually settled by the Supreme Court two years later, songwriters were guaranteed recompense if their music was played in public establishments as a way of enticing customers.

Tin Pan Alley was the beginning of a revolution of technology and popular taste that would mean a bonanza for songwriters and their publishers. The brightly illustrated promise of the fifty-cent piece of sheet music would soon give way to the more obstreperous fanfare of the gramophone record, the radio console, and the talking picture.

Crossroads of the World

THE THEATER DISTRICT

Broadway . . . the great thoroughfare is ablaze with the electric light, which illumines it with the radiance of day. . . . The crowd is out for pleasure at night, and many and varied are the forms which the pursuit of it takes. Then the theaters pour out their audiences to join it and for an hour or more, the restaurants and cafes are filled to their utmost capacity. Then, as midnight comes on, the street becomes quieter and more deserted. New York has gone to bed and Broadway enjoys a rest of a few hours only to begin at daybreak a repetition of the scenes from the previous day.

When journalist James D. McCabe Jr. penned this paean in 1882, the city's thriving theatrical community could indeed be found along Broadway, but much farther downtown from the Theater District of the twentieth century.

With the end of the Civil War, New York City slowly began to evolve as the center of theatrical activity in America, so much so that, by the time of McCabe's encomium in 1882, the city not only had its own theatrical industry, but a national reputation. Touring shows were still extremely popular by the turn of the century, but they had to begin some-where and Broadway developed as its logical locus. Union Square, on 14th Street and Broadway, became a kind of open-air market for producers to assemble touring companies, managers to book tours, actors and singers to acquire material, and so forth. A handful of theaters nestled around Union Square, and so did the various auxiliary businesses that keep the theater alive and vice versa: wigmakers, press agents, scenic artists, restaurants, bars, publishers, agents, ticket brokers. The theaters and their allied businesses moved uptown several times in the nine-teenth century, including sojourns at Madison Square in the East 20s and Herald Square in the 30s. By the time the new century began, however, the Theater District stretched from West 37th Street along Broadway to 40th Street, culminating at the Metropolitan Opera House. Spoofing the Venetian promenade and marketplace, the area was now known as the Rialto, for all the theatrical goods and services available south of 42nd Street.

Goods and services of another kind were avail-able north of 42nd Street. Originally developed as land parcels for tony townhouses, the area north and west of Broadway and 42nd had degenerated by the 1890s into the brothel capital of Manhattan, known officially as Long Acre Square and unofficially as the Tenderloin.

Famous as a showcase for operettas, the Casino Theatre, at the southeast corner of Broadway and 39th Street, was the northernmost landmark of the Herald Square Theater District at the turn of the twentieth century.

It was a kind of non-descript neighborhood on the northern edge of [42nd Street] with prostitution, stables, and ordinary buildings around it, a neighborhood for vice and sex that got its name because a crooked policeman once was transferred there and he said, "I've been getting by on chuck steak all my life now I'm going to get a bit of the tenderloin."

—Robert W. Snyder, Historian

Broadway north of 42nd Street was a no-man's-land; anyone thinking of opening a theater there, where families attending popular middle-class entertainment would be surrounded by prostitution and corruption, should have had his head examined.

The pioneer architect of the current Theater District was a chimerical dreamer, a Prussian immigrant, an inventor of cigar machines, a self-made businessman, with a dollop of the con artist about him. Oscar Hammerstein, the grandfather of the famous lyricist and librettist (who called himself Oscar Hammerstein II—not "junior," because he wasn't), used his money to indulge his passion—building theaters—and he bought up several parcels of land from 43rd Street to 45th Street on the east side of Broadway. It was there, in 1895, that he built an Olympian conglomeration of theaters with a roof garden, a bowling alley, and restaurants called, naturally, the Olympia. Within a few years, he lost control of the Olympia to creditors who subdivided it (foreshadowing our current multiplexes) into smaller entertainment centers, but, undeterred, Hammerstein opened the Victoria Theatre in 1899, on the corner of 42nd and Seventh. It ultimately became a vaudeville house—the country's biggest. By 1900, Hammerstein had staked his claim and proved that Long Acre Square was a fertile frontier for developers with theatrical real estate on their minds.

As was the case in the rest of the country, the turn of the century offered unparalleled opportunities to New York businessmen with the vision and ambition to dominate their fields. Marc Klaw and Abraham Lincoln Erlanger were producing partners with a background in the legal profession and in booking tours nationwide. In the 1890s, they realized that if they controlled product (plays and actors), distribution (tours), and outlets (theaters across the country), they could command a previously unheard-of share of the American entertainment business. By 1896, Klaw and Erlanger combined with

Marc Klaw (l.) and Abraham Lincoln Erlanger, whose ruthless business tactics earned him the nickname Dishonest Abe.

four other producers across the country to parcel out their show tours coast to coast; they became known informally as the Theatrical Syndicate and wrung extraordinary concessions out of almost a thousand theater owners from Boston to Seattle.

Even as the Syndicate indulged the capitalist rapacity for monopoly found at the time in the steel, railroad, and oil industries, they encountered another aspect of the free market: competition. Lee, J.J., and Sam Shubert descended on New York from Syracuse in 1900, determined to break the Syndicate's stranglehold on theaters and contracts. As the Syndicate built new theaters in Long Acre Square and across the country, the three brothers built more; by 1910, there were thirty-four theaters north of, or near, 42nd Street, most of them new, many of them the result of the bidding war between the Shuberts and the Syndicate. What both sets of producers knew in 1900 is what every producer knows today: "Direct from New York" was the best branding a touring show can have. The race was on to produce shows that originated in New York.

In 1900, a decision was made by the city of New York that would bring the most enduring change to the young Theater District along Long Acre Square. The city committed to a series of underground railways—subways—to be built by the Interborough Rapid

Transit Company, under the direction of August Belmont, a wealthy New York banker with ties to City Hall. By the time the subway was nearing completion in 1904, the *New York Times* had moved its headquarters to a triangular patch of land north of 42nd Street, bounded on either side by Broadway and Seventh Avenue. The publisher, Adolph D. Ochs, had erected an Italianate campanile on the spot as the new home for his paper. Ochs had failed in his attempt to make the Times Tower New York's largest building of its day (it came in second); he had to settle for the fact that it would become one of the city's immortal landmarks.

The IRT subway construction at the northeast corner of Broadway and 42nd Street, 1903. Shanley's would be a popular Theater District restaurant for the next quarter century.

The northwest corner of 42nd and Broadway, April 1898—an uncharted frontier of the Theater District and the future site of the "Crossroads of the World."

By 1904, Oscar Hammerstein would build his Victoria Theatre at the corner of Seventh Avenue and 42nd Street. This is currently the site of the Reuters building, with the renovated New Victory Theatre on the site of the Belasco.

With the addition of the renovated Grand Central Terminal astride Park Avenue, 42nd Street had now become one of the city's busiest thoroughfares. As Ochs was building the Times Tower, the IRT was moving its major line uptown on the east side and having it turn west along 42nd, and then uptown again along Broadway. There would have to be a major subway stop at this corner of 42nd and Broadway, and on April 9, 1904, the triangle of land supporting the Times Tower officially became Times Square. In one of the cleverest entrepreneurial schemes of the young century, Ochs and August Belmont had convinced the city to name the new subway stop not "Broadway" or even "Long Acre Square," but "Times Square." One hundred years later, the Times Square subway stop is the only one out of hundreds in New York City to be named after a still-functioning commercial enterprise.

Once it was established around Times Square in 1904, the Theater District never moved from its domain in the West 40s. Although only a fraction of its theaters are actually *on* Broadway (yet another of its charming anomalies), the Theater District encompasses something larger than the sum of its parts. For a century, the phrases "Live from Times Square," "Direct from Broadway," and "On Broadway" have been understood by the whole world to represent the gold standard for theatrical hip hooray and American ballyhoo.

Looking south from 45th Street, the new Times Tower dominates the four-year-old Times Square. On the right stands the Hotel Astor, the reigning post-theater hangout for the next thirty years.

New York was laid out in 1811 in a very severe, brutal, pressing down of a gridiron upon a naturally marvelous island of hills and dales and streams. . . . So Broadway broke the gridiron wherever it crossed it on its way up to the Hudson River. And wherever Broadway broke the gridiron, there was extra energy, something happened, and that was always the theatre district.
—**Brendan Gill,** Critic

Glorifying the American Girl
FLORENZ ZIEGFELD AND THE *FOLLIES*

Florenz Ziegfeld reviewing the troupers.

It is necessary for a girl selected for the Follies to have personality and have grace. I do not care if the hair is long or short, blond or brunette, as long as it frames the face becomingly. The eyes should be large and expressive. A regular profile is a decided asset. Back and shoulders, of course, should be beautiful, and a rounded neck is also essential, while graceful hands are quite necessary. The legs must be shapely, and last but not least, the proportions of the figure must be perfect.

—Florenz Ziegfeld, 1928

At the beginning of the twentieth century, when Americans were setting new standards for themselves—what their homes should look like, how they should dress, even what it meant to be an American—Florenz Ziegfeld took it upon himself to set the standard for female sexuality. In producing his annual *Follies*—nearly two dozen editions from 1907 to 1931—he reflected for the country an image of its most refined ideals of female beauty, an image that still exists, a century later, as a complex amalgam of sex, exploitation, and the unobtainable. His daughter put it simply: "That was his role in life, to make women as beautiful as they could be. And he could find them anywhere and everywhere. It was his life's work." Ziegfeld expressed his mission in a simpler phrase: Glorifying the American Girl.

Ziegfeld's accomplishments went far beyond the creation of the chorus girl; with an uncanny sense of what the American public wanted, he created a polished commercial product for new Americans out of a patchwork of disparate musical and ethnic traditions. Musical theater historian Miles Krueger says, "Simply the greatest producer for musicals in the history of the American theater is Flo Ziegfeld. He's the man who really guided the American musical theater to maturity."

The producer who would become famous for middle-class entertainment was born into a temple of high art in Chicago in 1867. He was the eldest child of German immigrants; his father, Florenz Ziegfeld Sr., was a concert pianist and founder of the Chicago Musical Academy (now the Chicago Musical College). Despite his father's best intentions and European pretensions, young Flo was far more enamored of the American brand of ballyhoo practiced by showmen such as P.T. Barnum and Buffalo Bill Cody. He literally ran off to join the circus, hooking up with the likes of Buffalo Bill, until his father ordered him to come home. Working for his father at Chicago's visionary World Columbian Exposition in 1893, Ziegfeld set himself up as a promoter of a German strongman named Sandow, who performed his feats of Herculean strength in as little clothing as the law allowed. By creating a special velvet glove for society matrons who wanted to feel Sandow's muscles, Ziegfeld—not for the last time—combined the allure of physical beauty with his unerring instinct for show biz publicity.

Ziegfeld's first big star, German strongman Eugen Sandow, 1894.

With his pockets stuffed with a percentage of Sandow's earnings, Ziegfeld decided his next move was to conquer New York, which was humming with theatrical energy by 1896. He brought over his next attraction from London, a petite Polish-born, Paris-based entertainer named Anna Held, who was short on talent but long on charm. He produced her in

Ziegfeld's star entertainer, muse, and common-law wife, Anna Held, mobbed by stage-door johnnies outside her dressing room, 1906.

various showcases on Broadway during the early years of the century, and pulled off several publicity coups based on Held's mildly provocative poses and numbers. Ziegfeld clearly knew whereof he promoted; Held became Ziegfeld's lover and common-law wife. If Ziegfeld made Held a star, Held returned the favor and made him a legend. Around 1907, Ziegfeld was casting about for a new project and Held suggested he import some of the spirit of the French *Folies-Bergère,* with its seductive dancing ladies of the chorus. Ziegfeld veiled the Continental sexuality with a thin chiffon of American respectability, then he put together all the things he liked best—songs, showgirls, and scenery—into a tasteful production, suited for all audiences, called a "revue." In July of 1907, at the behest of theater owners Klaw and Erlanger, who were looking for a summertime booking for their Jardin de Paris, atop the Liberty Theater, he launched his first revue, called the *Follies,* supposedly after a chatty New York newspaper column titled "Follies of the Day."

Ziegfeld was successful enough to launch another edition the next year, and by the time the decade came to an end, he had perfected his formula for popular entertainment. Ziegfeld poached the funniest comics, the most beautiful girls, the best composers and sketch writers from the worlds of vaudeville, burlesque, minstrel shows, and Tin Pan Alley. Rather than follow a conventional story, his revues combined various acts, songs, and dance numbers, alternating in a non-narrative structure that would provide audiences with one laugh, gasp, and thrill after another. Songs were written by various hands or borrowed from other shows or commissioned to make fun of some topical issue. Sketch writers crafted skits on demand for specific comics or stars, always careful to tailor the length of the skit to be no longer—and certainly no shorter—than a costume change for the girls. What the various *Follies* all had in common was Ziegfeld's tasteful and commanding eye. He oversaw the design, came up with the numbers, hired the performers; no director in the musical theater—even in the 1960s heyday of powerful directors—would ever have as much creative power as Florenz Ziegfeld. Whatever cachet a comic or a starlet had before was multiplied tenfold by appearing in the *Follies.* Ziegfeld was able to legitimize a performer simply by inviting him or her to join his exclusive club; he singlehandedly created the concept of the crossover artist.

Of course, what people remember most about the *Follies* is the girls. Using the shapely legs of attractive women to sell tickets was hardly a Ziegfeld invention; he simply perfected an art that had begun on Broadway in the fall of 1866 with the presentation of a dance spectacle titled *The Black Crook.* As Leonard Bernstein explained in one of his lectures in the *Omnibus* television series in 1956:

> Someone named Barras had written a Germanic melodrama called *The Black Crook,* which called for no music at all. Meanwhile, a French ballet company had arrived on these shores to find the theater where they were to dance burned to the ground. Then the great idea was born: in order to provide a theater for the ballet company, it was decided to merge the two productions. *The Black Crook* was attached to song and dance with spit and chewing gum, and the show was on.

The dancing girls' "immodest dress, short skirts, flesh-colored tights and exceedingly indelicate attitudes," as one nineteenth-century clergyman characterized them, created a mild scandal and then, as usually happens, a popular success for *The Black Crook,* considered by some critics, largely by default, to be the first American musical comedy.

Poster for the arrival of a revival of The Black Crook, *1873.*

Ziegfeld was interested in more than mere chorus girls; in fact, the ladies of his ensembles could be divided into four categories (five, if you count the rare comedienne like Fanny Brice): the stars; the dancers (or ponies, as they were called); the statuesque beauties of the tableaux; and that special attraction called a Ziegfeld Girl. Showgirls have a more complicated relationship to the prurient twenty-first century; they can seem exploited, clichéd, or laughable, but in the *Follies*, Ziegfeld gave them pride of place.

Mr. Ziegfeld loved beautiful girls and he didn't object to presenting the girls in a sensuous manner—but not a vulgar manner. His sensuousness was like a painting of the Renaissance period. You couldn't take offense; it was beauty and that was the way that he presented his girls. They may have had some scant costumes on, but they moved beautifully and they looked beautiful, not vulgar.
—Doris Travis Eaton, Ziegfeld Girl

Billie Burke Ziegfeld.

LEFT: *Ziegfeld had more luck with the cards of his chorines' costumes than his cards at the gaming tabless.*

OVERLEAF: *A bevy of Ziegfeld Girls.*

The things Flo cherished as a showman were color, music, spectacle and fun. . . . His genius was his towering ability to play one against the other, matching his palette to his music, his comedy to his spectacle, stirring and mixing the whole until he produced out of the utter conflict that unique work of art, a great musical comedy. No one, indeed, ever knew how he accomplished it.

—Billie Burke Ziegfeld, 1948

Program, 1916.

Ziegfeld's house designer, the incomparable Joseph Urban, contrasted the gleaming Broadway of 1916 with the sedate theatrical charms of Shakespeare's Stratford-on-Avon.

One might say that if Ziegfeld hadn't existed the American consumer culture of the early twentieth century would have had to invent him, but the reverse is probably the truer statement. In an era when New Yorkers began to enjoy leisure time, gained the ability to travel throughout the city, could promenade after dark thanks to the harnessing of electricity, and grew curious about themselves and other Americans, Ziegfeld offered them a glamorous playground where they could be thrilled without being offended, enlightened without being lectured, entertained without being cheated.

As was the case with many Americans of the time, and most entertainers in his shows, Ziegfeld's greatest creation was himself. He was the Big-Time Producer, imperious and grandiose, penny-wise and pound-foolish. His elegant dress and noble mien commanded respect from moneymen and stagehands alike. He serially bedded his leading ladies with a droit du seigneur, until he found happiness with performer Billie Burke (best known as Glinda in the film of *The Wizard of Oz*), whom he wed in 1914, and who would carry on his legacy. From his offices towering over Times Square he shot off telegrams to his employees with a careless alacrity that we would now reserve for Post-Its and e-mails. He was a gambler who lost more than he made, both offstage and on, and however foolishly he himself behaved with his money, he never suffered fools gladly when they were in his employ. The Hollywood moguls of the 1930s—with whom he briefly flirted before his death in 1932—all cast themselves in the manner of Ziegfeld. A hundred years after his first *Follies,* his name is still synonymous with a unique brand of American self-promotion, and it's safe to say that Atlantic City and Las Vegas would be drab gambling joints without the flashy floor shows and brassy pulchritude inspired by Ziegfeld's pioneer vision. He gave his eager customers two and a half hours of the American Dream.

A Salome tableau from the Ziegfeld Follies of 1919.

He glorified beauty, but he really sort of hymned the general abundance of the culture. . . . When you went to a Ziegfeld show, it was abundance at play, it was an abundance of talent, abundance of fabric and design—everything was absolutely the best that money could buy, and that's what he sold. . . . What was being eroticized was not sexuality but possession. —**John Lahr**, Critic

Dolores in her famous peacock costume, 1916.

The showgirls were exquisite. They came from all over the country, and they were selected, they were all about six feet because they carried those beautiful costumes, and they had to learn a certain walk in order to balance the hats, the hats were huge, and their arms were outstretched. . . . Then they found out to call it "the Ziegfeld walk." —Dana O'Connell, *Follies* Girl, 1921–23

FANNY BRICE

IN 1909, AN EIGHTEEN-YEAR-OLD COMEDIENNE named Fannie Borach came to Irving Berlin with a problem. Her career hadn't been going so well—George M. Cohan had fired her from the chorus of one of his shows two years before and she was reduced to performing from one burlesque hall to another. She needed a specialty number for a benefit performance the next night; she had lied to her producer about having one. Berlin took the girl to the back room of the Ted Snyder Music Publishing House and played her a tune he had, about a Jewish girl who improbably joins the stage to play one of history's most famous vamps.

> Sadie Cohen left her happy home
> To become an actress lady,
> On the stage she soon became the rage,
> As the only real Salome baby.

Brice continued with the Follies, *even after the Shuberts produced them in the 1930s. Here she portrays her Baby Snooks character opposite Bob Hope in the 1936 edition.*

It became Fanny Brice's passkey to fame.

Brice grew up in far more comfortable surroundings than Berlin had, moving from her native Newark to Coney Island to Harlem, and from a young age, she was taken by her mother to every show they could catch. Quitting school to perform on the low-down burlesque circuits outside of Manhattan (burlesque being a form of satirical physical comedy, not the strip joints of later years), Brice did not specialize in any particular brand of comedy. When he played "Sadie Salome" for her, Berlin insisted a Yiddish accent was needed to put it over. Fanny had her reservations—she didn't know any Yiddish—but it soon became her trademark dialect.

> **I breathed and ate and drank and lived theater—in my neighborhood were all the nationalities of all of Europe. That is where I learned my accents; the Polish woman with her intonation rising up like chant. I saw Loscha of the Coney Island popcorn counter and Marta of the cheeses at Brodsky's Delicatessen and the Sadies and the Rachels and the Birdies at the Second Avenue dance halls. They all welded together and came out staggeringly true to type in one big authentic outline.**
> **—Fanny Brice, 1936**

When Fanny got a telegram to come down to see Florenz Ziegfeld a year later, she thought it was a joke. She had a friend, a secretary named Helen Ziegfeld, and every time they had a date for lunch, Fanny would say, "Ziegfeld wants to see me." This time it was no joke. Impressed by his scouts' reports of Brice's success in local burlesque houses, Ziegfeld signed her for two years—at $75 a week, then $100. Fanny ran down the street with the signed contract, showing it to everyone on the corner of 47th and Broadway. It grew so tattered, Ziegfeld had to draft a new one. He didn't mind; Ziegfeld never had much of a sense of humor himself, but he knew his audience went for comics and, once again, he gave the public the best his money could buy.

Under her new stage name—Fanny Brice—she proved her comic versatility, slaying the audience in her *Follies* debut with another Yiddish number and even a blackface song—both by Irving Berlin. She always credited Ziegfeld with her success: "I'd rather work for him than any person in the world. If he's the only person in the room, I can sing to him as if I had an audience of ten thousand!" Over the

next two decades, she was a fixture in the *Follies*, appearing in seven different editions, and two more after the Shubert Brothers appropriated Ziegfeld's name in the 1930s. She was at her best spoofing the grand pretensions of middle-class art—classical ballet, the Barrymore acting style, ragtime, and even herself. When her husband was convicted of gambling, her bad luck made it into the act. But Ziegfeld saw something else in Brice, beyond her goofy elasticity. On a trip to Paris, he bought the rights to a heartbreaking *chanson* called "Mon Homme" and had an English lyric made for his 1921 *Follies*. Fanny thought she would play it for comic effect, but Ziegfeld would have none of it.

Brice became the first crossover performer of the new century, eventually conquering not only Broadway but films, and most successfully radio, where she played the character of an aggressively precocious child, Baby Snooks, until she was well into her fifties. That Broadway and America would have adopted such an obvious ethnic type into their hearts is an immense tribute to Brice's talent.

In anything Jewish I ever did, I wasn't standing apart making fun. I was the race and what happened to me on stage is what could happen to my people. They identified with me, which made it all right to get a laugh.

—Fanny Brice, 1936

In 1964, she would be immortalized in a lavish stage musical and film based on her complicated life, starring Barbra Streisand, but a fellow member of the *Follies*, chorus girl Dana O'Connell, understood the simplicity of her appeal: "Fanny Brice was just a delightful individual; we all got to know her quite well and we just loved her—the way she said things and moved with them, she was just funny. She was just a funny girl."

WILL ROGERS

ROGERS WAS OKLAHOMA'S greatest contribution to the American musical until Rodgers and Hammerstein came along. Born in 1879 in Oolagah, Indian Territory (now Oklahoma), Ziegfeld's most unlikely star was part Cherokee Indian and made a living in vaudeville and tent shows with his expert rope tricks. Ironically, he was about to be sacked after his debut in Ziegfeld's 1915 *Frolic* when his wife realized the problem was that the nightclub's audience kept returning and were getting bored by the same routines. The next night, Rogers made an impromptu crack about Henry Ford, based on something he had read in the newspapers, and it brought the house down. Ever after, he scanned the dailies each morning for topical humor and it made him the most famous monologist in America. Interspersing his trenchant observations—"You can be killed just as dead in an unjustified war as you can defending your own home"—with his virtuosity with a lasso, he moved downstairs to the *Follies* for five seasons, and by the 1920s he had a daily newspaper column which made him one of the most quoted and admired performers in American history. The fellow who "never met a man he didn't like" was beloved by his *Follies* castmates for his kindness and generosity. He became a film star and died tragically in a plane crash in 1935; like Fanny Brice, he was given his own stage musical biography, *The Will Rogers Follies*, in 1991.

Will Rogers with an adoring chorine.

W.C. FIELDS

ZIEGFELD SPENT FORTUNES ON COMEDIANS but never liked them," said W.C. Fields. "Why he tolerated me for so long, I do not know." Fields, who gained a worldwide reputation as a master pantomime juggler in vaudeville, was a last-minute entry to the 1915 *Follies*, performing his silent "Pool Sharks" sketch. Fields's ability to wreak havoc on inanimate objects was put to use in skits in other *Follies*, where he summarily made comic hay out of tennis, croquet, golf, and the family Ford. But Ziegfeld, who was particularly averse to pantomime comics, stuck Fields in other skits and songs, and soon the bulbous, bibulous comedian had to expand his repertoire by speaking; hawking peanuts from a cart in one sketch, he elaborated his one line to "Seeking sustenance from peanuts, friend? Those small yet succulent morsels of tastiness?" A rogue was born. Free to ally his uniquely arcane vocabulary to his miraculous comic timing, Fields played and toured with the *Follies* off and on for a decade, always battling over contracts with his producer, until he broke away to become a full-fledged star in his own stage vehicle, *Poppy*, in 1923. Sound film was the perfect medium for his eccentric misanthropy and by the 1930s, he was tippling gin, oppressing little children, and convulsing audiences all over the world.

W.C. Fields, confounded by physics, in his Follies *days.*

EDDIE CANTOR

WHEN CANTOR MET ZIEGFELD for the first time, he was bucking to get a one-night shot in the *Frolic*. "I'm marvelous!" he told Ziegfeld. When the producer wondered why he should believe him, Cantor shot back, "Why, Mr. Ziegfeld, I wouldn't lie to you." Cantor's gig at the *Frolic* stretched to twenty-seven weeks and by 1917, he was performing downstairs in the *Follies* and would become practically a ward of Ziegfeld's state. A fatherless waif born Edward Israel Iskowitz in 1892 and raised by his grandmother in dire poverty on the Lower East Side, Cantor began as a streetcorner entertainer, just like

Irving Berlin, and broke through the ranks of vaudeville with a brash confidence that bordered on unmitigated gall. A hyperkinetic comedian, dancer, and singer, Cantor performed in blackface for his early *Follies* appearances, but gradually gave it up to cultivate a more accessible persona as a neurotic wisenheimer who could punctuate a corny line with a roll of his inimitable "banjo" eyes. Adopted offstage as the "third musketeer" by his older colleagues W.C. Fields and Will Rogers, Cantor developed into a versatile and popular comedian under Ziegfeld's guidance and eventually starred in several vehicles of his own for the producer in the 1920s. Cantor's specialty numbers, like "Margie" and "Makin' Whoopee," made him a successful recording artist, and he found a second career in movies and radio in the 1930s.

Eddie Cantor as an eager beaver golf caddy in Kid Boots, *a Ziegfeld-produced vehicle in 1923.*

"Give my regards to Broadway"

GEORGE M. COHAN AND VAUDEVILLE

At the turn of the century, you didn't go to some academy or drama school to learn how to be a performer; you enrolled in the nationwide school of hard knocks called vaudeville.

Vaudeville had achieved a preeminence in New York City after 1881, when impresario Tony Pastor opened a vaudeville house on 14th Street that featured material suitable for women and families, who were not welcome at music halls or variety theaters. Vaudeville shows featured almost a dozen different artists or acts at a time, performing all kinds of material in programs called bills. The bill was repeated several times a day for a week or two, and then the performers moved on to the next town. Ticket prices were cheap, but the variety was enormous. From the 1890s until the 1920s, vaudeville was the country's most popular form of entertainment, and many performers devoted their whole lives to breaking into the best theaters on the best circuits, "the big time"—one of the many vaudeville phrases that have entered the American lexicon.

> **In the arrangement of the ideal vaudeville program, there is one or more sources of complete satisfaction for everybody present, no matter how "mixed" the audience may be. In vaudeville, there is always something for everybody, just as in every state and city, in every county and town in our democratic country, there is opportunity for everybody, a chance for all.**
>
> **—E.F. Albee,** Vaudeville Producer, 1923

The Four Cohans put young George front and center, 1888.

A performer had to define and refine his or her skills in a hotly competitive world and come up with something that no one else could do—or at least do as well.

It was really the culmination of a proving ground for people interested in the performing arts. Some of these people would spend their whole lives developing twelve minutes of material so it was absolutely perfection by the time it reached the Palace in New York.

—Al Hirschfeld, Illustrator

If the audience didn't "get" you, you were through and on the next train out of town. To be a success in vaudeville, you had to know how to roll with the punches, how to appeal to a broader audience, in other words, how to break out of your ghetto and become an American.

Vaudeville proved to be the ideal school for a bantam-size Irishman with an ego larger than the Flatiron Building.

Cohan at his dressing table, c. 1910.

In the middle of the nineteenth century when Irish-Americans were newcomers to this country, they were always looked down on as being un-American, their loyalty was doubted in all sorts of ways, but by the time Cohan gets to be a star, he's defining what it means to be American.   —Robert W. Snyder

Cohan as the center of attention in The Little Millionaire, *1911.*

He sang through his nose, carried a jaunty cane, wore his hat to one side of his head, and danced exuberantly.
—**Brooks Atkinson,** 1973

George M. Cohan was born to a husband-and-wife variety team, Jerry and Nellie Cohan, in 1878 in Providence, Rhode Island, though probably not on the Fourth of July, despite his sentimental embellishments. He had no more than six months of schooling, and his violin training ended after two weeks when the teacher sent him back to his father with a note that read: "Impossible to teach this boy any more. HE KNOWS IT ALL." As an infant, George was carried onstage, and not too long afterward he joined the family act along with his older sister Josie, playing the fiddle, tearing tickets, and selling autographed pictures during intermission.

By the mid-1890s, the Four Cohans were a top vaudeville draw, touring across the country. Their act was a crude amalgam of specialty dancing, bald Irish humor, and corny skits, but the Cohans knew how to pack a socko finish; frequently, they would get a rise out of the crowd by brandishing American flags and singing patriotic songs. Young George was the center of it all, often playing his old man's old man in one skit and then his son in another, or stealing the spotlight for a buck-and-wing dancing solo. "What the fifteen-year-old, clean-faced, fresh-minded, full-of-life American boy or girl likes, the average American audiences will like," Cohan once said. He had the all-American seat warmer in mind, a fictional audience member called Joe Blatz, to whom he always geared his performances. Being a hit in two-a-day houses was fine, but to Cohan, "Broadway was the only one bell I wanted to ring."

After a brief taste of New York City in his teens, Cohan spent years trying to craft the right vehicle to bring him to Broadway. At one point, he tried to steal away from his folks' act in the middle of the night with a train ticket to New York. But by 1904, his family relented, and he struck out on his own in spectacular style, with a vehicle he wrote for himself called *Little Johnny Jones*, which premiered on November 7 at the Liberty Theatre.

As an American jockey who travels to London to win the big race, Cohan had the perfect platform for his insouciant patriotism. Singing his own words, he immortalized himself:

Cohan in Forty-five Minutes from Broadway, *1906.*

I'm a Yankee Doodle Dandy,
A Yankee Doodle do or die;
A real live nephew of my Uncle Sam's,
Born on the Fourth of July.

The show missed its mark in its initial engagement, but after fine-tuning it in Philadelphia, Cohan brought the show to Broadway one more time in 1905 and never looked back. He became a fixture in the Theater District, trotting out his love for the red, white, and blue in songs like "You're a Grand Old Flag," sung in a show with the characteristic title *George Washington, Jr.* Some critics were immune to his charms. James Metcalfe wrote in a 1906 *Life* article:

Mr. Cohan is naturally the highly patriotic youth who is the hero of the piece. . . . He makes him a vulgar, cheap, blatant, ill-mannered, flashily dressed, insolent, smart aleck, who for some reason . . . appeals to the imagination and apparent approval of large American audiences. . . . If he can bring himself to coin the American flag and national heroes into box office receipts, it is not his blame, but our shame.

But critiques like these were mostly expressed by people who had considered themselves "American" for several generations. For Cohan's fans, who reflected the city's immigrant mix, that fellow had missed the point entirely.

It would be nice to report that Cohan's fame had tempered his personality, but that was hardly the case. Cohan's smart-aleck style was something that worked offstage as well as on-stage. "On what lines have you usually constructed your plays?" a well-known playwright once asked him. "Mostly on the Pennsylvania and New York Central," he replied. His vindictiveness would become legendary; when his hometown paper once gave him a bad review, he refused to play there again for many seasons.

Sheet music for "You're a
Grand Old Flag," 1906.

None of this hampered his energy or industry. "Speed, speed—and lots of it! That's my idea of the thing!" he exhorted his family while in vaudeville. He became the first famous song-and-dance man, setting the standard for "wowing" an audience by drawing on a feral instinct for putting over a song by any means necessary. It was a style of performance emulated by Fred Astaire, Gene Kelly, Sammy Davis, Bob Fosse, Gregory Hines, and countless others since. Fanny Brice once said that "George M. Cohan was Broadway's fullest expression—a vital exclamation of its mood, its pulse!" and if his passion was patriotism, his religion was showbiz. The titles of some of his more than forty shows say it all: *Forty-five Minutes from Broadway; The Man Who Owns Broadway; Hello, Broadway!* His most famous valentine to his favorite neighborhood came in the second act of *Little Johnny Jones:*

Give my regards to Broadway,
Remember me to Herald Square;
Tell all the gang at Forty-second Street
That I will soon be there.
Whisper of how I'm yearning
To mingle with the old-time throng;
Give my regards to old Broadway
And say that I'll be there, ere long.

It is worth remembering that the lead character in the show is not a song-and-dance man, nor even an entertainer, but a jockey. Cohan was apostrophizing the *society* of Broadway which, in the 1900s, extended from 23rd Street up through Herald Square on 34th Street to 42nd Street. It was a fraternity of bonhomie, where famous people met each other after the show in taverns, bars, and roof gardens, joined private theatrical clubs, raised toasts, bought drinks for the house, played practical jokes on each other, showed each other their clippings and generally strutted their fame and their glory. That social Broadway, now utterly, utterly lost, was a world that Cohan loved perhaps more than being onstage, and he made it immortal.

Only one musical theater performer in American history has a statue in New York City. Tourists rushing to catch a matinee can still see the first great song-and-dance man at the corner of 46th and Broadway, where he always wanted to be, mingling with the old-time throng.

"I ain't never done nothin' to nobody"
BERT WILLIAMS AND THE MINSTREL TRADITION

One of the most influential sources of the American musical was one of its most shameful.

The minstrel show got its start in the early nineteenth century, when a number of white entertainers, mostly of Irish descent, found they could connect with their more raucous audiences by applying burnt cork to their skin and caricaturing black people in various songs, dances, and skits. White audiences—the vast majority of whom had never met a black person in any socialized situation—lapped up the litany of corny jokes and silly songs put across by white entertainers pretending to be shiftless plantation slaves, or later in the century, feckless black arrivistes insinuating themselves into urban life. The popularity of these entertainments stretched across the country and beyond the shores of the Atlantic for most of the nineteenth century.

Apart from its perpetuation of negative stereotypes, the minstrel show contributed numerous mimetic aspects to popular entertainment, including the master of ceremonies, the spoof of popular songs with humorously rewritten lyrics, cross-dressing, and probably most durable of all, the double act. Derived from the two comic "endmen," who placed themselves on opposite ends of the minstrel line, the double act required two comedians who fed each other setups and served as the foils for each other's material. Without this precedent, the vaudeville patter of white entertainers such as Burns and Allen, or Abbott and Costello, would never have existed. Comic double acts could be found at the center of Broadway musical entertainment from the 1910s on, making stars out of the black duo of Flournoy Miller and Aubrey Lyles in the 1920s, William Gaxton and Victor Moore in the 1930s and extending all the way up to the twenty-first century with the antics of Nathan Lane and Matthew Broderick in *The Producers*.

Sheet music from the 1848 Christy Minstrels. Leading and finishing the minstrel line were the two end men, a double act known as Mr. Tambo and Mr. Bones.

In the late nineteenth century, blacks questioned the assumed supremacy of the white minstrel entertainers. Contemporary African-American entertainer Ben Vereen explains:

African Americans didn't talk like that. But [white entertainers] created this dialogue, it became very fashionable, it became the "in" thing, so now the African Americans are sitting out there, looking at these white entertainers, and they go, "Wait a minute—I can do me better than they're doing me," so they get together and they form a troupe. But the white audiences in this country told them, "If you want to be on our stage, in this country, you better black up. We don't want to see your black skin." And that's where the minstrel show came from. And so out of that, from behind that mask, genius was born.

Bert Williams, 1922.

Bert Williams was the funniest man I ever saw and the saddest man I ever knew.

—W.C. Fields

One man transcended minstrelsy's denigration of his race and became not only the most popular comedian of his day, but the most famous African American since Frederick Douglass: Bert Williams. The genius of black minstrelsy was born Egbert Austin Williams in the West Indies in the 1870s and moved to California in 1885. After he was denied entrance to Stanford University, he worked as a banjo player in saloons and minstrel shows. By 1889, he had teamed up with George Walker to form a popular blackface double act. But, where Walker was the slick and sporty one, Williams played the comic one, the butt of the jokes. As Walker and Williams became the famous act on the segregated black vaudeville circuit, Williams refined his characterization into a kind of high art.

Walker and Williams eventually made a hit on Broadway with their trademark cakewalk, a high-stepping spoof of white audiences' vision of black dancing, and by 1903, they headed the cast of *In Dahomey,* the first full-length musical written and played by blacks to be performed at a major Broadway house. They performed in several other shows until Walker became ill in 1909, leaving Williams to try his luck as a solo act; it was not successful.

In 1910, Florenz Ziegfeld took one of the greatest gambles of his career and offered a contract to Williams to star in his annual *Follies.* It would be the first time a black entertainer performed as an equal with a white ensemble on Broadway. Most of Williams's white castmates threatened to quit or boycott the show rather than appear with a black man. Ziegfeld called their bluff. "Go if you want to," he supposedly replied. "I can replace every one of you, except the man you want me to fire." Williams was a huge hit in 1910 with the *Follies,* and continued to delight audiences for seven nearly consecutive editions.

Although by all accounts Williams was beloved by his fellow *Follies* comedians Will Rogers, W.C. Fields, and Eddie Cantor, Rogers reputedly demanded to know why a black man got better billing than he did; Ziegfeld replied that it was because a black man brought in more money. Still, in his contract with Ziegfeld, Williams stipulated that he never appear alone with a white woman on stage, out of concern for his audience's sensibilities and his own safety; while in return, Ziegfeld released Williams from touring in the South. When traveling across the country during the *Follies'* annual spring engagements, Williams was treated as one of the gang but, in order to spare his colleagues any embarrassment, he would always insist on using the rear entrance of hotels.

Although his comic skits had him entertaining the crowds in front of the curtain while the girls changed their elaborate costumes and he always stayed behind the burnt-cork mask, Williams presented an enormous variety of comic material in the *Follies.* In 1911, Irving Berlin wrote a spoof of the classic sentimental poem "Woodman, Spare That Tree" for him, in which he played a henpecked husband hiding in a tree from his wife. Williams would go on to play, among many other characters, a minister in a haunted house, a cabdriver saddled with a drunken passenger, a stevedore humiliated by his effeminate son,

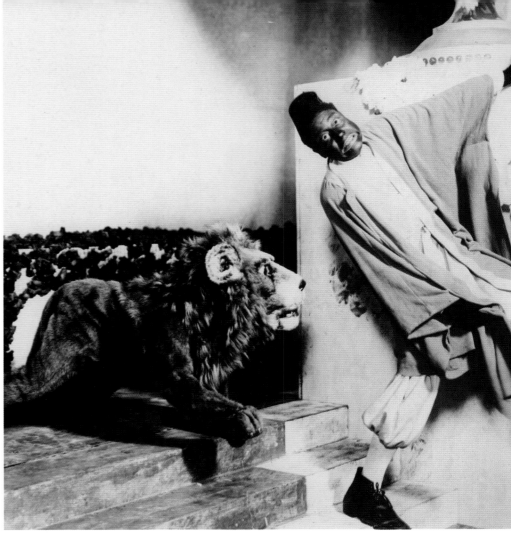

Williams in a Follies *sketch, 1918.*

He was able to bring a humanity to what he called the "shuffling coon" character that had not existed before. Everyone else played that character as a total buffoon and it was totally derogatory. Williams invested some humanity into the character, made him a living human being and made him someone that people could be sympathetic to. You laughed at him, but you also sympathized with his plight.

—Mel Watkins, Cultural Historian

and, in a burst of astonishing virtuosity, a one-man poker game. Yet Williams, a soft-spoken, well-read autodidact, was always politely bewildered by the dichotomy between his reception onstage and off. Theater historian Max Wilk observed:

> He had the humor of pain. . . . There is an apocryphal story about him. The story is he walked into a bar and he asked the bartender for a martini, and the bartender looked at him and said, "That'll be a thousand dollars." And Bert Williams without saying a word opened his coat, took out his wallet, and put five thousand-dollar bills on the bar and said, "I'll have five." There's the pain story of all time.

As with so many performers of his day, Williams was best summed up by his signature number, the kind of song that seamlessly blended his public persona with his personal philosophy. "Nobody" (1905) was a number for which Williams had written the music; he perfected it in his vaudeville act and performed it in almost all of his *Follies* appearances.

> When life seems full of clouds and rain,
> And I am filled with naught but pain,
> Who soothes my thumpin', bumpin' brain?
> Nobody!

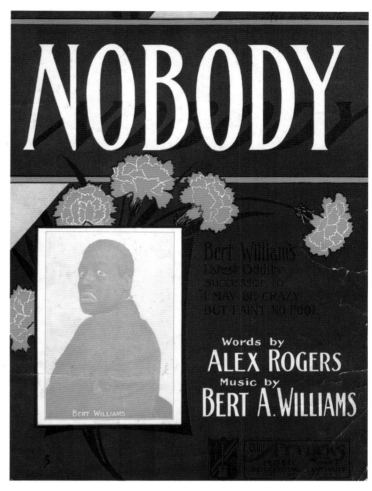

Sheet music for "Nobody."

When all day long, things go amiss,
And I come home to find some bliss,
Who hands to me a glowin' kiss?
Nobody!

I ain't never done nothin' to nobody;
I ain't never got nothin' from nobody, no time!
And until I get somethin' from somebody, sometime,
I don't intend to do nothin' for nobody no time.

Although later black entertainers like Stepin Fetchit may have borrowed Williams's sad-sack elements, they left out his dignity entirely. Williams's onstage persona—the decent soul triumphing over adversity through humble, dogged persistence—can be found in white comedians such as Buster Keaton and Harpo Marx; Jackie Gleason's Ralph Kramden would have been unthinkable without Williams, and Redd Foxx's Sanford is Williams's Nobody, but finally allowed to speak his mind. Who knows whether Williams would be happy to hear of his influence? Nobody.

And there's just a little hint that someday he's not gonna do anything for "nobody" himself, so that he's both saying "I am a black man, and I am depressed in this society," and there's a little hint, "And someday I may stop playing your game. I may refuse to perform." There is nothing more enticing to an audience than someone who says, "I'm here tonight singing and entertaining you, and I'm a little unwilling, and I may not go on doing this. You really have to pull me by your energy into this performance."
—Ann Douglas, Social Historian

"For 'tis love, and love alone, the world is seeking"

VICTOR HERBERT AND AMERICAN OPERETTA

Operetta was tailor-made for the tastes and habits of the turn-of-the-century consumer of refined amusement. Middle-class audiences hankering for an evening's lyrical entertainment found the boisterous attractions of the Bowery too rough-and-ready (and perhaps unfortunate reminders of whence they came), and the boxes of the Metropolitan Opera House and the Brooklyn Academy of Music were available only to the select Four Hundred of the Edith Wharton circle. Operetta provided a fanciful in-between world of romance and escape; it was the most popular brand of musical theater for the first two decades of the twentieth century.

Americans in the nineteenth century usually took their cue from Europe and England when it came to musical entertainment, warmly embracing the comic operettas of Gilbert and Sullivan, as well as those by the French composer Jacques Offenbach. Soon, there were many American versions or imitations of these shows and operetta—original or,

Babes in Toyland (1903) was Victor Herbert's first great commercial success; its innocent songs are still played and sung.

even better, imported—developed into its own successful genre. Operetta didn't ask much of its audience; the story was big and romantic, the score was accessible and soaring, the tenor and the soprano center stage, with a supporting cast of incongruous comedians and a large male chorus, and a happy ending was always promised. The setting was usually some exotic European country or mythic utopia or a combination of the two. In operetta, it was never simply boy meets girl, but rather prince meets gypsy girl, or duke meets countess. The conventions (or less kindly, clichés) of operetta were so immutable that in the late 1920s Groucho Marx could get a big laugh by announcing that a soprano's next selection would be "'Somewhere My Love Lies Sleeping' with an all-male chorus."

New York's infatuation with imported operetta would reach a fever pitch in 1907, when Franz Lehár's *The Merry Widow*—already the toast of Vienna, Paris, and London—arrived on these shores and, in the words of Leonard Bernstein, "swept the Broadway public off its feet" by creating a mania not only for its music, but for various fashions inspired by the operetta's eponymous heroine. But thirteen years earlier, a composer of Promethean proportions had already made the reputation of the homegrown American operetta. Victor Herbert, like many figures in early musical theater, was an immigrant whose formative years were spent in Europe. Born in Dublin in 1859 and raised in Stuttgart, where he got his classical training, he played the cello in some of the most highly regarded orchestras of Austria and Germany. Like one of his own characters, he fell in love with the leading lady, a soprano who told the Metropolitan Opera that she would sing there only if her young husband were made first cellist in the orchestra. A happy ending; she got her wish.

Upon his arrival in New York in 1886, Herbert began playing, conducting, and composing at a furious pace, and by 1894 he had his first operetta staged on Broadway. Over the next twenty-two years, he would compose more than forty more. An enormous, affable fellow with a huge appetite for work and food, he was the Diamond Jim Brady of the musical theater; the story goes that in 1898, Herbert was composing and orchestrating four scores simultaneously, while constantly refreshing himself with a different wine from the countries where each of his four shows was set. His 1903 hit, *Babes in Toyland,* brought a childlike innocence to the usually ardent operetta and also gave the world, as his shows usually did, a hit song or two: the lullaby "Toyland" and "March of the Toys," which is still played by battalions of high school marching bands who have never heard the term "operetta."

Critic Deems Taylor wrote, "Think of a Herbert score and ten to one you can't quote the words beyond the first line. It's the music that counts, frequently in spite of lyrics that are appallingly pedestrian." Taylor's case is proven by Herbert's 1910 hit, with lyrics by Rida Johnson Young:

> Ah! sweet mystery of life, at last I've found thee;
> Ah! I know at last the secret of it all;
> All the longing, seeking, striving, waiting, yearning—
> The burning hopes, the joy and idle tears that fall!

This is what passed for passionate (and moving) encounters in 1910, but the song did enter the American repertoire (at least the first line) and became infamous sixty-five years later in a rather climactic moment in the Mel Brooks movie *Young Frankenstein.* The song

Herbert was the greatest celebrity composer of his day; "Ah! Sweet Mystery of Life" was arguably his most famous piece, and Naughty Marietta *earned the distinction of being the first operetta set in America, although its eighteenth-century Louisiana milieu might as well have been Versailles or Gerolstein.*

proved even more integral to its show, *Naughty Marietta,* where it actually figured in resolving the plot—a rare occurrence in operetta.

The operetta is an easy target for mockery, but Herbert gave his scores an integrity and rhapsodic fervor that would long outlive the productions of his shows. Herbert's operettas allowed romance to be taken seriously by American audiences; and although it is, ironically, less sexy to talk about romance than the influence of comedy or dance on the musical, love stories have clearly been at the center of the vast majority of musical theater pieces for the last century. By the teens, Herbert was clearly the dean of American show music. He contributed several finales to the *Ziegfeld Follies,* especially in the patriotic days of World War I, and was also a tireless conductor of show, band, and symphonic music. Herbert managed to churn out a show or two a year up until his death in 1924, but by 1914, Herbert had passed the baton to another composer, one who valued his own musical integrity as much as Herbert valued his.

"And I'm certn'ly going to tell them"
JEROME KERN

Jerome Kern, c. 1910.

Jerome Kern was born in New York City in 1885, and unlike most of his musical contemporaries had never known a day's poverty. His father was the executive of a fashionable department store in Newark, who preferred that young Jerry go into the family business rather than pursue his conservatory training. When the teenaged Kern accidentally ordered two hundred pianos for the store—rather than the two requested—his father hastily packed him off to the Heidelberg conservatory, and both Kerns were the happier for it. His musical education continued in England; in 1905 he returned to New York to become a song plugger, rehearsal accompanist, and musical jack-of-all-trades. He was also cursed with a persistent ambition; the trite European operettas that he was asked to accompany in rehearsal provided him with his first chance to get ahead.

His first big hit came in a 1905 British show. "How'd You Like to Spoon with Me?" (lyrics by Edward Laska) was a tune that perfectly captured the carefree chasteness of the turn of the century. Between 1905 and 1912, almost a hundred Kern songs were interpolated into thirty Broadway musicals, including several editions of the *Ziegfeld Follies.* Kern became known as "the Red Cross for the imported musical comedy." By 1910, he was prominent enough for one music critic to query, "Who is this Jerome Kern, whose music towers in an Eiffel way above the average primitive hurdy-gurdy accompaniment of the present-day musical comedy?" Praise was fine, but what Kern really wanted was a chance—not just for himself, but for a liberation from the automatic sycophancy of American producers toward English and European scores.

> **What I would like to see is an opportunity given to American talent to express itself. . . . I contend that the producer might have saved the expense of all the middlemen and been given a good product by letting Americans do the work to begin with.**
>
> **—Jerome Kern,** 1913

History contends that Kern's career-making opportunity to express himself came in 1914, when a British show called *The Girl from Utah* was imported to Broadway. Kern was asked to give an American flavor to the mostly British score. The result was "They Didn't Believe Me" (lyrics by Herbert Reynolds), a number that seamlessly moved from dialogue to song and back to dialogue—a revolutionary idea in 1914.

And when I tell them,
And I certn'ly am goin' to tell them,
That I'm the man whose wife one day you'll be—
They'll never believe me,
They'll never believe me,
That from this great big world you've chosen me!

After 1915, Kern had an even better chance to show his gifts in the musicals he wrote for Broadway's tiny Princess Theatre. Their original and American settings allowed him to produce melodies without artistic compromise. Along with other discriminating theatergoers in New York, teenagers George Gershwin and Richard Rodgers moved to the edge of their seats and listened closely when a Kern tune wafted its way up to the Princess balcony.

The Girl from Utah *(1914) was the showcase for Kern's groundbreaking song.*

> **The sound of a Jerome Kern tune was not ragtime; nor did it have any of the Middle European inflections of Victor Herbert. It was all his own—the first truly American theater music—and it pointed the way I wanted to be led.**
>
> **—Richard Rodgers,** 1975

Kern's career had an odd kind of patient intolerance; he would grind out mediocre or unsuccessful shows for years and then explode—as if under mounting pressure—with an extraordinary fount of melody and invention. His long stint as a dogged interpolator abruptly ended with the highly original Princess Shows, but after some other huge successes in the early 1920s he spent most of that decade toiling on rather underwhelming material. One can only suppose he was simply gaining the necessary strength to explode again in 1927.

BILL

Words by P.G. Wodehouse
Music by Jerome Kern
Cut from Oh Lady! Lady!! *(1918)*

I N 1914, THE 299-SEAT PRINCESS THEATRE on West 39th Street had ground to a financial halt and desperately needed something new on its boards, or the management would have to get rid of it. An agent named Elisabeth Marbury countered with a suggestion: Scale everything down (the number of sets, the size of the orchestra and chorus), keep the costumes contemporary, and get some younger artists on the cheap to write the shows. By 1915, she had settled on thirty-year-old Jerome Kern as composer. He was more than happy to oblige.

His good fortune continued with his eventual collaborators: librettist Guy Bolton and lyricist P.G. Wodehouse (who would go on to write the *Jeeves* stories). Both gentlemen were British-born, had a civilized if pleasantly sophomoric wit, and were dedicated to writing shows about recognizable romantic couples in contemporary situations—something that set them apart from the operetta librettists of their day. Kern, Wodehouse, and Bolton became famous collaborating more than a half dozen times on various projects from 1915 to 1918, most of them for the Princess Theatre.

The shows were limited by the scope of the Princess stage to stories about honeymoons, mistaken identities, and country house guests; whereas romantic couples in an operetta might sing about mountain ranges in Ruritania, those in the Princess Shows sang about the charms of waiting for the Long Island Rail Road to bring their swains home for the weekend. The sheer charm of the stories and sexual innocence of the characters, abetted by Kern's sprightly melodies, captured the town.

"Bill" was written in 1918 for the heroine of *Oh Lady! Lady!!* but dropped out of town at the last minute, possibly because leading men in musical comedies, even in the groundbreaking Princess Shows, couldn't be quite as riddled with flaws—however endearing—as Bill was. The song resurfaced a year later, in a flop called *Zip Goes a Million,* sung, in a test of credulity even by musical comedy standards, to a dollar "bill." Again it was cut. But nothing dies forever in the American musical theater. The song was again resurrected in 1927 for *Show Boat,* which Kern wrote with Oscar Hammerstein II. With some further doctoring by both men (and a contractual credit to Wodehouse), the song found a happy home as a second-act torch song for Helen Morgan and became an immortal standard.

"Bill" contains the faint tremor of a songwriting revolution. Previously, musical theater characters had *always* known how to express themselves—and with perfect grammar. However, in "Bill," Wodehouse adds the miraculous line "I don't know" to the heroine's explanation of her lover's attributes in the final refrain. The heroine's shrug of ineffability seems so human, so touching, so *normal,* that this lyric alone demonstrates how influential the unpretentious style of the Princess Shows would be on the next generation of Broadway songwriters.

Vivienne Segal leading the chaste chorines of Oh Lady! Lady!!

I used to dream that I would discover
The perfect lover
    Some day:
I knew I'd recognize him,
If ever he came 'round my way.
I always used to fancy then,
    He'd be one of the god-like kind of men,
With a giant brain and a noble head
Like the heroes bold in the books I read.
But along came Bill
Who's quite the opposite of all the men
In story books.
In grace and looks
I know that Apollo,
Would beat him all hollow;
And I can't explain
It's surely not his brain
    That makes me thrill.
I love him
Because he's wonderful
    Because he's just old Bill.

He can't play golf or tennis or polo
Or sing a Solo
    Or row;
He isn't half as handsome,
As dozens of men that I know.
He isn't tall or straight or slim,
And he dresses far worse than Ted or Jim,
And I can't explain why he should be
Just the one, one man in the world for me.

He's just my Bill.
He has no gifts at all:
A motor car
He cannot steer;
And it seems clear
Whenever he dances,
His partner takes chances,
Oh I can't explain
It's surely not his brain
    That makes me thrill.
I love him
Because he's—I don't know
    Because he's just my Bill.

P.G. Wodehouse, Guy Bolton, and Jerome Kern.

Sheet music for "Till the Clouds Roll By" from Oh Boy!, *1917.*

The Princess Theatre program, c. 1915.

"Someday I'm going to murder the bugler"

BROADWAY AND THE GREAT WAR

Operetta was doomed to temporary obscurity on June 28, 1914, the moment two shots rang out halfway across the world in Sarajevo. With the assassination of Archduke Franz Ferdinand, war broke out in Europe, and no one was interested any longer in the romantic escapades of fictitious *mittel*-European aristocrats when real ones were being killed. In April 1917, the United States itself was at war and all of Broadway rallied to support the war effort. Of course, Florenz Ziegfeld let the public know where he stood immediately; the finale to the *Follies* of 1917 was a patriotic number titled "Can't You Hear Your Country Calling?," written by none other than Victor Herbert, with lyrics by Gene Buck. It featured Paul Revere and Abraham Lincoln, and, to top it off, President Woodrow Wilson himself, impersonated by a stock Ziegfeld comedian, reviewing the troops—troops composed of Ziegfeld Girls in Continental Army uniforms.

LEFT: *Sheet music for "It's a Long, Long, Way from Here to Old Broadway," 1917.*

BELOW: *A* Follies *number during the Great War.*

The patriotic fervor inspired by the Great War caused an immense change down in Tin Pan Alley. The ethnic songs that had been such a staple of popular music for twenty years were replaced practically overnight by a flood of all-American rousers, many of which, such as "Good-bye Broadway, Hello France," spotlighted Broadway as the center of American culture; for the many doughboys shipping out of New York Harbor, a night on Broadway was indeed the last frivolous excursion of their young lives. George M. Cohan, always Broadway's most fervent flag-waver, came to his country's aid and composed a song specifically for the war effort; inspired by the first three notes of a bugle call, "Over There" became the most famous hit to emerge from the Great War.

RIGHT: *Sheet music for "Goodbye Broadway, Hello France!," 1917.*

BELOW: *Ever the patriot, George M. Cohan marches up Broadway, flag in hand.*

No one on Broadway did his part more enthusiastically than Irving Berlin. In 1918, he became an American citizen and was promptly drafted into the Army ("UNITED STATES TAKES BERLIN" read the most amusing headline of the entire war). Banished to a desolate training camp among the potato fields of Yaphank, Long Island, Private Berlin promptly discovered that serving your country dictated a different time clock for someone used to catting around Broadway until all hours. Berlin poured his frustrations into a song mocking the relentless assault of reveille that has found kindred spirits among soldiers and schoolchildren alike for nearly a century:

Oh! How I hate to get up in the morning!
Oh! How I'd love to remain in bed!

Program for Yip! Yip! Yaphank.

Irving Berlin on K.P. duty with two of the "girls" from the show Yip! Yip! Yaphank, *1918.*

The popularity of the song reputedly allowed Berlin to get an even more delicious revenge on Army life. Pointing out to his commanding officer that there were a lot of show folk in the Army—and wouldn't it be great if we all put on a show!—Berlin got special dispensation to write a revue about the armed forces. And if he could sleep in, the composer added, it would help him write the songs faster.

The all-military revue *Yip! Yip! Yaphank* quickly transferred from Camp Upton to the Century Theater on Broadway, where it was staged and performed by members of the U.S. Army, now under the supervision of Sergeant Irving Berlin. It was a massive success, with soldiers in uniform, in drag, or in blackface spoofing the drudgery of Army life. Not all of it was pure comedy, however; the finale required the cast of nearly three hundred to march up the aisles to a ship onstage, singing a Berlin song called "We're On Our Way to France."

Now picture this. In the middle of one of the performances, the soldiers actually got their overseas orders. They marched up the aisle onto the ship, they couldn't say good-bye to their folks in the audience, they were embarking for France with the stage boat pulling away.
—Eddie Cantor, 1928

The show not only made Berlin famous all over again, it gave him his first intoxicating taste of what it meant to be a producer. He cut one number from the show when a friend, songwriter Harry Ruby, suggested it might be drowned out in the sea of patriotic songs of the era—so the stately "God Bless America" was put into the trunk for another day. But what audiences and historians remember most about *Yip! Yip! Yaphank* was Berlin himself, making his appearance as a skinny Army private in, as theater critic Brooks Atkinson recalled, "tight leggings and a huge campaign hat that threatened to unbalance him" and singing "Oh! How I Hate to Get Up in the Morning." Cantor thought his friend looked like the picture on an ad that reads "Help send this boy to camp," but what Berlin really looked like most was a real live nephew of his Uncle Sam's.

FOLLIES OF 1919

BY THE TIME the Great War was "over, over there," nearly three million New Yorkers converged along Fifth Avenue to welcome home the victorious soldiers and sailors with unparalleled enthusiasm.

Florenz Ziegfeld was never one to be upstaged. He planned for his 1919 *Follies* to be the greatest victory party New York had ever thrown. Before the show opened at the New Amsterdam on June 16, Ziegfeld had completely undone his famously loose pursestrings: his weekly payroll was $20,000 and the costumes alone cost $17,000. Although not innovative in terms of structure or story, the *Follies of 1919* was sparked by a compelling blend of old-fashioned show biz traditions confronting the uncertainty of changing times.

A tribute to minstrelsy, of all things, wrapped up the first act. Bert Williams and Eddie Cantor—both in blackface—acted as minstrel endmen in a new Irving Berlin number, "I'd Rather See a Minstrel Show." Another of the nearly dozen tunes Berlin provided for this edition was "Mandy," originally written for *Yip! Yip! Yaphank*. The production number featured specialty singers Van and Schenck (for whom the song would be a hit), backed up by the Ziegfeld Girls unfortunately referred to as "the Follies Pickaninnies."

Comedy was served up by Williams in a sharp-shooting sketch and Cantor being mangled into a human pretzel by a sadistic doctor in what became the famous "Osteopath Scene." Berlin gave Cantor his own comic solo song, the mildly risqué "You'd Be Surprised." Cantor's recording of the song would sell more than a million copies, signaling the shift in popularity from sheet music to recorded sound.

The *Follies* girls, as always, were at the romantic center of the show. Dave Stamper and Gene Buck, two of Ziegfeld's more reliable house composers, came up with "Tulip Time," a much-admired production number ladled with Hollandaise.

After the overture, the curtains parted on a Ziegfeld "salad." The girls are portraying, l. to r., Paprika, Oil, Spice (arms outstretched), Sugar, Lettuce, and Chicken. While this number was going on, Marilyn Miller was dressing.

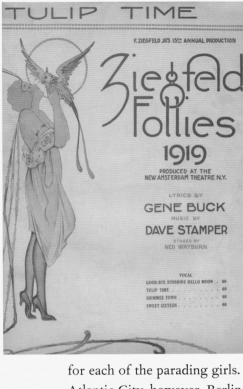

But Ziegfeld needed a second-act number. Stuck with five gorgeous gowns he wanted in the show but for which he had no song, he approached Berlin and asked him to bail him out, even though the songwriter had already fulfilled his contractual obligations. Since the tune was to be sung by the show's tenor, John Steel, to show off his voice, Berlin constructed five popular opera arias, one for each of the parading girls. When the show tried out in Atlantic City, however, Berlin realized the number needed a tune to connect the opera sequences.

A pretty girl is like a melody
Who haunts you night and day,
Just like the strain of a haunting refrain,
She'll start upon a marathon
And run around your brain.

"A Pretty Girl Is Like a Melody" became the anthem of all subsequent *Follies*. Years later, Berlin would write, "Today they play it when a pretty girl walks across a stage. And strip teasers disrobe to it. That's show business."

The modern world of 1919 intruded in several numbers. Another Berlin song, "Look Out for the Bolsheviki Man," never made it to New York, but the incipient adoption of the prohibition of alcohol in January 1920 inspired an entire second-act sequence. Bert Williams, still in blackface, sang Berlin's "You Cannot Make Your Shimmy Shake on Tea," part of which ran:

On the day they introduced their Prohibition laws
They just went and ruin'd the greatest shimmy
      dancer because:
You cannot make your shimmy shake on tea;
It simply can't be done.
You'll find your shaking ain't taking
Unless you has the proper jazz
That only comes with such drinks as
Green River, Haig and Haig, and Hennessy.

A perfect amalgamation of everything Ziegfeld had mastered in the previous twelve years, this edition would play for a smashing 171 performances. Irving Berlin was also prescient enough to conjure up the next era of the Broadway musical in a number called "A Syncopated Cocktail," to which Ziegfeld Girls paraded by in the guises of Lemonade, Sarsaparilla, and Coca-Cola:

Now that your drinking days are through,
Come along with me;
I've got a brand-new jag for you—
It's a melody.
Syncopated music
Goes right to your head . . .
Come along and have
A syncopated cocktail with me.

The greatest musical comedy cast ever assembled in a single show, I believe, was in the *Follies of 1919*. . . . [It] was one of those ideal organizations that bespoke the last word in stage generalship and the most perfect harmony of actors and material. Everyone in the cast clicked. Each specialty, no matter what its character, was performed by the acknowledged master of that field.

—Eddie Cantor, 1928

"A Pretty Girl Is Like a Melody," one of the most popular songs to come out of the Follies.

"And we won't come back till the managers are fair!"

THE EQUITY STRIKE

As the year 1919 began, labor issues dominated the American political consciousness. After the war, the cost of living rose precipitously and Congress seemed unwilling to tax the businesses and corporations that had made so much money off the war itself. Profits rose but wages didn't, and the workingman was caught in the middle. Primed by the increasing, if inaccurate, news of the Bolshevik revolution in Russia, the country braced itself for a showdown between capital and labor. Strikes and threats of them exploded from coast to coast; in March 1919, there were 175 strikes nationwide. New York City, with its large immigrant working class and cadres of socialist theorists, was considered by the government to be particularly flammable; it instituted the Palmer raids in November to weed out any Communist insurgents.

There had been grave abuses in the producing business. Actors would rehearse for ten and twelve weeks without pay; then the show might play a week or two, and they'd have to start rehearsing in a new piece all over again. On the other hand, if a show was a success, a manager could play as many extra shows as he pleased without compensating the actor for extra performances. . . . There were producers who ordered special performances in honor of their own birthdays. Chorus girls were particularly hard hit. . . . When their show finally opened, they got as low as twenty-five dollars a week, and out of that they had to pay for their stockings and shoes.
—Eddie Cantor, 1928

Vaudeville star and popular stage comedienne Marie Dressler joins the throng in support of the strike, 1919.

Actors on Broadway had been moving toward union representation as early as 1912, but many performers were against the idea, feeling that they were professional artists who shouldn't be grouped with manual laborers. Despite this opposition, an organization calling itself the Actors' Equity Association affiliated with the American Federation of Labor in 1916. For three years, they were locked in frustrating negotiations with the Producing Managers' Association, and on August 6, 1919, Actors' Equity voted to go on strike, half an hour before curtain time. Twelve shows closed immediately, another six a few days later.

The strike hit Florenz Ziegfeld where it hurt the most: at the box office. The strike had come just six weeks after the debut of his *Follies of 1919*. He obtained temporary injunctions prohibiting cast members from striking, claiming the walkout would cost him almost a quarter of a million dollars. The chorus girls formed their own union and left. Ziegfeld promised Eddie Cantor, who had always thought Ziegfeld to be a fair employer, that he wouldn't join the PMA, but five days later, on his way to the theater, Cantor discovered that the producer had. Cantor stood on 41st Street, across from the New Amsterdam stage door, and signaled to his fellow actors that the jig was up; they all left the show and joined Equity that night. Ziegfeld cabled Cantor:

HOW COULD YOU DO THIS TO ME WHEN I'VE BEEN LIKE A FATHER TO YOU ALL THESE YEARS STOP WE NEVER HAD A DISPUTE ABOUT SALARY OR ANYTHING STOP

Ethel Barrymore gets into the act, posing as Justice for the Actors' Equity Association, 1919.

But it was no use. It would be several seasons before Ziegfeld forgave Cantor and put him in another show.

The strike affected all of Ziegfeld's stars—W.C. Fields was performing upstairs in the *Frolic*, but still joined the union—but not in the same way. Bert Williams told Fields: "Do you know what happened to me the night of the strike, Pops? I went to the theater as usual, made up and dressed. Then I came out of my dressing room and found the stage deserted and dark, the big auditorium empty and the strike on. I knew nothing of it: I had not been told. You see, I just didn't belong." Williams took off his makeup, went home, closed the library door behind him, arranged some chairs in a semicircle, and had what he called the "Bert Williams Equity" meeting. "I held briefs for both sides, because, you see, I don't belong to either side." With Fields's support, Williams would eventually join Actors' Equity in 1920, but the *Follies of 1919* would be the last time he'd grace the stage for Ziegfeld.

George M. Cohan had no illusions about the theater of hard knocks either. Until the strike, actors had worshiped the legendary song-and-dance man, but Cohan's vehement opposition to the union caught everyone off guard. His beloved Friars and Lambs Clubs

OVERLEAF: A parade of stagehands and actors marching up Broadway to Columbus Circle during the strike, fall 1919.

Actors gather on the steps of the Actors' Equity Association, 1919.

snubbed him, so he resigned and vowed to fight Equity with every penny he had. He announced that if Equity won, he would quit the theater and run an elevator. Eddie Cantor responded, "Somebody better tell Mr. Cohan that to run an elevator he'd *have* to join a union." Even worse, the striking actors—clearly having the time of their lives, enjoying immense public support and the unspoken approval of the police—mocked Cohan with new lyrics to his beloved anthem "Over There":

> Over fair, over fair,
> We have been, we have been, over fair. . . .
> So beware, have a care,
> Just be fair, on the square, everywhere,
> For we are striking, yes, we are striking,
> And we won't come back till the managers are fair.

The striking actors put on vaudeville extravaganzas with the most famous names in show biz to benefit their cause; they marched in parades and created street theater to keep audiences from entering those PMA theaters that kept giving performances. Comedian Ed Wynn explained to a gathering crowd what he would have done onstage by performing his act then and there. The Equity strike was that rare thing: agitprop with gags. Soon, the strike spread, to other cities and other unions, but it wasn't until the musicians, stagehands, and electricians walked out in support that the producers agreed to recognize Actors' Equity as the legal bargaining agent for stage performers. The strike was over, one month after it began. Membership in Actors' Equity after the strike went from 2,700 to 14,000. Nine years later, Cantor would write, "Equity is now recognized by both sides as a monument to the growing dignity and stability of the American theater."

George M. Cohan continued to nurse a grudge. He eventually rejoined the Friars and Lambs Clubs, but still refused to join the union. Actors' Equity wasn't nearly so vindictive; it looked the other way, and so Cohan became the only actor ever to be allowed on the modern Broadway stage without an Equity card.

Finale

Most of the really good stories of the 1920s begin in 1919. It was a year in which the country itself would undergo cataclysmic change. America had become, in the wake of the Great War, the most powerful nation in the world; it would enact legislation to prohibit the manufacture, sale, and consumption of alcohol, give women the right to vote, and dedicate itself to stemming the tide of socialist politics, labor unions, and foreign immigration. The romance of the Harlem Renaissance would begin in February when the 369th Infantry, an all-black regiment from Harlem, marched triumphantly up Lenox Avenue to the beat of the ragtime marches of James Reese Europe. Millions of youngsters and their parents were devastated to learn that the World Series had been fixed.

In the New York theater, changes were emerging from every corner that year. One venerable show biz tradition, minstrelsy, was on its last legs, sustained by only a handful of entertainers; another, operetta, was in temporary eclipse. Still, the vaudeville stages across the country and across the city poured a seemingly endless stream of talent onto Broadway, and the revue form that Flo Ziegfeld had pioneered was poised to exploit that talent, exploding the stage with energy and invention. Producers were promoting their own newly minted stars, who would burst out of their featured status in revues to headline their own vehicles, slightly plotted shows full of song and dance, called "musical comedies." The *Follies of 1919* responded to the hunger of consumers for ever-increasing spectacle, while the Equity strike responded to the hunger of performers for better conditions. In the fall, a Ziegfeld dancer named George White would break away from the Great Glorifier and start his own revue, called the *Scandals*. The nonmusical theater began to create its own powerful American identity in 1919 as well. An avant-garde theater group in Greenwich Village, called the Provincetown Players, would produce short plays by a famous actor's young son, Eugene O'Neill. Another group of Village artists would move uptown, call themselves the Theatre Guild, and become Broadway's most prestigious producers.

By 1919, Jerome Kern was finished with the Princess Shows, and Irving Berlin had written a half dozen hits for the *Follies*. He also had the presence of mind to tell the rehearsal pianist for the 1918 *Follies* to break out on his own as a composer; by May of 1919, George Gershwin had written his first complete score for a Broadway show, *La, La, Lucille*. An aspiring composer-lyricist with only a 1916 flop to his name returned from Paris to write a revue called *Hitchy-Koo of 1919*; it gave Cole Porter his first hit song. And in July 1919, a seventeen-year-old composer named Richard Rodgers teamed up with twenty-four-year-old lyricist, Lorenz Hart, and had their first song placed in a Broadway show. "Any Old Place with You," from *A Lonely Romeo*, was a typical song of the period in which the hero declared his devotion to his leading lady, but one couplet ran:

> I'd go to Hell for ya,
> Or Philadelphia,
> Any old place with you.

The lyric was nothing to write home about, but it had a kind of confident pugnacity that dared the listener not to admire its cleverness. The song was a perfect overture for a decade that would dare audiences to be as clever, as fresh, and as young as the astonishing battery of songwriters that would rhapsodize the bright, noisy, whirling playground called Broadway to the rest of the world.

THE COMIC SIDE OF TROUBLE
By BERT WILLIAMS

American Magazine (excerpt), January 1918

ONE OF THE FUNNIEST SIGHTS in the world is a man whose hat has been knocked in or ruined by being blown off—provided, of course, it be the other fellow's hat! All the jokes in the world are based on a few elemental ideas, and this is one of them. The sight of other people in trouble is nearly always funny. This is human nature. The man with the real sense of humor is the man who can put himself in the spectator's place and laugh at his own misfortunes.

That is what I am called upon to do every day. Nearly all of my successful songs have been based on the idea that I am getting the worst of it. I am the "Jonah Man," the man who, even if it rained soup, would be found with a fork in his hand and no spoon in sight, the man whose fighting relatives come to visit him and whose head is always dented by the furniture they throw at each other. There are endless variations of this idea, fortunately; but if you sift them, you will find the principle of human nature at the bottom of them all.

Troubles are funny only when you pin them to one particular individual. And that individual, the fellow who is the goat, must be the man who is singing the song or telling the misfortunes, fielding flatirons with his head, carrying large bulldogs by the seat of his pants, and picking the bare bones of the chicken while his wife's relations eat the breast, and so forth.

It was not until I was able to see myself as another person that my sense of humor developed. For I do not believe there is any such thing as innate humor. It has to be developed by hard work and study, just as every other human quality. I have studied it all my life, unconsciously during my floundering years, and consciously as soon as I began to get next to myself. It is a study that I shall never get to the end of, and a work that never stops, except when I am asleep. There are no union hours to it and no let-up. It is only by being constantly on the lookout for fresh material, funny incidents, funny speeches, funny traits in human nature that a comedian can hope to keep step with his public.

I find much material by knocking around in out of the way places and just listening. For among the American colored men and negroes there is the greatest source of simple amusement you can find anywhere in the world. But Americans for the most part know little about the unconscious humor of the colored people and negroes, because they do not come in contact with them. A short while ago I heard an argument between two men. One of them was pretty cocky and tried to bulldoze the other, who was trying his best to be peaceable, and kept saying, "I don't want no trouble with you now." Presently it got too warm for him, and the peaceable man turned to the other and said, "Looka hyah, nigga, you better get away fum me, 'cause I'm jes' going to take this bottle an' bathe your head with it." Of course I put that line into the *Follies* the next day.

Every comedian at some time in his life learns to curse the particular stunt of his that was most popular. Before I got through with "Nobody" I could have wished that both the author of the words and the assembler of the tune had been strangled or drowned or talked to death. For seven whole years I had to sing it. Month after month I tried to drop it and sing something new, but I could get nothing to replace it, and the audiences seemed to want nothing else.

In picking a song I always consider the words. I should feel sorry for a song that depended on its tune if I had to sing it! I study carefully the acoustics of each theater I appear in. There is always one particular spot on the stage from which the voice carries better, more clearly and easily than from any other. I make it my business to find that spot before the first performance, and once I find it I stick to it like a postage stamp. People have sometimes observed that I practice unusual economy of motion and do not move about as much as other singers do. It is to spare my voice and not my legs that I stand still while delivering a song. If my voice were stronger I would be as active as anybody, because it is much easier to put a song over if you can move about.

I hope nothing I have said will be mistaken to mean that I think I have found a recipe for making people laugh, or anything of that sort. The man who could find that recipe would be bigger than Klaw and Erlanger and the Shuberts put together. Humor is the one thing in the world that it is impossible to argue about, because it is all a matter of taste. If I could turn myself into a human boomerang: if I could jump from the stage, fly out over the audience, turn a couple of somersaults in the air, snatch the toupee from the head of the bald man in the front row of the balcony, and light back on the stage in the spot I jumped from, I could have the world at my feet—for a while. But even then I would always have to be finding something new.

People sometimes ask me if I would not give anything to be white. I answer, in the words of the song, most emphatically, "No." How do I know what I might be if I were a white man? I might be a sand-hog, burrowing away and losing my health for eight dollars a day. I might be a street-car conductor at twelve or fifteen dollars a week. There is many a white man less fortunate and less well equipped than I am. In truth, I have never been able to discover that there was anything disgraceful in being a colored man. But I have often found it inconvenient—in America.

Frankly, I can't understand what it is all about. I breathe like other people, eat like them—if you put me at a dinner table you can be reasonably sure that I won't use the ice cream fork for my salad; I think like other people. I guess the whole trouble must be that I don't look like them. They say it is a matter of race prejudice. But if it were prejudice a baby would have it, and you will never find it in a baby. It has to be inculcated on people. For one thing, I have noticed that this "race prejudice" is not to be found in people who are sure enough of their position to be able to defy it. For example, the kindest, most courteous, most democratic man I ever met was the King of England, the late King Edward VII. I shall never forget how frightened I was before the first time I sang for him. I kept thinking of his position, his dignity, his titles: King of Great Britain and Ireland, Emperor of India, and half a page more of them, and my knees knocked together and the sweat stood out on my forehead. And I found—the easiest, most responsive, most appreciative audience any artist could wish.

Each time I come back to America this thing they call race prejudice follows me wherever I go. When Mr. Ziegfeld first proposed to engage me for the *Follies* there was a tremendous storm in a teacup. Everybody threatened to leave; they proposed to get up a boycott if he persisted; they said all sorts of things against my personal character. But Mr. Ziegfeld stuck to his guns and was quite undisturbed by everything that was said. Which is one reason why I am with him now, although I could make twice the salary in vaudeville. There never has been any contract between us, just a gentlemen's agreement. I always get on perfectly with everybody in the company by being polite and friendly but keeping my distance. Meanwhile I am lucky enough to have real friends, people who are sure enough of themselves not to need to care what their brain-

less and envious rivals will say if they happen to be seen walking along the street with me. And I have acquired enough philosophy to protect me against the things which would cause me humiliation and grief if I had not learned independence.

It was not people in the company, I since discovered, but outsiders who were making use of that line of talk for petty personal purposes.

Meanwhile, I have no grievance whatsoever against the world or the people in it: I'm having a grand time. I am what I am, not because of what I am but in spite of it.

STEPHEN SONDHEIM ON JEROME KERN

Liner notes for The Columbia Album of Jerome Kern *(excerpt), 1971.*

IT IS DANGEROUS, and perhaps foolhardy, to try to pin down in words the qualities of musical style, since the essence of music is that it is an abstract and therefore highly personal expression. If music could be described in language, there would be no need for it. But in trying to pursue the style of a composer, we may come closer to a common understanding of his art and its meaning. The "style" is the composer's personality come to fruition; it is what differentiates him from all others, like a face or a way of speaking or a nervous habit. The leading, and only the leading, American theater-composers (by whom I mean writers of integrated scores rather than individual and unconnected songs) such as Jerome Kern, George Gershwin, Richard Rodgers, and Cole Porter, have "styles"—their songs are more often than not recognizable immediately as *theirs* and no other composer's. Their imitators as well as their competitors cannot duplicate all the earmarks, hallmarks, trademarks and other marks which go in to the making of their styles.

For instance, the most striking characteristic of Gershwin's songs is their harmonic decoration and (in the faster ones) their rhythmic drive. In Rodgers' music, "deceptive simplicity" (in *Time* magazine's phrase) is the trademark—sudden surprising shifts of spare block harmonies under essentially diatonic, often repeated note melodies with occasional unexpected chromatic leaps. The

ARCHIVES

impressive feature of Porter's songs is their "sophistica-tion"—the frequent use of Latin-American rhythms, the lush chromatic harmony, and the lengthy extensions of standard chorus forms (as in *Night and Day* and *Begin the Beguine*, the two longest and most famous examples).

The style of Kern's songs is subtler and far more elusive to trap in words. Is it the simple diatonic structure of their melodies? But Rodgers's melodies are just as simple and diatonic, for the most part. The high standards of Kern's craftsmanship in construction? Gershwin's standards were just as high and just as well met. Kern's long fluid vocal lines? Porter's are just as long.

Still, a Kern song is almost always recognizable, even to the untrained ear. It has a "feel," a "sound" that is distinct and unique. The melody has an enduring freshness. The harmony is usually simple and not very inventive or event-ful, yet graceful and clear and full of air. The melodic rhythm is perhaps the strongest point—a direct and simple motif developed through tiny variations into a long and never boring line. There are few syncopations in a Kern melody and when they occur, they are of the most elemen-tal sort. And yet a Kern line is seldom dull. Each phrase grows out of the preceding one—Kern knew the technique of small-form composition so well that, like any trained composer, he was able to utilize it unconsciously. All of his best songs have that economy indigenous to the best art: the maximum development of the minimum of material.

Antoine de St. Exupéry pointed out in "Wind, Sand, and Stars" that the history of the airplane from Kitty Hawk on was the gradual development of its shape into a cigar. The more knowledge gained, the more additions required, the more flexibility, versatility, refinement, the simpler the shape. Complexity leads paradoxically to simplicity. And this hard-won simplicity is, I think the keynote of Jerome Kern's style. His melodies are as smooth, rounded, stream-lined, simplified and undecorated as a cigar. The price of the cigar may vary as the quality of his inspiration may change, but his inferior work has the same cigarlike perfection as his best. (And what this country needs is a good five-cent song.)

In his introduction to *The Jerome Kern Song Book,* Oscar Hammerstein II points this out:

His smooth and effortless melodies . . . are the result of unstinting and meticulous work. . . . [Kern] was a worker who would never stop polishing until he was satisfied that a melody had reached its destined and perfect shape. . . . I have seen him struggling hours over a modulation. . . . Smoothness is achieved only by scraping off roughness.*

This smoothness, this cigar-shape economy, is what identifies a Kern song. It is true simplicity, not the "simplic-ity" of the familiar, of the tunes which you whistle going into the theater, but the simplicity of a fresh musical thought spun out and transfigured into a rounded and complete form. It's easy to believe that Kern, as Oscar Hammerstein noted, struggled for "hours over a modulation," because his modulations are so uncomplicated. Even the more unusual transitions (like the ends of the releases of "The Song Is You" and "All the Things You Are") are simple enharmonic relationships.

Kern's music over the years probably changed less than the music of most other American composers. He has less variety, in the usual sense, than Gershwin or Porter or Rodgers. The types of songs he wrote remained, through-out his career, essentially the same. The melodies vary (Kern steals from himself less than any of his peers) but they are always cut from the same cloth. There's an almost symphonic homogeneity of style, as if all his motifs and melodies had been taken from one enormous melodic line, one endless song.

As with all good music, no matter how large or small, subtleties begin to shine through the second time around, and new ones appear the third, fifth, tenth and fiftieth times. That is why no American songwriter has written so many standards as Kern. Small and simple and subtle as they are, his songs stand up under countless rehearings. And this is also why Kern's music survives the fads of American popu-lar taste—from "jazz" (musical comedy style) to rock-and-roll. His music deals with the essentials, not the decoration. And the essentials are timeless.

The Jerome Kern Song Book, edited by Oscar Hammerstein II. Copyright 1955 by Simon and Schuster, Inc. This and all other quota-tions are used by kind permission of the author and publishers.

WHENCE THE SONG
By THEODORE DREISER

The Color of a Great City *(excerpt), 1923*

Dreiser's brother was Paul Dresser, a songwriter with such hits as "On the Banks of the Wabash" and "My Gal Sue" to his credit.

ALONG BROADWAY in the height of the theatrical season, but more particularly in that laggard time from June to September, when the great city is given over to those who may not travel, and to actors seeking engagements, there is ever to be seen a representative figure, now one individual and now another, of a world so singular that it might well engage the pen of a Balzac or that of a Cervantes. I have in mind an individual whose high hat and smooth Prince Albert coat are still a delicious presence. In his coat lapel is a ruddy boutonnière, in his hand a novel walking-stick. His vest is of a gorgeous and affluent pattern, his shoes shiny-new and topped with pearl-gray spats. With dignity he carries his body and his chin. He is the cynosure of many eyes, the envy of all men, and he knows it. He is the successful author of the latest popular song.

Along Broadway, from Union to Greeley Squares, any fair day during the period of his artistic elevation, he is to be seen. . . .Well-known variety stars nod to him familiarly. Women whose sole claim to distinction lies in their knack of singing a song, smile in greeting as he passes. Occasionally there comes a figure of a needy ballad-monger, trudging from publisher to publisher with an unavailable manuscript, who turns upon him, in passing, the glint of an envious glance. To these he is an important figure, satisfied as much with their envy as with their praise, for is not this also his due, the reward of all who have triumphed?

In Twenty-seventh or Twenty-eight Street, or anywhere along Broadway from Madison to Greeley Squares, are the parlors of a score of publishers, gentlemen who coordinate this divided world for song publishing purposes. There is an office and a reception-room; a music-chamber, where songs are tried; and a stock room. Perhaps, in the case of the larger publishers, the music-rooms are two or three, but the air of each is much the same. The walls are hung with the photos of celebrities, neatly framed, celebrities of the kind described. A boy or two waits to bring *pro-fessional* copies at a word. A salaried pianist or two wait to run over pieces which the singer may desire to hear. Arrangers wait to make orchestrations or take down newly schemed out melodies which the popular composer himself cannot play. He has evolved the melody by a process of whistling and must have its fleeting beauty registered before it escapes him forever.

For the time being, then, this little center of song-writing and publishing is for him the all-inclusive of life's importance. From the street organs at every corner is being ground the one melody, so expressive of his personality, into the ears of all men. In the vaudeville houses and cheaper concert halls men and women are singing it nightly to uproarious applause. Parodies are made and catch-phrases coined, all speaking of his work. Newsboys whistle and older men pipe its peculiar notes. Out of open windows falls the distinguished melody, accompanied by voices both new and strange. All men seem to recognize that which he has done, and for the time being compliment his presence and his personality.

Then the wane.

Of all the tragedies, this is perhaps the bitterest, because of the long-drawn memory of the thing. Organs continue to play it, but the sale ceases. Quarter after quarter, the royalties are less, until at last a few dollars per month will measure them completely. Meanwhile his publishers ask for other songs. One he writes, and then another, and yet another, vainly endeavoring to duplicate that original note which made for all his splendid success the year before. But it will not come. And, in the meanwhile, other song-writers displace him for the time being in the public eye. His publishers have a new hit, but it is not his. A new author is being bowed to and taken out to dinner. But he is not that author. A new tile-crowned celebrity is strolling up his favorite Broadway path. At last, after a dozen attempts and failures, there is no hurry to publish his songs. You may see the doubles of these in any publisher's sanctum at any time, the sarcastically referred-to *has been*.

It seems strange, really, that so many of them should have come to this. And yet it is true—authors, singers, publishers, even—and yet not more strange is it than that their little feeling, worked into a melody and a set of words, should reach far out over land and water, touching the hearts of the nation.

CHAPTER TWO

SYNCOPATED CITY

(1 9 2 0 – 1 9 3 0)

Overture

Al Jolson, among his many other attributes, was the most restless man in show business. His nonstop energy gave patrons a show and a half; offstage, he could be even harder to contain. Once, claiming he needed a vacation, he took one of his pals, a former ukulele player whom he had brought to New York, a lyricist named Buddy DeSylva, to Atlantic City. After a few days in a deck chair, Jolson had had enough: "I'm just tired of looking at the Atlantic. Let's go to California where I can get a glimpse at the Pacific," he said, and off they went. Even in his off-hours, Jolson was always on, holding court at theatrical restaurants, cracking jokes, picking up the tab, surrounded by cronies, acolytes, and yes-men. One evening in the fall of 1919, he was dragged to a party by DeSylva, who wanted Jolson to hear an up-and-coming songwriter with whom he'd just written a show.

George Gershwin was almost as restless as Jolson. He had spent the preceding year as the rehearsal accompanist for the *Ziegfeld Follies,* had placed several songs in two Broadway shows, had written a full-length score with lyrics by DeSylva in May, and was preparing another show for December. Gershwin and lyricist Irving Caesar had also written a song in 1918 that was finally being performed nightly as a movie lead-in at the Capitol Theatre on Broadway and 51st Street. "Swanee" was a jaunty tune in the minstrel tradition, put across by sixty chorus girls, dancing in the dark with electric lights on their tap shoes. The song itself, however, failed to light up any interest along Tin Pan Alley.

PAGE 64: *The phrase "Great White Way" was reportedly coined by public relations maverick O.J. Gude in 1901. In this photo of Broadway and 46th Street, c. 1925, trolley tracks can be seen as well as a glimpse of the Capitol Theatre in the distance.*

Al Jolson (second from right) clowning with friends, including George Gershwin, right.

OPPOSITE: *Jolson on bended knee, performing "Swanee."*

The spectacle of Jolson's vitality had the same quality as the impression I got from the New York skyline—one had forgotten that there still existed in the world a force so boundless, an exaltation so high, and that anyone could still storm Heaven with laughter and cheers.

—Gilbert Seldes, 1926

Then again, the show at the Capitol didn't have the piano virtuosity of Gershwin himself to deliver the number. When Jolson heard Gershwin's rendition of "Swanee" at the party, he knew he had to have the song as his own. How could he resist lyrics that included:

> I know my mammy's
> Waiting for me, praying for me,
> Down by the Swanee.

Jolson immediately stuck the song into his touring version of *Sinbad*, and in January 1920 he recorded the number. It became a hit beyond anyone's wildest expectations, selling more than a million copies of sheet music—Jolson's face adorning the cover—and even more remarkably, 2 million gramophone recordings. The song would become the biggest hit of Gershwin's entire career—even bigger than the remarkable collaborations with his lyricist brother, Ira. Jolson's performance was one that viewers would remember for years. Critic Gilbert Seldes recalled: "Hearing [Jolson] sing 'Swanee' is what book reviewers and young girls loosely call an experience. I know what Jolson does with false sentiment; here he was dealing with something which by the grace of George Gershwin came true."

This, then, was the overture to the '20s. A minstrel song, a remnant of a dying performance style, would be reinvigorated by a Jewish boy from the Lower East Side and put across the footlights nightly by a Russian-born Jew pretending to be a black man. Cultural boundaries were shifting all over Manhattan. Jewish musical traditions from the Lower East Side and a brand-new kind of music coming from uptown in Harlem would collide at the corner of 42nd and Broadway. The explosion could be heard across the country. Gershwin would go on to reinvent the musical language of Broadway, and Jolson would ride the crest of his fame through the Crash at the end of the decade, becoming the first American superstar of the mechanical age. New York City would become, in Prohibition parlance, an "open town": open to lax enforcement of the drinking laws, open to gangsters and their easy money, but, more than that, open to the innumerable pleasures and possibilities of the Jazz Age.

"Hello, suckers!"

PROHIBITION AND NEW YORK NIGHTLIFE

The bar at the Savoy ballroom in Harlem:

In the 1920s, everyone had permission to visit each other's lands and see what they were doing. There was this period in which everybody was leaping across borders and boundaries with complicated results. You had people who said, "There's an energy source. Let me go explore that."

—George C. Wolfe, Director

At midnight on January 16, 1920, New York City officially went dry. The state's adoption of the Volstead Act meant that it was illegal to sell or transport beverages with more than one-half of one percent of alcohol. Although Prohibition brought mock funerals for John Barleycorn all over Manhattan, it had very little effect on Broadway. Shows might make fun of Prohibition, but certainly no musical was ever closed because of it. A new species of entertainment called the speakeasy proliferated, but most of those were in the West 50s, somewhat removed from the Theater District (although speakeasies did provide figures of

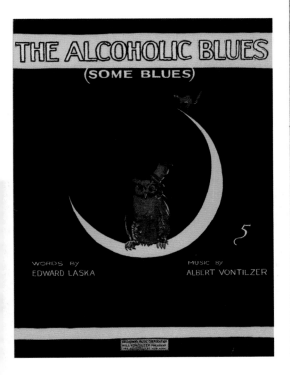
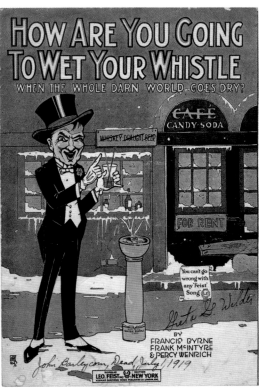
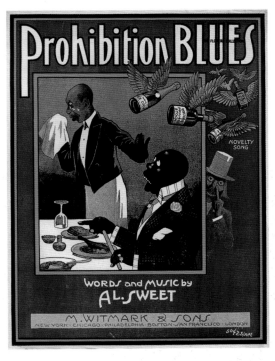

Popular songs cried the blues over the prohibition of alcohol.

fun such as Texas Guinan, hostess of the El Fay Club, who was gently parodied in several 1920s musicals). Harlem, where liquor could be more easily purchased in effervescent night-clubs owned by white mobsters, became a new center for singing and dancing entertainment. As the decade wore on, Harlem was able to incubate talented performers who would eventually find a venue downtown on Broadway.

If anything, Prohibition allowed Manhattan nightlife to flourish. Shows began much later in the 1920s—the curtain went up around 8:45 most evenings—and were often just a prelude to nightclubs, supper clubs, and speakeasies. Mayor James Walker, known to be available for a good time himself, was so worried about the effect of partygoing on his citizens' workday that he insisted something be done; he asked the clubs to close their doors by three in the morning.

The Broadway musical was still the main event for a night on the town, and the decade saw an exponential increase in the number of shows, with the highest number in history—264 plays and musicals—debuting in the 1927–28 season. In the West 40s, a building boom sprang up to house the sheer volume of this product: almost twenty new theaters were constructed in the Theater District. American dramatic playwrights had finally found their voice, but the ebullient energy of the musical is what dominated the age. Now there were more stars, more producers, more songwriters and, most crucially, more backers with ready money than the American theater had ever seen, or would ever see again. All those forces would combine to create the decade that defined Broadway for the rest of the world.

Posterity has not been particularly kind toward Al Jolson, which is a shame, because no one ever worked harder to make the public happy. Between the blackface that makes him anathema to today's public—so much so that many of his performances are simply deleted from films if and when they are shown at all on television today—and his over-the-top style that now seems downright garish in the medium of sound film which he made famous, it is difficult to imagine how transcendently popular Jolson was. Not only did he bestride the theatrical runway of the 1920s like an eight-cylinder Colossus, he was the decade's most ubiquitous superstar. And not only was he a superstar, he was the first to behave like one, making his private life public, throwing tantrums, using his huge paychecks to purchase an entourage, a racehorse, and all the other perquisites of stardom.

The origins of the man who would be billed as "The World's Greatest Entertainer" could not have been humbler. He was born Asa Yoelson in Srednik, Russia in 1886, the son of an itinerant cantor who sent for his family in 1894 after he settled himself in Washington, D.C. Asa came to this country in 1904 and, along with his older brother Harry, faced a hardscrabble existence as their father tried furiously to make ends meet in the capital's meager Jewish community. That same year, Jolson endured the first shock of his young life when his mother died unexpectedly. It traumatized him and, in many ways, the emotional journey of his life can be seen as a relentless quest for love—from his departed mother, from his wives, but most voraciously, from his audience.

When his overbearing father wasn't watching, Jolson and his brother danced and sang popular songs for pennies in front of Washington hotels. The lure of show biz was too great and at the age of eleven, Jolson did what many boys dream of, but few accomplish: he ran away and joined the circus. As he got older, he adopted blackface as a way of relating more easily to an audience (legend is obscure as to how and when) and the convention suited him well; soon, he was part of Lew Dockstader's Minstrels, touring the country in one of America's last, but most popular, minstrel troupes. During a summer layover in 1909, he was booked into Hammerstein's Victoria Theatre, the crown jewel of the vaudeville stage at the time, and became an immediate sensation.

When the Shubert Brothers built their commodious Winter Garden Theatre at 52nd and Broadway in 1911, they selected Jolson to appear in its opening production, *La Belle Paree*. The story goes that audiences were cool to Jolson in the first few performances, so, throwing off the constraints of his blocking and character, he appealed to the crowd directly: "What's the

OPPOSITE: *Jolson, as a contemporary valet sent back in time to the world of the Arabian Nights in* Sinbad, *1918. The show included songs such as "Rock-A-Bye Your Baby" and "Swanee."*

Variety *was known as the bible of show business and Jolson devoured it, chapter and verse.*

Jolson applying blackface. Jolson's blackface also disguised a neurotically tortured offstage personality; when other acts were on, getting laughs, he would run the faucets of his dressing room sink to drown them out.

matter, you come into this classy joint, you think you shouldn't have a good time?" When it came to his first Broadway audience, to paraphrase one of the songs he popularized, he made them love him. So began an unprecedented string of successes for Jolson, often at the Winter Garden, usually in the employ of the Shuberts, nine consecutive hit shows from 1911 to 1926.

By 1922, he was earning $10,000 a week from his salary, a percentage of the gross, and his recordings combined—more than any entertainer ever had. Jolson might have also been the first to qualify as "the hardest-working man in show business." In addition to his Broadway smashes, he toured his productions enthusiastically around the country, and at a time when Sunday performances were against the law in New York City, he gave special one-man "recitals" at the Winter Garden on his Sunday nights off; he often sang more than thirty songs in these programs. In most of the Winter Garden shows, he played the role of Gus, a wily servant in blackface, always quicker and smarter than his master. No matter if Gus was placed on an island with Robinson Crusoe (*Robinson Crusoe, Jr.*, 1916), or on the *Santa Maria* with Columbus (*Bombo*, 1921), he always found a way to sing about his mammy or the South, from the Mason-Dixon line ("Rock-A-Bye Your Baby with a Dixie Melody") to the Gulf ("Miami"). Anyone eager to point out these wild inconsistencies had bought a ticket to the wrong show.

Jolson's devotion to blackface was religious. He carried the convention into the '20s, when other artists such as Eddie Cantor had either dropped or minimized their use of it, and would have eagerly continued it into the 1930s (he famously wanted to play Porgy in *Porgy and Bess*). To watch him assiduously apply burnt cork to his features was like intruding on an Orthodox Jewish ritual. When one considers that those rituals include covering up and washing off, one approaches culturally complicated territory, but Jolson's Jewishness—he never pretended he was anything but—and his onstage blackness merged into something larger, and more complex, than its two parts.

> **Here's this Lithuanian Jew from the shtetl singing about [his] homeland in Dixie and [his] lost mother. Well, of course the lost mother was very real to him, but the homeland was a homeland of the mind, a place where his sadness would be healed. Jolson never would have done that on his own, in his own persona—but hiding behind the black mask he could go there and audiences were intensely moved.**
> **—Stephen Mo Hanan,** Performer, *Jolson & Company*

Sentimentality was key to the Jolson alchemy. When he was in Hollywood filming *The Singing Fool* in 1928, he telephoned his "house" composers, DeSylva, Brown, and Henderson, in New York and asked for a new song for the picture: "Listen, fellas, it's gotta tear the hearts outta the people." As a gag, the team crafted the most sentimental bilge they could, called "Sonny Boy." Lew Brown sang it to Jolson over the phone. Jolson was crying so much he couldn't talk—it was exactly what he wanted. When Eddie Cantor went to see *The Singing Fool*, two women in front of him were bawling—as was the rest of the audience—when Jolson sang the number. Suddenly one stopped, turned to her friend, and said, "What are we crying about? Here he is, married to beautiful Ruby Keeler, they're on their honeymoon, he's got fame, fortune, and love—and we're killing ourselves crying!"

His fame was so vast that he would repeatedly demand a colyricist credit on many of the songs he performed. Eager young songwriters were happy to share the royalty with him, just to be associated with Jolson. Few of the major songwriters of the 1920s worked with him directly, however. Berlin seems to have politely disdained him, Kern (with

Jolson as Gus in Robinson Crusoe, Jr. *(1916), which included the inevitable song, "Where Did Robinson Crusoe Go with Friday on Saturday Night?"*

lyricist Edward Madden) wrote him one song—"Paris is a Paradise for Coons"—for his Broadway debut, Gershwin never really wrote for him, and when Rodgers and Hart wrote an original movie score for him, *Hallelujah, I'm a Bum* (1933), his career was tapering off.

When Jolson knelt down on the Winter Garden runway to sing his tailor-made rhapsodies to the South and flung his arms wide open, he didn't leave much elbow room for anyone else. If any performer was ever "larger than life," it was Jolson; by the end of the decade, that wouldn't be just a metaphor.

INTRODUCE MYSELF to you as New York's most notorious gossip, in case you have never read my drivel in the *Daily Mirror* or the other papers with which I've been associated. I'm the Peek's Blab Boy who turns the Broadway dirt and mud into gold." When Walter Winchell first met radio audiences as the host of his own fifteen-minute program ("Saks Broadway with Walter Winchell") in May 1930, he had already been the unofficial voice of Broadway for six years, popularizing its quotidian myths and legends in his column, "Your Broadway and Mine." What radio eventually gave him was a national audience, a chance to extol Broadway over the airwaves as a mythical kingdom of imperious producers, spoiled actresses, gifted songwriters, bright lights, and broken hearts. Now you could sit in your living room in Appleton, Wisconsin, and feel like you had house seats to opening night at the Music Box Theatre.

The 1920s saw the advent of three major technologies that would not only influence the quality of American domestic life but reconstruct the entire edifice of show business: broadcast radio, electronic sound reproduction, and talking pictures. In 1920, two radio stations sprang up, carrying snippets of the news, and by 1926, the National Broadcast Company, operating out of New York City, aired the first national broadcast, a variety show that was carried by two dozen affiliate stations across the country. By the end of the decade, 40 percent of all Americans had radio consoles in their homes; not surprisingly, the number reached 58 percent of households in New York City. The sound of America had completely changed.

What Americans listened to most of all was music. Almost three-quarters of radio programming was devoted to music, much of it classical, but popular songs were making tremendous inroads over the air waves. In the 1920s, practically every major urban hotel had a dance band in its ballroom, and live broadcasts were extremely popular, turning bandleaders such as Paul Whiteman and Fred Waring into overnight celebrities. As jazz became more popular, performances were broadcast from Harlem's Cotton Club and other hot spots. Large sections of America were listening to black performers—without necessarily being aware of the musicians' race—for the very first time. Of course, jazz and show tunes proved to be the fount of popular broadcast music.

Radio delivered the young century's second uppercut to the Tin Pan Alley music publishing business. Gramophone recordings had severely undermined the sales of sheet music in the late 1910s, and by 1920, a publisher considered himself lucky if a song sold a hundred thousand copies of sheet music. However, the firms in Tin Pan Alley, in conjunction with ASCAP, realized there was royalty money to be made in the recording industry, and their fortunes began to rally in the early 1920s. Just then, however, radio cut into gramophone recordings as well; listeners were disenchanted with the tinny sound provided by acoustic recording and record purchases slumped drastically. But, by 1925, advances in electronic sound recording allowed studios to capture their recording artists with better range and fidelity. Sales began to pick up, and recording companies such as Victor realized that the radio could be more friend than foe. Rather than squeeze out the popularity of a recording, if artfully promoted, radio could enhance the exposure of an artist or a song. Thus began the recording industry's long (and often complicated) affair with the broadcast media. "The music you want when you want it," trumpeted the recording industry.

Outside of the odd novelty song (and some were *very* odd), the music that people wanted was largely from Broadway. For example, in 1927, out of the top ten songs played on the radio, five were from Broadway shows: "Blue Skies," "Hallelujah," "Ol' Man River," "S'Wonderful," and "The Varsity Drag." Two others, "Me and My Shadow" and "Russian Lullaby," were by Broadway composers. The songs were usually performed, or "covered," by popular bands or crooners rather than by original cast members. Many Broadway songs were rescued from obscurity by radio performers. Irving Berlin's "Say It Isn't So" languished until collegiate idol Rudy Vallee sang it repeatedly on his show. The traffic could go the other way as well: Walter Donaldson and George Whiting's "My Blue Heaven" was such a big radio hit that Eddie Cantor used it in the *Ziegfeld Follies of 1927*. When their songs weren't filling the airwaves, the songwriters were themselves: Rodgers and Hart, Sigmund Romberg, and most successfully George Gershwin (promoting Feen-a-Mint laxatives) hosted their own radio programs.

But the voice that meant "Broadway" for Mr. and Mrs. North America was Walter Winchell's. Winchell, born in 1897 and raised in Harlem in a poor Jewish family, climbed up the ladder as a kid entertainer and, later, a hoofer in vaudeville. Show business ran so thick in his blood, it's a wonder there was any room left for hemoglobin. His Broadway column (originally in the tabloid *Evening Graphic*) doled out gossip, predictions, homilies, picks, and pans in a staccato burst, often with items separated by ellipses. As a reviewer, he was a mediocre writer (although he was banned by the Shuberts for a while and had to watch the opening of *Animal Crackers* from the wings, after being sneaked through the stage door disguised as Harpo Marx), but as a chronicler of his age, he was peerless.

Winchell's streetcorner neologisms are legendary: sex was "making whoopee," pregnancy was "infanticipating," booze was "giggle water," wives were the "ball and chain," and divorcing couples were being "Reno-vated." But he saved his linguistic passion for Broadway, which he called "the slang capital of the world." He created, used, or cited from Sime Silverstein's *Variety* magazine such theatrical expressions as "hit," "flop," "turkey," and "wow" (as a verb), and starlets had to have "S.A." (sex appeal) in order to "pay off at the gate." His beat was immortalized as "The Main Stem," "The Hardened Artery," "Baloney Boulevard," or most famously, "The Big Apple: the goal of all ambitions, the pot of gold at the end of a drab and somewhat colorless rainbow . . ."

Eventually, Winchell saw himself as a kingmaker and delved into politics and gangbusting with embarrassing results; he made the fatal mistake of believing his own publicity. But in the 1920s in print and throughout the 1930s on radio, there was no one like him.

Broadway gave him the dubious honor of basing characters in at least three musical comedies on him: Wally Winston (who "Knows All, Sees All, Tells All" for the *Traffic*) in *Animal Crackers* (1928); Max Mencken in *It's a Bird, It's a Plane, It's Superman* (1966), where he is driven half-insane by Superman's superior publicity; and as J.J. Hunsecker in *Sweet Smell of Success* (2002), a musical adaptation of the classic 1957 film. All three versions give the Winchell character a chance to show off his soft-shoe technique. "Did you ever know I used to be a hoofer?" asks Max Mencken of Lois Lane. "You killed vaudeville, Max," she responds. "Can't you leave journalism alone?" Had the line been about anybody else, Winchell would have found it screamingly funny.

Walter Winchell, broadcasting his scoops.

"Say it with music"

THE RISE OF THE REVUE

Nothing on Broadway catered to Manhattan nightlife like the revue. During the Roaring '20s, nearly 120 revues opened on Broadway. Their flash, color, topicality, and brazenness caught the spirit of the age, and they had their conveniences, too: unlike later musical comedies, you could miss the first act and it wouldn't make any difference. Revues could be assembled easily, and there was always room for an additional investor, whether it was a newly wealthy Wall Street broker with a crush on a showgirl or a bootlegging gangster who wanted to see his moll installed at the end of a chorus line.

What the revue also provided in abundance was opportunity. It offered songwriters so many chances to get a number placed in a show that the revue became the greatest conservatory for popular music the country has ever seen. The question often arises, "Why did so many great songwriters pop up in New York in the 1920s?" The answer may be simply that there were so many shows in which they could pop. Composer Arthur Schwartz and lyricist Howard Dietz gave America some of its most memorable songs during this period: "Dancing in the

George White and his "Scandal"ous chorines.

Dark," "Alone Together," "Something to Remember You By." All went into revues, a genre they mastered, yet they failed to have any successful shows in the musical comedy format. Without the revue as a springboard for their talents, the Gershwins, Rodgers and Hart, and DeSylva, Brown, and Henderson might have found their road to fame infinitely more arduous or downright impossible.

Here, then, is a scorecard for the more important revues of the period, excepting the *Ziegfeld Follies*, which are in a category all their own.

ON THE LEVEL YOU'RE A LITTLE DEVIL
(BUT I'LL SOON MAKE AN ANGEL OF YOU)
WORDS BY JOE YOUNG MUSIC BY JEAN SCHWARTZ

DOROTHY L. DODSON

AS SUNG IN
The WINTER GARDEN
PASSING SHOW OF 1918

THE PASSING SHOW

The Shubert Brothers began producing their own annual revues at the Winter Garden in 1912, out of sheer spite for Ziegfeld's success. The thirteen editions were distinguished largely by their lack of distinction. The comedy end of things was frequently held down by the Jewish comedy team of Willie and Eugene Howard, while stars launched by the *Passing Shows* included the Astaires, Fred Allen, and chorus girl Lucille LeSueur—the future Joan Crawford.

GEORGE WHITE'S SCANDALS

Hoofer White irked his former employer Florenz Ziegfeld no end when he broke away from the *Follies* in 1919 to start his own revue. White's sharp eye for sleek design and emerging hot talent made his *Scandals* the only real rival to the Master's productions. He had the novel idea of using only one composer for each of his thirteen editions, and his particular passion for the latest dance craze allowed his leading dancer, Ann Pennington—whom he lured from the *Follies*—to introduce several popular new steps to Broadway. Stars such as Helen Morgan, Ethel Merman, and Ray Bolger were given a huge stepping stone from White.

THE MUSIC BOX REVUE

Irving Berlin got into the producing game in 1921 by joining with producer Sam Harris to build the jewel-like Music Box Theatre as a showcase for his newest tunes. Before he and Harris tired of mounting an annual edition every season until 1924, Berlin placed such timeless songs as "Say It with Music," "What'll I Do?," and "All Alone" in his revues, which also featured sketches by such prized humorists as Robert Benchley and George S. Kaufman.

EARL CARROLL VANITIES

Anyone who wondered where producer Earl Carroll's passions lay had only to glimpse one of his innumerable voluptuous tableaux, with dozens of sexy women draped all over the set wearing as little as possible. Carroll tweaked Ziegfeld by placing a sign over his stage door that read "Thru These Portals Pass the Most Beautiful Girls in the World." His shows favored raciness over sophistication, and his comedians included Sophie Tucker, Jack Benny, and Milton Berle. Throughout his nine editions, the most interesting thing Carroll ever did was to get arrested in 1926 when, in one number, a girl was bathing nude in a tub filled with champagne. It wasn't the nudity that annoyed authorities; Carroll was indicted for perjury when he falsely claimed the tub was filled with ginger ale.

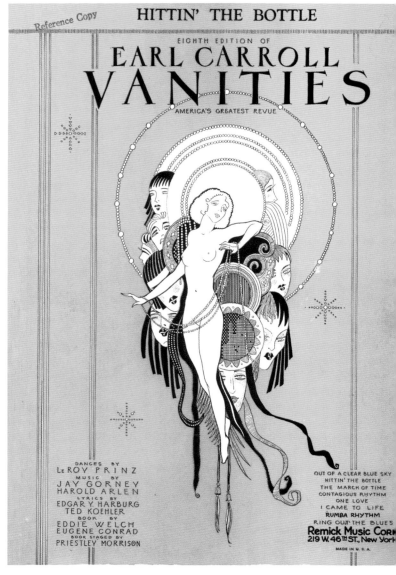

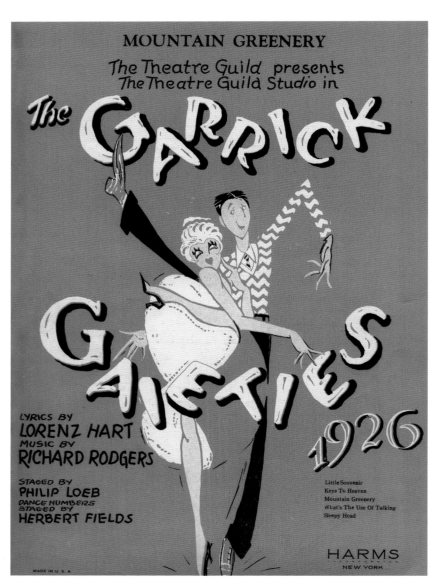

THE GARRICK GAIETIES

The *Gaieties* were the "Hey! let's put on a show" of the revue world. First produced in 1925 by the Theatre Guild as a way of raising money, the three editions of the *Gaieties* emphasized youth, wit, and parodies of contemporary shows. The initial edition was famous for giving Rodgers and Hart their start; other songwriters who got their break here included Vernon Duke and Johnny Mercer.

DIETZ AND SCHWARTZ

Composer Arthur Schwartz was trained as a lawyer, and lyricist Howard Dietz had a day job as M-G-M's advertising manager (he created the famous lion), but when they collaborated at the end of the decade, they made beautiful music together. They rode in with the *Little Shows*—intimate, sophisticated revues that gave audiences an alternative to the bombast of Ziegfeld and George White. The team found its true voice in four revues from 1930 to 1935: *Three's a Crowd, The Band Wagon, Flying Colors,* and *At Home Abroad.* Dietz also contributed sketches and direction to many of their shows.

THE BLACKBIRDS REVUES

Lew Leslie was a white producer-director who brought some of Harlem's best black talent to Broadway and to the West End. The 1928 edition featured the incomparable machine-gun tap technique of Bill "Bojangles" Robinson, as well as the singer Adelaide Hall. The songwriting team of Jimmy McHugh and Dorothy Fields contributed a breakout score that included "Doin' the New Low-Down" and "I Can't Give You Anything But Love." Later editions spotlighted the performing talents of Ethel Waters. Another black revue of the period, 1929's *Hot Chocolates,* transferred directly from Harlem to Broadway and featured Louis Armstrong in the pit band and onstage performing Fats Waller's "Ain't Misbehavin'."

Hot Chocolates
*(1929) spotlighted
some of Harlem's
best talent.*

Chorines from George White's Scandals, *1925.*

OPPOSITE: *Former hoofer George White
rehearses his chorus for the* Scandals, *c. 1925.*

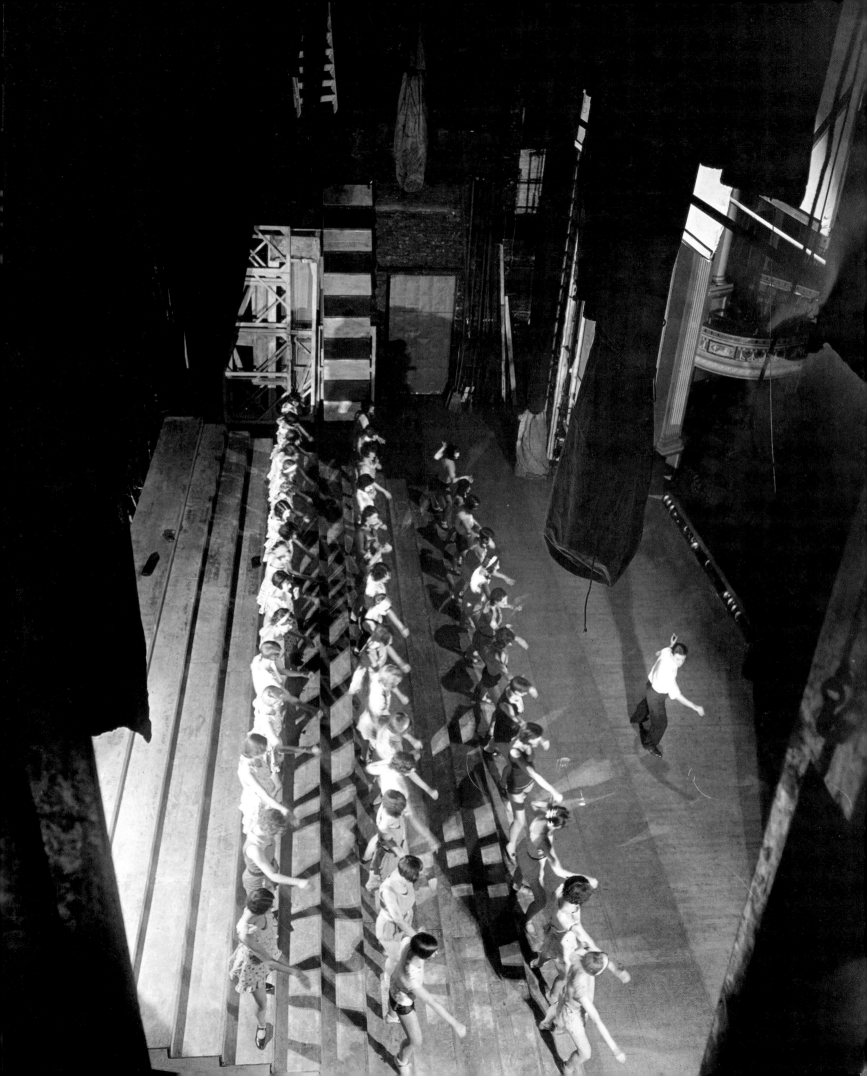

"Look for the silver lining"

MARILYN MILLER

This is an age of modernization, and perhaps nothing is modernized more dramatically than feminine identity. If you look at what the woman was wearing in 1914 and what she's wearing in 1922, her hair is gone, her skirts are gone, her breasts are bound, her hips have disappeared, back is in view, much more skin, but kind of in different places, she looks more boyish, she looks more androgynous, she's smoking, she's drinking, she has kind of trashed the past and just thrown it in a garbage can en route to the party at the speakeasy—and what would attract theater and musical comedy more than something changing that fast? You had a number of plays about the flapper, or the would-be flapper; she becomes a new variant on the older Cinderella story.

—Ann Douglas

A Park Avenue Prince Charming in one of the greatest Cinderella stories of its day, Irene *(1919).*

OPPOSITE ABOVE: *A rare article written by Miller (or her press agent), c. 1914.*

OPPOSITE BELOW:

Sally *required Marilyn Miller to live out a Broadway version of the Cinderella story, first as a scruffy dishwasher (l.) and then, in the finale, as a stage princess with comedian Leon Errol (r.).*

In 1920, after a long and difficult struggle, American women earned the right to vote. Coincidentally or not, that same year, spunky shopgirl Irene O'Dare was toe-dancing her way out of the Hell's Kitchen slums to become a successful dress designer and marry the hero. Irene was the eponymous heroine of a rags-to-riches musical that would, at 670 performances, become the longest-running musical of the decade and set the tone for the innumerable Cinderella stories on Broadway during the 1920s.

Stories in which the "pluck and luck" of the heroine triumphs at the end were embraced by audiences of the period and became a central myth of the musical theater that continues to the present day with such pieces as *Thoroughly Modern Millie* and *Hairspray*. A quick glance at the titles of several 1920s shows—written by the greats along with the hacks—gives a clear picture of how the "typical American girl" was placed front and center: *Irene; Mary; Manhattan Mary; Sally; Sunny; Peggy-Ann; Betsy; Rosalie; Oh, Kay!; Helen of Troy, New York; La, La, Lucille; No, No, Nanette; Sweet Adeline; Treasure Girl; Show Girl; The Gingham Girl; The Five O'Clock Girl; The Girl Friend;* and *Two Little Girls in Blue.* The Shubert Brothers even had the temerity to produce a brand-new show in 1922 called *Sally, Irene and Mary*, which is akin to a modern-day film producer releasing a movie called *Batman, Spider-Man and Wolverine* without acquiring the rights.

None of the hardworking ingenues who played these little ladies embodied the onstage magic of Cinderella better than Marilyn Miller. Born Mary Ellen Reynolds in 1898 in Evansville, Indiana, she was, legend has it, the first woman to coin the name "Marilyn" (actually, it was initially "Marilynn") by putting two family names together. She was pushed out of the wings in toe shoes at an absurdly early age and was billed as "Mademoiselle Sugarlump" in her parents' vaudeville act. As a teenager, she debuted in the Shuberts' *Passing Show* revues, starting in 1914; Ziegfeld himself spotted her, lured her away to the 1918 *Follies*, and quickly became infatuated with his dancing soubrette.

As the 1920s began, Ziegfeld started grooming his *Follies* attractions to become break-out stars, showcased in full-fledged book musicals, and his affection for Miller gave him extra incentive. He enlisted the Princess Theatre team of Guy Bolton, P.G. Wodehouse, and Jerome Kern to rework an earlier show into *Sally*, the tale of a gamine dishwasher who dances her way into an elegant Long Island party, wins the hearts of all, and winds up in, of all places, the *Ziegfeld Follies*, clearly the *ne plus ultra* of happy endings. The plot allowed Miller to display her dance specialties and she had the audience in the palm of her dainty hand. It seems that Miller's greatest quality was ineffability; Bolton describes her "wistful charm," Wodehouse her "curious enchantment." A Kern melody, imported from another show (with lyrics by Buddy DeSylva, as Wodehouse had left the project), became Miller's signature song. It suited both her guileless onstage persona and the hopes of an audience entering a decade of promise.

"Mademoiselle Sugarlump"

BEING AN INFANT PRODIGY AND LIVING IT DOWN

By Marilynn Miller

Child toe-dancer and mimic who is featured in "The Passing Show of 1914"

Photograph by White, New York

Marilynn Miller

BEING an Infant Prodigy and living it down is no easy matter. For twelve years I was under the spell; but my emancipation—my escape, as it were—came on the tenth day of last June, when I appeared at the Winter Garden, New York. Up to that night I was a prodigy, with no hopes of escape till my final day of rest came. But after that night—after that ordeal—I was just myself, Marilynn Miller, mimic and dancer. The slate was wiped clean, the stigma was removed; I was free.

But how did I come to be a phenomenon in the first place? It was the most natural thing in the world, for my father and mother and sisters are all of the stage. To begin away back, my father, Caro Miller, has been on the stage since he was a boy. He was living at Findlay, Ohio, when the juvenile "Pinafore" craze broke out. So, possessed of a good voice, he escaped from home and played the part of *Sir Joseph Porter*. He has been at it ever since.

He has played in all sorts of things—opera, farce, drama, and even tragedy. I think that Father hasn't escaped anything as a showman. 'Way back in 1885, he traveled with the Sells Brothers and Forepaugh Circus—sang in the concert, sold reserved seats, did a single turn on the trapeze, and then a high-school "manage" act. Then Father got married and finally went into vaudeville. His act was known as The Columbians. It consisted of Father and my sisters, Ruth and Claire. Mother being along, they lured her on the stage and changed the name of the act to "The Columbian Four." My sister Ruth was a wonderful soft-shoe dancer and was known as the feminine George Primrose. Claire was a prodigy as a pianist.

Then I came along and joined the family. I was to have been born in Memphis, Tenn., but destiny and yellow fever drove my mother northward, a fugitive to Evansville, Ind. So it is that Evansville has the honor of be-

Look for the silver lining
Whene'er a cloud appears in the blue.
Remember, somewhere the sun is shining
And so the right thing to do
Is make it shine for you.

After a hugely successful run in *Sally*, Miller was lured away by Ziegfeld rival Charles Dillingham to star in *Sunny* (1925), the first collaboration of Kern and Oscar Hammerstein II, and an obvious copy of *Sally*, only this time the heroine is an equestrian star. For her final show of the decade, Miller played the title character in *Rosalie* (1928), a Cinderella in a mythical kingdom. Critic Alexander Woollcott described her star entrance in that show:

Down in the orchestra pit, the violins chitter with excitement and the brasses blare. The spotlight turns white with expectation. Fifty beautiful girls in simple peasant costumes of satin and chiffon rush pell-mell onto the stage, all squealing simple peasant outcries of "Here she comes!" Fifty hussars in fatigue uniforms of ivory white and tomato bisque march on in columns of four and kneel to express an emotion too strong for words. The lights swing to the gateway at the back and settle there. The house holds its breath.

And on walks Marilyn Miller.

Marilyn Miller makes her grand entrance for the finale of Sally.

OPPOSITE: *Marilyn Miller. Ziefgeld's infatuation with Miller is a subject of much discussion, but his wife was not so threatened by Miller that she couldn't appreciate her talents:*

> **She does her hair all wrong. She isn't costumed properly. She has a sweet voice, but not much of it, and I've seen better dancing . . . but a delightful thing happens when she comes on stage.**
>
> **—Billie Burke Ziegfeld**

It is sad, but somewhat predictable, that her life offstage had no silver lining. Her first great romance was with a *Follies* singer named Frank Carter; the jealous Ziegfeld had him fired. Miller married Carter anyway, but only months later he was killed in a car crash; her next two marriages ended in divorce. Miller's "wistful charm" appears to have vanished the moment she crossed offstage, up left. Oscar Hammerstein recalled that after he and Kern played the score of *Sunny* for her and described the plot in painstaking detail, she merely paused and asked, "When do I do my tap specialty?"

In the end, the quintessential Jazz Age Cinderella was perhaps more Jazz Age than Cinderella: she favored loud parties with plenty of drink and unsavory customers and became an alcoholic herself. Her attempts at breaking into sound film were met with a shrug. Her evanescent style would have been out of favor in the 1930s in any event; by the time she died in 1936 at age thirty-seven, following surgery for a sinus infection, the clock had long since struck twelve and her enchanted evenings were only a memory.

"It's Getting Dark on Old Broadway"

SISSLE AND BLAKE AND *SHUFFLE ALONG*

Songwriter Eubie Blake was concerned about his new musical. "We were afraid people would think it was a freak show and it wouldn't appeal to white people," he reflected years later. "Others thought that if it was a colored show, it might be dirty." He had every reason to be concerned; his show, written with lyricist Noble Sissle, would be the first black production on Broadway in nearly a decade. Times had changed since the end of World War I: African American culture was flourishing up in Harlem, and the country was tentatively sampling the black rhythms of jazz. But, white culture could never be taken for granted—even Woodrow Wilson had backed a formal plan to segregate theater audiences. There was a chance, however, that *Shuffle Along* might find a place among mainstream New York theatergoers.

> **The creation of jazz by black artists gave this country a language that it was searching for and gave it a rhythmic identity, and so it makes perfect sense that the composers would use this inventive language and rhythm for the theater.**
> **—George C. Wolfe,** Director

Sublime to the ridiculous (l. to. r.): songwriters Sissle and Blake with performers Miller and Lyles (on piano).

If any songwriters could crack the color bar on Broadway in the 1920s, it was the team of Sissle and Blake. Their musical pedigrees were impeccable. James Hubert Blake was born in 1883 and raised in Baltimore by a fanatically religious mother and a hard-drinking father. Eubie first syncopated church hymns on an organ, and moved on to playing piano in brothels. He eventually performed in black vaudeville with vocalist Noble Sissle, and both men joined the esteemed "Hell Fighters" Jazz Band of the 369th Infantry led by James Reese Europe, famous for marching the band up Fifth Avenue to Harlem in 1919 to celebrate the Armistice. When Europe set up his band commercially in postwar New York, he hired Sissle to sing and Blake to manage the office. Tragically, Europe was stabbed to death during the intermission of a concert by a deranged member of his own band in 1919, but his vision for his colleagues to make something of themselves as a cultural force stayed with them. Sissle and Blake soon began touring as an elegant vaudeville act—"America's Favorite Society Entertainers"—and eventually crossed paths with another black vaudeville team, the comedians Flournoy Miller and Aubrey Lyles.

The two teams were considerably different in their styles. Miller and Lyles joked in minstrel fashion, wearing blackface and speaking garbled argot, while Sissle and Blake played the sophisticates in tuxedos and sans burnt cork. But the four of them thought they might have a show if they all pitched in together, and in 1921, using an old sketch of Miller and Lyles's called "The Mayor of

Jimtown" as the basis for a thin scenario about the comic complications of a three-way mayoral race, they cobbled together *Shuffle Along*. The show was produced on a wing and a prayer, with musical numbers occasionally written to suit some extra costumes that came the producer's way at bargain prices. Even when *Shuffle Along* made it into New York after some desperate tryouts, it was kept at arm's length by the Theater District, debuting far uptown at the 63rd Street Theatre, near Columbus Circle. To make matters worse, the show was nearly $20,000 in debt before the curtain went up.

But the extraordinary musical excitement of *Shuffle Along* didn't owe the audience anything. The jazzy syncopation of "The Baltimore Buzz" was a new sound on Broadway. *The New York Herald Tribune*'s critic wrote: "It is when the chorus and principals . . . get going in the dances that the world seems a brighter place to live in. They wriggle and shimmy in a fashion to outdo a congress of eels, and they fling their limbs about without stopping to make sure that they are securely fastened on." Blake adored the music of Victor Herbert and wrote his own lyrical waltz for the production. When one cast member questioned the appropriateness of a waltz in a "colored show," Blake simply turned it into a fox trot, and "I'm Just Wild About Harry" became one of the most popular songs of the decade, coming back into style in 1948 as Harry Truman's presidential campaign song.

Amid the bustle and energy of the score, Sissle and Blake found an opportunity to open yet another window onto the African American experience with the ballad "Love Will Find a Way."

Noble Sissle and the girls of
Shuffle Along.

The proudest day of my life was when *Shuffle Along* opened. At the intermission, all these white people kept saying, "I would like to touch him, the man who wrote the music." At last, I'm a human being. —**Eubie Blake**

> Love will find a way
> Though skies now are gray
> Love like ours can never be ruled
> Cupid's not schooled that way
> Dry each tear-dimmed eye
> Clouds will soon roll by
> Though fate may lead us astray
> My dearie, mark what I say
> Love will find a way.

[Blake and Sissle] were introducing a kind of romantic quality about black performers that had never before been allowed onstage. There was a great question about whether or not "Love Will Find a Way" should be included in the show because how would our white audiences respond to the idea that we are no longer grotesque, that we can speak with a human heart, that there is gentility as part of our makeup? The day was won, however, by including that song, because not only did *Shuffle Along* prove that whites would go to see blacks perform on Broadway, it made them say, "Oh wow, maybe these dusky people are more like us than we think."

—Andre De Shields, Actor

Whatever anxiety Blake and the producers felt about the show's reception vanished after the May 23 opening, when the major white critics found their way to cover it and discovered that *Shuffle Along*'s charms were abundant and transcendent. One social boundary could not be transcended, however:

> **In the 63rd Street Theater, in the prime seats of the orchestra section, sat whole rows of matinee ladies who had detrained from the society register, surveying through lorgnettes the Negro antics and agonies of which the play was wrought. Meanwhile, the Negroes who had ventured to come see this piece about themselves—a piece written, produced, directed, and performed by members of their own race—were shunted up to the balcony.**
> **—Alexander Woollcott,** in the *New York Times,* 1921

But both black and white audiences were entranced enough by the show to make it a sensation downtown, where it played, and uptown, where it created a new sense of race pride in the burgeoning Harlem community.

Shuffle Along also became a performing arts academy for some of America's finest emerging black talent. Paul Robeson sang in the chorus, as did Adelaide Hall. As the ingenue, Florence Mills would launch her career as Harlem's favorite showgirl (the funeral following her untimely death in 1927 brought uptown to standstill) and a sixteen-year-old Josephine Baker made her professional debut as a wisecracking chorine. More than any single entertainer, Baker would go on to export the follies (lower-case "f") of jazz-based Broadway performance style to Europe in the 1920s and '30s.

Comic shenanigans surrounding a mayoral race were nominally at the heart of Shuffle Along.

For nearly two years it was always packed. [*Shuffle Along*] gave a scintillating send-off to that Negro vogue in Manhattan. . . . It gave the proper push—to the vogue that spread to books, African sculpture, music, and dancing.
—Langston Hughes, *The Big Sea*

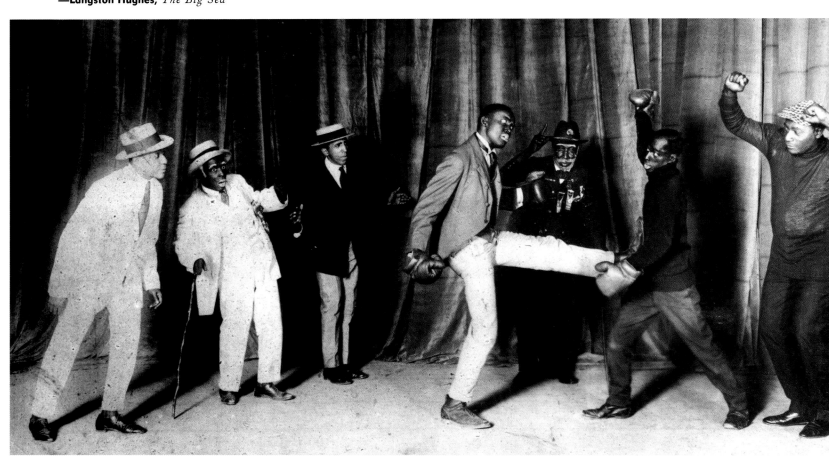

Shuffle Along inspired more than a dozen new black musicals and revues on Broadway, many of which mined the abundance of talent available north of 125th Street. One number in the 1922 *Ziegfeld Follies* was prescient and condescending enough to exploit it. Dancer Gilda Gray led "It's Getting Dark on Old Broadway," with a special lighting effect that managed to turn all the white chorines into sepia-toned versions of their dancing selves. It was a potent metaphor. Producers, choreographers, and composers were cabbing it up to Harlem in record numbers, looking to access this new performance energy, hoping to sepia-tone their own work.

Broadway's most enduring exploration of African American culture in the 1920s came in the area of dance. George White, with his background as a hoofer, always put innovative dance numbers at the forefront of his *Scandals*, and in 1923 he produced the next show by Miller and Lyles, called *Runnin' Wild*. The all-black production highlighted a brand-new step that went on to conquer the world: the Charleston. The origins of this groundbreaking (literally) dance are complicated to untangle—it either originated in the black enclaves of the South Carolina city or perhaps Flournoy Miller had observed some black youngsters performing an unusually energetic and percussive dance on the street corner outside the theater. What matters is that composer James P. Johnson wrote an infectious melody that was served up by dancer Elizabeth Welch and a team of male dancers. Its natural athleticism was a boon for young dancers of both sexes; by 1924, it had become a national craze, pounded out on dance floors in contests, shows, and marathons everywhere.

White, who reportedly wanted the Charleston cut from *Runnin' Wild* so he could debut the dance in his own more prestigious *Scandals*, got his chance to initiate a craze of his own in 1926 with the Black Bottom, performed in his revue by Ann Pennington. The

Ann Pennington, of the fabled dimpled knee, demonstrating the Black Bottom.

name of the dance—a fairly simple sideways step punctuated by a slap on the rear end—was said to have been inspired by the "deep muddy waters of the Swanee," but that didn't fool anyone. The dance had its origins in Nashville, was claimed by several artists as their own, and became a brief but nationwide sensation.

The vogue for black entertainment in the 1920s would seem to spell a bonanza for the greatest black entertainer of his era, Bert Williams. Sadly, this was not to be the case. On tour, it was one thing to pal around with his white colleagues over dinner, but afterward, he still returned to his hotel room through the back entrance. Such stupid inequities ground down his spirit, and Williams started drinking heavily. After the 1919 *Follies*, he tried to create several starring vehicles for himself, such as *Under the Bamboo Tree*, but he collapsed during its out-of-town tryouts. He died at age forty-six in March, 1922.

> **When in the calm afterday of thought and struggle to racial peace, we look back to pay tribute to those who helped most, we shall single out for highest praise those who made the world laugh: above all, Bert Williams. For this was not mere laughing: it was the smile that hovered above blood and tragedy; the light mask of happiness that hid breaking hearts and bitter souls. This is the top of bravery.**
> **—W.E.B. Du Bois, 1922**

Williams lived just long enough to see a new generation of black talent—most of them showing their own faces and their own souls—make a hit on Broadway.

"I'll Build a Stairway to Paradise"
GEORGE GERSHWIN

The piano was supposed to be for the other brother.

The Gershovitz family had never been flush, but by 1910 they had scraped together enough money to buy a used upright piano for their Lower East Side apartment. Fourteen-year-old Ira was the family's resident intellectual, and a piano would seem just the thing to round out his liberal education, but, to everyone's surprise, it was Ira's twelve-year-old brother, George, who took to the instrument immediately. He had shown some musical aptitude around a family friend, but no one could have predicted how quickly he mastered the piano. The Gershovitzes somehow found the requisite fifty cents a pop for music lessons, but within three years, George had "played out" all his local teachers.

Luckily, he hooked up with an instructor named Charles Hambitzer who could push the boy into more complex musical territory. By 1914, George was accomplished enough to take a job as a song plugger at Remick & Co., which meant that, to his own and his family's dismay, he had to quit high school. As Ira entered City College, George was spending bone-grinding hours arranging songs, fiddling with orchestrations and key changes, cutting piano rolls, and working as an all-around musical expert for Remick. Although the job paid him only $15 a week, it became, as he would later admit, an invaluable education in the practical requirements of writing songs for the stage. He longed for the day when a tune of his own would hit Broadway.

That day came in 1916, when Gershwin placed his first songs in various revues, a practice he continued over the next four years. The success of "Swanee" in 1919 led to a unique job with the young impresario George White, who, alone among all revue producers, decided that his shows would have songs by a single house composer rather than the various interpolations that constituted most revues. Gershwin wrote the complete score for White's *Scandals of 1920*, and would go on to write forty-five songs for White over the next five seasons. Gershwin came into his own with the *Scandals of 1922*, when he wrote the majestic, swirling first-act finale, "I'll Build a Stairway to Paradise." Accompanied by the Paul Whiteman Orchestra, the jazz anthem contained the following lines written by Buddy DeSylva and George's brother Ira:

> I'll build a stairway to Paradise
> With a new step ev'ry day.
> I'm gonna get there at any price—
> Stand aside, I'm on my way.

Gershwin also exercised his considerable compositional ambition in a remarkable twenty-five-minute jazz opera, set in Harlem, called *Blue Monday*. Plunked down into the middle of the lighthearted revue's second act, the opera made it through exactly one performance before White ordered it cut.

Gershwin's discontent with White reached a peak in 1924, when the composer asked for a raise beyond the $125 a week (plus royalties) he was getting. White refused and Gershwin walked. For Gershwin, it was just as well, for 1924 was shaping up to be one of the most remarkable years any composer would ever have. In February, challenged by bandleader Paul Whiteman, who was keen to bring jazz to a larger, more prestigious audience, Gershwin wrote *Rhapsody in Blue* for a concert called "An Experiment in Modern Music" at New York City's Aeolian Hall. The program included pieces by Kern, Berlin, and Herbert, among many others, but it was Gershwin's "jazz concerto," which, accompanied by Whiteman's orchestra, he played

George Gershwin, c. 1924.

George is distinctly of his day, of his city. His roots, if not his branches, are in the present, and of Gotham. His jazz is more complex than that of his early brothers in Tin Pan Alley because his nature is restless and experimental.
—Isaac Goldberg, 1930

GEORGE GERSHWIN

RHAPSODY IN BLUE

FOR JAZZ BAND AND PIANO

Piano Solo and Second Piano

HARMS

on the piano himself, that created a sensation and made Gershwin a celebrity overnight. By the end of the year, he and his brother Ira had written their first musical comedy score to reach Broadway, *Lady, Be Good!*, and it became a huge hit. He was on his way.

In person, my brother was a good deal like his music: vibrant, dynamic, and honest. And, if I may, charming. He was full of life and lived a full day. Although most of it was devoted to the piano and his music, it was a continual source of amazement to me that he found time to engage in so many other activities. . . . George moved fast, lived fast, studied hard, and learned fast.
—Ira Gershwin

Gershwin's natural ease and ebullient energy made him the perfect ambassador to introduce the slightly mistrusted jazz to a wider audience. He wrote about jazz frequently (see page 126), championed it ardently, but most important, he could play it like nobody's business. He frequently visited Harlem's various saloons and nightclubs to absorb jazz from its source. Eubie Blake remembered that "James P. Johnson and Luckey Roberts told me of this very talented ofay piano player at Remick's. They said he was good enough to learn some of those difficult tricks that only a few of us could master."

Gershwin was as accomplished a concert pianist as anyone in New York; in fact, with the possible exception of Duke Ellington and Vernon Duke, he was the best piano player among any of the show composers of the twentieth century. His virtuosity ingratiated itself into his scores, constantly raising the bar for what dancers such as Fred Astaire and singers such as Gertrude Lawrence could do, and frequently it took two piano players in the pit orchestra to do justice to his work. Paul Whiteman recalled that "whenever we'd go to anybody's house, he'd be the last one to play the piano, and it might as well just be that way because he played so long that nobody else could." It became a benevolent addiction for Gershwin.

Anywhere [George Gershwin] went, he was the center of attention. He had the energy of the devil, he was enormously attractive, he was charming, and he made it his business to be the center of attention. When he would go to a party, he would say to a young lady who took his fancy, "I'm inspired to write a song for you. Come." And he would put her down on the piano bench next to him and he would play this song, that presumably, he'd just composed just for her. But the song had a blank space in it for the girl's name—*any* girl.
—Kitty Carlisle Hart

Where the slightly bumptious Irving Berlin made the perfect celebrity songwriter for the early days of the rough-and-ready century, Gershwin embodied the pace, the energy, the sleekness of the 1920s; he underscored the beat of the entire decade. His potential seemed limitless: Carl Van Vechten, one of the key chroniclers of the Harlem Renaissance and the '20s in general, said it with potent simplicity in 1925: "What he will do in the future depends on no one but George Gershwin."

OPPOSITE: *Gershwin's most famous piece*, Rhapsody in Blue.

FASCINATING RHYTHM

Words by Ira Gershwin
Music by George Gershwin
From Lady, Be Good! *(1924)*

THE MAIN REASON RHYTHM figures so prominently in Ira Gershwin's lyrics must be that his brother George gave him so much trouble with it. Practically every other composer of the time wrote in a more accessible, more formulaic rhythm that was easier to create a rhyme structure around. A bookworm who attended high school and college, Ira was the quieter and more disciplined of the two. But, whereas Ira, with a devotion to the lyrics of W.S. Gilbert and P.G. Wodehouse, was incisive with words, his brother was promiscuous with melody.

George had written the first eight bars of this song, originally titled "Syncopated City" (a logical extension of his love for New York City and its pace) for *Primrose,* the first show he created with his brother under Ira's real name (previously, Ira had used a pseudonym, Arthur Francis—the first names of their brother and sister). George was persuaded to save the fragment for another show.

When the Gershwins began working on *Lady, Be Good!,* the song fragment was pulled out of the trunk and given a new title. Ira begged his brother to let him end the fourth lines with a masculine, or one-beat, ending. George liked it his own way, with the emphasis on the penultimate syllable of the two-beat ending. It made no sense as poetry, or even spoken English, but it made plenty of sense as 1920s jazz. This was the kind of challenge that Ira was thrown daily by George, but he hardly minded; he loved his brother and knew they would meet somewhere in the middle. Ira admirably combined the music's jazz-based theme with the street language of the 1920s—"on the go," "make it snappy"—and juxtaposes such Victorian anachronisms as "all a-quiver" with that omnipresent 1920s car, a rat-trap jalopy, or the "flivver." The syncopation of George's music required Ira to boil down his language in a lyrical crucible—the lines had to be short, sharp, and pointed in order not to be overwhelmed by the frenetic music.

The song was sung in the show by Cliff "Ukulele Ike" Edwards, a specialty artist later known as the voice of Jiminy Cricket, and danced by Fred and Adele Astaire. It became a song that Astaire would record throughout his career. "Syncopated City" was, by the way, not the song's only alternate title. George and Ira's father, who had a tendency toward malapropism, often referred to it as "Fashion by the River."

Got a little rhythm, a rhythm, a rhythm
    That pit-a-pats through my brain;
        So darn persistent,
        The day isn't distant
When it'll drive me insane.
        Comes in the morning
        Without any warning,
And hangs around me all day.
        I'll have to sneak up to it
        Someday, and speak up to it.
I hope it listens when I say:

Fascinating Rhythm,
    You've got me on the go!
        Fascinating Rhythm,
        I'm all a-quiver.

What a mess you're making!
    The neighbors want to know
        Why I'm always shaking
        Just like a flivver.

Each morning I get up with the sun—
    Start a-hopping,
    Never stopping—
To find at night no work has been done.

    I know that
    Once it didn't matter—
But now you're doing wrong;
    When you start to patter
    I'm so unhappy.

Won't you take a day off?
    Decide to run along
        Somewhere far away off—
        And make it snappy!

Oh, how I long to be the man I used to be!
    Fascinating Rhythm,
Oh, won't you stop picking on me?

OPPOSITE: *Astaire with chorines in* Lady, Be Good!

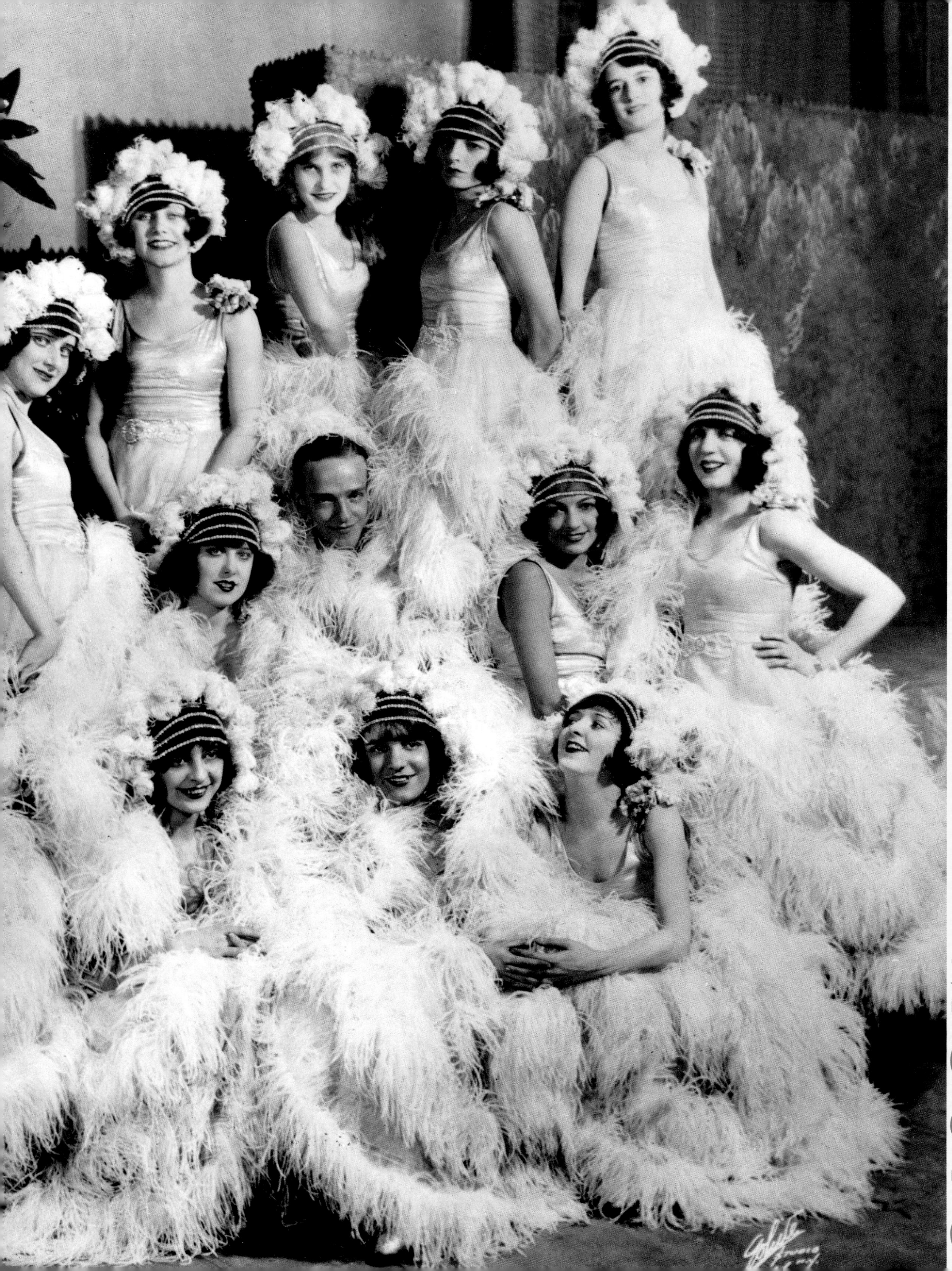

"The best things in life are free"

DeSYLVA, BROWN, AND HENDERSON

When George Gershwin walked out on *George White's Scandals*, he left the door open for a trio of songwriters who would come closer to capturing the rambunctious spirit of their times than even he would himself. Composer Ray Henderson, along with lyricists Lew Brown and B.G. "Buddy" DeSylva, were so keyed in to the Roaring Twenties that the moment the decade faded, their tremendous popularity faded with it. But until the Depression came along they were, in the words of an early Henderson hit, sittin' on top of the world.

They were a ragtag bunch, inexorably drawn to Tin Pan Alley from diverse corners: Henderson (born Raymond Brost in Buffalo) was a song plugger at Leo Feist's who had written music for such hits as "Five Foot Two, Eyes of Blue" and "Bye, Bye Blackbird"; Brown was a veteran lyricist who hailed from Odessa, Russia; and DeSylva was a Santa Monica lifeguard who came to New York at the insistence of Al Jolson. Their collaboration was, by all accounts, a joyous and egalitarian one—the ideas flowed freely from one writer to another. When George White assembled them for his *Scandals of 1925*, their work was rather undistinguished, but the following season, they contributed two standards out of a thirteen-number score: "The Birth of the Blues" and "Black Bottom." While they continued their association with White, they branched out of the revue format and, in 1927, hit pay dirt with one of the most successful musical comedies of the era.

In the 1920s, college life meant pep, vigor, excitement, and youth, youth, youth. It was also, thanks to the stories of F. Scott Fitzgerald and various well-publicized campus fads, very much part of the public consciousness. DeSylva, Brown, and Henderson turned all this into *Good News!*, a bouncing divertissement about a football star and the girl who tutors him for the astronomy final. During the run of the production, the theater ushers and the orchestra members all wore college jerseys, and the show's big number, "The Varsity Drag," gave the songwriters their second national dance craze hit. Everybody was, indeed, doing the Varsity Drag.

For the rest of the decade, the team had a new show every year, transforming fads of the day into musical comedy scenarios. Boxing inspired *Hold Everything!*; golfing turned into *Follow Thru*, a "musical slice of country club life"; and aviation became the theme for *Flying High*. The shows themselves were negligible (although, along with *Good News!*, they each ran very near or

Brown, DeSylva, Henderson, and their music publisher, Robert Crawford (seated), c. 1927.

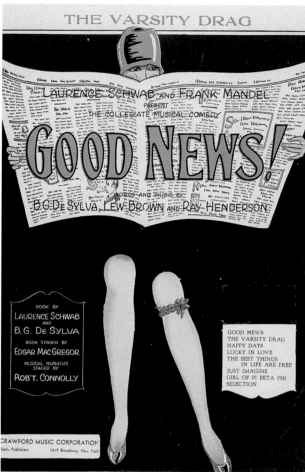

Good-natured high jinks abound in Good News!, *which spawned a dance craze with "Varsity Drag."*

beyond four hundred performances—an astonishing string for the time), but the songs were anything but. The titles alone bring a smile to the face, cheery Victorian bromides re-embroidered as football pennants: "The Best Things in Life Are Free," "Life Is Just a Bowl of Cherries," "Button Up Your Overcoat," "Keep Your Sunny Side Up," "You're the Cream in My Coffee." In fact, their songs are so affable, they make you feel like DeSylva, Brown, and Henderson have just bought *you* a cup of coffee.

When the '30s arrived, the team headed west and wrote for Hollywood, then went their separate ways, with Brown and, especially, DeSylva becoming successful film producers. As songwriters, the team suffers from contemporary neglect, perhaps because that brand of optimism doesn't travel well to a cynical age. Experimentation, sophistication, cleverness, or salaciousness were not for them—they left that for other songwriters. They were happy enough to sell tickets.

> **One Sunday morning in late 1927, 1928, [composer Burton Lane] was at the home of the Gershwins on 103rd Street and they're all having brunch and Mrs. Gershwin—the mother of George and Ira—comes in and she looks at George and she says, "George, why can't you write hits like DeSylva, Brown, and Henderson?" George was so annoyed at his mother, he didn't know what to say—he just got up and left the table.**
>
> **—Robert Kimball,** Theater Historian

FRED AND ADELE ASTAIRE

THE DANCING PARTNER WHO MADE FRED Astaire famous isn't the one most people remember. Fred, born in 1899, and his sister, Adele, a year his senior, were the children of an Austrian immigrant named Austerlitz who had settled in Omaha, Nebraska. Their mother had a notion that they should learn to dance and so they journeyed east to New York in 1903 and began a long vaudeville career as a boy-and-girl specialty duo. The transition to adulthood was an awkward one for the Astaires; it was not until 1917 that their charm and dancing specialties reached a Broadway audience. They were featured in several revues from then on, and it was the gamine Adele, not her more serious and disciplined brother, who usually got the better notices. He didn't care; he'd rather spend his time crafting new numbers or innovative steps for them to master.

One of the steps, incorporated into most of their shows, was the "oompah trot," or the runaround, where Adele and Fred, side by side, would ape riding in huge circles on an imaginary bicycle. Audiences went wild for this particular antic, especially in London, where the bright-eyed, exuberant Americans were welcomed even more enthusiastically than in their own country.

Fred had known George Gershwin since 1916, when he went to the composer looking for a vaudeville number. They had vowed they'd work together someday; that day came on December 1, 1924, when the Astaires headlined George and Ira's first full-length New York musical, *Lady, Be Good!* Playing a brother-and-sister dance team down on their luck, the Astaires had found the perfect vehicle for their talents. George not only provided them with some of their best tunes, he suggested a couple of dance steps to help Fred with the ending for "The Half of It, Dearie, Blues." Fred got his first solo, while the romantic end of

Adele and Fred Astaire in Lady, Be Good!, *1924.*

things was held down by his sister and the leading man. It proved to be such a felicitous match that critic Alexander Woollcott later wrote, "I do not know whether Gershwin was born into this world to write rhythms for Fred Astaire's feet or whether Fred Astaire was born into this world to show how the Gershwin music should really be danced."

The Astaires followed up that success with another Gershwin smash, *Funny Face* (1927), where Adele got to introduce "'S Wonderful." When the show made its inevitable visit to London, Adele met a stage-door Johnnie from the B-list of the British aristocracy and was soon engaged to be married. Mindful of her incipient retirement from the stage, the duo made sure their 1931 appearance in *The Band Wagon* would be an appropriate finale to their partnership. It was one of the finest revues of the period, with an impeccable Schwartz-Dietz score including

Lady, Be Good! *poster, 1924.*

"A New Sun in the Sky," in which Fred dressed for a night on the town. The number highlighted Fred in an attempt to beef up his stage presence so that his transition into a solo career would be easier. That transition occurred in 1932 with Astaire's introduction of "Night and Day" in Cole Porter's *Gay Divorce*. "Fred struggled on without [Adele] for a while," wrote Guy Bolton and P.G. Wodehouse years later, "but finally threw his hand in and disappeared. There is a rumor that he turned up in Hollywood. It was the best the poor chap could hope for after losing his brilliant sister."

THE MARX BROTHERS

THERE WOULD SEEM TO HAVE BEEN more than enough insanity in 1920s Manhattan without anyone having to pay for it, but Broadway audiences couldn't get enough of the Marx Brothers. The Marxes began their arduous career in vaudeville in 1907, when Minnie Marx, an indomitable stage mother who would make Ethel Merman's Rose look like a wallflower, put her teenage sons Milton (Gummo) and Julius (Groucho) together with a girl into a singing act called the Three Nightingales; the next year Adolph (Harpo) became the fourth Nightingale. Brother Leonard (Chico) joined the act in 1912, and they quickly—and mercifully—turned their talents to antic comedy. Now with brother Herbert (Zeppo) replacing Gummo, the Four Marx Brothers were socko at the Palace in 1915. By 1922, Chico, despite his propensity for gambling, had become the act's manager and decided the time had come for them to go legit—in other words, to star in an actual revue or musical comedy on Broadway.

"Hooray for Captain Spaulding!" (Clockwise from center) Groucho, Zeppo, Harpo, and Chico Marx from Animal Crackers.

Their Broadway debut was in a piece of hackwork called *I'll Say She Is* in 1924. It was the first time Broadway critics reviewed them, and the show became a huge hit as influential critic Alexander Woollcott fell in love with Harpo "in a nice way," as Groucho would put it years later. The boys were flooded with offers from Broadway producers, including Ziegfeld, but Chico held out again, this time for a first-class musical written expressly for them by real Broadway hands. He got the best: George S. Kaufman as librettist and Irving Berlin to write the music and lyrics. *The Cocoanuts* opened in 1925 and ran for more than a year on Broadway, and longer on the road. Kaufman was pressed into service again, along with colibrettist Morrie Ryskind and the songwriting team of Bert Kalmar and Harry Ruby, to write *Animal Crackers*, which opened in 1928 and became another hit. During its run, the boys were commuting daily to Astoria, Queens, where they were filming a version of *The Cocoanuts;* eventually they filmed *Animal Crackers* there, too. Between the financial drain of the Crash and their obvious appeal in sound film, it only made sense for them to ship their brand of craziness out to Hollywood.

Although Kaufman continued to write for them, he was constantly exasperated by the boys' lack of respect for the written word. Once, while standing in the lobby during a performance of *The Cocoanuts*, he broke away from a companion with whom he was having a conversation. "I'm sorry," said Kaufman when he returned, "I just thought I heard one of my original lines."

BEATRICE LILLIE

SHE WAS AN ELFIN PIXIE equipped with the sharp elbows of a bargain shopper. Toronto-born Beatrice Lillie had been a fixture on the British revue scene since 1914. When she made her American debut along with Gertrude Lawrence, in *André Charlot's Revue of 1924*, she launched a transatlantic career that placed her front and center in more than a dozen Broadway revues over the next thirty years. As a comedienne, she was nonpareil. Hopelessly lost in a lunatic world of her own devising, she could play a haughty customer tying her tongue in knots while placing an order for double-damask dinner napkins, or an obstreperous audience member gossiping away while poor John Gielgud tried to play Hamlet, or a superstitious dresser driving her leading lady to the brink of madness. As

a singer, she was a veritable arsenal of comic technique: she entered the stage armed with an extravagant character, performed the song with sharpshooter precision, tossed a bomb of surprise to the audience at the end of each number, and exited quickly. In one number, she famously lifted her evening gown to reveal a pair of roller skates and barreled offstage; in another, "There Are Fairies at the Bottom of Our Garden," she swung a rope of pearls around her neck so violently that it turned into a hula hoop.

In *This Year of Grace* (1928), she not only performed with Noel Coward, she sang several of his songs to incom-

Bea Lillie in
At Home Abroad.

parable effect and the two became close, if irascible, colleagues for the rest of their careers. It was Coward who cast her in her first—and last—book musical as late as 1964, as the "happy medium" Madame Arcati in *High Spirits*. She enjoyed a major triumph in it. Sadly, as time went on, Lillie was unable to leave her lunacy onstage and she put herself and her colleagues through trying times. Although she never achieved her lifelong dream of playing Mary Poppins (she was a dead ringer for the original illustrations), she did appear opposite Julie Andrews as the white-slave trader Mrs. Meers in the 1967 film *Thoroughly Modern Millie*. A film of her own life would have been aptly titled *Thoroughly Maddened Lillie*.

ED WYNN

BORN ISAIAH EDWIN LEOPOLD in Philadelphia in 1886, Ed Wynn joined the *Ziegfeld Follies* in 1914, but it was not until the next year that he butted heads with W.C. Fields. Wynn was mugging behind Fields's back during his pool hall sketch and Fields let the back end of the pool cue down on Wynn's head with a mighty thwack. After that, Wynn preferred to work as a solo act. A Category Four comic whirlwind, he starred in, and in many cases produced and wrote, eight different revues in the 1920s and '30s in which he introduced the shows, played in most of the sketches, and frequently hung around to greet the audience as they left the theater.

Wynn's onstage persona was the Perfect Fool (which became the title of his 1921 show): a giggling, lisping, prancing duffel bag of a fellow sporting outrageous hats and spouting even more outrageous puns. Explaining to the audience one night that all of the performers in his show were chosen solely for their experience on Mississippi showboats, he told them "I bred my cast on the waters" and then laughed at his own joke. He sprouted inane inventions, like a pair of eyeglasses with a windshield to protect you when you ate grapefruit, and threw himself into non-sequitur lines and routines with the abandon of a kiddie-show host lost in a Samuel Beckett play. With Guy Bolton, Wynn wrote the book for Rodgers and Hart's *Simple Simon* (1930), in which he starred as a naif who dreams in fairy tales, and Wynn allowed the real world to intrude briefly into his playpen with a 1937 antiwar satire, Yip Harburg's *Hooray for What!*, but mostly he followed the beat of his

Ed Wynn, c. 1930.

own tin drummer. "He has found a little odd corner of life which no one else cultivates," wrote critic Gilbert Seldes. "He is a perpetual immigrant obsessed by hats and shoes and words and small ideas, instead of bothering about skyscrapers."

In the '40s and '50s, Wynn's brand of silliness no longer found favor on the stage and he moved to television, where he eventually reinvented himself as a gifted and poignant character actor. Perhaps he was finally able to access his own deep melancholy; explaining his real-life personality, he once said, "Maybe I used up all my happiness on the stage." His last performance was as the levitating Uncle Albert in the film *Mary Poppins* (1964). His one number was "I Love to Laugh," and, for more than four decades, so did Ed Wynn's audience.

"*Lover, come back to me*"

OPERETTA IN THE 1920s

The musicals of the 1920s may seem to be all about syncopated rhythms and toe-tapping adolescents, but a far deeper, far more romantic strain could also be heard along Broadway. The operetta had a surprising resurgence, as a new generation of songwriters created some of the most popular and enduring musical theater pieces of the decade. Before the First World War, operettas were set in the colorful kingdoms of Austria, Hungary, and Czechoslovakia, and in the 1920s those very countries yielded two gifted composers who achieved their fame and fortune, not in their native lands, as an earlier generation had, but on the Great White Way.

Rudolf Friml was a piano virtuoso from Prague who came to New York to stay in 1906, and Sigmund Romberg, trained as an architectural engineer, turned his talents to songwriting after emigrating from Bucharest in 1909. Despite their nobler callings, both men were quickly swept along in the currents of musical theater, creating rapturous melodies for producers such as the Shuberts and Arthur Hammerstein. As the 1920s began,

The Desert Song (1926) parlayed the contemporary fascination with Rudolph Valentino's sheik and Lawrence of Arabia into a Moroccan romance featuring a masked marauder and his emotionally ravished fair lady. It achieved enormous popularity in New York and London; here Edith Day stands her ground against Harry Welchman in the British production.

both Friml and Romberg already had several hits under the belts, but their fortunes were made when they started working with lyricist Oscar Hammerstein II.

Hammerstein, the grandson of the man who created the Theater District, was born in a rather impressive trunk, but his family despaired over his theatrical ambitions. His father, William, begged him to study law, which Oscar did at Columbia University, but clearly his passions lay elsewhere. Uncle Arthur gave him a job stage managing one of his operettas, and as Oscar worked his way through the Hammerstein organization, he learned about the craft of lyric writing and the general architecture that goes into creating a piece for the stage—a hands-on education usually reserved for painters' apprentices of the Italian Renaissance.

Hammerstein began his collaboration with Friml in 1924 (Uncle Arthur had given Friml his first break with *The Firefly* in 1912) on *Rose-Marie*, an elaborate production set in the Canadian Rockies. The operetta, better known to modern audiences through the oft-parodied Jeanette MacDonald–Nelson Eddy movie (where they're "calling yoo-oo-oo-oo, oo-oo-oooo"), had a uniquely North American setting and managed to weave murder and revenge into its plot. Its tremendous success, both here and abroad, made the composer and lyricist millionaires.

Hammerstein crafted even more sophisticated successes with Romberg later in the decade. They followed up their 1926 hit *The Desert Song* two years later with *The New Moon*, a swashbuckler set in eighteenth-century New Orleans that interjected a subplot about class warfare and utopian social experiments into a good deal of requisite bosom-heaving. This last show contained some of operetta's most sweeping melodies: "Stout Hearted Men," "Softly, as in a Morning Sunrise," and "Lover, Come Back to Me," songs that have lived on in record albums, jazz interpretations, and fond hearts everywhere.

Romberg and Friml had their share of hits with other lyricists (*The Student Prince, The Vagabond King*), but the shows with Hammerstein can be seen, apart from their pure rhapsodic pleasure, as early experiments in expanding the conceits of the romantic musical—as opposed to the musical comedy—form. In all his collaborations with Friml and Romberg, Hammerstein brought something new to the party, some aspect of construction, plot, or setting that gently nudged the operetta form into something more poignant or more pertinent. The librettos themselves do not quite stand the test of time; they tend to overdose on testosterone, and modern audiences prefer their heroes and romantic episodes to have more psychological complexity. That is, perhaps, why *The Desert Song*, among all of them, can still place one tentative foothold in the modern era. Its heroine despises the bespectacled milquetoast who loves her, completely unaware that, at night, he transforms himself into the heroic masked Red Shadow, who spirits her away—ecstatically—into the secret camp of his desert rebels. (And this was more than a decade before the appearance of Superman!) Whether he or his peers were aware of it or not, the one librettist on Broadway who could lay claim to being a dramatic craftsman was Oscar Hammerstein II; his skills were soon to be put to the greatest test of his relatively brief but already accomplished career.

The dapper Sigmund Romberg, c. 1930.

THERE ARE TWO THINGS of immediate interest to the musical theater fan at the Baseball Hall of Fame in Cooperstown, New York. One is some sheet music from *Damn Yankees;* the other is the story of Harry H. Frazee. Frazee was a cantankerous alcoholic who worked his way up from being a box office manager to managing athletes. His attraction to theater, wagers, and money made him a born producer; he had the first hit of his new career with *Madame Sherry* in 1910. He also liked ball teams. In 1916, Frazee purchased the Boston Red Sox, but he was far more interested in making fast money than building a tradition. In the last week of 1919, he sold one of his crankier pitchers to the New York Yankees for the unheard-of sum of $100,000, plus a loan of $300,000 more. As far as Boston fans are concerned, Frazee's selling of Babe Ruth hexed the Red Sox with "the Curse of the Bambino," which has kept them from winning a single World Series between 1918 and 2004. One sports reporter wrote, "There are two things every New England schoolchild can recite: 'Paul Revere's Ride' and the sins of Harry Frazee."

In 1924, Frazee recycled a successful farce he owned called *My Lady Friends* as a three-act musical called *No, No, Nanette.* He brought together his *Madame Sherry* lyricist, Otto Harbach, one of Broadway's most successful wordsmiths, and an up-and-coming composer, Vincent Youmans, who had had a huge hit the previous year with *Wildflower. No, No, Nanette* was the innocuous tale of a middle-aged Bible salesman, his inquisitive wife, and Nanette, their pretty young ward. When Nanette gets it into her pretty young head to go off to Atlantic City for the weekend unchaperoned (oh no!), innocent complications ensue. The show lay there lifeless during its New York rehearsal period, so the genteel Harbach brought in another lyricist, the boisterous Irving Caesar, to write some new songs with Youmans.

Frazee took the show to Detroit and then to Cincinnati for two languishing tryouts. The only thing really accomplished there was the introduction into the show of two Youmans/Caesar collaborations; luckily, the songs just happened to be "I Want to Be Happy" and "Tea for Two." Those numbers turned the entire show into one jolly affair, made the rest of the score look good, and went on to become two of the most popular tunes of the decade.

But none of that would have happened without the Chicago tryout, which occurred in May 1924. Critics were lukewarm, but Frazee kept replacing actors and kept the show running at a loss through sheer bloodymindedness. It was a smart move—eventually the show caught on, sold out its performances, and became the longest-running musical in Chicago history, playing the Windy City for just shy of a year.

By the time *No, No, Nanette* opened in New York on September 16, 1925, Frazee had already sent several touring companies around the United States and opened a London production that had a two-year run. The Broadway run was a comparative disappointment, largely because the public had been hearing "I Want to Be Happy" for more than a year and the novelty had worn off. Frazee could not have cared less; he was already a millionaire from the show, which went on to play in productions all over the world.

Harry H. Frazee, the bane of Boston, c. 1926.

OPPOSITE: *Pretty, young Nanette makes a big splash in Atlantic City.*

The story of *No, No, Nanette* ended happily—twice. In 1971, a revival made it to Broadway, after another much-troubled tryout. No one expected much from the production—the musical theater had moved in several other directions since 1924, and unlike the venom-tipped nostalgia of Prince and Sondheim's *Follies*, this *Nanette* served it up straight: flappers and tap dances in pastel colors, helmed (in name only) by Busby Berkeley, who was brought out of retirement, along with 1930s film star Ruby Keeler, who played the Bible salesman's wife. Riding the crest of the nation's nostalgia craze of the early 1970s, *No, No, Nanette* thoroughly enchanted older Broadway audiences (it ran for 891 performances, nearly three times longer than the original) and also helped initiate the revival movement that is still prominent on Broadway.

H.H. Frazee dropped dead at the age of forty-eight in his Park Avenue apartment, two years after mounting a failed sequel to *No, No, Nanette* called, with a straight face, *Yes, Yes, Yvette*. He lost far more on that show than he made selling the Bambino to the Yankees—a fact that might make Red Sox fans want to be happy, too.

"Thou swell, thou witty"
RODGERS AND HART

Portrait of Rodgers (l.) and Hart, 1927.

Their songs were thrilling. No one had ever heard anything like it; the lyrics were articulate, witty, personal, intimate, heart-wrenching, and the music was all of those things too. There wasn't a wrong choice made by Rodgers. Now, when you consider the fact that these gentlemen wrote show after relentless show through the '20s and the '30s, all theoretically encouraging wrong notes, because the notes were being applied to these ridiculous little stories, you would think that Rodgers would have dropped his guard: "I'll just take this E-flat because it's easier for me today." Nothing like that ever crossed his mind.

—Jonathan Schwartz

As the 1920s roared to life, Richard Rodgers was given an opportunity rarely presented to eighteen-year-olds; he and his partner, Lorenz Hart, were to write their first full Broadway score. The show, *Poor Little Ritz Girl,* was being produced by the legendary Lew Fields, of the vaudeville team Weber and Fields, who was also the father of their Columbia University chum Herbert. For an eager beaver like Rodgers, the opportunity seemed too good to be true. It was. While the show was trying out in Boston, young Rodgers had resumed his annual job as a summer camp counselor. When Rodgers and his family arrived at the Central Theatre in New York in July of 1920 and opened their programs, they had an unpleasant surprise: half of the team's score had been thrown out and substituted with numbers composed by Sigmund Romberg. No one had bothered to tell Rodgers. "Even now," he wrote in 1975, "more than fifty years later, I can still feel the bitter disappointment and depression of that opening. My parents and I sat and suffered together until they took me to the train to go back to camp."

Rodgers was nothing if not determined and ambitious. He knew at that moment he had to take control of his own career, and by and large he did, over the course of six unprecedented decades. He knew he would never let the *Poor Little Ritz Girl* experience happen to him again, just as he had known from an early age that he had to be a show composer.

They always sold the printed score [of 1910s operettas] in the lobby of the theatre and my parents used to buy it and bring it home and up it would go on the piano, and my mother would play it again and again and again, starting with the overture—not doing the whole thing in one night—but eventually reaching the exit march.
—Richard Rodgers, 1963

Rodgers had enrolled at Columbia University in 1919, not to further his education but to write the fabled Varsity Show. Two earlier graduates from Columbia would become his most indelible collaborators: Oscar Hammerstein II and Lorenz Hart. Rodgers wrote a few school songs with alumnus Hammerstein but soon realized he needed a full-time partner. A mutual friend introduced him to Lorenz Hart, seven years older, who had been translating Hungarian plays for the Shubert Brothers. Dick and Larry seemed to be a good match: they were both from well-off Jewish families on the Upper East Side and had the benefits of a liberal education. After spending an afternoon with Hart, being taught rhyme structures, masculine versus feminine endings, and how good songs should go, Rodgers famously wrote, "I left Hart's house having acquired, in one afternoon, a career, a partner, a best friend, and a source of lasting irritation." What irritated Rodgers was that he could never find Hart. Years later, he elaborated: "He would disappear and he had to be found and he had to be locked up in a room and I had to stay with him there until he wrote."

For the first half of the 1920s, the team sat and watched Broadway hit after Broadway hit from the sidelines, but with the terrific success of "Manhattan," Rodgers and Hart became a permanent fixture on the musical scene. The Theatre Guild brought them back for a second *Garrick Gaieties* in 1926, and despite the fact that they wrote a song called "We Can't Be as Good as Last Year," they proved that they could be. In "Manhattan," Rodgers and Hart wrote of a couple who were blissfully impoverished in the city; with "Mountain Greenery," they transposed the sentiment to the country:

> In a mountain greenery,
> Where God paints the scenery,
> Just two crazy people together.

To understand the genius of Larry Hart, one has to understand that once a lyricist commits to ending a rhyme scheme with a word such as "greenery," he is left with precious few options. "Scenery"—well, that only makes sense, as does "life's machinery," a handy antithesis, but it was Hart's solution at the end of the first refrain that was utterly inspired:

> Beans could get no keener re-
> Ception in a beanery.

Part of the Rodgers and Hart alchemy derived from the difference in their personal styles that Rodgers had helplessly decried. Rodgers was businesslike, diligent, focused, and brilliant at what he did. Hart was an alcoholic, unreliable, profligate, and brilliant at what he did. Their mutual brilliance helped; Rodgers's jaunty melodies (always written first, because Hart could never be counted on to get cracking) were the perfect counterpart to Hart's essential melancholy. Most writing teams try to be on the same page, as it were, but Rodgers and Hart's perpendicularity created some terrific sparks. The other thing they had going for them was the thing

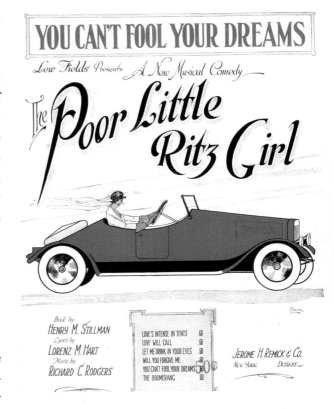

Dearest Enemy *(1925) was Rodgers and Hart's first musical hit after "Manhattan" landed with audiences. Written with Herbert Fields, it was a risqué spoof set during the American Revolution; there wouldn't be another hit musical set in that period for nearly fifty years.*

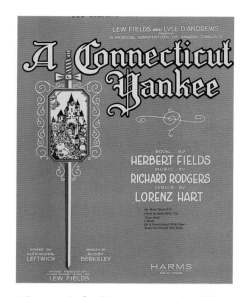

Sheet music for "My Heart Stood Still" from A Connecticut Yankee.

RIGHT: *Nana Bryant and William Gaxton in* A Connecticut Yankee, *1927.*

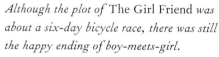

Although the plot of The Girl Friend *was about a six-day bicycle race, there was still the happy ending of boy-meets-girl.*

that drove them crazy: their late entry into the field. By the time "Manhattan" debuted, shows such as *Lady, Be Good!* and *No, No, Nanette,* not to mention the Princess Shows, were already proven successes. Like it or not, Rodgers and Hart were a new generation, and it gave them their edge. They were determined to bring something different to the Broadway stage. "The one possible formula," said Rodgers, "was don't have a formula. The one rule for success: don't follow it up."

Rodgers and Hart took that formula to heart and, from 1925 to 1930, wrote scores for an incredible eighteen shows—both book musicals and revues, in New York and in London. *Peggy-Ann* incorporated Freudian dream sequences and *Dearest Enemy* was set during the American Revolution. The Prince of Wales hummed "My Heart Stood Still" to a British bandleader and it became a hit song on two continents. *A Connecticut Yankee,* which debuted in November 1927, was an exceptionally ambitious piece for its time. Herbert Fields's libretto was based on a source with real literary merit—a story by Mark Twain—and it provided Hart with a chance to mix high speech and low art with "Thou Swell."

Although trying to be innovative, they could not always escape the "boy-meets-girl" scenarios of the previous generation. "We wanted to write shows that had different settings," Rodgers recalled in a 1963 television appearance. "*The Girl Friend* was about a big thing at the time, a six-day bicycle race, and so the fellow meets the girl there. In *A*

Connecticut Yankee, it was a fantasy in the days of King Arthur and the fellow goes back in time and what do you think happened? He fell in love with a girl." Yet through all the giddy times and zippy productions of the 1920s, Rodgers and Hart never grew pretentious or hackneyed, an achievement in itself.

On October 25, 1929, Rodgers and Hart were out of town with a new show, *Heads Up!* It seemed an apt title. Whatever problems they were having with their first act curtain paled next to the crisis on Wall Street, where it was—simply—curtains. Despite the Crash, Rodgers got engaged to be married in 1930, and in 1931, Rodgers and Hart were spoofing talking pictures in *America's Sweetheart*. The score contains one of the first songs to mine hope from the Depression:

> I've got five dollars;
> I'm in good condition;
> And I've got ambition—
> That belongs to you.
> Six shirts and collars;
> Debts beyond endurance
> On my life insurance—
> That belongs to you.

A year later, Rodgers and his wife had a baby daughter and times were getting tough, so he suggested to Hart that they go west to work in those talking pictures they had ribbed so mercilessly in *America's Sweetheart*. Berlin, Gershwin, and Kern had all gone to Hollywood. Rodgers needed the paycheck. Hart, true to form and to the difference between the two men, thought it would be a lark. Paramount Pictures called and off they went.

In Present Arms *(1928), a musical about Marines stationed in Hawaii, the military background of Busby Berkeley came in handy. Here Berkeley (left, with Joyce Barbour and Charlie King) performs as well before his own exodus to Hollywood.*

MANHATTAN

Words by Lorenz Hart
Music by Richard Rodgers
From The Garrick Gaieties *(1925)*

I F THE PHONE HADN'T RUNG in Richard Rodgers's parents' house one night in 1925, the world might have gained a mediocre underwear salesman, but it would have lost one of the greatest composers of the twentieth century. The 1924–25 theater season was "the most miserable period of my life," Rodgers later wrote. It had been four years since he had had a song on Broadway, and doubt gnawed away at him: "I had been a boy wonder. I had gotten a show to Broadway at an earlier age than Gershwin. It all seemed to be falling apart." Rodgers had been offered a job—at an impressive $50 a week—selling children's underwear. He asked the man for a day to think about it; that night the phone rang.

The call was from the prestigious Theatre Guild, the leading producer of straight plays on Broadway, asking Rodgers and Hart to contribute a couple of songs to *The Garrick Gaieties*, a semiprofessional revue being mounted to raise money for the elegant tapestries that would adorn its new Guild Theatre. This time Rodgers didn't need a day to think it over: "Literally overnight, I was lifted from despair," he wrote in his autobiography. It would be the first of two times the Theatre Guild would change his life; almost twenty years later, they would ask him to write a little show called *Oklahoma!*

"Manhattan" was written as a duet between a boy and a girl (although it is rarely performed that way) and was resurrected from an earlier show, *Winkle Town*, from Rodgers and Hart's Columbia days. The song is a perfect marriage of tune and lyrics, with the sauntering air provided by Rodgers, redolent at first of "The Sidewalks of New York," then gently rhapsodic as it progresses; Hart's way of getting a listener to bend his or her ear around certain rhymes ("what street/Mott Street") demands a friendly complicity; the lines at the end of each second A-section contain no less than five exquisitely unforced rhymes. Most impressively, where other songs about New York apostrophize skyscrapers, Broadway, and expensive nightspots, Rodgers and Hart take the listener on a subtle journey through the city's more frugal charms. Of all the songs that glamorized the Big Apple in the 1920s (and beyond), none is as delightful as the one that sought glamour simply through the eyes of a "boy and goil"—from Brooklyn, obviously—in love.

Years later, when Rodgers and Hart were unconditionally successful, they attended a show at the Guild's new theater. Spying those expensive tapestries out of the corner of his eye, Hart said, "See those tapestries? We're responsible for them." Rodgers, ever the paternal of the two, responded, "No, Larry. They're responsible for us."

Rodgers and Hart, c. 1930.

Summer journeys to Niag'ra
And to other places aggra-
Vate all our cares.
We'll save our fares!
I've a cozy little flat in
What is known as old Manhattan,
We'll settle down
Right here in town!

We'll have Manhattan
The Bronx and Staten
Island too.
It's lovely going through
The zoo.
It's very fancy
On old Delancey
Street, you know.
The subway charms us so
When balmy breezes blow
To and fro.
And tell me what street
Compares with Mott Street
In July?
Sweet pushcarts gently gliding by.
The great big city's a wondrous toy
Just made for a girl and boy.
We'll turn Manhattan
Into an isle of joy.

We'll go to Greenwich,
Where modern men itch
To be free;
And Bowling Green you'll see
With me.
We'll bathe at Brighton;
The fish you'll frighten
When you're in.
Your bathing suit so thin
Will make the shellfish grin
Fin to fin.
I'd like to take a
Sail on Jamaica
Bay with you.
And fair Canarsie's lake
We'll view.
The city's bustle cannot destroy

The dreams of a
girl and boy.
We'll turn Manhattan
Into an isle of joy.

We'll go to Yonkers
Where true love conquers
In the wilds.
And starve together, dear,
In Childs.
We'll go to Coney
And eat baloney
On a roll.
In Central Park we'll stroll,
Where our first kiss we stole,
Soul to soul.
Our future babies
We'll take to *Abie's*
Irish Rose
I hope they'll live to see
It close.
The city's clamor can never spoil
The dreams of a boy and goil.
We'll turn Manhattan

"*There never was and never will be a show like this!*"

SHOW BOAT

It was lucky for Florenz Ziegfeld, and the American musical theater, that Jerome Kern was such a devoted bibliophile. In October 1926, Kern had just read Edna Ferber's new epic novel about a showboat called the *Cotton Blossom*, which traversed the turbulent waters of the Mississippi with its various show folk over several generations, from the 1870s to the present. It was exactly the kind of textured, serious, yet inherently musical material he had been searching for. During the intermission of a Broadway show, Kern asked critic Alexander Woollcott to arrange an introduction to the often imperious novelist; Woollcott did just that, by whistling over Miss Ferber from across the theater lobby.

Although Kern was one of the most respected composers in his field, Ferber blanched at the idea of her serious work being turned into her notion of a musical comedy, but she allowed him to go ahead. He needed a librettist, so he called on the best: his collaborator on *Sunny*, Oscar Hammerstein II. Hammerstein didn't have to think twice; he said yes.

The team wrote most of the first-act songs and took their work to the only man on Broadway with the vision and resources to take on the project. The day after Ziegfeld heard the material, he called his secretary Goldie Clough into his office to take a letter to a tenor named Harry Fender:

> Last night I heard the first act of the *Show Boat* and Jerome Kern's music. This is the best musical comedy I have ever been fortunate to get a hold of; I am thrilled to produce it, this show is the opportunity of my life, and is an opportunity that comes once in a lifetime [for the leading actors].

The serious undercurrents of Ferber's Mississippi River, however, put Ziegfeld in uncharted waters. His daughter, Patricia Ziegfeld Stephenson, recalled:

> *Show Boat* was really a step for him that was terrifying. And although he loved doing it, it was rather a sad story, and he said, "We cannot do this musical with all this sadness." . . . He was so afraid that people would not like what he was doing, because it wasn't the kind of *Follies* the audience expected. They expected laughter, and beautiful girls.

Ziegfeld's experience with getting shows up and onstage quickly had not prepared him for the care and time that Kern and Hammerstein would need to adapt a sprawling novel to the stage, so the creators and the producer argued frequently about the schedule.

> **Ziegfeld was a man who had no equal when it came to taste in the theater . . . for visual effects. . . for the beauty of girls, for the beauty of scenery and costumes, and for what the audience saw. . . . I think that before we opened he expected Show Boat to be a pretty big bore and he thought all that story stuff would be cut out . . . and what would remain would be pretty costumes and scenery and the tunes and the girls and the comedian.**
>
> **—Oscar Hammerstein II,** 1954

Jerome Kern plays the piano while Oscar Hammerstein II looks on.

What Oscar did was to marry European operetta and American musical comedy tradition. One of the reasons *Show Boat* turned out as well as it did is that Kern knew what Oscar was trying to do, and he was just as interested in doing it—attempting to tell some kind of story about character.

—Stephen Sondheim

OPPOSITE ABOVE: *Joseph Urban's three-dimensional set model for the interior of the show boat.*

OPPOSITE BELOW: *Scene-within-a-scene from* Show Boat.

In dealing with the "story stuff" Hammerstein's task was unlike any challenge faced by a librettist or lyricist for the American theater up to that point. No musical had ever been adapted from a serious novel, none had had to deal with a three-generation time span in the story, none had to bring a story from the past to the present, and certainly none had dealt with white characters and black characters sharing the stage as full dramatic entities. As if that weren't enough, *Show Boat* also had to sing with a score that not only honored the traditions of its entertainment milieu, but engaged the audience in its lighter and more romantic moments.

Hammerstein's libretto was remarkably faithful to Ferber's novel. Cap'n Andy's showboat, the *Cotton Blossom*, travels up and down the Mississippi for decades. Among its colorful passen-

In the show's famous "miscegenation" scene, Julie (Helen Morgan, center) faints as the secret of her mixed-race past is revealed.

It was seismic then. There was this incredible centerpiece of a scene in the first act, which had all of the leading characters interrelating— no songs—and an incredibly complex political plot about miscegenation. . . . Suddenly along comes a show with issues and politics and serious stories.
—Harold Prince

gers are his brittle wife, their glowing daughter, Magnolia, her gambler husband, and a troupe of complicated supporting characters.

The most complicated is Julie LaVerne (Dozier, in Ferber's novel), a mulatto performing on the showboat and married (illegally, by the laws of the South) to a white man; her secret revealed, she leaves the boat and winds up, in the second act, a wasted alcoholic version of her earlier buoyant self. *Show Boat*'s height of invention—among many highlights—is the revelation of her secret, which comes not in dramatic exposition, but when she sings "Can't Help Lovin' Dat Man" to the smitten Magnolia. Halfway through the song, Queenie, the showboat's black cook, recognizes the tune. "Ah didn't ever hear anybody but colored folk sing dat song—sounds funny for Miss Julie to know it." Julie's defensive reaction—"What's so funny about that?"—tells the audience everything it needs to know and sets the stage for a dramatic showdown two scenes later. To put this in perspective, the dramatic dilemma at the core of the biggest hit musical at the time, *Good News!*, was whether the football captain could win the big game, pass his astronomy exam, and get a date with the girl.

Yet all of Hammerstein's ministrations would have mattered little if the music had not also risen to the occasion. Kern's score to *Show Boat* is certainly the grandest and most ambitious of its time—arguably the greatest ever written for the musical theater. Hammerstein had to weave characters in and out, but Kern had to weave musical idioms and exploit his audience's knowledge of genres and fads in order to propel the narrative's complicated storytelling without falling into clumsy pastiche. His surefootedness is breathtaking. African American folk idioms ("Ol' Man River," the deleted "Mis'ry's Comin' Aroun'") mix with operetta ("Make Believe"); comedy numbers ("Life Upon the Wicked Stage") frame Latin convent hymns; torch songs hold their own with upbeat ensemble numbers; even the "traditional" "Can't Help Lovin' Dat Man" is turned on its head in its reprise—"tricked" into a ragtime number to bring us into 1904. Kern even had the guts to use other composers' songs, such as "After the Ball," just to set the proper period and mood.

At its Washington, D.C., tryout, the show ran more than four hours. Ziegfeld and his creative team started hacking away at it, and after several brief out-of-town stops, *Show Boat* finally docked in New York on December 27, 1927, at the stunning new Ziegfeld Theatre, which had been conceived by the producer's celebrated scenic designer, Joseph Urban. Ziegfeld had abruptly evicted his theater's first tenant, *Rio Rita*, so that *Show Boat* could have its premiere in his eponymous showcase. Ziegfeld was giving the audience the same values he had offered them for two decades: a huge cast, comic songs and dances, black actors performing with white actors, breathtaking design, soaring music, overwhelming spectacle, all burnished to a golden sheen. But this time, the show had a story. An American story. A story with heart.

During the opening night performance, Ziegfeld sat on the back stairs of the theater with his secretary Goldie. He didn't know what the audience would think and, for most of the performance, the audience didn't know itself—it had never seen anything like this before, and certainly not from the man who had brought them a glorified girlie show every season. Hammerstein, who had overseen the direction of the show, decided against putting in the customary curtain calls, so when the final curtain came down, there was absolute silence. The audience got up, put on their coats, and shuffled quietly out into the night. Ziegfeld turned to Goldie and said, "Well, now I've really done it." Only the next morning, when he read the reviews and witnessed, incredulously, the lines at the box office, did he know what kind of hit he had on his hands.

Ziegfeld was rewarded for his gamble with something that meant more to him than artistic prestige: box office receipts. Not only was *Show Boat* more than a *succès d'estime*, it was an out-and-out hit, running 572 performances, and proved so beloved by audiences and so lucrative to Ziegfeld that he revived it as early as 1932.

Show Boat has been revived nearly a half dozen times on Broadway and still routinely plays around the globe. It is undeniably one of America's most revolutionary musicals, and its grandeur cast a long shadow throughout the twentieth century. However, unlike Hammerstein's other revolutionary show, *Oklahoma!*, it was not immediately influential. Times changed very quickly after the show's opening, and even if Kern and Hammerstein had found a comparably rich subject to musicalize (their next collaboration, *Sweet Adeline* in 1929, was much lighter in tone), there was no guarantee that Depression audiences would have been galvanized in quite the same way. *Show Boat* had to wait almost two decades for a worthy successor to its ambitions.

Oscar Hammerstein II, Florenz Ziegfeld, and Jerome Kern in front of the theater, 1927.

OVERLEAF: Show Boat'*s epic structure begins at a Natchez levee in 1890 and ends at the same place, in the year it was written, 1927. In a still from the London 1928 production, Paul Robeson, far right, as Joe reprises "Ol' Man River."*

OL' MAN RIVER

Words by Oscar Hammerstein II
Music by Jerome Kern
From Show Boat *(1927)*

ALTHOUGH *SHOW BOAT* IS A MUSICAL EPIC with many storylines, the most important character of all wasn't even onstage. "Ol' Man River" was one of the last songs written for the score. It's been said that Hammerstein needed the number to cover a set change and borrowed a snatch of Kern's opening "Cotton Blossom" number and slowed down the tempo. But in an interview later in his life, he revealed a deeper motive:

> The motive for writing "Ol' Man River" was not even a song-writing motive. It was my anxiety about the story itself, Edna Ferber's novel, which I admired very much, and loved and wanted to adapt. It was a sprawling kind of novel, it didn't have the tightness that a play requires. I thought that we lacked something to make it cohesive. . . . I wanted to keep the spirit of Edna's book. And the one focal influence I could find was the river. I decided to write a river theme, which would hold the play together. . . . I put the song about the river into the voice, the throat of a character who is a rugged and untutored philosopher who hung around the wharves and the showboat. Possibly there's an implied protest.

The song was not without controversy. The second verse appears as the first lyric of the show, heard the moment the curtain rises on a group of black stevedores on a Natchez levee: "Niggers all work on de Mississippi." This is how Paul Robeson sang it when he played Joe, the "untutored philosopher," in the 1928 London production, but over the years, in various productions and renditions, the original lyric has been altered. In the 1936 film, Robeson sang "Darkies all work . . ."; the 1946 revival, which Hammerstein worked on, had "Colored folk work . . ."; subsequent versions attempted a half-baked neutrality with "Here we all work . . ." In some productions, the verse has been omitted altogether. One can only assume that Hammerstein, one of musical theater's most liberal souls, deliberately chose his words not to offend but to telegraph to his audience that what they were about to see onstage was a realistic world, not an operetta fantasy. In using the word *nigger,* however, he embroiled his song, and the show, in one of the most emotionally charged cultural arguments of the twentieth century. Controversy over the word dogged Broadway revivals of *Show Boat* as late as 1995.

None of this, however, has kept the song from becoming an American standard. When Kern played the song to the still-skeptical Ferber in 1927, tears came to her eyes. "I knew this wasn't just a musical comedy number," she later wrote. "This was a great song. This was a song that would outlast Kern and Hammerstein's day and your day and my day." Hundreds of singers and musicians, black and white, have used it in a variety of ways to express themselves musically, emotionally, or politically. It just keeps rolling along.

Jules Bledsoe as the original Joe, singing "Ol' Man River."

JOE:
Dere's an ol' man called de Mississippi;
Dat's de ol' man dat I'd like to be!
What does he care if de world's got troubles?
What does he care if de land ain't free?

Ol' Man River,
Dat Ol' Man River,
He mus' know sumpin'
But don' say nuthin',
He jes' keeps rollin',
He keeps on rollin' along.
He don' plant taters,
He don' plant cotton,
An' dem dat plants 'em
Is soon forgotten,
But Ol' Man River,
He jes' keeps rollin' along.
You an' me, we sweat an' strain,
Body all achin' an' racked wid pain—
Tote dat barge!
Lif' dat bale!
Git a little drunk,
An' you land in jail.
Ah gits weary
An' sick of tryin',
Ah'm tired of livin',
An' skeered of dyin',
But Ol' Man River,
He jes' keeps rollin' along.

JOE and MALE CHORUS:
Niggers all work on de Mississippi,
Niggers all work while de white folks play,
Pullin' dem boats from de dawn to sunset,
Gittin' no rest till de Judgment Day.

MEN:
Don' look up
An' don' look down,
You don' dast make
De white boss frown.
Bend yo' knees
An' bow yo' head,
An' pull dat rope
Until yo' dead.

JOE:
Let me go 'way from de Mississippi,
Let me go 'way from de white man boss;
Show me dat stream called de river Jordan,
Dat's de ol' stream dat I long to cross.

MEN:
Ol' Man River . . . (repeat)

JOE and MEN:
Ah gits weary
An' sick of tryin',
Ah'm tired of livin',
An' skeered of dyin',
But Ol' Man River,
He jes' keeps rollin' along.

A color rendering of the scenery for Act One.

MUSIC

"You ain't heard nothin' yet!"

THE TALKIES AND THE CRASH

A lobby card shows Jolson selling "Dirty Hands" to an adoring crowd.

In 1926, Rodgers and Hart wrote *Betsy* as a vehicle for an actress named Belle Baker. When its producer, Flo Ziegfeld, decided that the show needed a big hit ballad, he went straight to Irving Berlin and asked him for one; "Blue Skies" was quickly dropped into *Betsy* and on opening night Rodgers and Hart—who never countenanced interpolations into their shows—sat in their house seats, fuming. Perhaps they would have accepted their humiliation better if "Blue Skies" had simply made the rounds for a season and faded away, but Berlin's number was destined to become not just a popular standard but part of show business history.

On October 6, 1927, the Warners' Theatre on Broadway and 52nd Street was the launching pad for one of the most spectacular skyrockets in American popular culture. It was at this movie palace that Warner Bros. debuted the first talking picture, *The Jazz Singer*, starring Al Jolson. Jolson plays Jakie Rabinowitz, the son of a cantor, who escapes from his Orthodox home, changes his name, and becomes a huge star in vaudeville and on Broadway. Any other star might have consulted his lawyer, but Jolson was immensely flattered and was eager to do the picture.

The studio had been experimenting with sound film technologies for some time and finally cast their lot with Vitaphone, which synchronized film with giant phonograph disks. The technology was not advanced enough to allow for a full-length sound feature, so *The Jazz Singer* alternated several sound sequences with huge stretches of silence.

That evening in October, fifteen silent minutes into the movie, the audience all of a sudden heard Al Jolson belt out the song "Dirty Hands, Dirty Face" and finish by telling the crowd "Wait a minute, folks, wait a minute, you ain't heard nothin' yet!" When his character comes back to the family tenement to visit his long-suffering mother, Jolson plays "Blue Skies" on the piano twice, jazzing up the reprise. The song was added after shooting had already started because Warners wanted to feature a surefire hit; Jolson turned it into one a second time.

No one could predict how this experiment with sound would land, but audiences couldn't get enough of *The Jazz Singer*. The theater was forced to screen the movie around the clock and it became the second-highest-grossing picture of the year, remarkable for a film in limited release for only eleven weeks. Jolson and Berlin had shown producers and the public alike that movies could bring musical theater to audiences far beyond Broadway. In 1929, *The Cocoanuts*, starring the Marx Brothers, with a score by Berlin, became the first Broadway musical that was adapted to the screen.

It is difficult to assess how deeply sound film might have affected Broadway if another earth-shattering event hadn't occurred two Octobers later. The stock market crash of 1929 ushered in an era of extraordinary change in American society; as far as the make-believe world of the Broadway musical was concerned, sound film and the Depression were a one-two knockout punch. It wasn't enough that the deleterious effects of the Depression made shows harder to produce—now actors, singers, directors, and songwriters were fleeing the gray canyons of the Theater District for the one place where money seemed to grow on trees, just like the oranges. Hollywood's ability to produce new musicals and steal the best stage talent of the 1920s brought something to the Broadway musical it had never really known before: competition.

Finale

"Satire is what closes Saturday night" was one of George S. Kaufman's most incisive witticisms. Although he was the decade's most successful comic playwright and had written the book for several musical hits, his luck ran out in Philadelphia in September 1927. Kaufman had teamed up with the Gershwins to write the first musical antiwar satire, *Strike Up the Band*. The story, which would not have seemed out of place in a Marx Brothers show, was about a megalomaniacal Midwestern cheese manufacturer who offers to pick up the tab for a war against Switzerland—as long as the conflict is named after him.

Kaufman provided an adroitly absurdist book and the Gershwins wrote a distinguished score. Ira's verse for the title song went, in part:

> We fought in 1917.
> > Rum ta ta tum, tum, tum!
> And drove the tyrant from the scene.
> > Rum ta ta tum, tum, tum!
> We're in a bigger, better war
> For your patriotic pastime.
> We don't know what we're fighting for—
> But we didn't know the last time!

Paul McCullough and Bobby Clark in the denatured Strike Up the Band, *1930.*

Such trenchant humor went over the heads of the Philadelphia audience, and after *two* Saturday nights, the satire closed out of town. Kaufman and the Gershwins slunk back to New York, regrouped, and moved on to other triumphs.

Two months after the stock market crash, the original producer brought the show back to Broadway, in a drastically revised version. Kaufman, feeling played out, as it were, graciously allowed his recent collaborator Morrie Ryskind to rewrite the book. Silliness was still in vogue for musical comedies, so Ryskind denatured the satire, substituted chocolate for cheese, and turned the whole war into a dream sequence, tailored to the knockabout antics of the comedy duo Clark and McCullough. "What I had to do, in a sense, was to rewrite *War and Peace* for the Three Stooges," said Ryskind later. It looked harmless enough to be a hit.

The revised *Strike Up the Band* premiered on January 14, making it the first musical of the 1930s. As Kaufman (who maintained a friendly and financial interest in the show) and Ryskind stood at the back of the Times Square Theatre on opening night, they watched the audience eat up the more palatable high jinks on stage. It might well have been the last carefree evening the crowd would have in a long time. The tremors of the Depression were just beginning to rumble the floorboards of every house on Broadway. Kaufman and Ryskind counted themselves lucky this time out; they were savvy enough to know that, in the months ahead, theatergoers might no longer buy such a giddy piece of fluff. As the curtain came down, they promised each other that it would be different next time—no compromises. They would write their next show just for themselves. By the time they sat down to write their new musical, the politically turbulent decade of the 1930s would prove to be their most potent collaborator.

The Jazz Singer convinced moviegoers that
talking films were more than a novelty, and
fires under exhibitors to get their features
for sound.   The film earned over $3,000,0
the Warners. . . . Thus, already a legend wit
his own time, did Jolie complete the cycle f
vaudeville to minstrelsy, to star at the Wint
Garden, to the historic impetus that gave
soundpix their start and finally to glorificati
in celluloid as the subject of two biopix
[*The Jolson Story* and *Jolson Sings Again*].
—Abe Green and Joe Lau
Show Biz

EDDIE CANTOR ON AL JOLSON

Take My Life (*excerpt*), 1957, by Eddie Cantor with
Jane Kesner Ardmore

WHILE I WAS STILL A STOOGE for Bedini and Arthur, still rushing around backstage at Hammerstein's taking suits out to be pressed or seeing that Jean Bedini's laundry was back on time—a fellow in blackface wandered onto the stage one day. He was from Lew Dockstader's Minstrels. Now he was doing a single and there was something electric about him that sent a thrill up your spine. He sang and talked; but he was more than just a singer or an actor—he was an *experience*, and he was to become the most romantic figure of a romantic era, the King of it. Al Jolson.

From the time I heard him at Hammerstein's, he was my idol. I somehow saw every show he was in, and always, for minutes after he'd left the stage, you sat still, knowing that a great presence had been there. And I saw him at the Winter Garden where he was at his best, a real one-man show. Oh, there were some other people occasionally on the stage; a line of dancing girls, enough of a company to keep the thing going while Jolie took a glass of water or mopped his brow off stage. But he was the show and many's the night he'd look at the audience about a quarter of eleven and say, "The girls are waiting backstage and they have some songs and dances, but they've worked pretty hard tonight, let's let 'em go home, huh? I'll stay here as long as you want but let the poor kids go home, huh?" And he'd send everybody home while he stood there maybe another hour, singing, clowning, giving the audience the time of its life and having the time of his own. For this was Jolson's big love affair. Through all the years, the love of his life was—the audience. . . .

Jolie and I were friends from that night. He didn't like actors, actually, but of all actors he minded me least, maybe because he knew I worshiped him. . . .

We were good friends and competitors. During the years when Jolson was with the Shuberts and I was with Ziegfeld it would sometimes happen that we'd open in the same town the same night. This was tough. We'd stay at the same hotel, take our meals together, and send spies to each other's houses to find out the grosses. I should add here that Jolson would have been a sellout if all he'd done was read the telephone directory. I had to have a show, and my shows were better than Jolie's because it was Jolson people went to see, and the rest of his show didn't matter.

The rivalry was at its height when we opened on the same day and date in Chicago, he in *Bombo* at the Apollo, I in *Kid Boots* at the Woods. We both did fine. Professionally, that is. Personally, we were both hypochondriacs and for once both had reason to be. We'd been playing for about sixteen weeks when that cold Lake Michigan breeze caught up with me and I developed my old stand-by, pleurisy.

As the days went by, the pain was such that I could scarcely breathe. The doctor strapped me with adhesive tape and the show went on. *Kid Boots* was a rough show. I bounced all over the place, and it got to the point where I could barely bounce through a performance. The doctor wanted me to drain the fluid, but I wouldn't let him. Ida begged me to close the show. Jolie talked to me like a big brother.

"Eddie, show business ain't worth it. You need sun, kid. Go to Miami, close the show, get some rest and heat and get well."

I thanked him sadly, but the show must go on. Why? Because in my mind's eye I could see the headline in *Variety:* JOLSON DRIVES CANTOR OUT OF CHICAGO. Finally one night between the first and second acts I quietly collapsed. The doctor stepped in and the show was closed, and I was trundled to the train for New York.

"You're doin' the right thing," Jolie said. "Get a rest, Eddie. No show has to go on."

I arrived in New York, picked up the *New York Times*, and on the front page read: JOLSON ILL, CLOSES SHOW.

What I hadn't know—all the time I was suffering with pleurisy, Al was sicker than I was, with a throat infection. But Jolie wouldn't close the show, because in his mind's eye he could see a headline in *Variety:* CANTOR DRIVES JOLSON FROM CHICAGO.

He won that round. . . .

Gay one moment, morose the next, the King was unpredictable. I'll say this. No one has ever had the drive and confidence of Jolson. I'll never forget the Liberty Bond benefit at the Century Theatre during World War I. Highlight of the evening came when the great Enrico Caruso sang and the audience almost tore down the building. The applause was thunderous and you didn't think it would ever end. Jolson was scheduled to follow Caruso. It wasn't a spot anybody'd envy, but Jolie rushed out onto the stage, loosened his tie, and said, "Folks! You ain't heard nothin' yet."

On the other hand, in a show of his own he couldn't stand for anyone else to be a hit. Did I say in his own show? In any show. He could sit in his Winter Garden dressing room and read that somebody'd been a hit in Detroit—and he'd take it as a personal affront.

His death left a real gap in the heart of show business. I was in Mobile, Alabama, when NBC in New York phoned at 4 A.M. They had just received the news of Jolie's death and were paying tribute to him on a special broadcast. Could I be at the studio at 6 A.M. ? They'd cut me in from Mobile. That night I went on with my one-man show. Everything went along as usual until I got to the spot for my regular parody of the King.

> Ole man Jolson, that ole man Jolson
> He's older than Johnson, together with Olsen
> But ole man Jolson, he just keeps goin' along.
> He don't plant cotton, he don't plant 'taters
> He just plants corn in the picture the-aters.
> But ole man Jolson, he just keeps goin' along.
> Al gets down on bended knee, sings that 'Mammy' melody
> Can't get up from off the ground, his moneybags just weigh him down.

The music started, but I couldn't sing it. Instead, I talked to the audience of the Jolson I knew. I was crying, and so were they. The King was gone, the greatest minstrel of them all.

LORENZ HART ON RICHARD RODGERS

New York World (*excerpt*), *April 7, 1929*

OF ALL THE PEOPLE ENGAGED in any kind of artistic work Dick Rodgers is the most methodical and the least temperamental, but he becomes infuriated if a cat walks across the carpet while he is composing. He has regular working hours and never varies his schedule—from eleven in the morning until six at night. He is practically the Beau Brummel of Broadway. His ties are a perpetual delight and an everlasting enigma. He adores chorus girls. Blondes. And very innocent-looking. Brains not essential, but they must be innocent-looking.

His reticence on matters romantic is a continual provocation and impregnable. He loathes but two things—dialect comedians and my cigars. He really has never said anything about my cigars, but I have noted that he immediately opens a window when I light one of them. His secret passion is to conduct an orchestra. And he has a weakness for George Gershwin's music. His favorite opera is "Tristan." He is tremendously modest about his work and success and lives with his father and mother, sincerely enjoying home life. If he has an avocation it is for teas and dinner parties. He does love society. With a capital S. However, with strange inconsistency he gets equally as much pressure from an impromptu gathering of harum-scarum friends.

He is an excellent, even an exceptionally good, traveler, and he is fond of Italy and London. The easiest way to send him into a rage is to say the orchestra is too loud. He doesn't want it to play too loudly, but he never thinks it is playing too loudly. And I know it is. He indulges in everything with moderation. He drinks, smokes, stays out late, falls in love, but with moderation. Richard Rodgers might be called the conservative modernist. The discerning discover this in his music. I can't tell the most amusing thing I ever saw him do, but it happened in Washington and it was a wow!

ARCHIVES

OUR NEW NATIONAL ANTHEM
By GEORGE GERSHWIN

Theater Magazine *(excerpt), August 1925*

THE TRUE IMPORTANCE OF JAZZ in American music is a subject over which controversy has raged back and forth. There are those who condemn the new idiom, root and branch, and there are those who profess to see in it the new musical evangel. The former brand jazz as expressive of all that is ugly in modern life, condemning it as destructive of beauty, taste, and all that goes towards artistic progress; the latter hail it as the germ of a new school of music, a school essentially American. I myself tend more to the latter than the former, but I am far from going to the extreme limit of believing that jazz is going to revolutionize music or even American music. Jazz will in time become absorbed into the great musical tradition as all other forms of music have been absorbed. It will affect that music, but it will be far from being a predominant element. It will in short find its place.

Indeed, there are many signs that it is already finding its place. The blatant jazz of ten years ago, crude, vulgar, and unadorned, is passing. In my *Rhapsody in Blue* I have tried to crystallize this fact by employing jazz almost incidentally, just as I employ syncopation. I realize that jazz expresses something very definite and vital in American life, but I also realize that it expresses only one element. To express the richness of that life fully, a composer must employ melody, harmony, and counterpoint as every great composer of the past has employed them. Not, of course, in the same way, but with a full knowledge of their value. The future lies with the composer who, without forgetting the innate impressions of his youth, can employ in their expression the full resources of the masters of the past. It is only in this way that jazz can become of lasting value.

In speaking of jazz there is one superstition, and it is a superstition which must be destroyed. This is the superstition that jazz is essentially Negro. The Negroes, of course, take to jazz, but in its essence it is no more Negro than is syncopation, which exists in the music of all nations. Jazz is not Negro but American. It is the spontaneous expression of the nervous energy of modern American life. . . .

The more one studies the history of jazz during the last fifteen years the more one realizes that it is following precisely the same course that all dances of the past have followed. Beginning with crudity and vulgarity, it has gradually been freeing itself and moving towards a higher plane. At first it was mere discord for the sake of discord, a simple reveling in animal vigor. But slowly the meaning of that discord, its color, its power in the depiction of American sentiment, has been brought to life. The discord of jazz is today no mere succession of meaningless and ugly grunts and wheezes. That these are still there is no doubt true, but then modern life is, alas! not expressed by smooth phrases. We are living in an age of staccato, not legato. This we must accept. But this does not mean that out of this very staccato utterance something beautiful may not be evolved. We all remember the ugliness of the early skyscraper architecture. We all remember the attacks hurled against this architecture, attacks justified in themselves yet oblivious to the beauty possible in the future. Today with such structures as the Woolworth Tower and the new Hotel Shelton we begin to realize that the skyscraper can be as beautiful as it is original. The same result will happen, I feel certain, in the case of jazz.

It is then as useless to deplore the triumph of jazz as it is to deplore the triumph of machinery. The thing to do is to domesticate both to our uses. The present craze for dancing will pass as everything human passes. The evil which that craze brought in its wake will also pass, but a residuum of good will remain. The employment of jazz will no longer dominate but only vitalize. It is for the trained musician who is also the creative artist to bring out this vitality and to heighten it with the eternal flame of beauty. When this time comes, and perhaps it is not so far away, jazz will be but one element in a great whole which will at last give a worthy musical expression to the spirit which is America. Meanwhile we can but do our best by writing what we feel and not what we think we ought to feel. And no one who knows America can doubt that jazz has its important place in the national consciousness.

Jazz is, in short, not an end in itself but rather a means to an end. What the end will be the future musical development of the country will determine.

YOUR BROADWAY AND MINE

By WALTER WINCHELL

Daily Mirror *(excerpt)*, March 31, 1928

BROADWAY IS A STATE OF MIND, a comedy, a tragedy, a smile and a frown. With one hand it bestows and with the other it takes away. Broadway is a cynic and an optimist, a royal good fellow, a pretty woman, a highball and a headache. The underlying spirit of Broadway is the spirit of carnival. Less concentrated places separate their fete days with long, heavy periods of commonplaces. Broadway's holiday is perpetual.

The great thoroughfare is all things to all men. It yields to all men what they have the strength to take, and then, like the water that is drawn from the sea, Broadway takes its own again. It is the street of opportunity, of gilt paint, of color, of high lights and deep shadows. It countenances the vulgar, when the vulgar is rich, it tolerates art, but does not indorse it. It laughs with the spendthrift while his money lasts, and forgets him when he has ceased to be interesting.

Broadway's chief lure is its life. It lives hard, it lives gaily; but it lives. The dynamic activity of the greatest street in the United States represents the quick beating of the heart of a speeding nation. Broadway breathes with the breath of a runner and speeds with the great strides of progress. It is as restless as a troubled sleep. It demands new life to feed its life, new forms to people its sidewalks, new faces for its red and gold playhouses and its upholstered restaurants. It demands new money, new laughter, new buildings, and gets them all in each succeeding fortnight. Those who require the concentrated essence of lighter life come to the carnival places to get it. Those who are young of heart and free of purse like Broadway better than all that the best of the provinces can provide.

The outlanders rail at Broadway, but their shoutings are drowned by the din of the cabaret shows. Broadway doesn't care who likes it. It asks nobody to its party. It bars no man because of his past, and greets no man because of his future. It is the street of the present. It is a series of ephemeralities. Like the four o'clocks of the garden, it has fresh blooms every day. Broadway is a juggernaut and a flowery chariot. It is an arena that doubly crowns its victors and turns its face from the defeated. It is not typical of New York, nor of Manhattan, nor of any section, locality or place. It is typical only of itself. Its code and its costs are of its own making.

Broadway's dialect is a mingling of the jargon of many tongues blent with a patois individual and distinct. Broadway is a mosaic contrived of living fragments. Its elements are one and many. It is united in the intensity of its life. It breathes and speaks and moves and rushes on with a concerted rhythm that defies definition. Broadway is loved and cursed, admired and scoffed. It responds not and resents not. It burns its candle at both ends, but takes thought to have fresh candles to light the flickering wicks of the old.

To omit Broadway is a calamity, to survive Broadway is an achievement. Broadway is a strong wine of which all may sip, but of which only the strong may drink deeply. Its lure is its life and its carelessness of life. Its vulgarities are incidental, not material. Its camaraderie is as free as the air, yet costly as jewels. Men have conquered the professions, but have fallen in the hurry of the feet on its crowded surface. Broadway welcomes heroes and proves them clay. Its people are the high, the middle and the low. It loves a clown better than a king and prefers a song to a sermon. Broadway is cold to the failure, adamant to the prude, pitying to its critics and hearty to all new life.

The spirit of Broadway is the spirit of the child. A bauble pleases it as mightily as a masterpiece. It caters to each of the senses rather that to the head, to the heart rather than to the soul.

Song, laughter, wine, beauty, color and life—always life—these are the good things of Broadway. The bitterness, the failures, the tragedies—these are for the side streets into which are crowded those whose steps have grown heavy in the swift dance. Broadway is the light that never grows dim, the fire that never burns low—the heart that always palpitates.

CHAPTER THREE

I GOT PLENTY O' NUTTIN'

(1 9 3 1 – 1 9 4 2)

Overture

Tuesday, October 29, 1929, found Florenz Ziegfeld Jr. in a courthouse downtown. Just as Ziegfeld could dream larger than anyone on Broadway, he could also be astonishingly petty, especially toward rivals, employees, and creditors, and by the late 1920s the creditors were growing more numerous. Ziegfeld was on the stand, testifying against a vendor over a $1,600 bill for a marquee sign. A short walk from the courthouse, the stock market was beginning an alarming plunge, and Ziegfeld's friend and broker, E.F. Hutton, was frantically trying to get him on the phone. It was no use: to ensure an airtight case, Ziegfeld had insisted that his entire staff come to court to testify. The Ziegfeld office, the busiest on Broadway, was left completely unattended.

By the time Ziegfeld returned to his office, the stock market had crashed. The market value of $10 billion worth of stocks and shares had vanished that day, more than twice the amount of total currency in circulation throughout the country. Broadway's greatest showman had lost almost $3 million. He staggered home to his wife, Billie Burke, who later recalled, "I had never seen Flo like this before. I pulled his head down and took him into my arms. 'Well, poor old darling, what is it?' Flo sobbed. They were great, struggling sobs. 'I'm through,' he said. 'Nothing can save me.'"

That night, New York's mayor, the one-time Tin Pan Alley songwriter Jimmy Walker, appealed to the movie companies to "show pictures that will reinstate courage in the hearts of the people." Ziegfeld himself had been flirting with motion pictures. It was a financial necessity, for gambling was not merely a show-biz metaphor with him; throughout his career, he lost as much at the gaming tables as he did on a flop show, and Burke went through tremendous trials to wean him from his habit. When sound pictures came in, Ziegfeld was able to sell the screen rights to some of his properties, such as *Show Boat*, and

PAGE 128: *The Astor Theatre, on Broadway between West 45th and 46th Streets, had been a barometer for changing tastes in the Theater District since it was built as a legitimate theater in 1906. In 1925, it was turned into a movie theater and became the showcase for major M-G-M films throughout the 1930s. It was a commercial space in the 1970s and was razed in 1982 to accommodate the Marriott Marquis Hotel.*

William Powell became Hollywood's embodiment of the great Ziegfeld in two films: this one and Ziegfeld Follies *(1946).*

even the slogan "Glorifying the American Girl," for record sums, but the income just vanished. There were too many people to pay off. In 1930, Ziegfeld tried his hand at movies, coproducing the film version of *Whoopee!*, starring Eddie Cantor, with Hollywood mogul Sam Goldwyn. But the master showman learned quickly that even though Hollywood aped his gift for self-promotion and ballyhoo, it didn't really want any big-shot Broadway producers. Ziegfeld eventually ended his fifteen-year relationship with Cantor, selling the comedian's contract to Goldwyn for ready money.

Nothing seemed to offset Ziegfeld's debts; the creditors, sensing doom perhaps, fell upon him at an alarming rate; even the fortunes of his 1932 revival of *Show Boat* amounted to pocket change when the bills were paid. Billie Burke went to Hollywood in 1932, to jumpstart a film career in order to bring in some family income, and Ziegfeld, ill with pleurisy, followed her out there. One afternoon in July 1932, she was at the studio, reading lines in a screen test for actor Walter Pidgeon, who, thirty-five years later, would portray Ziegfeld in the film version of *Funny Girl*. The phone rang on the set, asking her to come home quickly. When she walked through the door, she was told her husband had died minutes earlier.

The newspapers estimated Ziegfeld's debt at somewhere close to $2 million. Burke had no choice but to sell the name "Ziegfeld Follies," to the Shubert Brothers, who then produced a series of revues in the 1930s that were only a shadow of their former glory. Several months after Ziegfeld's death, the Palace Theatre on Broadway and 47th Street, "the Valhalla of Vaudeville," threw out vaudeville altogether and started showing movies all day long. Movie houses overran the Theater District, and soon all the legit theaters on 42nd Street—even Ziegfeld's beloved New Amsterdam—would turn to showing cheap talkies.

By 1933, Hollywood had mastered the art of putting glamorous girls, buoyant comedians, and dazzling production numbers on celluloid. In 1936, M-G-M released such an elegant, star-studded, tuneful musical blockbuster that it won the Academy Award for Best Picture.

It was called *The Great Ziegfeld*.

"*Just around the corner, there's a rainbow in the sky*"

BROADWAY AND THE DEPRESSION

The Depression struck New York City with a hardship that bordered on cruelty. By 1932, one-third of the city's factories were forced to close. Out of a population of seven million, 1.6 million were on relief—an early and inadequate form of welfare—and nearly a third of all New Yorkers were unemployed, or accepted some form of job cut or partial pay. Shantytowns, dubbed "Hoovervilles," popped up along the East River and in the middle of Central Park (where authorities removed the sheep from Sheep Meadow, for fear they would be killed and eaten), and there were breadlines in even the highest-profile public places. Theatergoers could not ignore the defeated men lining up behind Bryant Park at 42nd Street and Sixth Avenue, or along Duffy Square at 47th and Broadway, as they pushed past them to make an 8:40 curtain.

My mom and dad [actor Bert Lahr] told me a story once about how, at the height of the Depression, they were walking from the Tavern on the Green, a very chic nightclub, across Central Park in evening dress, and as they passed a couple of hoboes warming themselves in a fire in a garbage can, the hoboes turned and waved to them. And I said, "Isn't that amazing that they did that, Mom—they're there living in Hoovervilles." And my mother said, "John, we gave them hope." And as appalling as that answer is, it's true. That's how stars function in the culture, and always have, and always will. They are part of the system of belief, the big survivors, the icons who have achieved what America has always promised: to fulfill the destiny of self and to push that self to the limits of its accomplishments in a lifetime. That's what America is, and that's what stars act out every day.
—**John Lahr**

Breadlines were prevalent throughout the city; four decades later, theatergoers would line Duffy Square again, this time queuing for discount tickets at the TKTS booth.

Whereas the Broadway fare of the 1920s supplied a seemingly endless stream of jaunty, somewhat relevant, fun, the 1930s created an entertainment schism. Effervescent musical comedies still took audiences' minds off the country's misery for three hours at a time, but a strong vein of social criticism and political satire was also emerging in the American musical. Escapism and engagement became the dueling stars of the Broadway stage.

The business itself was severely affected. Theaters closed down or were turned into far more financially successful movie houses. It was harder to raise money for a new production. In 1927–28, there were a record 264 productions on Broadway; in the 1930–31 season, there were 187. During the Depression, there were five thousand Equity actors and twenty thousand theater artists desperate for work on Broadway.

To be working was the main thing. To survive was the main thing. We weren't thinking so much of the art of the theater, believe me. I knew a lot of people who worked and lived in that period—everybody was working for minimum. And it wasn't altogether bad, because people did shows that they wouldn't have done had it been a normal time.

—Jerome Chodorov, Playwright

Out of this adversity came an extraordinary decade of artistic growth for the Broadway musical, which, next to the daily newspaper, became the most vibrant and incisive indicator of what was going on in America. Never again would Broadway reflect its country's concerns with such crystal clarity.

BY THE EARLY 1930s, the theater capital of America and the film capital of America were separated by an entire continent. Broadway and Hollywood were now individual commercial entities in competition with each other; while they might offer the same type of entertainment (sometimes under the same title), they had different standards, different regulations, different resources, different budgets, different lifestyles, and often different audiences. In London, Paris, and Berlin, stage and film production occurred in the same city, so the contrast was not as stark. Now, in the hungry days of the Depression, artists had to make a choice: stay in New York, with its harsh winters and gray, shuffling breadlines, working in a business staggered by layoffs and cutbacks, or move to California, where it was sunny all year round and smelled of eucalyptus, and money was thrown at you in fistfuls by studio executives. Who would stay in New York?

That is, of course, a trick question. Early film musical production was no bed of eucalyptus. Although the motion picture studios jumped at the chance to add musicals to their rosters after the introduction of sound, it was several years before the technology of filming a musical was mastered. The actual sound quality was tinny and false, and the camera, whose whirring gears were all too easily picked up by rudimentary microphones, was often sealed off in a soundproof refrigerator box, severely limiting the camera movement that silent-film audiences had grown to appreciate.

None of this kept the Hollywood studios from exploiting the novelty of sound musicals. From 1927 to 1932 the studios acquired and filmed an enormous amount of material. Flexing their financial muscles and creating some symbiotic relationships that would redefine the business of Broadway, studios approached Tin Pan Alley firms for the rights to use songs in their pictures. The simplest method was to buy them out, and soon Warner Bros. subsumed the publishing firm of Remick & Co. Film musicals were either portmanteau revues such as *The King of Jazz, Hollywood Revue of 1929*, and *Paramount on Parade;* awkwardly filmed stage adaptations such as *The Cocoanuts, Sally,* and *Show Boat* (1929), or newly crafted stories, often with a backstage theme that glamorized the genre's source: *The Broadway Melody, Broadway Babies*, and *Footlights and Fools.* Unfortunately, Hollywood glutted the market with an inferior product, and the slogans such as "All-Talking! All-Singing! All-Dancing!" that enticed audiences into the

theater in 1928 soon turned to "Musical Films Are Taboo," according to *Variety* in 1930.

It was up to a former Army drill instructor and Broadway dance director to turn all this around. In 1933, Busby Berkeley conceived the dances to the quintessential backstage film musical, *42nd Street,* and his visual skill at manipulating both chorus girls and the camera finally made movie musicals as dynamic as their stage counterparts. He followed up this triumph with a string of backstage yarns for Warner Bros., such as *Gold Diggers of 1933* and *Dames,* and achieved an iconographic immortality for his over-the-top concepts and overhead photography. Soon, the other studios were churning out their own musical styles (Paramount, elegant and sophisticated; M-G-M, glossy and overblown; RKO, Astaire and Rogers) and the Hollywood musical was glorying in its heyday, enrapturing Depression America.

Gradually the Hollywood musical became less indebted to Broadway. Early on, everything was imported from the East Coast: stars, songwriters, properties. Some Broadway stars clicked immediately in front of the camera (Al Jolson, Eddie Cantor, Fred Astaire, Ginger Rogers, and the Marx Brothers); others were more or less plucked out of the metaphorical chorus and became stars (Irene Dunne, Ruby Keeler, and Betty Grable). Once successful in Hollywood, these stars rarely, if ever, performed again on Broadway. Hollywood was also cultivating its own kind of musical star, personalities who never had appeared on Broadway—and never would.

For songwriters, Hollywood proved to be an even riskier roll of the dice. By the early '30s every major Broadway songwriter was under some kind of film contract. Their response to the temptations of the West Coast were no more uniform than their personal styles. Irving Berlin was initially distrustful of film technology and studio interference; his misgivings were confirmed when United Artists butchered his 1931 *Reaching for the Moon.* Eventually, he was lured back to write *Top Hat* for Astaire and Rogers and began a healthy relationship with various studios, which returned his old songs to the public consciousness for three decades. (The greatest hit he ever wrote—that *anyone* ever wrote—"White Christmas," came out of the 1942 film *Holiday Inn.*) The Gershwins loved the Hollywood lifestyle, but frequently commuted to the East Coast, until George's experience with *Porgy and Bess* on Broadway sent him back into the arms of RKO. Jerome Kern, never one to suffer fools gladly, surprisingly liked Tinseltown and moved there permanently in 1936, while freelancing for various studios. He was given

Hollywood sent an impossibly grandiose version of Broadway to American audiences; here, in a "Follies" number from The Great Ziegfeld *(1936), M-G-M promotes a vision of a Broadway spectacle that no theater in New York could possibly contain, let alone produce.*

the chance to team up with various studio-contracted lyricists like Dorothy Fields, Johnny Mercer, even Ira Gershwin, and produced some his most extraordinary songs, including the Oscar-winning "The Way You Look Tonight," "I'm Old-Fashioned," and "Long Ago and Far Away." Cole Porter was easily amenable to the assembly-line method of creating songs in Hollywood; he was always content to toss out one song and start over again on another. He reveled in the sybaritic social life of Hollywood and, despite failing health, always ventured every year to

Marilyn Miller, hoofing it in front of the cameras, during the filming of Sunny. *Watching on the sidelines is the composer of the score, Jerome Kern (standing, center).*

his house on Rockingham Drive to enjoy the sunshine, parties, and gay subculture.

Writing songs in Hollywood, however, could not have been more different from the creative process of Broadway. In New York, Rodgers and Hart called the shots on their shows, inventing storylines, bringing in collaborators, and so forth. In Hollywood, they were shunted around from studio to studio, doctoring pictures, writing songs that were either rewritten by other hands or cut. Often, they had no idea what kind of story their song was for until they saw the finished film itself—if they could bear it. Oscar Hammerstein II also had a miserable time in Hollywood, going about his dreary studio assignments without much enthusiasm. (He did, however, win an Oscar in 1941 for "The Last Time I Saw Paris," music by Kern.)

Although Hollywood has little to do with Nature, it too abhors a vacuum, and it soon assembled its own stable of songwriters, some of whom created immortal standards. Harold Arlen and Johnny Mercer had some early Broadway notoriety, but it was on the West Coast that their talents really blossomed. The most spectacular songwriting team bred in Hollywood was Harry Warren and Al Dubin, whose scores for the Busby Berkeley movies included such legendary numbers as "I Only Have Eyes for You" and "Lullaby of Broadway." Warren, the dean of studio songwriters, also always longed for a Broadway hit, but was also stymied in his attempts, although he lived long enough to see the stage version of *42nd Street*, which contained his best

songs with Dubin, become a huge success. Other writers like Dorothy Fields, Frank Loesser, and Jule Styne were nurtured by the studio system and were able to extend their successes to Broadway in the late 1940s and '50s when Hollywood musical production was slowing down.

When Hollywood did buy the rights to a Broadway property, the show rarely, if ever, made its way to celluloid intact. The list of depredations that the film studios inflicted on Broadway musicals would take up an entire book, but frequently whole scores were thrown out or reduced, with new songs written by new songwriters, sometimes by different teams of songwriters. In general, even the most faithful versions were shorn of several songs for length; wholesale revisionism was typical of Hollywood, especially with shows from the 1930s. Obviously, the demands of film are different from those of the stage, and it is very rare that a movie version captures the spirit, let alone the letter and the cast, of the original show. Even small changes to the book musicals of the 1940s and '50s can alter their tone: the 1949 film of *On the Town* throws away the World War II setting so crucial to its meaning, and *Kiss Me Kate* in 1953 keeps most of the score, but idiotically has someone pretending to be Cole Porter sort of introducing the movie.

Broadway producers, songwriters, and librettists cried all the way to the bank as film options on their material became more and more frequent in the 1950s, with record sums for the rights to shows like *My Fair Lady* topping several million dollars. Eventually Hollywood would have the last laugh on its East Coast detractors by flooding Broadway in the 1980s and '90s with stage versions of original Hollywood musicals—a complete inverse of the situation decades earlier—such as *Gigi, 42nd Street, Singin' in the Rain, Meet Me in St. Louis*, and *Footloose*, as well as the Disney animated films *The Lion King* and *Beauty and the Beast*.

One thing Hollywood never had, however, was creative freedom. In addition to the interference of studio chiefs and tone-deaf line producers, Hollywood had its own form of self-censorship: The Production Code, better known as the Hays Code, introduced in 1934, made it impossible for sophisticated Broadway material to be reproduced unaltered. The most benign lyrics were tweaked with idiotic regularity by inane sensibilities.

Despite the sunny blandishments of Hollywood, at the end of the day, if a songwriter in the 1930s wanted to challenge his own imagination—and the imagination of the audience—he had to heed the cry of a song Rodgers and Hart wrote for their last picture: "I Gotta Get Back to New York!"

"*There's an, oh, such a hungry, yearning, burning inside of me*"

COLE PORTER

With a million neon rainbows burning below me

And a million blazing taxis raising a roar

Here I sit while deep despair

Haunts my castle in the air

Down in the depths of the ninetieth floor.

"Down in the Depths," *Red, Hot and Blue!* (1936)

Oxymoron—the poetic device of juxtaposing two contradictory ideas—is difficult to pull off, but in the hands of Cole Porter, it seemed as natural as, well, night and day. Millionaires are despondent, great fun is just one of those things, flying high in the sky is simply nothing to do, and, in an early song, the heroine has to decide which, for her, is the right man—"Walt Whitman or Paul Whiteman." Perhaps Porter's skill was the result of the fact that he was a walking oxymoron himself. In an age when the most brilliant songwriters were either from New York, Jewish, from humble backgrounds, or inconsistently educated, he was emphatically none of the above—except, of course, brilliant.

Cole Porter was born in 1892 in Peru, Indiana, the son of a cowed drugstore owner who loved Browning and an ambitious mother, whose own father was worth more than $8 million. The grandfather pushed the boy toward the best educational and social circles in the East, and young Porter had to temporarily abandon his musical ambitions in order to stay in the old man's good financial graces. After prep school he went to Yale, where he fell in with the white-shoe crowd, sang, wrote the football fight song, and traveled with pals on the New Haven Railroad to catch the latest shows on Broadway.

Still chafing under his grandfather's imprecations to continue a conventional education, Porter disobeyed him one more time by writing songs for a Broadway "comic opera" in 1916, soon after his graduation. Critics were not impressed: "*See America First* Last," wrote one. Considerably chagrined, in 1917 Porter hightailed it to Europe, where he served, apparently without much distinction, in the French Foreign Legion. France was a lucky break for Porter and a haven for his high spirits—he wrote more songs set in or about Paris than any Anglophone composer ever—and it was there, in 1918, that he met the intoxicatingly gay divorcée Linda Lee Thomas, eight years his senior but considered to be the most beautiful woman in Europe. Even though Porter was homosexual, they were married the next year and stayed together for the rest of her life. Porter loved her deeply, and she overlooked his many affairs as long as the men in his life were well mannered. A homosexual with the perfect marriage—another oxymoron.

Linda's fortune—double the size of Cole's own considerable funds (his mother gave him $2 million of what she inherited when her father died in 1923)—made them "rich-

So nice to come home to: Cole Porter and wife, Linda, in New York, 1935.

He was determined to become a Broadway writer. He wanted to be like Irving Berlin; he wanted to be like Jerome Kern. At the same time, he was rich and idle and a playboy and liked to be on the Riviera and liked his nice apartment in Paris. So he tried to have both worlds at once—and he got them.
—Brendan Gill

rich," as Porter liked to put it, and they lived the high life in Europe throughout the 1920s, with the perfectly appointed apartment in Paris, a rented palazzo in Venice, and summers on the Riviera. Eventually the charm in playing his witty songs for dinner guests began to wane. Noel Coward, Rodgers and Hart, and Irving Berlin—all of whom knew him at least by reputation—visited him in Europe during the '20s and wondered why he was wasting his genius on underscoring for canapés and Veuve Clicquot.

Porter's return to Broadway was largely engineered by Berlin. When Berlin sought to marry Ellin Mackay, her gentile millionaire father disapproved, but Mr. Mackay was a former beau of Linda Porter's and she interceded on Berlin's behalf. Berlin returned the favor and recommended Porter as the composer/lyricist for a new Broadway musical about the City of Light starring Irene Bordoni, the wife of E. Ray Goetz, the show's coproducer. *Paris* debuted in May 1928 and made Cole Porter an immediate sensation. A racy number called "Let's Do It" replaced an even racier one called "Let's Misbehave."

> Cold Cape Cod clams, 'gainst their wish, do it,
> Even lazy jelly-fish do it,
> Let's do it, let's fall in love.
> Electric eels, I might add, do it,
> Though it shocks 'em, I know.
> Why ask if shad do it?
> Waiter, bring me shad roe.

If Porter had done nothing else for musical theater, he made it safe for sex—never depicted, of course, but wittily implied. His risqué material often got him in trouble with the censors and the bluenoses—the lyrics to "Love for Sale," a prostitute's torch song, were banned from the radio for twenty-five years—but it was rarely gratuitous. Porter's view of sex is unapologetic, passionate, and healthy; after all, everyone knows what the leading characters in a musical are going to do after the final curtain comes down.

"I GET A KICK OUT OF YOU"

Verse:-

My story is much too sad to tell
But practically everything leaves me totally cold
The only exception I know is the nights
That I'm out on a quiet spree
Fighting vainly the old ennui
And I suddenly return and see your fabulous face.

Refrain:-

I get no kick from champagne
Mere alcohol doesn't thrill me at all
So tell me why should it be true
That I get a kick out of you
Some get a kick from cocaine
I'm sure that if I took even one sniff
That would bore me terrific'ly too,
Yet I get a kick out of you.
I get a kick every time I see you
Standing there before me,
I get a kick though it's clear to me
You obviously don't adore me
I get no kick in a plane
~~I shouldn't care for those nights in the air~~
~~That the fair Mrs. Lindbergh goes through~~
But I get a kick out of you.

*Flying too high with some
guy in the sky
Is my idea of nothing to do*

He had two more hits in two more seasons, and as the 1930s began, critics recognized that someone new and remarkable had arrived. In 1932, his score for Fred Astaire's first solo venture, *Gay Divorce*, included "Night and Day," which went on to become one of the ten most popular songs of the twentieth century. *Anything Goes* in 1934 proved to be a carefree tonic for Depression-weary audiences; at 420 performances, it became Porter's longest-running hit of the decade.

Porter's shows were rarely experimental or distinguished, but the songs that came out of them were unlike anything heard on Broadway. He had a gift for deeply yearning, aching ballads, often using Latin rhythms and unexpectedly long and complicated musical structures, as in "Begin the Beguine." His patter songs, catalogues of metaphorical or topical ideas spun out endlessly in refrain after refrain, proved him to be the wittiest lyricist since W.S. Gilbert. Those comic numbers are time capsules, the whole spectrum of elite art and popular culture of the day, seen through the eyes of Cole Porter. Something for everyone—Upper East Side and Lower East Side.

Porter's lyrics seemed as effortless as his lifestyle. He wrote his songs in luxurious European apartments, on transatlantic liners, and in his aerie in the magisterial Waldorf Towers on Park Avenue, where he worked in a separate bedroom from his wife, long into the night, after the baccarat and the Courvoisier had been cleared away. "The jaunty and debonair world of Cole Porter disappeared completely when he was at work," wrote Moss Hart, who wrote the book for *Jubilee* while accompanying Porter on an around-the-world cruise. His superb manners both hid and enabled his fear of confrontation; he would rather start over on a song than argue about it with a collaborator or producer. He often felt that critics resented the fact that his was not a rags-to-riches story; then again, his propensity for giving engraved cigarette cases as opening-night presents and living so conspicuously well didn't do much to alter that perception. Porter was the most successful composer-lyricist of the 1930s and gave audiences—and the Broadway musical itself—the glamour they so desperately craved. He knew how to put it into his songs and he knew how to wear it to the opening-night party.

Moss Hart (l.) contributed the book to Porter's score for Jubilee *(1935), about the British Royal Family traveling on an incognito holiday.*

"Posterity is just around the corner"

OF THEE I SING

When, in 1930, George S. Kaufman and Morrie Ryskind decided to write their new musical satire, they set their sights higher than folderol about cheese or chocolates and moved from the shadows of presidential power straight into the thick of it. Their new show, provisionally titled *Tweedledee,* was to be about a running battle between two indistinguishable political parties over a new national anthem. There was no question that they would first approach the Gershwins to write the score; the brothers were suitably intrigued, but were contracted to go to Hollywood in late 1930 to supply the songs for the film *Delicious.* Kaufman and Ryskind agreed to write a scenario that George and Ira could take with them to the West Coast.

The librettists soon realized that their premise gave them only about a scene and a half of plot. Sooner or later, as Ryskind pointed out—to the unsentimental Kaufman's dismay, no doubt—some boy-and-girl stuff had to make an appearance. In order to find material for a political satire, however, they had only to go to the newsstand and pick up one of the dozen daily newspapers then published in Manhattan. The Republican president, Herbert Hoover, declared in May 1930 that the worst of the Depression was over—"prosperity was just around the corner"; one did not need to be a satirical playwright to be cynical about the government's competence. Also, in 1931, New York City politics were shaken and stirred when playboy-mayor Jimmy Walker was the subject of a corruption investigation by a committee organized by Governor Franklin D. Roosevelt. Walker's song-and-dance bonhomie was coopted by Kaufman and Ryskind for their leading character, and they also recalled that the reason Warren G. Harding was elected in 1920 was that "he looked presidential."

The plot of *Of Thee I Sing,* if for no other reason than it's practically the only plot of the 1930s that is worth repeating, is worth repeating. It centers around a presidential candidate named John P. Wintergreen, who, nominated on the 63rd ballot, intends to have "a good clean campaign without any mention of an issue." Wintergreen's handlers decide he will run on the "Love" platform—everybody loves a lover—and, anticipating modern-day reality TV series, the bachelor candidate will choose "Miss White House" in a beauty contest and marry her if he is elected. Wintergreen, to his credit and eventual chagrin, rejects the Southern bombshell who wins the contest and proposes instead to the no-nonsense organizer of the contest, Mary Turner. Wintergreen is swept into the White House, but both the country and the media turn against him when the Southern bombshell sues him for breach of promise. Eventually, he is brought up before Congress for impeachment hearings and is only saved at the last minute by the First Lady's announcement that she is pregnant. Congress refuses to impeach an expectant father and all ends happily.

ABOVE: *The winning ticket (clockwise from upper right): George Gershwin, Morrie Ryskind, George S. Kaufman, and Ira Gershwin.*

BELOW: *Appealing to demographics: Mary Wintergreen (Lois Moran) gives birth to twins—a boy and a girl.*

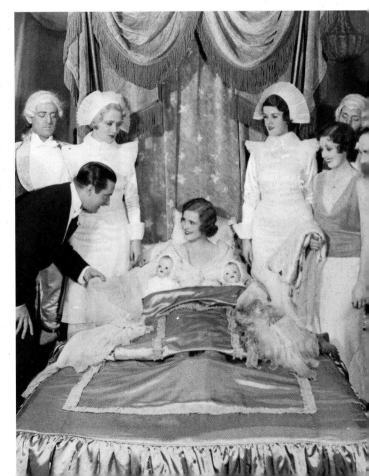

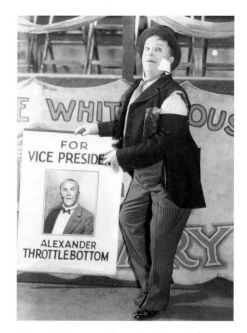

Victor Moore as Alexander Throttlebottom, a vice-president so vacuous that he is ejected from his own nomination proceedings.

Rounding out this merrily timeless scenario is an ancient and addle-pated Supreme Court (the combined ages of the nine actual 1931 Supreme Court justices was 624 years) and a vice president named Alexander Throttlebottom, a well-meaning fellow so innocuous and dispensable that he can gain admittance to the White House only by joining a tour group. Kaufman and Ryskind were especially astute in refusing to brand any of their characters as Republicans or Democrats; the rampant absurdity of American politics was clearly a bipartisan affair.

Although it frustrated Kaufman no end that the Gershwins had to prepare their part of the collaboration from the West Coast, the brothers were entirely simpatico with the show's point of view and threw themselves enthusiastically into satirical territory, creating the first score for an American musical that rivaled a Gilbert and Sullivan operetta in both ambition and craft. Ira opened the show with a campaign song that was terse, amusing, and drawn from his New York background:

> Wintergreen for President!
> Wintergreen for President!
> He's the man the people choose;
> Loves the Irish and the Jews.

George provided a stunning series of marches, pastiches, contrapuntal finales, and a soaring ballad that Ira brought down to earth by adding a happy sentiment to a phrase from a solemn national hymn:

> Of thee I sing, baby—
> Summer, autumn, winter, spring, baby.
> You're my silver lining,
> You're my star of blue;
> There's a love-light shining
> Just because of you.

When we first played this sentimental political campaign song . . . there were objectors who thought that juxtaposing the dignified "of thee I sing" with a slangy "baby" was going a bit too far. Our response was that, naturally, we'd replace it with something else if the paying audience didn't take to it. Opening night, and even weeks later, one could hear a continuous "Of thee I sing, *baby!*" in the lobby at intermission time.

—Ira Gershwin, 1959

The song that brought the Depression home to audiences and made the president and his wife seem like just another couple trying to make it through hard times occurs when, in the middle of a grueling press conference, Wintergreen declines to relinquish his presidency and reaffirms his love for his wife:

> Who cares
> What banks fail in Yonkers,
> Long as you've got
> A kiss that conquers.

The American theater had never seen a show like it. Certainly, there had been satirical material before, but only in the occasional revue sketch, where the point of view didn't need to be sustained longer than seven minutes. Here was a densely and cleverly constructed two-act musical comedy with a consistent and focused satirical viewpoint. Moreover, in an age where characters walked onstage simply to toss off a joke or to set up a song, *Of Thee I Sing* developed the stories of several characters and managed the difficult trick of allowing the audience to laugh at them and care about them at the same time. More than seventy years later, it remains as well constructed a musical comedy book—and as pertinent a satire—as Broadway has ever seen.

When the show opened on the day after Christmas in 1931, following a seamless Boston tryout, it was a triumph, running 441 performances, the longest run for any original Gershwin show. It was also the first musical to be published in book form and the first musical to win the Pulitzer Prize for drama.

> **Of Thee I Sing** is not only coherent and well-knit enough to class as a play, but it is a biting and true satire on American politics and the public attitude towards them. . . . The play is genuine and it is felt the Pulitzer Prize could not serve a better purpose than to recognize such work.
> **—1932 Pulitzer Prize Committee**

Infamously, the prize was shared only by Kaufman, Ryskind, and Ira Gershwin; the $1,000 prize money was split three ways, with Ira awarded the extra penny because he was the youngest. George Gershwin was left out because the prize was considered to be a "literary" honor—an oversight partially redressed by an honorary Pulitzer given to him in 1998—and George had to browbeat his brother into accepting the prize without him.

Before fictional president John P. Wintergreen was one year into his musical administration at the Music Box Theatre, the country placed its hopes for a better future in the hands of the newly elected Franklin D. Roosevelt, who in his inauguration speech on March 4, 1933, pledged to ask Congress for broad executive powers to wage war on the Depression. It would no longer be so easy to make fun of the government's incompetence. Posterity, to paraphrase Ira in one of his numbers, might well be right around the corner.

BROTHER, CAN YOU SPARE A DIME?

Words by E.Y. Harburg
Music by Jay Gorney
From New Americana *(1932)*

YIP HARBURG WAS THE RESIDENT SKEPTIC of Broadway, and he had plenty of good reasons to be skeptical. He was born in 1896 into poverty that was extreme even by the standards of most New York songwriters and grew up in what would become Alphabet City, the area immortalized in *Rent* a century later. He did odd jobs, including lighting streetlamps, to augment his parents' sweatshop wages. At Townsend Harris Hall, a select public high school affiliated with City College, Harburg became great friends with the boy who sat in front of him, Ira Gershwin. Ira turned him on to the work of Gilbert and Sullivan, and Harburg found a kindred spirit in the cantankerous whimsy of Gilbert's lyrics.

Inspired by songs and poetry, but even more moved to put food on the table, Harburg went into the electrical supply business with a college classmate. By September 1929, the business was worth a quarter million dollars; two months later, Harburg was penniless and deeply in debt. "All I had left was my pencil," he said. His nickname "Yip," which came from *yipsl,* the Yiddish word for squirrel, was particularly apt: he learned to jump from one branch to another pretty quickly. (An eventual victim of McCarthyism, he used to joke that the nickname was also the acronym for the Young People's Socialist League.) He immediately got hold of Ira, who lent him $500 and referred him to composer Jay Gorney. Harburg began working with Gorney at night; as he liked to say, he "gave up his dreams of business to go into the business of dreams." After some initial success with various revues, they landed a job in 1932, with a revue called *New Americana.* The show was centered on "the Forgotten Man," which FDR had made into a popular slogan as part of his presidential campaign. But it was another phrase, muttered by jobless men on street corners, that Yip Harburg used as his inspiration for what would become America's anthem in the Depression. He recalled:

> Along the street . . . you'd see bread lines. The biggest one in New York City was owned by William Randolph Hearst. He had a big truck with . . . big cauldrons of hot soup, bread. Fellows with burlap on their shoes were lined up . . . for blocks and blocks around the park, waiting. [In one of our sketches,] Mrs. Ogden Reid of the *Herald-Tribune* was very jealous of Hearst's beautiful bread line. It was bigger than her bread line. It was a satiric, volatile show. We needed a song for it. On stage, we had men in old soldier's uniforms, waiting around. . . . The prevailing greeting at that time, on every block you passed, by some poor guy coming up, was "Can you spare a dime?" or "Can you spare something for a cup of coffee?"

New Americana was not much of a success, but when Bing Crosby recorded it, "Brother, Can You Spare a Dime?" became a major hit. It continues to be the one song most closely identified with the Depression. Other songs of the period swung to the beat of tapping feet or gliding glamour girls—this one counted time through the inexorable shuffling of a million unemployed men, waiting silently for an end to their misery.

They used to tell me
I was building a dream
And so I followed the mob.
When there was earth to plough
Or guns to bear
I was always there
Right on the job.

They used to tell me
I was building a dream
With peace and glory ahead.
Why should I be standing in line
Just waiting for bread?

E.Y. "Yip" Harburg.

A somber chorus line for "Brother, Can You Spare a Dime?"

Once I built a railroad,
Made it run,
Made it race against time.
Once I built a railroad,
Now it's done.
Brother, can you spare a dime?

Once I built a tower
To the sun,
Brick and rivet and lime.
Once I built a tower,
Now it's done.
Brother, can you spare a dime?

Once in khaki suits
Gee, we looked swell
Full of that Yankee Doodle-de-dum.
Half a million boots went sloggin' thru hell
I was the kid with the drum.

Say, don't you remember?
They called me "Al."
It was "Al" all the time.
Say, don't you remember?
I'm your pal.
Buddy, can you spare a dime?

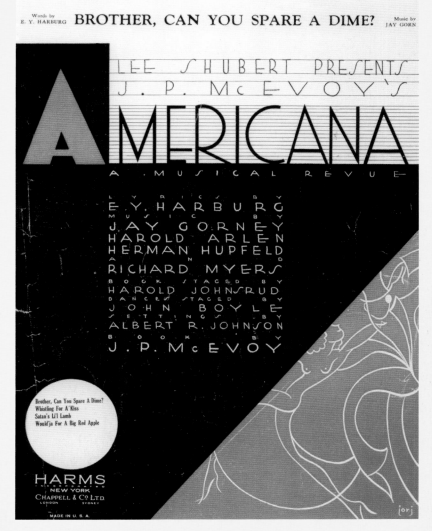

MUSIC

"Who could ask for anything more?"

ETHEL MERMAN

When Ethel Merman burst upon the scene at the beginning of the decade, she gave Broadway audiences something to shout about. She was pretty darn good in the shouting department herself—"She can hold a note as long as the Chase Manhattan Bank," went one famous quote—and was as different from the typical demure and accommodating Broadway ingenue of the time as the Chrysler Building was from a bungalow for two.

The alpha and the omega of Broadway divas was born Ethel Zimmermann in 1909 and raised in the working-class neighborhood of Astoria, Queens. As a child, she would sneak away from her doting mother to peer through the fence of the Paramount movie studio two blocks away in order to ogle the stars in their limousines. She made her singing debut at the age of five at the Astoria Republican Club, of which both her Scots-German parents were members, accompanied on piano by her father, a bookkeeper. On Friday nights, her folks took her into Manhattan, to the famed Palace Theatre, where they paid 46 cents to sit in the first row of the second balcony to hoot and holler at the vaudeville acts.

As she entered high school, Ethel had dreams of being a singer, but her "Mom and Pop," to whom she was immensely devoted, had instilled in her a bedrock of common sense; as a compromise, she learned shorthand, typing, and bookkeeping, and eventually took a job as a stenographer at B-K Vacuum Booster Brake. She often arrived at work late because she was singing in nightclubs, at $7.50 a night, and the gigs were becoming more frequent. Ethel realized "Zimmermann" would be a marquee buster and promptly shed four letters in order to gain immortality.

A month before the stock market crash, an agent caught her act and signed her up, and the rechristened Ethel Merman started appearing in the best vaudeville venues in New York. A favorite producer of the Gershwins', Vinton Freedley, was trying to cast a bright new show by the team called *Girl Crazy*, which would feature dancer Ginger Rogers. Freedley took Merman up to the brothers' shared penthouse apartment overlooking the Hudson River to audition for a supporting part.

Merman, 1934.

If you ever write lyrics for Ethel Merman, they better be good, because everybody's going to hear them. —Irving Berlin

I was taken into this gorgeous living room to meet this great composer. He sat down at the piano and played three songs, which I eventually wound up singing in the show. I was scared stiff. I should have been. He was the great Gershwin, and I was a nobody. . . . After George finished playing, this humble genius turned to me, a complete unknown, and said something I'll never forget. "Miss Merman, if there's anything about these songs you don't like, I'll be most happy to change it."
—Ethel Merman, 1978

She went into rehearsals in September 1930, while still performing at night at her beloved Palace Theatre. The Gershwin show, arrant nonsense about playboys and Jewish cabdrivers stuck in the middle of Arizona, featured Merman in the small part of a petty gambler's wife, but as her considerable talent emerged, her role kept getting bigger. The Gershwins thought it was hilarious when she took down her new lyrics in shorthand. "I didn't see what was so funny," Merman recalled. "What could have been more natural? I'd been a secretary, hadn't I?"

Opening night came at the Alvin Theatre on October 14. Merman's first number, "Sam and Delilah," was the ninth song of the evening. When the audience roared its delight at the sultry comedy number, Merman was concerned that her garter had snapped or something. The next number in the show was "I Got Rhythm," and Merman sang it within an inch of its life, at one point holding her "money note" for sixteen bars—almost ten seconds. As they would continue to do for four more decades, the crowd went berserk.

Merman discovered to her own surprise that she was now a somebody on the Great White Way, but what meant even more to her was the visit she received during intermission:

Ethel Merman (seen here with William Kent) made her big splash as a gambler's wife in Girl Crazy.

When I opened [my dressing room door], there stood George Gershwin. He'd climbed three flights. "Ethel," he asked, "do you know what you're doing?"

"No."

"Well," he advised, "never go near a singing teacher . . . and never forget your shorthand."

—Ethel Merman

Unfortunately, her newfound celebrity did not translate to the movies. The film industry didn't know what to do with her, so it threw up its hands and moved on to perkier and quieter soubrettes. Merman came back to Broadway to become the closest thing to a goddess the American musical ever had. Cole Porter wrote *Anything Goes* for her in 1934 and then went on to create the scores for four more shows for the voice he favored above all others. Irving Berlin composed two scores for her as well. She was a songwriter's dream.

She spent most of the 1930s sharing the stage with such improvisational clowns as Jimmy Durante, Bob Hope, and Bert Lahr, but as the 1940s began, she became the center of attention. It was probably just as well, for Merman disliked anything that distracted her from delivering the goods. Anecdotes about her are legion. During the intermission of a show late in her career, she berated a fellow actor for "doing something" onstage during the Act I finale. "I wasn't doing anything, Miss Merman," said the young actor, defending himself. "I was only reacting to what you were doing." "Listen, pal," she stated firmly, "let's get this straight: I don't react to *you*—you don't react to *me*."

Long before it became a pop psychology term, Merman was grounded; she'd plant her feet and let 'er rip. She was without artifice or forced sentimentality and could never really hide behind a dance step or even, with a few exceptions, a deep characterization. Her appeal is bewildering to some, usually people who never saw her perform live, but her sustained popularity, which verges on beatification, comes from a basic fact: At the eye of the make-believe cotton-candy hurricane that is the American musical, Ethel Merman was very simply the real thing.

Merman singing "Katie Went to Haiti" in Porter's Du Barry Was a Lady *(1939).*

I love Ethel. I hope it will not be considered ungracious of me, in the face of the other very talented artists who have sung my songs and helped them along to popularity, to confess that I'd rather write for Ethel than anyone else in the world. Every composer has his favorite, and she is mine. Her voice, to me, is thrilling. She has the finest enthusiasm of any American singer I know. She has a sense of rhythm which few can equal. And her feeling for comedy is so intuitive that she can get every value out of a line without ever over-stressing a single inference. And she is so damned apt.

—Cole Porter

YOU'RE THE TOP

Words and Music by Cole Porter
From Anything Goes *(1934)*

FOR LEADS ETHEL MERMAN AND William Gaxton, playing star-crossed lovers on an ocean liner, Cole Porter wrote the greatest of his "list" songs—a can-you-top-this? bit of stichomythia. The song itself, as theater historian Robert Kimball puts it, "came to represent the embodiment of the Roosevelt recovery. Roosevelt himself loved the song, and it became a national craze. It made America feel better in an awful time." Porter allowed P.G. Wodehouse to Anglicize some of the lyrics for the London production, and there were many parodies, including a rather lewd one, which ran, in part, "You're the breasts of Venus/You're King Kong's penis/You're self-abuse." Legend has it that this parody was presented to Porter before an ocean cruise by his pal and mentor Irving Berlin, who gets his own mention in the original song.

Porter's references to time and place were never casual. Here is a brief annotation of some of the song's highlights (selected from refrains one, two, three, and five):

- Henri Bendel is a Fifth Avenue boutique, known for its millinery.
- Vincent Youmans was the talented composer of *No, No, Nanette.*
- In 1934, Indian leader Mahatma Gandhi was in the midst of his ten-month walking journey to visit every province of India.
- Greta Garbo's salary in 1934 was $250,000 per picture.
- Cellophane, the clear plastic wrapping, had been introduced to the American market in 1923.
- The Ritz was Porter's favorite Paris hotel.
- A Packard Brewster was a limited-edition limousine in the early 1930s.
- Zuider Zee, an inlet in Holland, was part of an extensive drainage project in the 1920s.
- George Jean Nathan was the fearsome drama critic of the *American Mercury.*
- Bishop William J. Manning was the ambitious Episcopal bishop of New York, who built the Cathedral of St. John the Divine.
- Broccoli had only become a popular vegetable in the early 1930s.
- Sloe-eyed Irene Bordoni was the star of *Paris,* Porter's first hit.
- Waldorf salad, using chopped apples and walnuts, was the specialty of the restaurant housed in Porter's own luxury apartment building.
- The Roxy was an elaborate 6,000-seat movie theater in New York with an army of smartly uniformed ushers.

Porter and Merman.

At words poetic, I'm so pathetic
That I always have found it best,
Instead of getting 'em off my chest,
To let 'em rest unexpressed.
I hate parading my serenading
As I'll probably miss a bar,
But if this ditty is not so pretty,
At least it'll tell you how great you are.

You're the top!
You're the Colosseum.
You're the top!
You're the Louvre Museum.
You're a melody from a symphony by Strauss,
You're a Bendel bonnet,
A Shakespeare sonnet,
You're Mickey Mouse.
You're the Nile,
You're the Tow'r of Pisa,
You're the smile
On the Mona Lisa.
I'm a worthless check, a total wreck, a flop,
But if, baby, I'm the bottom
You're the top!

Your words poetic are not pathetic.
On the other hand, boy, you shine,
And I can feel after every line
A thrill divine down my spine.
Now gifted humans like Vincent Youmans
Might think that your song is bad,
But for a person who's just rehearsin'
Well, I gotta say this, my lad:

You're the top!
You're Mahatma Gandhi.
You're the top!
You're Napoleon brandy.
You're the purple light of a summer night in Spain,
You're the National Gall'ry,
You're Garbo's sal'ry,
You're cellophane.
You're sublime,
You're a turkey dinner,
You're the time
Of the Derby winner.
I'm a toy balloon that is fated soon to pop,
But if, baby, I'm the bottom
You're the top!

You're the top!
You're a Ritz hot toddy.
You're the top!
You're a Brewster body.
You're the boats that glide on the sleepy Zuider Zee,
You're a Nathan panning
You're Bishop Manning,
You're broccoli.
You're a prize,
You're a night at Coney,
You're the eyes
Of Irene Bordoni.
I'm a broken doll, a fol-de-rol, a blop,
But if, baby, I'm the bottom
You're the top!

You're the top!
You're a Waldorf salad.
You're the top!
You're a Berlin ballad.

You're a baby grand of a lady and a gent,
You're an old Dutch master,
You're Mrs. Astor,
You're Pepsodent.
You're romance,
You're the steppes of Russia,
You're the pants
On a Roxy usher.
I'm a lazy lout that's just about to stop,
But if, baby, I'm the bottom
You're the top.

Anything Goes *put Merman over the top as the musical comedy diva of her day.*

MUSIC

"Oh Lawd, I'm on my way"
PORGY AND BESS

DuBose Heyward (center) with George (at piano) and Ira Gershwin.

Considering the extent of George Gershwin's restless musical ambitions, it's no surprise that as early as the 1920s, he was contemplating writing an opera. At the time, it was nearly inconceivable that a Broadway composer would venture into that arena, but Gershwin was always far more than a Broadway composer. A variety of subjects and opportunities came his way over the years; he considered musicalizing such plays as the Yiddish classic *The Dybbuk* and Eugene O'Neill's Expressionistic *The Emperor Jones*—something with black characters always seemed to pique his interest—and the Metropolitan Opera patron Otto Kahn extended an open-ended commission to him.

Although an opera might have been at the top of Gershwin's to-do list, during the '20s a variety of other projects and challenges kept pushing it to the bottom. In 1926, however, he read a powerful novel published the previous year by an upper-class white South Carolinian, DuBose Heyward, called *Porgy*. It was a series of vignettes of life in a black Charleston ghetto called Catfish Row, where a cripple named Porgy falls desperately in love with a woman named Bess, whose inconstant affections both torment and inflame him. The white author's depiction of his segregated black neighbors was particularly insightful; Gershwin was immediately inspired by it and contacted Heyward.

Heyward was flattered, but had to respond, regretfully, that he and his wife, Dorothy, were adapting the book as a play for the Theatre Guild to produce in 1927. No matter, said Gershwin—he had other irons in the fire, they'd be in touch. The play, *Porgy,* was a huge success for the Guild, in an impressive production directed by the Russian émigré Rouben Mamoulian. Its impact led to several other attempts to musicalize the source material, including an improbable request by Al Jolson to play Porgy. Heyward, typically strapped for cash, considered the idea very seriously, especially as Jerome Kern and Oscar Hammerstein were mentioned to write the project. The author's dilemma: should he go for a sure commercial success, or the participation of the most accomplished composer in the business? Gershwin, to his credit, responded diplomatically:

> I think it is very interesting that Al Jolson would like to play the part of Porgy, but I really don't know how he would be in it. . . . The sort of thing that I have in mind is a much more serious thing than Jolson could ever do. . . If you can see your way to making some ready money from Jolson's version, I don't know that it would hurt a later version with an all-colored cast.

Luckily for the future of musical theater, the plans fell apart. Although it took several years to put all the pieces together, by the fall of 1933 Heyward (who would write his own libretto) and Gershwin had a deal in place. Ira Gershwin would collaborate with Heyward on the lyrics—Ira handling the snappy songs, Heyward taking the more lyrical ones, then polishing each other's work—in a kind of round-robin with George's music. It was an odd way to collaborate, but the gracious professionalism of all three men created an ego-free atmosphere of remarkable creativity. Gershwin also decided to spurn the advances of the Metropolitan Opera, which wanted to produce *Porgy*, in favor of a Broadway production that would play for an extended run at the Theatre Guild. It was, in many ways, to be his most fateful decision because his desire for a broad, popular audience outweighed his desire for prestige; the choice of production venue would blur the distinction between a musical and an opera for decades to come.

Further complicating the logistics was the fact that Heyward found New York too distracting and stayed in Charleston, while George was busy with a thousand other professional obligations. Still, he managed to make his way down to Charleston several times, including a sojourn to nearby Folly Island, to work with Heyward and soak up the musical ambiance of the black population, the Gullah people. Gershwin, who lived in a Manhattan penthouse with a private gym, decamped to a small cottage without running water and roamed the palmetto-dotted beach, shirtless and unshaven, for five weeks—he had the time of his life.

> **The most interesting discovery to me, as we sat listening to their spirituals, . . . was that to George it was more like a homecoming than an exploration. The 'Gullah' prides himself on what he calls "shouting." This is a complicated rhythmic pattern beaten out by feet and hands as an accompaniment to the spirituals, and is indubitably an African survival. . . . At a Negro meeting on a remote sea-island, George started "shouting" with them. And eventually to their huge delight stole the show from their champion "shouter."**
> **—DuBose Heyward,** 1935

When Gershwin returned to New York, the enormity of the task ahead confronted him straight on. He had to cast the show in an era when African American opera singers were consigned to recitals or small stages. He was supremely lucky in finding a Washington, D.C., music professor and baritone named Todd Duncan to play Porgy—"Imagine a Negro auditioning for a Jew singing from three Italian operas," Duncan said later—and a Juilliard-trained soprano named Anne Brown for Bess. Gershwin chose to orchestrate the score himself; the sheer mass of the piece nearly overwhelmed him, so a battery of arrangers and copyists was ensconced in his penthouse, still working on the music a week after rehearsals had started. Heyward and the Gershwins were more than happy to have Mamoulian back to direct the opera version, and as the entire troupe of nearly fifty took the train to Boston in September 1935, expectations there for *Porgy and Bess*—her name having been added late in the game to distinguish it from the play—were already running high.

The opera, though, was also running long, at more than three hours. Mamoulian prevailed upon the composer to make cuts; Gershwin took a deep breath and went about it with rigorous professionalism. The Boston crowd loved the show; now it was on to Broadway's Alvin Theatre. The Theatre Guild worried that audiences would be scared off by the work's ambitions. Gershwin explained his concept to the press one more time:

> *Porgy and Bess* is a folk tale. Its people would naturally sing folk music. I decided against the use of original folk material because I wanted the music to be all of one piece. Therefore I wrote my own spirituals and folksongs. But they are still folk music—and therefore, being in operatic form, *Porgy and Bess* becomes a folk opera. I have adapted my method to utilize the drama, the humor, the superstition, the religious fervor, the dancing, and the irrepressible high spirits of the race. If, in doing this, I have created a new form, which combines opera with theater, this new form has come quite naturally out of the material.

George Gershwin orchestrating the score to Porgy and Bess *in Florida, February 1935.*

Rouben Mamoulian (center of crowd) directs the cast of Porgy and Bess.

The newspapers sent their music critics as well as their drama critics, and although the reviews were not nearly as polarized as legend has it, the piece had its admirers and its detractors.

> **It is . . . one of the far-famed wonders of the "Melting Pot" that can be found. It is a Russian who has directed it, a Russian who has set it, two southerners who have written its book, two Jewish boys who have composed its lyrics and music, and a stageful of Negroes who sing and act it to perfection. The result is the most American opera that has yet been seen or heard.**
> **—John Mason Brown,** *New York Evening Post,* October 11, 1935

Composer and critic Virgil Thomson thought the show was "crooked folklore and halfway opera," and Duke Ellington objected to "Gershwin's lampblack Negroisms," but it was the audience whose opinion mattered most. The show ran for 124 performances, astonishing for an opera, but meager—one-third of the run of the original play—for a Broadway musical, even in the 1930s. A brief tour was mounted in Washington—Duncan refused to play there unless the owners of the National Theatre desegregated the

Georgette Harvey as Maria and John Bubbles as Sportin' Life, the show's slinky, sharp version of the devil.

audience—but that, too, lost money. It was not until its much-scaled-down revival in 1942 (minus Gershwin's recitatives and thus closer to a musical in this incarnation) that *Porgy and Bess* became a Broadway success. Soon, with a full-scale worldwide tour in 1952, it began claiming its place as a great American opera—really, *the* great American opera.

While some of its songs have become enduring standards, the milieu of Catfish Row—with its indolent gamblers, loose women, drug peddlers, petty criminals, and murderers—has vexed artists and audiences, black and white, in opera houses and theaters for nearly seventy-five years. Some of these legitimate concerns are aroused, as they always will be, by issues of provenance; others by the perpetuation of reductive stereotypes.

None of this should obscure the fact that at the generous heart of *Porgy and Bess* is a theme the musical theater has always embraced: Love will conquer all. At the end of the piece, Porgy, hearing that his beloved Bess has once again run off with another man, heads to New York, a place he has never heard of—"a thousand mile from here"—to find the woman who completes his soul.

> Oh Lawd, I'm on my way.
> I'm on my way to a Heav'nly Lan'—
> Oh Lawd, it's a long, long way,
> But You'll be there to take my han'.

After the run of *Porgy and Bess*, George Gershwin's immediate future seemed pretty clear; he and his brother closed up shop in Manhattan and settled in Hollywood to write songs for the latest Astaire and Rogers picture for RKO. George quickly took to the party circuit, rubbing elbows with some movie stars, romancing others, among them Paulette Goddard, and "seeing a great deal of Irving Berlin and Jerome Kern at poker parties." In February 1937, he was performing in two concerts of his own music, including the first selections from *Porgy and Bess* to be heard on the West Coast. At the second concert, he bungled some easy passages and complained of a sudden and strident headache.

The headaches got worse as the spring months went by; most of Gershwin's considerable circle attributed them to his depression over working within the studio system. By early July, his illness had accelerated rapidly. On July 9, he lapsed into a coma and it was discovered he had a brain tumor; surgery was attempted despite any likely positive result, and the thirty-eight-year-old Gershwin died on July 11, without regaining consciousness. Radio stations announced his passing with the opening bars of *Rhapsody in Blue*. He was mourned by his family, his colleagues, his peers, and the millions of Americans across the country who knew him only through the music that brightened their lives. "George Gershwin died today," said writer John O'Hara famously, "but I don't have to believe it if I don't want to."

Porgy may have "plenty o' nuttin'," but here he has his gal (Todd Duncan and Anne Brown).

Porgy's nemesis, Crown (Warren Coleman), exalts in his power over the denizens of Catfish Row.

GEORGE GERSHWIN'S AMERICAN FOLK OPERA
PORGY and BESS

PRODUCTION DIRECTED BY ROUBEN MAMOULIAN

A THEATRE GUILD PRODUCTION

It's the piece in which Gershwin's powers at their
absolute maturity are completely unleashed. As the
character Porgy at the end of the show goes off into
an unknown future, you have the sense of his
probable doom. You also hear this piece and have
the sense of Gershwin being on the brink of an unknown
future, which would have had colossal consequences
for the whole future of American music.

—Michael Tilson Thomas, Conductor

"Is it an earthquake, or simply a shock?"
COLE PORTER, ACT TWO

Cole Porter's loyal valet and chauffeur make sure that, despite his injuries, he arrives for opening night in style.

In October 1937, Cole Porter returned from a hiking vacation in the Austrian mountains to begin work on a new show, *You Never Know*. He was eager to rejoin the social whirl of his New York pals and quickly accepted an invitation to spend a weekend on Long Island. Cole impetuously decided the guests should all go horseback riding at the tony Piping Rock Club. "He hadn't been riding in a long time," said one of the fashionable crowd. "It was a sudden caprice, but Cole's caprices seemed sometimes to be made of steel."

As he went off along the bridle path, Porter's horse stumbled and fell and rolled over on him, broke one leg, then rolled over on the other side and broke his other leg. According to legend, as he lay there waiting for help, he took out his little notebook and went on working on the song he was in the midst of composing, "At Long Last Love." One of his legs had been smashed in nearly a thousand places. His wife, Linda, from whom he was temporarily estranged, came back from Paris immediately. She consulted with Porter's mother in Indiana and begged the doctors not to amputate; they knew that Porter could endure anything but that. He underwent dozens of operations throughout his life, but none of them did much more than delay the inevitable for the next two decades.

After the accident, Porter would have to be carried into the theater on opening nights by two strong men, looking like an immaculately dressed puppet, pained but never pathetic. Porter might grow suddenly quiet during a dinner party—it was a signal that he was in pain and his guests were to leave—but, in general, his amour propre was stronger than his discomfort. Although he remained a spirited socialite and adventurer, it was his devotion to his work that did what the doctors never quite could: it made him whole.

Though in excruciating pain, Cole still managed to create pieces in his trademark buoyant, sassy style. From the time of the accident until the end of World War II he would write eight shows, including three new musicals for Ethel Merman—*Du Barry Was a Lady*, *Panama Hattie*, and *Something for the Boys*—each of them a hit. In fact, he had one show on Broadway nearly every season during that time; five of them in a row each ran more than four hundred performances, a string unmatched by any songwriter in Broadway history. These shows provided springboards for the early careers of such emerging stars as Mary Martin, Gene Kelly, Betty Grable, Eve Arden, and Betty Hutton. He also contributed songs to revues and films, and although the vehicles were relatively mindless, Porter's work for them was among his very best: "My Heart Belongs to Daddy," "I Concentrate on You," "You'd Be So Nice to Come Home To."

Leave It to Me! *(1938) gave newcomer Mary Martin a chance to tell audiences that her "heart belongs to Daddy." Gene Kelly was an eager chorus boy in this number.*

Despite his nagging disability, theatrically at least Porter was still, in his own words, "ridin' high." However, the changing tastes of Broadway audiences after the Second World War curtailed his run of hit-making scores and rendered him nearly obsolete. He could surmount a cruel twist of fate through sheer willpower; the dismissal of the critics—"Porter not up to his usual standards"—would prove harder to endure.

A silly musical about an army training camp didn't stop Let's Face It *(1941) from making stars out of Danny Kaye (center), Eve Arden, (l.), and Vivian Vance (r.).*

ETHEL WATERS

IF ANYONE WAS BORN TO SING THE BLUES, it was Ethel Waters. She came into the world around 1900 after a man she never knew raped her mother at knifepoint. Young Ethel was shuttled from relative to relative in a Philadelphia neighborhood so poor and violent it was known as the Bloody Eighth Ward. She grew up a solitary and restless child, distrustful of authority, wary of kindness or commitment, but somehow she connected emotionally with the songs "her people" sang and the stories they carried with them. At the age of seventeen, she sang a solo at a local nightclub and finally began to envision a life beyond being a maid to a rich white lady—the previous height of her teenage ambition. For a decade, Waters sang in black nightclubs and on the segregated vaudeville grind known as the Chitlin Circuit. Her svelte figure earned her the nickname Sweet Mama Stringbean, but there was nothing demure about her; out of some deep inner source, she could produce gutsy and raunchy songs, delivered with impeccable diction.

Ethel Waters in On with the Show, *1930.*

As black performers enjoyed a vogue on Broadway in the mid-1920s, Waters was frequently courted by white producers, but was characteristically leery of their blandishments. "I ain't changin' my style for nobody or nothing," she once vowed. "The very idea of appearing on Broadway in a cast of ofays made me cringe in my boots." In 1927, she finally did debut on Broadway in an ambitious but unsuccessful black revue, *Africana*. Soon she was singing in other revues, including *Rhapsody in Black*, where she made an astonishing $2,500 a week. But it was a gig at Harlem's Cotton Club in April 1933, where she introduced a new Harold Arlen song (lyrics by Ted Koehler) called "Stormy Weather," that brought her unique talents to a wider audience. She recalled:

> One night Irving Berlin, the frail little Jewish man who has written the great love songs for two generations of Americans, came up to hear me sing that song. The following day he got in touch with [my management]. . . . "We're going to try to inject a serious note into [a musical and] we'd like to talk to Miss Waters about it."

As Thousands Cheer (1933) was a brave show in many respects, but perhaps bravest in the range of songs Berlin asked Waters to perform. She was blazing in a Latin number, singing of a young woman who started a "Heat Wave" by letting her seat wave; then she wittily mocked the pretensions of her uptown chum, the expatriate Josephine Baker, in "Harlem on My Mind." But nothing prepared audiences for the second number in Act II, which revealed Waters under the projected headline "Unknown Negro Lynched by Frenzied Mob." Behind her was the silhouette of a man with a rope around his neck hanging from a tree. She stepped forward and sang:

> Supper time,
> I should set the table
> 'Cause it's supper time;
> Somehow I'm not able,
> 'Cause that man o' mine
> Ain't comin' home no more.

The song's popularity as a generic torch song has obscured the pointed particularity of its roots, but Waters understood it perfectly:

> If one song can tell the whole tragic history of a race, "Supper Time" was that song. In singing it, I was telling

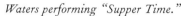
Waters performing "Supper Time."

Hitting 93°: Waters singing "Heat Wave."

Ethel Waters didn't have to sing. All she had to do was say "Hello" and I would weep. There was a quality in her voice and her appearance that's indescribable. She just had it.
—Al Hirschfeld

my comfortable, well-fed, well-dressed listeners about my people. I only had to think of the family of that boy down in Macon, Georgia, who had been lynched to give adequate expression to the horror and the defeat in "Supper Time."

During the show's out-of-town tryout, people begged Berlin to cut the number, but he had complete faith in Waters's ability to make it a transcendent moment. His faith would come in handy when the show's white leads—including Clifton Webb and Marilyn Miller—refused to take their curtain calls with Waters. "Fine," said Berlin. "There need be no curtain calls at all, then." They reconsidered.

Waters lent her versatile talent to the 1935 Dietz-Schwartz revue *At Home Abroad* and the 1940 book musical *Cabin in the Sky*, where she introduced Vernon Duke and John Latouche's "Taking a Chance on Love." She triumphed as a dramatic actress in plays like *The Member of the Wedding* and gradually turned her back on singing commercially, devoting enormous time and energy to various Christian evangelical charities. She remained her own person to the very end, still somewhat wary of others,

still revered, always relentlessly honest as a performer and a human being.

RAY BOLGER

RAY BOLGER KNEW HE WANTED to be a performer when, as a sixteen-year-old from a struggling Irish Catholic family in the Boston neighborhood of Dorchester, he attended a matinee of *Jack O'Lantern* in 1920. There, bouncing around onstage, was the acrobatic comedian Fred Stone. "I've never forgotten it," Bolger later said. "He bounded on a trampoline out of a haystack, looking just like a scarecrow." In order to support himself, Bolger took a job as a bookkeeper for a dance academy and gradually started taking lessons with the other students. He took his dancing so seriously that it made the other kids crack up, and he discovered that comedy was a way out of the Dorchester slums. Soon, his rubbery, gravity-defying hoofing made him a success in a vaudeville double act, "Stanford and Bolger: A Pair of Nifties," then as a single in *The Passing Show of 1926*. He was perfect revue material and made a wonderful comic partner for another former vaudevillian, Bert Lahr, in the 1934 revue *Life Begins at 8:40*. Bolger, however, was evolving into something more than a specialty dancer. "What is dance?" he asked in a 1942 interview. "I am dancing all the time. Every gesture, the body line of every pose, the way I get from place to place, the movement in the acting—none of it would be the way it is if I weren't a dancer."

In 1936, Rodgers and Hart gave him the lead in *On Your Toes*, where his sensational character-driven footwork in the Balanchine ballet "Slaughter on Tenth Avenue" solidified his stardom. At the end of the show's run, Bolger signed a film contract with M-G-M and fulfilled a long-held dream of playing the Scarecrow in *The Wizard of Oz*—his idol, Fred Stone, had played the part in a 1903 stage version.

Bolger returned to Broadway in 1942, winning accolades as the lead in Rodgers and Hart's *By Jupiter*, and in 1949 he became the second leading musical actor to win a Tony Award for his sprightly, infectious turn in Frank Loesser's *Where's Charley?* His star turn as the Scarecrow in *The Wizard of Oz* perfectly exploited his loose-limbed stage persona and made him a legend, but Bolger always had the brains to know what made him click with audiences: "I just play the little guy, except I play him through dance."

Bolger defying gravity as an epicene mythological king in By Jupiter.

Bert Lahr, clowning with Ethel Merman—the perfect blendship—in Du Barry Was a Lady.

BERT LAHR

PUT 'EM UHHHP! C'mawn, put 'em uhhhp!" Those unforgettably pugnacious lines, rendered in faux Brooklynese, may have made Bert Lahr famous in the movies, but ten years earlier he was already convulsing audiences as the punch-drunk boxer Gink Schiner in the DeSylva-Brown-Henderson musical *Hold Everything!* Lahr found his debut in a book musical a welcome change of pace from a grueling decade in which the high-school dropout (born Irving Lahrheim in 1895 in New York) toiled his way through every burlesque and vaudeville house on the national circuit, usually in a double act with his severely troubled first wife, Mercedes Delpino. After scoring big at the Palace in the late 1920s, Lahr, with his cartoon face, woofing out contortions of the English language with a hangdog bravado, caught the imagination of Broadway, starring in eight shows during the 1930s. He was equally adept in musical comedies and revues; in the revue *Life Begins at 8:40* he parodied lumberjacks, poetry lovers, and concert baritones alike with one swell foop of his mighty axe in the specialty item "Song of the Woodman." When its lyricist, E.Y. Harburg, was asked to write the songs for the movie musical *The Wizard of Oz*, he knew only one actor could get under the blustery hide of the Cowardly Lion and brought Lahr to Hollywood.

The film industry never knew quite what to do with Lahr, so he was more than happy to return east to star opposite Ethel Merman in Cole Porter's *Du Barry Was a Lady* in 1939, where their double-entendre shenanigans made audiences weak with laughter for more than a year. He continued acting for another quarter-century, neurotically fretting, as he always had, over which jokes would pay off, playing Shakespeare and Feydeau, introducing Samuel Beckett to Broadway audiences, and winning a Tony for a first-rate performance in the fourth-rate musical *Foxy* at the age of sixty-nine.

WILLIAM GAXTON AND VICTOR MOORE

THE DOUBLE ACT was the comic backbone of vaudeville, but whether it could make the transition to the book musicals of the 1930s was anyone's guess. Luckily, the best song and book writers had the knockout team of Gaxton and Moore at their disposal.

Victor Moore, born in 1876, had been a Broadway veteran since 1906, when he played the comic lead in George M. Cohan's *Forty-Five Minutes from Broadway*. He had mastered the character of a lovable, oblivious bumbler and resembled Elmer Fudd with the personality of Porky Pig (or even the other way around). William Gaxton, born Arturo Gaxiola in 1893, had been the romantic lead in Rodgers and Hart's *A Connecticut Yankee* in 1927,

introducing "My Heart Stood Still" to New York audiences. A needle-nosed charmer, Gaxton was not much of a singer and even less of a dancer, but he had a crisp, snappy energy that was perfect for the era's smart-alecky musical scenarios.

When Gaxton and Moore were paired as president and vice president in the Gershwins' *Of Thee I Sing*, they proved to be a winning ticket, with the suave Gaxton effortlessly leading the dithering Moore into various political misadventures. They reprised their roles in the show's unsuccessful sequel, *Let 'Em Eat Cake*, and became the hottest single-sex duo on Broadway when they joined Ethel Merman in *Anything Goes* in 1934. They continued their partnership into the 1940s with four more shows. Gaxton's appeal was somewhat of a mystery to critics; however, he introduced an astonishing number of standards on the American stage, including "Mine" and "You Do Something to Me." George S. Kaufman was so distressed by Gaxton's ad-libbing that he once sent him a telegram that read: "Am watching from back of house. Wish you were here." Moore, on the other hand, had a genuine innocence that made him one of Broadway's most beloved comedians; he acted in musicals and in straight plays long into the 1950s. Theatergoers lucky enough to have seen *Of Thee I Sing* could still be convulsed decades later by the incongruous image of Moore turning the reins of the administration back over to Gaxton, wheezing gratefully, "You can go back to being president and I'll go back to vice!"

Gaxton (r.) and Moore lead the nation in Of Thee I Sing.

"To reach the top, you've got to be up on your toes"

RODGERS AND HART IN THE 1930s

Rodgers waiting, characteristically, for Larry Hart to finish a lyric.

Hollywood's a great place if you like to tan by the pool, drinking orange juice and reading the newspaper. One morning in 1934, Richard Rodgers was doing exactly that when he came across an item in the Broadway column of the *Los Angeles Herald Examiner*. The lead: "Whatever happened to Rodgers and Hart?" hit him right in the solar plexus. After several years in Hollywood, the team of Rodgers and Hart had very little to show for their efforts beyond the adventuresome *Love Me Tonight* (1932), directed by Rouben Mamoulian and starring Maurice Chevalier and Jeanette MacDonald, and the hit song "Blue Moon," written from some studio discards on a dare. Otherwise, although Larry Hart enjoyed the sybaritic sunshine of Los Angeles, the team's grander ambitions were being frittered away by studio interference. "The studio might have lulled us into staying out there longer," Rodgers wrote forty years after the fact, "but that would have been the end of Larry Hart and Dick Rodgers. I'm sure I would have ended up as a neurotic, a drunkard or both."

When they got off the *Super Chief* at Grand Central Station in 1935, they were returning to a different Broadway than the one they'd left four years earlier. The Depression had severely curtailed the number of new productions—Rodgers and Hart could never hope to match their extraordinary run in the giddy 1920s. Their peers who had dominated the form when they left—Berlin, Porter, the Gershwins—were still there, producing more adventurous, more sophisticated, and more political work. But Rodgers and Hart were more than equal to the challenge. Over the next eight years, they would write, and in some cases coproduce, eleven shows—almost all of them hits, almost all of them raising the stakes of the musical theater—and raking in the chips each time.

> **We broke the form. Our motto was "This is what they don't like: let's try it." We were never without a show—production or rehearsal—and every song came out of situation, character, and relationship.**
> **—Richard Rodgers,** 1963

Their first stop was producer Billy Rose's ambitious and foolhardy attempt in 1935 to resurrect the 4,600-seat Hippodrome Theatre with a big-top romance called *Jumbo*. The show itself was elephantine and lost buckets of money, but in it Rodgers and Hart introduced such standards as "My Romance" and "Little Girl Blue." The next project, *On Your Toes*, was much more characteristic of their unique imagination. The show featured choreography by George Balanchine in a mixed-up world of gangsters and classical ballet, directed by George Abbott. The final ballet, "Slaughter on Tenth Avenue," with its sinewy low-down sound, had Rodgers flexing his Gershwinesque muscles; the number's relevance to the plot telegraphed the sensitive use of dance that would brand Rodgers's musicals for the next twenty years.

Onward and upward Rodgers and Hart moved, with two shows in the musically sparse year of 1937: *Babes in Arms* and *I'd Rather Be Right*. The first was the original hey-kids-let's-put-on-a-show show, inspired when the partners were watching some children bossing each other around on a playground. They decided to write the book themselves—nearly unheard-of for a songwriting team—and cast the whole show with unknown youngsters at a time when no musical comedy would dare open without a star. *Babes in Arms* also featured what is arguably the greatest single collection of sophisticated cabaret songs ever written, performed by a cast below the legal drinking age: "Where or When," "Babes in Arms," "I Wish I Were in Love Again," "My Funny Valentine," "Johnny One Note," and "The Lady Is a Tramp."

I'd Rather Be Right, with a book by George S. Kaufman and Moss Hart, the first full-length musical to spoof a sitting president, brought George M. Cohan out of retirement to star as a soft-shoe Franklin D. Roosevelt. (Rodgers and Hart had some cause to regret the casting; Cohan sneeringly referred to them as "Gilbert and Sullivan" and took it upon himself to rewrite some of Hart's lyrics during the Boston tryout until he had his wrists slapped.) *The Boys from Syracuse* followed the next season, the first

Ray Bolger dances with Tamara Geva in the ground-breaking Balanchine ballet "Slaughter on Tenth Avenue" for On Your Toes, *1936.*

George M. Cohan, as FDR, introducing his mother to the boy and girl leads in I'd Rather Be Right *(1937). The character of the aggrieved butler on the left turns out to be Alf Landon, whom FDR vanquished in a 1936 landslide election.*

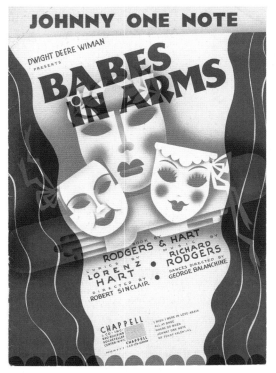

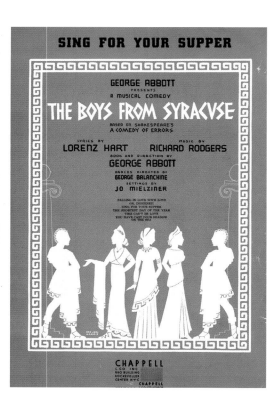

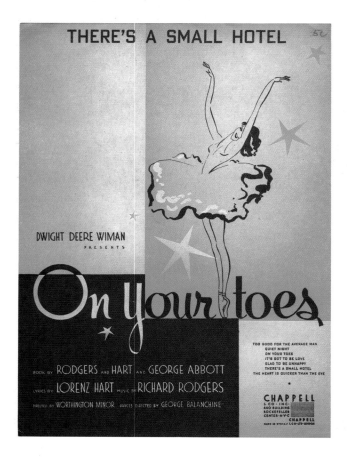

musical to be based on Shakespeare (*The Comedy of Errors*); it was a smash and gave the world such songs as "This Can't Be Love" and "Sing for Your Supper," which was sung by a female trio and spoofed the swing music vogue for tight-harmony girl groups. There seemed to be no end to Rodgers and Hart's inventiveness.

For Dick Rodgers, the '30s provided everything he liked: creative challenges, great collaborators, big hits, out-of-town tryouts with plenty of chorus girls. For Larry Hart, however, as the decade went on, getting back into rehearsal for a new show seemed less interesting than staying out all night with his cronies on a bender. Rodgers was famous for always coming up with some wry excuse for his partner's indolence—"Larry was the kind of guy who, if you had a meeting at noon on Tuesday, shows up on Friday"—but by the late '30s, it wasn't so amusing anymore. At one point, when Hart was drying out in a hospital, Rodgers had a piano brought up to his private suite to finish some songs.

None of this was making Rodgers happy, but Hart, forced to keep his homosexual lifestyle a secret, was even unhappier. His lyrics had always expressed skepticism about love and contentment; now they were not only melancholy, they were downright despondent. For *Pal Joey* in 1940, Hart wrote an eleven-o'clock number for the hero that was so sad it was cut in Philadelphia:

I'm talking to my pal,
Myself, my closest friend,
And that's the only pal
On whom I can depend . . .
I can't be sure of girls,
I'm not at home with men—
I'm ending up with me
  again.

Uneasy in his easy chair:
Larry Hart in the early 1940s.

"Sing me a song with social significance"

POLITICAL SATIRE ON BROADWAY

Irving Berlin's patriotic belief in his adopted county was an affectionate constant in his career, but as the crisis of the Depression deepened, even Berlin could see the box office potential of some good old-fashioned social satire. In 1932, he teamed up with the bright young playwright Moss Hart, who had become a rising star on Broadway when he coauthored the Hollywood satire *Once in a Lifetime* with George S. Kaufman two years earlier. Kaufman's own satirical musical, *Of Thee I Sing*, was playing to big business at the Music Box Theatre, which Berlin owned, and the composer thought there might be room for another sharp show in town—even if he had to rent out the New Amsterdam for it.

The plot of *Face the Music*, as concocted by Hart and Berlin, is really a triptych of slight social satires, tentatively stitched together: the Depression; the Seabury investigations, which forced Mayor Walker to resign; and the Ziegfeld Follies. The show's lack of conceptual clarity is obvious from its subtitle, "A Musical Comedy Revue," and it was not the smash return to Broadway that Berlin had anticipated. In the end, a musical comedy with an extended plot was beyond Berlin's interests and ambitions; he was more comfortable with the revue format—short, sharp, and quick— as he himself would be the first to admit.

The next season, Hart and Berlin tried again for a topical revue, but this time they kept their target well within sight and hit the bull's-eye. *As Thousands Cheer* was typical of the general trend in the 1930s in giving the revue form some kind of structural or thematic

As Thousands Cheer's amusing gimmick was to turn newspaper stories into revue numbers. Here, in "Noel Coward, Celebrated Playwright, Returns to England," the working-class hotel staff (l. to r.: Helen Broderick, Marilyn Miller, Ethel Waters, Clifton Webb, and Leslie Adams) are turned into cosmopolitan wits simply by cleaning the Master's room.

unity. In this, the team achieved a kind of brilliance: *As Thousands Cheer* had as its concept the daily newspaper, with each number and skit taken from (or performed in ironic contrast to) a headline or regular feature—which was projected across the proscenium. (This was several years before the Federal Theatre Project created a unit called "The Living Newspaper," which dramatized political stories in a documentary form.) This structure allowed Hart to parody such wet-ink-fresh subjects as Gandhi, evangelist Aimee Semple McPherson, the building of Rockefeller Center, and the outgoing Hoover administration (the sketch has the lame-duck ex-president and his wife running up a huge last-minute long-distance phone bill on the eve of FDR's inauguration). Berlin took a gentler swipe at society—with the extraordinary exception of "Supper Time" for Ethel Waters (see page 158)—by ribbing Josephine Baker ("Harlem on My Mind"), Woolworth heiress Barbara Hutton ("How's Chances?"), even the hoary conventions of the revue format itself ("Supreme Court Hands Down Important Decision"), which says that revues are forbidden to reprise their most memorable songs in the finale.

A month after *As Thousands Cheer* opened on Broadway in September 1933, Kaufman, Morrie Ryskind, and the Gershwins returned to the scene of their rhymes with *Let 'Em Eat Cake,* a rare musical sequel, reprising the cast of characters in *Of Thee I Sing.* This time, the team designed their political satire on a more international canvas. John P. Wintergreen gets voted out of office, but decides to overthrow the new administration, installing himself as dictator of the proletariat. The score was even more sophisticated than its predecessor's, but the book's often depressing take on fascism ground audiences down, rather than inspiring them. More egregiously, the show was simply a formalistic copy of the original—at one point, Wintergreen says to his wife, Mary, "Try it. It worked [in the first show]." It was a costly failure, closing after only ninety performances at the Imperial Theatre, while Berlin was clocking four hundred performances of *As Thousands Cheer* at his very own Music Box Theatre.

George Gershwin's manuscript page for a rehearsal draft of Let 'Em Eat Cake; *brother Ira's lyrics are framed by George's own self-portrait doodles.*

In 1933, as American newspapers get their fill of European fascists posturing on balconies, Let 'Em Eat Cake *turned ex-president John P. Wintergreen (William Gaxton, center) into the Dictator of the Proletariat.*

This was more a matter of craft than of sentiment; as the 1930s wore on, political satire on Broadway became more, rather than less, prominent. As times grew more complex, the Broadway musical became more adventuresome, reflecting national and international tensions. The last part of 1937 saw four intensely political musicals on Broadway—*The Cradle Will Rock*, *Pins and Needles*, *I'd Rather Be Right*—and an antiwar satire starring Ed Wynn called *Hooray for What!* The style of the shows ranged from the sublime to the ridiculous, but they each caught a different facet of the American consciousness. By the fall of 1937, it looked as if the Depression would be forever clouding the skies. After a landslide reelection victory in 1936, Roosevelt seemed to be having only partial success with the New Deal; besides coping with a severe budget deficit, FDR was trying to pack the Supreme Court. All over the nation, struggles between labor and management were exploding into dangerous and often fatal violence. Dominating this class warfare was the emergence of the Congress of Industrial Organizations, a breakaway of industrial unions from the more craft-oriented American Federation of Labor. It pushed for wage strikes against the automotive and steel industries, which were particularly harsh in instituting wage cuts and firings at plants across the nation. In Pittsburgh, Michigan, and Chicago, strikes ended in violence as workers were beaten and fired upon in the spring of 1937. The only ray of light in the union struggle was the adoption in 1936 of the Wagner Act, which opened a legal door for collective bargaining. Surprising as it may sound, all of these grim events made their appearance, one way or another, on the Broadway musical stage.

David Dubinsky, the powerful head of the International Ladies' Garment Workers' Union in the 1930s, was devoted to the betterment of its members, whose numbers had tripled since the New Deal was instituted, although he, too, was caught in the middle of the A.F. of L./C.I.O. warfare. One of his ideas was a Cultural Division, which made "good union members aware of the truth that man does not live by bread alone." The largely immigrant membership was soon being offered lessons in tap dancing, mandolin playing, and elocution. In the mid-'30s, the Division had the idea of creating a musical revue by and for the members of the ILGWU and hired a former architect turned songwriter, Harold Rome, to write it. Rehearsals for most Broadway musicals in 1937 usually involved four weeks in town, plus two on the road, but there was nothing usual about *Pins and Needles.*

Rome rehearsed his cast—assembled from the ranks of stitchers, seamstresses, and cutters—after their work shift three hours a night, three nights a week, over the course of an entire year. The show opened two days after Thanksgiving in 1937, and it took some time before New York theatergoers heard about it—it played only on weekends, as the cast needed to get to bed early to rest up for their day jobs.

Pins and Needles *stitched together a broad satirical canvas. Here, "Four Little Angels of Peace"— an unnamed Japanese general, Hitler, Mussolini, and Anthony Eden—sing about their ability to unleash devastation on other nations. The lyrics for this song were revised throughout the thirties to accommodate the changing political climate; when England went to war against the Axis powers in 1939, Eden's character was dropped altogether.*

Rome's score set the tone for the whole show, which was not really a condemnation of the world's evil, but rather a lighthearted look at young people in a changing society in the middle of America's most politically engaged city. The opening number let the audience know where the hearts of these young workers lay:

Sing me of wars and sing me of breadlines,
Tell me of front-page news.
Sing me of strikes and last-minute headlines.
Dress your observation in syncopation!
Sing me a song with social significance.
There's nothing else that will do.
It must get hot with what is what,
Or I won't love you.

The boy-girl duet invoked the running battle between the A. F. of L. and the C. I. O. as its metaphor ("No scabbing when I'm out of town / In our big union for two"), and the gathering storm in Europe was acidly mocked in a merry waltz called "Four Little Angels of Peace" in which Anthony Eden, Mussolini, Hitler, and a Japanese general kept insisting on their desire for peace. The show had an extraordinarily long run for the period—1,108 performances—but that was largely because its theater, the Labor Stage (formerly the Princess Theatre, of all things!), had only three hundred seats. The success of the show surprised its creator, Harold Rome. "I didn't realize that the big attraction was that the garment workers themselves were doing the show themselves and singing to the audience, creating a rapport which is very rare in the theater." Even the bluestockings in the audience found it all charming. Critic Heywood Broun wrote that "stout ladies in ermine must realize they are being kidded [for] few if any have rushed out screaming into the night. No dowager has been observed standing on a street corner waiting for a tumbril."

Perhaps no one was more pleased than Dubinsky, who must have been extremely grateful for this gentle respite in contentious times. He wrote:

With zest and disarming frankness, their songs and skits punctured economic platitudes, ridiculed political insincerity, satirized the seamier side of American life, and poked fun at overseas dictators. At the same time, with wonderful freshness, they sang of pay envelopes and picket lines, of romance in the shop and Sundays in the park. All of this they did with the enthusiasm and attractive amateurishness that drew the high and mighty to sit in their small theater among ILGWU members and to cheer performance after performance.

Opening three weeks before *Pins and Needles*, *I'd Rather Be Right* bypassed the

"It's Not Cricket to Picket" ran one number in Pins and Needles, *but labor issues turned this revue into an unlikely hit.*

middlemen of shop foremen and went straight to the top for its satirical target: President Roosevelt himself. In the modern television era, it is hard to imagine how revolutionary it was for Kaufman and Hart and Rodgers and Hart to put a sitting president onstage for two and a half hours of comic ribbing. To be fair, all four creators were good New York liberals, so the arrows sent FDR's way were not exactly tipped with venom, but the president was summarily chided for his attempt to pack the Supreme Court (all nine pop out of the bushes to shout down FDR every time he proposes a new law), his failure to balance the budget, his ambition for a third term, even his frequent browbeating by his overbearing mother. (Kaufman and Company were clever enough to leave Eleanor offstage for the evening.) All aspects of the WPA came under the fire, and it was perhaps inevitable when the Wagner Act appeared onstage—as a German vaudeville team. The high profiles of the creative partners, plus the electric performance of George M. Cohan (who despised the president's politics), made the show the hit of the season, despite—or perhaps because of—its sentimental closing speech, which had FDR rallying America with a fireside chat.

Jesters for hard times (l. to r.): Moss Hart and George S. Kaufman join Harold Rome (at piano) and director–sketch writer Charles Freedman onstage for a rehearsal of Sing Out the News.

A year later, Kaufman and Hart teamed up to produce (and rewrite) *Sing Out the News,* Harold Rome's first commercial Broadway revue. It had a less pungent liberal agenda than *Pins and Needles;* if that show played like a musical version of *The Nation, Sing Out the News* played more like the *New York Times* op-ed page. Sketch topics included the difficulties the Republican Party was having finding a candidate to run against FDR (he turns out to be an angel who loses his wings when he accepts the nomination), and a song is set at a Harlem block party where a new black baby is christened Franklin D. Roosevelt Jones, which, according to the joyous celebrants, augurs well for his future.

All this stage preoccupation with the president may appear unseemly or as a bald attempt to curry some kind of favor, but in the 1930s FDR was, simply, the greatest showman in the country. His voice (which emanated regularly, with great brio, from the radio), his conviction, and his keen sense of humor, often about himself, made him a highly theatrical character. As war became imminent in Europe, the satirical focus would shift from domestic problems and start to include unsettling developments across the Atlantic. With fascism becoming a clear and present danger, the Broadway stage's freedom to poke fun at whomever it chose was a gift that theatergoers—and Americans—could no longer take for granted.

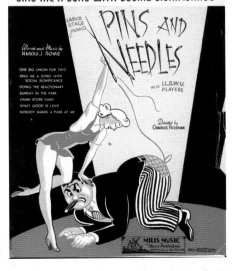

THE CRADLE WILL ROCK

IN 1935, THE NEW DEAL'S Works Progress Administration (WPA) added unemployed stage artists to the ranks of its relief efforts by creating the Federal Theatre Project, a nationwide producing organization that employed thousands within a network of smaller theater units that would put on all manner of plays and musicals for the public at popular prices. It was an unprecedented effort, eventually sponsoring almost twelve hundred productions for an audience of more than 30 million—one quarter of the United States population.

The most exciting unit by far was based in New York; focusing principally on classical theater, Project 891 was run by producer John Houseman and the twenty-one-year-old wonder boy of the American theater, Orson Welles. One of the three shows Welles and Houseman chose for its 1936–37 season was an extremely unconventional "play in music" written entirely by Marc Blitzstein, a left-leaning composer who had trained with Schoenberg. Blitzstein had visited Germany in the politically charged 1920s, where he fell under the spell of the powerful Marxist musical theater pieces of Kurt Weill and Bertolt Brecht. It was Brecht himself who encouraged Blitzstein in 1936 to develop his acid-tinged songs into the theater piece *The Cradle Will Rock*.

Cradle's ambitions exceeded those of anything before it. Blitzstein described it as a combination of "realism, romance, vaudeville, comic strip, Gilbert & Sullivan, Brecht and agitprop." His parable is set in Steeltown, USA, where a series of union meetings are undermining the authority of the domineering industrialist, Mr. Mister. A more sentimental (and more logical) playwright might have dramatized the growth of the emerging unions, but Blitzstein keeps any kind of rally offstage, preferring instead to emphasize, in a series of episodic flashbacks, the tyrannical grip of Mr. Mister as he manipulates the fears and weaknesses of Steeltown's residents, turning

the town into a snake pit of pious hypocrisy. Only the solidarity of the unions can "rock the cradle" of capitalistic complacency.

Director Welles knew he had a new and powerful piece in front of him:

> The arts of Music and the Play have had efficient business relationships in the past, an occasional partnership and few happy marriages. Here, finally, is their first off-spring. It is a love-child, and besides being legitimate, it looks like both its parents, and it is called a "music drama." As a matter of fact, it isn't easy to find a title for a new art form. Just now of course this one has only one real name: *The Cradle Will Rock*.

Project 891 prepared for its June 16 opening at the Maxine Elliott Theatre on 38th Street. The combined cast and orchestra of more than fifty rehearsed under Welles's typically grandiose vision, on an extraordinary set of transparent glass wagons, lit from underneath by floodlights.

Alas, nothing onstage quite became *The Cradle Will Rock* like the closing of it.

The Federal Theatre Project was not a favorite among the more conservative members of Congress, who could never reconcile themselves to the idea of the government "getting into show business." In early June, the FTP was told to cut the New York unit back by 30 percent just as *Cradle* was about to open with more than 18,000 tickets sold in advance. On June 12, the government closed the show, claiming "impending cuts and reorganization." Houseman and Welles would contend that *Cradle* fell victim because of its incendiary message, but it's unlikely that Congress contained many astute theater critics. On June 15, a dozen uniformed WPA guards took control of the theater and forbade the company to make use of the stage or sets, or even to sell tickets. Project 891 was, in essence, being repossessed by the United States government.

Welles and Houseman were not to be deterred and decided a day before the scheduled opening to reconstitute the show under their own commercial management, a decision that blew up in their faces. Houseman recalled:

> Then the next morning, Actors' Equity [decided that the company was no longer in the employ of the government]. Our actors were forbidden [to appear] for us on any stage unless we paid them for three full weeks of rehearsal and two guaranteed weeks of performance. And since we didn't have a penny, this was entirely out of the question.

Warriors of the Broadway world: Orson Welles (l.) and John Houseman.

Houseman later noted the irony of "the final, fatal blows" to the original production being "dealt by those very unions in whose defense the piece had been written." However, such defeats only served to strengthen the troupe's resolve. The evening of the opening, as the cast sat in the darkened Maxine Elliott awaiting instructions, Welles and Houseman had their assistant lighting designer rent a piano, hire a truck, and drive around town until they could find an available theater to put on their show. A crummy theater near Central Park called the Venice was located just before curtain time, and Welles and Houseman mobilized the cast and their growing audience to march twenty-one blocks uptown to occupy their new venue. Blitzstein jumped onto the truck carrying the piano and served as the Pied Piper for the crowd.

By nine o'clock, with the Venice packed to the gunnels with a fervent crowd, awaiting who knew what, Welles came out on the bare stage and announced that the composer himself would perform the entire show at the rickety rented piano. Blitzstein entered to applause, took his seat, and set the scene: "Scene One. Street corner. Steeltown, USA." Blitzstein recalled:

> I started, ready to do the whole show myself. I began the Moll's first song of the play, and then I heard the words taken from my mouth by the Moll herself seated in the right loge. . . . Again I heard an actor take my melody and my lines from me—only this time from mid-center in the orchestra. . . . As the play progressed, [the audience] turned as at a tennis match from one actor to another.

The company had been prohibited from performing onstage, but not in the house, and from the moment Olive Stanton, who played the Moll, courageously raised her voice to sing her song, the actors in the cast held the theater hostage for the next two hours, performing Blitzstein's entire show in an extended, inspired group improvisation. The brazenness of the whole impromptu exercise made front pages all over the country.

The Cradle Will Rock continued playing at the Venice for two weeks and, under the auspices of Welles and Houseman's newly constituted Mercury Theatre, reopened on a Broadway stage

The cast takes to the aisles at the opening night; Blitzstein can be seen at the piano.

Olive Stanton, the actress who started it all, in front of a poster for a production that never opened the way the poster promised.

for an extended four-month run early in 1938. In 1939, Congress finally pulled the plug on the Federal Theatre Project. Houseman and Welles went on to conquer Hollywood; Blitzstein remained at the fringes of Broadway success for the rest of his career. But for just about everyone in the audience on June 16, 1937, *The Cradle Will Rock* provided the greatest opening night of the 1930s, and of their entire lives.

George Balanchine and his then wife, ballerina Vera Zorina.

When Irving Berlin and Al Jolson came to this country at the turn of the century, there was no such thing as a Broadway musical. In the middle of the 1930s, another wave of immigrants would arrive in New York, mature artists in search of artistic and political freedom, inspired by the infectious bravado of the Broadway musical and eager to conquer it.

Choreographer George Balanchine had already left his native Russia and was working with an avant-garde ballet company in Paris when a wealthy New York arts patron named Lincoln Kirstein sailed to France in order to invite him to start a company in America. Balanchine needed little convincing; his Les Ballets 1933 was failing, and besides, he said, he would love to go to a country that produced such beautiful girls as Ginger Rogers. Soon after his ship docked in October 1933, Balanchine plunged into myriad new assignments: starting the School of American Ballet, running the corps de ballet of the Metropolitan Opera, and, by the beginning of 1936, creating dances for Josephine Baker and the Nicholas Brothers in the *Ziegfeld Follies of 1936* on Broadway.

Only four months later, in April 1936, Balanchine's gifts for sinuous dance, character work, and puckish parody were on display at the Imperial Theatre in Rodgers and Hart's *On Your Toes.* Rodgers, who could be rather intimidating himself, was utterly intimidated by the aquiline, imperious Russian who spoke little English. "But that was okay," Rodgers said. "He spoke a lot of dance." Balanchine's generous professionalism endeared him to Rodgers, and together, with the ballets "Princess Zenobia" and "Slaughter on Tenth Avenue," they set a new standard for how dance could be used to advance the narrative of a musical comedy. Balanchine asked the producer if his program credit could read "Choreography by," rather than the traditional "Dances by"; it became the first time the word was used in connection with a Broadway musical. (The first two of Balanchine's four wives, the exquisite ballerinas Tamara Geva and Vera Zorina, would each play the lead in *On Your Toes*, Geva in the original production and Zorina in the 1939 movie and the 1954 revival.) Balanchine would go on to choreograph more than a dozen other musicals before devoting most of his energy to running the New York City Ballet. More than any other choreographer, he paved the way for revolutions in musical storytelling that would be the cornerstone of the 1940s, '50s, and '60s.

When composer Kurt Weill sailed into New York Harbor with his wife, singer and muse Lotte Lenya, in September 1935, he was like many of the artistic refugees from Hitler's Germany: talented, provocative, and Jewish—the son of a cantor, just like Irving Berlin, Al Jolson, and Harold Arlen. Weill had two things that most refugees weren't always so lucky to bring with them, however: a reputation and a job. When Weill wrote the music for leftist playwright Bertolt Brecht's *Threepenny Opera* in 1928, it became the greatest sensation in modern Europe. A New York production in 1933 merely bewildered critics and closed in two weeks, but the German-language recording of its jazzy, discordant songs made Weill famous in New York artistic circles, and he had been brought to New York to write the music for *The Eternal Road,* a staged oratorio about the wanderings of the Jewish race. America represented, for Weill, an end to his own wanderings.

I decided to become a citizen the day on which I arrived here, six years ago. I remember very well the feeling I had as the ship moved down the harbor past the Statue of Liberty and the skyscrapers. All about us were exclaiming in amazement at the strange sights, but my wife and I had the sensation we were coming home.

—Kurt Weill, 1941

Kurt Weill (center) and his wife/muse Lotte Lenya (right of Weill) arrive in New York to begin work on The Eternal Road, *1935.*

Weill and Lenya plunged into the theater scene, socializing with as many people as they could. After meeting George Gershwin at a party in his penthouse apartment, Weill was invited to the dress rehearsal of *Porgy and Bess,* and it made him nearly heartsick with envy. It was just this kind of serious musical theater work that Weill had dreamed of creating as he traveled across the Atlantic. Soon, however, Weill got his chance. In 1936, New York's daring Group Theatre hired him to write the music for the stark antiwar parable, *Johnny Johnson.* With this respectable Broadway credit in hand, Weill ventured to Hollywood, but his idiosyncratic talents went unrecognized by producers. One doubted

A scene from the ambitious Johnny Johnson *(1936).*

Knickerbocker Holiday *gave the world* "September Song."

that he was "American" enough for a certain picture, and Weill responded that "the 'most American' composer, Irving Berlin, is a Russian Jew—and I'm a German Jew; that's the only difference." But it was clear that what he really needed to make it in Hollywood was a hit in New York.

In 1938, Weill traveled back east and teamed up with one of Broadway's leading playwrights, Maxwell Anderson, to create the political satire *Knickerbocker Holiday,* which yielded the elegiac and immortal "September Song," his first popular standard in America. The show itself, however, was not a huge success. Still frustrated, Weill wondered if his serious conception of musical theater would take hold. In a 1939 newspaper interview he said:

> You hear a lot of talk about the "American opera" that's going to come along some day. It's my opinion that we can and will develop a musical-dramatic in this country, but I don't think it will be called "opera," or that it will grow out of the opera, which has become a thing separate from the commercial theater, dependent upon other means than box-office appeal for its continuance. It will develop from and remain a part of the American theater—"Broadway" theater, if you like. More than anything else, I want to have part in that development.

Weill was fortunate that his next collaborator, Moss Hart, was equally eager to experiment. Hart stated in a 1941 press release:

> I refuse to waste any more time wracking my brain to provide a good excuse for the boy and girl to burst into a love duet. I've become much more interested in characters than stories. Over the last few years, I've sabotaged every serious idea I've had for a play. And my psychiatrist made me resolve that the next idea I'd had, I'd carry through.

Meeting one day for lunch in 1940 at the Hapsburg restaurant, Hart and Weill tried to brainstorm an idea. Hart's preoccupation with psychoanalysis—he went to a session every day—led to a natural proposition: Why not show someone in the process of being psychoanalyzed and dramatize the dreams? Weill's musical genius leaped ahead to the leading character's dream sequences, which he would conceive as "little one-act operas." But who would do the lyrics? On New Year's Day, they phoned Ira Gershwin in Beverly Hills. He was in self-imposed retirement after his brother's death, but he said yes to Weill and Hart on the spot.

Hart's conception of the show, retitled *Lady in the Dark* from its original *Are You Listening?,* grew from a play with incidental songs to a complex musical form. Heroine Liza Elliott, editor of a stylish fashion magazine, is cursed with an inability to make up her mind. Weill and Gershwin rejected the conventional alternation between scene and song and, instead, wrote three extended musical sequences of Liza's elaborate and complicated dreams: a Glamour Dream, a Wedding Dream, and a Circus Dream. The extraordinary score featured choral numbers, rhumbas, patter songs, vaudeville turns, and sentimental ballads. In the book scenes, through sessions with her psychoanalyst, Liza is able to retrieve a song from her childhood that eventually unlocks the key to her confusion.

> I do not care if that day arrives—
> That dream need never be—
> If the ship I sing
> Doesn't also bring
> My own true love to me.

Gertrude Lawrence as chic, chronically indecisive fashion magazine editor Liza Elliott, who is all business during the day . . .

Almost a year to the day after the phone call to Gershwin, *Lady in the Dark,* which Hart billed as "a musical play," opened in Boston, starring Gertrude Lawrence as Liza and a young comedian with his eyes on the prize, Danny Kaye. The two topped each other's dazzling performance to dizzying heights.

Audiences had never seen anything as sophisticated in scope and setting, as adult in its subject matter and treatment. After the show opened on Broadway, the morning review in the *New York Times* proclaimed Weill to be "the best writer of theater music in the country." It went on to run 777 performances—each of them with Gertrude Lawrence in the lead—and set a record for the sale price of a stage play to the motion pictures.

My old friend and teacher Ferruccio Busoni used to say: You don't feel at home in a new language unless you dream and count in this language. Well, there is not a word of German in my dreams any more, and since the success of *Lady in the Dark,* I even count in English.

Kurt Weill, 1941

It had been five and a half years since the composer had set sail from Berlin to Paris to London to New York to Hollywood and back to New York again. Kurt Weill's ship had finally come in.

but in her dreams . . .
Liza's explosive third-act Circus Dream:
Danny Kaye (far right) brought the house
down as a ringleader who glided his way
through Weill and Gershwin's tongue-
tangling "Tchaikovsky."

DEN OF INIQUITY

Words by Lorenz Hart
Music by Richard Rodgers
From Pal Joey *(1940)*

"IT WAS THE FIRST MUSICAL TO DEAL WITH THE FACTS OF LIFE," wrote Richard Rodgers. Indeed, sex—not burlesque sex, but complicated affairs among consenting adults—is at the center of *Pal Joey*. Most of the characters and atmosphere had been present in John O'Hara's original short stories, published in *The New Yorker* from 1939 to 1941. When O'Hara first had the idea of adapting a couple of them to the musical stage, the only team he thought capable of capturing the sophisticated world with wit and charm was Rodgers and Hart. For a major literary figure such as O'Hara to approach the musical-theater world was a big deal—Edna Ferber, remember, had to be convinced.

The slim story of *Pal Joey* concerns a second-rate nightclub singer in Chicago who, hoping to realize his dream of owning his own nightclub, becomes the kept man of Vera Simpson, an older, married socialite—which doesn't keep Joey from sleeping with all the cuties in the chorus line *and* trying to romance a decent working-class girl. The show's integration of musical numbers into the story wasn't quite revolutionary, but the story itself was. Within the first two pages of the libretto, Joey auditions at a seedy nightclub and is asked by the manager whether he's into booze, cocaine, little boys, and/or just plain chorus girls. It goes on like that for two and a half hours.

In his score, Rodgers alternated musical styles, providing saucy, snappy numbers appropriate for a Chicago nightclub and then switching to some of the most elegant songs ever written to express the emotions of the characters, such as the show's most famous ballad, "Bewitched, Bothered and Bewildered." The barroom habitué Lorenz Hart felt right at home in the milieu of the piece. "He knew there was a dark, sad, dirty story down there somewhere and that people are having fun because they know the words to that story," said historian Ann Douglas. Ironically, Hart was outmatched by the heavy-drinking O'Hara, who was so invisible during production that Hart himself was forced to send him a telegram begging him to phone in.

Vivienne Segal, a Rodgers and Hart favorite since the 1920s, played the socialite, but the part of Joey required someone who could be likeably unlikable. A young dancer from Pittsburgh, who had recently been a chorus boy backing up Mary Martin in Cole Porter's *Leave It to Me*, answered the call. Stanley Donen, who made his Broadway debut in *Pal Joey*, recalled:

In terms of a Broadway musical, Gene Kelly was playing a tricky role: a very brash, cocky, sure person, who was very randy for girls, but who was needy and not well educated, which made him funny. He was an energetic, fresh, aggressive, Irish American presence, which had a great charm, and I'm sure when they saw him for the part—John O'Hara being Irish American [as well]—they had to say that's the guy. There are those moments on Broadway when these people suddenly come forth—it's a big moment—and Gene was one of them.

When *Pal Joey* opened on Broadway on Christmas Day of 1940, it immediately alienated some critics, particularly the lead critic at the *Times*, who famously objected to its sordid characters. Rodgers felt there was some validity to that reaction. "*Pal Joey* was a good show about rotten people; everyone in it—the hero, the leading lady—they're all bad people. Except the girl. And she was stupid." But just as many critics recognized the show as a landmark. *The New Yorker*'s Wolcott Gibbs wrote in his opening-night review:

With *Pal Joey*, musical comedy took a long step towards maturity . . . the idea of equipping a song-and-dance production with a few living characters behaving like human beings may no longer strike the boys in the business as merely fantastic.

Few songs of the pre–World War II era, even those of Cole Porter, capture adult sexuality the way "Den of Iniquity" does. In the second act, Joey and Vera wake from a postcoital reverie and celebrate the joys of an illicit affair. Rodgers's dainty minuet provides just enough contrast to Hart's double—no, make that single—entendres.

Just two little lovebirds all alone
In a little cozy nest
With a little secret telephone;
That's the place to rest.
Artificial roses round the door—
They are never out of bloom—
And a flowered carpet on the floor
In the loving room.

In our little den of iniquity
Our arrangement is good.
It's much more healthy living here;
This rushing back home is bad my dear,
I haven't caught a cold all year.
Knock on wood!
It was ever thus since antiquity,
All the poets agree.
The chambermaid is very kind,
She always thinks we're so refined.
Of course, she's deaf and dumb and blind—
No fools, we—
In our little den of iniquity.

In our little den of iniquity
For a girly and boy,
We'll sit and let the hours pass;
A canopy bed has so much class,
And so's a ceiling made of glass—
Oh, what joy!

Love has been that way since antiquity,
Down to you and me.
The radio I used to hate,
But now when it is dark and late
Ravel's "Bolero" works just great—
That's for me,
In our little den of iniquity.
Oh, what joy!

We're very proper folks, you know.
We've separate bedrooms *comme il faut.*
There's one for play and one for show.
You chase me
In our little den of iniquity.

LEFT: *Hoofer Joey Evans (Kelly) making his umpteenth pass at his umpteenth chorine.*

RIGHT: *Gene Kelly and Vivienne Segal revel in their den of iniquity.*

MUSIC

"The Army's made a man out of me"

IRVING BERLIN'S *THIS IS THE ARMY*

On Sunday, December 7, 1941, the *New York Times* reported some earth-shattering news: Irving Berlin was writing a new revue for the coming year.

> Here is a wire from Mr. Irving Berlin on the Coast, sent in answer to a question about whether there is to be another revue: AM DEFINITELY PLANNING TO DO A MUSIC BOX REVUE TO OPEN SOME TIME IN THE SUMMER. . . . IDEA I HAVE IN MIND IS FOR A PERIOD REVUE OF PAST, PRESENT, AND FUTURE. MOSS HART HAS PROMISED TO WRITE A COUPLE OF SKETCHES. AM TRYING TO LINE UP SOME OF THE CAST OUT HERE.

When the events of the day that will live in infamy became known, Berlin was forced to change his tune. The Japanese attack on Pearl Harbor prompted the United States to enter World War II, and everyone was called on to pitch in. The Office of War Information, in charge of morale on the home front, immediately set about getting Tin Pan Alley to create the next "Over There"—a patriotic ballad that would galvanize the country. Berlin always maintained that such songs could never be written to the beat of a government edict; they had to evolve the same way any song would, out of the convictions and talent of the composer. Sensing that Broadway's tastes would change overnight, Berlin scrapped his plans for the Music Box revue and charged into the world he knew best: creating stirring material for a country in need of spirit rather than sophistication, in need of patriotism rather than psychoanalysis, soldiers and factory workers rather than gigolos and fashion editors.

Berlin journeyed to Washington to meet with General George C. Marshall and proposed a sequel to *Yip! Yip! Yaphank*, to be titled *This Is the Army*, and worked out a deal whereby the Army would release men to Berlin to perform in the show, with all the proceeds from the performances going to the Army Emergency Relief Fund. While commanding officers gathered talent from Army ranks around the country, Berlin returned to Camp Upton on Long Island, where he had written the earlier revue, to gather new material. By May 1942, the show was ready for rehearsal. The basic form was the same as the World War I extravaganza's: a cast of three hundred enlisted men spoofed Army life in skits, jokes, songs, and dances—usually in uniform, often in drag. In addition to attending rehearsal, many of the men were required to complete weapons training, so a typical day might involve dancing in the morning, firing rifles in the afternoon, and dressing up as a woman at night, all with the approval of the U.S. Army.

This time, however, there would be a crucial difference. Berlin knew that the Depression had changed the tenor of the times—the innocent fun of 1918 wouldn't play in 1942. His show had to reflect recent shifts in society, so he insisted on an integrated unit; the cast of *This Is the Army* would, in fact, be the only integrated armed services unit in World War II. Blackface minstrel numbers would be out of the question. Instead, Berlin wrote a number in which black Army officers showed up their zoot-suited civilian pals in "What the Well-Dressed Man in Harlem Will Wear."

Almost two thousand people, theater folk and Army personnel alike, were packed into the Broadway Theatre on opening night, Saturday, July 4, 1942—the first Fourth of July after the United States entered the war. The audience was stirred by the sight of the three hundred men marching in to "This Is the Army, Mr. Jones" and was moved when one corporal sang about leaving his heart at the Stage Door Canteen with a girl named Eileen. But their reaction was nothing compared to how they greeted the appearance of Berlin himself in Act II, dressed in his khaki puttees and oversize hat, just as in *Yip! Yip! Yaphank*, to sing "Oh! How I Hate to Get Up in the Morning." His daughter Mary Ellin Barrett recalled:

Cast members learning Berlin's new lead sheet—"What the Well-Dressed Man in Harlem Will Wear."

Irving Berlin immortalizes his contempt for the bugler in the film version of This Is the Army, *1943.*

There he was in his World War I uniform, a small, dark man with these huge dark eyes, opening his mouth to begin to sing, and at that moment the theater exploded, and there was a roar, cheers, applause, everybody on their feet, standing for my father. And finally he was allowed to begin his song, and there he sang, with that true, frail voice, a little nervous at first, and then beginning to pick up, really delivering it. And when he finished, a whole other round of applause and cheers. And I remember my feelings: I had never seen anything like this before—I saw something in that theatre which was more than the fame of my father, but it was love, real love from that audience, love for this man, for what he had given people, not just for *This Is the Army*—but that was enough—but for everything he'd done as a songwriter, as a showman, as an American, for this country.

The show played 113 performances on Broadway, and a special command performance was arranged for the president and the First Lady. As the cast marched its way to Penn Station, following a big brass band, onlookers cheered them, thinking they were going overseas to lick Hitler; in fact, they were just

taking the train to Washington. After Secret Service men checked the onstage rifles for real bullets, Roosevelt cheered them on from his private box—an act of some courage, when one considers what had happened to an earlier president at the theater. The show went on national tour, ringing up the cash register for the Relief Fund at stop after stop, although housing arrangements for the black members of the cast caused some complications.

Berlin refused to give it a rest. Still performing in the show, and writing new specialty numbers for each new tour of duty, he took *This Is the Army* to London, then North Africa and Italy, where he wowed the audience with Italian songs from his Lower East Side days, eventually embarking on a risky tour to the South Pacific. By the time it finished with a brief appearance in Hawaii, the show had been running—around the world—for more than three years. Berlin had been personally responsible for a staggering $9.8 million contribution to the war effort. Critic John Chapman had said, "The only thing that can stop *This Is the Army* is the end of the war." In fact, Berlin's show had a longer run—by two months.

In January 1943—as Roosevelt and Churchill met in Casablanca, Morocco, to coordinate battle plans against Germany, Italy, and Japan—before it began its European tour, *This Is the Army* was filmed in Hollywood, where the story was rewritten, women were added to the cast, and the talent included George Murphy, Sergeant Joe Louis, and Lieutenant Ronald Reagan. Berlin's own star turn as the infantry insomniac was recorded on film for posterity. The show's press director, Max Wilk, recalled that as Berlin performed the song for the cameras in his inimitable way, one stagehand turned to another and said, "If the guy, whoever wrote this song, ever heard *this* guy sing it, he'd turn over in his grave."

Finale

One morning in September 1941, Richard Rodgers was behind the wheel of his car. He had been in Philadelphia to shepherd the out-of-town tryout of director George Abbott's latest musical, a bit of college high jinks called *Best Foot Forward*. Rodgers was acting as a silent partner on the show; he was desperate for something to do, as Larry Hart seemed uninterested in pursuing any new project. He didn't want people to think he and Hart were through, so Rodgers agreed to help Abbott out, as long as his name was kept off the program. As he sped along Route 202, listening on the car radio to the dire news about the German invasion of the Soviet Union, he was considering a future without his partner of twenty years. He had an appointment for lunch at the Bucks County farm of Oscar Hammerstein.

Hammerstein had been more than happy to get Rodgers's call. He had nothing but respect for the composer, whom he had known for a quarter of a century, since Rodgers's older brother Morty had brought him backstage after a Columbia Varsity Show. Hammerstein was having a comparative dry spell. His last real hit on Broadway, *Music in the Air*, with a score by Jerome Kern, had been nearly a decade earlier, and his Hollywood career, with the exception of a few hit songs like "The Folks Who Live on the Hill" and "The Last Time I Saw Paris," was tedious and uninspiring. He was currently drudging his way through a new show with Sigmund Romberg, a bit of New Orleans nonsense called *Sunny River*, which would prove to be a Thanksgiving turkey when it opened in New Haven two months later.

Oscar Hammerstein, surrounded by pastoral serenity, works at his Bucks County, Pennsylvania, farm.

As they had their coffee on the veranda overlooking the meadows of Hammerstein's seventy-two-acre farm, with its split-rail fences and languorous cows, Rodgers explained the purpose of his visit, none of which came as a surprise to the lyricist. Larry Hart was simply not capable of collaborating in an effective manner anymore and Rodgers was at his wit's end. Hammerstein listened, thought for a minute, and responded: "I think you ought to keep working with Larry just so long as he is able to keep working with you. It would kill him if you walked away while he was still able to function. But if the time ever comes when he cannot function, call me. I'll be there."

I GET A KICK OUT OF COLE PORTER

By RUSSEL CROUSE

Stage Magazine (excerpt), August 1938

I'M NOT A MUSICIAN. I wouldn't know an arpeggio even if Walter Damrosch threw one at me and told me he was throwing it. All I know is that some of Cole Porter's music gives me a glow of satisfaction that makes me feel as though I had just dined on sunbeams with chocolate sauce, and the rest of it thrills me so that my spine tingles.

Just how Mr. Porter does this I am unable to state. If this is supposed to analyze the man I'm afraid I will have to call in the experts. Such works of genius as he dashes off should, of course, according to the traditional theory, come out of anguish, of which Mr. Porter hasn't any. Mr. Porter should be a sad little man who never smiles but just hides in a garret and writes great music.

But Mr. Porter isn't a sad little man at all. He is one of the gayest men I've ever known. I think he knows how to live better than any human being I have ever met. I have never seen him unhappy—even with two broken legs. He has a good time wherever he goes and if occasionally he doesn't he gets out of there, but quickly.

What exasperates me even more is that Mr. Porter can even go to his own first nights and have a good time. He will sit in the third row and enjoy himself immensely. On my own first nights I pace the back of the theatre looking for someone from whom I can borrow a few grains of cyanide or some other equally destructive poison. But Mr. Porter has a good time. Mr. Porter always has a good time.

Of course the perfect blend of word and note in his songs is brought about by the fact that he writes both words and notes. He is not easily satisfied in this respect and that is another good sign. I'll never forget the day during rehearsals of *Red, Hot and Blue* when he went for an entire day without speaking to me. By the time five o'clock had arrived I was sure I had offended him and lost a friend. I was just about to open negotiations for a restoration of an *entente cordiale* when he came up to me, looked me square in the eye, and said: "In my pet pailletted gown."

Isn't it a shame, I thought in my quiet way, that Mr. Porter has gone nuts.

But it turned out that it was a phrase he had been seeking all day, for a song. He hadn't had time to notice anyone. And it was the perfect phrase to fit the music. To me the greatest of the Porter words is "fabulous." He uses it frequently and always perfectly. When Miss Merman sang in the verse of "I Get a Kick Out of You"—"I suddenly turn and see—your fabulous face," no other word would have been right.

No other word is right for Mr. Porter either. His songs are just that. I would be content to sit quietly listening to them until such time as I am tuned in on that angelic chorus—and even then I'm afraid I'm going to ask the boys and girls with the harps to go into "I Get a Kick Out of You" pretty frequently, which may make me something of a problem-cherub.

NOTES ON THE MORNING AFTER AN OPENING NIGHT

By COLE PORTER

New York Times (excerpt), November 8, 1936

AM I MADE WRONG?

While Russel Crouse was pacing back and forth in the lounge of the Alvin Theatre during the opening performance of *Red, Hot and Blue!* giving a perfect take-off on all of the ten million ghosts, and Howard Lindsay was somewhere on his New Jersey estate getting quarter-hourly reports from his wife, I was in as good a seat as the management would give me, and, flanked by Mary Pickford and Merle Oberon, was having a swell time watching the actors. Russel claims this is being as indecent as the bridegroom who has a good time at his own wedding.

The morning after an opening of one of my own shows is more or less the same as any other morning—except that I sleep much later. In the case of *Red, Hot and Blue!* I broke my record by exactly ten minutes.

The reason for my behavior isn't that I'm confident of the play's success or that I'm totally without nerves. I'll put up my nerves against the best of them. But for some reason, the moment the curtain rises on opening night, I say to myself: "There she goes," and I've bid good-bye to my baby.

During the months of preparation the piece itself has a way of becoming something of a person to me—not always a nice person, perhaps, but at least some one that I've grown fond of. The minute it is exposed . . . however, I feel that it's no longer mine. It belongs to the performers. And I become just another $8.80 customer. That is why I take my friends along and make a night of it afterward.

The morning after is still a hangover of the holiday mood. One of the luxuries is to wake up to an inspired breakfast and then hunt for the notices. It is a pleasant feeling, this sensation of laziness which dictates that the entire day be dedicated to comfortable indolence, and nothing else but.

KAUFMAN AND HART

THE AMERICAN PRESIDENCY had been gently kidded in Broadway shows since the 1920s, but in the 1930s the team of George S. Kaufman and Moss Hart, both separately and together, bravely put the president onstage. The following are excerpts from the books from three shows. The first portrays Herbert Hoover in a sketch for Hart's *As Thousands Cheer*; the second shows a fictional president in a full-length musical (*Of Thee I Sing*, Kaufman and Morrie Ryskind); and, finally, a real-life president in a full-length show (*I'd Rather Be Right*, Kaufman and Hart).

From AS THOUSANDS CHEER:
"Franklin D. Roosevelt inaugurated tomorrow scene"
A room in the White House. It is littered with suitcases and boxes.
MR. HOOVER: [*Offstage*] Lou! Oh, Lou! Where do you want *this*, Lou?

MRS. HOOVER: [*Entering*] Bring it in here, Herbie.
MR. HOOVER: [*Entering with pedestal*] What do you want to lug that thing along for, Lou? It'll cost more than it's worth to ship it to California.
MRS. HOOVER: Never mind! I'm not going to leave anything for the Roosevelts, I can tell you that. Did you bring that electric toaster up from the kitchen, Herbie?
MR. HOOVER: No!
MRS. HOOVER: Well, go down and get it. I'd like to see myself leaving 'em a perfectly good electric toaster. Like fun.
MR. HOOVER: All right.
MRS. HOOVER: Oh, Herbie. Better take your fruit salts while you're downstairs, Herbie. You know what a long train ride does to you.
MR. HOOVER: All right. What's that?
MRS. HOOVER: This is nothing, Herbie—nothing at all. Just a little souvenir for my room at home.
MR. HOOVER: Let me see it.
MRS. HOOVER: But it's nothing, Herbie.
MR. HOOVER: Then let me see it. [*He uncovers the package—it is a painting.*] Now, Lou, you go right down and put that back. You can't take that. It's very valuable. It's Government property. You want to be stopped at the train?
MRS. HOOVER: Herbie, they'll never miss it. This house is lousy with pictures of George Washington.
MR. HOOVER: I don't care. You go put that back. Why, those Democrats are liable to pick on a thing like that and cause a whole Senate investigation.
MRS. HOOVER: All right, I'll put it back. We'll just go back to Palo Alto with nothing at all to show for your having been President of the United States.
MR. HOOVER: Nobody else in the country has got anything to show for it either.
MRS. HOOVER: That's right. Wise cracking is going to help us a lot.
MR. HOOVER: Now, Lou, things might have been a lot worse. Suppose I'd been re-elected.
MRS. HOOVER: You know what Palo Alto is. It's going to be very nice, isn't it, for me to go to bridge parties and luncheons and have all my old girl friends saying, "Herbie get anything to do yet, Lou? Well, don't worry. Something'll turn up sooner or later." I can just hear 'em.

MR. HOOVER: I've still got my Civil Engineer's license, don't forget that.

MRS. HOOVER: Oh, sure! Now you remember it, after fiddling away four whole years. I hate to say I told you so, Herbie—but you can't say I didn't warn you.

MR. HOOVER: But it seemed like such a good idea at the time—being President.

MRS. HOOVER: Not to me it didn't. We were doing so well too. Everything was going along beautiful for us. Then you had to go and become President. Herbie, there's a streak in you that makes you do the most simple-minded things sometimes. Had to become President. Couldn't leave well enough alone.

From *OF THEE I SING:*

(Vice-President Throttlebottom meets President Wintergreen outside the Senate chamber, where Wintergreen is about to be impeached.)

THROTTLEBOTTOM: Hello, Mr. President.

WINTERGREEN: *(Not recognizing* THROTTLEBOTTOM*)* How do you do?

THROTTLEBOTTOM: I'll bet you don't remember me, do you?

WINTERGREEN: *(After a moment's thought)* You're the fellow that gave me that dill pickle.

THROTTLEBOTTOM: That's right.

WINTERGREEN: What are you doing now?

THROTTLEBOTTOM: I'm Vice-President.

WINTERGREEN: You don't say? Lost your other job, huh?

THROTTLEBOTTOM: Well, I'm going to have a good job now, because I'm going to be President.

WINTERGREEN: *(Realizing it)* Say, that's right! If they kick me out that makes you President.
(Looks at him)
The country certainly *is* in a hole.

THROTTLEBOTTOM: Say, I wonder if you'd mind doing me a favor?

WINTERGREEN: Sure!

THROTTLEBOTTOM: You see, I don't know anything about being President. I just found out today how to be Vice-President.

WINTERGREEN: Well, that's something.

THROTTLEBOTTOM: Isn't there some book I could read?

WINTERGREEN: Sure—I'm writing one. *What Every Young President Ought to Know.*

THROTTLEBOTTOM: Has it got pictures?

WINTERGREEN: It's got everything. Tells you just what to do. Of course the first four years are easy. You don't do anything except try to get re-elected.

THROTTLEBOTTOM: That's pretty hard these days.

WINTERGREEN: The next four years you wonder why the hell you wanted to be re-elected. Then you go fishing.

THROTTLEBOTTOM: Well, couldn't I save a lot of time and go fishing right now?

WINTERGREEN: No, you got to wait until an important matter comes up and then you go fishing.

THROTTLEBOTTOM: Well, do you ever catch any fish?

WINTERGREEN: Well, I'm the President.

THROTTLEBOTTOM: Yeah, but it's a pretty hard job being President. You've got to keep writing those Thanksgiving proclamations, no matter what—and then there's that other bunch, Congress—What about those messages that the President is always sending to Congress —who reads those, anyway?

WINTERGREEN: The fellow who prints 'em.

THROTTLEBOTTOM: Well, wouldn't everybody read them, if you made 'em funnier?

WINTERGREEN: Some of them have been pretty funny.

THROTTLEBOTTOM: Couldn't you make a speech instead? Then they'd have to listen.

WINTERGREEN: No, no! You've got to be careful about speeches. You only make a speech when you want the stock market to go down.

THROTTLEBOTTOM: What about when you want the stock market to go up?

WINTERGREEN: *(Fairly throwing himself on his neck)* Oh, boy! Wouldn't I like to know!

From *I'D RATHER BE RIGHT*:

(President Roosevelt convenes a meeting of his cabinet, in order to help two new young friends, Peggy and Phil.)

ROOSEVELT: No, no, no. I want everybody's attention, please.

(A chorus of disappointment)

Now I've already introduced you to these two young people, haven't I? Now, you're not going to like this. It's something that we said we weren't ever going to talk about again, but I've got a special reason. I've got to talk about it. Gentlemen, it's the budget.

(A great chorus of "Aw's")

I know, but wait till I tell you. This boy and girl are in love with each other, and they want to get married. But they can't get married unless Phil gets a raise, and he won't get the raise unless we balance the budget.

MORGENTHAU: Well, they're awfully nice young people, Mr. President, but you know as well as I do that we can't balance the budget.

ROOSEVELT: Now, wait a minute. We've *got* to balance it. You just listen to these two young people and see if you don't feel as I do.

(He turns to the youngsters)

Phil, Peggy—I want you to tell the Cabinet your story. And, gentlemen, if this doesn't make you want to balance the budget, I don't know what will.

(And, with the CABINET *as audience,* PHIL *bursts right into "*HAVE YOU MET MISS JONES?*" The* CABINET *members thereof listen attentively, and are obviously moved when it is all over)*

ROOSEVELT: *(When* PHIL *has finished)* Well, gentlemen?

MORGENTHAU: Mr. President, if we don't do something about this, we're just a bunch of dirty Republicans!

FARLEY: *(Choked up)* He's right, Frank. Let those Democrats wait.

MISS PERKINS: As a woman, perhaps I can speak for all of us. We *must* balance the budget.

(She wipes away a furtive tear)

ROOSEVELT: Thank you, Miss Perkins. . . . I take it for granted that you all feel the same way.

MORGENTHAU: Of course we do.

HULL: We just can't talk.

ROOSEVELT: *(To* PHIL *and* PEGGY*)* There! Is this a nice little Government or isn't it?

PEGGY and PHIL: Oh, yes, Mr. Roosevelt! It's wonderful!

ROOSEVELT: *(To the* CABINET*)* Now then, I'm open for suggestions. *How* are we going to balance the budget?

(He looks around the table, hopefully)

SECRETARY OF THE NAVY: *(Belligerently)* Can't cut the Navy!

SECRETARY OF COMMERCE: Mustn't touch Commerce!

FARLEY: Don't look at me!

ROOSEVELT: *(Reproachfully)* Now, gentlemen, that wasn't what I meant at all. All I meant was—what *new* taxes can you think of?

(Great relief all around, naturally. "Well!" . . . "Why didn't you say so?" . . . "That's different!")

FARLEY: *(Rubbing his hands)* Hot dog! New taxes, boys! Wheeee!

ROOSEVELT: Jim, you ought to be able to think of something. What about the Post-office Department? How about some hundred-dollar stamps?

FARLEY: Frank, that gives me an idea. Suppose every letter has to be sent air mail? That would double the revenue from stamps. If it only goes from the Bronx to Brooklyn, it has to go air mail.

ROOSEVELT: No. Nobody in the Bronx has anything important enough to send air mail.

FARLEY: They wouldn't *go* air mail—we'd just sent them the regular way. But it would double the revenue.

ROOSEVELT: No, no, Jim. That wouldn't be honest.

FARLEY: Oh! I thought we were talking about taxes.

CHAPTER FOUR

OH, WHAT A BEAUTIFUL MORNIN'

(1 9 4 3 – 1 9 5 9)

Overture

The bright lights of Broadway had always been one of the city's—one of the world's—great attractions, but on May 18, 1942, the U.S. Navy decided otherwise. Once America went to war, New York became the greatest port city in the nation for the construction and shipping of materiel and cargo for the war effort, and the Navy was acutely aware that ships embarking from docks on the Hudson River were easily silhouetted by the brilliant diffusion shed by midtown's Times Square. A complete blackout of all lights above street level was ordered, and the colorful incandescence that defined the Theater District went into patriotic hibernation for most of the war's duration.

Two weeks later, the *Herald-Tribune* reported on the first big opening night since the blackout: Rodgers and Hart's latest musical comedy, *By Jupiter.* "Theatregoers were completely baffled by the lack of familiar West Side landmarks and were feeling their way from Sardi's to the Shubert Theater and back by an elaborate system of navigation based on the Braille system and dead reckoning." Waiters at Sardi's acted as "harbor pilots," guiding customers to their seats, and, after intermission, one couple accidentally found themselves in the right seats for *By Jupiter,* but in the wrong theater. That's too bad, for they missed the second act of the biggest hit Rodgers and Hart would have in their entire career. It was also the last original show they would write together.

As 1942 stretched into 1943, Rodgers found it increasingly difficult to get his partner back to work on any new project. Rodgers hoped that the two of them might adapt the play *Green Grow the Lilacs* into a musical, but when Hart professed disinterest in the show, Rodgers decided it was time to take Oscar Hammerstein up on his offer to collaborate on a project. That musical, *Oklahoma!,* was a triumphant success, but, to the world of Broadway, Rodgers and Hart were still a partnership. Even though Hart's infamous

PAGE 191: *In July of 1942, the northern side of 47th Street between Broadway and Seventh Avenue became the Pepsi-Cola Center, where soldiers were given a free Pepsi-Cola to go along with their nickel hamburgers. Here, a couple of servicemen on the town get a view of the sights—as well as Broadway, what would now be the Duffy Square TKTS booth.*

A new song for an old show: Rodgers and Hart's A Connecticut Yankee.

indolence had degenerated into functional paralysis, Rodgers still felt compelled to find some new project for them to write together. He sagely acknowledged that it would have to be a manageable one and proposed to Hart that they revive their 1927 hit, *A Connecticut Yankee*, and add a couple of new numbers. It would be an opportunity to get "Rodgers and Hart" back where it belonged, on a theater marquee, but Hart would have to promise to remain sober. Hart realized that, in the wake of Rodgers's success with Hammerstein, this was his last, best chance to make it up to his partner and agreed. He went on the wagon while he wrote lyrics to six new songs; one of them, "To Keep My Love Alive," the comic confessions of a serial murderess, was one of his best ever.

Rodgers kept his love for Hart alive through the November 1943 opening of *A Connecticut Yankee*, which had been updated to make its hero a naval officer, but Hart could not stay on the wagon. As soon as Hart turned in his lyrics, he started drinking again, and on opening night, after giving all his house seats away to the wrong people, he showed up at the top of the second act, drunk, and singing along with the actors onstage. Rodgers's patience, stretched to the breaking point, snapped, and he had Hart ushered out of the theater. Hart's brother and sister-in-law brought him home, but the next day, he walked out of their apartment into a snowstorm, without a topcoat. Two days after the opening of *A Connecticut Yankee*, Larry Hart was found wandering the streets and was admitted to Doctors Hospital for pneumonia. Rodgers and his wife went to see him immediately, but he never regained consciousness. Three days later, on the evening of November 22, there was another blackout, and by the time the lights came back on, one of the brightest sparks of the musical theater had been extinguished.

Rodgers was both devastated and relieved. He was never the most effusive of men, and it would have been uncharacteristic of him to mourn the death of his partner of twenty-six years excessively. Besides, the antidote to any of Rodgers's problems had always been work. With Hammerstein, he finally had a partner as willing and ready to roll up his sleeves as he was. Despite the blackouts imposed by the government, the lights were shining brightly for Richard Rodgers as 1944 began. He had just opened a hit show, with lyrics by Larry Hart, at the Martin Beck, on Eighth Avenue at 45th Street. On the other side of Eighth Avenue, at the corner of 44th Street stood the St. James Theatre, where *Oklahoma!*, with lyrics by Oscar Hammerstein, had been playing to standing-room audiences since April. Rodgers's career was literally and figuratively at a crossroads, and so was the American musical theater.

A new show by a new team:
Rodgers and Hammerstein's Oklahoma!

Times Square and its legendary marquees
were particularly inconvenienced by the
wartime blackouts.

"*There's no business like show business*"

THE POSTWAR WORLD OF BROADWAY

The Broadway that emerged when the lights came on again over Times Square was a near mirror image of postwar American culture. The country became settled, comfortable, and well-appointed, and so did the musical. The separate strands of escapism and social criticism that epitomized the musicals of the 1930s gave way to cohesive commodities of consumer culture.

For the first time, the musical developed into a cultural export, extending its boundaries beyond the Theater District. Certain shows became so popular that they spawned several touring productions each; for the first time, you could see a perfectly good production of a show like *Oklahoma!* in Oklahoma. New technology gave millions of theatergoers across the country the chance to see their favorite Broadway stars in carefully selected cameos on television and to hear the latest Broadway songs in their very own living rooms. Even the living room changed: the spread of suburbia extended the audience for a Broadway show; by the end of the 1950s, the population of the outlying suburbs was more than half that of the city itself. Seeing a Broadway show became an all-day family outing; producers and restaurant owners saw the potential profits of family audiences and adjusted their curtain times and hours accordingly.

In other aspects of cultural relevance, however, Broadway was playing catch-up. The most glamorous events in Times Square during the 1940s and '50s were not the opening nights of Broadway shows, but the premieres of motion pictures (shot with flashy new techniques such as Cinerama and Todd-AO), attended by klieg lights and movie stars. Imitation would become the sincerest form of competition.

On Easter Sunday evening, April 6, 1947, a night most Broadway performers had off, the American Theatre Wing paid homage to its former chairman, Antoinette Perry, who had passed away the previous year. The tribute, presented at the Grand Ballroom of the Waldorf Astoria, came in the form of awards given for achievements on Broadway for that current season; they would be called, in honor of Perry, the Tony Awards.

The evening was a casual affair, by contemporary standards. There were no "bests"—just outstanding achievements; the honorees were given useful items (silver compacts for the women, gold-plated money clips or cigarette lighters for the men) rather than trophies; and there was some brief entertainment courtesy of several running musicals, plus performances by Frank Fay, Ethel Waters, and David Wayne. The restaurateur Vincent Sardi was recognized for providing an informal "post office" and "rest room" for actors who were in the service during the war; the list of award winners was broadcast at midnight for fifteen minutes on a local radio station. Although the Tonys kept their elastic integrity well into the '50s, honoring whatever number of people it deemed worthy from season to season, by eventually replicating the format and the promotional value of the Academy Awards, which had grown into a worldwide phenomenon since its inception twenty years

earlier, Broadway quietly conceded its role as the dominant center for creative achievement in the performing arts.

But Broadway conceded nothing as far as the quality of its product was concerned. The 1940s and '50s provided audiences with an impressive series of well-crafted, beautifully scored shows, with strong narratives and memorable characters. Towering above their peers was the partnership of Rodgers and Hammerstein. They mastered the form of the American musical and dominated their field in much the same way that Shakespeare ruled the Elizabethan stage, or the Beatles topped the charts with rock and roll in the 1960s. Rodgers and Hammerstein provided a new kind of commodity, a show that could work on its own dramatic merits, and not be held hostage to a gifted star or contemporary tastes. They influenced not just the form of the musical, but the way it was disseminated throughout the world. More than forty years after the musical first took shape, the 1940s and '50s yielded up something more than interesting or compelling shows, they yielded up a series of classics. It was the Golden Age.

Times Square in 1948; by then, Danny Kaye and Gene Kelly had become major film stars. Angela Lansbury— Kelly's costar in Three Musketeers— *would have to wait two more decades to conquer the Great White Way.*

"And the land we belong to is grand!"

OKLAHOMA!

The Theatre Guild had given Rodgers and Hart their big break in 1925, and almost two decades later, it would, unwittingly, deliver the final blow to their collaboration. The Theatre Guild had been suffering some lean years in the late 1930s, momentarily rescued by Katharine Hepburn's appearance in *The Philadelphia Story;* a big hit was the only thing likely to save them.

In 1941 one of the Guild's producers, Theresa Helburn, saw a summer-stock revival of a play the Guild had produced a decade earlier, *Green Grow the Lilacs,* by an Oklahoma native named Lynn Riggs. Something about its simple story of settlers on the western fringes of Oklahoma's Indian Territory as it stood on the brink of statehood appealed to Helburn. Perhaps because this production had traditional folk songs and square dances, perhaps because Helburn was sentimental about the play—although it had not been a success for the Guild—she decided it would make a good musical, and a hit musical might provide the revenue stream the Guild so desperately needed.

Helburn approached Rodgers, who immediately took to the material. The difficult part would be convincing Hart. Contemporary, slick, snappy shows were Hart's cup of Jack Daniel's, and a musical about cowhands, farmers, and their gingham-dressed ranch girls would be a hard sell. He turned Rodgers down flat, realizing, in a moment of clarity, that the material would never excite him enough to get back to work. Besides, he had other plans. "He wanted to go to Mexico," Rodgers recalled in 1975. "He wanted to take a vacation. And I told him that if he didn't stay home and work, I was going to Oscar. And he told me I was right— he didn't blame me a bit. So I did; I had to." Felicitously, Hammerstein had always admired *Green Grow the Lilacs* and had even sought the rights for a musical version with Jerome Kern, so he accepted Rodgers's proposition immediately. By the spring of 1942, they were officially a team.

Collaboration in musical theater requires the trickiest alchemy— Ira Gershwin called it "marriage without sex"—and no two partnerships are alike. From the beginning, the collaboration of Rodgers and Hammerstein was going to proceed differently. Hammerstein would write the lyrics first and Rodgers would set them to music, the opposite of Rodgers and Hart's approach. The first words Hammerstein submitted were the first lines to the opening song: "There's a bright, golden haze on the meadow." Rodgers said he had to get straight to a piano, that "you couldn't resist those words, they were so lovely, and musical and theatrical . . . we hit it off terribly well, we understood each other, I knew what his words meant, and I felt that I could match them."

With Hammerstein adapting Riggs's play, the team now turned its attention to the libretto. The approach to the source material was so simple that it was revolutionary: keep it true. In 1942, there were not nearly as many adaptations of other material on the musical stage

An old song from a new show: "Boys and Girls Like You and Me" was an ensemble number cut early from Away We Go!, Oklahoma!'s original title. The sheet music (signed by members of the original cast) was printed in advance of the Boston engagement.

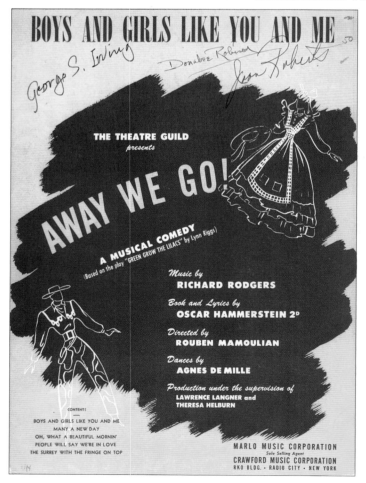

as there would be a decade later, and what adaptations there were (usually of inferior material) could be rather cavalier, primarily serving the conventions of the musical comedy. Rodgers and Hammerstein were faced with a challenging question—how to evoke a pioneer spirit of turn-of-the-century Oklahoma? Start with a bang-up opening number—a square dance, or a traveling medicine show, or some rope tricks? Any of those ideas would have been a conventional solution, but they all seemed false to Hammerstein. The charm in *Green Grow the Lilacs* lay in its bucolic milieu and its characters: Curly, the amorous cowhand; the plainspoken Laurey, the object of his affections; Jud, the sociopathic farmhand, who also loves Laurey; Aunt Eller, the no-nonsense matriarch. Rodgers and Hammerstein agreed that these people's stories had to be respected before anything else; the trajectories of their lives had to be conveyed without any concession to show biz. There would be no specialty dances, no clever-for-the-sake-of-being-clever songs, no extended gags for the supporting comic—just a relentless narrative drive.

Hammerstein decided to begin the musical exactly the way the original play did: in front of a farmhouse, with Aunt Eller seated behind a butter churn, looking out over the meadow, while, "like the voice of the morning," Curly sings from offstage about the bright golden haze on the meadow, and, continuing as he saunters on:

Oh, what a beautiful mornin'!
Oh, what a beautiful day!
I got a beautiful feelin'
Ev'rythin's goin' my way.

The opening heard round the world: Curly (Alfred Drake) greets Aunt Eller (Betty Garde) on the morning of the day where everything's going his way.

This simple beginning, two people alone on stage, one of them singing *a capella*—sans chorus girls, sans production number, sans anything predictable—signaled to the audience that this show was going to unravel its narrative differently. It is unlikely that jaws dropped in amazement, as legend would like to have it, but it was immediately clear that *Oklahoma!* was going to be a personal story, centered around its characters. There had been musicals before *Oklahoma!* that had experimented with musical narrative—*Show Boat, Of Thee I Sing,* and *Pal Joey* among them—but even these groundbreaking shows either relied on the odd musical comedy specialty number or used dance as pure entertainment, rather than as a storytelling medium.

It was the use of dance as a means to advance the story that would distinguish Rodgers and Hammerstein's premiere show from its predecessors. After the Theatre Guild committed to producing the new musical—originally called, by a kind of default, *Away We Go!*—it hired Rouben Mamoulian, the director of *Porgy and Bess,* and asked Rodgers and Hammerstein to look at the work of choreographer Agnes de Mille, who had just created a "Wild West" ballet called *Rodeo.* Even a folk treatment of classical ballet seemed like a big leap, so to speak, for their little musical, but after some hemming and hawing, Rodgers and Hammerstein accepted de Mille. After such marquee names as Shirley Temple and Groucho Marx were rejected in favor of an unknown cast, the show went into rehearsal in February 1943.

As the conjured "dance-hall girls" of Jud's French postcards pair up with the boys,
the Dream Laurey (Katharine Sergava) is trapped in a conflict of her own uncertainty.

There's nothing like a Box Social to bring the farmer and the cowhand—not to mention their gals—together.

The tryout in New Haven was definitely a stressful one. Mamoulian and de Mille argued incessantly about rehearsal time, and the Theatre Guild was stretching every dime. Luckily, the strong narrative backbone of the show enabled the creators to make quick and incisive decisions. Mamoulian immediately cut two solo specialty dances from the second act—this was a show that was determined not to use them. As the production moved to Boston, Helburn asked Hammerstein to write a song about the land—that was as clear as she could be—*something* about the land. He got the point and wrote the words to "Oklahoma":

> We know we belong to the land,
> And the land we belong to is grand!

Hammerstein, de Mille, and Rodgers would collaborate on three musicals, beginning with Oklahoma! *The story goes that Walter Winchell's secretary cabled from New Haven exactly how far off the show was from a conventional show of the early 1940s: "No gags, no gals, no chance."*

The song was hurriedly orchestrated during the train ride to Boston by Robert Russell Bennett, and when, during a rehearsal in the lobby of the Colonial, the song was arranged for the entire cast to sing in harmony, it galvanized everyone. Suddenly the second act crystallized into something brilliant. The number also necessitated a title change for the show. Despite the fact that posters and reams of sheet music had already been printed with the title *Away We Go!*, when it left Boston, the show was now called *Oklahoma!*

The unconventional nature of the show caused some hand-wringing among the producers and staff, but Rodgers appeared serene as *Oklahoma!* made its way to the St. James Theatre for its March 31 opening.

> I was sure of it. I don't know who else agreed with me—Oscar had had a bad time; the Theatre Guild had had a bad time; Agnes de Mille, who did such a wonderful job, had never had a Broadway show; nobody expected the show to work, but we had a runthrough one time, when we were in rehearsal, and my wife was there. When I got home about three hours later, there was a little note on my pillow that said, "Darling, this is the best musical show I've ever seen." So I had some idea that we had hit it.

Posterity proved Rodgers correct. The show was jubilantly embraced by the press, with particular praise for the psychological perception of de Mille's dances, appealingly idiosyncratic chorus girls, and the melodious score.

There was no dearth of acclaim for the show—even the Pulitzer Prize committee awarded it a special citation—but, for Rodgers, one comment on opening night stood out from the rest. As he was on his way to Sardi's, Rodgers recounted, "I suddenly saw a little man break through the crowd. It was Larry Hart. 'Dick,' he said, 'I've never had a better evening in my life! The show will still be around twenty years from now!' And I knew he meant it." Although Hart genuinely loved Rodgers, the overwhelming success of a show written in collaboration with another lyricist must have weighed heavily upon him.

One night, he was sitting in a Manhattan living room listening to the radio with a young protégé from Harvard, Alan Jay Lerner, and his collaborator, Frederick "Fritz" Loewe. There was a wartime blackout that night and Lerner recounted what happened next:

> The only light came from Larry's cigar. Fritz turned on the radio and an orchestra was playing something from *Oklahoma!* The end of the cigar flashed brighter and brighter with accelerated puffs. Fritz immediately switched to another station. Again, someone was playing a song from *Oklahoma!* And Larry's cigar grew brighter and the puffs became faster. It happened three times. . . . The moment the lights came on, Larry continued the conversation . . . without a trace of what had happened.

The songs that Hart heard on the radio, the same songs that Rodgers and Hammerstein worked so hard to keep within the context of the setting, broke out to achieve extraordinary popularity; the self-defensive love song "People Will Say We're in Love" was the number-one song of 1943, and "Oh, What a Beautiful Mornin'" and "The Surrey with the Fringe on Top"—an ode to a buggy with brown leather upholstery—also topped the charts. Most of the score was recorded on a historical series of 78 rpm disks, bringing the sound of the new team of Rodgers and Hammerstein to homes all across the country.

The difficulty in obtaining tickets to *Oklahoma!* became a national joke, and if you had been browbeaten enough by Theresa Helbrun to invest $1,000 in the show, your return would have amounted to $2.5 million. In 1947, the show opened in London, where it was a tremendous success, and eventually become the first American musical to play all around the world. In the decade before it opened, not a single hit show ran more than 500 performances, but *Oklahoma!* would go on to run for 2,212. It was more than a hit—it was the first real phenomenon in modern Broadway history.

"Plen'y of heart and plen'y of hope": a brand-new state and a brand-new state of affairs for the American musical.

Why We Fight: a June 1944 special performance of Oklahoma! *for U.S. servicemen.*

Oklahoma! had a potent appeal for the various fighting men shipping out from New York City. In violation of the fire code, visiting servicemen who couldn't get a ticket to *Oklahoma!* were smuggled into the St. James to watch the show from the wings. Celeste Holm, who played the comic second lead, Ado Annie, recalled what it was like performing the show:

> The war was very immediate, very present. So many people since then have said, "You know, it was the last show I saw before I went overseas and it made me prouder to be American than I had been, because it really talked about the unselfconscious courage of the people who settled the West." And then people would say, "It was the first show I saw when I came back and I brought my girl and it gave me the courage to ask her to marry me and she said 'yes' and we've never been sorry."

In the musical theater, onstage and off, timing is everything. Had *Oklahoma!* opened before the war, its homespun sincerity, which made the creators themselves apprehensive, would have seemed irrelevant. Had the show opened during the first year of the war, it might have been buried by the avalanche of pure patriotism that burst upon the stage, screen, and airwaves; had it opened as the war was ending, the country might have been too exhausted to embrace it. But, as it was, it opened just when audiences, after a year of combat losses and a complete retrenchment of daily domestic life, needed to be reminded of what they were fighting for—*something* about the land.

"Out of my dreams and into your arms"
AGNES DE MILLE AND THE BIRTH OF NARRATIVE DANCE

When *Oklahoma!* premiered in 1943, it was the fullest expression to date of a movement toward the greater integration of a musical's component parts: dialogue, song, and dance. This last crucial element was supplied by a petite, determined, often querulous, perennially anxious choreographer named Agnes de Mille.

De Mille was born in 1905 into a distinguished and complicated artistic family; her father was a successful playwright, and her uncle, Cecil B., was a Hollywood pioneer and one of its most famous directors. As a girl, she was shuttled between two stimulating environments—her family's artistic retreat in upstate New York and the film colony in Hollywood—and soon developed a passion for dance. Her career choice was frowned on by her imperious father, which only exacerbated de Mille's intense desire to please him. Her mother smiled more kindly on her ambitions and sponsored an endless series of ballet lessons and recitals for Agnes, in both America and England. It soon became apparent that Agnes's talent lay more in choreography than in performing—she never had the ideal ballerina figure—and by the early 1930s, she was choreographing dances for musical comedies in the West End and on Broadway, as well as a brief and disastrous sojourn in Hollywood doing dances for a film directed by her uncle.

In October 1942, Agnes staged a piece of her own for the Ballet Russe de Monte Carlo at the Metropolitan Opera House. *Rodeo*, with music by Aaron Copland, was pure folk Americana—a popular trend in the war years—about a cowgirl, played by de Mille herself, who incites the dueling passions of two champion riders. The fresh, passionate athleticism of the ballet created a sensation. *Rodeo* was the perfect audition piece for *Oklahoma!*, and five months later de Mille found herself putting a full chorus line of cowgirls through their paces.

De Mille plunged right into the creative development of the show without a shred of deference to her collaborators. She defied Mamoulian by casting strong, idiosyncratic dancers from her corps, rather than a line of gooey glamour girls. More famously, she contradicted Hammerstein over the end of the first act. The focus was to be on Laurey, the ingenue, as she contemplates going to the box social with either Curly or Jud. Hammerstein wanted a circus ballet, with an idealized gilded surrey to spirit Laurey away, but de Mille was of another opinion:

> I said [to Hammerstein], this is the kind of dream that young girls who are worried have. She's frantic because she doesn't know which boy to go to the box social with. And so, if she had a dream, it would be a dream of terror, a childish dream, a haunted dream. Also, you haven't any sex in the first act. He said, haven't I? I said, goodness, no. All nice girls are fascinated by [the darker side of sexuality]. Mr. Hammerstein, if you don't know that, you don't know about your own daughters.

De Mille cast herself as the cowgirl temptress in her 1942 ballet, Rodeo.

In de Mille's psychological vision of the Dream Ballet, the Id (Jud) strangles the Superego (Curly).

The truly revolutionary character of the dance that became "Laurey Makes Up Her Mind" would change the American musical. In this dream ballet, Laurey imagines herself on her way to her wedding with Curly, only to be abducted by Jud and brought to his Expressionist den of iniquity full of dance-hall girls, inspired by the dirty French postcards that adorn his bunkhouse. Laurey is repelled by Jud's unapologetic earthiness, but also strangely drawn to him; when he "kills" Curly and carries her away, her worst fears—if, indeed, they *are* her worst fears—are realized. The genius touch in the piece is that at the very end of the act, Laurey, awakened from her dream/nightmare, confronts the real-life Jud, who escorts her to the social. It is as if the anxieties of the dream have not simply reflected reality, but conjured it up. It is pure Freud—de Mille herself had been in psychoanalysis, trying to resolve her own conflict between two very different men in her life—but served up in a tasteful and accessible manner. More to the point, it brought the expressive possibilities of dance in the musical to a new narrative level. There had, in fact, been dream ballets in musicals prior to *Oklahoma!* but, as in *Pal Joey*, where the leading character declares he wants to own a big nightclub and then the dream ballet shows the big nightclub, these earlier ballets only told the audience what it already knew. In de Mille's groundbreaking vision, the characters are revealing not only something the audience doesn't already know, but something the characters don't even know about *themselves*.

The success of *Oklahoma!* made de Mille the preeminent choreographer of the musical theater. In the next two years, she had three other hit shows on Broadway: Kurt Weill and Ogden Nash's *One Touch of Venus*, Arlen and Harburg's *Bloomer Girl*, and *Carousel*, which reunited her with her *Oklahoma!* collaborators. All of these shows allowed de Mille to demonstrate her narrative skills in various dream ballets. *Bloomer Girl* had a particularly disturbing ballet that portrayed women awaiting the return of their menfolk from the Civil War; some of the creative staff found it too dark, but de Mille stuck to her guns, the collaborators stuck with de Mille, and it became the dramatic highlight of a rather unfocused show. In *Carousel*, her pièce de résistance was a twelve-minute ballet (cut down from an hour in rehearsals) that told the story of the hero's daughter's adolescence: her tomboyishness; her ostracism from the community because of her father's past; her wistful, near-Freudian infatuation with the father she never knew. What would have taken painful pages of exposition in a conventional narrative was rendered by de Mille in a manner that made strong men weep.

People were always leaving Agnes: Her father left her; in the 1940s, her husband, Walter Prude, was off in the Army. She never felt like a very attractive young woman, there's a degree of pathos in anything Agnes does that has to do with saying goodbye. She was very empathetic about that—she felt those things very acutely—and it shows up in everything she does.

Mary Rodgers, Composer, daughter of Richard Rodgers

For Lerner and Loewe's *Brigadoon* in 1947, de Mille applied herself diligently once again to a mixture of folk tradition (Scottish, in this case) and romantic yearning; this show, probably the one musical of the 1940s that borrowed the most from Rodgers and Hammerstein, gave de Mille another hit. That same year, she became the first director-choreographer in Broadway history with Rodgers and Hammerstein's complex *Allegro*. Unfortunately, the show's clogged dramaturgy, and the logistical nightmare of running rehearsals, confounded her, and Hammerstein had to intervene, directing the book scenes.

De Mille's furiously busy career seemed incapable of outpacing her own basic dissatisfaction with her work, her times, herself. She was relentless in her quest to gain respect for her craft within the Broadway community, lobbying for better-paying contracts for dancers and residual payments for choreographers. As time went on, her flinty determination cost her several important collaborators, including, eventually, Rodgers and Hammerstein. Once, after creating some misguided bit of choreography, she was berating herself harshly, when Hammerstein enfolded her a big, bearlike hug: "Come now, Agnes," he said. "You're talking about the woman I love." Unconditional love like that came to de Mille only in small doses; perhaps that is why the yearning of her heroines still seems so rich, so sad, and so compelling.

De Mille would continue to choreograph ballets for both the musical and classical dance stage for another quarter of a century, as well as direct the occasional show, but her style of choreography, particularly the dream ballet, was copied and diluted by so many diverse hands that her own original work lost some of its appeal. Still, no one has ever been able to match the status she achieved in the 1940s.

Agnes de Mille.

Today, those of us who want to use dance and story as one, we all stand on the shoulders of Agnes de Mille.

—Susan Stroman,
Director–Choreographer

In Lerner and Loewe's Brigadoon *(1947) de Mille brought her incisive understanding of the folk milieu to a mythical Scottish village. Here is the traditional sword dance.*

SOLILOQUY

Words by Oscar Hammerstein II
Music by Richard Rodgers
From Carousel *(1945)*

ALTHOUGH *Carousel*'s run of 890 performances was less than half that of *Oklahoma!*, it was Rodgers and Hammerstein's favorite show and represented the perfect coalescence of their narrative skills. It also showcased a number of innovations: an opening scene, set entirely to music, but without lyrics or dialogue, that told the audience everything it needed to know about the New England fairground setting and its characters; a twelve-minute scene in the first act, alternating dialogue and music, centered on the song "If I Loved You" that set into motion the tragic love affair between the virginal mill worker Julie Jordan and the braggart carnival barker, Billy Bigelow.

Carousel also gave Billy an extraordinary number toward the end of the first act. A soliloquy is, by its very Shakespearean nature, a moment of private thought externalized in front of an audience. Billy has just learned that Julie is pregnant, and he bursts into an extended free association. He immediately assumes his child will be a boy, that he will inherit his father's name and his (to the audience, dubious) qualities. Midway through the song, though, by the sheer repetition of the word *girl*, Billy comes to realize that it might all turn out differently; that he might have to be responsible; that perhaps he's not such a big shot after all; that he's willing to die for his child—which, in fact, he will, in the second act.

The song is a miracle of dramatic construction. It was also the first time in a musical that a character begins in one emotional place and finishes in a completely different one during the course of a song.

I wonder what he'll think of me!
I guess he'll call me
"The old man."
I guess he'll think I can lick
Ev'ry other feller's father—
Well, I can!

I bet that he'll turn out to be
The spit an' image
Of his dad,
But he'll have more common sense
Than his puddin'-headed father
Ever had.

I'll teach him to wrassle,
And dive through a wave,
When we go in the mornin's for our swim.
His mother can teach him
The way to behave,
But she won't make a sissy out o' him—
Not him!
Not my boy!
Not Bill . . .
Bill!

Jan Clayton as Julie Jordan and John Raitt as Billy Bigelow in the famous bench scene, as the blossoms fall:
"Jest their time to, I reckon."

My boy, Bill!
(I will see that he's named
After me,
I will!)
My boy, Bill—
He'll be tall
And as tough
As a tree,
Will Bill.
Like a tree he'll grow,
With his head held high
And his feet planted firm on the ground,
And you won't see no-
body dare to try
To boss him or toss him around!
No pot-bellied, baggy-eyed bully'll toss him
    around!

I don't give a hang what he does,
As long as he does what he likes.
He can sit on his tail
Or work on a rail
With a hammer, a-hammerin' spikes.

He can ferry a boat on the river
Or peddle a pack on his back
Or work up and down
The streets of a town
With a whip and a horse and a hack.

He can haul a scow along a canal,
Run a cow around a corral,
Or maybe bark for a carousel—
Of course it takes talent to do *that* well.

He might be a champ of the heavyweights
Or a feller that sells you glue,
Or President of the United States—
That'd be all right, too.

His mother would like that. But he wouldn't be
President unless he wanted to be!
Not Bill!
My boy, Bill—
He'll be tall
And as tough
As a tree,
Will Bill!

Like a tree he'll grow,
With his head held high,
And his feet planted firm on the ground,
And you won't see no-
body dare to try
To boss him or toss him around!
No fat-bottomed, flabby-faced, pot-bellied, baggy-eyed
    bastard'll boss him around!

And I'm hanged if he'll marry his boss's daughter,
A skinny-lipped virgin with blood like water,
Who'll give him a peck and call it a kiss
And look in his eyes through a lorgnette . . .
Say!
Why am I takin' on like this?
My kid ain't even been born yet!

I can see him
When he's seventeen or so,
And startin' in to go
With a girl.

I can give him
Lots o' pointers, very sound,
On the way to get round
Any girl.

I can tell him—
Wait a minute! Could it be—?
What the hell! What if he
Is a girl!
Bill!

Oh, Bill!
What would I do with her? What could I do *for* her?
A bum—with no money!
You can have fun with a son,
But you got to be a *father*
To a girl!

She mightn't be so bad at that—
A kid with ribbons
In her hair,
A kind o' sweet and petite
Little tintype of her mother—
What a pair!

My little girl,
Pink and white

As peaches and cream is she.
My little girl
Is half again as bright
As girls are meant to be!
Dozens of boys pursue her,
Many a likely lad
Does what he can to woo her
From her faithful dad.
She has a few
Pink and white young fellers of two or three—
But my little girl
Gets hungry ev'ry night
And she comes home to me!

I got to get ready before she comes,
I got to make certain that she
Won't be dragged up in slums
With a lot o' bums—
Like me!
She's got to be sheltered and fed, and dressed
In the best that money can buy!
I never knew how to get money,
But I'll try—
By God! I'll try!
I'll go out and make it
Or steal it or take it
Or die!

ABOVE: *Billy comes back from "up there" to watch over his little girl, Louise.*

OPPOSITE: *The innovative opening sequence of* Carousel.

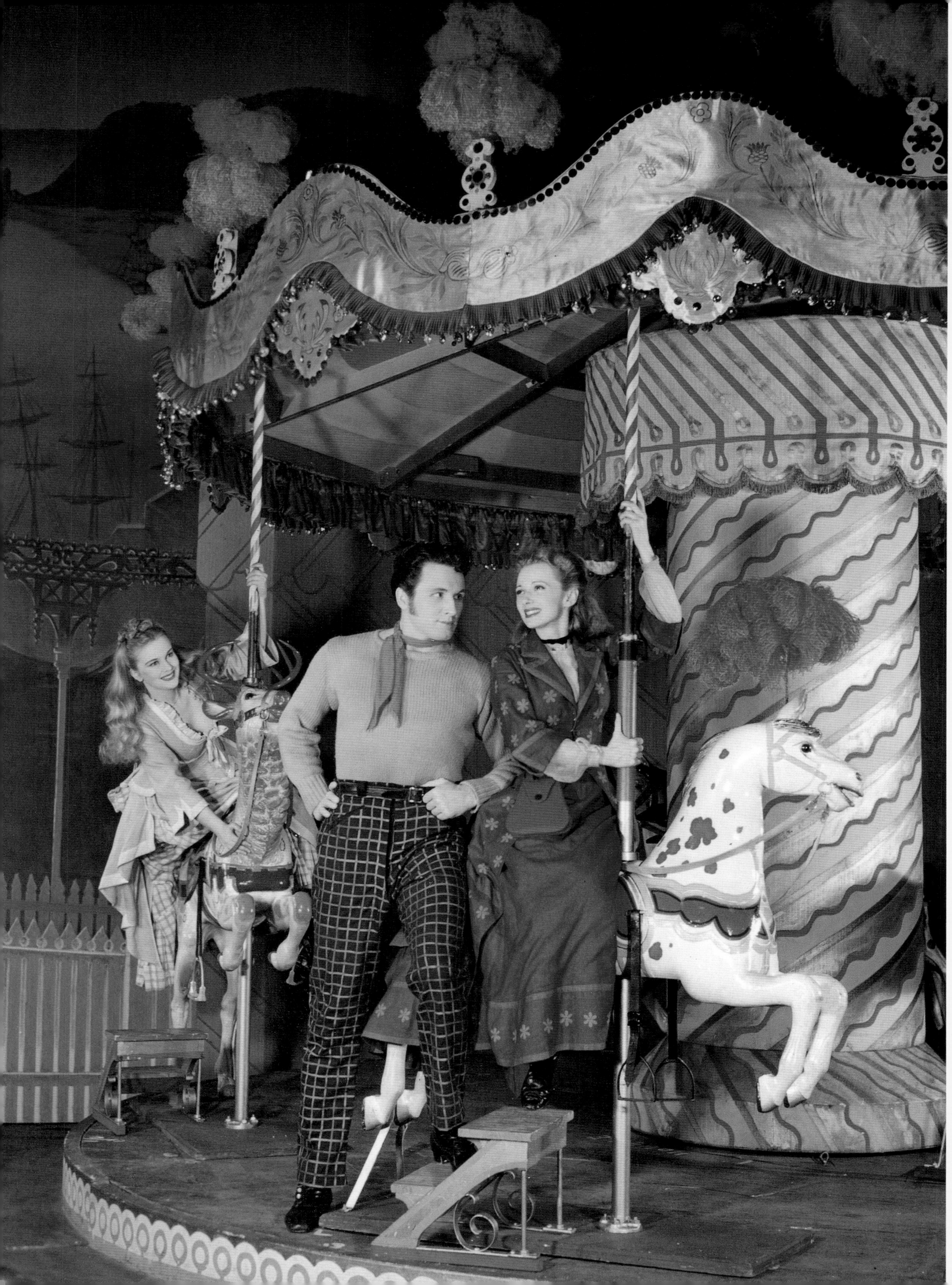

MUSIC

"New York, New York, it's a helluva town!"

ON THE TOWN

A new generation of musical comedy artists enlist with the Grand Old Man (l. to r.): Writer and performer Betty Comden; actor Cris Alexander; actor Nancy Walker; writer and actor Adolph Green; dancer Sono Osato; commanding officer, director George Abbott; choreographer Jerome Robbins (seated); and composer Leonard Bernstein (behind Robbins).

I was dancing at the old Met Opera, which was down on 41st Street, and when you left the stage door, you walked out and there were thousands of sailors all over the place—that was 1944—all around New York. And they were all looking for a good time. And all the girls were out on the town. And I thought, gee, that would be a wonderful subject.

—Jerome Robbins, Choreographer, *On the Town*

New York City had always been a hub for servicemen. Half of those who fought and half the cargo used during the Second World War shipped out from either the West Side or the Brooklyn Navy Yard. Broadway and Times Square provided a glittering and amusing distraction for thousands of soldiers and sailors. At the Stage Door Canteen, created by the American Theatre Wing in the basement of the 44th Street Theatre, enlisted men would line up around the block to get free food and drinks, served to them by the brightest stars on Broadway, and perhaps even wangle a dance with Ruth Warrick or June Havoc. The USO, on 43rd Street, offered free tickets to Broadway shows, and the orchestra of every musical played "The Star-Spangled Banner" before the curtain went up.

When Jerome Robbins debuted his short ballet piece "Fancy Free," with music by Leonard Bernstein, in April 1944, it was apparent that his scenario of three sailors out on a spree in the city had, to use a Broadway expression for longevity, "legs." Scenic designer Oliver Smith prevailed on Robbins to expand the idea into a full-length musical. Bernstein, who at the age of twenty-six was already a musical celebrity, having stepped in to conduct a New York Philharmonic concert on a moment's notice, called in two friends of his with whom he had written some nightclub material, Betty Comden and Adolph Green. Thrilled by the chance to collaborate on a real live Broadway show, and inspired by the strides made by *Oklahoma!*, the four of them—all in their twenties—sat around a West Side apartment and planned their futures. Comden recalled:

We just decided to write down what we wanted to do or not do. We did call it "Credo," it's a little embarrassing to talk about, but we wanted the show to be integrated, we wanted everything in it to serve the show, and everything should tell the story, and we didn't want anything pretentious. We wanted things to be direct and simple and honest and not fancy, not phony.

The collaborators were a new generation of songwriters, but they were young and needed someone older and wiser to guide them, so they sent the script to master director

George Abbott, who was twice as old as they were. He agreed to direct, and they were on their way.

The plot of *On the Town* is more of a premise: three sailors are on twenty-four-hour leave in New York and they each hook up with a different girl. There were a lot of bumptious gags, and two of the three couples—one of which was played by Comden and Green themselves—had a corny brashness to them. But Bernstein's music captured the city's cacophany, utilizing a sophisticated blend of symphonic themes, jitterbugs, rumbas, wrenching ballads, and socko show tunes, especially in the opening number:

> New York, New York, a helluva town.
> The Bronx is up, but the Battery's down.
> The people ride in a hole in the groun'.
> New York, New York, it's a helluva town!

Robbins, in his first choreography job on Broadway, created six major dance sequences, including not one but two requisite dream ballets. His eye for detail, for human psychology,

When the three sailors hit New York, all Chip (l., Chris Alexander) wants to do is follow his grandfather's old guide book and see the famous sights; Ozzie (Adolph Green) and Gabey (John Battles) want to check out some curvier attractions.

Betty Comden and Adolph Green (center) were clever writers—clever enough to write parts for themselves. Claire de Loon hooks up with Ozzie for an afternoon of being carried away at the Museum of Natural History.

was apparent in the way he had the three sailors and their girls ride the subway or dance in a nightclub or drink orangeade from Nedick's. It looked just like life, only ten times more fun.

In the first draft of *On the Town*, the war was specifically cited; at one point, the sailors read news of a naval battle in the South Pacific off the "zipper" on the Times Tower. But Abbott wisely maintained that mentioning the war was not only jarring, it was redundant. The war is made manifest in every moment of *On the Town*. One of the girls, Hildy, is a sexually aggressive cabdriver and the other two are refreshingly open to romantic encounters. After all, three million women entered the workforce during the war, and every available single man left on the homefront had two and a half women competing for him. A great deal of the show's charm comes from the fact that the girls are just as happy to be pursued as the boys are to pursue them.

On the Town, which opened at the very end of 1944, ran long enough to see the boys come home from both Europe and the South Pacific, while igniting the Broadway careers of its youthful quartet of creators. New York was a helluva town, indeed.

Cabdriver Hildy, short for Hildegarde (the irrepressible Nancy Walker), uses her charms to lure Chip up to her place.

Laurey in *Oklahoma!* was invented in 1943 and one year later you have Hildy and Claire who are, like, "Come here. I need a man." These women have sexual drives, are assertive, are in command, and that, of course, was reflective of the day, because of the war, but still, they're very, very, very fascinating characters.

—George C. Wolfe, Director

Times Square ballet, end of Act One, courtesy of Robbins and Bernstein. One of On the Town's *lesser-known achievements was its use of a racially integrated cast.*

SOME OTHER TIME

Words by Betty Comden and Adolph Green
Music by Leonard Bernstein
From On the Town *(1944)*

IN AN EVENING filled with high jinks and high spirits, "Some Other Time" took its audience on an unexpected detour in the real world of a nation at war. Late in the second act, two of the show's couples are about to take a subway ride to Coney Island to rendezvous with the third couple, and as they wait in a lonely station, they reflect on what might happen after their dizzy twenty-four-hour adventure comes to an end. "It's about the feeling of what a brief moment life and joy can be," said lyricist Adolph Green, who also played Ozzie.

The song never joined such forlorn ballads of wartime longing as "I'll Walk Alone" or "I Don't Want to Walk Without You" on the Hit Parade, but in later years, cabaret artists and jazz musicians turned it into a cult favorite (pianist Bill Evans rendered the tune in various interpretations throughout his career). "Some Other Time" was also deleted from the 1949 M-G-M film version of the show; perhaps its subtle references to the "morning after" were too adult for a general audience. But, in New York City itself, everyone understood that, in the words of Jerome Robbins, "the boys're gonna go off the next day and they may not come back."

Well, we were all in the middle of the war, of course, and my husband was in the Army, and of course there was this painful separation. It was also a time, on the other hand, of tremendous energy. You felt it, people united in a common purpose, that the war seemed to have some meaning and that there was a kind of galvanized feeling of people working toward winning the war. And it absolutely colored all our lives tremendously. And I think that the song has the feeling of poignancy, that you cram as much as you can into the few hours you've got, 'cause you don't know whether you'll have any more.

—Betty Comden

CLAIRE:
Twenty-four hours can go so fast,
You look around, the day has passed.
When you're in love
Time is precious stuff;
Even a lifetime isn't enough.

Where has the time all gone to?
Haven't done half the things we want to.
Oh, well—
We'll catch up
Some other time.

This day was just a token,
So many words are still unspoken.
Oh, well—
We'll catch up
Some other time.

Just when the fun is starting
Comes the time for parting,
But let's be glad for what we've had
And what's to come.

There's so much more embracing
Still to be done, but time is racing.
Oh, well—
We'll catch up
Some other time.

HILDY:
Didn't get half my wishes,
Never have seen you dry the dishes.
Oh, well—
We'll catch up
Some other time.
Can't satisfy my craving,
Never have watched you while you're shaving.
Oh, well—
We'll catch up
Some other time.

HILDY, CLAIRE, OZZIE, CHIP:
Just when the fun's beginning,
Comes the final inning . . .

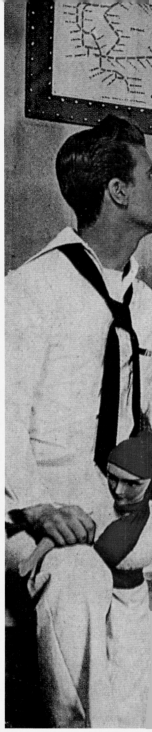

In a posed promotional shot for On the Town, *Gabey summons up his dream girl, while Claire, Ozzie, Chip, and Hildy dream of the day they'll all meet again.*

OZZIE:
Haven't had time to wake up,
Seeing you there without your makeup.
Oh, well—
We'll catch up
Some other time.

ALL:
Just when the fun is starting
Comes the time for parting,
But let's be glad for what we've had
And what's to come.
There's so much more embracing
Still to be done, but time is racing.
Oh, well—
We'll catch up some other time.

"Stand up and fight like hell"

THE POSTWAR BLACK MUSICAL

After his triumph with *Oklahoma!*, Oscar Hammerstein turned to an even more improbable project, something that had preoccupied him for years: a new version of the 1875 opera *Carmen*, reimagined in the American South, with his own lyrics set to Bizet's original music, for a cast composed entirely of black actors. Producer Billy Rose enthusiastically took up the idea, hired a first-rate director and designer, and made plans to book the Broadway Theater for the end of 1943.

What Hammerstein and Rose didn't have was a cast. The vocal and acting demands of *Carmen Jones* required performers equally adept at opera and musical comedy, but the opportunities for black actors to learn their craft in these genres were limited. For years, roles for black talent had been in short supply, so the talent pool dried up, and as a result there was not enough talent to fill the roles. Rose engaged a music promoter named John Hammond (who managed the early careers of such artists as Billie Holiday and later Bruce Springsteen) to round up whatever singers he could; Hammond found his leads working in a camera store, on the police force, and in a shipyard.

"Goin' Home Train" in Harold Rome's Call Me Mister *featured soldiers and sailors of all races coming back home to face an uncertain future. For black veterans like Lawrence Winters (center), there would be trying times ahead.*

Carmen Jones was a spectacular hit, opening half a year after *Oklahoma!* It was also the advance guard for a brief but impressive vogue for Broadway musicals that gave new prominence to black performers, sometimes in all-black shows, sometimes as part of an integrated company. Although these new shows were written, composed, and produced almost entirely by white artists, Broadway had not welcomed so many black actors since the early 1920s. The number of black performers in plays and musicals in 1946 was more than five times the number before the war began. In some ways, the increased professional opportunities for African Americans mirrored the social changes that occurred during the war. Although black army units were still segregated, some war production jobs formerly closed to blacks were opened up; black women also had an opportunity to move out of domestic jobs into factories; the membership of the NAACP quadrupled; and such polar opposites as Eleanor Roosevelt and Hollywood worked to promote racial tolerance and inclusion.

On Broadway, the results of this inclusion were mixed, both in style and quality. The trend had a brief prologue in 1940 with Vernon Duke's simplistically drawn allegory, *Cabin in the Sky*, but it was Hammerstein's adaptation of *Carmen*, with its steamy seductress, obsessed army officer, and macho prizefighter, that really packed a punch. As a bookend to *This Is the Army*, Harold Rome wrote a 1946 tribute to returning veterans, the revue *Call Me Mister*, which contained a musical number, "Red Ball Express," that portrayed a returning black serviceman who had run a successful supply line during the war being denied a job back home because of the color of his skin. That same season, Harold Arlen and Johnny Mercer journeyed to the turn-of-the-century racetrack scene in *St. Louis Woman* (see page 220), and in 1949, Kurt Weill and

ABOVE AND BELOW: Carmen Jones *transplanted the passions of Seville to the American South. Carmen (center) makes her sexual presence known in front of an army garrison; Joe, an army corporal, loses his heart to Carmen (Luther Saxon and Muriel Smith)—"Dat's love."*

Kurt Weill's final score for the theater,
Lost in the Stars *(1949), with book and*
lyrics by Maxwell Anderson, was a
powerful adaptation of Alan Paton's
Cry, the Beloved Country.

Maxwell Anderson ventured to South Africa for *Lost in the Stars,* the tragic journey of a black preacher and his son, which featured a haunting title tune. Weill also wrote the score to 1947's *Street Scene,* an adaptation of Elmer Rice's urban panorama. This time, his lyricist was the renowned African American poet Langston Hughes, who added several black characters to the material. Although Hughes felt his contributions were gradually whittled down, it was the first interracial collaboration on music and lyrics between artists of such magnitude.

The most provocative look at race relations came from the pen of Yip Harburg, who in *Finian's Rainbow* (1947), turned racism on its head or, more accurately, inside out. The show, which featured lilting words and music by Harburg and Burton Lane and a book cowritten with Fred Saidy, was set in the mythical Deep South state of Missitucky. In one of the subplots, a local racist senator (the papers at the time were filled with the real thing) is turned into a black man through a bit of misplaced Celtic magic. The senator's journey to enlightenment—he is forced to sing along with three black men in a traveling gospel troupe—makes for a wickedly satirical second act, but, sadly, the blackface requirements of the role kept a wonderful score from a major Broadway revival until 2009.

While the increased employment opportunities for African American performers were definitely appreciated, the roles themselves—often menials, lowlifes, or exotics—were less so, especially since they were written by whites. Facing criticism from black performers and political organizations, white writers virtually stopped creating black roles by the early 1950s. Even Rodgers and Hammerstein, among the most progressive writers of their time, failed to create a significant role for a black performer during their collaboration. The explosion of shows that put blacks back on Broadway stages during the late 1940s dissipated as quickly as it began. Such a concentration of talent wouldn't be seen again for nearly thirty years.

In Finian's Rainbow *(1947), David Wayne as Og, a leprechaun with a witty sense of social justice, attempts to reverse the race-baiting senator, Billboard Rawkins (Robert Pitkin), out of his worst nightmare—life as a black man.*

ST. LOUIS WOMAN

IF, IN THE 1940S, YOU WERE TO BET on one songwriting team other than Rodgers and Hammerstein to write a hit score for Broadway, the smart money would have been on composer Harold Arlen and lyricist Johnny Mercer. Both men had begun their careers in New York, but they really hit their stride in Hollywood, writing such songs as "My Shining Hour," "Ac-Cen-Tchu-Ate the Positive," "One for My Baby," and "Blues in the Night," songs that transcended the forgettable movies which featured them. Each man wrote with other distinguished partners, but there was something about their collaboration that brought out the most thoughtful, thrilling, and profound work in both of them. The first of their two Broadway collaborations, *St. Louis Woman*, contains not only their finest work, but one of the finest scores from the heady Golden Age.

Sadly, Arlen and Mercer entered the Broadway game at a point when wonderful songs were no longer enough to sustain the public's interest, let alone a thousand-performance smash hit. Before the Second World War, an enchanting score by Cole Porter, for example, could easily turn a show with a second-rate book into a success, but even the most skilled songwriters were now at the mercy of the book scenes that set up and followed their gems. Arlen and Mercer were denied the success their glorious score for *St. Louis Woman* deserved through a strange confluence of events, trends, and bad luck that was harsh even by the capricious standards of the Broadway musical.

St. Louis Woman has one of the most intriguing cultural pedigrees of any musical, up to its time. It began life as a 1931 novel called *God Sends Sunday*, about the peregrinations of a black jockey named Li'l Augie in the turn-of-the-century South. Its author, Arna Bontemps, was one of the leading lights of the Harlem Renaissance, who, after the Depression, became the chief archivist at Fisk University, where he built one of the world's finest collections of African American literature. In 1937, Bontemps teamed up with another Harlem celebrity, the Harvard-educated poet Countee Cullen, to turn the novel into a play. Now called *St. Louis Woman*, it concentrated on Augie's adventures with femme fatale Della in St.

Louis (which took up only one-third of the novel). The play had a brief run at the Lafayette Theatre in Harlem.

After World War II, Arlen contributed to two successful all-black Hollywood musicals, *Cabin in the Sky* and *Stormy Weather;* there seemed to be a market for popular dramatic entertainment with African American characters. A producer named Edward Gross optioned the Bontemps-Cullen play and hired them to write the libretto, then hired Arlen and Mercer to return east to do the score. It was the first time in Broadway history that black and white writers would collaborate together on a musical. That would seem to be a felicitous beginning, but plans quickly went from good to bad to worse. Lena Horne was signed to play the title character, but she soon objected to her "painted woman" character and quit; indeed, the NAACP complained about the show's lowlife gamblers and kept women. Horne's replacement was fired, then reinstated after the cast protested. The original director was let go, along with the choreographer, and Rouben Mamoulian, who had worked magic in a similar milieu with *Porgy and Bess,* took over, but to no avail. Worst of all, in a show about bad luck and omens, Cullen died two weeks before rehearsal began. After several out-of-town engagements, it limped into New York on March 30, 1946.

But other shows have surmounted worse odds; *St. Louis Woman* was mostly undone by its attempts to force a complex and unwieldly story into the form of a conventional musical. Bontemps's original story had the jockey Li'l Augie living openly with Della after taking her from her pimp and, thinking himself hexed, plunging headlong into doom. The revised book mixed this near-Shakespearean story with a good deal of incongruous comedy and happy endings. On the road, it was transformed from two acts to three—a length rarely sustainable in a musical. The famed acrobatic dancing Nicholas Brothers were hired, but only the pint-sized Harold had a real part—Li'l Augie—so his brother Fayard was assigned a contrived comic role, and they were given a dancing duel that had no narrative point. Augie's tragic romance with Della was

sugared over and a requisite comic subplot uncomfortably added. The lusty, louche atmosphere of East St. Louis was turned into the happy-go-lucky world of a musical comedy.

What transcended the 113-performance train wreck was the score. Arlen, the son of a cantor in Buffalo, New York, and Mercer, a privileged son of Savannah, Georgia, had a particular knack for writing in a black idiom; separately and together, they created signature numbers for such prominent African American artists as Lena Horne, Ethel Waters, the Mills Brothers, Louis Armstrong, and Joe Williams. *St. Louis Woman* gave Arlen a chance to write a sparkling cakewalk contest and a searing funeral eulogy called "Leavin' Time." Mercer wrote hilarious patter lyrics for the feisty young Pearl Bailey. Della's entrance song, "Any Place I Hang My Hat Is Home," is one of musical theater's greatest introductions, and the brooding, mournful "I Had Myself a True Love" has assumed a rightful place in recital halls around the world. Any of these would have ennobled an evening in the theater, but one song transcended them all. When Augie and Della pledged their affections to each other, Arlen and Mercer gave them one of the finest of American standards:

> I'm gonna love you
> Like nobody's loved you
> Come rain or come shine. . . .
> Happy together
> Unhappy together
> And won't it be fine?
> Days may be cloudy or sunny
> We're in or we're out of the money
> But I'm with you, Della/Augie,
> I'm with you
> Rain or shine.

"Come Rain or Come Shine" is the most successful song to come out of the least successful show.

There have been several attempts to get the show back up on its horse; Arlen himself adapted it as a "blues opera," *Free and Easy,* which had a European tour produced by Quincy Jones, and there have been concert versions in New York and Philadelphia. In the end, *St. Louis Woman* is a thoroughbred of a score that simply ran with the wrong field at the wrong track. No horseracing tout ever tore up his losing ticket with more regret.

OPPOSITE: *Pearl Bailey, as the no-nonsense comic lead Butterfly, lets her man Barney (Fayard Nicholas) know in no uncertain terms that he'd better "Legalize [Her] Name" by seeking out a justice of the peace. And, she reminds him, she "spells peace with an E–A!"*

Everything about it was appealing:
Annie Get Your Gun *worked hard under Joshua Logan's direction to give audiences the thrill of a Wild West Show.*

With *Oklahoma!* and *Carousel,* the team of Rodgers and Hammerstein gave the public something it greedily devoured: musical stories, with depth, character, and artistry. They set the tempo of the time, and it became increasingly clear that to have a hit of their own, their colleagues had to write to that beat.

Not content with dominating the artistic life of Broadway, Rodgers and Hammerstein set about changing its commercial life as well. Rodgers had always been moving toward financial autonomy with his shows. Producers were the bane of his existence, starting with the hacks who cut his first Broadway score in half; now he had the clout to exercise control without compromise. While *Oklahoma!* was in rehearsal, Rodgers and Hammerstein set up a publishing firm to publish the score themselves. By 1944, they were full-fledged producers, with an office and a staff on Madison Avenue. They now had the means to finance their next projects—and those of others—while maintaining artistic control over the casting, promotion, and quality of the various tours and foreign productions of their work.

About the same time, lyricist Dorothy Fields had a brainstorm for a new musical project. Hearing about a young Army rifleman with a chestful of medals who had won an armful of dolls at a Coney Island shooting gallery, she immediately thought of Buffalo Bill's ace female sharpshooter. And just as quickly, she hit another bull's-eye: Ethel Merman as Annie Oakley. Fields brought in her brother Herbert, who had written numerous shows with Rodgers and Hart in the 1920s, to cowrite the book. She took the idea straight to Rodgers and Hammerstein, who agreed on the spot to produce the show, provided Fields could get Merman. Merman was recovering in the hospital from a caesarean delivery, but Fields barged into her room and told her about the project. Merman, in no condition to do much of anything, asked for some time to think it over; a $4,500-a-week salary, plus a portion of the gross, soon kindled her enthusiasm. The project now had a title—*Annie Get Your Gun*—two producers, a lyricist, two librettists, and a star. And just as soon as it acquired a composer, it lost him.

Jerome Kern wasn't particularly eager to leave Hollywood for New York, but he and Dorothy Fields had collaborated on some wonderful films, so he cast his lot with the new show. Only three days after his return in November 1945, he collapsed on Park Avenue. He was carrying no identification, so he was taken to the Welfare Island hospital, where he lan-

Folks may have been dumb where she came from, but Ethel Merman's Annie Oakley was nobody's fool.

guished in a ward filled with indigents and drunks. One hospital official noticed Kern's ASCAP card in his wallet and tracked the number down. His family and friends arrived to comfort him, but it was no use; within a few days, Jerome Kern was dead of a coronary thrombosis at the age of sixty.

"You're broken-hearted—but you go on." Rodgers thought only one person was capable of picking up where Kern left off: Irving Berlin, who had just finished his final tour of duty with *This Is the Army*. There was one complication—Berlin wrote both words and music; Fields would have to relinquish her role as lyricist. She graciously agreed. It was Berlin, however, who balked at the idea—he was used to originating and producing his own projects. More problematic, the show already had a concept, a plot, and characters, and Berlin was a songwriter, not a dramatist. He was worried that he wouldn't be able to write songs to fit "a situation show," as he called it, with a touch of awe and apprehension.

Yet Berlin was savvy enough to know which way the wind was blowing, and Rodgers was encouraging. He suggested that Berlin look at what Fields had already prepared. Accounts differ as to whether Berlin took five days or a week or a week and a half to write the first five songs, including "Doin' What Comes Natur'lly," "You Can't Get a Man with a Gun," "They Say It's Wonderful," and "The Girl That I Marry"—but each was a brilliantly crafted comedy song or ballad, each perfectly keyed, not only to Merman, but to the culture, psyche, and conflicts of Annie Oakley.

LEFT: *Berlin and Merman had immense admiration and affection for each other, but when he tried to revise some lyrics during the out-of-town tryout of* Call Me Madam, *she famously told him: "Call me Miss Bird's-Eye of 1950—this show's frozen."*

BELOW: *Berlin's legendary paean to show biz almost didn't make it into the show when he felt the song didn't appeal to his collaborators.*

Miss Bull's-eye of 1946: Annie Oakley's sharpshooting routines brought the house down.

So prodigious was Berlin's skill at churning out terrific songs that Broadway's greatest anthem, "There's No Business Like Show Business," was nearly filed away by him as an interesting failure after he thought his colleagues seemed nonplussed when he played it for them. In fact, they were so impressed by the song, they hardly knew what to say.

But audiences knew. *Annie Get Your Gun* opened in May 1946 and produced the longest run of Berlin's career—1,147 performances—and yielded at least eight pop standards. Berlin had some initial reservations about Merman, considering her too brassy a personality, but their collaboration became a lovefest. In her opinion, Berlin had written the best character she ever played, and they went on to do several more projects, including a 1950 hit, *Call Me Madam*, and a 1966 revival of *Annie* with additional songs, his last work for the theater. Someone told him that critics thought the show was old-fashioned. "Yep," Berlin replied, "full of good old-fashioned hits."

"Another op'nin, another show"

KISS ME, KATE

Let's be buddies:
Cole Porter and Bella Spewack.

If Berlin had qualms about writing a "situation show," Cole Porter was uninterested in writing any kind of show. The mid-forties had only brought him two major disappointments on Broadway, a revue and a weak score to Orson Welles's gargantuan version of *Around the World in 80 Days*. He preferred to stay in Hollywood, write film scores at his own pace, and be near the doctor who attended to his crippled condition. There was a sense among Broadway wags that, in the postwar musical world of big themes and complex characters, Porter and his effervescent style were passé.

In September 1935, the Theatre Guild gave Broadway a version of Shakespeare's *Taming of the Shrew*, starring their golden duo, Alfred Lunt and Lynn Fontanne. Arnold Saint-Subber, a starstruck production assistant for the 1940 tour, marveled at how the Lunts carried their onstage feuding in the play back to their dressing rooms, where their egos clashed nightly. Almost a decade later, he was a producer who thought these star turns might be musical comedy material. Teaming with *Oklahoma!*'s designer, Lemuel Ayers, he approached comic playwright Bella Spewack about creating a book that folded together Shakespeare's play with the backstage antics of a hyperbolically self-centered thespian couple. Spewack turned to the songwriter with whom she and her estranged husband, Sam, had written *Leave It to Me*—Cole Porter.

Porter, however, was at best skeptical. Shakespeare seemed like a highbrow, commercially unappealing idea; besides, he didn't want to come back east. Spewack wore down his resistance through repeated pleading, and by the spring of 1948 Porter pronounced himself enchanted by the drafts of her libretto about the out-of-town tryout of a musical *Taming of the Shrew*, directed by and starring a Wellesian ham named Fred Graham alongside his ex-wife Lilli Vanessi. Nothing about the story of *Kiss Me, Kate* required Porter to master the sweeping narrative of the Rodgers and Hammerstein musicals; he confined himself instead to the sweeping emotions of the leading characters. Banking on the convention of two lovers who can't live with each other and can't live without each other, one that had neatly served authors from Shakespeare to Noel Coward to Preston Sturges, Porter brilliantly captured the self-delusion and overwrought masochism of romantic egotism:

> So taunt me and hurt me
> Deceive me, desert me,
> I'm yours till I die,
> So in love, so in love,
> So in love with you, my love,
> Am I.

Petruchio/Fred (Alfred Drake) gets to act out his frustrations on Kate/Lilli (Patricia Morison); no wonder she hates men.

Jack Diamond and Harry Clark are gangsters who know what will start the girls in society simply ravin': the Bard of Stratford-on-Avon.

When Sam Spewack was called in to add a silly subplot about a pair of gangsters, Porter matched his low comedy with high style. The second-act soft-shoe showstopper, "Brush Up Your Shakespeare," has nothing to do with an integrated musical, a good deal to do with old-fashioned specialty numbers, and everything to do with Porter's ability to flirt playfully with downright obscenity.

If she says your behavior is heinous,
Kick her right in the "Coriolanus.". . .
When your baby is pleading for pleasure,
Let her sample your "Measure for Measure."
Brush up your Shakespeare,
And they'll all kowtow.

Paradoxically, Porter's renderings of the outsize, melodramatic personalities of Fred and Lilli were the most truthful things he ever wrote, perfectly embodied by Alfred Drake and Patricia Morison. The show opened in Philadelphia in early December 1948 and worked like a charm from that moment on. It moved practically intact to the New Century Theatre on Broadway, premiering two days before the beginning of 1949. *Kiss Me, Kate* gave Porter the greatest hit of his career—it ran 1,077 performances and won five Tony Awards, including Best Musical. It also gave Porter a new lease on life. He had two more hits in the 1950s, *Can-Can* and *Silk Stockings,* an underrated contemporary adaptation of the 1939 Ernst Lubitsch film *Ninotchka,* with some blisteringly perceptive critiques of the Cold War.

As Porter tangled with the narrative demands of the Golden Age musical, he surely must have known that the dramatic heavy lifting of the Rodgers and Hammerstein "musical play" was not for him; his musical comedies might now be pitched at a higher level, but they were still always musical comedies. The thrilling achievement of *Kiss Me, Kate* was only temporarily eclipsed when *South Pacific* opened four months later, earning the lion's share of critical bouquets. When Porter and an acquaintance heard that show's hit song, "Some Enchanted Evening," emanating from the radio, his friend remarked what a powerful song it was. "Yes," Porter twinkled in reply, "if you can imagine it taking two men to write one song."

"So, come on and kiss me, Kate":
a glorious finale on a glorious set by
Lemuel Ayers.

GWEN VERDON

THE EISENHOWER YEARS had two favorite redheads. Across the country, Lucy ruled on the television console, but in the West 40s, another redhead was champ, one who could not only do comedy like Lucy, but also sing with an unforgettable tear in her voice and dance up a tornado. And, frankly, Gwen Verdon was a hell of a lot sexier, too. She was the perfect seductive siren for the 1950s: spicy enough to be titillating, yet vulnerable enough to be unthreatening.

Gwyneth Verdon was born in Los Angeles in 1925 and raised by a stage mother who ran a dance studio; when two-year-old Gwen developed rickets, her mother immediately enrolled her in ballet class so she could get stronger.

Victorian England never saw a dish like Gwen Verdon in Redhead.

Verdon stayed on the West Coast and became an assistant to choreographer Jack Cole, working briefly in a few of his shows on Broadway before settling back in Hollywood. In 1953, choreographer Michael Kidd was looking for the right dancer for a second-act specialty number in Cole Porter's *Can-Can* and brought Verdon to New York for an evening that would change her life. Kidd recalled:

> Opening night in New York, she does the classic apache dance in slow motion with another dancer, which ends up with her taking a knife and sticking it into him, and he rolls back, ends up on a chair, a waiter comes walking by carrying a tray of cheese, she sticks the knife into the cheese and slowly walks offstage. As she left the stage the audience broke into unbelievable applause, they applauded and applauded and applauded and I ran from the back of the theater, all the way down into her dressing room, and said "Gwen, you've got to come out here this minute, the audience won't stop applauding, we can't continue with the show." She says "But I'm not dressed, I'm getting ready to change my costume," so I pulled a little bathrobe off her clothes rack, stuck it around her. "Here, hold this, go out there." And she went out there and the audience applauded tumultuously, the kind of a thing that you only see in the movies. And that moment you could see a star being born.

Verdon immediately incurred the wrath of the show's leading lady for purloining the evening and later took home a Tony for her supporting performance. When Harold Prince's production office was casting the part of Lola, the temptress from Hell in *Damn Yankees* (1955), they summoned Verdon:

> I remember her walking into the office. She was just dazzling, with a whole lot of red hair teased way up, what a glamorous figure, and she wore a dress that just looked sensational. I remember saying to the designers, "Copy that dress for her entrance dress in the show." And they did. . . . It is not uncommon in musicals for a performer not to appear for the first thirty minutes of the show and then come in, and you're so glad they're there, and they just take the whole show with them. And that's what she did.

She walked away with another Tony as well as the show's choreographer, Bob Fosse. They were immediately entranced with each other; she became his muse and, five

Verdon in one of Fosse's spoofs for Redhead, *"The Pick-Pocket Tango."*

years later, his wife. (Separated in 1971, they continued to work with each other, and Verdon was with him when he died in 1987.) Fosse created the dances for her next show, *New Girl in Town* (1957), where she played Eugene O'Neill's waterfront prostitute, Anna Christie, and audiences who already knew her as a brilliant dancer discovered a fine actress as well. "She gives a complete characterization . . . a woman of silence and mysteries," wrote the *Times*. "It would be an affecting job on any stage." Another Tony, followed by a slight vehicle in 1959, whose title, *Redhead*, did not refer to Lucy. It provided Fosse with his first directing credit and Verdon her fourth Tony.

After a six-year break following the birth of their daughter, Verdon dazzled audiences as *Sweet Charity* (1966); conceived for her by Fosse, it was a tour de force that brutally required her to sing and dance a half-dozen numbers. She played her final temptress in *Chicago* in 1975 and the idea of audiences seeing her as a "hot honey" always made her, characteristically, giggle: "I never thought my dances sexy—I suppose that's because I see myself with my face washed, and to me I look like a rabbit." The most electric triple threat of her time—maybe of all time—she needed three separate understudies to cover her in *New Girl in Town*. In only one instance did she seem false: in *Redhead* when she sang about being "Merely Marvelous.' There was nothing "merely" about Gwen Verdon.

ALFRED DRAKE

IN AN ERA WHEN CHARACTERS ACQUIRED new depth, the American musical was lucky to have a leading man who brought panache, masculinity, and dash to some of the most challenging roles of the Golden Age. Alfred Drake, with his commanding mahogany baritone, was equally adept at romance, comedy, Shakespeare, and period pieces—sometimes combining all four skills in one show. He was born Alfred Capurro in the Bronx and sang in church choirs before making his Broadway debut at the age of twenty-two, understudying William Gaxton in *White Horse Inn* (1936). He quickly went into Rodgers and Hart's *Babes in Arms* and, after a number of mediocre revues, made musical theater history with his portrayal of Curly in *Oklahoma!*, belting out five songs that would become some of the most famous of all time, with a range that could climb clear up to the sky. After a failure as Macheath in *Beggar's Holiday*, Duke Ellington's modern version of *The Beggar's Opera*, he played the dual role of Fred Graham and Petruchio in *Kiss Me, Kate*, a difficult part he embraced so indelibly that it took more than fifty

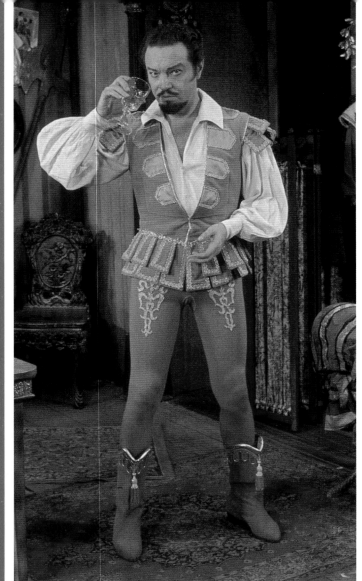

Alfred Drake as Edmund Kean in a 1961 musical version of the actor's life.

PHIL SILVERS

DURING THE TRYOUT of one of his shows, Phil Silvers was checking in to his Philadelphia hotel. "Now, my wife will be joining me between eight and ten tonight," he confided to the desk clerk, in his inimitably ingratiating hi-how-are-ya style. "But she works in disguise for the FBI, so she might check in as a blond or a brunette—ya never know." The con man extraordinaire was born Fischl Silverstein in the Brownsville section of Brooklyn in 1911 and worked his way up telling cheap gags in stale burlesque joints. His big break came in 1939, when, during the run of *Yokel Boy,* the leading comedian quit and Silvers's minor part was beefed up. It led immediately to a film contract, but Silvers hated playing the hero's best

years to find another actor who could fill his boots. Equally vain, sententious, and lecherous, Drake's Graham was utterly convincing as the greatest Shakespearean actor-director on Broadway (perhaps because Drake himself would act in and direct Shakespeare throughout his career), and to hear him defend his amour propre when slighted by his ex-wife—"I *beg* your pardon, Lilli; I was the *underrrr*-study!"—is to get a lasting lesson in musical-comedy acting. Turning down the lead in the *The King and I* for a bigger paycheck, he won his first Tony as the wily poet in *Kismet* (1953) and combined his love of the bard and musical theater by playing the impossibly demanding role of nineteenth-century actor Edmund Kean in a labor of love called *Kean* (1961). An actor's actor and an insomniac, he could be found holding court at Sardi's into the night, quoting Shakespeare and telling backstage stories, just like one of his characters.

"What's TV but burlesque with an antennae?" asked Phil Silvers in Top Banana *(1951).*

friend in all his pictures. He came back east to create his first Broadway lead, con artist Harrison Floy in *High Button Shoes* in 1947, and three seasons later, he had another starring vehicle, *Top Banana* (a phrase coined by songwriter Johnny Mercer for the occasion), a spoof of television, where he played an egomaniac closely modeled on Milton Berle. Silvers played it for more than two years, on Broadway and on tour, and won a Tony, after which he was lifted to television immortality himself as the ever-conniving Sergeant Bilko. After the series ended, Silvers returned to Broadway in a Comden and Green musical about the music business called *Do Re Mi,* which required him to stretch his considerable dramatic muscles. When, in 1962, the creative team of *A Funny Thing Happened on the Way to the Forum* adapted the Roman farces of Plautus into a burlesque homage, they had only Silvers in mind as the manipulative slave, Pseudolus. Alas, Silvers passed on the first go-round, but led a 1972 revival back to Broadway, winning a second Tony, twenty years after his first, at the age of sixty-one. A debilitating stroke curtailed his run, but the fast-thinking, fast-talking Silvers was at his best on opening night, when the set accidentally collapsed. After the stagehands rushed out to lash the set back together, Silvers turned to the audience, beamed his thousand-watt grin, and ad-libbed, "Well, Rome wasn't built in a day!"

One of many magic moments in Barbara Cook's career: The Gay Life *(1961).*

BARBARA COOK

BROADWAY'S FAVORITE INGENUE got her first glimpse of New York City at the age of twenty, on a trip with her mother from her native Atlanta in 1948. After seeing *Oklahoma!,* she sent her mother back alone. The silver-throated soprano soon made her Broadway debut as the ingenue in Yip Harburg's satirical flop, *Flahooley,* in 1951, following it with a series of other roles on tour and on Broadway. Cook finally made a name for herself in 1956 as the much-maligned Cunegonde in *Candide.* Her showcase number in Leonard Bernstein's demanding score, "Glitter and Be Gay," in which she essentially makes a compelling case for being a kept woman, required her to hit twenty-one high Cs.

Her porcelain skin, blue eyes, and vocal purity made her the golden girl next door, but it was never as easy as it looked. "Very early in my career, I was standing in the wings, waiting to audition, and I thought everybody who sang before me had a better voice, looked prettier, had a better figure. I was always a mess," she recounted. "For some reason, it occurred to me that if I could find a way to really learn who I am and put that into my work, then there could be no real competition—because there's only one of me." That "me" won hearts as a Midwestern librarian searching for her "White Knight" in *The Music Man* (1957); an ardent bride-to-be in *The Gay Life* (1961); a lovelorn shopgirl in *She Loves Me* (1963); and in several Rodgers and Hammerstein revivals. She brought a feisty determination to all her roles—one way or another, she was going to get the guy before the end of the second act, and isn't that what musical comedy is all about?

The second act of her own life proved to be more interesting than those of her shows. After dropping out of the Broadway scene in the late 1960s, she returned to a triumphant recital debut at Carnegie Hall in 1975. Since then, she has built a second career as the most accomplished cabaret and concert singer of her generation. In the 1950s, no one could match the buoyancy of her innocence; now, no one can match the poignancy of her experience.

"You've got to be carefully taught"

THE MORAL VISION OF RODGERS AND HAMMERSTEIN

During the late 1940s, novels, plays such as *All My Sons* by Arthur Miller, and the occasional movie (*The Best Years of Our Lives*) were addressing the serious, less glorified ramifications of World War II. One short novel called *Mister Roberts* took a hard look at the boredom and incompetence aboard a Navy ship stationed in the South Pacific. Director Joshua Logan agreed to adapt the book for the stage, and while he was preparing for the show, someone slipped him the galleys of James Michener's collection of short stories, *Tales of the South Pacific*, thinking it might serve as background research. It did more than that. Realizing the stories would make a great musical, Logan knew there was only one team capable of capturing the exotic locale and sweep of the stories: Rodgers and Hammerstein. Although the negotiations were protracted (and painful, in Logan's case), the team, with Logan as coauthor and director, embarked on their new show, now called *South Pacific*. Opening in April 1949, only two months after the premiere of *Death of a Salesman*, the musical offered, like Arthur Miller's play, a candid portrait of what kind of America had emerged from the crucible of the Second World War. No one in the audience could have been oblivious to seeing the same servicemen that they may have said good-bye to (perhaps forever) only a few years earlier, now cavorting and, in some cases, dying onstage.

The adaptation was a difficult one, even for Hammerstein's narrative gifts. The focus was on three of Michener's stories, and only the third, the least of them, was in any way musical-comedy material. Rodgers, Hammerstein, and Logan therefore decided to put the comedy on the back burner and, instead, intertwined two serious romantic plots. One involved a middle-aged French planter and his nascent romance with a young Navy nurse from the American South; the second was about a WASPy lieutenant who falls in love with a native Tonkinese girl. What tied the two plots together was not just romance, but the undercurrent of prejudice that threatens to destroy each couple's happiness.

Before the effects of such conflicts could be rendered dramatically, however, there were some practical questions. By a stroke of good fortune, the writers acquired a full-fledged opera singer to essay Emile, the French planter, a Metropolitan Opera basso named Ezio Pinza. Besides being thrillingly handsome with a voice to match, Pinza gave the production some clout by being the first vocal artist of his rank to appear in a Broadway musical. When Rodgers and Hammerstein thought next of

S.R.O. for Rodgers and Hammerstein's second-biggest hit: South Pacific.

their Arkansas-born nurse, Nellie Forbush, they turned quickly to Mary Martin. Martin was an unofficial protégée of Hammerstein's; they had met in Hollywood after she was signed to a studio contract following her success introducing Cole Porter's saucy "My Heart Belongs to Daddy" in 1938's *Leave It to Me*. Martin was the bubbly, reassuring embodiment of musical comedy and, after touring in *Annie Get Your Gun*, was more than ready to come back to Broadway to play the corn-fed girl raised just across the border from her native Texas. Martin had a particularly low vocal range for a musical comedy ingenue. "What on earth do you want," she demanded of her collaborators upon hearing who her costar would be, "two basses?" But Rodgers and Hammerstein artfully solved the problem by giving both Pinza and Martin some of the most gloriously rhapsodic music ever sung on the Broadway stage— but they hardly ever sang it at the same time.

Nellie's romance with Emile grinds to a halt when she learns that he has fathered two children with a native woman; her Southern background prevents her from accepting any mixing of the races (she is from Little Rock, where one of the country's worst segregationist battles would be fought in 1957). The Navy lieutenant, battling his own misgivings over his affair with the Tokinese girl, responds:

> You've got to be taught before it's too late,
> Before you are six or seven or eight,
> To hate all the people your relatives hate,
> You've got to be carefully taught!

However blunt Hammerstein's appeal for tolerance seems today, one has to remember that race relations were of interest to practically no one in the late 1940s. The story runs that James Michener was accosted by a friend after a preview performance of *South Pacific*. The friend raved about the show, but begged Michener to get rid of that "prejudice" song. When Michener relayed the encounter to Hammerstein, the liberal-minded lyricist was thrilled to hear it—"You've Got to Be Carefully Taught" was the whole reason for the show, in his opinion, and of course his collaborators backed him up.

Twin romances: William Tabbert as Lt. Cable sings "Younger Than Springtime" to Liat (Betta St. John), and Ezio Pinza as Emile De Becque reconciles with Mary Martin's Nellie Forbush in the subtle climax to South Pacific.

Like *Oklahoma!*, *South Pacific* captured the American spirit, only this time in its postwar zeitgeist—and won every award in sight, including the Pulitzer Prize for Drama, the first for Rodgers and Hammerstein, and only the second one awarded to a musical. Of course, audiences didn't beat down the doors for nearly two thousand performances to be hectored about bigotry; they thrilled to the romance and the extraordinary score. The cast album sold more than a million copies; twenty years after its opening, the show had netted its producers—Rodgers and Hammerstein, plus Logan and Leland Hayward—more than $7 million; and the song "Some Enchanted Evening" forever raised the temperature of every crowded room.

"Once you have found her, never let her go." Pinza and Martin in South Pacific.

"You've Got Be Carefully Taught" would not, however, blend quietly into the Hit Parade. When *South Pacific* played Atlanta during its national tour in 1953, it was denounced on the floor of the Georgia state legislature. Two state representatives targeted the song specifically, saying that it was offensive. "Intermarriage produces half-breeds. And half-breeds are not conducive to the higher type of society. . . . In the South, we have pure blood lines and we intend to keep it that way." Furthermore, they criticized Atlanta for "permitting such propaganda to be foisted upon Southern men and women." Hammerstein replied quickly: "I meant every word in that song. The play was not written as propaganda, but the propaganda, if they want to call it that, comes naturally."

By the time this brouhaha occurred, Hammerstein was enjoying the second year of a long run of another project drawing on the contrasting cultures of East and West, *The King and I.* Rodgers and Hammerstein had been approached by the English musical-theater diva Gertrude Lawrence to adapt the story of Anna Leonowens and her job in nineteenth-century Siam as the schoolmistress to the King's royal court. The way was fraught with obstacles, not the least of which was how to render the culture of Siam in convincing musical idioms and dignified dramatic language. It was an unconventional musical in that its central couple were not typical romantic leads. Anna and the King are at loggerheads for most of the play and have only one moment of sexual frisson, in "Shall We Dance?" She teaches him a polka and he, literally and figuratively, sweeps her off her feet. The real love story in *The King and I* is one of diplomacy, not conjugality. Anna's Western ideas of freedom and what we would now call empowerment carry the day, and the show ends on a hopeful note for the prospects of suffrage and participatory democracy. The show was another huge hit for the team, running for 1,246 performances; eventually it was made into an award-winning film that immortalized Yul Brynner in the role he originated (he went on to play the King on tour and revivals throughout his life, for more than 4,500 performances).

The influence of *South Pacific* and *The King and I* cannot be over-estimated. In both their stage and film incarnations, they reached an audience of millions, not only in America but around the world. The glossy cinematic versions of the Rodgers and Hammerstein shows became international film successes in the 1950s and exported a vision of America (in *Oklahoma!* and *Carousel*) and American values (the latter shows) around the world, inculcating a generation of movie-goers who had never been to a Broadway show and might not ever get to attend one.

Oscar Hammerstein was, as his protégé Stephen Sondheim once said, "judgmental, a true moralist." He may well have been the most influential dramatic moralist of his time, constructing a commercially successful bully pulpit that allowed his sermons to be given in the form of glorious songs. His strong beliefs are implicit in all but his least success-ful shows and he was lucky that Rodgers's politics were equally sym-pathetic. Hammerstein embraced such values as fellowship, tolerance, and faith; he believed that understanding was better than ignorance, that hope was better than despair; that love was better than hate. He would continue to explore his musical version of conflict resolution with a look at generational tensions in San Francisco's Chinatown in *Flower Drum Song* (1958), and he addressed, somewhat facilely, freedom and persecu-tion in *The Sound of Music* (1959). Hammerstein could be preachy—a cardinal sin in the eyes of sophisticated theatergoers—but America has always relied on its preachers. In the 1950s, when the world turned to this country again and again for guidance, Rodgers and Hammerstein were promoting in their musicals a new American worldview, devoid of cant and hypocrisy, where everyone is given a chance to embrace, as Lincoln said, "the bet-ter angels of our nature."

"Shall I tell you what I think of you?" Never the twain shall meet between Gertrude Lawrence (Anna) and Yul Brynner (the King).

Nothing brought the Rodgers and Hammerstein musicals to life like a clash of cultures. Here, Anna confronts the multiple wives and children of the King of Siam; they will be charmed by her, and she, in turn, will slowly change the social structure of Siam.

"The oldest established permanent floating crap game in New York"

GUYS AND DOLLS

My time of day is the dark time,
A couple of deals before dawn,
When the street belongs to the cop
And the janitor with the mop,
And the grocery clerks are all gone,
When the smell of the rain-washed pavement
Comes up clean and fresh and cold,
And the street lamp light fills the gutter with gold.

Frank Loesser, "My Time of Day"

By the late 1940s, Times Square had been utterly transformed into a twenty-four-hour outdoor bazaar. The influx of movie theaters along 42nd Street in the early 1930s had been only the beginning. Soon, burlesque theaters dotted the landscape (although Mayor Fiorello La Guardia tried to ban them in the late 1930s), as did other seedy forms of amusement such as flea circuses, tattoo parlors, taxi-dance halls, peep shows, and penny arcades. Movie houses—dubbed grind houses—played double and triple bills of squalid "B" movies into the wee small hours. The elegant theater restaurants of yesteryear had been supplanted by cheap all-night food joints: Nedick's, with its famous orange drink and hot dogs, Childs, Walgreen's, Lindy's. Newspaper stands on each corner offered up to three editions—morning, afternoon, or very late—of almost a dozen city papers; one could also get local papers from all over the country. The Madison Square Garden sports emporium had moved to the western boundary of the Theater District in 1925, and prize-fighters, their managers, and various hangers-on clogged the bars and taverns of the West 40s, rubbing elbows with dancers, actors, publicists—all manner of public personalities, struggling or successful. Broadway defied the diurnal rhythm of a great city: it provided round-the-clock entertainment—whatever you wanted, whenever you wanted it.

The poet laureate of this beat was Damon Runyon. Born in 1880 in Manhattan, Kansas, Runyon spent his early years in Colorado, working hard as a journalist, playing hard as a night owl and a drinker. He came east at the age of thirty and forswore alcohol, only to become addicted to coffee—forty cups a day—and cigarettes. Caffeine and nicotine fueled his nocturnal wanderings along the West 40s; by the 1920s, Runyon and Walter Winchell were the city's greatest chroniclers of its nightlife. In a series of articles for the *New York American,* in numerous short stories, and in sports columns, Runyon immortalized the driven, sad, ambitious, and in some cases criminal denizens of New York after dark. In a unique and imitable style, he combined gutter argot with an incongruous delicacy of expression, giving the world a glimpse into the secret world of gamblers, gangsters, and their girls. In one story, he referred to West 47th Street as "Dream Street":

[In] Dream Street are always many hand-bookies and horse players, who sit on the church steps on the cool side of Dream Street in the summer and dream about big killings on the races, and there are also nearly always many fight managers, and sometimes fighters,

OPPOSITE: *Set designer Jo Mielziner's extraordinary renderings of the streets of Times Square and (below) a sketch of what lies beneath them in* Guys and Dolls.

GUYS: *Late in the show's run, B.S. Pully (center) as the committed craps shooter Big Jule . . .*

hanging out in front of the restaurants, picking their teeth and dreaming about winning championships of the world, although up to this time no champion of the world has yet come out of Dream Street.

In this street you see burlesque dolls, and hoofers, and guys who write songs, and saxophone players, and newsboys, and newspaper scribes, and taxi drivers, and blind guys, and midgets, and blondes with Pomeranian pooches, or maybe French poodles, and guys with whiskers, and night-club entertainers, and I do not know what all else.

Runyon's characters had provided fodder for Hollywood since the late 1920s, and it was only a matter of time before his guys and dolls were enlisted to perform on the street that gave birth to them.

When producers Cy Feuer and Ernest Martin optioned some of the Runyon material in 1949, they turned immediately to Frank Loesser, the colorful and explosive songwriter who had given them a hit in 1948 with *Where's Charley?* Loesser, born in 1910, began his career as a lyricist and had an impressive string of successes in Hollywood during and after the war. Working with other composers or writing his own music, Loesser had nearly a dozen number-one hits from the movies, including "Heart and Soul," "I Don't Want to Walk Without You," "On a Slow Boat to China," and "Baby, It's Cold Outside," which would earn him an Academy Award for Best Song. Loesser, Feuer, and Martin; the eventual book writer, Abe Burrows; and the choreographer, Michael Kidd, shared something else besides their devotion to the works of Damon Runyon—they were all native New Yorkers and understood Runyon's urban milieu perfectly. "When we met, we all spoke the same language—at a very high pitch, mind you," recalled Kidd. "We all shouted at one another because that's the way you communicated in New York."

. . . AND DOLLS: Vivian Blaine (center) leads the Hot Box showgirls in loving their guys "A Bushel and a Peck."

The early days of the new musical's development required a fair amount of shouting. Loesser took off to write the score before a script was even completed; that turned out to be a good idea, because the first writer, Jo Swerling, had submitted a book that was nearly unusable (although he would, contractually, always receive a credit for it). Abe Burrows, a radio comedy writer, was brought in, and he worked in deferential tandem with the show's director, the dean of stage comedy, George S. Kaufman. The adaptation for *Guys and Dolls* leaned heavily on one short story, "The Idyll of Sarah Brown," which depicted an incongruous romance between an inveterate gambler named Sky Masterson and a worker for a Salvation Army–type mission, headquartered in the Theater District.

The prevalent formula of the time required a comic subplot. More loosely suggested by some other Runyon characters, this story concerns another hustler, Nathan Detroit, who is always leaving his chorine fiancée, Miss Adelaide, at the altar while he seeks out another crap game. To the credit of Burrows, Loesser, and Kaufman, the romantic plot and the comic subplot are beautifully interrelated, and they drive the musical straight to the finish line. Other colorful characters—gamblers and racketeers with names like Harry the Horse, Nicely-Nicely, and Big Jule—were drawn from a variety of Runyon stories, and the universe of the show was generously and jocularly fleshed out.

The love interest (romantic version): Pat Rooney Sr. as Brother Arvide, Robert Alda as Sky Masterson, and Isabel Bigley as Sarah Brown.

The creators were faced with a real challenge: how to make such unsavory types into acceptable, affection-inspiring musical-comedy characters. In the '30s, perhaps, such characters might have appeared without compromise in a Blitzstein show, for example, or late Rodgers and Hart, but tastes had changed. The producers hit upon a simple solution:

It spoke to me as a New Yorker, because I knew prototypically all those people, and I just thought it was wildly funny and immensely gifted. The show is downright funny, and it's intellectual, and it's observed, and it's true, and it's fabulous. That whole score of Frank Loesser's is just a testament to how brilliantly he wrote and captured everything.

—Fred Ebb, Lyricist

We subtitled the show "A Musical Fable of Broadway." It was on everything: "Guys and Dolls: A Musical Fable of Broadway." It was as though all of our mugs and tough guys were the seven dwarfs, Disney characters. They were all lovable; even our worst villain was a big teddy bear.

—Cy Feuer

Still, there was enough grit to the story to make it recognizable, not only to Runyon fans, but to the theatergoers who spilled out onto the sidewalk of the 46th Street Theatre. Choreographer Michael Kidd created a fifteen-minute street ballet for the top of the show called "Runyonland," filled with cardsharps, con men, and racetrack touts. A crap game set in a sewer became the dance highlight of the second act, and Miss Adelaide performs her chorus routines in a nightclub with the eyebrow-raising moniker the Hot Box.

Loesser worked his own particular magic with words and music. No musical since *Pal Joey* moved so effortlessly from the tawdry to the rhapsodic. He invented a true-to-life language for his creased, raffish characters. In one song, "Sue Me," Nathan apologies for the thousandth time to his long-suffering girlfriend:

The love interest (comic version): Sam Levene (Nathan Detroit) tries to convince Vivian Blaine's Adelaide to forgive him for the fourteenth— no, the fourteen-hundredth—time.

All right already, I'm just a nogoodnik.
All right already, it's true, so Nu?
So sue me, sue me,
What can you do me?
I love you.

The blend of street argot, fractured grammar, and Yiddish (*nu* means "what are you going to do about it?") was unprecedented. "That didn't exist in songs up to that point, people didn't talk that way in songs, they used songwriter language," said Michael Kidd. "Loesser used real language of real people and that's what made it so unique."

After its opening in November 1950, *Guys and Dolls* became one of Broadway's most enduring successes, running 1,194 performances, and inspiring successful revivals all over the world, including three to date on Broadway. The show was miraculously able to mock the desperate denizens of Dream Street and celebrate them at the same time; it took Runyon's Broadway of legend and turned it into a legend of Broadway.

A N ALBUM, by its very definition, is a storehouse of happy memories. The original cast album—the recording of the score to a Broadway musical—has, over the last sixty years, preserved happy memories for millions of theatergoers, while making millions for a few smart record companies.

The cast album took a while to appear on the scene. Since the technology became available, stars from various revues and shows on Broadway recorded their popular or specialty numbers, but there was not sufficient technology to capture many songs in their entirety, much less an hour's worth of show music. Certain stars and composers, such as Ethel Merman and George Gershwin, might record several selections from a particular work, but these came nowhere near to capturing the experience of being in the theater.

The first Broadway production to have most of its score captured on record was *The Cradle Will Rock*, with Marc Blitzstein accompanying the original cast on piano for the Musicraft label in 1938. However, it was not until the unprecedented success of *Oklahoma!* that the recording companies really got into the act. More than half a year after the show opened, Decca Records producer Jack Kapp decided to record twelve songs, using not only the original cast, but the show's full orchestra. The six disks were packaged in brown cardboard sleeves, bound by a cover with a photo of the cast—hence the term "original cast *album*." The 1943 *Oklahoma!* album was such an instant success that in 1944 a second volume containing the rest of the score was released. Soon, Decca would record *Bloomer Girl* and *Carousel*, while Columbia Records made a revival of *Show Boat* its first cast recording. Capitol followed with *St. Louis Woman* and RCA Victor with *Brigadoon;* these four labels in their various incarnations would remain the major recording studios for cast albums over the next sixty years.

The recording of a cast album is an art unto itself, and musical-theater fans have such unsung heroes as record producers Kapp, Goddard Lieberson at Columbia, and Thomas Z. Shepard (at various labels) to thank for their sensitive transfers of shows from stage to disc. Productions are rarely recorded exactly as they are heard in the theater. Listening to a score in a living room is a much different event from seeing the show onstage, so songs are often trimmed, rearranged, or reorchestrated to provide a more self-contained experience. On record, short finales can be added or important lead-in dialogue cut out; it can be disorienting to see a show onstage when one knows it only from the cast album.

Frank Loesser's effusive and prodigious score to
The Most Happy Fella *deserved—and received—*
a rare three-LP treatment.

Traditionally, shows are recorded in an all-day studio session on the Sunday after the Broadway opening. For working on their day off, actors are compensated with one week's salary for each recording day; it's rare that they participate in any royalties. The makeup of a cast recording has changed as technology has advanced. The long-playing 33⅓ format, in 1948 (*Kiss Me, Kate* was the first new cast album released on LP), allowed for approximately fifty minutes of score, just about enough for most shows. Occasionally, a show was bursting at the seams with so much music that it required two LPs (*She Loves Me, Sweeney Todd*) and in 1956, Columbia paid Frank Loesser's melodious *The Most Happy Fella* the ultimate compliment: three LPs. On the other hand, certain scores suffered from temporal expediency; Stephen Sondheim's glorious score for *Follies* was eviscerated by Capitol in 1971 to fit on a single LP. Still, there was always something about a cast album that was bigger than the sum of its parts. In the golden age of the cast album LP, colorful elaborations such as photographs, specially commissioned liner notes, souvenir booklets, and lyric sheets all added to the effect of cramming an entire show into one thin, twelve-inch-square package.

From a commercial point of view, an original cast album is the parking lot of recording projects: build it once and lease it forever. The costs are relatively minimal, but the returns can be enormous. The original cast album of *My Fair Lady* spent 480 weeks on *Billboard*'s charts, making it the third-longest-selling album—in any category—of all time. This is an impressive achievement, when one considers that the album was competing against pop stars from Elvis Presley to the Beatles. Also, until the early '60s, there were fewer than 50 positions available on the charts, compared to 200 now, so for *My Fair Lady* to stay on the charts its first five years meant being in rather select company. In terms of albums holding the number-one position for weeks on end, *My Fair Lady* was rated nineteenth as of 2000. The movie soundtrack for the film of *West Side Story* is the number one album in this category, surpassing records by Michael Jackson or the Eagles.

CBS, which owned Columbia Records, put up the entire investment for the stage production of *My Fair Lady* in 1956 in exchange for the recording rights and made millions in the bargain. Based on *My Fair Lady*'s success, other companies rushed into the field, backing Broadway shows in exchange for the exclusive rights to record them. As the '60s went on, many companies only bought themselves a flop for their trouble, and they just as quickly stopped investing in Broadway. (However, those albums could keep an underrated score in the popular consciousness for decades.)

Still, a Broadway score can provide a huge revenue stream for a recording company and the ways in which a company can exploit the music of a Broadway show are infinite. Over the years, pop and jazz artists have had successful albums by "covering" Broadway numbers—hardcore jazz saxophonist Cannonball Adderley released a *Fiddler on the Roof* album in 1964, for example. In the 1970s, before they were put on the stage, the scores of *Jesus Christ Superstar* and *Evita* debuted first as concept studio recordings. The introduction of vinyl allowed for an additional ten minutes or so of show music per side, and once, as a gag, a disco version of "The Ballad of Sweeney Todd" was stamped in blood-red vinyl. Disco even discovered Ethel Merman: her 1970s album of Broadway standards sung to a Bee Gees beat

was the zenith (or nadir) of kitsch. Going from the ridiculous to the sublime, the 1980s saw recordings of classic Broadway scores with distinguished opera stars such as Kiri Te Kanawa and Placido Domingo.

The advent of the compact disc allowed for even more music to be packed into a recording; some scores, either original casts or studio re-creations, include every note of music in the show; however, whether this is a good thing is a matter of individual taste. It is now possible, with the accessibility of compact discs, to purchase practically every theater score from every conceivable venue; smart record producers have repackaged and rereleased the most popular cast album titles in their catalogs over and over again, along with their esoteric failures. A quick glance at the racks of the Broadway section of any major record store now reveals classic shows side by side with one-week floperoos; technology, hand in hand with a specialized market, has provided the ultimate democratization of the Broadway score.

Yet, for anyone of a certain generation, there was nothing quite like hearing the phonograph needle drop for the first time on the overture track to a brand-new cast album. Whether you bought the record in the theater lobby, or at Korvette's, or were given it as a birthday, Christmas, or graduation present, that effect was always the same: it sounded like you had the best seat in the house.

Rex Harrison (r.) records "A Hymn to Him" for the bonanza cast album of My Fair Lady *in the Columbia Records studio. Castmate Robert Coote pitches in, while producer Goddard Lieberson enjoys Harrison's delivery.*

The Abbott Touch

THE PAJAMA GAME AND DAMN YANKEES

> Abbott didn't say much. He was laconic, terse. He'd say, "All right, sit on the couch now. Now, kiss the girl and grab a piece of cake. Let's see: Where you tumble over and the couch falls on toppa ya, that's not funny. Why'n't you try it without the couch falling on toppa you?" And that *would* be funny.
> —**Walter Matthau,** Actor

The master director, watching a rehearsal in the late 1950s.

> I was discussing the fact that everyone calls him "Mr. Abbott" with an actress who had been on intimate terms with him. She assured me that, as close as they were, there were only specific moments during which she felt free to call him "George," then she went back to "Mr. Abbott."
> —**Ethel Merman,** 1978

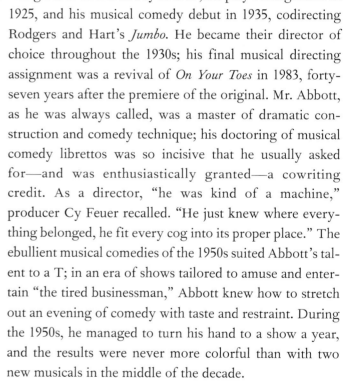

In the world of musical comedy, where artists like to show off with press agents, billing, program credits, and personal imprints, one man eschewed all forms of showboating. "The Abbott Touch" left no fingerprints; it was an ineffable something that turned lead into gold. Actually, George Abbott defined it once himself: "I make the actors say their final syllables."

The actor-writer-director who had the longest show biz career of the twentieth century was born in 1887. He made his acting debut on Broadway in 1913, his playwriting debut in 1925, and his musical comedy debut in 1935, codirecting Rodgers and Hart's *Jumbo*. He became their director of choice throughout the 1930s; his final musical directing assignment was a revival of *On Your Toes* in 1983, forty-seven years after the premiere of the original. Mr. Abbott, as he was always called, was a master of dramatic construction and comedy technique; his doctoring of musical comedy librettos was so incisive that he usually asked for—and was enthusiastically granted—a cowriting credit. As a director, "he was kind of a machine," producer Cy Feuer recalled. "He just knew where everything belonged, he fit every cog into its proper place." The ebullient musical comedies of the 1950s suited Abbott's talent to a T; in an era of shows tailored to amuse and entertain "the tired businessman," Abbott knew how to stretch out an evening of comedy with taste and restraint. During the 1950s, he managed to turn his hand to a show a year, and the results were never more colorful than with two new musicals in the middle of the decade.

The Pajama Game had what was, in its day, a provocative subject for a musical: based on a comic novel by Richard Bissell, called *7½ Cents*, it was about a strike at a pajama factory and the star-crossed romance between management (the boy) and labor (the girl). Far more contentious union issues had turned *The Cradle Will Rock* and *Pins and Needles* into successful musicals, but the political engagement of the Depression had given way to the timidity and fear of the McCarthy era. The book had been

Tempus fugit: *Eddie Foy Jr. as a "time study man" in* The Pajama Game; *his director was a similar model of efficiency (chorine Shirley MacLaine is to Foy's right).*

From Abbott, I learned discipline; I learned respect for the craft, for no nonsense; show up on time; do your job well; don't indulge yourself; don't suffer fools, not for one minute; don't indulge histrionics; apply to it many of the same rigid criteria that you would any job you do. Then have fun.

—Harold Prince, Director

optioned by Abbott's frequent stage manager, Robert Griffith, and his assistant, a precocious young man named Harold Prince. If Abbott would only consent to work on the project, Griffith and Prince were assured of partial financing and they could realize their dreams of becoming Broadway producers. Abbott was initially lukewarm, but he saw a way to develop the plot into something that could sustain an evening's worth of song and dance. The tyro producers were thrilled.

Finding a score was more difficult. Several songwriters turned them down, including Frank Loesser, but he recommended two of his protégés: Richard Adler and Jerry Ross. Adler and Ross, still in their twenties, wrote music and lyrics together in a truly collaborative way, each being credited for both, and they were among the last of the commercial Tin Pan Alley songwriters. Their spirited ingenuity made them ideal for the new show, and they supplied a score that had all the richness of the pop charts in the 1950s: soaring ballads such as "Hey There" (sung as a duet between the hero and himself, via a Dictaphone), the tango spoof "Hernando's Hideaway," even what was called a "hillbilly" number back then, the love duet "There Once Was a Man," that burst with sexuality.

Mr. Abbott gave Bob Fosse his first big break. Here, in "Steam Heat," Fosse's trademark derbies make their first appearance.

Other composers, of course, had previously brought diverse musical styles into a show, but that was usually to set a scene in a time and place; Adler and Ross just exploited what was on the airwaves for a show set in the here and now. It worked like gangbusters. "Hey There" was a hit before the show even opened, in a rendition by Rosemary Clooney.

Prince and Griffith wanted Jerome Robbins to choreograph, as he had for several other Abbott shows, but Robbins was not content with being the most imaginative young choreographer of the postwar generation; what he really wanted, as the saying goes, was to direct. A young dancer named Bob Fosse was recommended to do the dances, and Robbins agreed to supervise Fosse's choreography debut—so long as Robbins got a codirector credit. Prince was appalled at the request, but Abbott, with his typical equanimity, simply shrugged okay and said: "Everybody'll know who directed the show." When it premiered in May 1954, Abbott's name was practically the only thing that audiences *did* know; it had a minuscule advance and everyone involved with the production was understandably nervous. Still, "Hey There" had been on the charts for a while, and the fun, buoyant choreography (including Fosse's signature "Steam Heat") and bubbly score—all refined by Abbott—enchanted the audience. The opening-night response was so thunderous that the applause after each number added ten minutes to the show, and Prince, still stage-managing *The Pajama Game* in order to save money, knew that his life was changed forever.

The Pajama Game ran for more than a thousand performances and won Tonys for Best Musical and Choreography, and its program credits still induce jaw-dropping awe among Broadway cognoscenti: Abbott, Prince, Robbins, and Fosse, all working on the same show.

The next season, Prince and Griffith reunited Abbott and Fosse with Adler and Ross for the first successful musical about baseball, *Damn Yankees*. Surprisingly, the title came from the usually reserved Abbott. The show established Gwen Verdon as the hottest vamp on Broadway, in the role of a seductive witch hired by the Devil to lure a powerhouse ballplayer away from his wife. *Damn Yankees* proved to be only a handful of performances less successful than *Pajama Game*, but it was a damn sight sexier than the usual Abbott show. This may have been because of the onstage and offstage sparks between Verdon and Fosse, and both shows got a good deal of mileage out of their respective posters, which displayed the heroines in what were—for the 1950s—provocative stages of deshabille. *Yankees* also demonstrated to Broadway insiders that the producing team of Prince and Griffith was no fluke. The one dark cloud was the sudden death of Jerry Ross from a bronchial condition, only a year and half after the debut of *The Pajama Game*. One can only wonder what shows Adler and Ross might have gone on to write in an era that so valued their sassiness and sense of humor.

Taking a risk on an unknown team was part and parcel of the Abbott Touch. He gambled on more young talent than anyone since Ziegfeld. The partial list of artists who got their first big break under Abbott includes Tom Bosley, Carol Burnett, Liza Minnelli, Comden and Green, Kander and Ebb, Bock and Harnick, and, as a composer, Stephen Sondheim.

There was no one quite like him: he was well-read and an expert ballroom dancer, preferred Florida to Sardi's, was famously parsimonious (Walter Matthau remembered Abbott watching the World Series through an appliance-store window rather than pay for a television in his Philadelphia hotel room), and his only addiction was golf. He died at the age of 107, with every marble intact. The shows he directed get revived more often than any other director's—a testament to the quality of his craft—and any revival director who tampers with the alchemy of the Abbott Touch does so at his or her peril.

Whatever Lola wants: Gwen Verdon got her second Tony as the eternal temptress, vamping Stephen Douglass, in Damn Yankees.

"*I could have danced all night*"

MY FAIR LADY

When Oscar Hammerstein tells you a show won't work, odds are it probably won't work. Lyricist Alan Jay Lerner encountered Hammerstein at a Democratic rally in 1952 and mentioned that he and Frederick Loewe were struggling to adapt George Bernard Shaw's social comedy *Pygmalion* into a musical. Hammerstein acknowledged that he and Rodgers had tried to crack the same property for more than a year (although there is no documentation of their attempt) and gave up; despite its appeal, *Pygmalion* was simply not musical-comedy material. Lerner had to sigh and agree; however, two years later, he and Loewe took another shot at it. The result was the greatest success the American theater had ever seen.

Lerner and his partner came together by chance at New York's Lambs Club, a watering hole for show biz types, in 1942. They were the most unlikely pair since Rodgers and Hart. Loewe, seventeen years Lerner's senior, was a German émigré with an Austrian background, who had studied piano with Kurt Weill's teacher. Loewe was also a seemingly effortless fount of rhapsodic melodies, and a confirmed old bachelor who sought the company of undemanding young ladies to cheer him on at his beloved chemin-de-fer tables. Lerner was the son of New York Jewish privilege, educated at Choate and Harvard, an obsessive-compulsive go-getter with an addiction to serial monogamy (he had two more wives than Henry VIII). The team doctored an out-of-town flop in 1942 but went on to write several other Broadway shows, including *Brigadoon*, a huge hit in the 1947 season.

Lerner and Loewe were but one of several teams approached in the early 1950s by an eccentric movie producer named Gabriel Pascal, who owned the film rights to numerous plays by Shaw. No one was able to give Pascal the musical he wanted, which raises the questions, why was it so hard to adapt the play, and, if it was so hard, why would anyone keep trying? The answer to the second question is George Bernard Shaw, one of the theater's true titans, a prodigious playwright, critic, speechmaker, social philosopher, and resident intellectual to the world. His new plays were eagerly awaited in London and New York and his older plays were revived frequently because they always offered wonderful parts for great actors.

Pygmalion, written in 1912, was a popular success in its day, playing around the world. It was made into a well-regarded 1938 film (for which Shaw received an Academy Award for his screenplay), and it had been revived on Broadway as recently as 1945 with

Frederick Loewe and Alan Jay Lerner, an odd couple who made Broadway magic.

Gertrude Lawrence. Like of all Shaw's plays, it was written as a social critique. A phonetics professor named Henry Higgins wagers that he can "make a duchess" of a young Cockney flower girl by instructing her in the socially acceptable standards of the English language. A pioneering socialist, Shaw was far more concerned with breaking down the arbitrary boundaries of the British class system than he was in writing a romantic lark, but to his continued dismay, from the moment the play opened, audiences wanted the misogynistic Higgins to renounce his ways and run off with the transformed flower girl, Eliza Doolittle, at the final curtain.

The chief difficulty in adapting the play was that it was never a love story. Its only passion was for social equality, not between its leading characters. When Lerner returned to the project, after Pascal's death in 1954, he approached the problem from a different angle. Rather than attempt to shoe-

horn Shaw's play into musical-comedy conventions—a romance, a comic subplot, a colorful dancing chorus—Lerner realized "there was enough variety in the moods of the characters Shaw created, and we could do *Pygmalion* simply by doing *Pygmalion* . . . and adding the action that took place between the acts of the play." Lerner fought the adaptation battle on two fronts: he developed the needs and desires of the main characters, while dramatizing events that are only referred to, or occur offstage, in the play.

This liberating approach allowed Lerner to create scenes that expressed Shaw's intentions in more theatrical ways. For example, in the play, Eliza's mastery of the King's English is given a disastrous test run at a small tea party; Lerner transposes the scene to the highly public Ascot racing day, allowing Eliza to commit a similar verbal gaffe in front of a company of aristocrats resplendent in Cecil Beaton's exquisite Edwardian costumes. Lerner also knew that at its heart the play contained that ageless musical-comedy scenario, the Cinderella story. No one in the audience could be immune to the sight of the former "draggle-tailed guttersnipe" dressed to the nines, about to take her place among dukes and duchesses at the Embassy Ball. The project began to seem irresistible.

Such sophisticated effects would have fallen flat without the perfect company of actors and creative staff. Lerner and Loewe flew to London to enlist the services of England's redoubtable comedian of manners, Rex Harrison. But Harrison came with two problems: he was a prickly perfectionist and he had never sung in a musical; he was convinced he never could. Lerner and Loewe solved the latter problem by creating songs for Higgins that trod lightly on the melody, allowing the words to skip along. The kind of talk-singing

Moss Hart brought his legendary taste and style to My Fair Lady; *he had his work cut out for him between Julie Andrews's relative inexperience and Rex Harrison's tightly wound arrogance.*

*"Wouldn't It Be Loverly?" A Cockney Cinderella
dreams of her Prince Charming.*

required was just right for Harrison and allowed for a greater verbal dexterity that also suited his character. Harrison's personality would remain a problem, but that could be solved with diplomacy.

For the role of Eliza, given by theatrical tradition to grand actresses far older than the character's eighteen years, Lerner turned to a bright new face who was close to Eliza's age. Julie Andrews, who began her career as a child entertainer in England, made her Broadway debut in 1954 in a British musical pastiche called *The Boy Friend*. Lerner and Loewe were easily persuaded that Andrews had the requisite poise and charm to embody their leading character. She turned down an offer to star in Rodgers and Hammerstein's *Pipe Dream* (their only huge flop) and eagerly awaited a firm commitment from Lerner and Loewe.

Over the course of 1955, the team, through trial and error, kept developing the songs and dramatic vocabulary for the new show, helped immeasurably by their newly signed director, Moss Hart, whose taste, craftsmanship, and admiration for Shaw brought the project to a high level. On January 3, 1956, the cast assembled for their first rehearsal, and a month later, *My Fair Lady* (which, like *Away We Go!*, acquired its title by default)

In front of her busker mates at the Covent Garden market, Eliza rides what will be the first of many carriages.

Higgins laboriously teaches Eliza the difference between "cuppatay" and "a cup of tea"; all she wants is the tea itself.

opened during a blizzard in New Haven. Harrison, spooked by the live orchestra accompanying him, locked himself in his dressing room; Hart then threatened to tell the audience that "Rex Harrison is yellow and refuses to open." The star reconsidered and the audience, with snow dripping off their topcoats and furs, sat through a magical, if overlong, evening and stood at the end and cheered and cheered.

Expectation ran absurdly high when *My Fair Lady*, trimmed and refined, opened at the Mark Hellinger on March 15. Hart and Lerner panicked under the pressure at the last minute—out of town was one thing, but this was Broadway. Loewe, however, was almost Zen-like in his calm. He went and had a drink at a nearby bar during the first act; as far as he was concerned, there was no doubt that this was the best show Broadway had seen in ages. The next morning's papers left no doubt about it, either; Walter Kerr in

"By George, she's got it!" Andrews and Harrison, joined by Robert Coote as Colonel Pickering, in "The Rain in Spain," a number that, according to Lerner, took ten minutes to write, but on opening night "the applause exploded like nuclear fission."

"Come on, Dover, move your blooming arse . . . !" Eliza commits her fatal gaffe at Ascot.

the *Herald-Tribune* told his readers to stop reading the review and immediately write away for tickets. The doubters and naysayers could only agree with the characters at the top of the second act and sing to Lerner and Loewe:

You're the one who did it,
Who did it, who did it!
As sturdy as Gibraltar,
Not a second did you falter.
There's no doubt about it,
You did it!

My Fair Lady would run for more than six years—2,717 performances—and would make a Broadway star out of Julie Andrews and transform Harrison into an international celebrity. It was the most eagerly awaited show ever to arrive in London's West End; when Harrison, Andrews, and other members of the New York company opened at the Drury Lane Theatre there in 1958, they launched a four-year run. It has played in almost every capital in Europe and South America, was recorded in nearly every language and sold to the movies for $5 million. Columbia Records had put up the show's entire investment— $400,000—in order to procure the recording rights; according to Lerner, twenty years after the show opened it had grossed $800 million for the record company and its creators. *Oklahoma!* might have been the musical theater's first phenomenon, but *My Fair Lady* was its first blockbuster.

It was also immensely influential. Although Rosalind Russell, a nonsinger, had led *Wonderful Town* three seasons earlier, it was Rex Harrison's musical debut that changed producers' perceptions about what kind of actor could front a musical. In the next fifteen years, such nonmusical actors as Richard Burton, José Ferrer, Robert Ryan, Vivien Leigh, Melina Mercouri, Katharine Hepburn, and Lauren Bacall were given starring roles in Broadway musicals. The very improbability of the Shaw source material proved more of an incentive than a warning—musical adaptations of the most unlikely properties became commonplace.

What *My Fair Lady* did most of all, perhaps, was to bring British elegance to the American musical stage for the first time in three decades; the sensible-cloth-coated Eisenhower years were temporarily transformed by a silk-clad, high society fantasy. *My Fair Lady* took its audiences—and the country—to the ball.

OPPOSITE: *As with all great Cinderellas, it's the entrance to the ball that counts. Here, Andrews stops the show dead with her glamorous entrance.*

I'VE GROWN ACCUSTOMED TO HER FACE

Words by Alan Jay Lerner
Music by Frederick Loewe
From My Fair Lady *(1956)*

HOW DO YOU WRITE A LOVE SONG that is not a love song? This was the challenge that Alan Jay Lerner faced in giving Henry Higgins his eleven o'clock number in *My Fair Lady*. It would have been completely out of character for him to admit that he was in love with Eliza (and impossible for him to tell *her*), so Lerner had to get underneath Higgins's own arrogance and denial. In this, he was inspired by the one instance of real kindness toward Eliza that exists in Shaw's original play, in the fifth act:

> HIGGINS: (*arrogant*) I can do without anybody. I have my own soul: my own spark of divine fire. But (*with sudden humility*) I shall miss you, Eliza. I have learnt something from your idiotic notions: I confess that humbly and gratefully. And I have grown accustomed to your voice and appearance. I like them, rather.
>
> LIZA: Well, you have both of them on your gramophone. . . . When you feel lonely without me, you can turn the machine on. It's got no feelings to hurt.
>
> HIGGINS: I can't turn your soul on. Leave me those feelings; and you can take away the voice and face.

The song summed up Higgins's dilemma perfectly without compromising his character, and audiences were satisfactorily moved. "I've Grown Accustomed to Her Face" went on to become a romantic standard, without ever using the word love.

I've grown accustomed to her face!
She almost makes the day begin.
I've grown accustomed to the tune
She whistles night and noon.
Her smiles. Her frowns.
Her ups, her downs,
Are second nature to me now;
Like breathing out and breathing in.
I was serenely independent and content before we met;
Surely I could always
Be that way again—and yet
I've grown accustomed to her looks;
Accustomed to her voice;
Accustomed to her face.

Harrison and Andrews perform what is, essentially, Shaw's fifth-act scene.

Marry Freddy! What an infantile idea! What a heartless, wicked, brainless thing to do! But she'll regret it! She'll regret it. It's doomed before they even take the vow!

I can see her now:
Mrs. Freddy Eynsford Hill,
In a wretched little flat above a store.
I can see her now:
Not a penny in the till,
And a bill collector beating at the door.
She'll try to teach the things I taught her,
And end up selling flow'rs instead;
Begging for her bread and water,
While her husband has his breakfast in bed!

In a year or so
When she's prematurely gray,
And the blossoms in her cheek have turned to chalk,
She'll come home and lo!
He'll have upped and run away
With a social climbing heiress from New York!
Poor Eliza!
How simply frightful!
How humiliating!
How delightful.
How poignant it will be on that inevitable night
When she hammers on my door in tears and rags.
Miserable and lonely, repentant and contrite.
Will I let her in or hurl her to the wolves?
Give her kindness, or the treatment she deserves?
Will I take her back, or throw the baggage out?

I'm a most forgiving man;
The sort who never could,
Ever would,
Take a position and staunchly never budge.
Just a most forgiving man.
But I shall never take her back,
If she were crawling on her knees.
Let her promise to atone!
Let her shiver, let her moan!
I will slam the door and let the hellcat freeze!

Marry Freddy! Ha!
But I'm so used to hear her say
Good morning every day.
Her joys, her woes,
Her highs, her lows
Are second nature to me now;
Like breathing out and breathing in.
I'm very grateful she's a woman
And so easy to forget;
Rather like a habit
One can always break—and yet
I've grown accustomed to the trace
Of something in the air;
Accustomed to her face.

LEFT: *Shaw never intended* his *hero to get in this deep.*

The Abominable Showman

DAVID MERRICK

David Merrick in his office. Perhaps the stack of scripts is a gag, or props out of The Producers; *he nearly always built the shows from scratch.*

The logistics of being a Broadway producer—and the energy required—had changed considerably by the mid-1950s. The increasing costs of musicals sometimes required a consortium of investors, who often had to be acquired through a prolonged series of "backers'" auditions. Negotiations to sell blocks of tickets to charity fund-raisers or "theater party ladies" became necessary to create a financially comfortable advance for a show. Properties had to be negotiated with film studios or literary estates, and other industries, such as recording studios and broadcasting networks, frequently had to be approached for capital, in exchange for certain residual rights. The days of the gentleman producer of the old school, whose word was his bond, who would diligently work on one project at a time, and who could capitalize a production with his own money, were over. David Merrick was definitely not of the old school; there were times when he wasn't even a gentleman.

Born David Margulois, he arrived in New York in 1940 from St. Louis, with an ambition to make a name on the Great White Way. He apprenticed with several producers and mastered the public relations game early on, but what he wanted was his own smash hit. He created it from the ground up in 1954, flying to France to option a trilogy of French films by the director Marcel Pagnol, and hiring Joshua Logan and Harold Rome to turn them into a romantic musical called *Fanny*. The show was no classic, but it was a success, attributable to Merrick's determination to get the property put on and his diabolical talent for publicity. Merrick did whatever he could to brand *Fanny* into the theatergoing consciousness. He employed skywriting planes, publicity stunts, advertisements in out-of-town and foreign newspapers, and even tried to get the U.S. Weather Bureau to rename the next oncoming hurricane "Fanny."

Only five seasons after *Fanny*, Merrick was able to open four productions in less than a month, two of which were hits. In the late 1950s and early '60s, he often had at least four plays and musicals running at the same time. As time went on, he was successful enough to invest all his own money in a show, usually a blockbuster musical, anchored by a star and a creative staff who had worked with him before (although they usually swore never to repeat the mistake). "Sometimes, I think I'm producing just for mischief," he once said, and he earned the sobriquet "The Abominable Showman" for his tendency to feud with his leads, humiliate his writers and directors into quitting, or nickel-and-dime one star's contract, while he was spending record amounts on another's. When he wanted a song cut from one of his shows, he was not above stealing the sheet music from the musicians in the orchestra pit.

Merrick knew that there was no such thing as bad publicity. He infamously publicized a flop musical called *Subways Are for Sleeping* in 1961 by treating seven average citizens to the show, each of whom had the same name as a leading Broadway critic, and writing rave reviews for them to endorse. The intended full-page ad only ran in one paper, the *Herald-Tribune*, but it engendered a tremendous amount of publicity. At the very least, Merrick understood that, as the nation's attention was turning to other sources of entertainment—widescreen movies, television, rock and roll—it would take some extraordinary efforts to put the focus back on Broadway.

ABOVE: Fanny *was Merrick's first big hit in 1954: here are Florence Henderson and William Tabbert as lovers in Marseilles.*

7 OUT OF 7 ARE ECSTATICALLY UNANIMOUS ABOUT SUBWAYS ARE FOR SLEEPING

 HOWARD TAUBMAN .... "ONE OF THE FEW GREAT MUSICAL COMEDIES OF THE LAST THIRTY YEARS, ONE OF THE BEST OF OUR TIME. It lends lustre to this or any other Broadway season."

 WALTER KERR .... "WHAT A SHOW! WHAT A HIT! WHAT A SOLID HIT! If you want to be overjoyed, spend an evening with 'Subways Are For Sleeping.' A triumph."

 JOHN CHAPMAN .... "NO DOUBT ABOUT IT. 'SUBWAYS ARE FOR SLEEPING' IS THE BEST MUSICAL OF THE CENTURY. Consider yourself lucky if you can buy or steal a ticket for 'Subways Are For Sleeping' over the next few years."

 JOHN McCLAIN .... "A FABULOUS MUSICAL. I LOVE IT. Sooner or later, every one will have to see 'Subways Are For Sleeping'."

 RICHARD WATTS .... "A KNOCKOUT, FROM START TO FINISH. THE MUSICAL YOU'VE BEEN WAITING FOR. IT DESERVES TO RUN FOR A DECADE."

 NORMAN NADEL .... "A WHOPPING HIT. RUN, DON'T WALK TO THE ST. JAMES THEATRE. It's in that rare class of great musicals. Quite simply, it has everything."

 ROBERT COLEMAN .... "A GREAT MUSICAL. ALL THE INGREDIENTS ARE THERE. As fine a piece of work as our stage can be asked to give us."

Evgs. Mon. thru Thurs. Orch. $8.60, Mezz $6.90 Bale. $3.75, 4.80, 2nd Bale. $3.60, Fri. & Sat. Evgs. Orch. $8.40, Mezz $7.50, Bale. $6.90, 5.75, 4.80, 2nd Bale. $3.60, Wed. Mat. Orch. $4.80, Mezz $4.30, Bale. $4.05, 2.60, 2nd Bale. $2.00, Sat. Mat. Orch. $5.50, Mezz $4.80, Bale. $4.30, 3.80, 2nd Bale. $3.00

MAIL ORDERS FILLED THRU JAN. 1963

ST. JAMES THEATRE 44th St., W. of B'way

LEFT: *The most infamous ad in Broadway history; it ran only once, in the* Herald-Tribune; *at the last minute, copy editors at the* Times *recognized that the critic named Richard Watts was not black and pulled it.*

"Something's coming, something good"

WEST SIDE STORY AND THE "MUSICAL SERIOUS"

In 1948, on the heels of his success choreographing George Abbott's production of *High Button Shoes*, Jerome Robbins took his first steps to becoming a director and auditioned for New York's fabled Actors Studio. It would become legendary for training a generation of performers to express a greater degree of emotional truth than the stage or film had ever seen. The studio classes, run by Robert Lewis, director Elia Kazan, and, later, Lee Strasberg, stressed personal history and the importance of dramatic intention and employed techniques such as sense memory and improvisation. If Robbins could go anywhere to learn how to direct actors it was the Studio, and among his classmates were the finest in the theater, including Marlon Brando, Julie Harris, and Karl Malden.

The story goes that classmate Montgomery Clift, having trouble with a scene from *Romeo and Juliet*, talked to Robbins about how to make Romeo more contemporary, more relevant; eventually, they discussed the ethnically polarized gangs of New York City—Italian, Irish, Catholic, Jewish. The idea stayed with Robbins and in 1949, he called composer Leonard Bernstein to see if he would be interested in writing a musical about two star-crossed lovers, just as in Shakespeare's play, only the lovers would be Catholic and Jewish, and it would take place on the Lower East Side; in fact, it would be called *East Side Story*.

Robbins and Bernstein brought in playwright Arthur Laurents to do the libretto, but the combined work schedules of the three collaborators—Bernstein touring with the Philharmonic, Laurents in Hollywood, and Robbins at the New York City Ballet—delayed any progress for nearly six years. By then, when Laurents and Bernstein met again in Hollywood, the Catholic-Jewish conflict seemed old hat. In the meantime, the papers had been filled with stories of juvenile gang warfare among the burgeoning Hispanic populations in Los Angeles and Spanish Harlem. The idea finally seemed vibrant and timely. The rival gangs would be Puerto Rican and white ethnic—Poles, Italians, Germans. Bernstein and Laurents quickly persuaded Robbins to move the setting to the West Side of Manhattan, and they were on their way.

All three collaborators wanted to push the boundaries with this project; luckily their talent kept pace with their ambition.

Lyricist Stephen Sondheim (l.) helps out composer Leonard Bernstein (r.) at the piano; Carol Lawrence (Maria) is far left.

Why do we always have to do rather cheapish stories in musical comedies? Why can't we do something where we use the best part of ourselves? Why do I have to go over to the ballet company?. . . Why did Lenny have to write a symphony? Why did Arthur have to write [a serious play]? I said why can't we put those all together into a work that we like and try our best to put our best features that we're capable of into a work?. . . So we did.

—Jerome Robbins

The team also acquired a new lyricist when Bernstein gave up the notion of writing the lyrics himself. Stephen Sondheim, who wanted to compose his own music, originally expressed interest in the project simply because he wanted to meet Leonard Bernstein. Sondheim's most recent show, *Saturday Night,* which would have been his Broadway debut, had collapsed, and his mentor, Oscar Hammerstein, convinced him that the experience would be invaluable. Working with Bernstein was certainly a challenge, especially as he still tried to keep his hand in writing lyrics of his own. Sondheim recalled:

Something's coming along (l. to r.): producers Robert Griffith and Harold Prince, director–choreographer Jerome Robbins, Sondheim, Bernstein, and other production associates.

When I would bring in lyrics to Lenny, he was always looking for poetry, he would call it—purple prose, is what he really wanted. He wrote [a lyric] of such intense poetic coloration that you couldn't believe any character in any milieu would have said it, much less the characters in our show. It went, "Once in your life, only once in your life, comes a flash of fire and light. And there stands your love, the harvest of your years." And that's the kind of thing you read in freshman English. . . . But I can understand why Lenny thought it was poetic. It's just not my idea of poetry.

As work continued through 1956, the piece developed its own style: a clear-eyed investigation into the ethnic divisions and hatred of urban gangs, rendered with a lyricism, grace, and economy that lifted the material out of any lurid sensationalism. Laurents's book even invented its own youthful slang—it sounded like the voice of untutored teenagers—never overly hip or easily dated. The dramatic intensity of the show proved to be an obstacle in getting it off the ground, however. The show's initial producer, Cheryl Crawford, one of the leading lights of the Group Theatre, found that she couldn't raise a penny—the subject matter was just too depressing for backers—so, after casting had begun, only weeks before rehearsals were to start, Crawford pulled out.

Harold Prince was in Boston, struggling with the tryouts for *New Girl in Town,* when Sondheim called him late one night. After kvetching about the problems with his own show, Prince "politely" asked Sondheim how *Gangway,* as it was still called, was going. He was shocked to hear the show was in jeopardy. Prince and his partner, Robert Griffith, came straight to New York, listened to the score (Sondheim had already played some of it for Prince), loved it, and agreed to produce it, if the creative team would only wait until *New Girl* opened. They likewise agreed, and on May 15, 1957, the show had a new set of eager producers. Robbins caused some initial difficulties, having suddenly developed cold feet. He wanted only to direct, then he agreed to choreograph as well, then he wanted an associate choreographer, then an exorbitant eight-week rehearsal period, then three rehearsal pianos. Prince listened patiently to his pleas:

> Robbins would like the opening-night reviews in his hands before he goes into rehearsal. He is gun-shy. He hates to go into rehearsal. He's the fellow standing on the edge of the precipice; you, the producer, have to push him over. . . . But when he finally goes, of course, it's galvanic.

Prince gave Robbins everything he wanted—except the pianos.

Not one moment of the unprecedented eight weeks of rehearsal was wasted. *West Side Story* called for an ensemble of young performers who could sing Bernstein's challenging score, act Laurents's tragedy convincingly, and go through the rigorous paces of Robbins's choreography. A generation later, that combination of talents would be expected of all Broadway performers, but not in 1957. To get his rival gangs up to speed, Robbins put his Actors Studio training to good use. He asked the cast to refrain from hanging out with members of the other gang: the two groups were to square off in their respective camps for breaks, meals, outside socializing. It seemed shocking and innovative at the time. Years later, cast members admitted they were simply having too much fun to obey completely; besides, some of them were dating each other.

Much more effective was Robbins's commitment to the context of the musical. He would festoon the callboard with articles about gang violence in Spanish Harlem and scrawl "This is your life!" atop the clippings. And, however severely he could treat his corps of dancers, he gave them something no other choreographer had deigned to give the chorus: individual integrity.

Nowhere was this more palpable than in the show's kinetic, tense prologue, done wordlessly to Bernstein's aggressive music with plenty of brass and percussion.

It's an entire history, a prelude to the events. It's a true prologue—a Shakespearean prologue. You know who these gangs are, you know their rivals, that's all you need to know. It's all done in a style that says, "You're going to see an evening of a kind of choreographed movement that's neither ballet or traditional musical comedy dance, but you're going to see action in movement." It was in a zone of choreographed movement that had never been done before. That was what was new about Jerry's work in *West Side Story*.

—Stephen Sondheim

West Side Story received a rapturous reception at its Washington and Philadelphia tryouts, and its opening at Broadway's Winter Garden on September 26, 1957, was treated like a Hollywood premiere. Most reviews were extremely positive, but the show's tragic plot—two deaths at the end of the first act, one at the end of the show—was off-putting to some; ticket buyers were not immediately enthusiastic, either. That year, it lost all of the major Tony Awards to another show with a dance in a gymnasium: *The Music Man,* whose homespun, heartland cornpone struck a familiar and comfortable chord with theatergoers. Robbins, at least, won a Tony for choreography. He also noted that his show had a different kind of appeal for non-Broadway types. Before rehearsals began, he

West Side Story*'s tragic ending—along with* New Girl in Town*'s seamy milieu—made audiences wonder about the future of musical comedy. "A funny thing happened to the musical the other night," wrote George Kaufman in "Musical Comedy or Musical Serious?" "It met a joke." Al Hirschfeld's accompanying illustration imagines the future of the American musical.*

The rumble: Oliver Smith was revered for his elegant, colorful set designs; here, he does an about-face with a gritty urban landscape.

visited Spanish Harlem and checked out the dancing at some of the clubs there, befriending the gang members who ran them. He eventually invited a bunch of tough characters to come downtown and see the show once it opened on Broadway. He recalled:

> They watched the show up till the end of act one, which ended with two dead bodies on stage. And they came out and said good-bye. I said, What do you mean, good-bye? They said, Well, wasn't that the end of the show? I said No, that's only the first half. Don't you

want to see what happens after that? And then strange expressions crossed their faces. Oh, there's more than just death. They didn't expect any more. There's something after, so back they went into the theater again.

West Side Story ran for nearly two years, then went on a brief national tour, and came back to Broadway for another year, totaling nearly one thousand performances. Yet it was the movie sale to United Artists, for the paltry sum of $315,000, that really secured the

OVERLEAF: *"Mambo!" Some of Bernstein's most thrilling music gave Robbins the opportunity to display the sexual and athletic prowess of the rival gangs.*

ABOVE: *Lawrence and Larry Kert (Tony) break all the boundaries of the respective enclaves.*

LEFT: *When Renaissance Verona became the Upper West Side, the lovers' balcony naturally became a fire escape. Here, Robbins directs Kert and Lawrence in the scene.*

> I remember when everybody dies at the end of *West Side Story*, and you sat there and you just couldn't believe it: they killed people in a musical. And it was so sad, 'cause they were such decent kids and you thought, "Oh my God, what is this? What can a musical do?"
> —William Goldman, Screenwriter

show's place in American culture. The 1961 film, which Robbins codirected (until he was let go for his costly perfectionism) and choreographed, went on to win a record ten Academy Awards and finally captured the imagination of the public.

Just as there had never been a show like *West Side Story* before, there would never be another one like it. There would never be a score that would lend such symphonic grace to such a sordid subject, and there would never be such dramatically

ABOVE: *Robbins teaching the mambo. Chita Rivera (Anita) is at his left.*

RIGHT: *"I Have a Love": Lawrence tries to explain to her brother's girlfriend, Anita (Chita Rivera), what happens when love comes along.*

He made us go back and make up stories about our families that belonged to the story. You felt suddenly that dancers weren't just physical, they were using their own minds, and a lot of us came out of that, thanks to Jerry, better actors, better dancers, better understanding ourselves.

—Chita Rivera, Original Cast

intentioned dancing again—skillful, perhaps, but not as dramatic. Robbins's contempt for the limits of musical comedy would inspire a new generation to vault over the chain-link fences of convention with the agility of the dynamic young gang members in *West Side Story*. For Harold Prince and Stephen Sondheim, it was the beginning of a professional relationship that would land them in the uncharted territory of a new Broadway tradition.

Finale

In late April 1959, Oscar Hammerstein went to Philadelphia at the request of Stephen Sondheim and Arthur Laurents. Their new show, *Gypsy*, starring Ethel Merman, with music by Jule Styne, was trying out there, and as always, Sondheim found his mentor's advice invaluable. After seeing the show, Hammerstein concluded that there were two problems: an errant doorknob on a first-act set, and the lack of applause for Merman at the end of her big eleven o'clock number, "Rose's Turn." The problem wasn't Merman's performance, which was glorious; the problem was that Laurents, Sondheim, Styne, and the director, Jerome Robbins, had purposely not given Merman the applause-getting "button."

At the Bucks County Farm. (l. to r.): James Hammerstein, Dorothy Hammerstein, Nedda Logan, Oscar, and the teenaged Stephen Sondheim, c. 1946.

Her character was having a nervous breakdown; to give her a conventional show biz moment would have been, in Sondheim's words, "dishonest." "Yes, it's dishonest," Hammerstein argued, "and it's the kind of dishonesty that you have to take into account in the theater, particularly the musical theater." The audience wanted to applaud, *needed* to applaud. "It's dishonest psychologically," he continued, "but there's another kind of honesty, and that has to do with theater honesty." The writers conceded Hammerstein was right, made the change, and the number brought down the house for the rest of the run. Theatrical convention could only be defied so much.

Five months later, in the middle of rehearsals for his latest musical with Richard Rodgers, *The Sound of Music*, Hammerstein was diagnosed with stomach cancer. An operation was quickly scheduled in mid-September, and Hammerstein had to miss the New Haven tryout of his new show. He caught up with it in Boston and was called on, as he had been sixteen years earlier, to write a new song—*something* about the land. "Edelweiss" poignantly described a hardy flower that flourished in the Austrian alps. It would be the last lyric he would ever write; although no one in his family could bear to tell him, his operation was not successful—Hammerstein was dying.

In July of 1960, six weeks before his death, he had a party at his New York apartment to celebrate his sixty-fifth birthday. Sondheim was among his guests, and before they went in to lunch, Hammerstein gave Sondheim a framed photographic portrait of himself. Sondheim recalled:

I said, "Would you sign it?" And he looked at me—he didn't know what he wanted to write. Everybody went in to lunch and he stood, and suddenly he got a smile on his face and he signed it. And he went in to lunch, and I looked at it, and it said "For Stevie, my friend and teacher." If you remember in *The King and I*, he talks about how by your pupils you are taught. That's what he meant, and of course it was a major moment for me, and still is. He was that kind of man.

The night Hammerstein died, the lights were turned off on London's West End, and a week later, all the lights along Broadway—from 42nd Street to 53rd Street, between Sixth and Eighth Avenues—were extinguished at 9:00 P.M., in honor of the man who lived such an exemplary life of personal and theater honesty.

In the words of his song from
Me and Juliet *(1953), to Oscar*
Hammerstein, *the theater was*

> That big black mass
> Of love and pity
> With troubles and hopes and fears,
> Will sit out there
> And rule your life
> For all your living years.

PETER STONE ON WRITING THE MUSICAL BOOK

Interview from

Broadway: The American Musical *(excerpt)*
Peter Stone (1930–2003) was the award-winning book writer for 1776, My One and Only, *and* Titanic, *among others.*

THERE WERE BOOK SHOWS in the '20s and '30s, but they were usually about wealthy people having a good time on a weekend in Connecticut and then some interloper who came into it. They had great fun with the clash of the lower classes or the middle classes and the upper classes, and they had good jokes and good dialogue. Wodehouse and Bolton were fabulous, and Herbert Fields was very, very good. However, the book had been following the score around somewhat like the elephant keeper and cleaning up after it, to make it a show. What book writers did in those days was basically to create glue between the songs, which was not always that easy, because the songwriters would write songs unfettered by any sense of plot or any sense of character development; it was up to the book writer to string the songs together.

The book show, as we know it now, never really happened until Oscar Hammerstein invented it, refined it. There were people who played with it and people who did it without realizing what they were doing, but Oscar literally invented it. It started to take form in *Show Boat;* when he got finally to *Oklahoma!*, he was dealing with a book that was quite difficult. *Green Grow the Lilacs* had some very difficult things in it. He didn't touch them very deeply—the Jud Fry aspect is very dark and very strange—but he made the *score* follow the *book* instead of the other way around. The songs had to enlighten the story. He also had to figure out what to do with the ballad in the first act. In all shows, the ballad appeared in the first act and then was reprised in the second act. But the fact is that the ballad cannot be sung until the characters know each other and the love affair begins—you cannot sing undying love to someone you've just met, which is what happened in the old days. But Oscar invented something that I've called the conditional ballad. The first one I know about was "Only Make Believe" in *Show Boat*. (Just *make believe* we're in love.) Then there is *Oklahoma!* with "People Will Say We're in Love." (We're

not, but people will *say* we're in love.) And then *Carousel* comes along with "If I Loved You." (Well, I don't, but *if* I loved you . . .) This continues all the way through "Some Enchanted Evening"—all of the love is in the future or conditional. This way, you could have a wonderful ballad in the first act.

Bookwriting is not the same as playwriting. They are obviously connected, but there are certain things that must be either developed or learned in order to write a book. When I was offered a chance to do my first musical, I went to Frank Loesser for advice—he could articulate everything. I said, "Where does a song go?" And he would say, "Well, when a character gets to a point where he can't express himself in normal language and has to use an interjection, that's where the song goes." That's why there are so many good songs that begin with interjections. "Oh, what a beautiful morning." When a character comes to a point where all he can say is, "Gosh," "Golly," "Gee," or something stronger, at that moment he becomes inarticulate with prose and has to move into something more emotional or more interesting—into lyric, into rhyme and so forth.

But the most important aspect in writing a book to a musical is to tell two hours of story in one hour. The score does not really help your story—it is not supposed to. It fills in emotional moments, comedy moments, all sorts of things, but it does not really tell the story. Some musicals do have the score advancing the story, but not by much. If a song lasts four minutes, it might do twenty seconds of story. So you have to be very, very economical and terse about it. The other thing you cannot do is fight the lyrics—you cannot tell the song before it is sung. Now, that involves a certain ego adjustment.

I am often asked if the book is written first and then the score, or the score first and then the book. Neither one of those works—you have to write them together. If you write the book first, the songwriters are going to take every one of your best moments, because that is where song goes. It is very painful and very upsetting.

Collaboration is what really differentiates bookwriting from playwriting. You have to make the collaboration work. The only collaboration a playwright has is with the director, and then through him, or her, to the actors. But in a musical you have a very, very large collaboration. The primary collaboration is the three creators—the bookwriter, the lyricist, and the composer. It could be two people in some cases—in Meredith Willson's case, one person—but it's still that collaboration between book, lyrics, and music.

When you finish that, the collaborative group starts to grow—you don't just get a director, you also get a choreographer, designers, and so forth. Loesser had a word for this. He said, "*Level* is the secret word of putting together a musical." You all have to be on the same level. It is a very hard concept to define, but the fact is, if everyone is not on the same level, regardless of the talents involved, the collaboration is never going to work.

A DISCUSSION WITH RICHARD RODGERS AND OSCAR HAMMERSTEIN II

Youth Wants to Know (excerpt),
Sunday, April 1, 1956
Moderator: Stephen McCormick

SM: You gentlemen have made many movies. I know *Oklahoma* and *Carousel* are touring the country right now and on Broadway you have *Pipe Dream* playing. Which medium do you prefer?

OH: Our principal medium is the theater and most of our movies have been adaptations of our stage plays. Although each one of us has written movies, and together we wrote *State Fair,* especially for films. I think our answer would have to be we like the theater best.

RR: I think that eventually, Broadway is more gratifying because you have a live audience and this is not simply a reproduction every night of what you once did.

SM: Why do you prefer adaptations instead of writing original musicals?

OH: You have a great head start when you start off with a group of characters and a story and know just where you are going. Obviously that gives you a great advantage because writing a musical is so much more difficult than writing a straight play. It is technically a very much more difficult thing so we welcome all the help we can get and of course I am not a bit ashamed of that because Shakespeare wasn't ashamed of doing it either. Most of the grand operas are adaptations of famous books or plays.

SM: With all your success have you ever been so discouraged with the theater that you wanted to give up?

RR: Oh no. That would be awful. You couldn't. You just couldn't.

OH: That is true of me too. And I have been tested too. I have had lots of failures but I have never felt like giving up the theater. There is a kind of inner conceit that most people have who work in the theater. They always feel that tomorrow is going to be all right and very often it is.

RR: Then there is love too. It is just like giving up food. You just don't.

SM: We all know what a great influence you have had on the theater since you have collaborated together. I was wondering, Mr. Rodgers, whether any composer influenced you greatly and Mr. Hammerstein any author.

RR: I think there are two who have had tremendous influence on my thinking musically. One is a composer of light music who happened to be a collaborator of my collaborator Mr. Kern. Jerry Kern. He influenced me tremendously when I was a child. And in so-called serious music I think Brahms. You know this is deeply sentimental and I have no reason to be ashamed of this.

OH: I was brought up and tutored by another librettist called Otto Harbach who is a couple of decades older than I but with whom I collaborated. I started to work with him when I was about twenty-three and I learned a great deal from him directly. And then of course I have been influenced by certain poets—Walt Whitman and Shakespeare although it might be very difficult for you to see any similarity in our work.

SM: Have you ever been discouraged by your parents from entering into the profession?

OH: I was, although I come from a theatrical family. No members of the family wanted me to go into the theater and yet I have encouraged all my children to go into the theater.

RR: Now my experience is exactly the opposite. My father was a doctor and wanted to do nothing but music. He loved music. My mother loved music. She was a very good pianist. When I was a baby they used to go to the operettas and bring home the scores and for weeks they would play the "Merry Widow Waltz" and the "Chocolate Soldier." They were dying to have me go into the theater and they won.

SM: We all know that an artist in order to be a success has to cater to the public taste. Have you ever had to compromise between artistic inspirations and pressures of today's entertainment?

RR: I had deep convictions about this. If you and the public have the same mind you are successful. I think it is a disaster to try to do what the public wants if you don't feel that way yourself. You are doomed or you are fixed. One way or the other. If the public doesn't understand what these eight bars mean you are dead. If they do, you are successful. And there is nothing you can do to change it.

OH: It is a coincidence. It is not deliberate. You can't deliberately say, "I will please the public although I don't like what I am doing." I don't think that is possible. I think sometimes when cheap things succeed the man who wrote them believes they are great. He doesn't think they are cheap. If he did they couldn't succeed. There must be a faith behind every work.

SM: I wonder if you ever wrote a song for a particular person that you wanted that person to sing.

OH: I did. I wrote a song for Paul Robeson and he didn't sing it. He did eventually but when we wrote *Show Boat* Jerry Kern and I we wrote "Ol' Man River" with Paul Robeson in mind. He was unavailable and was making a concert tour.

SM: Why are your productions called musical plays instead of musical comedy?

OH: In our own minds they are very definite classifications. The operetta, the musical comedy, and the musical play. I think in the operetta and the musical comedy the songs and the entertainment are uppermost and you wait in between. The dialogue scenes are the intermissions between the musical numbers and the requirements of reality are as great. In musical plays, however, we are meeting a challenge of reality in motivation and in characters and in the events of the story.

SM: The soliloquy in *Carousel* has so many beautiful themes running through it each of which could be a separate song. I was curious about how you happened to write that together.

OH: We didn't write it together. I wrote it all out first and it took me several weeks. Then I gave it to him and two hours later he called me and said, "I've got it." I could have thrown a brick through the phone.

SM: Could you play it for us?

RR: (*Rodgers at the piano*) You know we talked about "It Might As Well Be Spring" and how you make the music and the words come together. Now what is the lyric?

OH: "I'm as restless as a willow in a wind storm. I'm as jumpy as a puppet on a string."

RR: Now what do you do with a puppet on a string?

SM: You dangle it up and down?

RR: (*Playing the first part*) It is a jump. It is the hop. This is the interpretation of the words. You couldn't do this without the words.

SM: In other words the words come first?

RR: Not always. I have done a lot of these tunes first and then Oscar Hammerstein has written the words. But one must interpret the other.

SM: Do you gentlemen work separately all the time when you go to compose a song?

RR: Yes.

SM: Do you talk about things?

OH: We talk a great deal. Whether the song is going to be in a story and what it is going to do for the story. What the title might be. But then the actual lyrics or the actual music is written apart and one is worked into the other.

SM: Mr. Hammerstein, have you written any music or you, Mr. Rodgers, have you written any lyrics?

OH: I have never written any music because I know enough about music to know that I can't write it. I think I know a good tune when I hear it and I have a feeling for music but not for the creation of music. When I try to write dummy sometimes to my own words it is always I discover later stolen from somebody else. I have too many tunes of composers going around in my head.

RR: You are not being fair to yourself. You write simply terrible music. Just awful. I once made him sing some of the stuff that he makes up for dummies and it is awful. But where he is unfair is that he has the most superb sense of form that you have ever seen in your life. This is what makes it easy for me.

SM: What do you mean by form, Mr. Rodgers?

RR: The architecture of a lyric. A lyric has architecture. Great big fat architecture. It has to be built like the Lever Brothers Building. And this he knows, you see. So you get this lyric and it is laid out and it has form, it has substance, it has a foundation, it has embellishment. All the things that you need. And he hands me this. This is a great help.

SM: Has there ever been a song that you didn't particularly think would be a hit and was?

RR: Oh, I am sure yes. "Bewitched." That took ten years before it became a hit.

SM: What is your opinion of rock and roll?

RR: I love rock and roll. I am just crazy about it because I think all this racket sends people right back to Rodgers and Hart, Rodgers and Hammerstein. I think we are just cashing in on rock and roll. I hope it lasts forever. I love it.

FRANK LOESSER
1910–1969
by ABE BURROWS

Obituary from the New York Times, *August 10, 1969*

When "The Most Happy Fella" was trying out in Philadelphia, Frank asked me to come down and take a look. This was his first show since "Guys and Dolls." He had been working on it for three years. We had done "Guys and Dolls" together, but this time he was flying solo. Music, lyrics and libretto. Pretty nervous about it, too. And so was I, for him. The show was remarkable. New kind of musical? Opera? Whatever it was, it was something special. I came out of the theater in great excitement, dashed up to Frank and began chattering away about the marvelous, funny stuff. Songs like "Standing on the Corner Watching All the Girls Go By," "Abbondanza," "Big D." Suddenly he cut me off angrily. "The hell with those! We know I can do that kind of stuff. Tell me where I made you cry."

This was Frank. The public Loesser was a cerebral, tough, sharp man with wit and charm. In a working relationship, he was a demanding perfectionist with a short fuse on his temper, his anger directed against himself as much as anyone else. But all of these qualities were surface. Somewhere, buried very deep, was a gentle something that wanted to "make them cry."

Here was one of the greatest writers of musical comedy songs of all time. Yet he was never completely happy with his work or its effect on people. He kept reaching out and up in a passionate striving for something else. In his reaching he sometimes casually dismissed the value of many of the great things he had done. "Guys and Dolls" had many ballads that were lovely and moving, but most of the raves were for the comedy songs. I think this bothered him. So he proved he could do the other things in "The Most Happy Fella." I remember how it was in "How to Succeed in Business Without Really Trying." His work was brilliant, musically and lyrically. A tough, abrasive score. The satire was savage and funny. He and I got a Pulitzer for that one. But a week later, when we met at lunch to search out a new project, he was once more hunting for romance and tears. I respected him for that. That big talent had to be respected.

Frank was one of the men in the musical theater who "did it all." A man with the technique and talent to cover the whole range of what is needed to get a musical show on. Ballads, character things, group songs, comedy numbers, and anything else, including a good overture. There haven't been many men who could "do it all" and, among the few who could, Frank ranks with the greatest.

Outside of his musical and lyrical genius, the thing that placed him among the greatest was the tremendous range of his interests. He was intellectually curious, a great reader, a language buff, a skillful painter. He even made fine furniture. He knew something about everything and something from everything always found its way into his work. To cap it all, he was a man of deep emotion. In whatever he wrote, ballad, comedy or marching song, these emotions always came through.

I remember the first time we met. It was in California. He was Private Frank Loesser. This was after Pearl Harbor and he had just written "Praise the Lord and Pass the Ammunition." He was a cocky private, dressed in a tailored uniform that a general would have given four stars for. I began to tease this slick, songwriting private by improvising a few songs which kidded the maudlin sentiments of many songwriters. One of the songs I did was "I Am Strolling Down Memory Lane Without a Single Thing to Remember." This was at a party and all us were drinking. The next morning I had completely forgotten all of the lyrics. Two days later I saw Frank and he handed me a sheet of paper with all my words typed out. He encouraged me to do more. I did. We became friends and for the next almost 30 years we saw each other, helped each other, worked together, fought together. And now . . .

1943–1959

CHAPTER FIVE

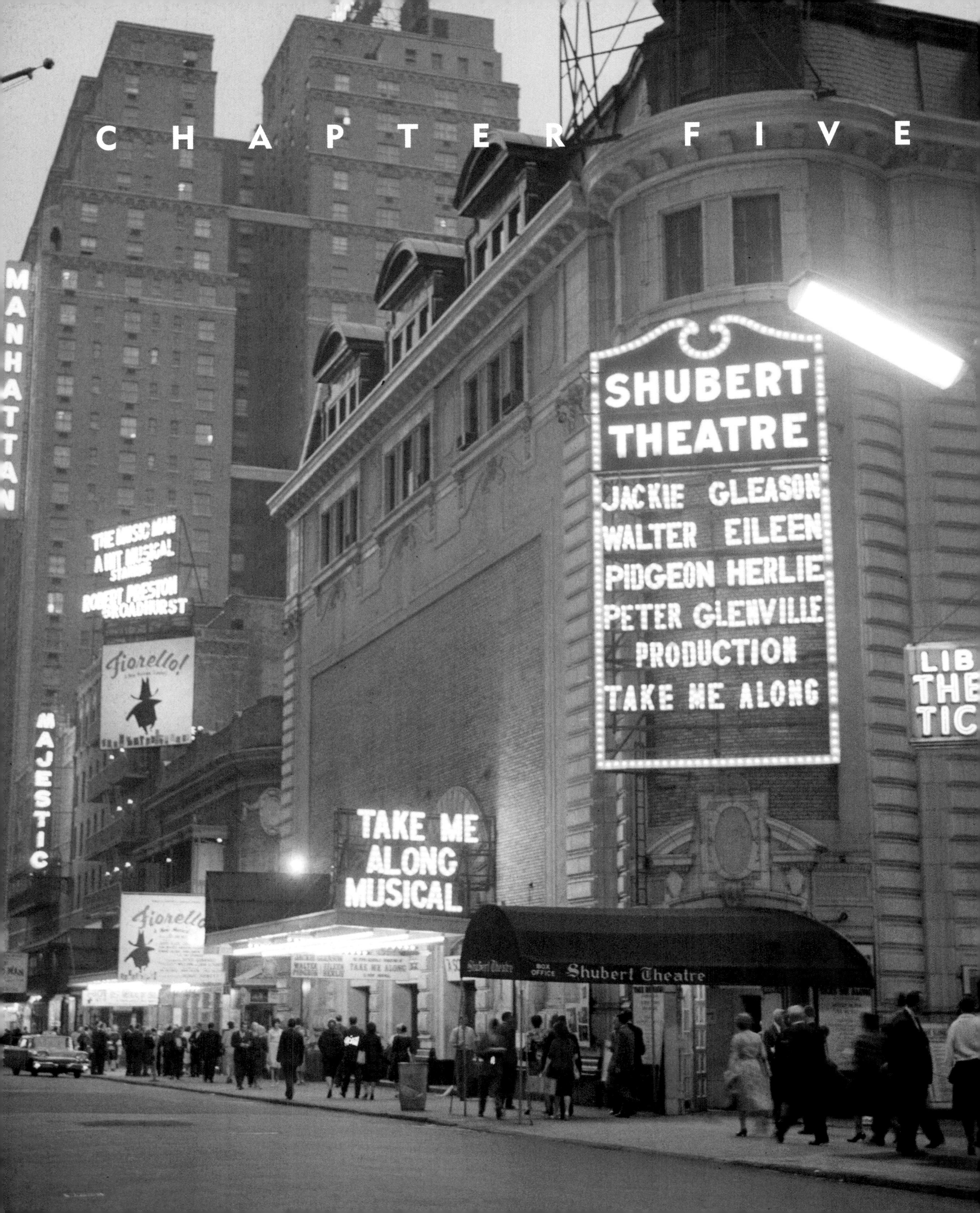

TRADITION
(1 9 6 0 – 1 9 7 9)

Overture

And I'd like to have you know
What the show is all about.
With the title *Mr. President,*
You've wondered, no doubt,
Just who it can be.
Don't jump to conclusions—
It's not who you think. . . .
Not the Roosevelts,
Not the Trumans,
Not the Eisenhowers, no—
This is not that kinda show.
Not the Kennedys,
No, not the Kennedys,
Just a family of four,
So it couldn't be the Kennedys—
With the Kennedys
There'd have to be more than four.

Irving Berlin, "Opening," *Mr. President* (1962)

It was the most glamorous opening night in the theater that Washington had ever seen. Irving Berlin had "resigned from his retirement" and bounced back to write his first new musical in twelve years, *Mr. President,* a backstage look at the White House with an attractive but fictional president and First Lady at its center. After a disastrous preview period in Boston, Berlin hoped to repair the show and its reputation by opening at the National Theatre in the capital on September 25, 1962. Luckily for Berlin (and Leland Hayward, the show's producer), the Kennedys—the attractive but real president and First Lady—were charmed by the idea of a Broadway musical even slightly suggested by their personas. They not only agreed to attend the premiere, but decided to buy out the National and use *Mr. President* as a charity fund-raiser. The cream of Washington society turned out; most of the audience was happy enough to be attending an Irving Berlin premiere, but everyone was especially hoping to catch a glimpse of the actual Mr. President, sitting in a favored rocking chair, in his box with Mrs. Kennedy.

Alas, that would only be the beginning of their disappointments that night. Although the curtain was held for some time, Kennedy did not join his wife until well into the second act; he had been preoccupied with watching the Floyd Patterson–Sonny Liston prize-fight on the television back home. The Kennedys even left before the final curtain (although they did appear at the post-show reception at the British Embassy). The production itself was little consolation to the crowd. Howard Lindsay and Russel Crouse had cooked up a toothless book, neither satirical nor perceptive, and Berlin's score, with its sentimental ballads and gung-ho final curtain flag-waver ("This Is a Great Country") seemed anemic and out of touch. Berlin and his collaborators had banked on the reflected glory of the Kennedys to give their show some punch, but *Mr. President* felt instead like it was about the Eisenhowers, only duller.

The show dragged its weary bones to Broadway's St. James Theatre in October. Berlin hoped that the New York crowd might receive him with more open arms; the show already had a $2,650,000 advance (the largest in Broadway history up to that time) so he figured the worst that could happen was a two-year run. Unfortunately, New York was just as underwhelmed as Boston and Washington, and when the advance ran out eight months later, the show closed. Irving Berlin, now three quarters of a century old, had to look obsolescence square in the face. "You can't sell patriotism unless the people feel patriotic," he said.

Perhaps it was a blessing that *Mr. President* closed during the dog days of summer 1963. Its genial enthusiasm for a good-looking president and his glamorous wife would have been horrifyingly inappropriate by the end of November.

A week after President Kennedy's assassination, *Life* magazine managed an interview with his widow in Hyannis Port, in which Jacqueline Kennedy told the reporter, Theodore H. White:

> When Jack quoted something, it was usually classical, but I'm so ashamed of myself—all I keep thinking of is this line from a musical comedy. At night, before we'd go to sleep, Jack liked to play some records; and the song he loved most came at the very end of this record. The lines he loved to hear were: "Don't let it be forgot, that once there was a spot, for one brief shining moment, that was known as Camelot."

When lyricist Alan Jay Lerner read the interview, he practically blacked out. He had known Kennedy since they attended private school together and had even produced one of Kennedy's presidential birthday parties, but he had never heard about the president's affection for *Camelot,* the musical Lerner wrote with Frederick Loewe in 1960. The show had been dogged by criticisms that it was not as good as *My Fair Lady,* and it did suffer

from structural problems, but it was continuing to tour around the country at the end of 1963. This heartbreaking information about Kennedy's interest in the show and his favorite lines from the final scene was to change the complexion of *Camelot* forever. Lerner said it best in his memoirs: "From that moment on, the first act became the weak act and the second act, the strong one. God knows I would have preferred that history had not become my collaborator."

Trouper of troupers Nanette Fabray kicks off her shoes and kicks up her heels as the First Lady in Mr. President; *Robert Ryan comports himself with dignity in his only starring musical role.*

New York Times *advertisement for* Mame *and* Sweet Charity, *1966.*

The spirit of the traditional American musical in the early 1960s could be quickly captured by turning to the second page of the Sunday "Arts and Leisure" section of the *New York Times.* This was where a new musical announced itself to the world, in a full-page advertisement with an amusing or striking graphic; the names of the stars emblazoned over the logo; often the familiar name of a reliable producer toward the top; a score by the new generation of Broadway songwriters; perhaps a tag line that read "Based on the novel by" or "Adapted from the film"; or even the logo of the record company that would release the original cast album. The most exciting line of text, however, was reserved for the banner stretching across the entire ad: "Mail Orders Accepted Now!"

By the time the 1970s ended, however, that tradition, like so much else in America, had been stretched nearly to the breaking point. Ads for new musicals were still placed in the Sunday *Times,* but as time went on there would be fewer of them. Sometimes the reader already knew about the show; it might have had a successful run in London's West End or transferred from a small Off Broadway venue. But the stars were less recognizable, the names of the producers were often either unfamiliar or part of a list containing a dozen names, the songwriters might be obscure or from the world of rock. Even the mail-order address had given way to a phone number, the mention of credit cards, or a strange new method called "Tele-Charge."

At the beginning of the 1960s, a perceptible changing of the guard was taking place. Oscar Hammerstein had died in 1960, Cole Porter would pass away in 1964, and Frank Loesser followed in 1969. The Lerner and Loewe stage partnership essentially ended in 1960 with *Camelot.* These giants gave way to new hit-making songwriters, like Jerry Herman, Charles Strouse and Lee Adams, Jerry Bock and Sheldon Harnick, John Kander and Fred Ebb, Cy Coleman, and Stephen Sondheim. This new era yielded many satisfying traditional shows and a decent amount of good fun on the musical stage.

The success of *My Fair Lady* in 1956 ushered in an era of adaptations. Producers and writers turned into tomb raiders, ransacking every conceivable topic or classic for a musical libretto. Literary characters such as Oliver Twist, Elmer Gantry, Sherlock Holmes, Superman, Billy Budd, Don Quixote, Cyrano de Bergerac, Auntie Mame, Zorba the Greek, and Snoopy were given musical vehicles, as were such historical personages as Caesar and Cleopatra, Henry VIII, Ben Franklin (twice), Thomas Jefferson (twice), Fiorello La Guardia, Coco Chanel, Anastasia, Joan of Arc, and Mata Hari—not to mention the less recognizable sources that provided fodder for the musical stage.

The economic realities of the Broadway musical could no longer be ignored. There were warning signs in the mid-'60s when shows such as *High Spirits* and *Golden Boy,* with great reviews and respectable runs, just missed edging into the black-ink column. Musicals had gotten larger and more costly to produce (about $500,000 by 1965), and they took longer to recoup ("A musical has to run six months at absolute capacity to break even, and how many musicals have done that?" moaned one investor in 1968). Despite a rise in ticket prices that outpaced inflation—in 1960, you could get an excellent orchestra seat on a Saturday night for a Broadway musical hit for less than $10; by 1975, it might cost you $17.50; by 1981, it would be $40—only one out of five musicals was a hit. When the Harold Prince/Stephen Sondheim musical *Follies* closed in July 1972, it had lost $685,000 of its $800,000 investment, despite a run of a year and a half. When *Seesaw*, an infinitely less inspired musical, closed in December 1973 after ten months, its loss was $1.25 million.

Broadway made some attempts to lure customers back by adopting some of the marketing techniques and consumer inducements available elsewhere—television commercials, promotional packages, the ability to purchase tickets with a credit card—but they were late in coming.

As the 1960s wore on, it became increasingly clear that the events that riveted the country—the Vietnam War, civil rights, the generation gap, the sexual revolution, drug use, political corruption—were nearly impossible to find on a musical stage, or when they were, they were often simply the butt of cheap jokes. Ironically, it was during this period that Hollywood finally cast off its self-imposed Production Code, and one by one, films such as *The Pawnbroker*, *Who's Afraid of Virginia Woolf*, *Bonnie and Clyde*, and *The Graduate*, with adult language and themes, not to mention sex and violence, appeared. By the beginning of the 1970s, films, not plays and certainly not musicals, were speaking most incisively and provocatively to the American public. As Broadway's once relevant storytelling tradition crumbled, other traditions stepped forward to take its place, but things were falling apart faster than they could be reinvented. No fiddler on any roof found himself in a shakier position than the Broadway musical by the close of the 1970s.

Broadway in the late 1960s: blockbuster Hollywood musicals—one original, Goodbye, Mr. Chips; *one adaptation,* Oliver!—*are the latest bill of fare.*

"Everything's coming up roses"

GYPSY

Just before the decade began, one show ushered in the '60s with the perfect culmination of star power, integrated score, and narrative skill pioneered in the Golden Age. Three different show biz traditions collided in *Gypsy*: vaudeville, musical comedy, and the integrated musical. But what could have been a train wreck produced instead a creative detonation of atomic proportions. Producer David Merrick had optioned the stage rights to stripper Gypsy Rose Lee's memoirs about her early days in vaudeville and saw the property as a perfect vehicle for the embodiment of musical comedy, Ethel Merman, as Lee's maniacal stage mother, Rose. For the creative team, Merrick and coproducer Leland Hayward brought in the golden boys of the integrated musical: Jerome Robbins to direct, Arthur Laurents to transform the memoirs into a libretto, and (at Laurents's suggestion) Stephen Sondheim to write the score.

Merman was thrilled by the idea. She wanted material that would allow her to *act:* "Nobody's ever given me the chance before," she claimed. She was less enthusiastic about the composer. Her most recent show was a rare flop, written by an inexperienced songwriting team, and she didn't want to go with Sondheim, who hadn't yet composed the music to one song that had made it to Broadway. He wasn't thrilled with the prospect of only writing the lyrics for a show, either, but Oscar Hammerstein persuaded him to take that job, noting that writing for a star such as Merman would be an education in itself. Sondheim agreed and Jule Styne was brought in to supply the music.

Styne had far more in common with Merman than his other colleagues did. He was four years older than she, born in London and transplanted to Chicago at a young age. A child prodigy at the piano, Styne forswore his classical calling to run a Chicago dance band in the 1930s and wended his way to Hollywood, where he became a house composer for Twentieth Century–Fox. Styne churned out a number of hits during and following the Second World War, including (with lyricist Sammy Cahn) "I'll Walk Alone," "Let It Snow!," and "Three Coins in the Fountain." He made his Broadway debut in 1947 with *High Button Shoes* (again with Cahn as lyricist) and went on to become one of the most prolific composers of the postwar era, penning such hits as *Peter Pan* and *Bells Are Ringing*. At times, it seemed like Styne's personality, in addition to his career, was straight out of a Hollywood movie about Broadway: a cigar-chomping sparkplug of a man, he possessed a bottomless trunk of songs—if someone didn't like a melody, back it went into the trunk, so fast it made your head spin, and Styne would pull out another tune on the spot.

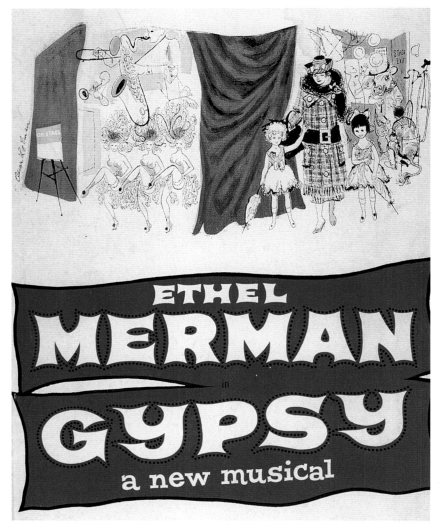

Poster for Gypsy, *1959.*

Ethel Merman as Momma Rose tries to sell her kiddie vaudeville act to the reluctant Uncle Jocko.

Composer Jule Styne, happily sandwiched between two Annie Oakleys: Ethel Merman (l.) and the movie's Betty Hutton.

The way some people sweat, that's the way melody poured out of Jule. He was the most enthusiastic person I've ever encountered. Very natty, he was. He was always in debt, a real gambler. He came into my house one night, rang the bell, came in, slammed the door. He said, "They're after me. They wanna break my legs. Got twenty thousand?"
—Arthur Laurents

From the moment the brassiest of trumpets ever heard in a Broadway musical pealed out in the thrilling overture, *Gypsy* announced itself as something different: it was razzmatazz for the Method-acting crowd. Although Gypsy Rose Lee's highly embroidered memoirs were about her own career, the musical shifted the focus of the story so that it became that rare show biz bio about the person who *doesn't* make it to the top, Lee's obsessive mother, Rose, a character the critic Walter Kerr called "the very mastodon of stage mothers." Even Merman's entrance was different for her: "stalking down the aisle . . . carrying my dog, and looking most unattractive as I interrupted [her young daughter's audition for a children's vaudeville spot], shouting 'Sing out, Louise!'" as she recalled. "It was new and it was terrific and it immediately told you what kind of person Momma Rose was."

Jerome Robbins had worked theatrical magic conjuring up, first, the tawdry onstage world of small-time vaudeville, and then its backstage world, which was even tawdrier. And yet it was entertaining, even elegant, thanks mainly to Laurents's incomparable libretto, which focused the drama on the universal need for recognition. Despite reports of disagreements, Merman took to Robbins: "I called him 'Teacher'. . . I'd never been presented to better advantage. I loved working with him."

The score was one of Broadway's snappiest and most sophisticated. Styne and Sondheim made an odd couple as collaborators, but the younger man brought out some real depth in Styne, who returned the favor by giving Sondheim the most accessible melodies of his career. They created a bone-chilling moment at the end of act one, when Rose's younger daughter quits the children's vaudeville act and she transfers her affections—and her obsessions—onto her older daughter. The song, "Everything's Coming Up Roses," with Merman's powerhouse delivery, captured the terrifying depths of Rose's ambition and introduced a phrase that passed into the English language.

The show opened at the end of the 1958–59 season, received some of the best reviews of the decade, ran 702 performances, and became a Broadway classic, with four subsequent revivals starring, respectively, Angela Lansbury, Tyne Daly, Bernadette Peters, and Patti LuPone. However, at Tony Awards time, the show was left out in the cold, losing every one of its nine nominations. Even Merman, in the role of a lifetime, lost out to her chum Mary Martin, who was playing the novitiate-turned-folksinger in *The Sound of Music*. Here, too, Merman revealed her inimitable common sense; when someone offered her sympathy, she shot back, "How are you going to buck a nun?"

Amigos—together. Sandra Church, Merman, and Jack Klugman as her long-suffering beau decide to stick it out in their quest for the Big Time.

"And we'll have a real good time, yes sir!"
Sandra Church as Gypsy Rose Lee, the butterfly
sprung from the cocoon at the end of Gypsy.

The real Gypsy Rose Lee attends rehearsal with
Church and Merman.

I think Gypsy Rose Lee was allergic to the
truth. I would go see her and say, "Tell me
something: Where did you get the name?"
She said, "Oh, honey, I've had fourteen
versions of it. Yours will probably be better."
All she cared was that it was called *Gypsy;*
that was in the contract. She once said to
me about the last scene between mother
and daughter, "Don't you think I'm a little
too tough there?" I said no. She said "Okay."
She was charming, but the relationship to
real life is problematical.

—Arthur Laurents

WORDS AND

ROSE'S TURN

Words by Stephen Sondheim
Music by Jule Styne
From Gypsy *(1959)*

THE TERM "ELEVEN O'CLOCK NUMBER" was coined during the decades when the curtain went up at 8:30. (Nowadays, any number beginning at eleven would run into expensive overtime.) Nevertheless, over time it has come to refer to the song toward the end of the show in which the leading character would sing his or her heart out, choosing which fork in the road to follow, or letting the audience discover the character's secret dreams.

In *Gypsy,* the audience knew the leading character's secret dreams all along; Momma Rose has always wanted to be a star and she has transferred those dreams to her two daughters. But after she is rejected by her older daughter when she herself becomes a star, Rose has a turn of her own (*turn* having a double meaning: a chance and a solo spot in vaudeville). Sondheim and director Jerome Robbins cobbled the number together late one night in their rehearsal hall on the roof of the New Amsterdam, home to Ziegfeld's *Frolics* in the 1910s. Robbins wanted a nightmare ballet, but there wasn't enough time to create one, so Sondheim improvised at the piano, using themes that appeared earlier in the show, and submitted the song to Jule Styne for his approval the next morning; it was given enthusiastically.

The next person who had to approve was Ethel Merman. The story goes that she seemed pleased after Styne and Sondheim played the number for her in the rehearsal room, but she didn't know quite what to do with one part of the song, where she stutters and stumbles on the word *momma.* Was she able to come in on the downbeat or the upbeat? Sondheim replied that "she could come in whenever she felt like it because the orchestra would continue the vamp underneath until she felt the moment." She then nodded sagely and said, "Yeah, but do I come in on the upbeat or the downbeat?" "Rose's Turn" became the most dramatic moment of Merman's career and the eleven o'clock number by which all Roses—and all eleven o'clock numbers—are measured.

Here she is, boys!
Here she is, world!
Here's Rose!

Curtain up!
Light the lights!
Play it, boys!

You either got it,
Or you ain't—
And, boys, I got it!
You like it?
Well, I got it!

Some people got it
And make it pay,
Some people can't even
Give it away.
This people's got it

When Louise becomes a star as Gypsy Rose Lee, her mother's job will be over.

And this people's spreadin' it around.
You either have it
Or you've had it!

Hello, everybody! My name is Rose! What's yours?
How d'ya like them egg rolls, Mr. Goldstone?

Hold your hats,
And hallelujah,
Momma's gonna show it to ya!
Ready or not, here comes Momma!

Momma's talkin' loud,
Momma's doin' fine,
Momma's gettin' hot,
Momma's goin' strong,
Momma's movin' on,
Momma's all alone,
Momma doesn't care,
Momma's lettin' loose,
Momma's got the stuff,
Momma's lettin' go,
Momma—
Momma's—
Momma's got the stuff,
Momma's got to move,
Momma's got to go—
Momma—
Momma's—
Momma's gotta let go!
Why did I do it?
What did it get me?
Scrapbooks full of me in the background.
Give 'em love and what does it get you?
What does it get you?
One quick look as each of 'em leaves you.
All your life and what does it get you?
Thanks a lot—and out with the garbage.
They take bows and you're battin' zero.
I had a dream—
I dreamed it for you,
June,
It wasn't for me, Herbie.
And if it wasn't for me
Then where would you be,
Miss Gypsy Rose Lee!

Well, someone tell me, when is it my turn?
Don't I get a dream for myself?
Startin' now it's gonna be my turn!
Gangway, world,
Get offa my runway!
Startin' now I bat a thousand!
This time, boys, I'm takin' the bows and
Everything's coming up Rose—
Everything's coming up Roses—
Everything's coming up Roses
This time for me!
For me—
For me—
For me—
For me—
FOR ME!

*Not by a long shot:
Merman's gonna let go!*

"I ain't bowin' down no more"
GOLDEN BOY AND THE CIVIL RIGHTS ERA

Richard Rodgers's first show as composer and lyricist, No Strings *(1962), allowed for Diahann Carroll and Richard Kiley to begin an interracial romance.*

Throughout the country in the 1960s, the issues of civil rights—of voter rights and registration for blacks, of integration, of fairness and equality in the workplace—were in the news and on television on a near-daily basis, but on Broadway they were virtually absent. Miscegenation, such a seismic event in the middle of *Show Boat* in 1927, made a tentative reappearance on the Broadway musical stage as the '60s began. Richard Adler's *Kwamina*, which took place in Africa, had a black doctor in an unconsummated love affair with a white Englishwoman. It was a quick failure in 1961. The next year, Richard Rodgers produced his first musical since the death of Oscar Hammerstein, an original piece entitled *No Strings*, for which he would write both the lyrics and music. Set in contemporary Paris, *No Strings* was about a love affair between two expatriate Americans, a writer, played by Richard Kiley, and a fashion model, played by Diahann Carroll, an exquisite and talented black actress and singer who had made her Broadway debut at the age of nineteen in 1954. Although the interracial aspect of the romance was apparent to anyone who was watching the show, it was never mentioned specifically in the script; Rodgers had Carroll's character refer to her growing up, not in Harlem, but euphemistically "up north of Central Park." A show that looked to be socially progressive appeared, upon reflection, to be finicky at best, cowardly at worst.

Producer Hillard Elkins had an obsession with signing Sammy Davis Jr. to a Broadway contract. Davis, one of the biggest nightclub and concert attractions of the 1950s and '60s, had starred in a Broadway musical in 1956, a semi-revue called *Mr. Wonderful* about a talented, young, black nightclub singer, dancer, and impressionist. It was not a stretch. Elkins caught up with Davis in London and dangled before him the prospect of playing the lead in a musical based on Clifford Odets's 1937 play *Golden Boy*, one of the Depression's great dramas, about a boxer who in his quest for glory loses his soul—and his life. It would be a serious musical, and in signing Davis, Elkins was determined that the book would not only be updated, but would reflect the struggles of an ambitious young black man in America. The songwriting team of Charles Strouse and Lee Adams was engaged, and Odets himself came out of semiretirement to adapt the book.

As *Golden Boy* moved toward its 1964 opening, the project was shaped to accommodate its star and, more compellingly, its times. Davis's character was originally named Joe Bonaparte, the son of poor Italian American immigrants, with a disapproving brother who works as a labor organizer; here, he is cleverly renamed Joe Wellington, a Harlem resident, whose brother now works as a civil rights organizer. Strouse and Adams provided a score that banked heavily and effectively on urban jazz. One of Davis's nine numbers (nine numbers, plus a prizefight at the show's climax, is an unfathomably large load for a performer—even Davis) has him returning as a success to his old neighborhood. In a funky gospel number, Davis and his cohorts mock both white attitudes and George M. Cohan:

> Don't forget One Hundred and Twenty-seventh Street—
> Don't forget your happy Harlem home!
> Don't forget One Hundred and Twenty-seventh Street—
> No, siree! There's no slum like your own! . . .

> Don't forget the cultural life on this here street—
> Richer than the outside world suspects!
> Hark! the cheerful patter of all the junkies' feet—
> And the soothing tones of Malcolm X!

It was undoubtedly the first time a Broadway audience had heard Malcolm X mentioned in a musical; it was also the first time an audience was confronted with anger, real anger, in a musical for a long time. The social and political frustration in *Golden Boy*—its hero asks "Who do you fight / When you want to break out / But your skin is your cage?"—was undeniable.

There were moments when that anger spilled over into the audience. In the original, Joe has a doomed love affair with the self-effacing mistress of his manager. In 1964, the woman was still the mistress of the manager, still had low self-esteem, but now her lover was black. This was a complicated image for the show, exploited in the original logo, which featured two black arms embracing a white woman, and made more resonant by the fact that, as everybody knew, Davis had a Swedish wife offstage. The kiss between Joe and Lorna in act two set off shockwaves during the show's tryouts. In Detroit, the entire balcony erupted, the police had to be called in, and the cast was escorted out of the theater.

Although its tryouts were troubled by other creative issues (Odets died suddenly and playwright William Gibson stepped in; the original director was fired), *Golden Boy* eventually opened as a slick, stark, well-intentioned piece of Broadway craftsmanship, with a knockout performance by Davis at its center. Despite its socially conscious message, the show also wowed audiences with its sheer performance quality, and Elkins insulated Davis and the company from the various death threats and other hostilities leveled against them. Soon after the opening, Martin Luther King Jr. came to see *Golden Boy*. He admired its message, particularly a number called "No More." As the civil rights movement gathered steam, Davis and Elkins canceled the show one night in March 1965 to allow Davis to perform in Montgomery, Alabama, at a "Stars for Freedom" rally in

Sammy Davis Jr. and Paula Wayne in a backstage moment from Golden Boy, *1964.*

SAMMY DAVIS
IN THE NEW MUSICAL
GOLDEN BOY

Photo by Milton Greene

support of the voting-rights marchers. When King was assassinated in April 1968, Davis was still playing Joe Wellington, during its post-Broadway engagement in Chicago. The words of the song that King so admired resounded harshly; it would be more than a decade before Broadway would support African American voices again in quite the same way:

> Well, you had your way!
> No more!
> Well, it ain't your day
> No more!
> Well, I'm standing up,
> I ain't on the floor.
> I ain't bowin' down
> No more!

ABOVE: *Despite a grueling role—and constant other gigs in nightclubs and concerts while in rehearsals—Davis was a consummate professional. Here, he clowns with producer Hillard Elkins as composer Charles Strouse looks on.*

"*Oh, Lorna—why couldn't you love me right?*" Paula Wayne as Lorna Moon and Davis as Joe Wellington, in one of the American musical's most tormented romances.

Some of the show's most telling lines were ad-libbed by Sammy Davis, who hauled me out of more than one pitfall: he said to me one night, "I leave you with two words," and paused for me to guess what they were, but I was wrong as well as indelicate, for he then divulged them: "Write colored."
                    —William Gibson, Colibrettist

OPPOSITE: *Davis and Johnny Brown stop the show with "Don't Forget 127th Street," a deeply ironic hymn to Harlem:*

"H—is for heroin they sell here;
A—is for the alleys where kids play.
R—is for the rats that run pell mell here
L—is for the landlords far away
E—is for the endless clean-up projects, and
M—is for the moldy rooms above—
Put them all together, they spell
H–A–R–L–E–M
The place that white folks think we love!"

"*You may ask, how did this tradition get started?*"

FIDDLER ON THE ROOF

"Too Jewish" is an odd criticism for a musical. Jewish songwriters and performers have been the backbone of the American musical since Irving Berlin arrived in this country in 1893. William Goldman, in *The Season,* his seminal book about Broadway theater in the mid-1960s, reasoned that if the attendance of Jews at Broadway shows were based simply on their presence in the population of the tri-state area, it would be 25 percent, but a conservative guess based on reality, he suggested, was more like 50 percent. Although many musicals have a Jewish sensibility, or at least a New York ethnic sensibility, very few musicals had ever dealt with specifically Jewish stories, certainly not since the late 1930s. *Fiorello!* (1959) had a few scenes among Yiddish-speaking garment workers (La Guardia himself was half-Jewish), and in 1961, Jerry Herman set his Broadway debut, *Milk and Honey,* in Israel. But that was about it.

That's what made *Fiddler on the Roof* such a winning improbability. The idea originated with the composer-lyricist team of Jerry Bock and Sheldon Harnick, along with Joseph Stein, who had written the book for their first collaboration, *The Body Beautiful,* in 1958. The broad range of settings for the many adaptations so prevalent in the late 1950s and 1960s proved to be bread and butter for Bock and Harnick. Bock could write a score that reflected the teeming ethnic world of Lower Manhattan in the 1910s (*Fiorello!*) or the Gilded Age rambunctiousness of the *Tenderloin* (1960) or czardas-shaded romances of Budapest in the 1930s (*She Loves Me,* 1963) but still sounded like melodious, charming Broadway theater music. Bock had gotten his start writing songs for television shows and revues, and Harnick came to New York from Chicago in the early '50s to write songs for revues such as *New Faces of 1952.* Harnick had the puckish humor of Yip Harburg and the love for words of a Larry Hart, and he had a particular gift for turning a lyric around in the last line to give the whole song a new meaning.

In 1960, Bock, Harnick, and Stein turned to a series of short stories by Yiddish writer Sholom Aleichem about Tevye, a garrulous Jewish dairyman in a Russian shtetl at the turn of the twentieth century. Tevye's struggle to survive, along with the conflicts involving his eight daughters and his argumentative relationship with the Almighty, seemed like fertile musical material.

Scenic designer Boris Aronson naturally inclined toward his fellow Russian Jewish émigré, painter Marc Chagall, for his Fiddler *designs.*

We felt that the material might be very special; we thought, "This will be a labor of love, and if we do our job right, maybe it will run a season, maybe."
—Sheldon Harnick

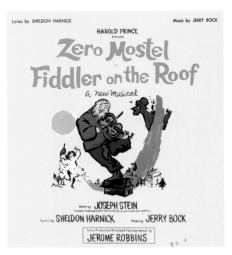

Chagall even found his way to the show's graphic: a Main Stem homage to his painting "The Green Violinist."

The three men brought the material to Harold Prince, who was just beginning his directing career; he realized that he just didn't connect to Russian Jewish peasant life, but he knew someone who did: Jerome Robbins.

Robbins's Judaism was very important to him as an individual and an artist. As a child, he had gone to Poland to see the shtetl his ancestors had come from (Robbins's family name was Rabinowitz), but it had been eradicated by the Nazis. The idea of rediscovering the world of his fathers (particularly his own father—Robbins had been trying most of his adult life to achieve a rapprochement with him) appealed to him enormously. He would need his customary eight weeks of rehearsal to choreograph and direct, and Prince, as producer, gave them to him. Many different character actors were considered for the pivotal role of Tevye, but it became clear that whoever played him had to be Jewish and, Robbins thought, larger than life. The logical choice was Zero Mostel. Mostel, an uncontainable spirit, was known to be tough on directors and Robbins was known to be tough on actors. Worse, Robbins had been a friendly witness before the House Un-American Activities Committee in 1953, naming names, including that of comedian Jack Gilford and his wife—both friends of Mostel, who had suffered under the blacklist himself. Luckily, Robbins and Mostel had already confronted each other, when Robbins was called in to doctor *A Funny Thing Happened on the Way to the Forum*, which starred Mostel in 1962. "You're not asking me to have lunch with him?" Mostel responded when he heard Robbins was called in. Each knew how to engage the best parts of the other professionally. Mostel was signed to a nine-month contract to play Tevye. Now all they needed to do was raise the $375,000 capitalization. As Tevye himself might say, it isn't easy. Sheldon Harnick recalled:

> We did many backers' auditions for the women who sell theater parties, and many of them were Jewish because they represented Jewish groups who, thank God, are wonderful theatergoers, very interested in the theater. And they were perhaps even more sensitive than non-Jews would be to the fact that this was a show about Jewish persecution and about Jews generally. So I would explain what the book was in brief, and Jerry Bock and I would then sing maybe three quarters of the score. Then after we did that, Harold Prince would get up and he would address the audience a little frantically, because the audience had just heard that there's a pogrom that ends act one, and act two ends with everybody being exiled, so Harold would get up and say, "You know, there's gonna be a lotta humor in this show, too, and we're gonna have Zero Mostel," and he would really have to try and sell the notion that it wasn't just going to be a Jewish tragedy.

Once rehearsals began in June 1964, Robbins was in his element. He had researched the vanished world of Russian Jews with an obsessive drive. He organized improvisations in rehearsals around contemporary civil rights issues. He encouraged the talented cast of mature actors to create specific, deeply drawn characters, without resorting to cliché. Most of all, Robbins knew that, in Oscar Hammerstein's dictum, the first ten minutes of a show have to spell out for the audience what the focus of the evening is going to be. *Fiddler's*

ABOVE: *"Be happy, be healthy—long life."* Here, Zero Mostel's Tevye toasts *"L'Chaim"* to his daughter's marriage to the butcher, Lazar Wolf (Michael Granger).

BELOW: *"It's a perfect match!"* Fiddler's creative team (l. to r.): lyricist Sheldon Harnick, book writer Joseph Stein, composer Jerry Bock, and director–choreographer Robbins.

problem was compounded by the fact that the opening also had to introduce the audience to an esoteric and vanished way of life. Robbins constantly hectored his writing team for an opening theme; Bock, Harnick, and Stein kept telling Robbins what *happened* in the course of the show, but he really wanted to know what the show was *about*. Finally someone replied that it was about the changing of a way of life, a set of traditions. That got Robbins excited, according to Harnick; he answered, "That's right. The opening number has to be a tapestry against which the whole rest of the show will play." The team created one of the strongest openings any musical had ever seen. "Tradition" had Tevye introducing "our little village of Anatevka" to the audience: its families, its rituals, the ancient mysteries of its traditions. Robbins physicalized the show's theme by constructing the number around a circle, the oldest of folk images, with the villagers dancing in the circle; at the poignant finale, as the villagers are dispossessed, the circle disintegrates and everyone goes off in their own direction.

During the out-of-town tryouts, the team was still concerned that audiences would find the material "too Jewish," a comment that had dogged them frequently. But something miraculous happened after the show opened at the Imperial Theatre on September 22. The specificity with which the creative team went about reproducing the life of an inconsequential Jewish village halfway around the world in 1905 revealed something deeper about the culture of their own time. Although Stein had been scrupulous about excising any Yiddish phrases that might serve to pander to (or alienate) the audience, Bock had written many of his evocative melodies with certain Hebraic harmonies (which were brought to life by Don Walker's klezmer-accented orchestrations), and Robbins had stayed true to the folk character of the dances. Audiences, Jewish and otherwise, flocked to the show in record numbers: *Fiddler* went on to have the longest run of its time, the first musical ever to run more than 3,000 performances, ending with 3,242. It was a success around the world—London, Paris, Warsaw, Tel Aviv, and Vienna, a city that had more than a passing acquaintance with anti-Semitism. It was even a huge hit in Tokyo, where a young Japanese man told Joseph Stein that he couldn't believe it was a hit in America, because it "was so Japanese"; indeed, *Fiddler* shared much of the ethos of the traditional familial structure in Japan. Even when other actors replaced Mostel during the run, the show's basic story still touched audiences.

ABOVE: *"Without our traditions, our lives would be as shaky as—as a fiddler on the roof!" Mostel leads the villagers of Anatevka in one of the greatest opening numbers in history.*

RIGHT: Fiddler*'s transcendent family saga made it a hit in the most unlikely of places: the Japanese equivalent to Hirschfeld captures the Tokyo production in 1966.*

Although the term *generation gap* wasn't coined until 1967, the increasing disparity between parents and their children was a central issue throughout the 1960s. That conflict was onstage in *Fiddler on the Roof;* Tevye watches the first three of his five daughters leave the family circle one by one, each causing a wider breach until, as Yeats said, the center cannot hold. Another circle was broken at the end of *Fiddler;* it would be the last time Robbins would be involved in creating an original musical for Broadway. Although the show was successful beyond any director's wildest dreams, the collaborative nature of the Broadway musical and its oppressive economic necessities broke the uncompromising artistic spirit of Jerome Robbins. Sheldon Harnick recalled:

It was very difficult for him to make up his mind: "Is this the best it can be? Is this the best it can be?" He would drive everybody crazy, himself most of all . . . . Shortly before the show opened, he and I were walking somewhere, and I asked him, I said, "What's your next musical going to be?" and he said, "I don't know whether I'll ever do another musical." He said, "It's too painful. I have this image, this vision, of what a show should be, and when I can't get onstage what I know it should be, it's so painful for me that I can't bear it." So he said, "I think I'll stick to ballet."

The end of the saga, the end of the show, the end of an era: Tevye and his family pack their belongings and leave the circle. So will Jerome Robbins.

WHEN THE TALKING MOTION PICTURE proved to be a threat to Broadway, there was some consolation in the fact that Hollywood was a continent away. The new threat of television was not only in everyone's apartment, it was right up the block. When the television industry came of age in the late 1940s, the studios of CBS, NBC, ABC, and the DuMont network were all within a stone's throw of the Theater District. The biggest Broadway stars were initially dismissive of committing to a series in the new medium, with its small screen, commercial advertisements, and limited production resources, but they were open to the promotional value of guest spots, both of the dramatic and musical variety. With such talent only blocks south, television could gingerly begin the same kind of mating dance that Hollywood had initiated with Broadway twenty years earlier.

Television was dependent on Broadway not only for talent, it drew on the Great White Way for a kind of cultural imprimatur. As a way of bolstering its own derided integrity, television invoked the glamour of the musical stage for many of its programs. The variety show—one of television's earliest popular successes—did the most damage to the Broadway musical. With titles such as *Texaco Star Theater Vaudeville Revue* (Milton Berle's original show), *The Admiral Broadway Revue* (Sid Caesar's vehicle), *Broadway Jamboree*, *Broadway Spotlight*, and *Broadway Open House*, the shows borrowed heavily from the vaudeville and revue tradition (early critics called it "vaudeo"). Television could put together comics, production numbers, dancers, and singers with a speed and celebrity that Broadway couldn't match. As Broadway lyricist Sheldon Harnick points out, "Weekly variety shows could do topical humor that was genuinely topical, and get the biggest stars to do it, whereas if we were creating a stage revue with topical sketches, we were lucky if the sketch was only six months old by the time the show opened."

By far the most successful and influential of these programs was Ed Sullivan's *Toast of the Town*, which had its debut on CBS in June 1948. Sullivan, the show's host, was a former Broadway gossip columnist for the *Daily News* who subsisted on Winchell's discards, but he loved Broadway and took every opportunity to promote its shows, its creators, and its stars. Rodgers and Hammerstein appeared on Sullivan's first broadcast, and it was a rare Sunday night between 1948 and 1971 that he didn't feature some song or show from Broadway. When he began, producers were afraid to allow a number from their musical on *The Ed Sullivan Show* (as it was eventually called)—it might keep customers from paying money to see it. But in 1952, a failing Harold Rome musical called *Wish You Were Here* had nothing to lose, and on its day off, the producers sent the set and the cast to the TV studio at Broadway and 52nd. The next morning, there were lines around the block and the musical went on to run for nearly two years. In 1961, Sullivan asked Lerner and Loewe to appear in a tribute to their work; in return, they asked if he might present some numbers from their new show, *Camelot,* which was doing only mediocre business. Twenty minutes of the show, featuring Richard Burton, Julie Andrews, and Robert Goulet, went on the air, reversing the musical's fortunes overnight. Sullivan became the best promoter Broadway ever had, sometimes presenting up to twenty minutes of selections of shows like *Fanny* and *Do Re Mi*, with full costumes and minimal settings. So vast was his influence, he was even honored in a Broadway musical, *Bye Bye Birdie:* an average family gets to appear on his show and rhapsodizes about their hero in a madrigal ("We'll be coast-to-coast / With our favorite host—Ed Sullivan!").

In 1955, NBC got seriously into the musical-theater act by broadcasting Jerome Robbins's production of *Peter Pan*, starring Mary Martin, live from its studio in Brooklyn. Its Broadway run was curtailed so the show could be televised, and the program was so successful—65 million viewers—that it was restaged and rebroadcast with the same cast ten months later and won an Emmy for best television program of the year. (By 1960, it was possible to preserve the program on tape, and Martin faced the cameras for a third production—in color.) Not to be outdone, CBS commissioned Rodgers and Hammerstein to write an original musical for television. With an eye to a family audience, they chose Cinderella as their subject and Julie Andrews to play her. When the heavily promoted, ninety-minute musical debuted—live—on March 31, 1957, it was watched by the

largest audience up to that time in television history: 107 million people, or three people for every set in North America. (Rodgers and Hammerstein could draw a big audience on their own; in 1954, all the major networks canceled their evening programming to broadcast jointly a star-studded tribute to the team on the *General Foods Special*.) Other original TV musicals followed, such as Sammy Cahn and Jimmy van Heusen's singing version of *Our Town*, starring Frank Sinatra, as well as programs written by the likes of Cole Porter, Burton Lane, and Jule Styne, but the fad had passed by the mid-1960s (although *Cinderella* would be remade successfully for television in 1965).

What did not pass, what would never pass, was television's unique ability to create and promote celebrity. Early in their careers, Jackie Gleason, Phil Silvers, and Sid Caesar all got their big break in revues on the Broadway stage. Television then lured them away and made them stars, such big stars that they each came back to Broadway between 1959 and 1962 to play the leads in hit musical comedies. Sometimes, producers' yearning for a bankable name resulted in musical vehicles being created for television stars who lacked the necessary chops: Lucille Ball, Mary Tyler Moore, Richard Chamberlain, not to mention the innumerable "personalities" who became Broadway cast replacements in the 1990s and beyond. On the other hand, many television stars of the 1960s and '70s had impeccable Broadway musical pedigrees, among them Dick Van Dyke, Carol Burnett, Alan Alda, Jean Stapleton, Beatrice Arthur, Linda Lavin, Angela Lansbury, Florence Henderson, and Jerry Orbach.

The 1960s saw few experiments involving musical theater on television, although a few studio versions of shows such as *George M!* were televised. More influential was stage producer Alexander H. Cohen's project to have the Tony Awards televised nationally, beginning in 1967; for decades, the broadcast became Broadway's best

commercial. Eventually, Broadway shows would have their *own* commercials. Bob Fosse codirected the first one, for his 1972 show, *Pippin* ("This was one minute from *Pippin*. The other one hundred nineteen minutes can be seen at the Imperial Theatre"), and it did much to extend the run of a lackluster show. Soon, incessant ads for *The Wiz* and *Shenandoah* appeared and another consumer tradition was born. Public television, created in 1966, stepped in to preserve and present some of the best musicals. In particular, the Culture and Arts division at Thirteen/WNET New York, headed by executive producer Jac Venza, has been an enthusiastic and prolific producer of many classics from the American musical stage.

In the 1980s, several of the new cable companies sought to enhance their prestige by broadcasting Broadway shows, but it was a losing proposition. Broadway has recently received a video boost from television personality Rosie O'Donnell, a self-professed musical-comedy buff who used her daytime talk show repeatedly to promote Broadway musicals, turning several of them, notably *Titanic*, into successes—giving her clout unmatched since the heyday of Sullivan. Following in that tradition, television host Oprah Winfrey went so far as to produce a musical on Broadway: *The Color Purple* in 2005. Another recent trend reminiscent of the 1950s has been the television versions of classic musicals such as *Gypsy*, *Annie*, and *The Music Man* produced in prime time by the team of Craig Zadan and Neil Meron, using first-class Broadway talent. Even Rodgers and Hammerstein's *Cinderella* was remade a second time by them and was a ratings blockbuster—who'd have ever thought that Broadway's Fairy Godmother would be waving a wand that looked a lot like a TV antenna?

FAR LEFT: *Gertrude Lawrence, fresh from* The King and I, *gets to know television and Ed Sullivan, on his show, 1952.*

LEFT: *Rodgers and Hammerstein understood the power of TV nearly from its inception. Here they are with Julie Andrews, the evening of their popular* Cinderella *broadcast.*

ABOVE: *Jerome Robbins takes Mary Martin for a spin—or is it the other way around?—in the TV version of* Peter Pan.

TELEVISION

"I'm the greatest star"

THE BLOCKBUSTER MUSICAL AND THE SOUND OF MONEY

In order to gain entry to the private club of the blockbuster musical, a show needs to run at least the magic number of 1,000 performances. The 1960s was the decade that nurtured long-running blockbusters in unprecedented quantities: ten musicals passed the rarefied 1,000 performance mark, three of them passed the 2,000 mark (*Hello, Dolly!*, a Merrick smash, grossed $27 million on Broadway), and one, *Fiddler on the Roof*, passed the 3,000 mark, earning back $1,574 for every dollar put into it. Blockbuster status meant that producers could also send out numerous profitable road companies and foreign productions. It also meant they got a phone call from Hollywood.

Hollywood adaptations of Broadway musicals had a resurgence in the 1960s with considerable consequences to the industries on both coasts. The crowd-pleasing nature of stage musicals during this period, with their strong narratives, colorful locations, and

BELOW: *"A pad is to write in, not spend the night in—"* The chorus of the ultimate show for the tired businessman— How to Succeed in Business Without Really Trying—*reminds the audience that "A Secretary Is Not a Toy." Only one man could have choreographed his dancers this way: Bob Fosse.*

buoyant good humor, made them a natural for the screen. The expanding widescreen technology of the movies seemed ideally suited to giving audiences the equivalent of an expansive cinematic proscenium arch, and the movie musicals of the 1960s are crowded with visuals and casts of thousands. Hollywood once again borrowed some of the theater's more prestigious techniques and frequently accompanied their blockbuster musical films with special road show bookings, colorful programs—even overtures and intermissions.

The genre of musical comedies for the "tired businessman" often enjoyed their last hurrah in their cinematic translations. These silly escapades made it to the screen with a surprising number of their original stars intact: *Bye Bye Birdie* with Dick Van Dyke and Paul Lynde; *How to Succeed in Business Without Really Trying* with Robert Morse and Rudy Vallee; *A Funny Thing Happened on the Way to the Forum* with Zero Mostel and Jack Gilford. Less successful were the overblown, lumbering versions of more serious material like *Gypsy*, *Camelot*, and *Man of La Mancha*. All of these screen adaptations were conspicuous in the misuse of their casts—none of them used any leading actors from the Broadway productions—and although, in typical Hollywood fashion, numbers were deleted from the score, these films seemed even longer than their stage antecedents.

Director–choreographer Gower Champion uses the stage (and Robert Randolph's hilarious set) to magical effect, capturing Bye Bye Birdie's *teenagers in* "The Telephone Hour."

ABOVE: *Julie Andrews charms Richard Burton as King Arthur in* Camelot; *she charmed Broadway audiences, too, before she conquered Hollywood with her incomparable talent and thousand-watt smile.*

LEFT: *A glorious Act One finale for a mythical tale that ennobled the mythical world of Broadway: Lerner and Loewe's* Camelot *(1960), directed by Moss Hart.*

In the 1930s and '40s, screen adaptations routinely substituted Hollywood stars for their Broadway counterparts and tailored the material around them, but the strong narratives of the blockbuster musical made that nearly impossible. Still, decades of show biz history had proven that a stage star and a film star are not necessarily the same thing, and the guessing game around Broadway quickly became which stars were going to make it into the film version. With her Broadway success in *My Fair Lady*, Julie Andrews was, of course, waiting for the chance to reprise her role in the multimillion-dollar 1964 Warner Bros. film, but she was not considered a big enough star and was denied the opportunity to make her name internationally in a big-budget movie. Her savior was an unlikely one. Walt Disney had seen Andrews in *Camelot* and was determined to cast her in the title role of his latest, prized film project, *Mary Poppins*. She accepted the part and began filming the live-action/animated musical on the Disney lot just as the cameras were whirring over at Warners, with Audrey Hepburn playing Andrews's part opposite Rex Harrison. Advance word on *Mary Poppins* was so strong that Andrews was offered two more movies, one of which was the Rodgers and Hammerstein musical *The Sound of Music*.

Only weeks after Andrews won the Best Actress Oscar for *Mary Poppins*, *The Sound of Music* was released in March of 1965 and shot into the stratosphere, becoming the highest grossing film of its time. For the next three years, Andrews was the number one box office draw in America;

On the other hand, nobody calls Miss Marmelstein "bubbele"—or even "passion pie"! Barbra Streisand in her Broadway debut as the much-maligned secretary in 1962's I Can Get It for You Wholesale.

she was not only a film star—she was *the* film star. The immense success of *The Sound of Music*— it made more money than any movie in history until *Star Wars* debuted in 1977— jumpstarted the rush in Hollywood in the mid-'60s to film more Broadway blockbusters, and the immediate beneficiary was a brassy, gawky, neurotic Jewish girl from Brooklyn.

When Barbra Streisand landed her first Broadway job—an eye-catching supporting role in Harold Rome's 1962 *I Can Get It for You Wholesale*—she was so thrilled that she told Rome, "Great. Now I can get a phone." *Wholesale* was a David Merrick show, but when he announced he was going to coproduce a musical biography of Fanny Brice called *Funny Girl*, with Brice's son-in-law, Ray Stark, he didn't have a star in mind. The creative team considered Mary Martin and Anne Bancroft, but the obvious person to play the young, goofy, idiosyncratic Fanny was right under Merrick's, you should pardon the expression, nose. Stark refused to have anyone so patently unglamorous play his mother-

The height of nonchalance: Streisand becomes a real leading lady, playing Fanny Brice about to have a midnight supper with her future husband, gambler Nicky Arnstein, in Funny Girl *(1964).*

in-law, but the show's composer, Jule Styne, knew what a powerhouse voice Streisand had, and how well she could sell a potential hit song like "People." He prepped her, pushed for her, promoted her. The disagreement seems now like such wasted time—it was *beshert;* Streisand was fated to play Brice. In March of 1964 Streisand opened in *Funny Girl,* after an incredibly tumultuous series of tryouts, and she became a brand-new Broadway superstar. With her recordings on the radio and her unique profile on television specials, Streisand was a ubiquitous presence in New York in the mid-1960s; she was a local-girl-made-good and her combination of off-kilter personality with virtuoso vocal chops caught the imagination of the era.

Julie Andrews had to watch such nonmusical talents as Twiggy, Audrey Hepburn, and Vanessa Redgrave in the movies play the parts she had originated onstage, but Streisand was determined not to fall into the same celluloid disappointment; she consented to the London engagement of *Funny Girl* only in return for a commitment to play Fanny in the movie. Stark, who would produce both, agreed, and in 1967, Streisand went to Hollywood with a history-making deal; although she had never made a movie, she was contracted for the film versions of three Broadway shows: *Funny Girl; Hello, Dolly!;* and *On a Clear Day You Can See Forever.*

No one begrudged Streisand her role in the film of *Funny Girl*—in fact, she won an Oscar for her performance—but the lead in *Hello, Dolly!* was another story. Dolly Gallagher Levi, the eponymous heroine of Jerry Herman's musical, is a meddling, middle-aged, widowed matchmaker. The role was originated on Broadway by Carol Channing, and other notable Dollys followed, always assayed by ladies of a certain age: Ginger Rogers, Pearl Bailey (in an all-black version), Ethel Merman (for whom the role was written), Mary Martin (on tour and in a special version airlifted to Vietnam during the war). Streisand beat out Channing and other film stars, like Elizabeth Taylor, for the movie role: she was twenty-six when filming began.

Hello, Dolly! made a decent amount of money in its cinematic release, but not enough to cover its considerable costs. At about the same time, Julie Andrews made an expensive biopic about Gertrude Lawrence; it was a huge failure and Andrews fell off her exalted perch. By the end of the 1960s, the public was no longer buying the toothy ebullience of the blockbuster musical. The trend had ended with a whimper, but in its heyday, it had turned Andrews and Streisand into two of the biggest superstars the movies had ever seen. Andrews returned to her roots in 1995, reprising her 1982 film role in *Victor/Victoria* for an inferior stage vehicle, but her appearance was a day late and a dollar short. "Streisand will return to Broadway when Hollywood comes to Dunsinane," said William Goldman in 1968 and he was right. One can only imagine the roles both ladies might have played had they returned to Broadway in the sixties and seventies. Broadway never quite recovered from the loss of two of its greatest stars.

Dolly will never *go away. Six ladies make their grand entrances into the Harmonia Gardens.*
CLOCKWISE FROM ABOVE: *Carol Channing, Ginger Rogers, Pearl Bailey, Ethel Merman, Barbra Streisand, and Mary Martin.*

"What good is sitting alone in your room?"

HAROLD PRINCE AND *CABARET*

When he went into rehearsal in the fall of 1966, director Harold Prince had no idea how *Cabaret,* the first musical to deal with the emergence of Nazi Germany, was going to turn out, but he knew how he was going to begin:

> I took a leaf from the Jerry Robbins book on *West Side Story*. . . . It was very stormy in our country when I started work on *Cabaret,* and I brought in a photograph from *Life* magazine, a two-page spread of a bunch of blond Aryan Nazi boys snarling at the camera, some wearing religious icons, and all stripped to the waist, and I said, "Who are these people, and where is this?" No one guessed. [They were demonstrators in Chicago the previous month protesting the integration of a housing development.] And so I used that to support the contention that wherever human beings are, terrible things potentially can happen. We were able to pitch ourselves right into it the same way the *West Side Story* kids pitched themselves into Jerry's exercise.

Prince by now was one of Broadway's finest producers, but as he himself admitted, that was also a means to an end, a way to create opportunities for himself as a director. He had observed the best—George Abbott and Jerome Robbins—not as an intern, but as their boss. After an initial foray in 1962, he took over a flop show called *A Family Affair* out of town, but by 1963, with the critical success of *She Loves Me,* he was making a reputation.

Nazi Germany—or America in the 1960s? The photo from Life *magazine that Harold Prince brought to the first rehearsal.*

He directed two clever musicals in the mid-'60s, each about a hero of fourteen-year-old boys everywhere, Sherlock Holmes and Superman, but his personal enthusiasm was most excited by a musical version of *I Am a Camera*, a 1951 play based on Christopher Isherwood's *Berlin Stories*. The stories, heavier on atmosphere than plot, dealt with the seamier side of life in Berlin—nightclubs, prostitution, anti-Semitism, libertinism—during the Weimar Republic when Hitler was beginning his brutal climb to power. It appeared to be even less likely musical comedy material than a shtetl in Russia.

But it was the very intensity of the material that appealed to Prince. His background was German Jewish; he had been stationed with the U.S. Army in Stuttgart in 1951. His collaborators were Joe Masteroff, who wrote the book for *She Loves Me*, and a young songwriting team, John Kander and Fred Ebb, who had just composed *Flora the Red Menace* for the Prince office, an Abbott-directed flop that nevertheless won a Tony for Liza Minnelli in her Broadway debut. Kander, a quiet Midwesterner, was one of Broadway's top dance arrangers, while Ebb, a brash New Yorker, had written a good deal of revue material. They had collaborated on a pop hit, "My Coloring Book," and their knack for sentimental ebullience and show biz snap, crackle, and pop made them one of the most enduring teams of the century.

As the team started to sort through the material, they were drawn not only to Berlin, but also to its cabaret

Composer John Kander and lyricist Fred Ebb wanted their chum Liza Minnelli to play the British chanteuse Sally Bowles, but Prince preferred—and got—a real British actress, Jill Haworth.

scene, the milieu of Isherwood's most compelling character, Sally Bowles, a gamine British chanteuse with frayed cuffs who shares a flat in Berlin with a homosexual male writer. Initially, the show had an extended "Welcome to Berlin" sequence, where a Master of Ceremonies imitated famous stars of the Weimar cabaret scene. Then it was decided to put all the cabaret songs at the end of the show. Regardless, a conceptual problem confronted Prince: there seemed to be two shows—a traditional book musical with a romance between Sally and the writer (now butched up to be a leading man), and a revue of numbers from the Kit Kat Klub, which were, in keeping with the period, mordant, tart, and mocking. Unable to come up with a solution, he temporarily shelved the piece.

Visiting Moscow some time after, Prince caught a play at the famed Taganka Theatre. It was an admitted piece of propaganda, but he was mesmerized by "the techniques, the vitality, the imagination to make every minute surprising, *involving*, yet consistent with a concept." A particular lighting effect, a row of movable floodlights buried in the deck of the stage floor, gave him the key to unlocking the structural door to his *Cabaret*. There would be separate areas of narrative space—a realistic area for book scenes and a limbo area, a kind of cultural "id," where shifts in the attitudes of German society could be charted— delineated by a curtain of light. It enabled *Cabaret* to traverse the territory of a book show with the commentary of a Brechtian cabaret.

The trajectory of the title song, "Cabaret," was as follows: What the girl's found out at the beginning of the song is that she's pregnant. She comes out to sing an idle frippery about herself and her old roommate, and then she walks downstage into an area that she's never been in before, namely the limbo area that we used to comment on the story, and she proceeds to get rather overwrought, and she sings "Cabaret" as we best know it. At the end of that song, she goes and gets an abortion. What she decides at the end of the song is that she doesn't want to have the baby or go on with the romance that caused the baby. That's pretty powerful material for a Broadway musical comedy.

—Harold Prince

The techniques Prince brought to the show were by no means new. European directors had been experimenting with nontraditional forms of stagecraft for decades, and British directors such as Peter Brook had even staged some of their work on Broadway by the mid-'60s, but no one had ever applied such techniques to a musical. This approach would be called a "concept"—a term Prince chafes at—but as his statement about the Taganka reveals, he was more than aware of how a concept could reframe a musical narrative. When Rodgers and Hammerstein first took on *Oklahoma!*, they adjusted the traditional musical conventions to focus essentially on the story, which would be the touchstone for all creative decisions. With the concept musical, the touchstone would become something larger than the characters or the story, it was the theme of the show made manifest in a physical or theatrical way. Working in concert with his designers, especially the gifted, imaginative Russian émigré Boris Aronson, Prince would create a visual and emotional metaphor on the stage—the limbo in *Cabaret*, a café of bouzouki musicians in *Zorbá*, Plexiglas skyscrapers in *Company*, an oppressive factory in *Sweeney Todd*. This influential approach would be seminal in transforming the musical into an art form that could accommodate serious subjects and treatments.

Prince rehearses Bert Convy (l.) and the incomparable Lotte Lenya, 1966.

But in 1966, Prince was also a showman. He brought Lotte Lenya, the widow of Kurt Weill, back to the Broadway stage after an absence of decades to play the conflicted German landlady, Fraulein Schneider. Not only had Lenya lived in Berlin during the time depicted in the show, she was, for American audiences, the most recognizable performance voice of Weimar Germany next to Marlene Dietrich. For his omniscient, androgynous Master of Ceremonies, Prince turned to a young performer named Joel Grey and conceived his character along the lines of a forlorn, effortful cabaret entertainer he had seen during his Army tour in Stuttgart. For Prince, the MC, with his teasing, mocking descent into anarchy, was a metaphor for Germany.

Hitler presented himself as "There'll be food on every table, so come with me." I always thought my character was very similar in terms of what I offered the audience. I always thought he was a bad guy but there were people who come to see that show that keep thinking, "Oh, he's fun." People read into it what they like.

—Joel Grey

We all loved her and still love her in memory. She was our conscience. We were out of town, and the critics started talking about how this was some sort of watered-down Kurt Weill score. "No, no, darling, it's not Kurt," she said to me, "it's Berlin. When I am out on that stage singing those songs, it is Berlin."
—John Kander

During *Cabaret*'s Boston try-out, audiences read a bit too much into Grey's character. When the wave of anti-Semitism in Berlin starts to become unmanageably apparent, the MC sings a mock love song to a stooge in a gorilla suit: "If You Could See Her Through My Eyes." The zinger comes in the last line, when the MC, pleading with his listeners to accept his devotion to his beloved, tells them: "If you could see her through my eyes, / She wouldn't look Jewish at all." Grey described it as "a kick right to the groin of the audience." But when Ebb and Prince were accosted by some Jewish members of the crowd who threatened to organize a boycott of the show, they had to confront the unintended effect of the line. Grey thought that audiences didn't get that it was "anti-anti-Semitic"; Prince, who admitted he was swayed by the power of the Jewish theatergoing contingent, asked Ebb to substitute something much more neutral, which he reluctantly did. "But that wasn't Hal the director," said Kander. "That was Hal the producer." (The line was restored for the film and other subsequent versions, and even during the Broadway run, Grey would often "accidentally" let it slip out.)

In the end, Prince served *Cabaret* well as both producer and director, and vice versa. It opened at the Broadhurst Theater at the end of November 1966 and went on to win eight Tony Awards. Its success allowed Prince to be welcomed into the inner circle of Broadway musical directors, and the material went on to be filmed successfully in 1971 (by Bob Fosse) and achieve worldwide status. Its greatest success, however, lay in the fact that, more than any other musicals of the 1960s, *Cabaret* served notice that—potentially—there was nothing the American musical could not accomplish.

"If you could see her through my eyes." The eerie MC (Joel Grey) conjures up a streak of anti-Semitism.

"Leave your troubles outside."
Grey leads the ensemble of Cabaret
in the groundbreaking opening number,
"Wilkommen."

I was in high school and I was visiting
Boston in the fall of 1966 and there
were two shows running in downtown
Boston: *I Do! I Do!* was trying out with
Mary Martin and Bob Preston, at the
Colonial, and at the Shubert was a show
called *Cabaret*, about which we knew
nothing. We get seats in the last row of
the orchestra and we get in just as it's
beginning, so we don't even have a
chance to look at the *Playbill*. It begins
with this drum roll, and what seems to
be an empty stage with just a trape-
zoidal mirror that reflects the audience
and as I recall blinding lights along the
footlights. And then this guy, Joel Grey,
comes out and starts singing a song that
we all know now is "Wilkommen," but
my friend and I looked at each other
and said, what is this show—in German?
We didn't know what it was. But you
absolutely felt you were seeing something completely new. After the show,
we were talking about it a mile a minute
and we couldn't even quite describe
what we were seeing. We knew the
period, we got the references to Brecht
and Weill but, that said, this was very
much a glamorous Broadway musical
that was about the collapse of
the society, about Nazis taking over
Germany, and told through song and
dance and this sort of Brechtian
alienation and fantastic stagecraft
and it was mind-blowing.

—**Frank Rich,** Critic

ANGELA LANSBURY

IF THERE IS A STATUTE OF LIMITATIONS for Cinderellas, Angela Lansbury exceeded it when, on May 24, 1966, she walked down a staircase onstage at the Winter Garden, clad in gold pajamas and carrying a trumpet. As the habitually eccentric title character in *Mame*, she mopped up the town in her first starring role in a musical comedy; she was forty years old. Lansbury was not a complete stranger to musical comedy—born into a theatrical family in her native England, she had gotten her share of music hall experience at an early age—but she was primarily known as one of the most effective character actresses in Hollywood. She was nominated for a supporting Academy Award in her film debut at eighteen, but by the early '60s, her film career was proving to be a disappointment to her, as she was invariably cast as a villainess or an oddball or a mother, or all three in *The Manchurian Candidate* in 1962.

Lansbury jumped at the chance to perform in her first Broadway musical two years later, in a somewhat strident satire by Stephen Sondheim with a book by Arthur Laurents called *Anyone Can Whistle*. Lansbury, cast in the showy supporting part of avaricious mayoress Cora Hoover Hooper, played it as a cross between Kay Thompson and Eva Perón. The show lasted only a week, but for Lansbury, musicals were "like alcohol, they go to your head, and you think, 'That's what I want to do—get out there and perform!'" She also earned the admiration of Sondheim and Laurents, which would come in handy later in her career.

Rosalind Russell had a legendary run as Auntie Mame, both onstage in the 1950s and in the 1958 film, but she had no interest in the musical version being prepared by songwriter Jerry Herman, fresh from his blockbuster hit *Hello, Dolly!* Despite her lack of Broadway marquee value, Lansbury knew she was right for Mame, and so did Herman; he coached her on the side, and after three auditions, she swayed the apprehensive producers. For Lansbury, *Mame* proved to be the ultimate dress-up fantasy: in a role that required her to dance the Charleston, the tango, and the Lindy, plus sing in seven numbers, including a wrenching eleven o'clock torch song about her nephew, she had almost thirty costume changes. The part allowed her to access the sexy, glamorous leading lady she always knew was inside, and it proved to be a triumph: "I've finally arrived. I always knew I would hit on something that would unlock all the doors and hit all those people right between the eyes." She won her first Tony.

ABOVE: *Lansbury charms the husks right off the considerable corn as* Mame, *1966.*
OPPOSITE: *"Times is hard": as the downtrodden Nellie Lovett in* Sweeney Todd.
BELOW: *The delusional Countess Aurelia in* Dear World *gave Lansbury a chance to assume a Bernhardt-like pose.*

As the 1960s merged into the 1970s, the leading roles available to a middle-aged woman in a Broadway musical weren't all that abundant, but they did require a superior actress who could sing, dance, and convey a complicated character with equal conviction. Lansbury was the ideal star for this era; while other mature Hollywood actresses were having Broadway musicals nipped and tucked to accommo-

date their meager musical talent, Lansbury was pushing the boundaries. She starred as a delusional visionary in Herman's *Dear World*—her second Tony—and as a pathologically antisocial Southern matron in *Prettybelle,* which mercifully closed out of town.

Gypsy had never been staged in London, and Lansbury initially turned down the chance to originate the role in her native land; she thought her singing was nowhere near good enough to compare with Merman's. But she finally conceded, and in 1973 she applied her cunning theatricality to the part, creating a ferocious, utterly believable Madame Rose. She had the guts to bring her performance to Broadway, too, where everyone had seen Merman, and earned not only raves, but also a Tony Award, her third.

In 1976, Sondheim rang her with a novel idea: the role of Mrs. Lovett, a murderous barber's deranged accomplice and prospective paramour in *Sweeney Todd,* a legendary horror story that Lansbury had known, as every Briton did, from her youth. She initially resisted—the show was not called *Mrs. Lovett,* she pointed out—but happily, he convinced her by writing an extraordinary entrance number for her, "The Worst Pies in London," a comic whirligig of rapacity, rage, and resignation. She was hooked, and in 1979, she and Len Cariou became the most famous pair of

Joel Grey gives his regards to Broadway in George M!, *1968.*

body snatchers since Burke and Hare. As Mame, Lansbury was the height of glamour; as Nellie Lovett, she sank to the depths of folly, looking like Raggedy Ann cast in a remake of *Whatever Happened to Baby Jane?* "It was an opportunity to do something that really came from my roots," she explained. "I was quite prepared to go to town with it and play the total slattern. I felt there was something beguiling and pathetic about this lost soul who didn't know good from evil and was caught up in the maelstrom."

Alternately mischievous, murderous, and music hall, Lansbury gave the show its soul and was rewarded with a fourth Tony Award as Best Actress in a Musical—an achievement no one has equaled.

JOEL GREY

WHEN JOEL GREY STEPPED into stardom, *wilkomming* wary customers to the Kit Kat Klub at the beginning of *Cabaret*'s Boston tryout, even his own mother wouldn't have recognized him:

Out I came in this very extreme pink pancake—the name of the greasepaint actually was "juvenile pink." And with these very heavy eyelashes, patent-leather hair slicked back, and Clara Bow bee-stung, blood-red lips and some rouge. And a tuxedo and a pink bow tie. I don't think anybody had ever seen that before.

Thirty-four years old when he appeared as the MC, Grey had toiled in show business since the age of ten. Born Joel Katz in 1932, he grew up in Cleveland, the son of a successful nightclub entertainer and clarinetist, and eventually made it to Broadway as a replacement for such stars as Anthony Newley and Tommy Steele. When Harold Prince picked him to host his *Cabaret*, Grey was so comparatively little known that he was billed fifth, along with the supporting cast. But his dazzling, creepy, utterly unpredictable performance won him a Tony Award and gave the world a Broadway icon. He followed his triumph with his first starring role, as George M. Cohan in the musical biography *George M.!* (1968), where his singing, dancing, and acting talents could be fully exploited. Hollywood beckoned, with a reprise of his role in the film of *Cabaret*, which won him an Oscar. In the 1970s, he returned to Broadway to star in two more shows, both at the Palace Theatre: *Goodtime Charley*, in which he played the Dauphin of France, and *The Grand Tour*, where he gave his most poignant performance, as a Polish Jew trying to keep one step ahead of the Nazis. Neither show ran for very long, but Grey received Tony nominations for both. He returned once more as the MC—this time with his name above the title—in a 1987 revival of *Cabaret*, and performed the self-effacing showstopper "Mr. Cellophane" as the cuckolded husband in the revival of *Chicago* in 1996. In 2003, he appeared as the Wonderful Wizard of Oz in *Wicked*, making his transition from song-and-dance juvenile to beloved character actor complete. "For me to take a role, I read a script and I think wow, I don't know how I'm going to do this, but I want to try," said Grey. "That's where I go." In *The Grand Tour*, Grey's big number was called "I'll Be Here Tomorrow," a sentiment that seems pretty accurate.

ZERO MOSTEL

IF MUSICAL COMEDY IS LARGER THAN LIFE, only one performer was larger than musical comedy. The son of an itinerant rabbi, Samuel Joel Mostel was born in Brownsville, the same poor Brooklyn neighborhood Phil Silvers hailed from, in 1915. His dream was to be a painter, and he worked for the WPA as an artist and museum tour guide. During his museum tours, he would blast off into bizarre improvisations, pretending to be a Picasso painting or a coffee percolator. This led to a successful career as a nightclub comedian and to a couple of early

"Yes, but how often will we find ourselves in this position?"
Mostel *in* Forum.

appearances in the 1940s on Broadway in revues and as Peachum in Duke Ellington's *Beggar's Holiday*. Mostel's left-wing sympathies caused him great travails during the blacklisting of the 1950s, scotching a blossoming Hollywood career as a character actor and funnyman. He returned to Broadway in triumph in 1961, transforming into a pachyderm before the audience's very eyes in the absurdist drama *Rhinoceros*, for which he won his first Tony. Producer Harold Prince thought Mostel's desperate humanity would be ideal for the freedom-craving slave in *A Funny Thing Happened on the Way to the Forum*, and Mostel's ability to push the complicated farce to the final curtain made it into a hit. He won a second Tony, making him the first performer to win in both musical and dramatic categories.

Mostel's onstage energy was prodigious; he could bellow like a bull, sing like a choirboy, mince about with the grace of one of Disney's dancing hippos, pummel another actor like a Teamster, fawn like a coquette, roll, bulge, or cross his "eight-ball eyes," all the while sweating up a storm and swearing under his breath. Yet he projected a Talmudic thoughtfulness, and that served him in great stead in his most famous part, Tevye, in *Fiddler on the Roof.* Mostel, an extremely well read man who continued his painting career throughout his life, was an ardent fan of Sholom Aleichem and brought dignity to his exorbitant clowning. His comic elaborations drove the creative staff crazy, and to Mostel's amazement, his nine-month contract was not renewed. He won a third Tony for his role and revived it several times (including a 1976 national tour, for which he was paid an impressive $30,000 a week), although not in the film, a source of great disappointment to him. He did get the chance to give the world Max Bialystock, the unscrupulous producer in Mel Brooks's 1968 film, *The Producers,* the gold standard of outrageous farce. Mostel, who died suddenly in 1977 during a Philadelphia tryout of a serious play about Shakespeare's Shylock, was constantly reviled for the ad-libbing that disrupted the context of the show. In a typically Mostellian farrago, he took exception:

> There's a kind of silliness in the theater about what one contributes to a show. The producer obviously contributes the money . . . but must the actor contribute nothing at all? I'm not a modest fellow about those things. I contribute a great deal. And they always manage to hang you for having an interpretation. Isn't [the theater] where your imagination should flower? Why must it always be dull as shit?

When Zero Mostel was onstage, it was many things, but it was never, never *that* dull.

CHITA RIVERA

DOLORES CONCHITA FIGUEROA DEL RIVERO, born in Washington in 1933, was such a hellion that her widowed mother enrolled her in a local ballet school simply to keep her from breaking the furniture. The training provided just the right discipline for the tomboy, and at fifteen she won a scholarship to George Balanchine's School of American Ballet. Now called Chita Rivera, she met Jerome Robbins two years later when she auditioned for the chorus of *Call Me Madam.* Entranced by her classical training and her striking presence, he gave her a featured dancing part in the road company. In 1957, she auditioned for Robbins again for a musical about Puerto

Everything was Rosie when Rivera took to the dance floor. Here she wows the Shriners in Bye Bye Birdie.

Rican gangs; she sang "My Man's Gone Now" and figured, given her Puerto Rican background, she was a shoo-in. After four more auditions, Robbins cast her as Anita, and she electrified Broadway. She would go on to star in nine more Broadway musicals and several others that never made it to town; the material wasn't always first-rate, but Rivera was.

She was multicultural before the term was even coined: she exploited her Latin roots as "Spanish Rose" in *Bye Bye Birdie* (and its misbegotten sequel); became a gypsy for *Bajour;* Irish—or something—as Velma Kelly in *Chicago;* played Liza Minnelli's Italian mother in *The Rink,* winning a Tony; and a sultry South American movie star in *Kiss of the Spider Woman,* winning another Tony. Rivera shows no sign of stopping: in 2002, she was a calculating millionairess (Swiss) in Kander and Ebb's *The Visit,* which has not yet made it to New York; in 2003, she was a film producer (French) in the Broadway revival of *Nine.* For all her international characters, she'll always be especially remembered for her sinuous back-handed tribute to "America" in *West Side Story.* "Some Puerto Rican people did not understand that it was tongue-in-cheek, and I tried to explain that it was by no means putting down the beautiful island, but I do think they were lucky to have a Puerto Rican sing it."

They were simply lucky to have Chita Rivera sing it.

" *The Age of Aquarius* "
HAIR AND THE ROCK MUSICAL

Michael Bennett's view of hippie life in Washington Square: Henry, Sweet Henry *(1967).*

OPPOSITE: *The real thing, "down to here, down to there":* Hair *(1968).*

In October 1967, a new musical opened on Broadway that featured a group of hippies in Washington Square Park, smoking dope and singing about their lifestyle. The show, *Henry, Sweet Henry,* was a very traditional book show about two fifteen-year-old girls. The hippie sequence was a second-act number called "Weary Near to Dyin'," and critics gave good reviews to the show's choreographer, a young man named Michael Bennett. Bob Merrill's score, however, did not get good reviews. Clive Barnes, the *New York Times* drama critic, said that it "could have been written anytime within the last twenty or thirty years and takes no account of the enormous changes in popular music, even of the last five years."

Barnes had been on a crusade for some time to get Broadway scores to reflect more of what passed for popular music in the 1960s: rock and roll, or rock, as it was being called. He argued, somewhat ignorant of the financial improbability of the suggestion, that Lennon and McCartney or Bob Dylan should be pressed into service to write a Broadway show. Certainly the basic point was well taken; a schism between Broadway and commercially popular music had existed for more than a decade, a crucial decade. In 1954, Bill Haley and the Comets released a single for Decca called "Rock Around the Clock" and it became the anthem for an era. By 1957, every entry on the *Billboard* Top Ten was a rock song. Rock spoke to youth, it was about youth, and it was the pop-culture wedge that divided parents and children. After the Beatles landed in America in early 1964, their singles soon occupied the top five places on the *Billboard* charts—and the dominance of youth became complete. (They were temporarily unseated by Louis Armstrong's rendition of "Hello, Dolly!"—a brief

paroxysm of revolt from the old folks.) By 1967, the tunes of Broadway were considered Your Parents' Music, which gave young audiences yet another excuse to avoid it.

Broadway was basically trying to ignore the sixties. The confirmation of the Broadway musical falling out of sync with pop culture was that there was no attempt made to recruit a Simon and Garfunkel or a Laura Nyro or a Lennon or McCartney— whomever—someone who might have bridged that gap, and so they essentially lost a generation [of theatergoers]. They never recovered from that.
—**Frank Rich**, Critic

The kind of show Barnes was asking for actually appeared a week before *Henry, Sweet Henry,* downtown in Greenwich Village, a five-minute walk east from Washington Square Park. Maverick producer Joseph Papp was one of the New York theater community's most unconventional figures. Since 1956, he had challenged the city fathers by presenting free Shakespeare in the parks, but in 1967, he finally found the home base he wanted. He bought the Romanesque-style Astor Place Library on the Lower East Side from the city for one dollar and began renovating it into several theater spaces, calling it the New York Shakespeare Festival at the Public Theatre. A couple of unemployed actors, Gerome Ragni and James Rado, had cobbled together a musical script about life among the flower children in the East Village and kept badgering Papp with it. They found a Canadian composer named Galt MacDermot, who had worked in Africa but had never even seen a Broadway show, to supply the score. When MacDermot's eclectic score of hard rock, Motown, hymns, ragas, and ballads was presented to him, Papp was enthusiastic. He had to pick something provocative to open his theater; *Hair* seemed a reasonably unreasonable choice.

Hair didn't have much of a plot: a young man named Claude, set loose among a "tribe" of young hippies in Washington Square, faces being drafted in the Vietnam War. What was far more compelling was the phantasmagoria that exploded around him. *Hair* was, in many ways, simply a revue, showing practically every aspect of the counterculture in a variety of musical styles, dances, and stage effects. It had an encyclopedic quality that would have made the cast of *Pins and Needles* dizzy: everything from Antonioni to Zombie (a racial slur for black people), including mind-altering drugs, pollution, the Vietnam War, civil rights, astronauts, astrology, hairstyles, the Waverly movie theater on Sixth Avenue, lyrics by Shakespeare and Abraham Lincoln. Plus sex. *Hair* became internationally famous for a brief, dimly lit scene at the end of the first act when the entire company assembled in the nude. It also used the names of a litany of sex acts—sodomy, fellatio, and cunnilingus, to name a few—as lyrics to a song, rendered with a yearning innocence. For all its confrontational moments, *Hair*'s charm came from its basic naïveté.

The war wasn't really the main thing, the main thing was the lifestyle. The theme is individual freedom. The freedom in all things, mostly freedom of thought, and the right to say those things, to say anything in any way that you wanted, and there were people that walked out. We were in Vietnam fighting a war that everybody in the play certainly disapproved of, that made it look like an accusation against the country, so some people didn't like that. But it's just the way it happened to hit those people.
—**Galt MacDermot**, Composer of *Hair*

One of the show's creators, Gerome Ragni, was also one of the performers. Here, he spreads the power of love to an audience member.

They had the kids running down and talking to the people and I guess on Broadway that was unusual. But you know the whole idea of *Hair* was to be unusual, so the fact that they did that didn't seem unusual to me. I think people liked it though—the kids were nice, they weren't rude to people.
—**Galt MacDermot**

Still, people came down to the Public to discover the excitement underneath all that *Hair*. After two months of performances, the show was transferred to a discotheque called Cheetah, where it got a new director, Tom O'Horgan, and a more flamboyant—and to some, less compelling—production.

In April 1968, *Hair* transferred to Broadway's Biltmore Theatre on West 47th Street, officially breaking several taboos on the Great White Way. There was no curtain, and the cast roamed the theater aisles before it was time to start. The show's nudity was a first for a Broadway musical, as was its full rock score. Both intrigued potential customers, and "The American Tribal Love Rock Musical"—a subtitle coined as a gag—settled in for a run of 1,742 performances. Initially, the audiences were older, parents who wanted to know what this "free love" and LSD were all about; perhaps they might understand their children better. But there was something of a theme park about *Hair*. William Goldman in *The Season* quoted a backer of the show: "All the tourists want to see what hippies look like, but no one wants to go all the way down to the Village: it's too much trouble and it might be dangerous. Here we've got them all nice and safe and bottled for view on Forty-seventh Street."

The show's rock score pleased Clive Barnes enormously and soon some of its more accessible songs—"Aquarius," "Hair," "Let the Sun Shine In"—made it to the pop charts (where they were most emphatically *not* covered by Perry Como and Rosemary Clooney). Eventually, a younger audience started coming to the show, intrigued by the music they found so compelling on the radio or the cast album. Would *Hair* be the musical savior of Broadway, dragging other scores kicking and screaming into the Age of Aquarius? Goldman quoted another Broadway hand: "You better believe it's gonna change things. There will now be a spate of shitty rock musicals."

At the end of 1968, *Hair* found itself competing with a show that might have had an even more profound effect in renovating the sound of Broadway. When composer Burt Bacharach and lyricist Hal David were approached by David Merrick to score the musical version of Billy Wilder's movie *The Apartment*, they were, next to Lennon and McCartney, the most successful songwriting team in pop music. With hits such as "Walk On By," "What the World Needs Now Is Love," and "This Guy's in Love with You," they had, in many ways, defined the sound of American romance in the 1960s. They were also excellent storytellers with a unique sound, and Bacharach proved himself to be an imaginative innovator in the recording studio. Bacharach was thrilled to take on the new show,

Washington crossed the Delaware and Hair *eventually crossed 14th Street, making it the most successful Off Broadway transfer of its day.*

Promises, Promises. Although he had not grown up with dreams of working on Broadway, he was inspired by Neil Simon's comic and poignant book, and he and David were challenged by writing for consistent characters and their emotions. Except for a bout of pneumonia during the out-of-town tryout in Boston, Bacharach loved his first Broadway assignment. (Even his pneumonia gave David an inspiration for a lyric during the tryout: "What do you get when you fall in love? / You get enough germs to catch pneumonia / And when you do, he'll never phone ya.")

In concert with producer Phil Ramone, Bacharach restructured the traditional orchestra pit to separate different sounds. With orchestrator Jonathan Tunick, he added "pit singers"— backup vocal artists, the kind found in every recording studio—which allowed the choreographer, Michael Bennett, to hire more dancers who didn't have to double as singers. Even better, the score itself was biting, tender, and impulsive and practically shrieked with the sounds of contemporary Manhattan. Bacharach used a completely modern pop sound in the service of a narrative musical comedy. But Bacharach was frustrated by the lack of control that was part and parcel of the Broadway musical, such as the frequent substitution of orchestra players at any given performance. "The impermanence of Broadway gets to you because everything shifts from night to night. If you've got a great take on a record, it's there, it's embedded forever," he said, and soon he moved back to Palm Springs; to this date, he has not written another Broadway score.

In his wake, the "contemporary" sound could be found instead, in such musicals as *Dude, Via Galactica, Sgt. Pepper,* and *Rockaby Hamlet,* unsuccessful attempts to put rock on the commercial stage. The modern sound of Broadway would have to come from someplace else.

1776

I T WAS THE FIRST MUSICAL in which everybody knew the characters in the show, but nobody knew the people behind it.

Sherman Edwards was a history teacher, with a talent for writing treacly pop songs and a passion for the Founding Fathers. For years, between gigs accompanying singers, he had been researching the events leading up to the signing of the Declaration of Independence, fascinated by such figures as John Adams, Benjamin Franklin, Thomas Jefferson, their public passions, and their personal foibles. "I wanted to show these men at their outermost limits. These men were the cream of their colonies. . . . They disagreed and fought with each other. But they understood commitment, and though they fought, they fought affirmatively. They didn't fight negatively and leave it at that. [What] they came up with was never perfect. But it was as good as they could make it at the time." As impressive as that sounds, it seems like the most improbable idea for a musical there ever was.

Producer Stuart Ostrow took a liking to Edwards and his project in the mid-1960s, but he thought Edwards had stretched himself too thin by writing both the score and the book. Ostrow had to twist librettist Peter Stone's arm simply to get him to listen to Edwards's score, but from the moment Stone heard the composer barking out the lyrics to a complicated three-part opening number—"Sit Down, John," which introduces John Adams and his explosive frustration with the dithering Continental Congress—Stone knew the

project was something special: "The minute you heard that, you knew what the whole show was. You knew the level that you were writing on. You knew immediately that John Adams and the others were not going to be treated as gods, or cardboard characters, chopping down cherry trees and flying kites with strings and keys on them. It had this very affectionate familiarity; it wasn't reverential."

Stone and Edwards began one of the most demanding dramaturgical processes ever asked of a musical team. Setting their story in Philadelphia during the sticky, humid summer of 1776, when the Continental Congress, at war with England, but uncertain of its course or its identity, debated whether to embrace independence and become a new country, Stone and Edwards had to conflate historical characters, streamline events, delineate arguments that were centuries old—and add room for some singing and dancing. The only thing they knew they had going for them was a bang-up ending—the signing of the Declaration itself—but even that was a potential problem. Everybody in the audience—everybody in the *country*—knew how the story turned out.

The creative team eventually followed the same course as the creators of *Oklahoma!* and *My Fair Lady:* they let their story tell them where to go, and musical-comedy conventions be damned. Their hero would be John Adams, "obnoxious and disliked" by his own admission, and his embattled mission to convince his peers from thirteen colonies that they should sever ties with the mother country. Among the show's topics were the evils of slavery (Adams

BELOW LEFT: *Ken Howard as Jefferson, Howard da Silva as Franklin, and William Daniels as John Adams can see the eagle inside "The Egg"—a number inspired by Fay Gage's poster design, right.*

1776
A
New
Musical
Comedy

46th STREET THEATRE
West 46th St.   Mats. Wed. and Sat.

demands its abolition, to no avail) and the horrors of war (a ballad called "Momma, Look Sharp").

In its original run, it was also one of the few musicals to play without an intermission. Among its few concessions to theatrical tradition was the brief inclusion of two women—Abigail Adams and Martha Jefferson—but Abigail appeared only in "certain reaches of John Adams's mind." An inoffensive minuet or two also tiptoed into the show.

The congressional delegates were recruited from the ranks of New York's best character actors. William Daniels, who had played in everything from Edward Albee to *The Graduate*, was given the role of a lifetime as Adams. Lanky, young Ken Howard was pulled out of *Promises, Promises* to play Thomas Jefferson. In a delicious irony, Howard da Silva, the left-wing actor who had played the lead in *The Cradle Will Rock* and been blacklisted in the '50s, was given the role of Benjamin Franklin.

Under the guidance of Peter Hunt, a director better known as a lighting designer, the show had a dispiriting New Haven tryout, followed by a more encouraging response in Washington. (One supposes that, had the cast played Philadelphia, it would have seemed like a revival.) When *1776* opened on Broadway on March 16, 1969, it took a weary and jaded city by storm. The British-born critic for the *Times*, Clive Barnes, claimed that the show made "even an Englishman's heart beat faster." Singled out for particular praise was one of the most unconventional finales ever seen in a Broadway musical: with the Liberty Bell pealing from the rafters, the delegates each sign the Declaration and then assume the poses made famous by the Pine-Savage engraving as a scrim descends, reproducing the actual signatures on the document. The show ran for 1,217 performances, won the Tony Award for Best Musical, played in London ("the hit musical from the Colonies," read the advert), and was filmed with most of the original cast in 1972.

A musical about the Founding Fathers might have proved unpopular during the Vietnam War, but much of *1776*'s genius stemmed from the fact that it refused to wrap itself in the flag—thirteen stars or fifty. It was about driven, noble, flawed individuals, just as Edwards had conceived it. It was also a cracking good debate, which always makes for good theater.

Nearly a year into its run, the Nixon White House asked the cast to come to Washington and perform the show in the East Room of the executive mansion for an invited audience of 200. There was some initial trepidation about the antiwar song "Momma, Look Sharp," but producer Ostrow said he would bring *1776* to the White House only if it were performed in its entirety. On February 22, 1970, it was, becoming the first musical ever to do so, and received a rapturous response from President and Mrs. Nixon and their mostly Republican guests. While the rest of the cast went back to New York that night, Howard da Silva stayed in Washington at a hotel across the street. The next morning, he awoke to the sounds of an antiwar demonstration organizing outside the White House; da Silva promptly got dressed and joined the rally.

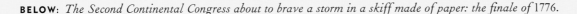

BELOW: *The Second Continental Congress about to brave a storm in a skiff made of paper: the finale of* 1776.

"It's a city of strangers"

COMPANY AND THE URBAN ANGST
OF STEPHEN SONDHEIM

Another hundred people just got off of the train and came up through the ground
While another hundred people just got off of the bus and are looking around
At another hundred people who got off of the plane and are looking at us
Who got off of the train
And the plane and the bus
Maybe yesterday.

It's a city of strangers—
Some come to work, some to play—
A city of strangers—
Some come to stare, some to stay

—Stephen Sondheim, "Another Hundred People"

Designer Boris Aronson's sketch for the unit set of Manhattan for Company *(1970).*

Boris Aronson observed about [Company] that the temptations in New York are so great. . . .That we're all exposed in the city to so many outside forces that are tempting and do not allow us to fulfill ourselves.

—Stephen Sondheim

For a writer who had two important hits at the end of the 1950s and who would go on to be the most important artist in the musical theater in the 1970s, the 1960s were a relatively quiet time for Stephen Sondheim. The first musical to feature both his music and lyrics, *A Funny Thing Happened on the Way to the Forum*, was a 975-performance hit in 1962; the second was the one-week flop *Anyone Can Whistle* in 1964. (As of this writing, not a single one of Sondheim's shows—music and/or lyrics—has run more than 1,000 consecutive performances.) His last show of the decade, in 1965, was the disappointing collaboration with Richard Rodgers, *Do I Hear a Waltz?*

After Sondheim's parents underwent a painful divorce when he was ten, his mother settled near Oscar Hammerstein's Bucks County farm, and Hammerstein became a surrogate father for the precocious young man, while also encouraging his desire to write for the musical theater with various informal tutorials. Before he died, Hammerstein suggested to Rodgers that he work with a younger man; and although he could not have predicted their lack of chemistry, he clearly had Sondheim in mind. Sondheim wrote lyrics only for the last time in his career with Rodgers, but the onstage and offstage disharmony of his collaboration with Rodgers simply proved that Sondheim was part of a new generation of musical-theater artists. The anxious years of the late 1960s could not have nurtured a more anxious and more appropriate poet laureate.

In 1969, Sondheim was busy planning a baroque backstage murder mystery with writer James Goldman, when a friend of his, actor George Furth, asked him to read a series of plays he had written. A member of the Actors Studio, Furth was always fascinated with character motivation. Sondheim was impressed with his series of one-act plays for two men and women, each a depiction of some kind of marital triangle, and brought them to Harold Prince. Prince was less impressed, but one day, while meeting with Prince and Sondheim, Furth blurted out that each of the plays featured a character who he had essentially based on himself. Prince saw the immediate possibilities of building a series of musical vignettes about relationships around one central character, rather than a group of separate stories. He asked Sondheim to write the score and put Furth on a small retainer to keep developing the material. It became *Company*.

Ironically, the show that had most influenced both Sondheim and Furth as youngsters was Rodgers and Hammerstein's *Allegro* (Sondheim was an assistant on the Broadway production, Furth had directed it in college), and the experimental form of that show with its Greek chorus and unconventional narrative inspired them to reinvent the structure of a musical. *Company* is more of a revue, a series of takes on married life in Manhattan in the

Robert (Dean Jones) surrounded by these good and crazy people, his married friends.

Whereas the city was a plaything for Gershwin, a fun place, a place where you got lucky, found a girl, stepped up in the world, in Sondheim's world, it's a place where you get lost, where you lose things, where you can't find yourself, where you're alienated, where another hundred people come out of the subway, and so it's people not meeting, not connecting.

—John Lahr

Table reading, first week of Company *rehearsal. Prince sits at head of table, to his left is book writer George Furth. Sondheim, far left, sits on his own.*

Robert, played by Dean Jones, finds a series of encounters among his married friends and with a number of single women; none of them are what he's looking for in life. Jones with Elaine Stritch, as the oft-married Joanne.

late 1960s that centers around a thirtysomething bachelor named Robert who is the hub for the five married couples who spiral around him. The plot is more circular than linear because it begins and ends on the same moment—one can read the whole sequence of events as happening in one brief moment in Robert's mind as he is about to enter a surprise party for his thirty-fifth birthday.

It examined people who don't want to get married. More importantly, it examined the willingness to commit yourself to another human being, marriage or not. That certainly was the central issue in our society, then. Since that day, think of all the people who live together and aren't married, so it has changed, big time.

—Harold Prince

Sondheim's score would be written almost perpendicularly, with characters commenting on scenes they weren't in, or stepping outside of the situation to comment on themselves, on love, on commitment.

All the numbers in Company are inserted like nuts into a fruitcake, they're inserted into the scenes, or they occupy, in the case of "Barcelona," the whole scene. But none of them just arises out of dialogue the way I'd been trained to do by Oscar Hammerstein.

—Stephen Sondheim

The show, as it developed, spoke both about and to the lives of upper-middle-class Manhattanites during the sexual revolution. "Swingers" didn't mean Dean Martin and Peter Lawford in 1970, it referred to the John Updike–type couples who experimented with open marriages and wife-swapping. Singles bars such as Maxwell's Plum sprang up in New York City in the late 1960s and became enormously popular. The same year *Company* appeared, the nonfiction best seller was the guide *Everything You Always Wanted to Know About Sex . . . But Were Afraid to Ask*, and it made millions of Americans eager to do so. Marijuana and martinis were both common forms of self-medication in Upper East Side apartments, and the apartment buildings themselves were transforming all along Lexington Avenue and Third Avenue into brand-new steel-and-glass multistory structures that were the latest in "In."

Company put all of this onstage, "side by side by side," to quote a Sondheim lyric, with sideburns, leather couches, and stewardesses. The show embraced a universal theme—"Only connect," as E.M. Forster put it—but its context was specifically "Fun City" during the Lindsay years. Prince and his designer Boris Aronson created a multilevel metallic skeletal apartment complex that required six tons of steel, one working elevator (Sondheim added bars of music in the opening number to cover its descent) and a barrage of slide projections. This was the city, the city of strangers, that everybody onstage was a part of and that was a part of everybody. No musical had ever portrayed Manhattan with such fantastic realism.

Critical reaction to the show was split down the middle, both at its Boston tryout and its New York debut, which occurred in April 1970. Audiences were split as well. For some, Sondheim and his crisp, critical contemporaneity were a tonic for a Broadway that seemed increasingly mired in adaptations of far-flung material in farther-flung settings. (Indeed, *Company* borrowed a fair amount of the sound of the Manhattan-set *Promises, Promises* by adding pit singers and utilizing its orchestrator Jonathan Tunick.) Others found the world too cold, too misanthropic. Still, *Company* eked out a decent profit during its 706-performance run, and Sondheim, Prince, Furth, Aronson, and the show all won Tony Awards.

Robert stuck between a battling married couple (Barbara Barrie and Charles Kimbrough).

> **Company does deal with a lot of so-called brittle people—upper-middle-class people with upper-middle-class problems, but I think the audience in those days was an upper-middle-class audience. . . . They couldn't say, "Oh, that's that world of people" 'cause they *were* that world of people. . . . It's no joke, that cliché that musicals are escapist entertainment and [audiences] really want to escape. And here we're bringing [their problems] right back in their faces. What they came to a musical to avoid, they suddenly find facing them on the stage.**
>
> **—Stephen Sondheim**

Sondheim, whose earlier lyric-writing attempts for *West Side Story* and *Forum* were ignored or politely dismissed, was finally being praised for his irony, his wit, his wordplay. Not since Cole Porter had any lyricist brandished a lexicon with such felicitous facility. But Sondheim brought something new to the ballgame. In the 1890s, the Russian playwright Anton Chekhov had developed the notion of subtext—dialogue that would capture the natural human instinct to say one thing while feeling another. By the late 1940s, using subtext to communicate emotions and contradictions in dramatic language was a technique mastered by such playwrights as Tennessee Williams and Arthur Miller, but it had never really made its way into the lyrical language of the American musical. Love songs had always operated from a place of utter truthfulness, but Sondheim kept the audience guessing about their emotional veracity. In one scene, portrayed entirely in the song "Barcelona," Robert awakes from a one-night stand with a stewardess, April, and discovers her getting dressed. He begs her to stay with him, but nothing he says convinces the audience that he really means it. In Sondheim's world, for the first time on a musical stage, we can never take what we hear for granted, which has made his theater a dangerous and exciting place to be. In a city of strangers, nothing is as strange and unpredictable as the human heart.

Robert desperately trying to remember the name of the stewardess played by Susan Browning—could it be "June"? Sorry, Bobby—wrong month, wrong girl—it's "April."

> **Musicals for decades have had no doubts about the efficacy of a happy ending. We were saying something ambiguous, which is, actually there are no endings, it keeps going on, that's what Company's really about. It's always difficult to make a contact with, commit to, and live with somebody, and at the same time it's impossible not to. But it's never going to be easy, and it's never going to be solved, because it's not a problem that has a solution. It's not even a problem; it's just what life is.**
>
> **—Stephen Sondheim**

BROADWAY BABY

Words and Music by Stephen Sondheim
From Follies *(1971)*

LIKE MOST OF SONDHEIM'S major work, *Follies* functions on several levels at once. The setting was a reunion of showgirls from the '20s and '30s in the shell of an old Broadway theater about to be torn down. Featuring ghostly lighting, faded scenery, and two sets of performers playing their older and younger selves, *Follies* was a musical about the death of the musical, as critic Frank Rich put it. But while it commented on a dying tradition, it celebrated that tradition at the same time. As part of the reunion, aged showgirls performed the routines and specialty numbers that had made them famous decades before. It required Sondheim to be true to the period in which the numbers might have been written and yet compose something that might be pertinent to a contemporary audience. He explained:

> I just picked my favorite composers, and each time I had to write a pastiche number I picked a different composer, different lyricist. You can call it, as they say in the movie business, an *hommage*, but in fact it was just an imitation. "You're Gonna Love Tomorrow"—that's my idea of Burton Lane. The verses of "Love Will See Us Through" are Kern. "Broadway Baby" is DeSylva, Brown, and Henderson.

"Broadway Baby" certainly sounds like a typical "I wanna be a star" song from the period, something that might have been sung in the '20s by Zelma O'Neal or Ruby Keeler or Ethel Shutta. In *Follies,* it was, in fact, sung by Ethel Shutta, who was seventy-five at the time. She had made her debut in the *Passing Show of 1922* and appeared in a number of Ziegfeld productions, most famously playing opposite Eddie Cantor in both the stage and film versions of *Whoopee!* "Broadway Baby" has become a cabaret standard, frequently rendered by soubrettes in their twenties, but that only makes it work on one level. Sung by an older woman, it tells the journey of a lifetime.

I'm just a
Broadway Baby,
Walking off my tired feet,
Pounding Forty-second Street
To be in a show.

Broadway Baby,
Learning how to sing and dance,
Waiting for that one big chance
To be in a show.

Gee,
I'd like to be
On some marquee,
All twinkling lights,
A spark
To pierce the dark
From Battery Park
To Washington Heights.

Some day, maybe,
All my dreams will be repaid:
Hell, I'd even play the maid
To be in a show.

Say, Mr. Producer,
I'm talking to you, sir:
I don't need a lot,
Only what I got,
Plus a tube of greasepaint and a follow-spot!

I'm just a Broadway Baby,
Slaving at a five-and-ten,
Dreaming of that great day when
I'll be in a show.

Broadway Baby,
Making rounds all afternoon,
Eating at a greasy spoon
To save on my dough.

Ethel Shutta in her 1920s incarnation as a real live Follies *girl.*

Shutta delivering her show-stopping number, half a century later.

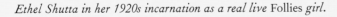

At
My tiny flat
There's just my cat,
A bed and a chair.
Still
I'll stick it till
I'm on a bill
All over Times Square.

Some day, maybe,
If I stick it long enough,
I can get to strut my stuff
Working for a nice man
Like a Ziegfeld or a Weismann
In a great big
Broadway show!

"My city, my city"
TIMES SQUARE IN THE '70s

It didn't look any better in the daylight: 42nd Street in 1970—the "world's greatest movie center"—but what movies!

By the late 1960s, one of Broadway's biggest obstacles in attracting customers was Broadway itself. To understand this paradox, one first has to picture Times Square during this period. It is not a pretty picture. West 42nd Street from Sixth Avenue to Eighth had been disintegrating as a theatrical venue for decades; once the U.S. Supreme Court liberalized the obscenity laws in 1967, the availability of pornography, plus potent drugs such as heroin, turned the patchwork quilt of movie houses, cheap food joints, and amusement arcades into an open-air market for degradation. The sex trade became a cash cow for organized crime, which "invested" in 42nd Street with the fervor of a chorus-girl-besotted financier of the 1920s. Movie theaters showed round-the-clock XXX-rated films with unrepeatable titles; hookers solicited passersby and "massage parlors" easily accommodated their transactions; peep shows and magazine shops catered to more self-reliant customers. As midtown New York's busiest thoroughfare, West 42nd Street allowed for a stream of anonymous access to these dubious pleasures; the Port Authority Bus Terminal became a freightyard for teenage runaways, easily susceptible to drugs or prostitution. Worst of all for anyone working in the Broadway theater, 42nd Street became synonymous with the entire Theater District. Movies and television shows such as *Midnight Cowboy* and *Kojak* sent indelible images of New York City street sleaze all across the country, and the evening news in the tri-state area broadcast urban horrors nightly. Customers stayed away in droves. The effect was insidious: the fewer shows, the emptier the street; the emptier the street, the fewer the shows.

Perhaps to insulate themselves from the reality of Times Square street life, Broadway musicals embraced the worlds of long ago and far away. Nostalgia became the rage in the early 1970s, and producers served it up in a variety of forms. The matinee ladies who didn't appreciate the acid-tinted nostalgia in *Follies* had other places on Broadway to relive their youth. The revival of *No, No, Nanette,* with its pastel colors and sunny disposition, provided a safe haven, as did Debbie Reynolds making her Broadway debut in *Irene,* a 1919 show reformatted to showcase her talents in 1973. *Good News!* reappeared briefly the following year, along with *Over Here!,* a new "Big Band Musical," starring two thirds of the Andrews Sisters. By the end of the decade, theatergoers of a certain age could enjoy the antics of Mickey Rooney and Ann Miller revisiting the world of burlesque in *Sugar Babies.*

Their baby boomer children might have been happier at *Grease*, the first of many pastiches of the rock and roll world of the Eisenhower years, which moved from Off Broadway in 1972. This innocent tribute to prom nights and drive-ins caught the imagination of undemanding audiences and became the longest-running musical on Broadway up to that time, with 3,388 performances.

As the cast of *Grease* was snapping its fingers at the Royale, Broadway was slowly beginning to snap itself out of its promotional stupor. Producers and civic leaders joined forces to make improvements in the Theater District. The most durable contribution was the creation, in 1973, by the city and the Theatre Development Fund, of the Times Square Theater Center, an open-air booth in Duffy Square at Broadway and 47th Street. The center, known more affectionately as the "TKTS" booth (for its logo), sells tickets for half-price, plus a small surcharge. It was an instant success; to this day, TKTS sales constitute roughly 12 percent of all sales on and off Broadway combined. In 1978, a glossy television advertising campaign, sponsored by the New York State tourism board, "I ♥ NY," showed clips from Broadway musicals, as did the annual, highly polished television broadcasts of the Tony Awards, supervised by producer Alexander H. Cohen; both helped bring increased tourist trade back to Broadway.

Still, it would take almost twenty more years to make profound changes in the Times Square area and reverse the negative national perception of the Theater District. For all the lobbying attempts at amelioration, only one thing could best revive the fortunes of Broadway: a new hit in town.

ABOVE LEFT: Irene *was the Broadway debut of Debbie Reynolds (center, with Ted Pugh),* in 1973.

ABOVE RIGHT: *Nostalgia is the word:* Grease *with Carole Demas and Barry Bostwick.*

"God, I hope I get it"

MICHAEL BENNETT AND *A CHORUS LINE*

We call them the gypsies—and they call themselves that. They are homeless, wandering people for the most part, defying all the conventions. They dress as they please—sloppy slacks and beat-up old sweaters seem to be the most popular street garments. As soon as they arrive at the theater, they change into rehearsal clothes of an unglamorous nature. The contrast between the lovely airborne creatures who will appear in music and light and color upon the stage, and these drab lackluster girls in their brown, black, and gray union suits known as leotards is always incredible. . . . Most of them live only for their art. They have turned to the dance because of a need to express themselves.

—George Abbott, 1963

Michael Bennett rehearsing
A Chorus Line *(1975).*

All Michael Bennett DiFiglia ever wanted was to be one of those wandering, convention-defying people—or better yet, the guy who showed them what to do. Born in 1943 in Buffalo, he was encouraged by his parents to pursue his early interest in dance; they bankrolled his dance classes and trips to Manhattan to see *Damn Yankees*. His preciosity was matched only by his talent; by his teens, Michael had his own dance company and was appearing on a local TV show. At the age of seventeen, he left high school and Buffalo ("To commit suicide in Buffalo is redundant," volunteers one of the characters in *A Chorus Line*) to tour in *West Side Story*. He made his Broadway debut in 1961, dancing in the chorus—and sometimes being featured—in several mediocre Broadway shows that at least displayed challenging choreography by the likes of Peter Gennaro and Michael Kidd.

Bennett made his debut as a Broadway choreographer in 1966 and worked his way through several flops, acquiring, as he went, a coterie of colleagues who would become invaluable to him in the future, among them Donna McKechnie, Baayork Lee, Tommy Tune, and Bob Avian. Bennett had his first big hit as choreographer with his fluid, discotheque-inspired dances for *Promises, Promises* and went on to choreograph *Company* in 1970 and to codirect and choreograph *Follies* in 1971. Bennett had a terrifically contemporary sensibility; he could combine character work, scenic movement, and virtuoso production numbers and still make it look like his characters were part of the fabric of New York in the 1970s. He was fortunate that, by and large, his shows were set in the here and now; Russian peasants or medieval knights were decidedly not his thing. Directing and choreographing his own musical from scratch *was* his thing, but, as of 1974, despite the immense praise (and a Tony) he had received for his earlier work, that particular prize had eluded him.

It was a fortuitous combination of Bennett's personal ambition and a larger professional desperation that created *A Chorus Line*. The Broadway scene in the early 1970s was discouraging for everyone in the musical field, but particularly harsh for dancers in the chorus line, the gypsies. The boffo shows of the 1960s, with their jolly dancing choruses, were curtailing their runs both in New York and on the road; it was getting harder and harder to find jobs, and, as George Abbott put it, a dancer's life "is an unending struggle against the body." In January 1974, two chorus dancers, Tony Stevens and Michon Peacock, were so dismayed by the prospects on Broadway that they set up a discussion session with a group of gypsies to explore their lives and future professional possibilities. They asked Bennett, who had been toying with the idea of a show about dancers for some time, to help run their session. Eighteen dancers, many of whom had worked with Bennett, gathered for an all-night discussion about what it meant to be a Broadway dancer. Another important participant was a reel-to-reel tape recorder. Donna McKechnie, who created the role of Cassie, recalled:

> In the tape sessions, Michael essentially asked the first questions that are put to the characters in the play: Step forward. Tell me your name, where you're from, when you were born, and why did you want to become a dancer. And we started talking and all of these things came out, beyond facts; it was all of everybody's secret passions and dreams and desires, and we found great delight and surprise that so many people felt the same way about so many things.

When the tapes were eventually transcribed, Bennett and his group, which included Nicholas Dante, a dancer with playwriting aspirations, knew they had something, but they weren't quite sure what.

Their problems were solved, or perhaps extended, by producer Joseph Papp. The producer had supposedly wanted Bennett to work at the New York Shakespeare Festival on a revival of Kurt Weill's *Knickerbocker Holiday*. Bennett turned it down (Papp produced a revival of *Threepenny Opera* instead), but asked Papp to help him develop the "dancers" project. Papp gave Bennett a rehearsal room for five weeks and money to hire some dancers and a creative staff at $100 a week each, and he demanded very little in return. Bennett recounted: "I don't think [Papp] always understood what we were doing, but he always understood that we were passionate about what we were doing, and he kept writing the checks." Bennett was the beneficiary of a trend Off Broadway to nurture and develop new projects. This modus operandi, called a "workshop," was central to the fortunes of the new project, called *A Chorus Line*, and to the subsequent history of the American musical.

The group that assembled downtown near Astor Place in August 1974 was a mixed bag. Bennett brought in Marvin Hamlisch to write the score; Hamlisch, a dance arranger for some earlier Bennett shows, had just astonished the entertainment industry by winning three Academy Awards in one evening for his music, but had never written a full show. Composer and lyricist Edward Kleban came aboard to write lyrics; Dante would function as a writer, alongside Bennett; and frequent Bennett collaborator Bob Avian was the cochoreographer. The cast was

Mr. Broadway meets Mr. Off Broadway: Bennett and his downtown angel, Joseph Papp.

I think the opening of *A Chorus Line* hooks the audience because they are in the back of the house in a dark theater and they are watching an audition that people are not usually allowed to go to—then, they become the judges and they start rooting for the characters that they like.

—**Baayork Lee,** Original Cast

At the first performance, Michael said his worry was that it was so inside that nobody would get it except dancers. And I said, well, everybody's gonna get it because everybody's tried to get a job, compete for a job, or be interviewed for a job—that's what's under it all and that's universal. And the fact that it's dancers instead of plumbers just makes it more theatrical.

—**Tommy Tune**

Early on in the show, people in the audience could identify with the characters even though the people in the audience weren't dancers; that to me was the absolute brilliance of the show. That you're doing a show ostensibly about dancers getting a job and what you're really doing is a show where the common denominator is "God, I hope I get it."

—**Marvin Hamlisch**

A Chorus Line told about an audition—it's not the greatest story in the history of the world, but it was that ability of Michael Bennett to show what that pure musical theater excitement is.
—**Frank Rich**

Everyone has dreams and hopes, and everyone gets disappointed and discouraged, and this show is kind of a prayer for starting over again.
—**Donna McKechnie**

I saw *A Chorus Line* at the Shubert Theater in Chicago, I was in the last row of the last balcony, I went back to my dancing school and I said to my teacher, you've got to teach me that opening combination. I had to be in the show—it moved me in a way nothing in my life had moved me. And when I went on the first time it was in Louisville, Kentucky, and I was doing the opening combination and I remember thinking to myself, "I wonder who's in the back row."
—**Jerry Mitchell,** Choreographer

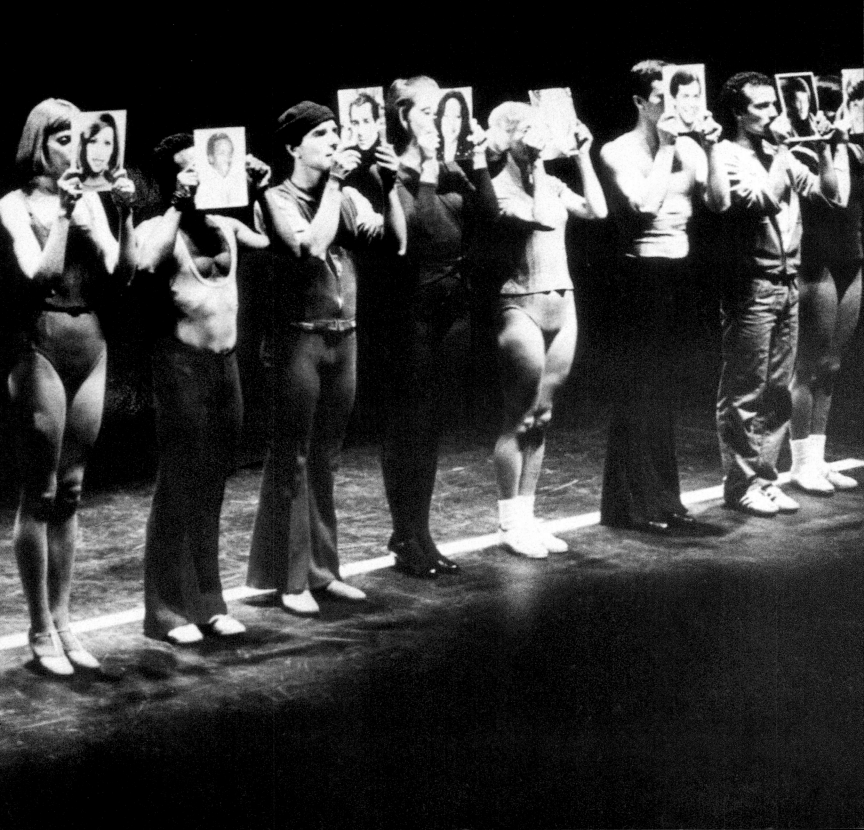

selected from many of the dancers who participated in the taped session—but not all of them; some dancers were not considered right to tell their own stories so several were reassigned to other dancers. The personal psyches of Bennett's cast and crew were but raw material to be shaped and molded unsentimentally by the director into the most original show anyone had seen in decades.

The Russian acting guru Constantin Stanislavsky wrote of a "super-objective," a need so overwhelming that all of a character's actions can be ascribed to that one need. *A Chorus Line* had the slimmest plot since *On the Town*, but it had one hell of a super-objective: twenty-five dancers desperately auditioning for eight jobs on the chorus line of a new musical. The passion of the piece came from Bennett's desire to make these seventeen dancers (eight get eliminated in the first ten minutes) represent the thousands upon thousands of gypsies over the years who sublimated their own careers to support the star. Bennett did for his dancers what Arthur Miller did for salesmen a quarter century earlier: he made sure that attention was paid. The first five-week workshop led to a second seven-week one at the beginning of 1975, where the exploration would go deeper, and with the addition of James Kirkwood as a colibrettist, elements of the show would finally be set.

The auditioning dancers (Donna McKechnie, center) rehearse the final combination with the director, Zack (Robert LuPone, r.).

One day in rehearsal, Michael Bennett took a chalk and—wham!—drew a line on the floor, and he said that's the line that we're all behind, we're all on the line. Well, now, with us all on the line it becomes: "Oh God, I need this job, I really need this job." Everything now changes, it's not just about dancers and their résumés and showing off, it's "I'm desperate, I am desperate for this thing in my life"—somehow or other, we're all in it together.

—Marvin Hamlisch

The finale of the show had the eight selected dancers performing (along with their rejected colleagues) a typical rousing showstopper—"One"— backing up a nonexistent star. At one point, Bennett thought of bringing someone different out of the audience every night to be the "Ann-Margret of the evening," but that was abandoned. The point was, as cast member Baayork Lee observed, "After two hours of spilling our guts out and just cutting our wrist and giving this choreographer everything that we have and begging him for the job, you finally get to see the job that we are auditioning for and we are all in the same costume and we all look alike and we all dance alike." That image was key to Bennett; it was a way of highlighting the anonymity of the chorus performer.

In April, the time came to open the show at the Public's 299-seat Newman Theater. Whatever the audience was going to see on April 16, it was certainly going to be different. The show received unprecedented word of mouth from the preview audience, and by the time the reviews came out, a commercial transfer to Broadway was a foregone conclusion. The Shubert Organization had contributed "enhancement money" to the project at the Public and quickly moved *A Chorus Line* to the Shubert Theatre on Broadway in July, only weeks after it closed its sold-out run at the Public. It caught the public's imagination and became Broadway's longest-running show in September 1983, continuing after that for

Many stories and many disappointments later, the final few get to sing about their star—"One Singular Sensation."

Sammy Williams in his Tony-winning performance as Paul, one of Broadway's first sympathetic gay characters.

another seven years, eventually notching a record-breaking run of 6,137 performances. *A Chorus Line* won every prize the theater can offer, including the Pulitzer and nine Tonys, two of which went to Bennett. He had overnight become the most desirable artist on Broadway.

The overwhelming success of the show is especially admirable because, in a history decorated with unlikely shows, *A Chorus Line* was in many ways Broadway's most unlikely. It is an anti-musical or, perhaps more accurately, the first counterintuitive musical. It had no scenery beyond some mirrors, no costumes but leotards except for a few spangles for the finale, no setting other than a nondescript theater, no intermission, and no star. Its very ethos was contrary to every convention the American musical had carefully built up over a century. As far back as *Sally* in 1920, musicals were about girls getting out of the chorus line to become stars; here, Cassie, Donna McKechnie's character, is a star *manqué* who is desperate to get *back* into the chorus line. The revelations of their pasts make the rest of the characters appear to be the most wounded, most damaged assemblage of individuals seen on a stage since the *Marat/Sade,* and the climax of the show celebrates only the dancers' uniformity, not their individuality.

None of which negates the show's immense popularity, nor its considerable influence on Broadway and beyond. The idiosyncratic, neurotic, often kooky characters and their rather clichéd psychological profiles were the first musical manifestation of a trend begun in the late 1960s, highlighted by Dustin Hoffman's appearance as a leading man in the film *The Graduate,* to glamorize unglamorous people. In Hamlisch's energetic, backbeat-heavy score, Broadway finally found the pop-rock sound it had been waiting for since *Hair.* The show provided the Broadway musical's first extended sympathetic portrayal of homosexuals; few will ever forget actor Sammy Williams, his hands crammed as deeply into his pockets as his shame, delivering the show's climactic monologue—a monologue, not a song—about his experience in a drag show.

A Chorus Line almost single-handedly raised the fortunes of Broadway. It certainly raised them for the Shubert Organization and became a cash cow for the nonprofit Shakespeare Festival, bringing it almost $50 million in exchange for a $500,000 investment in money and resources. It also shook the road out of its post–*Hello, Dolly!* coma by providing a reasonably inexpensive production without a star that could tour all over the country. The workshop would become the new method of developing musicals. The venerable outposts of New Haven, Detroit, and Boston would now be forsaken for two months in a rehearsal room littered with script drafts and cardboard coffee cups. Even though it was a rare creative mind who could mine a workshop as profitably as Bennett did—more often, workshops could be a way of artistically rearranging the furniture—the workshop has now become a Broadway institution.

The image of Bennett's heroic army of beautifully toned dancers, clad only in pre-spandex leotards, infiltrated nearly every aspect of pop culture. Television specials paid tributes to "gypsies," Hollywood rediscovered dance, producing movies such as *The Turning Point* and *All That Jazz* for the older crowd and *Staying Alive*, *Footloose*, and *Flashdance* for the younger crowd. Jane Fonda aerobicized on videotape, costumed like one of the eight dancers who get eliminated at the top of *A Chorus Line*, and became an idol to millions. Even the television exercise shows that have clogged the airwaves since the late 1970s tap in to the show's basic concept: if you work hard enough—in leotards—you too can make it.

Michael Bennett, who always had his eyes on the prize, finally "got it" in a way that eclipsed all others. The fact that he achieved his goal by introducing the world to the anonymity of the chorus line he so desperately sought to escape is but one of *A Chorus Line*'s many ironies. He had a theatrical magic that allowed him to create Broadway's most exorbitant success out of its humblest practitioners.

At the record-breaking 3,389th performance, September 29, 1983, Bennett brought back 332 A Chorus Line *alums and put them all onstage for an extraordinary special performance. "It was one of those rare occasions when the theater seemed to have gathered its past, present, and future into one house on one night," wrote Frank Rich in the* New York Times.

"The sun'll come out tomorrow"

NEW AUDIENCES FOR BROADWAY

If, in the early '70s, the Broadway musical was stymied to create a newly successful musical form, it was more successful in creating new audiences. At a time when the traditional audience of affluent, culture-minded white adults was winnowing down, it was necessary to expand the consumer base. Using new talent, new marketing techniques, and a combination of new and nostalgic material, Broadway opened its doors to a family audience for the first time in a decade, and to a black audience for the first time in nearly half a century. It was an audience that, the *New York Times* wrote in 1975, "the white theater establishment has for years been saying did not exist."

The few musicals in the '60s that dealt with the black experience were created by white writers and composers, but the early '70s saw the emergence of several shows whose creative staff and cast were predominantly African American. The shows had their roots in different genres. There were nonlinear musicals that put the urban black experience front and center, like Melvin Van Peebles's *Ain't Supposed to Die a Natural Death* (1971), and more traditional adaptations of earlier black plays, such as *Purlie* (1970) and *Raisin* (1973), a version of Lorraine Hansberry's groundbreaking *A Raisin in the Sun*. The fierce black militant movement of the late 1960s had faded from view, and it now seemed possible for white audiences to participate in the celebration of black life on stage.

The first completely black mainstream musical of the '70s came from a time-honored source, *The Wizard of Oz*. A black producer in New York, Ken Harper, saw the possibilities of reinventing the story in a manner that would access the popularity of Motown, *Soul Train*, Afrocentric fashion, and the black urban movies that were developing a crossover audience in the early '70s. If the material appealed to families as well, so much the better. He hired a black composer-lyricist named Charlie Smalls (who, tragically, died soon after the show opened) and got Twentieth Century–Fox to put up the $650,000 investment. "Ease On Down the Road" became the show's infectious theme, as Dorothy and her three friends ventured forth to see "The Wiz," but the musical's tryouts on the real-life road were anything but easy. After some near-disastrous detours, Geoffrey Holder, who had designed the costumes, stepped up to replace the director and the entire show developed elegance and style. When it arrived on Broadway at the very beginning of 1975, it met with apathy from the largely white critical community and was on the verge of closing.

To advertise the show, producer Harper bypassed the traditional print campaign and turned directly to television, with a joyous, bubbly commercial aimed at getting black seven-year-olds to ask their parents to "ease on down the road" called Broadway. Coupled with word of mouth, and the black community's skill at organizing theater parties and group sales, the television commercial turned *The Wiz* into a wow, running 1,672 performances, followed by an immensely successful national tour.

A plethora of revues brought the black music of the 1920s and '30s back to the Broadway stage. In 1976, *Bubbling Brown Sugar* relived the experience of the Harlem Renaissance, followed by *Ain't Misbehavin'* in 1978, whose amusing, talented cast of five was so expert at selling Fats Waller's music that it won the Tony Award for Best Musical. Eubie Blake had his moment in the spotlight—literally, onstage at the age of ninety-five—in *Eubie!* (1978), and Duke Ellington's song catalog was elegantly staged as *Sophisticated Ladies* in 1981. Other musical tributes to black cultural history followed in the 1980s.

OPPOSITE: *Andre De Shields in the title role of* The Wiz *(1975) greets the eager travelers who have eased on down the road to meet him.*

The Wiz dared to take white mythology, white genius, white brilliance and ask, Judy Garland, can you improve upon her? Can you improve upon the Wizard of Oz? Yes, if you want to take it from another point of view, an Afro-centric point of view. The Wiz said, this belongs to us too, this whole concept of there's no place like home, of depending on the magic inside your heart to achieve personal success. We claimed that.

—Andre De Shields, The Wiz,
Original Cast

Charlaine Woodard and Andre De Shields check out "How Ya, Baby?" and bring Fats Waller back to a new generation in Ain't Misbehavin' *(1978).*

If *The Wiz* was successful at bringing families—black, white, or otherwise—back to Broadway, it only exposed the paucity of material suitable for children. The 1950s and '60s provided genuine opportunities for parents to introduce their kids to the world of musical theater—*The Sound of Music, The Music Man, Fiddler on the Roof, Mame,* to name just a few—but in the '70s, the lack of family material was an immense cultural and financial oversight.

Into the breach stepped a red-haired moppet with a scruffy dog named Sandy to provide Broadway with its greatest Cinderella story in many seasons. Lyricist Martin Charnin had the idea of turning the 1930s comic strip *Little Orphan Annie* into a musical as early as 1972. He brought together composer Charles Strouse and book writer Thomas Meehan to develop a Depression-era journey for the spunky orphan who finds love, family, and, one assumes, a terrific stock portfolio with billionaire Oliver "Daddy" Warbucks. Annie had been a huge pop-culture figure in the '30s, with her own radio series and numerous commercial tie-ins, but in the early 1970s, she carried a tainted whiff of camp about her; producers turned down the musical version for years. Still, the team persisted, and after a brief run at the Goodspeed Opera House in 1976, director Mike Nichols stepped in as producer and took *Annie,* with an almost completely unknown cast, to Washington, D.C., for another tryout.

It received a welcome in Washington that would have been beyond even Daddy Warbucks's dreams of avarice. *Annie* also made a brief stop at the Carter White House, for a miniversion, and the ballad sung by the show's preadolescent heroine resounded through the East Room:

The sun'll come out tomorrow.
Bet your bottom dollar that tomorrow,
There'll be sun.

When the show opened in N.Y.C. on April 21, 1977, it was greeted with unambiguously open arms. Critics admired its craftsmanship, insiders were thrilled at its unabashed old-fashionedness, and little girls all over the tri-state area had a new media heroine. The show ran an impressive 2,377 performances, and *Annie*'s success was a surprise even to its creators. Thomas Meehan explained:

Paradoxically, a funny thing happened to America between the time we set to work on *Annie* and the time that it at last arrived on Broadway. We wrote the musical as a reaction to the Nixonian America of 1972, but now, with the Vietnam War ended, the economy on the upswing, and James Earl Carter in the White House, the message of hope in *Annie* is no longer antithetical to the mood of the country but is instead a mirror of it.

It's unlikely that the families who flocked to *Annie* over its impressive 2,377 performances were aware of such cultural subtleties, but it hardly mattered. *The Wiz* and *Annie* proved to producers that a decent family show could not only have its own unembarrassing integrity, it could be a gold mine.

OPPOSITE: *Annie (1977) brought back a beloved comic-strip character, as well as the glittering "N.Y.C" of the early '30s. Here, Reid Shelton as "Daddy" Warbucks and Sandy Faison as his secretary show Annie the high spots of midtown. Andrea McArdle, the original Annie, was soon replaced with a phalanx of preadolescent divas: here is Sarah Jessica Parker as the lizard-leapin' orphan.*

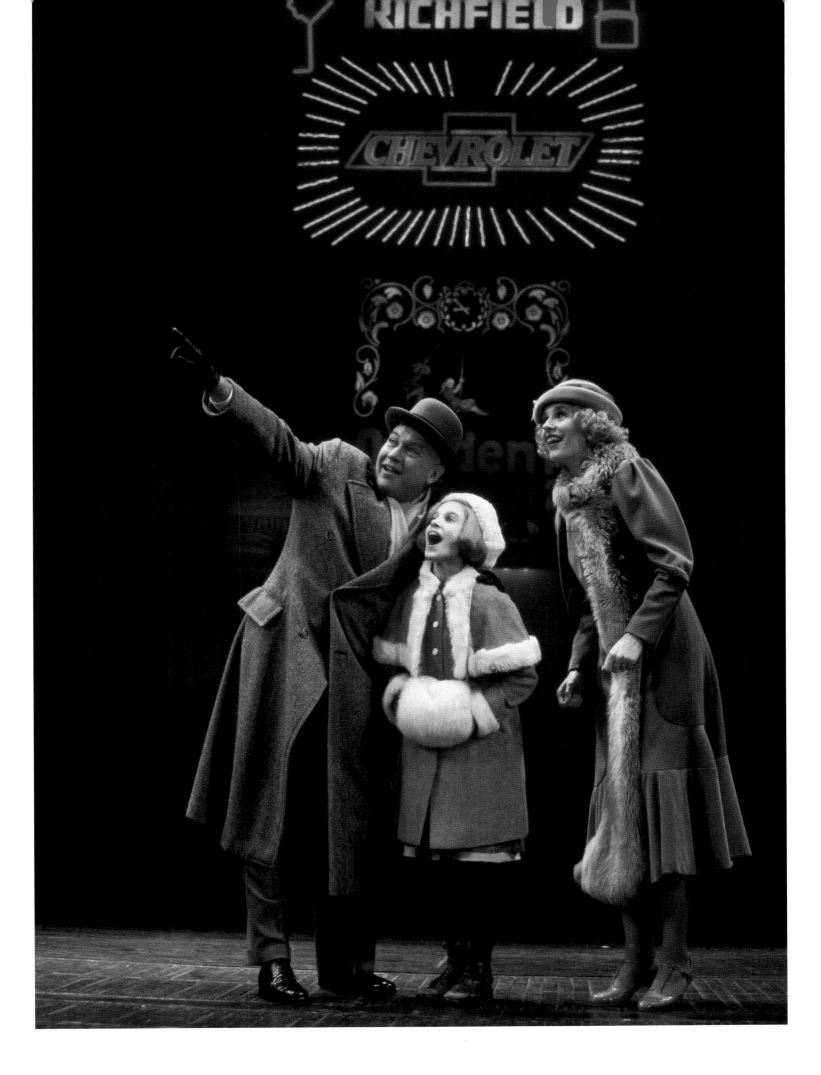

ON THE TWENTIETH CENTURY

We point with the deepest pride
To the grandest ride
On the New York Central Railroad,
The aristocrat of locomotive trains . . .

IN THE MIDDLE OF A DECADE that was looking for a musical language in every corner, an Art Deco stream-lined engine of a show sped onto Broadway like an express train straight from musical comedy heaven.

The original source material, *Twentieth Century,* had been a particular favorite of fans of the theater for decades. The 1932 play had been adapted by two of Broadway's snappiest writers, Ben Hecht and Charles MacArthur, from a stage farce by Bruce Milholland entitled *The Napoleon of Broadway,* and was directed by George Abbott, who was just beginning to sharpen his inimitable farcical skills. The story concerned a down-at-heels theatrical impresario, Oscar Jaffee, and his last-ditch attempt to win back his pro-tégée and former lover, movie star Lily Garland, as they zoom from Chicago to New York during their sixteen-hour excursion on the *Twentieth Century,* Depression-era America's most luxurious mode of railway travel. The com-edy became the granddaddy of all screwball comedies in its 1934 screen incarnation, which featured the ham-on-wry histrionics of John Barrymore and catapulted Carole Lombard to film stardom.

Betty Comden and Adolph Green were the perfect adaptors for the musical version. No other team was as adept at puncturing the pretensions of both Broadway and Hollywood (which their lyrics referred to as "ermine-vested, vermin-infested"). Their choice for a composer was unusual and adventurous—and new to them. Cy Coleman had been a Broadway fixture since 1960 when he made his name working with lyricist Carolyn Leigh on *Wildcat,* a vehicle for Lucille Ball. His subsequent scores—the vaude-villian *Little Me,* the swinging *Sweet Charity,* the funky *Seesaw*—all buoyed audiences with their infectious finger-snapping tunes. But Coleman's chameleon-like genius for mastering different musical idioms sometimes left his con-siderable depth unchallenged; when *On the Twentieth Century* came to Broadway in 1978, he already had a hit show running, *I Love My Wife,* a gentle extramarital farce in a Top 40s style, played by a tiny onstage band.

Coleman initially turned down the offer of *Twentieth Century* several times. "I didn't want to do twenties pastiche—there was too much of that around," he recounted. "But when I realized the main characters had these larger-than-life personalities, I thought—ah, comic opera! Even the tikka-tikka-tikka patter of a locomotive train has the rhythm of comic opera." It was an inspired decision and the creative team made the most of it. Instead of a DeSylva-Brown-and-Henderson retread, the score became a tribute to rhapsodical excesses of Romberg and Friml. Oscar Jaffee had not one but two over-the-top hambone songs, and Lily had an extraordinary number ("Babette") in which she was torn between appearing in a play about Mary Magdalene (a mock-religious oratorio) and a Somerset Maugham drawing-room knockoff (a Noel Coward parody). Together, the leads were given not only an extended rip-roaring feud ("I've Got It All"), but a breathtaking flashback duet ("Our Private World") built on exquisite harmonies.

The score had the breadth of *The Desert Song,* the sexy wit of *Kiss Me, Kate,* the rampant silliness of *On the Town,* and the potential to create a new musical language. Broadway had never heard a score like it.

Comden, Green, and Coleman were blessed with an ensemble of musically gifted farceurs. John Cullum as Oscar, fresh from his triumph as the lead in *Shenandoah,* ferociously channeled the zaniness of John Barrymore, and Madeline Kahn, whose comic film career hid an operatic soprano's range, channeled the zaniness of, well, Madeline

John Cullum, in a Tony-winning performance, taps into Barrymore's acrobatic histrionics as he tries to sell movie star Madeline Kahn on his latest project; she is not amused.

Kevin Kline also won a Tony—Best Featured Actor—for the show, as the aptly named Bruce Granit. Kahn displays looks that could kill—in a nice way.

Kahn. Beloved comedienne Imogene Coca played a deranged religious zealot, and Kevin Kline was introduced to the world at large as Kahn's current beau, a dense matinee idol who caromed off the walls like a billiard ball when she made an entrance in a low-cut silk dress. (Kline was cast instantly when, in a typical burst of enthusiasm, he kissed the male script reader during his audition.) In a daring change of pace, Harold Prince signed on as director. He recalled:

> After all, George Abbott directed it way back in the thirties. And I'd never directed farce and I wanted to see if I knew how to do it, and at the end of it I thought, I guess I knew how to do it. It's nice to laugh once in a while. You don't do a lot of laughing while you're rehearsing *Sweeney Todd*, you know.

Last but emphatically not least, scenic designer Robin Wagner provided the most elegant reimagining of the classic deluxe train, constructing it to break apart and reassemble in a thousand different ways. The set allowed Prince to stage the show as the theatrical equivalent of a Chuck Jones *Road Runner* cartoon, and the *Twentieth Century* was turned, by their inventiveness, from being a title into a title character.

Imogene Coca, as a lunatic zealot, had free rein of Robin Wagner's remarkable set.

On the Twentieth Century itself zoomed into New York in February of 1978, after a Boston engagement in the middle of the worst blizzard in decades (the show's producers had to operate the scenery that week). Although, by and large, the critics rolled out the red carpet, audiences were less enthusiastic. The big hit show that year, *Ain't Misbehavin'*, got most of the business and the Tony Award, and *On the Twentieth Century* was not helped when the inspired Kahn gave up her taxing role after a few months to be replaced by her understudy, Judy Kaye. It closed after 449 performances, which would have been a bonanza for the musical comedies of the '30s, but was a baggage car of red ink in the '70s. Perhaps it was simply the wrong time for a glorious piece of old-fashioned nonsense; or perhaps, as Prince once contended, the general populace is never really engaged by the problems of fictional artists and movie stars.

Still, for a season and a half, in the middle of a theatrically confused decade, the bravura intelligence and skill of *On the Twentieth Century* shot through Broadway like a comet in the evening sky.

"All I care about is love"

BOB FOSSE AND *CHICAGO*

In the spring of 1972, Bob Fosse won the Triple Crown of show business: the Tony for *Pippin*, an Academy Award for directing the film version of *Cabaret*, and an Emmy for the television variety show "Liza with a 'Z.'" It wasn't just unprecedented, it was unimaginable (actually, he won two Tonys that year—Best Director and Choreographer). A few weeks later, he checked himself into a discreet New York hospital for depression. "Pretty soon, they're gonna find me out," he once said to John Kander.

Fosse was always a complicated person. He could be devoted yet promiscuous, egotistical and insecure, attracted to the sleazier side of show biz but eager to be recognized and rewarded. Born in 1927 on the North Side of Chicago, Fosse started dancing at an early age. He formed a soft-shoe duo with another kid, and calling themselves the Riff Brothers, they played amateur shows, clubs, and burlesque revues all through high school. After his partner quit, Fosse enlisted in the Navy, in an entertainment unit for servicemen right after the Second World War (his commanding officer was Joseph Papp). Upon his discharge, he sought his fortune on Broadway in the late 1940s. All he wanted was to step into the dance shoes of Gene Kelly, and he did, after a fashion, playing Pal Joey in stock and getting a film contract on M-G-M's fabled musical lot in 1952.

A young Bob Fosse, at the beginning of his film career, ready to step into the tap shoes of Kelly and Astaire.

[In Hollywood,] he had no idea he was going to be a choreographer, or if he did, he certainly didn't talk about it. And in my opinion, he was going to be as good a song-and-dance man as any of the others, as Kelly and Astaire. I thought Fosse, this guy is going to be it. He was obsessed with dance and drama and acting and music and he could drive all of us into the ground with his determination and energy and constant work, more, more, more.

—Stanley Donen, Film Director

By the mid 1950s, he was back in New York, making a name for himself as a choreographer, and in 1959, with *Redhead*, he had earned the credit that was the Holy Grail for the dancers of his generation: "Entire Production Directed and Choreographed by." He adapted a Fellini film as a vehicle for his wife, Gwen Verdon, and they both took the town by storm with *Sweet Charity* in 1966. Fosse would eventually realize his ambition to be a film director, translating *Charity* to the screen, then shooting his own idiosyncratic vision of *Cabaret*. His favorite projects were about show biz, such as *Cabaret* and the film *Lenny*, or he found some way to make whatever he was working on feel like show biz. He frequently used hats and canes in his work, a holdover from his soft-shoe days, and constantly recycled a vaudeville vocabulary—emcees, slatternly showgirls,

BOTTOM: Pleasures and Palaces, *a rare flop by Frank Loesser—and his final show—at least had Fosse to direct and choreograph the troops (eighteenth-century Russian troops, in this case), 1965.*

onstage bands, working the crowd. Even Stephen Schwartz's *Pippin*, which on the page dealt with war in the Middle Ages, wound up looking like the Gaiety Village strip club on Western Avenue from his youth.

> **Bob Fosse saw the last twenty minutes of *Follies* and it changed his life. He thought, "Oh my goodness. Show business as a metaphor—you can write about war, but you can perform it as a song-and-dance trio."**
> **—Stephen Sondheim**

For years, Gwen Verdon had wanted to adapt a 1926 play called *Chicago* into a musical. It had been filmed in 1942 as *Roxie Hart*, a story about a murderess who shoots her lover, gets acquitted after a flashy trial, then tries to hit the big time in vaudeville. The woman who wrote the play, Maurine Dallas Watkins, was a former journalist who had actually covered a similar trial in Chicago, but in the ensuing years, she had had a spiritual conversion and renounced that part of her life. In other words, she wouldn't sell the rights. But by 1973, Watkins had died and Verdon bought the rights herself, envisioning it as a comeback vehicle for her to be directed by Fosse, from whom she had recently been separated.

"Spend a little time with me." During the cast recording of the cast album for Fosse's showcase for Gwen Verdon, Sweet Charity, *1966*.

Once upon a time, Velma Kelly (Chita Rivera) had an agent in her quest for show-biz fame: David Rounds, whose solo number, "Ten Percent," stopped the show dead—out-of-town. His part was cut out of Chicago *before the New York opening.*

OPPOSITE: *There is nothing like a Fosse dame: the female chorus of* Chicago *inspired set designer Tony Walton's watercolor rendering for the show's poster.*

Fosse brought Kander and Ebb on board to create something out of the material, but it didn't seem to have the makings of a typical book musical. The characters were interesting enough—Roxie Hart, another murderess-turned-vaudevillian named Velma Kelly, and their flashy, unscrupulous lawyer, Billy Flynn—but it wasn't until the team decided to make the whole evening into a "musical vaudeville" that it came together.

> **[The vaudeville format of *Chicago*] enabled us to present the characters in a fresh and unusual way by drawing an analogy between them and their vaudeville counterparts. When Roxie sings at the beginning, she's Helen Morgan, Billy Flynn becomes Ted Lewis, Amos [Roxie's cuckolded husband] is Bert Williams when he sings "Mr. Cellophane," Velma becomes Texas Guinan, and the prison matron is Sophie Tucker.**
> **—Fred Ebb**

Fosse was thrilled to be working on a project that allowed him to be as theatrical and cynical as he wanted, without having to worry too much about plot. He assembled a terrific cast; joining Verdon were Chita Rivera as Velma and Jerry Orbach as Billy Flynn. On the first day of principal rehearsals in November 1974, the usually driven Fosse was feeling woozy, and on the lunch break, he was quietly driven to the hospital. He had suffered a heart attack.

The show would be postponed for months while Fosse recovered. When he returned, his energy wasn't quite what it had been, but his point of view had sharpened drastically. *Chicago* was never intended as a "sunny, funny" look at the 1920s; its very nature was cynical, portraying the public's thirst for celebrity and entertainment as being completely unmitigated by any ethical distinctions or considerations.

Fosse threw himself into the darker underside of *Chicago*. It was no surprise to his colleagues that he felt the world was "all show biz" and pretense, but the show started to dance out of control with an unleavened view of corruption and sexual exploitation. Fosse's heart attack had taken an emotional toll, and it made him particularly harsh on his creative team, so much so that Kander dreamed of leaving the Philadelphia tryout and returning to New York, fearing that the stress of the production might actually kill him.

Fosse's colleagues eventually prevailed on him to scale back his more aggressive effects, and when the show arrived in New York on June 3, 1975, his unique magic was all over the stage. His "story of murder, greed, corruption, violence, exploitation, adultery and treachery—all those things we find near and dear to our hearts" was driven by the cast at full throttle, with sinuous, scantily clad chorines, fan dances, ventriloquist acts, transvestites, an onstage band, and a bravura finish for Verdon and Rivera.

Billy Flynn (Jerry Orbach) tries to convince reporter Mary Sunshine—via a ventriloquist act—that when Roxie Hart (Gwen Verdon) accidentally shot an intruder, "We Both Reached for the Gun."

OPPOSITE: Two of Broadway's hottest honeys: Rivera and Verdon work it in Chicago.

Critics were divided; in the post-Watergate summer of 1975, nine months after Nixon was pardoned and with New York City on the verge of bankruptcy, perhaps there was just too much corruption in real life without having to buy an orchestra seat to see more of it, no matter how masterfully it was served up. More to the point, A Chorus Line had opened downtown only weeks earlier, and Fosse's brilliant dance work would "place" to Michael Bennett's "win." Chicago managed an admirable 923-performance run, helped by Liza Minnelli's brief spell as a replacement for Verdon, but it failed to win a single Tony, despite eleven nominations.

Nothing obsessed Fosse more than mortality and posterity. Nine years after Fosse died of a heart attack in 1987, Chicago reappeared on Broadway in a scaled-down version, based on his choreography. It was still running when, the next season, Fosse, a revue of his greatest dances and supervised by Gwen Verdon, opened at the theater next door, and won the Tony for best musical. As an old-time vaudevillian once said, "The best gig of them all is immortality." Fosse would have liked that.

RAZZLE DAZZLE

Words by Fred Ebb
Music by John Kander
From Chicago *(1975)*

If cynicism ever had a theme song, it was this number from the second act.

They're about to go into the trial, and Roxie's nervous, and Billy says to her, "It's all gonna be all right, because it's all a circus, kid, and it won't matter what you know to be true and what you know to be not true, because, eventually, it's all a question of how you present it and how you razzle-dazzle 'em."
—Fred Ebb

Kander and Ebb had worked with Bob Fosse twice before, on the film of *Cabaret* and the television special "Liza with a 'Z,'" so they were familiar with his style and his predilections. Kander recalled:

It was certainly the heavily rhythmic stuff that appealed to Fosse a lot, as it does with most choreographers. There was a little vamp in it, and Fred said while we're writing it, "Put in two finger snaps": "Da-dum, da-dum (*snap, snap*) / dah-dah-dum." So I looked at him sort of funny and said, "All right, but why?" He said, "Bobby's gonna love that." And when we went to play it for him, we didn't get past the finger snaps, and Bobby started beaming.

Once the number was staged in rehearsal, Kander and Ebb were a good deal less enthusiastic. Fosse, in one of his darkest moments, had surrounded Jerry Orbach, who sang the song, with a chorus of couples simulating sex on the steps of the courthouse. The message, ostensibly, was that anyone seeking justice in the mid-1970s was in for a good screwing. The show's producers and the rest of the creative team were appalled when they saw the number in rehearsal. Fosse was skillfully talked out of his excesses by Orbach, who wisely realized the number was potent enough that it could be put over with a minimum of stage effects.

I was the sharp lawyer in the pinstripe suit with the little thin mustache and I explained that when we go to the trial, it's all show biz. I took off the jacket and I had suspenders underneath, pulled the shirt out of my pants to blouse it out, messed up my hair, and put on a little pair of wire-rimmed glasses on my nose, and I became Clarence Darrow, and then did "Razzle Dazzle." That's basically all it's about, fooling the jury, fooling the judge, making them believe one thing when something else is possible.
—Jerry Orbach

Give 'em the old razzle dazzle
Razzle dazzle 'em
Give 'em an act with lots of flash in it
And the reaction will be passionate.
Give 'em the old hocus pocus
Bead and feather 'em.

Clarence Darrow used his down-to-earth folksiness to get a number of murderers out of the Cook County death-house; Orbach plays the part in "Razzle Dazzle."

How can they see with sequins in their eyes?
What if your hinges all are rusting?
What if, in fact, you're just disgusting?
Razzle dazzle 'em
And they'll never catch wise!

Give 'em the old razzle dazzle
Razzle dazzle 'em.
Give 'em a show that's so splendiferous
Row after row will grow vociferous.
Give 'em the old flim-flam flummox
Fool and fracture 'em.
How can they hear the truth above the roar?
Throw 'em a fake and a finagle,
They'll never know you're just a bagel,
Razzle dazzle 'em
And they'll beg you for more!

Give 'em the old razzle dazzle
Razzle dazzle 'em.
Back since the days of old Methuselah
Everyone loves the big bamboo-za-ler.
Give 'em the old three-ring circus,
Stun and stagger 'em.
When you're in trouble, go into your dance.
Though you are stiffer than a girder
They let you get away with murder.
Razzle dazzle 'em
And you've got a romance.

Give 'em the old razzle dazzle,
Razzle dazzle 'em.
Give 'em an act that's unassailable
They'll wait a year till you're available!
Give 'em the old double whammy
Daze and dizzy 'em
Show 'em the first rate sorcerer you are—
Long as you keep 'em way off-balance,
How can they spot you got no talents?

Razzle dazzle 'em
Razzle dazzle 'em
Razzle dazzle 'em
And they'll make you a star!

Orbach warns Verdon—dressed up like a hausfrau for sympathy's sake—that "it's all show biz, kid."

"He never forgets and he never forgives"

SWEENEY TODD

Prince and Sondheim in rehearsal.

Commodore Perry's ships—portrayed in a Kabuki design, courtesy of Boris Aronson, violate the sovereignty of Japan in Pacific Overtures *(1976).*

On July 4, 1976, America celebrated its bicentennial, and New York Harbor was the scene of one of the nation's most glorious events. Operation Sail brought hundreds of ships from around the globe—three-masted clipper ships to tiny sailboats—into the harbor to remind the world of the voyages to freedom that defined the United States.

In the months before the event, Stephen Sondheim and Harold Prince had been using ships to remind audiences of America as well, but in typical fashion, they just did it a little differently. *Pacific Overtures,* their musical about the opening of Japan in 1853, has four American men-of-war under the command of Commodore Matthew Perry portrayed onstage in a Kabuki style as "Four black dragons / Spitting fire." The show, which closed one week before Operation Sail, was their most ambitious musical to date; with a book by John Weidman, it told the story of how American imperialism awakened the isolated culture of Japan, trammeled it underfoot, and turned it into a sleeping giant. Designed in the bold, sweeping strokes of the ritualized Kabuki theater, it was the kind of musical that used words like *détente* and *extraterritoriality* in its lyrics—and earned laughs with them. Broadway had never seen a show that even came close to the aspirations and scale of *Pacific Overtures,* with its nineteen male Asian American actors playing sixty-one roles.

It was not a commercial success, but success never came easily to the team of Prince and Sondheim. After their debut with *Company,* they created the glorious musical elegy *Follies,* which many musical aficionados regard as the greatest musical ever to reach Broadway. In 1973, they had their first big commercial success with *A Little Night Music.* Set in turn-of-the-century Sweden and based on an Ingmar Bergman film, it was the first anxious operetta, a roundelay of mismatched couples looking for love in all the wrong places. Sondheim had crafted a sensuous score, conceived in variations of waltz time, which brought forth his best-known song, "Send in the Clowns." In 1977 Prince imported a charming British four-person revue of Sondheim's work, *Side by Side by Sondheim,* which went a long way toward giving the composer a wider profile beyond his usual Broadway fans.

As creative, ambitious, and artistically bloodyminded as Prince and Sondheim were, audiences were unprepared for their next endeavor. The legend of Sweeney Todd means very little in this country, but in his native England, Todd is the fictional boogeyman par excellence, a cross between the Headless Horseman and Lizzie Borden. When Sondheim was in London in 1973 for Angela Lansbury's *Gypsy*, he attended a new stage version of the Victorian tale, produced in a small black-box theater. Since his debut in the nineteenth century, Sweeney Todd had been rendered on stage and page as a homicidal barber who slit his victims' throats, with his landlady and accomplice, Mrs. Lovett, baking the remains into meat pies for hungry Londoners. In the 1973 version, playwright Christopher Bond had given the old boy a new lease on life. Todd was no longer an obtuse monster, but a pathetic cog in the Victorian class system; sent to a prison colony by a venal judge who uses the barber's absence to rape his wife and adopt his daughter, Todd returns to London incognito to begin a reign of terror and revenge on the man who wronged him. Bond's version was a highly theatrical, gory mix of farce and melodrama—two of Sondheim's favorite genres. He explained why the story appealed to him:

> The piece is about being done an injustice and getting your revenge. And I think that's in everybody, from the day they're born—literally. Yanked out of the womb, slapped, and made to face this world, not to mention all of the vicissitudes we have in the next fifty, sixty years of our life, particularly when you're growing up. I think everybody has feelings of revenge. Sweeney acted on them and the audience senses that, and they identify with him.

"You know me. Sometimes ideas just pop into me head . . ." Sondheim reviewing the score with leads Angela Lansbury and Len Cariou.

It took several attempts for Sondheim to persuade Prince, who disliked old horror movies and dark farce as much as Sondheim enjoyed them, to direct the musical version. What eventually grabbed Prince was the inequity of Victorian society: "I needed to know that these people—chopping up humans and turning them into mincemeat pies, eating them—were the result of a soullessness brought on by the Industrial Age, by taking people off the farms and sticking them in the factories, by making them work sixteen hours a day and breathe filthy, soot-filled air, and so on."

Writing the piece took surprisingly little time even though it would be the most musically complicated score Sondheim ever attempted. It was operatic, almost entirely through-composed with quotes from the *Dies Irae* in the Mass for the Dead mixed in with the throbbing tension of a Bernard Herrmann film score. Sondheim also routinely juxtaposes moments of surpassing beauty with bloody chunks of terror, only to clear the palate with hilarious patter songs that Gilbert and Sullivan might have written for the Addams Family. The three songs that end the first act may constitute the most outrageous and finely crafted dramatic writing in the American musical theater. The soaring erotic reverie "Pretty Women" allows Sweeney and the corrupt judge to rhapsodize over female beauty before the Judge escapes Sweeney's murderous grasp. Then, in the bone-chilling existential aria called "Epiphany," Todd comes to the conclusion that he has been put on this earth to become its freelance executioner. It is the dark-mirror image of Hammerstein's "Soliloquy" (which also appears at the penultimate moment of the first act); while Billy Bigelow realizes he must raise his daughter or die, Sweeney Todd realizes he must release his daughter and kill. His homicidal broodings are then interrupted by Mrs. Lovett, who enterprisingly suggests how they might dispose of all the corpses that Todd will grimly

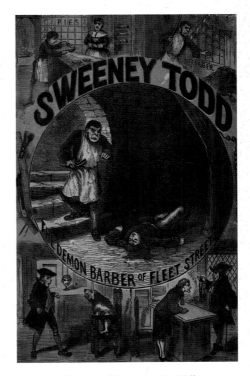

"Attend the tale of Sweeney Todd." The roots of the story stretched back to the "penny-dreadfuls" of the nineteenth century.

"At last my arm is complete again!"
Cariou as Sweeney Todd sees his future
in the sharpness of his razor.

reap:

MRS. LOVETT:
I mean,
With the price of meat what it is,
When you get it,
If you get it—

TODD:
Ah!

MRS. LOVETT:
Good, you got it.

The patter number "A Little Priest" continues in its merry music hall way, as Todd and Mrs. Lovett imagine all the members of Victorian society who will provide the tasty fillings for their meat pies.

TODD:
What is that?

MRS. LOVETT:
It's fop.
Finest in the shop.
Or we have some shepherd's pie peppered
With actual shepherd
On top.
And I've just begun.
Here's the politician—so oily
It's served on a doily—
     (Todd makes a face.)
Not one?

TODD:
Put it on a bun.
     (as she looks at him quizzically)
Well, you never know if it's going to run.

Lansbury and Cariou review their inventory in "A Little Priest."

With Eugene Lee's huge foreboding set (made from parts of actual nineteenth-century foundries shipped from Rhode Island), and the gleefully macabre performances of its leads, Len Cariou and Angela Lansbury, *Sweeney Todd* was one of the most delectably rich theatrical offerings ever seen on Broadway. To Sondheim's own amazement, the critics and audiences ate up the bizarre mixture of butchery and buffoonery onstage, and the show, which opened in March 1979, walked away with eight Tony Awards, including prizes for Prince, Sondheim, bookwriter Hugh Wheeler, Cariou, and Lansbury. Prince contended that you could not persuade someone to see a musical about cannibalism if they didn't want to see a musical about cannibalism, no matter how good it was, and therefore the show would always have a limited audience; it finished its Broadway run in the red (fittingly) at 558 performances. But *Sweeney Todd* has gone on to be revived in theaters large and small, opera houses and black boxes, around the world.

Although it was not the object of the exercise, Sondheim and Prince showed that there was nothing you couldn't put into a musical if you did it artfully and with integrity. You could gain the audience's sympathy for a serial killer; you could even get a couple of really boffo laughs out of his deranged accomplice. Sondheim and Prince were only the most daring of the Broadway practitioners who sought, throughout the last hundred years, to push the envelope. With *Sweeney Todd,* they slashed it wide open.

Although not a financial success in its Broadway debut, Sweeney Todd *has been resurrected time and again on theater and opera stages throughout the world, making it the most critically acclaimed musical-theater piece since* Porgy and Bess.

I think Steve Sondheim's best show is *Sweeney Todd,* **and I think part of the reason is he found something in the character of Sweeney that he identified with. And the show is enormously emotional because of that.**

—Arthur Laurents

Finale

For the first time in their careers, Harold Prince and Stephen Sondheim were looking backward.

In the fall of 1981 *Merrily We Roll Along*, a new musical adapted from a nearly forgotten play by Kaufman and Hart, went into rehearsal. A modern morality tale about a trio of friends who confront compromise in their artistic careers, *Merrily* told its story in reverse chronological order. Sondheim and George Furth, who wrote the book adaptation, made some dramatic changes to their source material. The time period was advanced from the early part of the century to the years 1977–1957, pretty much the era in which Furth and Sondheim grew to make their own significant marks in their field; the settings were changed to reflect the scenes of their own lives and triumphs: Greenwich Village, the Alvin Theatre (where *Company* premiered), Central Park West, and so on.

"Yesterday is done . . . " Harold Prince and Stephen Sondheim during the first week of rehearsal for Merrily We Roll Along *(1981).*

Most important, they changed the identities of the main characters. The musical became the story of friends who were also a successful musical-comedy team, conquering the same worlds their creators had with such distinction. Although the show is not truly autobiographical, it is intensely personal. Many of the incidents in the show's early years come directly from Sondheim's experiences writing and auditioning musical projects in the 1950s and '60s.

Prince's concept for the show was particularly unconventional. He cast the entire show with a company of actors in their teens and early twenties; it was to be a cautionary fable about the temptations of the material world, narrated by a chorus still young enough to take the correct road. The team made one other unconventional choice, and it proved to be calamitous: no out-of-town tryout. They sought to solve the show's problems while beginning previews at that same Alvin Theatre. Within the first five weeks, the leading man and the choreographer were replaced, full costumes were replaced by sweatshirts and jeans, and, out of a desperate need for clarity and to accommodate the young performers' limited range, the book and score were summarily overhauled. Presenting a raw, new show every night on 52nd Street laid Prince, Sondheim, and Furth open to every maven's criticism.

When the show opened on November 16, 1981, the reviewers' pens were sharp and ready. As Frank Rich put it in the *New York Times*, "Mr. Sondheim has given this evening a half-dozen songs that are crushing and beautiful—that soar and linger and hurt. But the show that contains them is a shambles." It closed after sixteen performances, barely enough time to record the cast album. One of the show's saddest casualties was the team of Prince and Sondheim; they would not work together again for the rest of the century.

The failure of *Merrily* inspired reflection for its collaborators and for the industry. Looking back over more than a decade of work, Prince and Sondheim could see the groundbreaking shows they brought to Broadway. Any aspiring historian could have seen the future of Broadway by looking further back—into the "dark backward and abysm of time," as Shakespeare puts it. One could have seen the shows of the Golden Age; most of them would be revived and revised on Broadway at the end of the century.

One could have seen Hollywood movies from the last fifty years turned into stage musicals. Looking back as far as the 1920s, one could have seen a Theater District when it was brimming with vitality and light.

And if one looked back a century, to the 1880s, one could have seen a time when— hard to imagine—imported British musicals ruled the American stage.

OVERLEAF: *At the top of the second act, Todd eagerly awaits the arrival of his new barber chair, while Mrs. Lovett rounds up hungry customers for her very special meat pies. Eugene Lee's set perfectly framed the callous Victorian society captured by Hugh Wheeler's book and Sondheim's score.*

HAL PRINCE ON
FOLLIES

Contradictions: Notes on Twenty-Six Years
in the Theatre *(excerpt)*, 1974

The Girls Upstairs was a totally realistic musical about two girls and the fellows they had married thirty years earlier, meeting at a real party in a real theatre, with real decorations and real food and drink. It dealt with the loss of innocence in the United States, using the Ziegfeld Follies (a pretty girl is *no longer* like a melody) as its metaphor. The extent of its realism diminished its size, reduced its four leading characters to selfish overindulged pains in the neck; whereas they might have represented the misplaced American Dream. (We never really licked that problem.)

I began looking for a concept. In *The Best Remaining Seats,* a history in photographs and text of the great movie palaces of the 1930s, there appeared a photograph, originally published in *Life* magazine, of Gloria Swanson standing in the rubble of what had been the Roxy Theatre. She had opened the Roxy in a silent film, and when they tore it down, Eliot Elisofon photographed her in a black chiffon dress against the gutted proscenium. . . . Elisofon had captured the metaphor.

It was to be surrealistic, inspired by *8½,* and rubble became the key word. Metaphoric rubble became visual rubble. A theatre is being torn down. On its stage a party in celebration of that. The celebrants for whom the theatre represents youth, dreams lost, a golden time, are to be orphaned. (Aronson: "There's no place for patina in the United States.") Is the theatre torn down? Will it be torn down tomorrow? Or was it torn down yesterday? Keep it ambiguous, a setting for the sort of introspection that reunions precipitate, a mood in which to lose sight of the present, to look back on the past.

[Book writer James] Goldman and Sondheim were about just such business, but not in surrealistic terms. However, they approved of our scheme and agreed to adapt it.

The title, *Follies,* suggested the *Ziegfeld Follies,* but also, in the British sense, foolishness, and in the French, "folie," which is madness. The show arced to a mini *Ziegfeld Follies,* giving the audience in the final twenty minutes what it had expected all along. The only difference was that the stars of our Follies would confront in lavish production numbers the lies that had led them relentlessly to the brink of madness. Defenseless, they would lay waste the past, leave the rubble of the theatre behind them, and start to live. It was clear what we wanted to do. But how to do it? . . .

We went into rehearsal without the Follies section, seventy pages of script culminating in a Goldman-inspired confrontation of eight people, the four principals and their young counterparts in a Lacoön tangle, screaming at one another on an empty stage and suddenly trapped in a Ziegfeld extravaganza.

The script quit abruptly with these words: "What follows is a capsule Follies—costume parades, comedy routines, specialty acts—traditional and accurate in all ways but one. Sets, costumes, music, movement; all this is faithful to the past. What's different and unusual about it is the content, what it's all about."

It was characteristic of *Follies* that there was an inordinate number of <u>potential</u> distractions. . . . Throughout *Follies* six-foot showgirls wandered around in incredible costumes, glittering and gleaming upstage of some very serious book scenes, the content of which was necessary to understanding the show. And they were not distracting. It was as though we set our own ground rules and lived by them. The audience knew what to listen to and where to look. We made them work in *Follies,* and some objected. For others, it was exhilarating.

Follies cost $800,000 to produce. It lost $685,000. There were fifty in the cast, thirty in the orchestra, and twenty-eight in the crew backstage. It cost $80,000 a week to break even. At capacity it would have taken approximately forty weeks to pay off. But it wasn't the sort of show that plays to capacity. We won seven Tony Awards in April of 1972 and our grosses rose to $91,000 for several weeks, but the summer was coming, so we moved to California and inaugurated the Shubert, the newest theatre in the United States, with a show about tearing down a theatre.

I am happy I did *Follies.* I could not do it again because I could not in all conscience raise the money for it. Perhaps it's best summed up by Frank Rich, who was the critic for the *Harvard Crimson* when we were trying out in Boston:

It is easy to avoid *Follies* on the grounds that it is, after all, a Broadway musical—and, given what Broadway musicals have come to mean, such a bias is understandable. But that is precisely why you should see it, for *Follies* is a musical about the death of the musical and everything musicals represented for the people who saw and enjoyed them when such entertainment flourished in this country. If nothing else, *Follies* will make clear to you exactly why such a strange kind of theatre was such an important part of the American consciousness for so long. In the playbill for the show, the setting is described as "a party on the stage of this theatre tonight." They are not kidding, and there is no getting around the fact that a large part of the chilling fascination of *Follies* is that its creators are in essence presenting their own funeral.

He titled his review "The Last Musical." An unanticipated metaphor.

MICHAEL BENNETT ON
A CHORUS LINE

Interview conducted on October 24, 1977, produced by the Theatre on Film and Tape Archive at the New York Public Library for the Performing Arts (excerpt)

I STARTED DANCING AT THREE, and I went to one class a week. By age four I was taking two a week and a private lesson. By five I was now studying tap, acrobatics, ballet; by six, it was jazz, modern, and I started teaching dancing by the time I was twelve. From about eight years old, I truly spent every day after school, and all day Saturday, in front of a mirror dancing. That mirror means a great deal to me.

Dancers are very honest, they're very truthful. Because when you go up in front of a mirror and you are in a room working on a combination or a step, you just look in that mirror, and you can see if you are doing it better than the person next to you or worse, or what you have to improve—you face the reality. You know, if you're too fat you know it and you lose weight, and an actor, unfortunately, doesn't have that kind of judge.

I trained all my life to be a Broadway director–choreographer—Jerry Robbins is my idol—and in the late '60s and early '70s, every year, people wrote pieces in the *New York Times* saying the theater is dying, Broadway is dying. I thought wonderful, here I am and the industry was dying.

When I turned thirty, I was very depressed about Broadway. When you try to sell an idea to backers for a show for Broadway, or to the theater owners, you have to go in and convince them that the theater-party ladies are going to love the show, that my mother's gonna love the show, that the young audience they want to build for the theater is gonna love the show, and the intellects will love the show, and the critics will love the show. So you are in the pleasing business.

Now the amazing thing about *A Chorus Line* was that there's a man by the name of Joseph Papp, who has the New York Shakespeare Festival, and he has created a unique situation in theater: you are allowed to go there and work on something that may not appeal to everybody. I came to Joe Papp with an idea. I said that I really don't quite know what it is yet, I don't know whether it's a play with music, or whether it's a full musical, I don't know.

I spent a summer really depressed just watching the Watergate hearings. Well, I thought, that's it for the American dream, because you're taught in school that you salute the flag and you trust the president. You trust, no matter who gets elected, once they're elected you trust the president. So if you take away those heroes from this country—and also the Vietnam War had been going on for so long—I didn't know a soul anymore who could believe that the Vietnam War was about anything else but economics. We didn't know if we were right or wrong anymore and that morally did a terrible thing to the country. We don't have heroes anymore, we don't have idols, who are the people going to look up to?

And I said, well, we better look to ourselves—whatever that is. We better just go, "Wait a minute, we're all all right."

You must know we rehearsed *A Chorus Line* for nine months. Everyone worked for $100 a week, we were real broke. And Joe would call up every five weeks and say, "How's it going?" and I would say, "Fine I think it's still worth trying, we're gonna go another five weeks." The composers ended up working right in the rehearsal, writing on the actors.

The trick, in a sense, of *A Chorus Line*, is that it is designed in a full circle. The first scene is not only about what happens in the play, it's about what it does to the audience, because the audience does go from associating with the director–character in the first scene, saying, "Oh, it's an audition, I get to judge who are the best dancers in the show." And what happens is by the end of the play they don't want to see anyone not get the job, and so they, of course, by that point they hate the director and love everyone on the stage, and every play of course needs a protagonist and a metaphoric death, all of which we have in this structure.

Chorus Line got millions and millions of dollars of free publicity because there's a thing in the program that says this is based on the lives of dancers.

You see, the media manipulated the statements I made about the show so that what got written was you were walking in and seeing the absolute truth of every one of those people who are playing absolutely themselves on the stage. In *A Chorus Line*, people walked in and said, "I'm really seeing these real people play their lives." Because that's what was interesting for the media to write about—a new slant for the media—but the show was written by the authors. The fact is that ten minutes of the tapes is what is actually in the show. Now there are ideas from the tapes that got written into songs and got written into scenes, and there are things that happened, for instance to me, that are not on the tapes.

The finale for me is typical Broadway—regimented, like the army. I mean the kick-line image that fades on for me is sad in a way because I have destroyed individuality in front of your eyes. But my mother loves the finale because for her it means that everybody got the job in spite of the ending of the play. And it emotionally lets her off the hook of feeling the devastation of the end of the play.

Most people leave the show, go home, and talk about themselves, not the show—and I love that! Everybody has a little flaw they never tell anyone about. Well, you put people on a stage who admit that they were really bugged about being too short, or that period through puberty when you have erections all the time. Boys don't talk about that with other boys because they think that that's something that just happens to them, and that they are just a sex fiend. Well, I mean, you suddenly bring those things back and release the guilt. I've heard about discussions between mothers and fathers and sons and daughters and families that have gotten close together, they go home and talk about when they were a child—the parents had been in the same situation with their parents. The audience watches *A Chorus Line*, and they trust it, and it makes them like people.

TOMMY TUNE ON A DANCER'S LIFE

Interview for Broadway: The American Musical *(excerpt)*

*Tommy Tune is the winner of nine Tony Awards in four separate categories, including Best Direction of a Musical (*Nine*), Best Choreography (*Grand Hotel*), and Best Leading Actor in a Musical (*My One and Only*).*

MY LIFE IS A CLICHÉ, because I'm this kid from Texas who came to New York and on the first day in New York, I went to an audition and I got the job. I danced in the chorus of Broadway shows and worked my way up. It's a cliché, but in New York City, dreams come true—it's as simple as that.

West Side Story was my first job. Here I am from Texas, the wide-open spaces, and now I'm dancing the part of an inner-city gang member. But [Jerome Robbins's] choreography was so specific, and the positions and the shapes and rhythms were so right, that I knew who I was. It was a thrilling thing to learn that choreography and have it transform you into a character.

When I first got to New York, dancers didn't have to sing. I always sang, so it was fine, but they hired eight [men] and eight [women] for a dancing chorus and there'd be ten and ten for a singing chorus. They would even tell the dancers not to sing, because they wanted those pure trained voices. Slowly, it changed around *West Side Story*, because it didn't really have a singing chorus. That's when I noticed that all of a sudden you went to the audition and you also had to sing. You started by singing eight bars, and then it became sixteen bars, and then they wanted you to sing a whole song, and so, with that, the fusion started—of course, there was also the economics of it—but you eventually had a dancing chorus that sang. And then of course *A Chorus Line* was the capper, because it was almost a through-sung piece. It was the dancers' story, but they sang and spoke.

Broadway dancers are different from any other kind of dancer in that they have to amalgamate character, vocal prowess, and dance and they have to do it eight times a week. Broadway is blue-collar work from the star down to the least working chorus member, who dances in the back. We sweat for a living. That's just the truth of it. We put on our uniforms, we get out on that stage, and we work as a team to win every night. To get the ball in the basket every night, because it's no good that we got one in last night— we have to do it *tonight*. That's tough, because in any sport, if you pull a muscle or something then you sit that game out. That doesn't work on Broadway. You have to show up; it's a life commitment. It's something that either you have inside of you or maybe you should go sell hamburgers instead, because it's not for sissies—contrary to popular belief. It's hard, hard work, but you do it because you have to do it otherwise you'll implode.

That was my energy coming to New York. They said you are too tall to dance in the chorus of a Broadway show and I knew I couldn't start out being a star—you've got to work your way up the ladder. I couldn't be bothered that I was too tall to dance in the chorus of a Broadway show. I had to do it, I had to do it—and I did.

GRACIELA DANIELE ON BOB FOSSE

Interview for Broadway: The American Musical *(excerpt)*

Graciela Daniele, a performer in Follies *and* Chicago, *went on to direct and/or choreograph* The Mystery of Edwin Drood, Once on This Island, *and* Ragtime, *among many other shows.*

BOBBY SAID TO ME that he didn't have too much technique, which I don't believe, because I've seen him dancing when he was young, and he did have it, so he was being modest about it. But he did say that he had certain physical things, like his hands or his shoulders, whatever, that were not to his taste, they were not great things for dancing. So he told me he used his handicaps to create a style. The lowering of the shoulders, the curved shoulder, the cigarette in the mouth, the small pelvis work; the vaudevillian attack too, because those were his beginnings; and then, his love, obsession almost, for women, his sensuality, and his great sense of humor. And he used all that to create a style. And this was the genius, because he is a stylist. When you see his work, you know immediately that it is Fosse. It's like when you see a certain period of Picasso, you know that it is Picasso.

I had never worked with Bob [until *Chicago*]. I had admired him for many years, but I was what was considered "a Michael girl"—as in "Bennett." The first day—I remember it so clearly—I was very excited, it was only the dancers, and he was going to start working on the opening, "All That Jazz." Gwen [Verdon] was in another room working by herself, and in one room there was Chita [Rivera] and all of the dancers, and we were at a place that he loved rehearsing in called Broadway Arts. They were not big studios, but he loved working there; all his steps were there, all his ideas were there. So we went in, and he showed us pictures, frozen pictures of dances from the twenties like the black bottom, Charleston, shimmy. Not steps, but different frozen images, and we did some of them.

Then he said, "Go over there. There is a trunk full of props"—like hats and boas and feathers—"Pick up anything you want." It's like children. So we went to the trunk and somebody picked up a top hat, another a derby, whatever, and I picked up a garter and a feather, and we went back onto the floor. He says, "Okay, now, everybody open up," and he says, "Okay, you do shimmy in slow motion, you do black bottom in slow motion, come in on this count and just come in slowly and stop there." So all of a sudden those frozen pictures had a movement to them, we came to life.

He was a great director; he instinctively believed you were going to go for something that was creating your character without thinking about it, as a child would pick something: "Oh, I like this." You were using that as part of the creation of that character—even though we were ensemble. It didn't matter to him. He treated people very individualistically. He is absolutely right.

I was playing the role of Hunyak [one of the murderesses of the Cook County Jail in the "Cell Block Tango"] and she only speaks in Hungarian, which I had to learn phonetically. "Of all the languages I know," I kept saying, "why do we choose the one I don't speak?" Anyway, the only words in English that Hunyak says are "Not guilty." That's all. So I had worked out my own history and I had made a decision that, even though she was a prisoner like everybody else in the cell, she was not guilty; she was actually saying the truth, that she had not committed the murder. We were in rehearsals for a week and he had his heart attack, and then we had to close shop for three months or so, and then we went back into it. So now we are into official rehearsals, and he starts working on "Cell Block Tango," which is a magnificent piece and where all of the prisoners have something to say. They explain the reason why they are in prison; Hunyak explains her reason in Hungarian. He continues staging, and little by little, I see that he's talking to every single girl, except he doesn't say a word to me. And, of course, as a performer, you're always insecure; you don't know if you're doing it right if somebody doesn't say "Good" or "No, you're in the wrong direction." You just need that. So a few days pass by, and then finally, because I was the dance captain, I had a moment with him and I said, "Bobby, by the way, am I on the right track?" He says, "What do I care?" I said, "What?" He says, "Well, you're guilty. I don't understand what she says, and therefore she's guilty." And then he turns around and he starts walking out of the room. And I swear, in that moment I felt like killing him, I felt so frustrated and desperate. And then he goes to the door, turns around, and he winks his eye, and he leaves. And I got it. He made me feel exactly how Hunyak felt. That's great direction. We never spoke about it any more.

Bobby was extremely specific, in his own style; it always was Fosse, while Michael wasn't so much of a stylist. He served the piece with different ideas. *A Chorus Line* was not similar to *Follies* or *Company*—they all had their own little flavor. They're both great, but to me, that's the difference.

CHAPTER SIX

PUTTING IT TOGETHER

(1 9 8 0 – 2 0 0 9)

Overture

No one would ever think of opening a $3 million musical during the sweltering dog days of August, weeks before the traditional beginning of the theatrical season, but David Merrick was always full of surprises. By the time his "song and dance extravaganza," *42nd Street*, had its opening night on the 25th, that August date would be the least of the surprises he would spring on the public.

Although he hadn't had a smash hit in a decade, Merrick was still the consummate Broadway gambler. When he optioned the stage rights for the 1933 Warner Bros. film musical *42nd Street*, only one other show had made the transfer from original movie musical to the stage, *Gigi*, in 1973—and it was a flop. In an era when producers were scaling musicals down in order to cut labor costs, Merrick had actually doubled the size of the chorus. And when *42nd Street* was out of town in Washington, he took over the full fiscal responsibility for the show by buying out its investors for $1 million each:

> **I was having a poker game one night and I saw him alone on the stage, looking around at the scenery on this empty stage, and I said, "David, we've got a big poker game going on tonight. Would you care to join us?" And he said, *"This* is my poker game."**
> **—Jerry Orbach,** "Julian Marsh," *42nd Street*

In only one instance did Merrick hedge his bets—he hired Gower Champion, who had worked for him six times before, as director and choreographer. Champion's instinct for showshoppers made him an ideal choice for the nearly dozen production numbers in *42nd Street*. Nothing would deter Merrick's dream of bringing a no-holds-barred, old-fashioned blockbuster back to Broadway.

A former ballroom dancer, Gower Champion became David Merrick's director of choice. Although the two would have bloodcurdling feuds, Champion delivered seven shows for Merrick: Carnival!; Hello, Dolly!; I Do! I Do!; The Happy Time; Sugar; Mack & Mabel; *and* 42nd Street.

Before the New York opening, Merrick had his share of characteristic spats and contretemps with the press, but this was just Merrick playing the PR game with his usual mischievous flair. Life on a Merrick show was always a roller-coaster ride of uphill battles and sudden descents into madness, but Merrick was always firmly in control of the offstage shenanigans. Not this time. This time, real life walked through the stage door and right past Merrick. While the show was trying out in Washington, Champion was wrestling with a rare form of leukemia. When the show was about to move to New York in mid-August, Champion's condition was so serious that he had to share the news with Merrick, who kept his confidence. Alternating his appearance at rehearsals with clandestine admissions to Memorial Sloan-Kettering Hospital, Champion still managed to craft a powerful show biz extravaganza, cleverly exploiting the irresistible appeal of two dozen enthusiastic youngsters tapping away to some of the finest tunes of the 1930s with military precision.

The morning of the opening, Champion succumbed to his fatal disease; Merrick asked Champion's family if he could withhold the news until later in the evening. No one in the packed house at the Winter Garden on August 25, 1980—including a young drama critic covering his first opening for the *New York Times*, Frank Rich—nor the cast was aware of Champion's death.

The show itself was a jazzy, noisy lullaby to the transcendent joys of Broadway. "Musical comedy—the two greatest words in the English language," barks the megalomaniac producer–director played by Jerry Orbach. When the curtain came down, the audience, having bought every second of its brash hokum, rewarded the show with ten curtain calls. When the curtain went up for the eleventh time, Merrick walked out onstage to cheers. He tried to subdue the applause, which only brought more. "No, no," he shouted. "This is tragic. You don't understand. Gower Champion died this morning."

The audience gasped and the cast stood onstage in stunned silence. Orbach shouted to the stagehands, "Bring it in! Bring it in!" and they closed the curtain on one of the strangest spectacles in Broadway history. Frank Rich recalled: "No one cared [about the reviews of the show] anymore. It was front-page news all over the world, that Merrick had announced Champion's death from the stage, and even people who didn't know what *42nd Street* was, or who Gower Champion was, or who David Merrick was, they all knew it now, and the show went on to run as long as *Oklahoma!*"

The opening night of *42nd Street* would bring in the final curtain for one era and serve as the overture for another. *42nd Street* would not only be the last new American musical to play the Winter Garden for the next quarter century, it would be the only American musical to play more than 3,500 performances for the next twenty-two years. Not even a deranged visionary such as Merrick could have created—or even foreseen—the new kind of musical that would revolutionize Broadway in the following decade. And as shocking as the death of the real-life director of the fictional *42nd Street* was, nothing could have prepared that opening-night audience for the resurrection of the real-life 42nd Street.

One of Champion's many showstoppers for 42nd Street—*Harry Warren and Al Dubin's "We're in the Money."*

RIGHT: *Merrick (l.) announcing the death of Gower Champion at the final curtain call. Stunned listeners include (l. to r.) Lee Roy Reams, Tammy Grimes, and Jerry Orbach.*

Now is [what Merrick did] perverse or was that good showmanship? A little of both—but he did what he had to do to make the show a hit.

—Tommy Tune

Gershwin revisited: Tommy Tune as the director, choreographer, and romantic lead in 1983's My One and Only, *swooning over Twiggy.*

If the world of Broadway seemed smaller in the 1980s, that is because, statistically, it was. The number of productions on Broadway reached a plateau of about thirty-five to thirty-eight per season from 1980 until 1990, out of which only six or seven every year were new musicals. When *La Cage aux Folles* and *Sunday in the Park with George* squared off at the Tony Awards ceremony in June 1984, they were the only two major new musicals still running to go head to head with each other. At the 1985 Tonys, there were so few offerings that the categories of best actor and actress in a musical and choreography had to be omitted—there was simply not enough competition.

Money, or the lack of it, became more and more the root of Broadway's evils. Labor unions, theater rent, advertising, and all the costs that were rising in the 1970s began to increase exponentially in the early 1980s. The revised Gershwin musical *My One and Only* cost a record $4 million to produce in 1983. To raise the capital for a show and sustain it through rocky times, a vast field of investors had to be tapped, and whereas once a producer was expected to have some artistic acumen, the job now was about cultivating the cash. In the 1983–84 season, ninety individuals were billed above the title as producers for a mere thirty-four productions. Producers came from everywhere: film corporations, record companies, real estate conglomerates, cable television networks, even a Japanese whiskey manufacturer. By the 1990s, many of these entities grew disenchanted with the slow rate of return and pulled out of Broadway, leaving the field to a few corporations that were in it for the long haul, such as the Walt Disney Company, and to a lesser degree, film producers such as David Geffen and Scott Rudin.

Even David Merrick had his last hurrah as a producer in 1980. In 1983 he suffered a debilitating stroke, and with his death in 2000, an American archetype passed from the scene. Producers in the '80s were better at importing shows from other venues—Off Broadway or the West End—than they were at developing new musicals from scratch. Broadway also increasingly relied on resident theaters across the country with built-in subscription audiences that could nurture a new musical until it seemed ready to move to New York. The workshop and the resident theater production almost completely absorbed the function of the out-of-town tryout. The Public Theater cultivated *Bring in 'Da Noise, Bring in 'Da Funk* and *The Wild Party;* the Old Globe in San Diego originated *Into the Woods* and *The Full Monty*, and the La Jolla Playhouse originated *The Who's Tommy, Big River,* and *Thoroughly Modern Millie*. Important regional theaters sprang up, all devoted to producing new musicals, such as the Goodspeed Opera House in Connecticut, which developed traditional shows, and the more cutting-edge Prince Music Theatre in Philadelphia.

Broadway audiences seemed more comfortable with material that was already familiar to them. Revivals became so prevalent, and were often produced with such care, that their resurgence was honored in 1994 with a new Tony Awards category, Best Revival of a Musical, and all too frequently, the revival so honored was preferable to the best new musical of that season. David Merrick was prescient in creating an audience for theatrically reconstituted film musicals; the next two decades would see almost a dozen familiar titles such as *Meet Me in St. Louis, Footloose,* and *Saturday Night Fever* making their debuts as Broadway shows.

There was an even greater strain among the creative personnel along Broadway. With fewer career-making original parts available for the current crop of performers, those who worked on Broadway often did so in revivals, or with short-term contracts, supplementing their profile by performing in concerts or nightclubs or on studio recordings. The corps of director–choreographers that defined the previous generation had suffered most. Both Michael Bennett and Bob Fosse died in 1987—Bennett of AIDS, Fosse of a heart attack. Their absence came exactly when Broadway needed their inventiveness and drive the most. At the end of the '80s, there was great hope when Jerome Robbins returned to the musical stage with the extended revue *Jerome Robbins' Broadway,* showcasing the choreographer's highlights. The production opened with an $8.8 million price tag and needed to run two years at capacity to recoup its investment. Despite enthusiastic reviews and a core audience, its high running costs and essential old-fashionedness caused the show to close prematurely. Robbins never returned to Broadway after that. Into the breach high-stepped Tommy Tune, a tall, lanky dancer who had worked with Bennett, and who lent his jolly razzmatazz as director–choreographer to conceptual material such as *Nine* and more hackneyed material such as *The Will Rogers Follies.*

But no matter how dire the state of the American musical seemed in the 1980s, there was one small consolation: no one in the world knew how to put on a smash musical hit like the producers and artists along Broadway. . . .

Hollywood repackaged: Thoroughly Modern Millie, *the 2002 Tony winner for Best Original Musical (starring Sutton Foster, center) had all the prerequisites for a musical to attract an audience at the end of the millennium: a period setting, a movie pedigree, and a known property.*

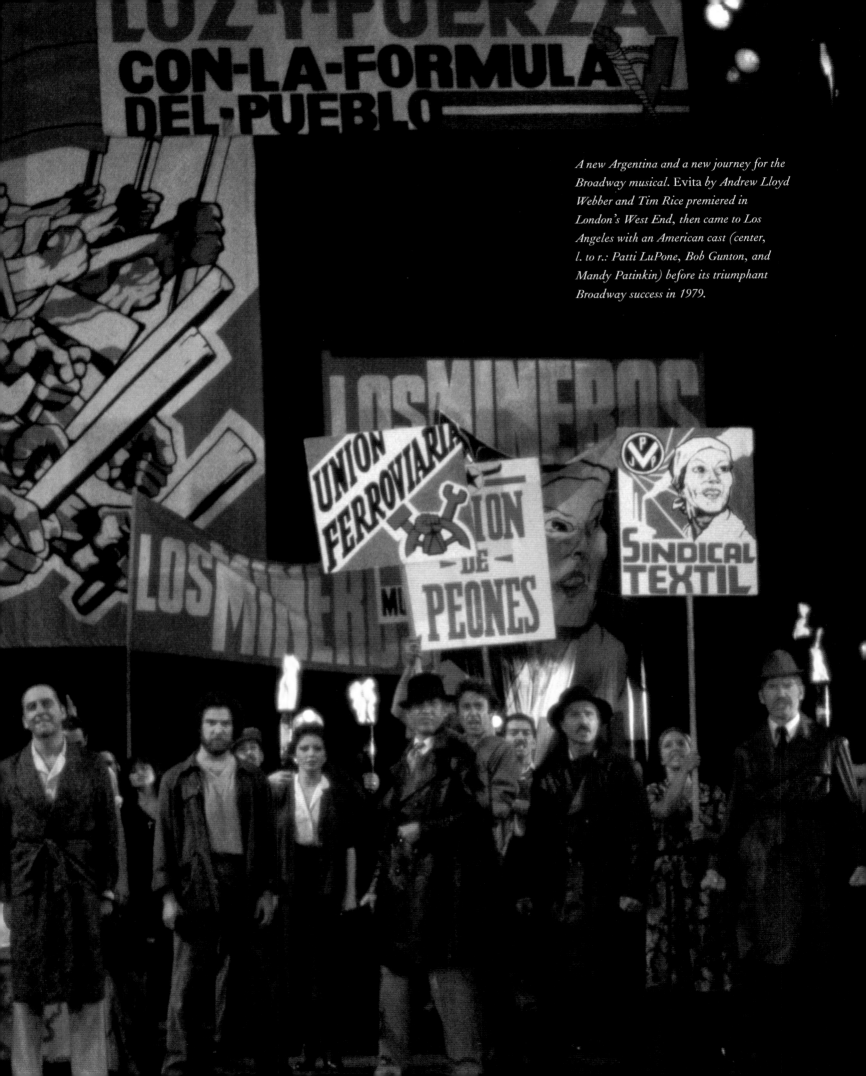

A new Argentina and a new journey for the Broadway musical. Evita *by Andrew Lloyd Webber and Tim Rice premiered in London's West End, then came to Los Angeles with an American cast (center, l. to r.: Patti LuPone, Bob Gunton, and Mandy Patinkin) before its triumphant Broadway success in 1979.*

"A cat's entitled to expect these evidences of respect"

ANDREW LLOYD WEBBER AND CATS

With cat-like tread,
Upon our prey, we steal
In silence dread,
Our cautious way we feel.

—W.S. Gilbert, *The Pirates of Penzance*

Lyricist Tim Rice (l.) and composer Andrew Lloyd Webber, the boy geniuses of the incredibly succesful contemporary sound of Jesus Christ Superstar *(below), c. 1971.*

Those lyrics had their professional debut on New Year's Eve 1879 in New York City. Gilbert and Sullivan were forced to premiere their new show, *The Pirates of Penzance*, in America because their previous one, *H.M.S. Pinafore*, was so popular that productions were "pirated" all over the States, due to a lack of copyright in this country. By premiering *Pirates* in New York City, they were able to receive a lucrative American copyright for their work. So began the first British musical invasion of America.

Over the course of the twentieth century, however, the invasion occurred in rather inconsequential fits and starts. By the 1960s and '70s, Londoners saw very little native product on West End stages that would encourage them to think they were revolutionizing the American form. Their stages were filled with American imports, or schematic attempts to harness the American musical form of storytelling to very British subjects. Revered British authors such as J.B. Priestley (*The Good Companions*) and P.G. Wodehouse (*Jeeves*) found their works inelegantly adapted to the West End musical stage.

The composer of *Jeeves* seemed, at first glance, to be an unlikely choice to write a musical comedy set in the 1930s. Andrew Lloyd Webber was his country's foremost apostle of the rock sound on the musical stage. Born in 1948, he was, like Ziegfeld, the son of the head of a classical music school, but young Lloyd Webber's tastes, as he was the first to admit, ran between Rodgers and Hammerstein and the Beatles, Puccini and Elvis Presley. With his lyricist collaborator, Tim Rice, he had his first success in 1968 with a "pop oratorio," *Joseph and His Amazing Technicolor Dreamcoat*. The show, based on the biblical story of Joseph, was a small-scale effort produced for a British boys' school, but it brought the team attention and the requisite funding to record their "rock opera," *Jesus Christ Superstar*, in 1970. The score met its international audience in waves; first as a single of the title tune; then a double-album set; finally, staged on Broadway in 1971. *Superstar*'s global success kept the writers busy supervising its many productions, but they went their separate ways in 1975, when Lloyd Webber wrote *Jeeves* with Alan Ayckbourn.

But Rice had been inspired by the epic soap opera journey of Eva Perón, the wife of Argentina's 1940s dictator, so the team regrouped for *Evita*, which was staged in the West End in 1978 and on Broadway the following year by master director Harold Prince. The show led a charmed life on both sides of the Atlantic, and soon Lloyd Webber turned to Prince with a proposition about a new project, based on a whimsical collection of poems by T.S. Eliot called *Old Possum's Book of Practical Cats*, a book virtually unknown in America but famous among British schoolchildren. The poems sounded like song lyrics to the composer, and he began to set them to music. He wasn't sure if these were a song cycle or a Broadway show, so he called Prince.

I listened to it all, and I said, "Andrew, is this something I don't get? Is this about Queen Victoria, she's the main cat, and Disraeli and Gladstone are other cats, and then there are poor cats, and am I missing this?" He took a terrible, painful, long pause and said, "Hal, it's about *cats*." And we never discussed it again.
— Harold Prince

Webber then turned to a compatriot, Cameron Mackintosh, a young producer whom he had only recently befriended. Mackintosh quickly recognized the larger theatrical possibilities and suggested they seek out a director from the prestigious Royal Shakespeare Company, Trevor Nunn. Nunn instinctively knew that the material needed to be shaped, that the disparate poems needed a through-line. Inspired by some stray lines of Eliot's poetry from another source, Nunn imagined the various brief cat biographies in Lloyd Webber's songs culminating in a nocturnal ceremony where one cat could be reborn into the next of its nine lives. This would become the show's emotional and visual climax, a glimpse into the mystical rituals of the feline tribe.

Cats said all of you human beings have arrived at our festival and you shouldn't be here, but I suppose we'd better get on with it, and try to explain to you what's happening, and we can instruct you and we can talk to you and we can appeal to you, we can reject you, we can be hostile, we can be seductive.
— Trevor Nunn

If that idea solved the narrative problem, such as it was, Nunn felt that the show needed an emotional spine, something that *motivated* their resurrected cat, Grizabella. Lloyd Webber found a tune in his trunk from a discarded idea for a show about Puccini. It only needed words, and some eleventh-hour entreaties went out to various lyricists, but nothing seemed to work. At the last minute Nunn himself tinkered with some lines from Eliot's "Rhapsody on a Windy Night":

"Look—a new day has begun." Betty Buckley inherited the role of Grizabella, the Glamour Cat, *from her British counterpart, Elaine Paige, who in turn inherited the role from Judi Dench in rehearsal.*

Every street lamp that I pass
Beats like a fatalistic drum,
And through the spaces of the dark
Midnight shakes the memory
As a madman shakes a dead geranium.

The poem was transformed, in part, into the following lyrics:

Memory, all alone in the moonlight
I can smile at the old days
I was beautiful then
I remember the time I knew what happiness was
Let the memory live again.

Burnt out ends of smokey days
The stale cold smell of morning
The street lamp dies, another night is over
Another day is dawning.

Nunn's version clearly fit the tune and the bill.

Cats' extraordinary finale (Ken Page and Betty Buckley) set the stage for a decade of astonishing stage effects.

OPPOSITE: *John Napier, also inspired by T.S. Eliot, designed an environmental wonderland for* Cats.

The show reached across perceived barriers of every kind, first of all, barriers between generations. It was entirely possible for a family of young children, parents, and grandparents all to go to the theater together in one great big party and all get something completely delightful out of the same show.

—Trevor Nunn

Even in London where a native smash hit would have been manna from heaven, the iconoclastic *Cats* was excoriated from nearly every corner while it was still in rehearsals. No one understood why a celebrated Shakespearean director was messing about with kitty cats. Lloyd Webber, Mackintosh, and Nunn inoculated themselves by hiring Judi Dench, a renowned classical actress, to star, but as the show leapt along to its West End debut in May of 1981, audiences were still skeptical. (Dench, injured in rehearsals, had to be replaced by Elaine Paige.) "'Catastrophe! It's the worst thing you've ever seen in your life! *Cats* is a dog.' All the great old puns—it was a perfect, wonderful title for all that," remembers Cameron Mackintosh about the show's preview period. However, after a few short weeks, it transformed into a phenomenon.

It was also a phenomenon that proved irresistible to American producers. Four of them, led by the Shubert Organization, bought the show for the Winter Garden. Here was a show that required no stars and had a presold market and a known hit composer. Even one problem that had bedeviled the casting of the British production, the relative paucity of singer–dancers in the West End, was easily solved in New York City. *Cats* was jet-propelled to New York; the transfer had cost $5.5 million but the show had already earned a $6.2 million advance sale, the largest in Broadway history. Its Broadway debut on October 7, 1982, earned grudging reviews. Few could ignore the spectacle provided by designer John Napier's fantastical Brobdingnagian trash dump (suggested to him by another Eliot title, "The Waste Land") or the whirling cat dervishes of Gillian Lynne's acrobatic choreography, all of it capped by the Spielbergesque levitation of Grizabella to the Heavyside Layer via an enormous used tire, but critics and intellectual audiences not only deplored its pop score and anthropomorphized felines, they downright sneered at the entire enterprise. "Aeschylus did not invent theater to have it end up with a bunch of chorus kids wondering which of them will go to Kitty Cat Heaven," comments the leading character in John Guare's play *Six Degrees of Separation*. The sheer spectacle of *Cats* seemed to represent, for many, its very emptiness. "These things were astounding to watch, but they have almost nothing to do with the kind of theater that we were developing under Rodgers and Hammerstein," commented Brendan Gill.

Although Rodgers and Hammerstein would never have created *Cats*, they certainly would have recognized it, at least from their earlier days. It's a revue, a revue about the world of cats, with a series of specialty numbers, dancing choruses, a swell eleven o'clock torch song, and a grand finale, all put together with dizzying showmanship. *Cats* honors a tradition that predates the narrative musical, a tradition that had kept Broadway in clover for more than forty years. Despite the scant respect it was given, *Cats*, as of its final and 7,485th performance on September 10, 2000, had grossed $380 million on Broadway (and nearly $3 billion worldwide). It solidified Andrew Lloyd Webber's reputation as the master of contemporary Broadway pop music and, in Trevor Nunn, gave him an inspired collaborator. "Memory" became the first show tune to appear on the pop charts in years; even more miraculously, it was recorded by Barbra Streisand *before* the show's move to Broadway. In a final irony, Nunn's royalty for the song's twenty lines—wrought with great difficulty though they were—earned him millions of dollars, a sum that exceeded his director's royalty on the show itself.

The second British invasion had begun in earnest. Mr. Gilbert and Mr. Sullivan, who held Barclays Bank in as much esteem as they did their beloved Savoy Theatre, would have been pleased indeed.

The evening Cats *became the longest-running show in Broadway history, composer Andrew Lloyd Webber serenaded colleagues Cameron Mackintosh, Gillian Lynne, Trevor Nunn, and the cast on the stage of the Winter Garden.*

"You'll love us once you get to know us"

LA CAGE AUX FOLLES AND THE GAY COMMUNITY

The American musical would be inconceivable—in fact, it never would have existed—without the contributions of African Americans, Jews, and homosexuals, but whereas *Fiddler on the Roof* put Jewish rituals onstage and *The Wiz* had an all-black production team and cast, even by the mid-1970s gay characters were nowhere to be found—on the Broadway stage.

The great irony is that the musical theater has always been defined by a large number of gay creators, among them Lorenz Hart, Noel Coward, and Cole Porter, and a vast gay following. In the early 1900s, Julian Eltinge appeared as a successful drag artist in a series of musicals, but for most of Broadway's history when onstage characters were identified as homosexuals, they were stereotypical "pansies," such as the hysterical magazine photographer played by Danny Kaye in *Lady in the Dark*. In 1970, Lee Roy Reams played Lauren Bacall's gay dresser in *Applause* (the audience knows his orientation because when he begs off an invitation from Bacall, saying he has a date, she replies, "Bring him along!"). Three years later, Tommy Tune played a gay choreographer in *Seesaw* and won a Tony for it. It was Tune, now a director–choreographer, who was announced in 1981 as heading up an adaptation of the 1978 French film *La Cage aux Folles*, a farce about a drag club in St. Tropez. The news that Tune would direct the show, with Maury Yeston writing the score, broke songwriter Jerry Herman's heart; reportedly, he had wanted to adapt the film to the musical stage the minute he left the movie theater.

But *La Cage aux Folles* had a number of false starts, and within months, Herman was offered the project. His new collaborators included director Arthur Laurents and playwright Harvey Fierstein, who had recently won two Tonys for writing and starring in *Torch Song Trilogy*, a relentlessly honest saga about gay life in New York. The musical *La Cage aux Folles* was conceived as a standard romantic musical comedy about a pair of mismatched lovers who, after leaping over the requisite obstacles, discover how deep their love really is; the basic plot would not have been out of place in a '20s musical comedy. But here the lovers—Georges, the owner of the St. Tropez drag-queen nightclub, and Albin, his star attraction—were a middle-aged homosexual couple.

For Herman, any anxiety over the show's subject matter actually ran second to his desire to have a hit; he had been the most successful songwriter of the 1960s, but the last sixteen years had yielded three flops in a row. Herman supplied a

The combination that works like a charm: Gene Barry (l.) and George Hearn as middle-aged lovers in La Cage aux Folles.

bouncy score, the production was beautifully clothed in the pastel hues of the Côte d'Azur, and the chorus line of drag queens was terrifically entertaining, but as the show was previewing in Boston, Herman felt that perhaps this was not the best of times or places to be breaking down barriers. He recalled:

From Albin to Zaza: George Hearn—a serious actor and singer who had great success replacing Len Cariou as Sweeney Todd—does an about-face, putting a little more mascara on.

About fifteen or twenty minutes into the play, Georges sang a love song to Albin. This was the first time in the history of musical theater that a man sang a love song to another man. And we were sitting frozen in our seats wondering what the audience was going to do, and right in front of us there was a typical Bostonian couple: he had a blazer and she had blue rinse on her hair; they couldn't have been more typical. And so we were glued to this couple. When the song started they sat very stone-faced, and as the song progressed, when it got to the line "I hear la-da-da da-da-da da / And I'm young and in love," this man took his wife's hand and squeezed it. That was the night we knew what we had.

What the creators had was a hit, which came to the Palace in New York in August 1983. The musical, which brought its final curtain down on two men embracing each other and dancing into the sunset, was, in turn, embraced by audiences of every kind.

The triumph of the show for its creators and cast was shadowed by the arrival of the terrifying AIDS epidemic. When the show was beginning its casting process, stories started appearing in the gay press and the national media about the onset of a new disease; "By the time *La Cage* opened, we knew," recalled Fierstein. "It had a name."

AIDS cut a devastating swath through the talent pool on Broadway. Michael Bennett and [choreographer] Ron Field come to mind—so many I can't even go back through the lists. I don't take their names out of my Rolodex because I want to remember, but there are so many people that worked on Broadway that are gone because of AIDS. In all fields, but a lot of choreographers, dancers, directors, designers, actors—it really did a number on what comes out on the street now.

—Tommy Tune

One of La Cage aux Folles' *cleverer gimmicks was to mix a couple of female chorines into the line of male drag queens, in order to keep the audience on its toes.*

Barry and Hearn.

Just as *La Cage* was responsible for breaking down barriers onstage, it was instrumental in uniting the Broadway community offstage. In the spring of 1984, members of the cast and company were the main event in one of the first charity evenings to raise consciousness and funds for people suffering from the disease. Broadway Cares/Equity Fights AIDS has since given more than $100 million to ameliorate the lives of its brothers and sisters in the Broadway community.

While the Broadway community was immediately active in dealing with the epidemic, the rest of the country was puzzling over the cause and effect of AIDS, and President Ronald Reagan was refusing to even articulate the word. Some observers have opined that the negative press around AIDS cut into the length of *La Cage aux Folles*'s run on tour and perhaps in New York, but it still played to sell-out crowds, at $43 a ticket, for 1,761 performances. As the chorus line of drag queens told the audience at the top of the show, "You'll love us once you get to know us.

This was a show that in the beginning when all the guys in drag came out onstage, the men who'd been dragged to see it by their wives covered their faces; at the end of the show they were standing and cheering two men dancing off into the sunset. I thought that was quite an accomplishment.

—Arthur Laurents

I AM WHAT I AM

Words and music by Jerry Herman
From La Cage aux Folles *(1983)*

A S "SOLILOQUY" in *Carousel* proved, an Act One closer is the best place in a show to interject drama and uncertainty into a musical: What will happen when we come back for Act Two? At the end of the first act of *La Cage aux Folles,* Albin, the drag queen, has just discovered that his adopted son has disinvited him to his wedding. Furious, humiliated, and confused, Albin has to work out his emotions as he's about to go on to perform his own eleven o'clock number at La Cage aux Folles. Jerry Herman felt "the hero of the show is a gay man who finds his pride by challenging his son's bigotry towards homosexuals. The moral of the piece is actually very wholesome, because it is about standing up for yourself and fighting bigotry."

At the end of the song, director Arthur Laurents had George Hearn, who won a Tony for the role, tear off his wig, storm up the aisle of the Palace Theatre, and go right out onto Broadway and 47th Street. The song resonated further because another version of the number, "We Are What We Are," with much gentler lyrics, is sung by the drag chorines at the top of the show. What was mildly provocative at 8:05 was excoriating at 9:30. Book writer Harvey Fierstein said, "The song has become sort of an anthem in our community: 'I am what I am. And I will be accepted this way or you don't get to be in my life.'" And the show had a happy ending.

I am what I am
I am my own special creation
So come take a look
Give me the hook
Or the ovation.
It's my world
That I want to have a little pride in
My world
And it's not a place I have to hide in
Life's not worth a damn
Till you can say, "Hey, world,
I am what I am!"

I am what I am
I don't want praise
I don't want pity
I bang my own drum
Some think it's noise
I think it's pretty
And so what
If I love each feather and each spangle?
Why not
Try and see things from a different angle?
Your life is a sham
Till you can shout—out loud—
"I am what I am!"

I am what I am
And what I am
Needs no excuses.
I deal my own deck
Sometimes the ace
Sometimes the deuces.
There's one life
And there's no return and no deposit.
One life
So it's time to open up your closet.
Life's not worth a damn
Till you can say—"Hey, world,
I am
What
I am!"

ABOVE: *Hearn's number helped earn him a Tony Award and it became an anthem for a community.*
LEFT: *"We are what we are / And what we are is an illusion." An opening number that took on greater significance at the end of the first act.*

"*At the end of the day, you're another year older*"
CAMERON MACKINTOSH AND THE BRITISH INVASION

Few producers ever took as much of a hands-on role in his productions as the incurably stage-struck Cameron Mackintosh, c. 1984.

The 1962 musical *Oliver!* was that rare thing in its time: a British musical that transferred successfully to Broadway. When Lionel Bart's *Oliver!* began its British national tour in 1965, it took on, as its assistant stage manager, a twenty-year-old theater enthusiast named Cameron Mackintosh, who was occasionally pushed onstage as an extra. By the time Mackintosh revived a production of his beloved *Oliver!* on the West End stage in 1994, he was worth almost three quarters of a billion dollars and owned an island off the coast of his ancestral Scotland. He had become, in only eight seasons, the most spectacularly successful producer of modern times, cleverly grafting the promotional wizardry of a David Merrick onto the exacting showmanship of a Ziegfeld, and combining both with a global vision Alexander the Great would have envied.

In the decade before his bonanza with *Cats,* the youthful Mackintosh made a name for himself producing first-rate revivals of Broadway musicals, such as *My Fair Lady,* in the British regions with the support of Arts Council money and bringing them in to the West End. On a whim, he also produced, in 1976, a small revue of songs by a composer–lyricist with a negligible following in England: *Side by Side by Sondheim.* By the mid-1980s, Mackintosh had developed close professional relationships with both Lloyd Webber and Sondheim, two very different songwriters who shared their admiration for Mackintosh:

SONDHEIM:	Isn't he rich?
LLOYD WEBBER:	Isn't he square?
SONDHEIM:	Isn't he counting the house
	Somewhere out there?
BOTH:	Send in the crowds.

Stephen Sondheim, "Dueling Pianos," from
the televised tribute *Hey, Mr. Producer!* (1998)

When the crowds came in for *Cats* in record numbers, it allowed Mackintosh to expand his reach. "I now would only do the shows I chose to do, and I could afford to nurture them for a very long time," he said. Upon his triumphant return to London after the tremendous Broadway premiere of *Cats,* Mackintosh listened to the demo tape of a concept album, all sung in French, brought to him by a Hungarian director. The unlikely musicalization of Victor Hugo's mammoth novel of indignity and hope in nineteenth-century Paris, *Les Misérables,* had been transformed by the French team of Alain Boublil and Claude-Michel Schönberg into a Lloyd Webber–type pop oratorio. Mackintosh instantly saw the epic potential and set about assembling an English-language team, composed of Trevor Nunn, his associate John Caird, and various English lyricists, to translate the piece to the stage.

The first stop, in October of 1985, was the Royal Shakespeare Company, which Nunn ran. Despite the powerful staging, the monumental scenery of John Napier, and the persuasive singing of the ensemble, it received negative notices from the British critics. Still, the narrative pull of the piece, centered on the redemptive journey of the ex-convict Jean Valjean, buoyed Mackintosh and his team, and the show made a risky transfer to the West End, where it became a solid hit. The now-inevitable transfer to Broadway happened in 1987, where the original Valjean, Irish singer Colm Wilkinson, was joined by an all-American cast. The $11 million advance fed a run of 6,680 performances; and the show, with its strong libertarian theme, melodramatic high points, and sympathetic characters, created legions of fans across the country and went on to win the 1987 Tony Award for Best Musical, the first ever for a creative team from Europe.

It was at that Tony ceremony when Andrew Lloyd Webber ran into Hal Prince backstage and asked him what he wanted to do next. Prince replied, "A romantic musical." Webber told him that he had one in his back pocket: a musical based on the 1911 French novel *The Phantom of the Opera*. Prince responded, "Great! Let's do it." Although Mackintosh, who would produce the show, initially thought that Prince's recent string of flops made him more a liability than an asset, he soon realized the property required a showman of the first order and he wisely signed him.

Phantom took the same route as its predecessors: a sumptuously mounted West End production, followed by an eagerly anticipated Broadway transfer. Fueled by good reviews in London, word of mouth from returning tourists, and a cast album, the show, starring Michael Crawford as its eponymous ghoul, had taken in an unprecedented $18 million in advance sales before its January 1988 Broadway opening. The Phantom's boat ride through

Colm Wilkinson was the heart and soul of Les Misérables, *playing Jean Valjean in the West End and on Broadway.*

"One day more . . ." The explosive force of social justice in nineteenth-century France made for a surprisingly popular show. Les Misérables *was a huge success around the country (here, a scene from the 2000 tour) and around the globe.*

an underground lagoon and the crashing chandelier became symbols for the new era of high-tech Broadway spectacles. They became grist for the critics' mill as well.

> It was the spectacle that beguiled us and we found thrilling—we began to applaud the chandelier for falling in *Phantom of the Opera*. We applauded the poor sons of bitches in *Les Misérables* who had to keep up with the turntable as they were singing. You're not supposed to feel ordinary human emotions at a spectacle, or indeed at the circus, you're aghast with admiration and wonder.
>
> **—Brendan Gill**

Mackintosh returned to Boublil and Schönberg for his next romantic epic, *Miss Saigon*, which reimagined Puccini's *Madame Butterfly* in the final tragic days of the Vietnam War. Once again, the show had a spectacular West End premiere and a spectacular special effect: this time, a helicopter airlifting desperate refugees. Its Broadway advance of $36 million set a record that has yet to be surpassed.

What Mackintosh created was something previously unknown in Broadway history, in terms of its breadth and influence: the megahit (or, as some called it, the pop-opera). Along with two other Lloyd Webber–Trevor Nunn shows that were less successful on Broadway, *Starlight Express* (1987) and *Sunset Boulevard* (1994), the four Mackintosh imports not only had the same West End–to–New York formula, they fed on one another's success for almost a decade. Mackintosh had achieved a dominance in the British, American, and global market that no one had dreamed of and no one will likely equal: four shows—*Cats, Les Misérables, The Phantom of the Opera,* and *Miss Saigon*—all running in the West End and on Broadway *simultaneously,* in addition to countless touring companies from Hartford to Helsinki, from Tokyo to Toronto.

Globalization would become a byword of the 1990s, placing a priority on the interconnectedness of international markets, and its theatrical application was mastered by Mackintosh. Perhaps because he did not learn his craft in New York's Theater District, he thought far beyond its borders. Mackintosh knew what audiences everywhere wanted, or more important, how much information an audience could absorb in the visually saturated world of the 1980s and 1990s. Perhaps his most radical innovation was in the marketing campaign for his shows, which represented a seemingly perverse rejection of Merrick-style ballyhoo. None of his advertisements would include any of the shopworn critics' quotes, nor would they carry any billing—not even for stars such as Michael Crawford or Jonathan Pryce—only the sleek, unforgettable logo for the show, at once instantly recognizable on a billboard over the Long Island Expressway or on a coffee mug. The process for designing the logos, usually done in creative concert with graphic designer Ross Eaton of DeWynters Limited, often took as much care and experimentation as the production of the show itself.

The marketing of the megahit may have been the most physically obvious manifestation of its success, but its artistic influences were also being felt. Frank Rich wondered in the *New York Times* in 1998, "Why pay the same high ticket price for a show, consumers asked, that didn't have a levitating spacecraft, or a falling chandelier, but only good songs, compelling characters or provocative drama?" Most importantly, there was now a kind of *style* to the megahit, something very different from the traditional Broadway musical. "They all have a furrowed brow," producer Cy Feuer remarked, "not the kind of fun that we used to have."

A more insidious aspect of the megahit was its influence on performance style. Megahits connected to their audience musically, tapping into a pop-rock synthesis of high-voltage ballads with ever-ascending key changes that required, first and foremost, singers who could belt the hell out of them. The old notion of an idiosyncratic Broadway character personality—an Elaine Stritch, a Robert Morse, even an Ethel Merman—would have been woefully inadequate to the demands of the megahit. As a result, a new generation of Broadway performers came of age during the 1980s: pop-inflected singers who could go from one megahit to the other—on the road, in New York—with ease. Performers, once the inimitable cornerstones of Broadway legend, were now becoming interchangeable parts.

In 1974, Hal Prince wrote: "I don't think a show will run longer than *Fiddler's* 3,242 performances on Broadway. It was like a rent-controlled apartment that you leased eight years ago. . . . If *Fiddler* were to open today, it would take [60 percent] more to operate each week, and that would curtail the run by more than three years." By the time *Cats* finally closed on Broadway, it had run nearly two and a half times longer than *Fiddler*. Broadway theaters themselves were undergoing a bizarre transformation; they now had the same tenants for *decades*. The *Cats* marquee had been plastered over the Winter Garden for the entire childhood of a generation; in fact, a child born on the opening night of *Cats* would have been old enough to become a featured dancer by the time it closed. Whatever one's aesthetic reservations, the megahits injected a much-needed vitality into the Broadway box office, and more impressively, they re-created the economics of the road: in 1995–96, the gross of the touring productions was $762 million—nearly double Broadway grosses for that season. A recent audience development survey claims that for every dollar spent on a Broadway ticket, fifteen additional dollars are spent on other goods and services; by that calculation, the megahits have brought billions of dollars to New York City. A more impressive calculation: *Cats, Phantom, Les Misérables,* and *Miss Saigon,* as of January 2010, had run a combined total of sixty-seven years on Broadway.

OVERLEAF: *The heat is on in Saigon:* Miss Saigon's *scenic wonders brought the tawdriness of the Vietnam War to audiences all over the world.*

BELOW: *"My power over you grows stronger yet": The Phantom (Michael Crawford) spirits the opera soprano Christine (Sarah Brightman) away to his subterranean lair. By 2006,* Phantom *had become the longest-running Broadway musical of all time.*

Phantom of the Opera **was not designed to be a spectacle; it was designed to serve the story it tells.**

—Harold Prince

SUNDAY IN THE PARK WITH GEORGE

IN 1982, after the failure of *Merrily We Roll Along*, a discouraged Stephen Sondheim announced his intention of giving up writing musicals to work on mystery novels, but a phone call from a graphic artist–turned–dramatist named James Lapine led to a new partnership. Soon, Lapine began a process that must be among the most provocative and coveted in the musical-theater world: batting around ideas for a new show with Stephen Sondheim. Lapine recalled, "I had just met him and was fairly new to the theater and so naively I said, 'Well, gee, I'm sure we could sit down and think of a show that could be popular, and could be successful.' And he looked at me like I was crazy, and said, 'I would never do that.'"

Lapine eventually brought up the French artist Georges Seurat's nineteenth-century pointillist painting *A Sunday on La Grande Jatte*. As Sondheim told biographer Craig Zadan, "And we realized that the painting was the setting of a play. All the people in that painting . . . when you start speculating on why none of them are looking at each other. . . . And then Jim said, 'Of course, the main character's missing.' And I said, 'Who?' And he said, 'The artist.'"

Seurat's obsessive creation of his masterpiece became the vehicle for exploring an artist's devotion to his work and the personal and social isolation it causes. Responding to the hostile environment on Broadway, Sondheim and Lapine chose to develop the new piece under the auspices of an Off Broadway theater, Playwrights Horizons, where audiences were eager for experimentation and where Lapine had been commissioned to write a new work. Eventually, a second act appeared that extended Seurat's fin de siècle journey into the struggle of his fictitious great-grandson, a conceptual artist derailed by the compromises and promotion needed to "put it together" in the contemporary art world.

Sondheim sought out a musical corollary for this most idiosyncratic of painters, the dean of the pointillist school. Seurat painted with only twelve colors, never mixing the tiny dots, but laboriously juxtaposing them; Sondheim adopted an analogous minimalist musical style. That also was grueling work, but both Sondheim and Mandy Patinkin, who played Seurat and his great-grandson, identified mightily with Seurat's perfectionism. Sondheim explained:

"White: A blank page or canvas. The challenge: bring order to the whole." Mandy Patinkin as the painter Georges Seurat, Act One.

"Art isn't easy": Mandy Patinkin as Seurat's great-grandson, Act Two.

He put hundreds of thousands of dots on that canvas. And every one was a separate decision. Some people say there were five million individual decisions. And that is what art is. You spend four days working out the flower of the hat, then you spend four days working on the hat. Then you have twenty other hats to do, then all the hats are a part of a pattern. Then you start working on the face. It is just . . . *hard . . . work.*

Rehearsals at Playwrights Horizons' 150-seat theater were somewhat chaotic, with many inches of the musical canvas left to be covered; in fact, there were several evenings when Sondheim would step in front of the preview audience before the show began to warn them there was no second act yet. "That whole process was just like watching a painting come together, particularly that painting, dot by dot," James Lapine remembered. "And as each song came in, as each lyric came in, the picture became more focused, and the storytelling clearer, and it literally didn't come together until a day or two before the critics arrived."

The show opened at Playwrights for the press on July 6, 1983, and with Shubert Organization money in hand, it transferred to the Booth Theatre on May 2, 1984. One element that eased the transfer considerably was the review in the *New York Times* by Frank Rich: "Stephen Sondheim and James Lapine demand that an audience radically change its whole way of looking at a Broadway musical. . . . *Sunday* is at once a culmination of past musical theater innovations and a rejection of them." But other critics—and audiences—were merely baffled.

At the 1984 Tony Awards, *Sunday in the Park*, which had garnered ten nominations, was in competition with *La Cage aux Folles* with eight; the evening unfolded as a competition between the two composers and their contrasting styles of show music. It was Jerry Herman who was given the Tony for Best Score, and as he ascended the podium, he remarked: "There's been a rumor around for a couple of years that a simple, hummable show tune was no longer welcome on Broadway. Well, it's alive and well at the Palace." Insiders considered that a reference to Sondheim, and although Herman eventually demurred, it seemed more and more that, as far as Broadway was concerned, Sondheim was caviar to the general. In April 1985, *Sunday* received the Pulitzer Prize for Drama, a first for Sondheim, and Broadway wags claimed that Rich and his paper had given the show so much coverage, the Pulitzer should have been awarded to the *New York Times*. Still, the show would go on to run for almost 550 performances on Broadway.

Perhaps even better, Sondheim found a new creative partner in Lapine; they would go on to do two more Broadway musicals together: the inverted fairy tale *Into the Woods* in 1987 and the epistolary romantic tragedy *Passion* in 1994. As the century closed, Sondheim found himself lionized and revered both in New York and London, which had consistently embraced his work with thoughtful revivals in the 1990s. But nothing quite epitomized his art of making art as that Sunday on the Grand Jatte.

BERNADETTE PETERS

ONLY ONE WOMAN has played both the child prodigy Dainty June in *Gypsy* as well as her indomitable mother, Rose. Only one woman could: Bernadette Peters. Born Bernadette Lazzara in a working-class Queens neighborhood in 1948, she made her stage debut at age nine, prodded by her own indomitable mother. With her boop-boop-a-doop looks and buoyant personality, she was a natural for the period-revival movement of the late 1960s. She performed her version of Ruby Keeler in the spoof *Dames at Sea* Off Broadway, then graduated to her Broadway debut as George M. Cohan's sister in *George M!* (both 1968). By 1972, she had earned a Tony nomination as Hildy in a revival of *On the Town* and starred as the ill-fated silent film star Mabel Normand (to whom she bore an astonishing resemblance) in Jerry Herman's *Mack & Mabel* (1974).

But her period looks began to limit her choices: "The shows being offered to me were so old-fashioned, always take-offs on the '40s, and '30s and '20s, like *No, No, Nanette*. I just didn't have any interest in tap-dancing my brains out." She branched out into television and Hollywood, but returned to New York in 1983 to work on the show that would alter the direction of her career: *Sunday in the Park with George*. As Georges Seurat's mistress (and as her own daughter in Act Two), Peters tapped into her humor and her rage and earned her third Tony nomination.

She captured her first Tony in Andrew Lloyd Webber's *Song and Dance* (1985), then returned to Sondheim again to play a beguiling witch in *Into the Woods* (1987). With that show, she burnished her reputation as Sondheim's most eloquent female interpreter and went on to perform his songs in various concerts, albums, and tributes throughout the next two decades. Although still impossibly beautiful and effervescent, she has, by her fifth decade in the business, made a rare and seamless transition from ingenue to leading lady to character actress.

Returning to revivals in 1999 to win a Tony for *Annie Get Your Gun*, Peters—the only musical-theater actress of her generation to get her name above the title eight times—finally took on the greatest dramatic role for a woman in contemporary musical theater: Rose in *Gypsy*. While her peaches-and-cream vulnerability worked against her, she certainly knew the territory of Rose's life. Although she lost the 2003 Tony for Best Actress in a Musical, she gave a

Peters as the Witch transformed in Into the Woods *(1987).*

performance of "Rose's Turn" at the awards ceremony that may have been the greatest of her career. It seemed as if she was finally bidding farewell to her trademark innocence to embrace, as she said in *Sunday,* "so many possibilities."

PATTI LuPONE

AS THE SAYING GOES, some roads are bumpy; for Patti LuPone back in 1976, the Road was especially bumpy. She was out of town, during the Washington tryout of *The Baker's Wife*, playing the ingénue in her first really big break. Producer David Merrick had just cut her bravura character song, "Meadowlark," out of the show. Furious and humiliated, LuPone raced back to her dressing room in tears. Along the way, she passed a fellow cast member on the backstage payphone. She proceeded to trash her dressing room—"like it was batting practice"—

when there was a knock at the door. It was her fellow cast member. "I don't know why you're going to all this trouble," he told her. "I was just on the phone with my agent. They're closing the show tomorrow."

But LuPone survived. (And so did the song, which became a signature number for her.) Her survival instincts would go on to serve her in good stead, both offstage and onstage, where LuPone was able to infuse characters with fire and steel for three decades. Born into a musical family on Long Island in 1949, LuPone was classically trained at the prestigious Juilliard School; it would give her the backbone to take on heroines of a Shakespearean dimension. She was plucked out of relative obscurity to play the coveted role of Eva Peron in *Evita* in 1979; LuPone won the Tony Award, but found Broadway diva-hood to be a grind and moved on. She played the resilient hooker in *The Cradle Will Rock* for The Acting Company in 1983, and during its London tour was signed to play Fantine in the RSC premiere of *Les Misérables* in 1985. She never reprised the role on Broadway, but tapped her way instead into *Anything Goes* (1987), where she had a triumph as the infinitely more upbeat Reno Sweeney.

Television and film took her from the stage for a while, until she was hired by Andrew Lloyd Webber to play the macabre silent film survivor Norma Desmond for his 1993 West End premiere of *Sunset Boulevard*. That boulevard turned into another bumpy road; despite strong notices in London, LuPone was replaced for the American production with Glenn Close. Hurt feelings and messy litigation abounded, and LuPone stayed away from Broadway for a while, sharing her talents in other venues: concerts, the Encores! series, and the Ravinia Festival outside of Chicago, which gave LuPone the opportunity to play a half dozen Sondheim heroines over the course of several summers. LuPone's talent for inhabiting complicated women fit Sondheim's writing perfectly, and in 2005, she returned to Broadway as Mrs. Lovett in *Sweeney Todd*. John Doyle's production allowed LuPone to play the tuba for the first time since high school, and her Weimar-esque Lovett, eking out a living in an inappropriate leather miniskirt and a gash of red lipstick, was another indomitable musical theater survivor.

But, of course, the greatest musical theater survivor is Rose in *Gypsy*, and after a couple of trial runs, LuPone brought her full-throttle portrayal to Broadway in 2008; the role enlisted both her dramatic and vocal prowess—it also

Starting here, starting now: Patti LuPone clears the decks as Rose in Gypsy *(2008).*

allowed her to give full vent to her appealing brand of shamelessness. John Lahr wrote in *The New Yorker*: "Thrilling from the moment she stalks onstage, the big-voiced and big-hearted LuPone plays Momma Rose more as a terrier than as a bitch—snapping, snarling, gnawing fiercely on the bone of opportunity." LuPone earned her second Tony and a fervent following (as well as notoriety for bawling out an errant shutterbug during her climactic number; it was downloaded endlessly on YouTube). As Rose herself bellows before her final turn, if she had been a star, "There wouldn't be signs big enough! There wouldn't be lights bright enough!" How about: "LUPONE GYPSY" two stories high above the St. James Theater?

MANDY PATINKIN

LIKE KURT WEILL, Harold Arlen, and Al Jolson—to whose high-voltage personality his has often been compared—Mandy Patinkin got his first taste of music in the synagogue. "That's how music got into my bones," he explained. "That's how I learned that if you felt something you went for it, you went for that place." After performing in several Off Broadway dramas, he was tapped by Harold Prince to play *Evita*'s peripatetic narrator, Che, in the 1979 Broadway production, which won him a Best Supporting Actor Tony. Like Bernadette Peters, Patinkin spent the early '80s in Hollywood, in a variety of supporting parts, eventually—again, like Peters—to be called back to star in *Sunday in the Park with George*.

The part of Seurat not only suited Patinkin's own neurasthenic intensity, the process allowed him to indulge in the highs and lows of creating a new work of art. As one of his mentors, Joseph Papp, said, "Mandy is worse than a perfectionist. A perfectionist reaches for some degree of satisfaction." *Sunday in the Park* gave him a Tony-nominated role and an introduction to the music of Sondheim. He has

since become the composer's most ardent and acute male interpreter, as when he decided to sing all the parts of a trio in "Buddy's Blues" in a 1985 *Follies* concert.

Since the mid-1980s, he has performed in frequent solo concerts, mixing Sondheim with Hammerstein, as well as old standards from the Jolson repertoire. His soaring tenor has reinvigorated countless tunes from the Broadway songbook—some as psychodramas, some as lullabies, but always deeply felt.

Patinkin returned to Broadway to play the leads in three failed musicals—*The Secret Garden* (1991), William Finn's *Falsettos* (1993), and *The Wild Party* (2000)—but his concert dates have taken the music of Broadway all over the country. Some audience members can find his interpretations a trial—he performed "Soliloquy" while doing chin-ups—but it's all part of a Broadway tradition that stretches back to Jolson sending the rest of the cast home and singing for another hour at the Winter Garden. "When I first heard people go on about my being 'over the top,' my initial reaction was, 'I've got to get rid of that,'" he says. "Then finally I realized, 'Get rid of it? That's who I am.' I understand that if you take that risk, there are times you will be very bad. But other times, something wonderful will come out of it."

NATHAN LANE

YOU GOTTA LOVE A GUY who took his stage name from a character in *Guys and Dolls*. While doing a dinner-theater production of the show in the 1970s, Joseph Lane discovered that someone else in Actors' Equity had his name, so he did the obvious: he adopted the first name of his character, Nathan Detroit. When Nathan Lane played his theatrical namesake in the 1992 Broadway revival of *Guys and Dolls*, he also took on the title "Clown Prince of Broadway."

"The theater was always the dream for me. The reason I was in most of the movies I've done is that they paid for me to be in the theater," he said in a *New York Times Magazine* interview. "I used to watch the Tony Awards and I was fascinated by those people—Robert Preston, Zero Mostel, Angela Lansbury. When I was a kid and my brother took me to the theater, that was the most exciting thing." Lane got his first Tony for reprising Mostel's role in *A Funny Thing Happened on the Way to the Forum* (1996) and his second in 2001 for adapting Mostel's film role in *The Producers* to the

Patinkin as the narrrator, Che, in Evita *(1979).*

BRIAN STOKES MITCHELL

The king of Broadway: Nathan Lane as Gomez, father of The Addams Family clan (2010). His Morticia is the slinky Bebe Neuwirth.

BRIAN STOKES MITCHELL (or "Stokes," as he likes to be called) is usually spoken of by critics and aficionados as a kind of Matinee Messiah, a full-throated masculine star in the manner of an earlier generation's Richard Kiley or, even earlier, Alfred Drake. These comparisons are aided and abetted by Stokes's appearance in revivals of *Man of La Mancha* and *Kiss Me, Kate,* playing roles that made those two stars into legends.

Upon his arrival on Broadway, he began a gradual but determined climb up the leading-man ladder, first in a musical called *Mail,* then in David Merrick's all-black version of Gershwin's *Oh, Kay!*—both flops. He went on to replace Gregory Hines in *Jelly's Last Jam,* then took over as the radical political prisoner in *Kiss of the Spider Woman.* His big break came in 1998 when he played Coalhouse Walker, a turn-of-the-century black man who is provoked into becoming an urban terrorist, in the musical version of E.L. Doctorow's *Ragtime* in 1997. Mitchell's considerable charm and the thrilling duets he performed with Audra McDonald transformed Coalhouse from a smoldering cipher (as he had been in the 1981 film) into the evening's hero and earned Mitchell a Tony nomination. For years, producers had been

musical stage.

Despite other blandishments, Lane has always come back to the Broadway stage: "I've been in seventeen Broadway shows—that must be more than Marian Seldes." His talent allows him to combine Mostel's four-dimensional energy with the staccato delivery of a Phil Silvers, but he brings his own neurotic skepticism to the proceedings, adding a modern note of tension to the tradition of buffoonery. There's an "I wouldn't want to belong to any club that would have me as a member" sensibility to Lane's performances, a kind of free pass for audiences, in this age of hype, not to take anything too seriously. When he was preparing for his upcoming role as the deranged *paterfamilias* Gomez Addams in *The Addams Family,* Lane said, "This process never fails to be exhilarating and nerve-racking. Some people climb mountains. Some jump out of planes. I get up onstage in front of 2,300 people and tell them a story. You just hope people respond."

Brian Stokes Mitchell comes to wive it wealthily in Padua: Kiss Me, Kate.

trying to revive *Kiss Me, Kate*, but in 1999, they had the real thing in Mitchell, and he finally won his Tony. In 2002, he starred in a Broadway revival of *Man of La Mancha*, for which he received his fourth Tony nomination. He had become that increasing rarity: a real Broadway leading man with a real Broadway sound.

But Mitchell is not just a leading man, he's a leading man for his times. Coming from a culturally diverse background—African American, German, Scots, and Native American—he lends himself naturally to a greater world of diversity on stage. Within eight seasons, he played a Latin American prisoner, an African American piano player, the all-American Fred Graham, and the seventeenth-century Spanish writer Miguel de Cervantes. To a twenty-first-century audience, that all sounds pretty good—just like Mitchell's booming baritone.

AUDRA McDONALD

SHE'S STUNNING. SHE'S CHARMING. But, in the end, with Audra McDonald, it's the voice. She broke barriers when she was still "Audra Ann McDonald" by being cast as the second lead in the 1994 revival of *Carousel;* it amused critics no end that a character named Carrie Snow was being played by a black woman. The production itself made no mention of her race; although she fainted in the middle of her audition, the director thought she was the best woman for the part. So, apparently, did the Tony nominating committee. She won the Best Featured Actress in a Musical in 1994, and then proceeded to win again two years later, this time for Featured Actress in a Play, *Master Class* by Terrence McNally. Two years after that, she claimed yet a third Tony in the featured musical actress category for her work as the yearning young mother in *Ragtime*, playing opposite Brian Stokes Mitchell. No performer since Gwen Verdon had won so many Tonys in so short a time; she was still in her twenties. (She won a fourth Tony for her featured role in *A Raisin in the Sun*.)

McDonald clearly needed a star vehicle, but after the failure of Michael John LaChiusa's *Marie Christine* in 1999, she chose to devote herself to the concert stage and a series of recordings. Backed up by some of the finest symphony orchestras in the world, she has sung the roles of Bess in *Porgy and Bess;* the Beggar Woman in *Sweeney Todd;* and

Raining on her parade: Audra McDonald as Lizzie Curry in the finale of 110 in the Shade.

Julie Jordan—the lead—in *Carousel*. Not content with mastering the works of Rodgers and Gershwin, she has turned her attention to the latest work of the new generation of musical composers: LaChiusa, Adam Guettel, Jeanine Tesori, Stephen Flaherty, and Lynn Ahrens. They could have no better ally than McDonald, who brings back the thrilling vocal virtuosity of the operetta era, marrying it to the psychological complexity of the twenty-first century.

Still, McDonald is used to doing things her way. When she appeared in the 2007 revival of *110 in the Shade*, she took on the part of Lizzie Curry, originally written as a white Depression-era heroine, and she was surrounded by a racially mixed cast. One of the lyrics required her to sing that she would "pour peroxide on my head," to which McDonald added her own, "No, I ain't gonna do that, no."

KRISTIN CHENOWETH

"**B**UBBLY." It's a word that Kristin Chenoweth has heard a lot, often about her personality, and probably more than she'd like. But when you get to make one of the grandest entrances in modern musicals by ascending from the heavens in a giant steel-framed bubble, it's hard not to make the comparison. "I get to arrive in a bubble," Chenoweth once said about her role as Glinda the Good in *Wicked* (2003). "That's why I took the job, everybody knows *that*." Her own bubble wasn't as effortless and transparent as it looked: "The bodice of [Glinda's] dress is reinforced with steel safety gear . . . likewise, the frothy character is reinforced with years of training, technique and plain hard work."

Chenoweth's own years of training take her back to her roots in Oklahoma, where she was a beauty pageant winner and a serious student of classical singing. A fluke audition for a regional revival of *Animal Crackers* in 1993 derailed her ambition to be an opera singer, but the Met's loss was Broadway's gain; after her debut in Kander and Ebb's *Steel Pier* (1997) as an ambitious dance marathon contestant, she quickly became the go-to girl for anything requiring period style or vocal chops or high-wattage personality or comic skills—well, for *anything*.

Her imaginative turn as Charlie Brown's fascistic little sister, Sally, created expressly for the 1998 revival of *You're a Good Man, Charlie Brown*, earned her a Tony Award and allowed her to cut to the front of the line of her generation.

A beautiful, glamorous, radiant, ravishing Broadway *star: Kristin Chenoweth in act three of* The Apple Tree *(2006).*

Chenoweth was skilled enough to take on two major Barbara Cook roles—Marian in *The Music Man* (for television) and Cunegonde (in concert and television)—as well as two Barbara Harris roles: the lead in *On a Clear Day You Can See Forever* (Encores!) and the three overwhelming roles in *The Apple Tree* (Encores! and Broadway, 2006). Jerry Bock, that show's composer, claimed there had never been a revival, "because until Kristin we haven't had the performer who could do it." Her excursions into film and television forced her to opt out of two high-profile projects developed with her in mind: *Thoroughly Modern Millie* and *Young Frankenstein*.

Even so, there are not a lot of missed chances in Chenoweth's career, which, in the words of journalist Jesse Green, "combines, in one tiny frame, faith in Jesus, sexpot allure, strict professionalism, insane girly-girliness, triple-threat talents and a steely, restless need to exploit them all to the fullest." When she emerged from her stage bubble, Chenoweth's Glinda asked the crowd—cheerfully, if rhetorically—"It's good to see me, isn't it?" Audiences—and producers—have to admit: yes, it is.

"It's still rock and roll to me"
RENT AND THE BROADWAY ROCK SCORE

By the mid-1990s, Broadway was still continuing its quarter-century-long search for a contemporary sound. The misbegotten experiments in rock musicals of the 1970s had given way to the accessible pop-rock rhythms of Andrew Lloyd Webber in the 1980s, and for a while, a younger generation of theatergoers was entranced by familiar electric guitar riffs appearing on Broadway. In addition, there were some other experiments; in 1985, country-western songwriter Roger Miller contributed an original, Tony-winning score to *Big River* and 1993 saw a popular theatricalized version of The Who's 1969 rock opera *Tommy*, but they were one-shot deals. But when the megahit scores of Lloyd Webber and his French counterparts began tapering off in the 1990s, Broadway producers desperately sought new ways of capturing the Generation X audience.

Luckily several big-name pop composers were contributing scores to Broadway. Elton John made his Broadway debut in 1997, working with Lloyd Webber's former partner, lyricist Tim Rice, on the transfer of his film score for the stage version of *The Lion King*. John's score was supplemented with songs by the South African composer Lebo M. When Disney offered John and Rice a chance to write a new version of Verdi's *Aida* for Broadway, they leaped at the chance, overjoyed at the opportunity to create a stage show from scratch. John applied his ebullient eclecticism to a score that he wrote at the amazingly fast rate of about one song per day: "It's truly a pop musical, with spoken dialogue. There are black songs, very urban based, rhythm and blues, gospel-inspired songs, and kind of 'Crocodile Rock' songs, and ballads, of course." *Aida* had its trials and tribulations on the road, but John was absent for most of them, and he barely participated in its Broadway previews, at least as compared with composers of the past. But, then again, Jule Styne was not a multimillion-dollar corporation who could play to a 100,000 sell-out crowd at Wembley Stadium. The same season that John made his debut with *Lion King*, another major figure in the pop world from the 1970s brought his first score to Broadway: Paul Simon.

Simon had often been invoked by critics as a natural for Broadway, for his sense of narrative was extraordinary and his songs had already provided strong emotional backgrounds for several films. Simon's Broadway project could not have been less conventional; it was based on the true story of a sixteen-year-old Puerto Rican gang member, dubbed "The Capeman," who had stabbed two white kids in 1959. Simon's look at urban history was both uncompromising and sympathetic. To a doo-wop beat, the opening song had the following lyrics:

> Let The Capeman burn for murder.
> Well, the "Spanish boys" had their day in court
> And now it was time for some fuckin' law and order
> The electric chair
> For the greasy pair
> Said the judge to the court reporter.

Simon had researched the story thoroughly and had provided a breathtakingly wide-ranging score of gospel, doo-wop, Afro-Cuban bop, and Latin salsa tunes. But whether it was the polarizing subject matter, two vastly different directors at the helm, or simply bad

Rock star Marc Anthony appeared as the teenage killer in Paul Simon's The Capeman *(1997).*

timing, *The Capeman* lasted only two months, costing $11 million, and when it folded, it took with it one of the most thrilling scores written for a Broadway show in the last twenty years. Fans of the music remain hopeful that *Capeman*'s original cast recording will eventually be released by Dreamworks to supplement Simon's own spellbinding version of its songs.

Billy Joel had grown up in the suburbs of New York City, and his cycle of songs in the 1970s and '80s about the boys and girls in his blue-collar community not only swung with an unforgettable pop beat, they were also great little one-act dramas. In 2000, choreographer Twyla Tharp wanted to create a large-scale theater piece and she knew that those songs of Billy Joel's held the answer. "[He] was clearly the best choice because he's such a good storyteller," Tharp said. "There is rage in his music and guts in his songs. I've always known that his music dances." Tharp's *Movin' Out* tells the story of three Long Island friends and the girls they leave behind during and after the Vietnam War, using only a large corps of dancers performing to the live accompaniment of thirty Billy Joel songs provided by a single singer and a backup band. Although the show hit some shoals on its way in from Chicago, it opened in New York in the fall of 2002 to ecstatic reviews. The only thing missing, in a way, was the composer himself. "It's been a collaboration with his music," Ms. Tharp said. "That's very different than a collaboration with him. We agreed from the beginning that his job was done when I started."

As variously effective as these four shows have been, their creative processes also provide the ultimate retort to anyone who wonders why there is not more of a rock sound on Broadway: a Broadway collaboration is a very different prospect from a date in the recording studio. Not only do rock and pop composers have to stretch their narrative range to produce songs that work together over the course of an evening, they have to surrender to the grueling politics and unpredictability inherent in creating a Broadway show. That unpredictability drove Burt Bacharach away in 1969, and there is no reason to assume that Elton John, Paul Simon, or Billy Joel really needs (or wants) to relinquish lucrative concert dates and recording contracts to spend the requisite four months in the day-to-day preparation of a new musical. Broadway babies are born, not made.

Neither Paul Simon's marquee value nor an $11 million budget could pull the creative team of The Capeman *together.*

Elizabeth Parkinson as a dazzling "Uptown Girl" thrills the suburban boys in Twyla Tharp's collage of Billy Joel tunes, Movin' Out *(2002).*

Jonathan Larson, however, *was* a Broadway baby. He grew up in suburban Westchester and was taken by his parents to see *Fiddler on the Roof* and *1776*. He took piano lessons and avidly followed the concerts and recordings of Billy Joel and Elton John, but Broadway was his first love. Once when a high school friend sent him to buy tickets to a Peter Frampton concert, he sheepishly returned with two tickets to *Sweeney Todd*.

In 1982, after college, he became a Greenwich Village starving artist, straight out of central casting, making the rent by toiling in a SoHo diner while trying to get myriad musical projects off the ground. One day, a friend brought an idea to him: a musical update of Puccini's *La Bohème*. Larson thought it should be relocated to Alphabet City in New York's East Village, an area he knew well; it was, indeed, the epicenter of bohemianism by the late 1980s. Larson eventually took over the book, music, and lyrics of the project himself and transformed Puccini's characters into people he knew, lived among, and loved. The characters were rock composers, video directors, and junkies, who were HIV-positive or danced in S-and-M bars. Performance art, rent strikes, transvestites, and second helpings of the zeitgeist filled in the rest (one lyric referenced both Stephen Sondheim and Susan Sontag). In Larson's own words, "*Rent* is about a community celebrating life in the face of death as it careers toward the millennium."

Larson hawked the piece to various producers, eventually finding a tentative home at the New York Theatre Workshop, an adventuresome not-for-profit theater located at the gates of the East Village, which committed to a series of readings and workshops in 1994 to

"La Vie Bohème," musical-theater style. The cast of Rent.

Jonathan was a very innocent, a very generous, a very open-hearted person. And very young. And his concerns were young. That's why the piece especially speaks to young people who are really finding their feet as adults.

—Michael Greif, Director

be directed by Michael Greif. Larson finally quit his day job at the Moondance Diner and threw himself into the arduous regimen of writing and rewriting the entire score and script to *Rent*. The ambitious score required him to orchestrate gospel numbers, hymns, tangos, patter songs, and character songs, all to a rock beat, and at times the onslaught of suggestions that comes from a developmental process got under Larson's skin. But by the time *Rent* prepared for its first workshop preview, on January 25, 1996, at the theater's home on East Fourth Street, the show was finally ready to rock and roll.

Larson, however, hadn't been feeling well. During the previous week, he had gone to the emergency room twice for chest pains; they were diagnosed as food poisoning or flu, and he was sent on his way. After the final dress rehearsal, Larson was interviewed by the *New York Times* in the theater's tiny box office. Then he went home, put some water on for tea, and died. His roommate found him on the kitchen floor. The cause was an aortic aneurysm. He was thirty-five years old. That night, the cast assembled and, in tribute to Larson and his friends, attempted to perform the show as a concert. It didn't last long; by the second act, the intense emotionalism had everyone on their feet, acting their parts and singing their hearts out. Practically every sentence of *Rent* now had a double meaning; its carpe diem philosophy seemed perfectly and horribly demonstrated by Larson's utterly unexpected death. Michael Greif, director, elaborated:

Composer, lyricist, and book writer: Jonathan Larson takes a break from Rent *rehearsals downtown.*

Larson's journal, ca. 1986.

> In those days following his death, he became a part of the musical, Jonathan and the musical united. The aspects of Jonathan's personality that were part of each character really came to the surface, and he felt very present to us. Those issues in the musical about loss pounded in our ears and beat in our chests. We all took a lesson from the musical about how to move forward and how to take care of ourselves in the face of that kind of loss, and it's unquestionable that that galvanized our process.

Word of mouth about the show was already strong, but the media avalanche after Larson's death created the biggest Off Broadway sensation since *A Chorus Line* opened at the Public Theater. But all the publicity would have meant nothing if audiences and critics hadn't liked the show. They loved it, and within days, and with the support of Larson's family, plans were laid to transfer *Rent* to the Nederlander Theatre on 41st Street. He would, of course, have been thrilled to have a show on Broadway, and it was a bittersweet consolation when the show won Tonys for Best Musical, Best Original Score, and Best Book, as well as the Pulitzer Prize for Drama. When it finally closed, twelve years after its 1996 transfer to Broadway, *Rent* had run 5,123 performances and has attracted a new, younger audience to Broadway, just the way Larson wanted.

> I am striving to become a writer and composer of musicals — I am 25 and am faced with a dilemma.
>
> Although I am a sentimental romantic who loves old fashioned musicals I am a member of a very unsentimental unromantic generation, who basically think musicals are too corny.
>
> I feel that if I want to establish myself with "the powers that be" in the theatre I must compose music that appeals to the older ears in the production houses & audiences
>
> But if I want to try to cultivate a new audience for musicals I must write shows with a score that MTV ears will accept.
>
> If you were me, which audience would you write for?

Many critics have compared *Rent* to *Hair;* both shows were nurtured in not-for-profit theaters, spoke to the contemporary counterculture, had a rock score and a four-letter title. But whereas *Hair* sent up its hermetically sealed world, *Rent* embraced its marginalized characters with compassion—and it had a plot. In many ways, *Rent* comes closer to the innovations of *Company. Company*'s characters were isolated by Upper East Side glass boxes; in *Rent*, the Lower East Side characters were isolated by video cameras, broken phones, and Con Edison. Both shows capture the anxieties of Manhattan with uncommon perception. More than that, all of the characters in *Rent* are *Company*'s Robert writ large, an entire ensemble of people desperate to make connections, to find love, to survive.

Rent's Broadway producers decided to grab a youthful audience by running ads that suggested something anarchic, hard-edged, and raw. "Don't you hate the word 'Musical'?" read the ad campaign. It is hard to imagine Jonathan Larson endorsing anything with the word *hate* in it. His death only complicated the debate about rock scores on Broadway—someone else will have to come along and bring the two together again.

"Getting to know you"
BROADWAY AND CULTURAL DIVERSITY

Broadway has always had a more comfortable relationship with ethnicity than Hollywood or television. When the broadcast media were still requiring ethnic artists to change their name or identity or hide in the background, on Broadway you could sometimes get further promoting your ethnic identity. It helped you get work—provided they were writing parts for your type.

Lea Salonga was brought at Cameron Mackintosh's insistence from the West End production of Miss Saigon *to Broadway.*

But in the summer of 1990, Broadway turned into a larger stage for a showdown over cultural forces that it had never really dealt with before. When Cameron Mackintosh was readying his New York transfer of *Miss Saigon*, Actors' Equity lodged a complaint against the show's lead actor, Jonathan Pryce, who was playing a Eurasian character called the Engineer. Equity was essentially asking Mackintosh to recast Pryce, a white British, Tony Award–winning performer who had international star status, with an American actor who had an Asian background. Mackintosh countered, "We passionately disapprove of stereotype casting, which is why we continue to champion freedom of artistic choice. Racial barriers can only undermine the very foundation of our profession," and threatened to pull the show completely. Equity ultimately backed down in its demands and Mackintosh compromised; future Engineers would be played by actors of Asian descent, and *Miss Saigon* eventually employed scores of Asian, African American, and Caucasian actors in its ranks for more than 4,000 performances.

Broadway was now plunged into the debate over cultural diversity. That same year, college campuses across the country were revising their curricula, displacing the dead white males who wrote most of Western Civilization's major works in favor of past and contemporary women and minority writers. The term *color-blind casting* became part of the theatrical debate: were actors of color forever condemned to appear only in roles that specifically typified their race? How would this affect the Broadway musical itself—almost exclusively the domain of white males, dead or

otherwise? Certainly opportunities for actors of color have existed on Broadway. There had been, for example, a semi-Asian company in Rodgers and Hammerstein's musical about the Chinese American experience, *Flower Drum Song* (which did, however, use some actors in yellow-face), and an all-black *Hello, Dolly!*, but in many cases these tales of the minority culture were created by writers of the dominant culture, or with simple substitutions—black actors as white characters—that denied the cultural truths behind the piece. In other words, performers of color had always been telling the stories—but where were *their* stories?

Jonathan Pryce, as the Engineer in Miss Saigon. *Pryce's previous Tony Award, film career, and "international star" status didn't keep the British actor from being embroiled in major controversy.*

> You are the one
> The sun's gonna rise on
> The one the world
> Is keepin' its eyes on
> The whole world's waitin' to sing your song
> —Susan Birkenhead, "The Whole World's Waitin' to Sing Your Song," *Jelly's Last Jam*

The 1970s had given Broadway a series of revues and musical biographies of great black songwriters, but *Jelly's Last Jam* in 1992 was something different. Composer Jelly Roll Morton would not simply be portrayed as a lovable rogue who wrote some catchy tunes but was a middle-class, light-skinned Creole who denigrated darker-skinned blacks as he distanced himself from his roots. Star Gregory Hines nearly bailed when an African

The incomparable Gregory Hines (r.) won a Tony as Jelly Roll Morton in Jelly's Last Jam; *here he does a tap duet with the brightest star of the next generation: Savion Glover, a Broadway vet from the age of twelve, as the younger version of Jelly.*

American writer–director with no Broadway experience, George C. Wolfe, was hired to direct the show. But by the early 1990s, Wolfe had made his reputation as a downtown director and a particularly acute observer of racial dynamics. Wolfe's unconventional desire to portray his black hero as a racist had surprising results: *Jelly's Last Jam* ran for almost 600 performances and earned a 1992 Best Actor Tony for Hines.

By 1995, Wolfe had earned a stellar reputation for directing plays as well as musicals, and after Joseph Papp's death in 1991, he had been running the Public Theater. It was there that Wolfe and the young dancer–choreographer Savion Glover translated the fury of the African American experience into musical theater, using the history of tap dancing as the narrative line. *Bring in 'Da Noise, Bring in 'Da Funk,* like *Hair* and *A Chorus Line* before it, quickly transferred from the Public to Broadway. Part 1920s revue, part Brechtian critique, *Bring in 'Da Noise* brought an urban, hip-hop-inflected sound to Broadway, and in Wolfe, uptown had discovered an artist with downtown sensibilities who also had an affinity for razzmatazz.

Bring in 'Da Noise was complemented the same season by *Rent,* another show whose downtown vision brought a culturally diverse cast to Broadway. It seemed as if Broadway was beginning to accommodate a new generation of ethnic talent who were finding their own voices. Jesse L. Martin, one of the African American leads in *Rent,* said, "The reason I don't like to do musicals is because you end up working in this world where you don't really fit. You're only there because they need some kind of color. In *Rent*, it doesn't matter. It's minority heaven. There's more minorities than anything else."

In the late 1990s, after beginning to diversify its casting and its stories, Broadway turned its attention to the works of its own legendary past.

The King and I is an infinitely fascinating musical to me simply because it's really about how to colonize a people. This woman comes in and she tries to affect this king. She really doesn't, but she trains his children so that by the time he dies, somebody whom she has trained has taken over. She just completely and totally violated an entire culture, all the while singing songs like "Getting to Know You." It was affirming this sort of optimism, and I think very specifically a white American optimism.
—George C. Wolfe

Ironically, Wolfe's thesis about colonialism and *The King and I* would be tested in 1996, when a revival of the show came to Broadway by way of another colony, Australia. The Broadway revival's director, Christopher Renshaw, developed his concept for an Australian production that reconceived the design and some of the musical settings to be faithful to the Thai culture of the nineteenth century. More important, with the exception of the show's four Caucasian characters, for the first time all of the roles of the Siamese court, including, of course, the royal children, were played by actors of Asian descent. The role of the king, so long associated with the Russian Gypsy Yul Brynner, was given to a half-Asian, half-Latino actor, Lou Diamond Phillips.

Savion Glover starred in Bring in 'Da Noise, Bring in 'Da Funk, *which he coconceived (with George C. Wolfe) and choreographed.*

ABOVE AND LEFT: *The 1996 revival of* The King and I *embraced the show's cultural conflict by supplying different cultures in the casting department. Lou Diamond Phillips takes on the role of the King, and Donna Murphy, who won a Tony for the role of Mrs. Anna, gets to know a royal court filled with Asian American child actors.*

There are two positions that one tends to take about *The King and I*: One is the Western influence coming to the East to try to modernize it, which is an offensive notion to a lot of people today; the other is a teacher who stands up to a man who just happens to be not only her employer, but the King of Siam, which could be viewed as a very feminist point of view.

—**Theodore S. Chapin,** President, Rodgers & Hammerstein Organization

Toward the end of the 1990s, Wolfe himself would revive *On the Town*, a show produced in 1944 with an integrated cast, with a panoramically diverse company. Even *Flower Drum Song*, a show that had simultaneously enthralled and embarrassed the Asian American community for decades, reappeared on Broadway in 2002, this time with a new book by the premier playwright of the Chinese American experience, David Henry Hwang. Hwang managed to contextualize the cultural references, while still allowing the show to have a sense of humor about itself. Artists of color were finally getting some say in how their stories were told on Broadway.

By 2009, four new musicals on Broadway—*In the Heights*, *Rock of Ages*, *Memphis*, and *Fela!*,—had culturally diverse casts, with actors playing racially specific parts, while five revivals also depended on racially specific casts to put their stories across.

The characters onstage are a bunch of animals, so when white audiences go to see *The Lion King* they don't think about race—they get the beauty and the talent of these great performers—and yet if a black audience goes, it's all about race, because imagine a young African American child going and seeing a king who's black.
—Julie Taymor, Director, *The Lion King*

Broadway seems to have confronted the cultural issues of the day in the most efficient and sensitive way possible: musicalize the best stories and hire the best performers.

"Fan Tan Fanny" was a San Francisco nightclub number in the 1958 Flower Drum Song *that made some Chinese Americans cringe. In David Henry Hwang's revision of the show (2002), he dealt with the racial stereotypes head-on and with a heavy dose of good humor.*

"There's a hell of a lot of stars in the sky."
Nicholas Hytner's production of Carousel,
which arrived at Lincoln Center's Vivian
Beaumont Theatre in 1994 with Michael
Hayden and Sally Murphy, captured
Hammerstein's universal vision.

Revivals have been around as long as there have been musicals. *The Black Crook* and *Evangeline* were revived regularly throughout the nineteenth century, and Ziegfeld himself revived *Show Boat* two seasons after its Broadway run, an event which finally gave Paul Robeson a chance to sing "Ol' Man River" on the Broadway stage. Operettas were routinely brought back to Broadway in the forties and fifties. In the mid-1960s, Richard Rodgers set up the equivalent of an opera repertory at Lincoln Center, favoring revivals of musicals with which he was associated. The most famous of these was a 1966 revival of *Annie Get Your Gun*, starring the then-fifty-seven-year-old Ethel Merman; it became legendary among theater fans as "Granny Get Your Gun." In the late 1970s, stars like Zero Mostel, Carol Channing, and Yul Brynner took a hefty percentage of the weekly gross to tool their famous vehicles around the country and back to Broadway.

But by the 1980s and 1990s, the percentage of Broadway theaters filled by revivals increased by a disconcerting number. Some of these were simply anemic restagings with the original stars, but gradually, a new generation of theater artists started to reimagine the classic texts of Broadway's Golden Age. Sometimes the most original idea was to cast the show in new ways (the 1996 revival of *The King and I*); other times, it was an inventive scenic concept that reframed the show (*Nine*, 2003). Often, due to the economics of changing times, the show's cast size, orchestrations, and scenery were simply scaled down (*Follies*, 2001). Many of the shows were altered dramaturgically; the creative staff would revise the structure of the original show, adding or subtracting numbers, sometimes sprinkling a dash more of the show's source material. This gave rise to a new term: the "revisal," although what makes for a revisal as opposed to a revival seems to have confounded critics.

The strength inherent in two classic shows by Oscar Hammerstein was such that they could benefit equally from a revival and a revisal. The mid-1990s brought both the British transfer of *Carousel* and Harold Prince's 1995 production of *Show Boat* to Broadway; each took a different route in re-examining the original material. Director Nicholas Hytner's version of *Carousel*, artfully conceived with his designer Bob Crowley for the Britain's Royal National Theatre, involved a bare minimum of textual revision, serving as a model for finding the dramatic values *inside* the text rather than imposing a "concept" on top of it. He stressed both the social reality of a nineteenth-century industrial coast town and the poetic universality of Hammerstein's vision; here, they were enthrallingly complementary.

Hammerstein himself had reworked the structure of *Show Boat* for its 1946 revival, but, in a way, the material was made for Harold Prince—the show was the first concept musical. When he directed the revival, he made many musical and textual revisions, as well as providing a cultural context for the show's racial divide and its epic structure. He made "Ol' Man River" into a recurring trope of melancholy destiny, using the character of Joe as something more akin to the Emcee in *Cabaret*. Prince's version also played like a modern

Lonette McKee as the tragic Julie in Show Boat, *a role she played in two separate Broadway revivals. Unlike the original Julie, Helen Morgan, McKee (here in Hal Prince's version) has a mixed racial background, just like the character.*

show in the way it moved scenically, and *Show Boat* ran for 947 performances, more than half as long as the original production.

Although he saw nearly his entire canon revived on Broadway in the last quarter century (some shows more than once), Stephen Sondheim told the *New York Times*: "Revivals encourage more revivals. Like kudzu, they are choking out new shows . . . Producers are unwilling to take a chance on new work, because so much of it doesn't become successful. They would rather put their money into pre-sold products." On the other hand, when composer John Kander was asked what he thought of revivals, he replied, laughingly, "I think a lot about my two revivals, I'll tell you *that*." The revivals of Kander and Ebb's *Cabaret* and *Chicago* would make their own kind of history.

Cabaret had been a convention-defying musical as far back as 1966, but even in the original production, there had always been a grittier, rawer show trying to break out. In 1997, *Cabaret* finally broke out—or perhaps "came out" would be a more fitting description. It fell to Sam Mendes, a young British director, to reimagine *Cabaret* in starker, more brutal terms. Taking his cue from the environmental theater of the early 1970s, he turned London's Donmar Warehouse into Berlin's Kit Kat Klub, with table service and a second-rate orchestra—doubled by members of the chorus. When the production transferred to New York, the Kit Kat Klub eventually took up residence in a renovated version of Studio 54, the once-notorious nightclub of the mid-1970s, infamous for its disco beat, drugs, and Liza Minnelli. It was an irony lost on absolutely no one. Mendes and his co-director, Rob Marshall, turned the chorus into a ragtag group of drug addicts and abuse victims. The ambivalent sexuality of the show's hero, Cliff Bradshaw, had always dogged the previous productions of the play; here, he was openly gay. What stood out was the Broadway debut of Alan Cumming as the Master of Ceremonies, who tied the whole concept together. With his bare torso, rouged nipples, and voracious omni-sexuality, Cumming pounced on the role, broke whatever boundaries were left, and made it his own. The production delivered its final coup de grace when the MC was revealed in the final

Alan Cumming as the compelling MC in Cabaret. *American journalists only wanted to ask him about Joel Grey; "I have never talked so much about someone I don't know," he said.*

tableau to be a concentration camp prisoner (wearing both a yellow star and a pink triangle).

While *Cabaret* doubled its original run, the other Kander and Ebb revival managed to run *six* times longer than its original counterpart—a Broadway record unlikely to be broken. It began with the Encores! series, initiated at City Center in 1993 by its executive director, Judith Daykin, as a way of reviving undervalued musicals in concert form, most of them from the '20s, '30s, and '40s. Encores! surprised its subscriber base when it presented *Chicago*, a show that was then only twenty years old. But Bob Fosse had been gone for almost a decade by then, and the vitality of his work seemed to be from a distant past. Fosse dancer and former girlfriend Ann Reinking not only took over the role of Roxie but also choreographed the show, as the program read, "in the style of Bob Fosse." The concert was scheduled for only four performances in the spring of 1996, but audiences were ecstatic at the new leaner, meaner *Chicago* in concert, and within six months, producers Barry and Fran Weissler had moved the show to Broadway in a scaled-down full production. Although no new material was interpolated into this Tony-winning revival, it seemed as if the show were ripped from the headlines of the day. In fact, *Chicago* made the front page on its own, with a rare front-page review in the *New York Times*. Critics and audiences alike realized that, in the age of instant celebrity, Court TV, and the O. J. Simpson trial, the 1975 *Chicago* was not just cynical, it was prescient. The score was finally given its due and touring companies played to packed houses all over America and the world.

The punch line for *Chicago* is that, like its heroine Roxie, it finally made good in show biz. Although film versions of the show had been bruited about since 1976 (one version was supposed to star Liza Minnelli, Goldie Hawn, and Frank Sinatra), it was the revival that finally jump-started the 2002 film version, produced by Martin Richards, who had backed the original stage show. *Chicago* became the first movie musical to win an Oscar for Best Picture since *Oliver!* thirty-four years earlier and brought a whole new worldwide audience to a show that, once upon a time, had been thought of—if at all—as a casualty of *A Chorus Line*. Rather than cutting the stage run short, the film version of *Chicago* only helped to resuscitate the Broadway box office; when film star Melanie Griffith stepped into the role of Roxie in the summer of 2003, the show was SRO all over again. The Broadway version shows little sign of slowing down—thanks in no small part to the revolving stage door of stunt casting, with celebrities such as Usher, Jerry Springer, and Ashlee Simpson appearing for limited engagements.

During the first decade of the new millennium, musical revivals continued at a furious pace; they usually constitute nearly half of the musicals that open on Broadway every season. The Roundabout Theatre Company, a not-for-profit theater, devotes a major part of each subscription season to revivals. Invariably, due to the size of the house and other financial considerations, the revivals are scaled down. Sometimes they catch fire anyway, as in a snappy new version of *The Pajama Game*, starring Harry Connick, Jr., and Kelli O'Hara; other times, as in a lugubrious *Pal Joey*, with Stockard Channing, or a tentative *Bye Bye Birdie*, they don't. The Roundabout has been a particular champion of Sondheim's work, offering several imaginative revivals, but two of the most notable Sondheim revivals came by way of the commercial theater, from an inventive director named John Doyle. While experimenting with musical revivals in a small English provincial theater, Doyle developed his *modus operandi*: to scale down the size of the show in every manner, while asking his cast to double as the orchestra (or asking his orchestra to sing the roles onstage, depending on how you look at it). Doyle brought *Sweeney Todd* to Broadway in 2005 with Patti LuPone and Michael Cerveris; the following season, he reconceived *Company* with Raúl Esparza. Whether Doyle's approach is revelatory, as some critics suggest, or annoying (the actors are limited as musicians; the musicians are limited as actors) is a matter of opinion, but the director has certainly shaken up the revival scene.

Such inventiveness becomes necessary when revivals revolve around the season schedule with such frequency that Broadway feels like, well, a carousel. *Guys and Dolls* has been revived on Broadway three times since 1950; *Gypsy* has been revived four times since

Ann Reinking and James Naughton performing "We Both Reached for the Gun" in the revival of Chicago. *At its concert debut at City Center for Encores!, 1,500 enthusiastic fans cheered the show. Its success stunned even its creators, Kander and Ebb: "I didn't think there were 1,500 people who had even heard of the show," remarked Ebb.*

Who can explain it? Paulo Szot, a matinee idol on the world opera stage, and Kelli O'Hara, a Broadway leading lady, in the revival of South Pacific *(2008).*

1959. Yet two major pillars of the musical theater canon had remained untapped for full-scale Broadway revivals for sixty years: *South Pacific* and *Finian's Rainbow*.

Although there had been waves of producers asking for the Broadway rights to *South Pacific* over the years, the original show was such a particular product of its time that it needed the proper context to put the show into perspective. A special one-night-only concert version at Carnegie Hall, starring Brian Stokes Mitchell and Reba McEntire in 2005, brought renewed interest in *South Pacific*, particularly from Lincoln Center Theater's artistic director, André Bishop. Ironically, it was a show presented at Lincoln Center Theater in 2006—*The Light in the Piazza*—that unlocked the door to a new *South Pacific*. The president of the Rodgers and Hammerstein Organization, Ted Chapin, reasoned that if the same production team could do such an impressive job staging Adam Guettel's score, imagine what they could do with a score by Richard Rodgers—who just happened to be Guettel's grandfather.

Bishop brought back *Piazza*'s director, Bartlett Sher, and his musical collaborators and design team, and threw the considerable resources of the Vivian Beaumont Theater at the new production; there would be a cast of 44 and a 30-piece orchestra in the pit—numbers normally unheard-of in a contemporary revival. Sher cast his leads in much the same manner as the original—a handsome leading man from the opera world (Paulo Szot) and a rising star from Broadway (Kelli O'Hara)—but went as far a field as Hawaii to hire his Bloody Mary (Loretta Ables Sayre) and to honor the racial specificity of the characters in the show. But perhaps the revival's greatest collaborator—and in some ways the most unfortunate—was the world itself. By the time *South Pacific* opened at the Beaumont on April 3, 2008, America was at war in two different countries on the other side of the globe (even the original production opened a year before America entered the Korean War). It also didn't hurt that the child of a racially mixed couple was on his way to becoming president of the United States.

But cultural relevance can only fill so many seats, and audiences and critics succumbed once again to *South Pacific*'s rhapsodic musical charms. Director Sher used the orchestra as the show's secret weapon, pulling back the stage floor of the Beaumont just as the overture reached the crescendo of "Bali Ha'i" to reveal every player in the pit sending Rodgers' lush melodies out to the crowd. The effect routinely stopped the show—even before it began—and was known in theater circles as the "802 reveal," referring to the musicians' union local.

The production also revealed how much audiences craved a full-throated, full-hearted show once more, and the revival took up permanent residence at the Vivian Beaumont.

If the country's increased sensitivity to racial issues made *South Pacific* more accessible to audiences in the twenty-first century, they only served to keep *Finian's Rainbow* off the boards for six decades. Although Yip Harburg and Burton Lane's score is one of the most glorious ever written, Harburg's satirical point of view—and his subplot of a bigoted Southern senator who is magically turned into a black man—struck many as ham-fisted, if not offensive, in the post–Richard Pryor age. "The use of blackface [to transform the senator onstage] really cursed *Finian's*, but over the years the show developed an even greater reputation as unrevivable due to matters of race, even though [the show] was so progressive," said Jack Viertel, who produced *Finian's Rainbow* as a part of the Encores! series in 2009, and then helped to revive it on Broadway.

In the 2009 version, the blackface issue is ameliorated by having a white actor (David Schramm) portray the senator before the transformation and a black actor of similar build (Chuck Cooper) portray him for the second half the show. Both actors are so engaging—and the rest of the musical is such a grab-bag of ideas (it does feature a leprechaun, after all)—that the audience goes along for the ride. Viertel's co-producer, David Richenthal, sees a deeper resonance in the audience's acceptance: "One of the senator's lines, after he has been both white and black, is, 'I can see both sides of it now'—which speaks very specifically, I think, to the age of Obama, to the ability to see both sides of the way people live in this country."

There's an apocryphal Chinese saying—or curse, depending on whom you believe— "May you live in interesting times." The Broadway motto might be: "May you live in interesting times—and have even more interesting musicals to revive."

Chuck Cooper (second from left) is the racist senator who begat a new wave of political correctness in the revival of Finian's Rainbow *(2009).*

NEW YORK CITY mayors and Broadway musicals just seem to go together. Irving Berlin spoofed City Hall in his 1932 *Face the Music*, and Peter Stuyvesant, Jimmy Walker, Fiorello La Guardia, and Edward Koch each found themselves as lead characters in Broadway musicals (technically, Koch was *Off* Broadway).

But it took until March 23, 1973, for a real New York mayor to appear on Broadway. For one evening, John Lindsay, nearing the end of his tenure, sang "My City," a backhanded paean to the charms of New York, in a performance of Cy Coleman and Dorothy Fields's *Seesaw*, because of his ostensible resemblance to the show's star, Ken Howard. Broadway seemed to like Lindsay—he was even given an honorary Equity card when he left office—and he considered himself a patron of the arts. But Lindsay's interest in reclaiming Times Square had far more to do with increasing tax revenue than with artistic patronage of the theater. His encouragement of development in the Theater District would spin out, over the next three decades, into a strange and tangled confluence of politics, economics, public relations, greed, and ego, where alliances shifted constantly and where decisions made in City Hall conference rooms could affect the scenic design of a Broadway show.

Mayor John V. Lindsay takes center stage to view a musical comedy hooker at the Uris Theater, eight blocks up from the real thing.

Lindsay's most complicated artistic legacy came in the guise of "tax abatements": financial incentives to encourage investment and development in the Times Square area. Developers were encouraged to build new office buildings in exchange for huge tax breaks from the city. One provision forced the developers to add a theater on the ground floor of their new buildings as part of the deal, and in the 1970s, the Minskoff, the Uris (later renamed the Gershwin), and the renovated Circle in the Square were added to the Broadway landscape, the first new theaters built in the Theater District since the beginning of the Depression. Unfortunately, the new theaters were cheerless and charmless, and despite these attempts, Times Square got seedier and sleazier; when a series of dire financial crises hit the city in the late 1970s, it brought an end to this brief period of redevelopment. By 1977, even the famous "zipper" sign that spun out headlines along the Times Tower for fifty years had turned out its lights.

When Koch became mayor in 1978, he saw both the PR and the financial potential in returning his office's attention to 42nd Street, and he eagerly accepted a Ford Foundation proposal for a complete renovation of Times Square. When the project was unveiled in 1980, however, Koch took one look at the plans, which called for West 42nd Street to be transformed into a tourist-oriented shopping mall, and told the public, "They want to build Disneyland," which was a devastating criticism back then. The project died. Koch and the city had another fish to fry, in this case a big barracuda from Atlanta, hotel magnate John Portman, who had contacted City Hall about building a multistory Marriott hotel on Broadway between 45th and 46th Streets. Koch put the project on the fast track in 1980. The Shubert Organization's Gerald Schoenfeld recalled:

> This area in the '70s was a sewer. This was the den of pornography, prostitution, felony crime, drug dealing— you name it. And along came Marriott and they wanted to build a new hotel here. Well, that hotel was advocated by everybody in this business, including us. We thought it represented a major signal that the area was alive and well.

The construction on that block of the Marriott meant that five theaters (including two beloved by the theater community, the Morosco and the Helen Hayes) would have to be razed, a decision that would obsess and polarize the theatrical community for years. Despite many protests and several court stays, the demolition began on March 22, 1982, and the Marriott Marquis, as it came to be called, is today the most successful hotel in America.

None of these maneuvers helped 42nd Street itself. During the mid-1980s, scandal and transition under the Koch administration shunted the renovation of the street to the bottom of the pile. By 1990, however, under the new administration of David Dinkins, an organization called the New 42 was constituted to try to resurrect 42nd Street one more time. The New 42 put its energy into returning the street to its fabled past as a center for legitimate theater, something it hadn't been since before the Depression. It would not be an easy task, for the street was still a grimy boulevard of porn and other sexual detritus.

The New 42 immediately set its sights on renovating a signature theater on the street. The Victory was an abandoned wreck that had begun life in 1900 as the Theatre Republic, eventually turning into both a burlesque house and, later, a porno house. The mission was to transform it into—of all things—a theater for young audiences. As planning began in 1992, attention turned to the New

A desolate lot on Broadway between 45th and 46th Streets, 1982. It had been the site of the Morosco Theater, among others.

The same lot in 2004, transformed into the Marriott Marquis Hotel.

Amsterdam, at the corner of 42nd Street and Seventh Avenue, Ziegfeld's grand aerie. Defunct as a legitimate theater since 1937, the New Amsterdam too had suffered the depredations of decay, neglect, and sleazy tenants.

The New Amsterdam had been dangled in front of developers and producers for years by the city, but no one had had the courage to seal the deal. Harold Prince, invited to look at the abandoned premises for a possible venue, witnessed a drug deal and a sex act in the five minutes he was waiting in front of the theater. But after the promising success of the stage version of *Beauty and the Beast*, the CEO of the Walt Disney Company, Michael Eisner, was interested in finding a theatrical venue that Disney could own, rather than having to rely on renting out from theater owners. A chance meeting on an airplane with New 42 chairperson Marian Heiskell convinced Eisner to take a look at the ruins of Ziegfeld's temple. "It was dark, and it was raining in the theater; birds were flying around," he recalled. "We had big flashlights and you aimed the flashlights at these frescoes that were falling down, but they were beautiful—you could see what it was."

In April 1993, Eisner began a series of cautious and elaborate negotiations with the city to restore and rent the New Amsterdam. The cost would be a hefty $32 million, with $24 million covered by the city in terms of loans that were extremely advantageous to Disney; Disney itself committed $8 million, and the terms of the lease would extend for forty-nine years. For reporters, critics, and mavens, the idea of Mickey Mouse on 42nd Street was a hilarious irony. For Eisner, it was a business decision fraught with catastrophic risk: what would it mean for a brand name of such wholesome family values to set up shop on the most decadent city block in the western world? He spoke with the new mayor, Rudolph Giuliani, who had made his career as a federal prosecutor crusading against the mob. Eisner says of their meeting:

I had a little concern about the adjacent nightlife and he [Giuliani] looked me in the eye and he said, "It'll be gone," and I said, "Mister Mayor, you know there is the American Civil Liberties Union and they're just not going to be gone." He said, "Look me in the eye." And I said, "What?" He said, "Look me in the eye." I said, "Okay." He said, "They will be *gone*." Scared *me*. I guess they were going to be gone. So that was that, and we said yes.

Disney's announcement that it would go ahead with the New Amsterdam in the winter of 1994 was met with derision, skepticism, and headlines with a lot of bad puns. But the floodgates were opened, just the way New 42 intended. By the end of 1995, the New Victory Theatre for young audiences, beautifully restored, had opened. Even more remarkable, there was a cappuccino bar next door. Retail outlets began to sign leases in the Times Square area, new bright and elaborate electronic signs began appearing in the Theater District for the first time since the beginning of the Second World War, and several business and communication firms announced plans to build new offices on, or adjacent to, West 42nd Street. Even the "zipper" was back, courtesy of *New York Newsday*.

In the fall of 1997, Disney opened *The Lion King* at the New Amsterdam, the first new musical there since Sigmund Romberg's *Forbidden Melody* in 1936. The show got wildly enthusiastic reviews, as did the theater itself, the result of a loving four-year restoration, masterminded by architect Hugh Hardy. Across the street that year, the Ford Motor Company as a corporate sponsor paid for the massive renovation of the Lyric and Apollo theaters, merging the two defunct spaces into one enormous musical house, the Ford Center for the Performing Arts, which debuted with *Ragtime* in January 1998. Later that year, the Empire Theatre on 42nd Street, which had housed musicals and burlesque shows, was rolled by engineers 168 feet west to begin life as a twenty-five-screen AMC multiplex. The renovation of the Selwyn as the American Airlines Theatre (a home for the Roundabout Theater Company) and the addition of a multistudio rehearsal space next door burnished the transformation of the new 42nd Street.

At certain moments in its history, the Theater District has been rudely awakened to the fact that it sits on some of the most desirable real estate in the free world. Critics attacked the city for giving tax concessions to a multibillion-dollar corporation like Disney, but what politician would have had the guts to walk away from the chance to resurrect a unique civic playground? It's also hard to wax nostalgic, as some writers have, for the "character" of the old 42nd Street. It's not likely to be mourned by any who as parents in the 1970s had to usher their children hurriedly from the matinee of *Annie* to the subway stop, past the Triple-X marquee for *On Golden Blonde*.

The unimaginable phoenix: the new, radiant, clean 42nd Street.

Theater has always been about transformation. In 2004, one could exit the revival of *42nd Street* at the Ford Center and walk right onto the real 42nd Street. The show sings of "naughty, bawdy, gaudy, sporty 42nd Street," but there isn't any of that now. Isn't it ironic that a song from 1933 would portray a grittier, seamier version of 42nd Street than the one you can see for yourself seventy-five years later?

"I just can't wait to be King"
THE WALT DISNEY COMPANY AND *THE LION KING*

To understand how Disney changed Broadway, one first has to understand how Broadway changed Disney.

In the 1980s, Disney had released a slate of moribund animated features, none of which had produced any characters or franchises that captured the Disney magic. But like any theater producer, the studio realized that what it needed was a good script and a good score. Executive Tom Schumacher drafted librettist Howard Ashman and composer Alan Menken, who had had a huge success with the Off Broadway musical *Little Shop of Horrors*, and asked them to develop a "little" project of their own: *The Little Mermaid*. With the 1989 release of that animated feature, Disney struck gold. It repeated the format for several films in the 1980s and 1990s, including *Beauty and the Beast*, *The Lion King*, and *Aladdin*, all of which used Broadway artists such as Tim Rice and Stephen Schwartz to craft their scores. Disney ingeniously adapted the formula of the Golden Age of Broadway for a contemporary audience and the films were the first Disney successes in more than a decade.

Under the stewardship of CEO Michael Eisner, Disney decided to get into the Broadway business. The critical and financial success of the 1991 feature *Beauty and the Beast* made it a natural for a stage adaption. Eisner decreed that Disney should produce the show on its own and enlist the creative contributions of its many theme park artists. An in-

Director Julie Taymor at work trying to create the proper balance between mask and actor for The Lion King.

I'm not trying to make this a technological feat—this is the most ancient, primitive means of theater that exists.
—Julie Taymor

house team, using additional songs written by Menken and Rice (Menken's lyricist, Howard Ashman, had died of AIDS soon after the film premiered), launched *Beauty and the Beast*'s stage incarnation in Houston in 1993, with the final destination of Broadway in its sights. It opened at the Palace in 1994 to negative press, industry resentment—and huge box office sales. Although the show seemed, at best, a competent exercise in putting a movie onstage, it far outpaced its only competitor that season, Sondheim's *Passion*, and in 2001, it pushed past *42nd Street* to become the longest-running American musical since *A Chorus Line*.

"How come we're not doing *The Lion King* as a stage show?" demanded Joe Roth, then chairman of Disney, of Michael Eisner. "It's the most successful film ever made and it has a huge built-in audience. If you don't, you're nuts." It fell to Thomas Schumacher, now executive vice president of the newly created Walt Disney

Cheetahs never prosper: Taymor's costume sketch for an actor-puppet for the opening number, "The Circle of Life" . . .

and its practical application onstage.

Theatrical Productions, to make sure Disney wasn't nuts. He hired an avant-garde artist with whom he had worked at a Los Angeles arts festival: a director, puppeteer, and designer, whose aesthetic was Disney Worlds apart from the company line.

Julie Taymor had one of the most eclectic backgrounds in the American theater. She had studied mime in Paris and went to Japan and Indonesia to learn the art of native puppetry there. She was obsessed with myth and folklore and was equally passionate about Latin music, commedia dell'arte, Zulu chants, and Balinese puppet theater. She had spent most of her career in not-for-profit theaters and arts festivals and she was consistently full of surprises. What surprised Schumacher the most was that Taymor had never seen *The Lion King*. When she did, she immediately tapped into the story of rebirth and redemption that was at the film's core. Taymor first went back to the text, beefed up the central story, gave more power to the female characters (including changing the baboon character Rafiki into a woman and the spiritual center of the piece), and added more of an African sound to the score. Then she tackled the real problem. "It doesn't make sense," Eisner himself opined, "to try and do Bert Lahr dressed up like the Cowardly Lion."

"Who wants to see a bunch of furry yellow lions up there?" she asked. "How boring." Instead, Taymor used everything she knew about puppetry. She explained:

[Puppetry] goes back to something very ancient. It's also very respectful of the audience because it's not trying to hide the strings and the rods, it's very transparent, it's out there. You see the human beings in the elephant legs, you see the two humans holding the rhinoceros suspended between them with birds on their heads and the audience goes back to something that we all did as children—make believe, where you needed very little to suggest quite a lot. Children are much more capable of comprehending an abstract image than adults are. The audience is not spoon-fed absolute reality, but they come and they finish the sentences with you.

Onstage, at Ziegfeld's showcase New Amsterdam Theatre, another form of stage extravaganza thrilled audiences three quarters of a century after the Great Glorifier developed the showstopper. Here is designer Richard Hudson's mastery of nineteenth-century stagecraft—a stampede of wildebeest.

Taymor shared her ideas with Disney in two workshop presentations, in 1996 and February 1997, giving executives a comprehensive demonstration of how she was going to use her unique brand of puppetry to banish Bert Lahr into the wings. Disney gave the green light to what would become one of the most technically complicated and visually astonishing productions in Broadway history. When *The Lion King* gave its out-of-town tryout in Minneapolis, audiences witnessed Taymor's magic, as the shamanesque Rafiki conjured all the animals out of the veldt to witness the birth of Simba, the future lion king, in the opening number, "The Circle of Life."

These giant puppets enter and people are going crazy. People are crying, to this day they cry because they're overcome. When you work in television, you don't feel a reaction—you see the ratings the next morning, it's a number—it's empty and it's sterile. But eighteen hundred and thirty-two people at this theater going crazy—it's awesome.

—Michael Eisner

When the show opened at the New Amsterdam on November 13, 1997, audiences and critics alike responded to the work onstage. "*The Lion King* makes you feel you are seeing something new and makes you happy to see it," wrote the *Times*'s Margo Jefferson. Other critics were less impressed. John Lahr said:

> You have this kind of schizophrenic experience where you're imposing onto very standard Disney material a very exotic sound and look—it has the look and feel of the avant-garde but the heart of a Hollywood production. It's the ultimate expression of business art, because you even leave the theater and they guide you right into the store.

Ziegfeld himself, no doubt the still haunting rafters of the New Amsterdam, would have admired a gifted artist at the helm, calling the shots, interpolating songs, and making sure that every dime could be seen onstage. Twenty-seven imposing chorus members magically appear upstage with gargantuan headdresses—this time, representing the Grasslands of Africa. For her skills as a modern impresario, Taymor made theater history by becoming the first woman to win a Tony Award for Best Direction of a Musical, and the show itself won for Best Original Musical.

Composer Elton John (l.) and lyricist Tim Rice were but two of the most accomplished pop and Broadway hands that Disney brought to the screen and the stage.

Sherie René Scott as Princess Amneris in Aida *(2000), a Disney stage original.*

Playing the Palace: Aida's stunning set designs by Bob Crowley turned the marshlands of Ancient Egypt into a Ziegfeldesque tableau.

We'll have giant failures like everybody else, but we'll have failures because the creative people fail, we will not have failures because the production side failed or the financing side failed. We're taking that out of the equation.

—Michael Eisner

With two commercial successes (and, finally, a critical success), Disney's theatrical division shifted into high gear, commissioning Elton John and Tim Rice to adapt *Aida* for the stage (which opened at the Palace in 2000), in addition to the complex job of exporting the shows to other theatrical venues here and abroad. There are nearly a dozen productions of *The Lion King* around the globe, and the show has grossed billions of dollars worldwide. Disney went on to produce, with varying degrees of success, other stage versions of their properties: *Tarzan*, *The Little Mermaid*, and *Mary Poppins*.

Eisner, guiding Disney's theatrical fortunes, understood something fundamental about Broadway, not the backstage part of it, but, as befits someone who is caretaker to one of the great trademarks in history, its *brand name*. "Broadway is the proving ground if you intend to be serious about theater. Commercial success in New York prompts the attention and buzz that then makes it possible to launch road companies in major cities around the country and around the world," he wrote in his memoir. No one except Disney really knows what *The Lion King* cost to produce—estimates run close to $20 million—but their corporate financing allows them to hang in there far longer than any Broadway producer ever dreamed. Many critics have derided Disney's influence and its marketing techniques (there's a Disney store right next to the lobby of the New Amsterdam), but this seems disingenuous—since the days of Ziegfeld, producers have always been prepared to make money in show business by any means necessary.

"Look out, Broadway, here we come!"

MEL BROOKS AND *THE PRODUCERS*

The big joke is not that Mel Brooks turned his 1968 film into a smash Broadway musical; the big joke is that *The Producers* was always a Broadway musical to begin with.

Ever since little Melvin Kaminsky was taken to see *Anything Goes* in 1935, all he ever wanted to do was work on Broadway, and, after he changed his name to Mel Brooks and became a television writer, he did, writing comic sketches for the revue *New Faces of 1952* and the books for two failed Broadway musicals in the early 1960s. His screenplay for his first film, *The Producers* (1968), quite cannily captured the Broadway scene he had observed firsthand:

I did work for a Max Bialystock [type of producer]. He had an office on 48th Street with a big half-moon window. I don't think he ever had a hit. I was his assistant, and he used to studiously, assiduously, make fierce love to eighty-five-year-old ladies on his old weather-beaten leather couch. He'd say, "Mel, go out and get me a White Owl." That's a cigar that he liked. And that was a clue to leave the office for forty-one minutes, so that he enough time to do the ladies and get proper again, you know. But they'd all give him money. And they'd dutifully write out the check to Cash, which was always the name of his latest play, *Cash*. That's a funny name for a play, and he'd usually say, "So is *The Iceman Cometh*."

"Mr. Tact"—Leo Bloom (Matthew Broderick)—stumbles onto producer Max Bialystock (Nathan Lane) in the middle of raising cash for his new show.

The movie's premise is well known: Flop-covered theatrical producer Max Bialystock realizes the key to financial redemption lies in producing the worst musical ever written, raising 25,000 percent of the capital, and pocketing it all when the show is a one-night-only disaster. Aided by a nebbishy accountant named Leo Bloom, Bialystock options the rights to a "Gay Romp with Adolf and Eva in Berchtesgaden" called *Springtime for Hitler*. Of course, if the show, by some insane stretch of credulity, becomes a hit, Bialystock and Bloom will be thrown in jail. And that is exactly what happens.

For all its farcical satire, the original film was, in many ways, one of the great time capsules of the Broadway musical in the late 1960s. Where Brooks really hit the bull's-eye was in the central absurdity of the premise. By the time he made his film, so many historical personages had recently been turned into musical-comedy characters, why not Hitler, too? *Cabaret* had made its own excursion into Nazi Germany, swastikas and all, the season before. By 1968, a musical about Hitler wasn't absurd—it seemed downright inevitable.

Brooks won an Oscar for his *Producers* screenplay, but the film itself tanked, earning a place only in the hearts of cult fanatics and Broadway camp followers. He had a huge film career bringing satire to movie screens in the 1970s, but by 1998, Brooks's career had begun eerily to resemble that of Bialystock. Then the phone rang. It was David Geffen, one of the savviest of the 1980s media moguls. Geffen was not the first to try to get Brooks to adapt *The Producers* to the stage, but Brooks had always demurred. This time, he was impressed by Geffen's acumen and said yes. All that was needed was a score. Brooks had written two numbers for the original film, including the unforgettable "Springtime for Hitler." ("We're marching to a faster pace / Look out here comes the master race" went one refrain.) Geffen insisted Brooks meet with Jerry Herman, but Herman passed on the project, believing Brooks himself to be the only person who could capture the spirit of the piece. Brooks then asked longtime collaborator Thomas Meehan to write the book with him. British director Mike Ockrent, who had displayed his knack for musical comedy with the Gershwin pastiche *Crazy for You* (1992), and his equally talented wife, choreographer Susan Stroman, joined the team. But when Ockrent succumbed to leukemia in December 1999, Brooks trusted Stroman to capture the spirit of the project, and she became the director as well as the choreographer.

For the role of Max Bialystock, so indelibly rendered by Zero Mostel on film, Brooks (and the rest of Broadway) knew there was only one choice: Nathan Lane. One night, when Lane was hosting *The Late Show* during David Letterman's heart surgery, Brooks browbeat him by bringing an actual contract with him onto the show. With Lane quickly—and happily—signed, the team managed another coup by landing Matthew Broderick, who had proven equally adept at film, straight plays, and musicals, to play the neurotic milquetoast Bloom. But even with such a stellar lineup, the show was no guaranteed success. After all, who wanted their favorite cult film tampered with? Here, Brooks and Meehan exhibited a kind of genius. Scenes, characters, and favorite lines were cut with ruthless abandon as the partners rethought their story as a live event. They also embraced the "old-fashioned" musical aspect of their material, keeping a traditional book-and-score structure, even backdating their story to 1959, a simpler, less jaded time.

As the show rocketed its way to Broadway after a sellout engagement in Chicago, it had lost Geffen as a producer but gained a large and eager consortium of fourteen actual producers. Its pre-Broadway advance was $18 million—less than half that of *Miss Saigon*, but huge for a musical originating in America. Audiences were helpless with laughter and the critics were rapturous. After its April 19, 2001, opening, the show quickly became not only the hottest ticket in town, but the hottest ticket in almost a decade. At the 2001 Tony Awards, Brooks, not content to let anyone vanish into the night unoffended, took a moment to thank Adolf Hitler. After Lane and Broderick left the show, business took a nosedive; it still did the kind of business that other producers dream of, but the producers of *The Producers* wanted their mojo back. Lane and Broderick returned to their roles on New Year's Eve, 2003, for a limited engagement, and a week after they reopened in the show, the papers reported that a film version of the stage version was being produced by Universal, starring Lane and Broderick. (When it was released, it failed at the box office.)

There were many reasons why *The Producers* became such a smash hit. Some of its success is due to the considerable artistry of the creative staff: Stroman's goofy ballet of Bialystock-besotted little old ladies tap-dancing with their walkers was a particular gem. Some of it may have been a reaction to the epic British musical that had so dominated Broadway. Nathan Lane observed: "People change, and the culture changes, and if the timing is right for something and something comes back that we used to like and we haven't seen in a while, then it's like welcoming back an old friend. In a sense, I think that's what happened with *The Producers*."

The Producers was new, but it was also old in a nice way, a throwback to a tradition where you went to Broadway to *laugh,* just like those shows in the 1930s that little Melvin Kaminsky watched from the second balcony.

"I'm the German Ethel Merman, don'tcha know?" Gary Beach playing Roger de Bris playing Adolf Hitler in the greatest stage entrance since Mame: *"Springtime for Hitler."*

I WANNA BE A PRODUCER

Words and music by Mel Brooks
From The Producers *(2001)*

MOST CHARACTERS IN SHOW BIZ MUSICALS wanna grow up to be big stars (*Sally, Gypsy, Funny Girl, Minnie's Boys*). Occasionally, they wanna be hit songwriters (*Merrily We Roll Along, Rent*), and every now and then, they wanna be both (*George M!*). But the milquetoast accountant Leo Bloom (played by Matthew Broderick) was the first musical comedy lead who actually wanted to be a producer.

In Mel Brooks's lyrics, one can see the myth of Ziegfeld, with all its perquisites of power and celebrity. In fact, if you wanted to be a producer of *The Producers,* here's what else you could have had:

- An $18 million preopening advance
- A record twelve Tony Awards
- A recoupment of your $10.5 million investment within seven months
- The right to charge $480 for each "VIP Dress Circle" ticket
- A Broadway record for the weekly gross of a show: $1.6 million
- A weekly gross on the road averaging $1.5 million
- A song in this book

LEO:
I have a secret desire
Hiding deep in my soul.
It sets my heart afire
To see me in this role.

I wanna be a producer
With a hit show on Broadway.
I wanna be a producer,
Lunch at Sardi's every day.
I wanna be a producer,
Sport a top hat and a cane.
I wanna be a producer
And drive those chorus girls insane.

*Broderick as Leo Bloom—an accoun
dreaming of becoming a Ziegfeld.*

Leo and Max—back on the Great White Way!

I wanna be a producer
And sleep until half-past two.
I wanna be a producer
And say, "You, you, you—not you."
I wanna be a producer,
Wear a tux on op'ning nights.
I wanna be a producer
And see my name, Leo Bloom, in lights!

SHOWGIRLS:
He wants to be the producer
Of a great big Broadway smash!
He wants to be a producer,
Ev'ry pocket stuffed with cash.
He wants to be a producer,
Pinch our cheeks till we cry "Ouch!"
He wants to be a producer
With a great big casting couch.

LEO:
I wanna be the greatest, grandest,
And most fabulous producer in the world.

GIRLS:
He wants to be a producer
He's gotta dine
With a duchess and a duke.

LEO:
I just gotta be a producer,
Drink champagne until I puke.

I wanna be a producer,
Show the world just what I've got
I'm gonna put on shows
That will enthrall 'em.
Read my name in Winchell's column.
I wanna be a producer
'Cause it's everything I'm not.

I wanna be a producer,
I'm gonna be a producer,
Sound the horn and beat the drum.
I'm gonna be a producer,
Look out, Broadway, here I come!

*Mel Brooks, accepting the Tony Award for Best
Original Musical, welcomed onstage fourteen other
producers— "a phalanx, an avalanche of Jews."*

"I'll make a brand-new start of it in old New York"

9/11 AND THE THEATER DISTRICT

Every savvy New York theatergoer knew that if the line at the TKTS booth on 47th Street was too long, there was another booth providing the same services down at the World Trade Center, in the lobby of Tower Two.

All that changed on the morning of September 11, 2001. The cataclysm of the World Trade Center attacks sent shock waves through the Theater District five miles uptown. Many Off Broadway theaters downtown were disrupted for months, and on Broadway, houses were dark for an unprecedented two days. Times Square was nearly deserted. When, at the insistence of Mayor Giuliani and Schuyler Chapin, commissioner of cultural affairs, the theaters were reopened on September 13, the drop in attendance at some shows was as great as 80 percent. It had been a successful summer for Broadway, but the week following September 11 saw a drop in box office income from $9 million to $3.5 million.

Those intrepid souls who did make it to the Theater District (which was not off-limits, the way everything south of 14th Street was) often joined the casts of the shows in singing "God Bless America" or "My Country 'Tis of Thee" at the curtain calls. Equity and the stagehands' union agreed to let employees of several shows take a 25 percent pay cut to help them stay open (ultimately, many producers repaid their employees when business picked up), but five shows folded immediately. Sondheim's *Assassins,* a musical about political assassination, was about to go into rehearsal on September 12 for its Broadway debut; it was wisely postponed until the mood was more receptive. (It was postponed again during a series of sniper attacks in Washington, D.C., in the winter of 2002.) The greatest commercial damage, relatively speaking, was done to the megahits, which depended so heavily on the tourist trade. No one was coming to New York.

"If you really want to help New York City, go see a play," Giuliani announced to the world at large on September 18. "You might even be able to get tickets to see *The Producers.*"

> **Historically, musical performers were always there during the war and during catastrophe, and Broadway seemed to be the only place that did thrive during these times, where people would reach out to go to the theater. And what ultimately happened after 9/11 is that people did indeed need relief. New York was grieving. You couldn't go anywhere where there wasn't someone else who was grieving. But to go to the theater and to be with another group of people, a group of people who were being entertained, by topnotch performers who were doing their best to give you a little relief from that grief, was not only appropriate, but completely healing.**
> **—Susan Stroman,** Director–Choreographer

One customer who showed up at the St. James on September 13 with his ticket for *The Producers* in hand summed up the general atmosphere: "I was determined to go. I was determined to laugh and determined to make my life as normal as possible."

The "I ♥ NY" campaign was restarted, and hundreds of working Broadway actors packed Duffy Square to film a commercial for Broadway, singing Kander and Ebb's "New York, New York." Eventually, despite further anxieties such as an anthrax scare in midtown, customers did come back, warily; there were not as many tourists, but they came. The box office for 2001–02 was only slightly less than the previous season's, and the next year it bounced back with an 11 percent increase. Finances and general good cheer along Broadway were encouraged that season by the appearance of three critically acclaimed shows: filmmaker Baz Luhrmann's version of *La Bohème; Movin' Out;* and the candy-colored shindig *Hairspray.*

ABOVE: *In the early 1980s, a second TKTS booth was set up at the World Trade Center to accommodate the demand for half-price tickets.*

OVERLEAF: *Broadway had never seen such a demonstration of affection for show business as the assembled forces at Duffy Square on September 19, 2001. Among the scores of celebrities who showed up to promote Broadway are (front row) Glenn Close, Valerie Harper, Michelle Lee, Bernadette Peters, Joel Grey, Dick Cavett, Elaine Stritch, Cady Huffman, Nathan Lane, Matthew Broderick, Roger Bart, and Gary Beach.*

"The Line King"

AL HIRSCHFELD

No one attended more Broadway shows over the last century than Al Hirschfeld. America's most acclaimed theatrical illustrator began his career in the late 1920s, becoming the official caricaturist of the *New York Times* and covering every major show and every major star to appear on Broadway. His teasing, elegant line drawings spun magic out of pen and ink; Hirschfeld didn't just capture the likenesses of Broadway, he captured its essence and communicated it to millions of readers.

On June 21, 2003, the Martin Beck Theatre on West 45th Street was renamed the Al Hirschfeld, in honor of the artist's 100th birthday. The usually skeptical Hirschfeld had been looking forward to the tribute, but he passed away five months shy of his centenary. He may have missed the event, but there wasn't much else he had missed in eighty years of theatergoing. He was the hieroglyphic Homer of Broadway.

I've been hearing about Broadway disappearing ever since I put on long pants. The form changes, and that's difficult for a lot of people to accept. They're stuck in one period, and they think that's the period that's important, but it isn't necessarily so. It could be just a passing fancy nobody even takes seriously in another fifty years. It changes, and you roll with the punches.

—Al Hirschfeld

The marquee for the Al Hirschfeld Theatre, 2004, which renders its namesake's likeness in neon.

RIGHT: *Hirschfeld's portrait of a Weber and Fields reunion (1925).*
OPPOSITE: *The last portrait drawn by Hirschfeld,* Tommy Tune: White Tie and Tails, *December 15, 2002, for the* New York Times.

"Defying gravity"

WICKED

Learning "For Good" in the studio, spring of 2004 (left to right): Idina Menzel, musical director Stephen Oremus, composer/lyricist Stephen Schwartz, and Kristin Chenoweth.

In a theatrical age when movies were routinely being turned into Broadway musicals, it was surprising when one potential movie stopped dead in its tracks and dropped down directly on Broadway instead. But then nearly everything about *Wicked* involved following its own particular yellow brick road.

Wicked began life as a complex novel written by Gregory Maguire in 1995 about power, historical revisionism, and destiny. If, as Churchill said, "history is written by the victors," this was history written by the losers, or more specifically, Elphaba, aka the Wicked Witch of the West, now recast as the lead in an inverted backstory to *The Wizard of Oz*. *Wicked* was compelling enough on its terms, but its relationship to one of America's most beloved movies made it a viable commercial property. Universal Pictures had thrown some money at a screenplay, but without a dramatic way to materialize Elphaba's tortured psychology, the script languished on the shelf.

In *The Wizard of Oz*, success depended on picking up the right companions along the yellow brick road; *Wicked*'s creative development followed, followed, followed the same path. Writer Winnie Holzman fell in love with the book; she was told it had been optioned by Universal. Composer/lyricist Stephen Schwartz, whose career had skyrocketed through the 1970s with shows like *Godspell* and *Pippin*, fell in love with the book; he was told it had been optioned by Universal. Schwartz, no stranger to the film industry, having scored several Disney successes in the 1990s, asked for a meeting with Marc Platt, the producer at Universal in charge of developing the *Wicked* material. Schwartz's enthusiasm and his pitch to theatricalize the novel as a musical instead made perfect sense to Platt; the complicated internal lives of Maguire's characters could easily be revealed in song—and, of course, the characters of Oz have been eternally intertwined with song and dance since the 1939 cinema classic. Platt, Schwartz, and Holzman would team up with experienced stage producer David Stone and travel down the road together. To Oz? To Oz!

Over a series of table readings on the Universal lot throughout 2002, the creative team, now guided by director Joe Mantello, refocused Maguire's narrative into something more accessible:

It became about Elphaba, who's a green girl growing up in Oz and obviously different. It's also about a girl who eventually becomes Glinda the Good. She doesn't really have as much raw talent for sorcery as Elphaba does; they're forced to become roommates in college, they immediately clash there and ultimately become very important in each other's lives—and change each other's lives.

—Winnie Holzman, book writer

Whether or not *Wicked* would have eventually come around to that particular story without the involvement of its two leading ladies is anyone's conjecture, but the project was blessed with two protean talents. The piquant Kristin Chenoweth added her vocal virtuosity and her chipper sense of humor to Glinda (and a couple of Glinda's wisecracks to the script, too), while Idina Menzel, an alumna of *Rent*, had the uncanny ability to nail a musical note straight up the middle with a laser-like precision that served her perfectly as

Chenoweth (as Glinda the Good) and Menzel (as Elphaba) tour the Emerald CIty of Oz; L. Frank Baum's novel had been adapted for Broadway as early as 1903.

Elphaba. Not only did Chenoweth's and Menzel's respective traits serve the musical's conflict, but they each represented two contrasting eras of popular entertainment: the crowd-pleasing vaudeville turns of the 1930s up against the intense vocal prowess of the modern pop-opera tradition.

As if that pop-culture battle of the titans weren't enough, Schwartz's score embraced the kind of contemporary sound that would engage a younger audience while honoring the materials' roots: "I wanted [the score] to sound otherworldly, but not inaccessible," he says. "At the same time, I wanted those who loved [Harold] Arlen's film score to feel that that my music was right for Oz." *Wicked* also exploited the very best of modern stage technology and craftsmanship, bringing the fantasy world of Oz to breathtaking, if nearly overwhelming, life. The demands of the physical production led to one of the more unique bends in the yellow brick road: "Joe Mantello felt that there were so many visual demands of the show—people fly and monkeys fly and there are magic tricks—you know, all this *stuff*—that it was going to be hard to tell much more from a workshop," said Schwartz. "Therefore, for better or worse, we had to do a production."

In May 2003, *Wicked* met the public for the first time at the Curran Theater in San Francisco; it had been years since a major new book musical opened out of town without workshop development—and this show was budgeted at $14 million. And rather than move the production straight to Broadway after the tryout, Platt and Stone put their production on a four-month hiatus, giving them time to fine-tune the script and score. They also replaced musical veteran Robert Morse, who played the Wizard, with Joel Grey. Appropriately, *Wicked* opened on Broadway the night before Halloween; the reviews were either extremely supportive or extremely dismissive: "I know we divided the critics," said Schwartz. "We didn't divide the audience, and that's what counts." Perhaps the most potent moment for the audience occurred at the end of act one, when story, score, scenery, and star all combined in one legendary moment: Menzel, discovering her gift for flight in "Defying Gravity," soared above the stage of the Gershwin Theatre while hitting a power note that made every other performer on Broadway green with envy. The crowd went wild every time.

However, despite the audience's invariable enthusiasm for the show, general approbation was harder to come by; the show won only three Tony Awards—one for Menzel as Best Actress in a Musical—but lost the grand prize to *Avenue Q*. "People ask if *Wicked* would be doing better business if it had won the Tony," said marketing guru Nancy Coyne. "It can't do bigger business." Indeed, all box-office rivals have had to surrender to the Wicked Witch of the West; with a twister-like ferocity, *Wicked* has set records in every place that it touched down. At one point, the four separate U.S. productions of *Wicked*—Broadway, Chicago, Los Angeles, and the Detroit stop on the national tour—earned a cumulative box office of $8.1 million in one week. During Thanksgiving week of 2009, the musical earned more than *two* million dollars at the Gershwin, the highest weekly gross in Broadway history. By the end of 2009, eight separate productions were breaking house records around the world, bringing *Wicked*'s take since October, 2003 to $1.75 billion. "We don't even know what the peak is [going to be]," said producer Stone. "The level of this success is beyond imagining. It doesn't compute."

Wicked was always about defying gravity—but defying *logic*? Only in Oz, and only on Broadway.

The stakes on Broadway are different and higher. A film can generate an awful lot of money very quickly, almost immediately over a three-day weekend, regardless of the reviews. Financially, a film can be very successful, and the copyright in that film lives on, and there are many ancillary markets. The scariest thing about the theater, it could open and nobody saw what you saw, and in a very short time, it's just gone.

—Marc Platt, producer of *Wicked*

"I am not dead yet"

SPAMALOT · **AND THE RESURRECTION OF MUSICAL COMEDY**

If, during the height of the through-sung pop-opera years of the mid-1990s, some theatrical soothsayer had predicted that, ten years hence, Broadway would be populated by cross-dressing *hausfrau*s, porn-addicted puppets, and outrageous hijinks on a Monty Python level—in fact, perpetrated by Monty Python—that prognosticating wag would have been tossed into a lunatic asylum. And yet, by the end of the first decade of the new millennium, the Theatre District resembled a high-spirited lunatic asylum. Broadway was waist-high in new shows that took dead aim at audiences' funny bones and wallets at the same time and succeeded in bringing back the good ol' days of unabashed musical comedy.

Clearly, the unparalleled success of *The Producers* in 2001 caught the attention of real-life producers, who realized that audiences would flock to an evening that provided a few good laughs. But trends on Broadway are only made by quality products, not by hunches; luckily, the following year, the musical adaptation of John Waters's film *Hairspray* hit the scene, providing an accessible demonstration of high camp within an homage to the candy-colored early 1960s. *Hairspray* was yet another Cinderella story in the Broadway tradition, only here the Cinderella in question was a plus-sized teenager named Tracy Turnblad who forsakes good manners and propriety to become the dancing queen of her Baltimore neighborhood. The show's putative romance concerned Tracy and the unattainable high school dreamboat, but the real love story was the unconditional support shown for Tracy by her

You can't stop the beat: Hairspray *kept it going for 2,642 performances.*

Camelot on the Broadway stage: **LEFT:** *First, as romance (*A Connecticut Yankee, *1927);* **CENTER:** *second, as revival (1943);* **RIGHT:** *third, as tragedy (*Camelot, *1960); and,* **FAR RIGHT:** *finally, as farce: Christopher Siebert (as Sir Galahad) and Sara Ramirez (as the Lady of the Lake) deliver "The Song That Goes Like This" in* Spamalot *(2005).*

mom, Edna—played by the Drano-voiced Harvey Fierstein, all dolled up in a Frigidaire-sized housecoat and a bouffant hairdo. Fierstein played the part straight, as it were (all the subsequent Ednas were played by men in drag), and won a Tony Award for Best Actor in a Musical. *Hairspray* coated its ebullient proceedings with a patina of social awareness but was mostly about giving its audience a whale of a good time; they responded by keeping the show running for six and a half years and returning the show to its cinematic roots in a 2007 release with John Travolta girdling his loins as Edna.

If *Hairspray* deployed everything in the contemporary musical's carpetbag to keep audiences amused, *Avenue Q* relied on nine actors, a finely honed snarky sense of humor, and a lot of foam rubber. Developed at the O'Neill Music Theatre Conference and the Off-Broadway Vineyard Theater, *Avenue Q* was a stealth musical that struck an immediate chord with Generation Xers. In fact, the show's premise—"plot" would be putting it too strongly—was that the Generation Xers who had grown up watching *Sesame Street* still lived among its puppets and its platitudes. Only now the adult world was proving too complicated to be solved by a bath with a rubber duckie. The show's Muppet-like characters (expertly yielded by singing actors who also played adults in the show) were beset by decidedly non-innocent problems such as confusion over sexual orientation and addiction to pornography—"The Internet is for porn," intones a character named Trekkie Monster, and no one seems able to contradict him.

The "real-life" denizens along *Avenue Q* had their own issues, too, such as racism and a disengagement from political activism. Yet *Avenue Q* conjured up the more innocent days

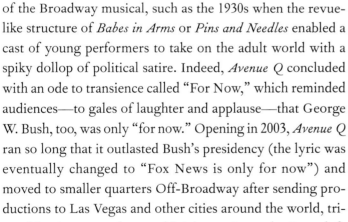

of the Broadway musical, such as the 1930s when the revue-like structure of *Babes in Arms* or *Pins and Needles* enabled a cast of young performers to take on the adult world with a spiky dollop of political satire. Indeed, *Avenue Q* concluded with an ode to transience called "For Now," which reminded audiences—to gales of laughter and applause—that George W. Bush, too, was only "for now." Opening in 2003, *Avenue Q* ran so long that it outlasted Bush's presidency (the lyric was eventually changed to "Fox News is only for now") and moved to smaller quarters Off-Broadway after sending productions to Las Vegas and other cities around the world, triumphing in venues that wouldn't know Oscar the Grouch from Oscar the Award.

One of the most outrageous laugh-fests in Broadway history was still to come thundering over the horizon—only the clamorous hoofbeats were created by pairs of cocoanuts being knocked together. The 1975 cult-movie favorite *Monty Python and the Holy Grail* was adapted for the Broadway stage by one of the five remaining members of the revered British group, Eric Idle. Idle had always been the most Gilbertian of the Pythons—in fact, he had played Ko-Ko in an English National Opera production of *The Mikado*—and could always be counted on to provide some witty parody lyrics for the troupe. The stage adaptation was inevitably titled *Spamalot* (after some initial litigious sputterings from the Alan Jay Lerner estate). Idle wrote the book and lyrics to music by John Du Prez, and it was the

David Hyde Pierce as the not-so-brave Sir Robin; he does offer some Talmudic wisdom to King Arthur, however. Hyde Pierce would go on to star in another show biz musical comedy, Curtains.

fulfillment of a longtime dream: "I've always wanted to write a musical. And the time is right for it. We've gotten past *Phantom*, the heavy musicals, the dramatic musicals, the visual musicals, and now it's time for comedy," he told *Newsweek* during the show's Chicago tryout in 2005.

Turning the film's anarchic (and anachronistic) take on King Arthur and his fellow knights' quest for the Holy Grail into something as organic and comprehensible as a Broadway musical would take some finessing, but Idle was lucky enough to enlist the services of the Merlin of the American comedy stage: director Mike Nichols. Nichols had only directed one other musical in his half-century career—*The Apple Tree* in 1966—but *Spamalot*'s antic disposition appealed to him: "The jokes are still based on people's heartlessness to one another, but they're buried a little deeper—because you have to be in a good mood to do a [musical] number." Those musical numbers were strewn all over the *Spamalot* lot, including a cheery chorus of reanimated plague victims, a parody of British Invasion–style power ballads, and a gentle imprecation from Sir Robin that King Arthur and Co. had better ramp up their *yiddishkeit* quotient if they want to be in a successful musical comedy:

> There's a very small percentile
> Who enjoy a dancing gentile
> But you won't succeed on Broadway
> If you don't have any Jews.

Nichols assembled a cast of adept farceurs from far and wide, including British film star Tim Curry and American television star David Hyde Pierce, and attuned their sensibilities to inhabit the characters legendarily created by the Pythons three decades earlier. Actor Hank Azaria, who played the temporarily closeted Sir Lancelot (who, of course, likes to "dance a lot") needed very little fine tuning; a huge fan of the movie, Azaria told Nichols that he'd "been off-book since I was twelve." Evidently, much of the *Spamalot* audience had also memorized the original film since they were old enough to shave; the show had captured the most sought-after demographic on Broadway: male ticket buyers between the ages of twenty-five and forty-five. All these unsentimental male Python fans—who wouldn't be caught at dead at *Hairspray*, let alone *Wicked*—were lining up to see these medieval maniacs bring out their dead and they helped to make *Spamalot* a worldwide hit. Every night, fans would shout out lines from the film before the stage actors could even open their mouths.

Such self-referential humor became *de rigueur* for the nearly dozen musical comedies that followed in *Spamalot*'s wake. Presupposing, perhaps, that if an audience member spent upwards of $100 to see a musical comedy, he or she must be pretty savvy about show biz, these musicals kicked the fourth wall down with can-can-like abandon and showered the crowd with in-jokes. *The Drowsy Chaperone* (2006) was a charming valentine to the knuckleheaded musicals of the 1920s that began by knocking Elton John's talent as a Broadway songwriter. The genially old-fashioned revue *Martin Short: Fame Becomes Me* elbowed jabs at everything from Sondheim to *The Vagina Monologues* to the preponderance of black female belters in the second act of Broadway musicals. *Curtains* was a detective spoof set during the out-of-town tryouts for a Broadway musical. The four-character *[title of show]* was a Broadway musical about four characters trying to create a Broadway musical; the show's obsessive compulsion about flop musicals was so intense that even its most *serious* number referred to two flops by Bock and Harnick and Kander and Ebb, respectively. (Perhaps *[title of show]* was too obsessed by Broadway flops; it turned into one after 102 performances.)

How the uninitiated theatergoer will react to the new school of "wink, wink, nudge, nudge" in the long run is anybody's guess, but at least the recent trend for musical comedy has certainly brought a new generation of comedians to Broadway. Talented musical comedy performers such as David Hyde Pierce, Christopher Siebert, Andrea Martin, Norbert Leo Butz, Mary Testa, and Christopher Fitzgerald found terrific showcases and brand-new careers inhabiting a time-honored Broadway genre that had been listed as D.O.A. only a decade earlier. Songwriter William Finn, whose gentle satire *The 25th Annual Putnam County Spelling Bee* ran over one thousand performances, commented on the resurrection of musical comedy back in 2005: "I think this is all happening because we really need to laugh right now," he says. "Bush is president and nobody can believe the world is as bad as it is—so we have to laugh at something."

Even into the first year of the Obama presidency, Broadway audiences are seeking out laughs wherever they could get them. The bus advertisements for *Shrek the Musical* featured a quote from a critic touting the 2008 adaptation of the animated comedy as "Far Far Away the Funniest New Musical on Broadway." Not too many critics—or audience members—agreed, but that's not the point: when it comes to the "funniest new musical on Broadway," at last there's finally some *competition*.

"Working my way back to you"
THE JUKEBOX MUSICAL

Karen Mason, Louise Pitre, and Judy Kaye are super-duper troupers in Mamma Mia! *(2001).*

Is it possible that the great Florenz Ziegfeld, the impresario who brought a new level of cultural prestige to the Broadway musical, would have anything to do with the genre derisively referred to as "the jukebox musical"? Bet your bottom three-plays-for-a-dollar he would.

For "jukebox musicals"—a term taken from the 1940s invention that allowed any customer with the right change to select his or her own playlist of popular music—are in many ways as old as the musical itself. Ziegfeld, for example, interpolated popular tunes into his annual revues whenever one caught his fancy—"My Blue Heaven" was drafted into the

Ziegfeld Follies of 1927 because it was a hit on the radio. The "And Then I Wrote" revues that dotted Broadway throughout the 1970s and 1980s, featuring the songs of Rodgers and Hart, Sondheim, Fats Waller, and others, were artful compilations of songs written over many different decades and for different contexts. Why, then, the recent explosion of catalog shows and why have these musicals tried the patience of the critical community?

The answer centers on two factors: the ongoing tension between narrative and non-narrative shows and a shift in generational tastes. Since the "Golden Age" of Rodgers and Hammerstein in the 1940s, the idea that songs should advance the story has become a kind of holy grail. "A musical is supposed to be a collaboration," said Arthur Laurents. "You don't have a finished score and then work up a script to push it around. It's not to my taste, and I think [the emergence of the jukebox musical] is hurting the musical theater." Still, one can't deny the charms and pleasures of a non-narrative evening, where good songs are served up entertainingly by an engaging cast. Thanks largely to the show's finger-popping songs delivered by a powerhouse cast of nine, the 1995 revue *Smokey Joe's Café*, based on the song catalog of Brill Building legends Leiber and Stoller, managed a run of over 2,000 performances (making it the longest-running revue in Broadway history). Even *Beatlemania*, an artless staged concert of Beatles tunes with Fab Four stand-ins that appeared on Broadway in the mid-1970s, entertained audiences for over one thousand performances.

As the baby boomer generation grew older, the potential theatergoing audience became more and more crowded with ticket buyers whose listening tastes were more attuned to "Lucy in the Sky with Diamonds" than "Diamonds Are a Girl's Best Friend." It didn't take producers long to realize that if they could marry the narrative comforts of the book musical with the pop chart hits of the 1960s and '70s, they could strike what the recording industry calls "solid gold." One such producer was England's Judy Craymer, who, in the late 1980s, became enamored with the Europop stylings of the Swedish band ABBA. ABBA, a quartet of two men and two women, had dominated the European pop charts for a decade since 1974, and their songs hits, written by the group's Benny Andersson and Bjorn Ulvaeus, were well-crafted, upbeat tunes that—uncharacteristically for the time—embraced optimism over angst. Craymer persisted in acquiring the rights to ABBA's catalog, and hired a playwright to devise a scenario that was loose enough to contain the band's songs. Borrowing liberally (and without credit) from a 1968 film, *Buona Sera, Mrs. Campbell* (itself the *credited* source for the 1979 Alan Jay Lerner musical, *Carmelina*), the new musical, called *Mamma Mia!*, was set on the Aegean coast and revolved around a mother, her daughter's wedding, and the visit of the girl's three possible fathers.

Opening on the West End in 1999, *Mamma Mia!* tapped into the audience's near-narcotic response to ABBA's familiar powerhouse songs and their strong female empowerment message. Critics were quick to point out that the story and the songs frequently crashed into each other with clanging non-sequiturs, but the musical was an instant hit and opened in Australia in the spring of 2001. *Mamma Mia!* was scheduled to open on Broadway a month after September 11, when critics and audiences weren't quite prepared to embrace its giddy inconsequence, but it soon became a huge hit in New York. By the end of 2009, it was still playing to full houses, even after a successful movie version; more than 40 million people have seen the show in 200 cities across the world and it has earned upwards of $2 billion. Such a potent combination of pop and popularity—how could other theater producers resist it?

The ensemble dancers weren't the only dancers in Mamma Mia!; audiences routinley took to the aisles during the show's finale.

The race was on; in the decade after *Mamma Mia!*'s premiere, most of the major song catalogs of the boomer era were optioned for some sort of stage production. By and large, they were all failures. Half of the jukebox vehicles were either contrived narratives, in which the songs were precariously propped up by rickety scenarios—*Good Vibrations* (the Beach Boys); *All Shook Up* (songs recorded by Elvis Presley); *The Times They Are A-Changin'* (Bob Dylan); *Hot Feet* (Earth, Wind & Fire); the other half were impressionistic hagio-biography (the eponymous *Lennon* and *Ring of Fire*, based on songs written or recorded by Johnny Cash). Although there were flashes of intelligence behind these shows, they begged an essential question: can you really take twenty-five songs from *any* catalog, each with different stories written at different times for different reasons, and succeed in shoehorning them into an organic narrative?

It would then seem to be the height of folly to option the catalog of a musical group that never developed any credibility with the critical intelligentsia. However, in the wake of *Mamma Mia!*'s success, two writers, Rick Elice and Marshall Brickman, were offered the opportunity to create a theater piece around the music of Frankie Valli and the Four Seasons, a highly successful quartet from New Jersey whose impeccably arranged doo-wop sound earned them coveted spots on jukeboxes all across the country for two decades. What it did not earn the group, however, was respect; even Elice and Brickman sneered at the opportunity to bring their catalog to life on the stage.

But once they had a "sit-down" with Frankie Valli, the band's falsetto virtuoso, and Bob Gaudio, their musical mastermind, the writers realized that the story behind the Four Seasons was as compelling as it gets —from their rough-and-tumble beginnings on the other side of Jersey's tracks through the various internecine struggles of creating heart-bending harmony onstage when there was nothing but discord offstage to their eventual immense but precarious success. The Four Seasons' turnpike to fame wasn't the usual "and then I wrote" rags-to-riches story; it involved organized crime, betrayal, payola, drug

abuse, gambling addiction, and, above all, the makeshift families that all artists create among themselves. The narrative ace in the hole was the fact that the Four Seasons' story had flown under the radar, just like the band itself. As the character of Bob Gaudio tells it in the show:

Bright lights of the big city across the Hudson: the act one closer of Jersey Boys *(2007).*

> Our people were the guys who shipped overseas . . . And their sweethearts. They were the factory workers, the truck drivers. The kids pumping gas, flipping burgers. The pretty girl with circles under her eyes behind the counter of the diner. They're the ones who really got us, who pushed us over the top.

Director Des McAnuff was brought on board to guide the project, a particularly apt choice because not only had he guided such diverse musicals as *Big River* and *The Who's*

Tommy to Broadway success, he fronted his own rock band. Even better, he was artistic director of his own theater, the La Jolla Playhouse, which provided a slot for the new show in the fall of 2004. McAnuff and his creative team threw out all the already clichéd rules of the jukebox musical and did something so obvious it was startling: they simply let the story go where it wanted to go and the music followed. Sometimes the characters narrated the story, contradicting each other; sometimes there were extended book scenes. Most often the Four Seasons' hits—"Sherry," "Big Girls Don't Cry," "Working My Way Back to You," "You're Just Too Good to Be True"—were delivered to the audience with a subtle surprise and, if a cinematic transition was required to move the story along, the songs were not even allowed to finish. The jukebox catalog of the Four Seasons was not the end in itself; in the accomplished hands of McAnuff and his gifted cast, the songs became the soundtrack that surged under the powerful narrative of the band's career, erupting full out at significant moments to give the audience what it wanted.

And what the audience wanted was *Jersey Boys*. The fact that the core audience for the show was only a few bridges and tunnels away from 52nd Street didn't hurt: *Jersey Boys* won the Tony Award in 2005 and has spawned several successful national tours. But the appeal of the show wasn't limited to fans of the band's music; audiences that liked a good story, they were the ones "who really got it, who pushed the show over the top."

Jersey Boys was a tough act to follow, but it gave the jukebox genre a fresh burst of street cred. An even more unlikely amalgam of non-narrative tunes, *Rock of Ages* found a successful niche among fans of the glam metal-rock bands of the 1980s. *Rock of Ages* (2009) went in the opposite direction of *Jersey Boys*, gleefully throwing sense and sensibility overboard to create a wild and woolly cross between a burlesque show and a stadium concert. Perhaps the fact that cocktail waitresses served drinks *during* the production made the show's incongruities go down a little easier.

The jukebox musical is probably here to stay on Broadway—at least for a while. The catalogs of Bruce Springsteen and Run D.M.C. have been optioned, and, for that matter, Broadway has recently seen shows built around the song catalogs of pioneers from earlier generations as well; *LoveMusik* was a new biography of Kurt Weill built around the songs he created on two continents and even *Irving Berlin's White Christmas* augmented the score with more than a few ditties from the warehouse. Still, as the first decade of the twenty-first century comes to a close, the jukebox musical's fortunes reside in a generational shift. "I think the Broadway demographic is now the boomer demographic," says Rocco Landesman, a producer who owns the theater where *Jersey Boys* has played SRO for four years (and presently the new head of the National Endowment for the Arts). "The people who are old enough and rich enough to afford a Broadway ticket grew up with this music. . . . The future of [shows like *Jersey Boys*] is dependent on audiences, rather than critics."

"*I will sing the song of purple summer*"
NEW VOICES, NEW SONGS

Ever since the mid-1960s, there has been an ongoing refrain from critics of the Broadway sound: will the musical ever really reject the traditions of Tin Pan Alley and embrace the kind of music that most of America listens to on its collective headphones? But towards the end of the first decade of the new millennium, that question was rendered moot by an explosion of new sounds on Broadway, brought forth by a battalion of new composers and lyricists, writing songs that come from a wide variety of backgrounds, but most importantly come straight from the heart.

In many ways, the diversification of the Broadway sound began with a show that sounded least like the latest iPod playlist—the 2005 production of *The Light in the Piazza*, with music and lyrics by Adam Guettel. Dynastic historians would smile at the fact that Guettel provides a break with the Tin Pan Alley tradition; he's the son of Mary Rodgers, composer of *Once Upon a Mattress*, and the grandson of Richard Rodgers. "Writing for musical theatre was not something I ever wanted to do, because it was the family business. . . . I played in a lot of rock bands and I played upright bass in a lot of jazz groups and I played out in New York in clubs," he told a reporter in 2001. "I went through all that stuff before I ended up realizing that writing for character and telling stories through music was something that I really loved to do, and that allowed me to express love."

Nowhere did Guettel express love better than in *The Light in the Piazza*, an anxious fairy tale set in the 1950s, when a young Italian man becomes infatuated with a frail and damaged American girl on holiday in Florence. The thirty-one-year-old Guettel threw himself into the rhapsodic contradictions of a thwarted love affair, scoring the soaring music with a full complement of strings and composing a dense but transcendent score— with some of the lyrics even playfully written in Italian. *The Light in the Piazza* wasn't for all tastes, but it was a serious modern work for the theater; it made aficionados equally frustrated that Guettel, a meticulous craftsman, takes so long to compose his work and patiently eager to hear what his next project will sound like.

If *The Light in the Piazza* sang about young love with a dash of Italian bitters, *Spring Awakening* (2006) treated the same subject with a heavy dose of Greek tragedy. Few musical subjects have ever seemed as initially unlikely as Frank Wedekind's intense early Expressionist play about sexual repression among a group of frustrated and bewildered German schoolchildren in the 1890s. The clouds of rape, pregnancy, masturbation, suicide— even resurrection from the dead—all lower heavily over Wedekind's play. But playwright and lyricist Steven Sater perceived a strong contemporary relevance in *Spring Awakening* and thought that music was the perfect medium to release the tension in its characters:

> It struck me that pop music—rock music—is the exact place that adolescents for the last few generations have found release from, and expression of, that same mute pain. . . . Caught in the relentless dramas of our adolescent lives, we are still rock stars in the privacy of our own bedrooms.

Sater teamed up with Duncan Sheik, a Grammy-winning singer and composer, and together they brought a hauntingly poetic rock sound to the score. Fuelled by Sheik's acoustic

It's a new old world: Victoria Clark as an American tourist waking up to discover the magic of Italy in The Light in the Piazza *(2005), with a score by Adam Guettel. Guettel's grandfather, Richard Rodgers, covered similar territory with lyricist Stephen Sondheim four decades earlier in* Do I Hear a Waltz?

The bitch of living: adolescent school-boys—and their frustrations—spring into action during Spring Awakening *(2006).*

guitar–inflected sensibilities, the tormented youngsters of *Spring Awakening* weren't singing a rock score as a *genre*—they were liberating their nineteenth-century selves by singing a rock score as a fantasy expression of their inarticulate feelings. In fact, all the songs in the show were exposed inner monologues, often sung as choral interludes; the narrative was contained only in the dialogue, a device that might have confounded Rodgers and Hammerstein, but that would have made Sophocles very pleased, indeed. Director Michael Mayer skillfully moved the small cast of talented young artists through their angst-ridden paces and although the staging often detached the characters from their physical environment (they pulled body mikes out of their jackets when necessary), there was nothing detached about their raging emotions. The inventiveness of the enterprise earned *Spring Awakening* eight Tony Awards, including two for Sheik: Best Original Score and Best Orchestrations.

Back in the late 1970s, producer Harold Prince lamented that there were no longer the opportunities for young songwriting teams to break into the Broadway club, but in the early twenty-first century, there seems to be more opportunities than ever—or at least more producers are taking creative gambles on new songwriters. Some of this is a by-product of an ever-evolving developmental world out there—the Sundance Institute, the Eugene O'Neill Theatre Center, the National Alliance for Musical Theatre—that is nurturing new voices at a pace that would have made even George Abbott's head spin. Still, more than a dozen new songwriting teams or songwriters debuted with Broadway musicals between 2004 and 2010. Often they garner attention away from much more accomplished songwriters—as in the case of the *Next to Normal* team of Tom Kitt and Brian Yorkey, who snatched a 2009 Tony Award for Best Original Score away from Elton John (who couldn't have been more gracious about it).

Perhaps the most improbable David and Goliath story (or Cinderella story, depending on how you look at it) was 2008's *In the Heights*, the first Broadway musical score—actually, simply the first musical score—written by Lin-Manuel Miranda when he was in his mid-twenties. Miranda grew up in Washington Heights—the largely Dominican American community at the northern tip of Manhattan—as the son of Puerto Rican immigrants. Still, he was completely assimilated—directing *West Side Story* at his high school, taking the 1/9 subway downtown to see *The Capeman* (four times) and *Rent* on Broadway. When he saw *Rent*, Miranda said, "A light bulb really went off and I was like, oh, you can write a musical about your life—and I can write a show that I would want to be in."

While attending Wesleyan University, Miranda wrote that show about his life—and put himself in it, too. *In the Heights* (with a book by Quiara Alegria Hudes) was set in Washington Heights and revolved around Miranda's character, a likable bodega owner named Usnavi, and the various complications of life in the 'hood. Nothing in the script was particularly confrontational or original—in fact, it bore a close resemblance to an innocent Comden and Green musical of the 1950s; think *Wonderful Uptown*—but the score brought a full-out Latin beat to Broadway. Miranda claims he had never written a Latin song before *In the Heights*, but he also added generous dollops of salsa, meringue, and hip-hop, all of which were ferociously arranged by Alex Lacamoire and Bill Sherman. Miranda even winked at an earlier Broadway tradition in the rap with which he opened the show:

> Me and my cousin
> Runnin' just another dime-a-dozen
> Mom-and-pop
> Stop-and-shop
> And, oh my God,
> It's gotten too darn hot,
> Like my man
> Cole Porter said.

A blackout in Washington Heights illuminates the lives of Usnavi (Lin-Manuel Miranda), his cousin Sonny (Robin De Jésus), and his pal, Benny (Christopher Jackson) up In the Heights *(2008).*

Miranda got an unprecedented chance to work with another great Broadway tradition after his score (and *In the Heights*) won the Tony Award in 2009. Arthur Laurents was planning a major Broadway revival of *West Side Story* and wanted to add passages of spoken Spanish for the Puerto Rican characters in both their dialogue and lyrics. He needed a translator for the lyrics and called on Miranda, who considered himself born for the job. Ultimately, Miranda got to work directly with Stephen Sondheim on the lyrics (Sondheim had come to see Miranda's high school production of the show years earlier) for four songs, including "A Boy Like That" and "I Feel Pretty" (Sondheim had never been thrilled with his own work on the original lyrics to the latter).

At one point, Miranda and Sondheim talked about translating the song "America" into Spanish, "but it would have thrown off the song. It didn't work." That's a shame, in a way, because the puckish wit of the original fits Miranda's sensibility perfectly. Still, Miranda had his own response to the culture clash on the "isle of Manhattan":

> There is a generation of us who either were born somewhere else and moved here or were born here but their parents came from somewhere else—whether it's from Latin America or Russia or the West Indies—and they don't know where they belong or what traditions you're supposed to bring with you; the question of finding your own island is not really a geographical one, but really an emotional one.

¡Fumalo en tu pipa y pontelo dentro!

"And suddenly I'm flying"

BROADWAY ENTERS THE TWENTY-FIRST CENTURY

"Theater has been a wonderful cottage industry, but always twenty or thirty years behind the times," said one theater producer in 1997, but a decade later, as Broadway entered its second millennium, it zoomed into interconnectedness, speeding to catch up with the self-promotion schemes of Madison Avenue, Hollywood, and television. In many ways, the digital age—which would hardly seem conducive to the world of live theater—has opened up a realm of possibilities for Broadway to communicate with the American public, and the American musical has penetrated the cultural consciousness in unprecedented ways.

An early signal of Broadway's renewed commercial potential came early in the new millennium as corporate sponsorship found its way into the Theater District; the Ford Motor Company, Cadillac, and American Airlines all paid top-dollar to advertise their wares by putting their names above three respective theater marquees, which also gave the companies a certain high-culture cachet (Cadillac and Ford ultimately decided against renewing their promotions and the Ford Center is now called the Hilton Theatre). Continental Airlines became "the official airline of Broadway" and Visa was its exclusive credit card. There were a lot of ticket charges in ten years. In the decade from the 1998–99 season to the 2008–09 season, Broadway came close to doubling its cumulative box office: from $588 million to over $943 million. A majority of the audience in 2008–09—64 percent—were tourists, but actual attendance only increased about 6% in during those years. Much of the increase was the result of the delirious cost of tickets; the average ticket in 1998 cost $51, and in 2008, it cost $78, with most musicals charging a top ticket price hovering around $125 for an orchestra seat. More prohibitively, a full-price ticket for some of the *worst* seats in the house went for upwards of $75. Perhaps it's a good thing that the average Broadway theatergoer—as reported in a 2009 demographic survey by The Broadway League—earned an annual income of nearly $200,000.

Money became Broadway's big story. As the risks have gotten bigger, so has the potential payoff; when both *Beauty and the Beast* and *The Lion King* have grossed more than $2 billion each in various worldwide productions—far more than their original animated versions—the gambler's blood starts to rush a little faster. No idea was too preposterous if it helped to narrow the extreme profit margin, even if it flew in the face of Broadway tradition. Sky boxes and other amenities had changed the financing of sports arenas, so producers and landlords adopted "Dress Circle" and other programs that allowed big spenders to get prime seats for hit shows, plus receptions, cocktails, and snacks. Premium or "V.I.P." seats for Mel Brooks' 2007 production of *Young Frankenstein* could be had for $450; this was a potential bonanza, but if lightning struck the show's Creature, it didn't strike the show itself—it closed after 485 performances. As the cost of each new major musical blockbuster escalated between $12 million to $16 million, any new financial enhancement, bell, or whistle was welcomed. "It takes a village to put on a Broadway musical," quipped Susan Stroman—or at least a village with very deep pockets.

The ascending costs of all these blockbusters had a circular, if not pernicious, effect on the artwork itself. New musicals needed to offer recognizable consumer-friendly properties with pre-sold titles, or stars, or visuals, or all three in order to attract audiences before the reviews came in; conversely, such components only drove up the budget, making it harder to recoup one's investment. *Thoroughly Modern Millie*, the 2002 Tony Award winner, was reconstituted from a dimly remembered 1967 film musical and, following on the heels of *The Producers*, ushered in a wave of commercially successful film properties from the last thirty years adapted to the musical stage.

There's nothing new about adapting musicals from the movies; the trend really began in the mid-1950s, with such screenplay-driven shows as *Fanny* and *Silk Stockings*. Critics who condemn the latest tsunami of movie-based musicals have short memories; as an example, from the 1966–67 season to the 1972–73 season, Broadway played host to numerous musicals derived from original screenplays: *Sweet Charity*; *Illya Darling*; *Henry, Sweet Henry*; *Golden Rainbow*; *Promises, Promises*; *La Strada*; *Georgy*; *Applause*; *70, Girls, 70*; *Sugar*; *A Little Night Music*. (This doesn't even include shows like *The Happy Time* or *Zorba*, which were based on plays or novels eventually made into movies.) However, in the past, theatrical producers went out of their way to distance themselves somewhat from the original source by rethinking the film creatively for the musical stage or at least by changing the title (it's hard to imagine how anyone buying a ticket for *Promises, Promises* thought they were seeing a musical version of Billy Wilder's film *The Apartment*).

The major difference in the twenty-first century is that the film studios that own the potential properties eagerly open up their vaults and actively produce or co-produce the stage musical version. (A generation ago, Hollywood studios briskly sold off the stage rights to a producer from the East Coast and could hardly be bothered to attend opening night.) Disney, of course, followed this course most aggressively and set the pace for others, setting up its own theatrical division and staging multi-million dollar versions of *Tarzan*, *The Little Mermaid*, and *Mary Poppins* (only the latter flew close to the box-office standard set by *The Lion King*—it had originated on the West End, co-produced by Cameron Mackintosh). Dreamworks followed in Disney's big yellow footsteps with *Shrek the Musical*; New Line Cinema helped underwrite its properties *Hairspray* and *The Wedding Singer*; MGM Onstage was behind *Legally Blonde* and *Chitty Chitty Bang Bang*; Universal Pictures holds the film rights to *Wicked* and brought *Billy Elliot: The Musical* in from the West End. The poster art and design concept for *Legally Blonde* was particularly close to its screen antecedent; one has sympathy for the patrons who spent $125 each for their tickets and were disappointed not to see Reese Witherspoon.

Of all these adaptations, the one that used the power of the stage most potently was *Billy Elliot*. It was certainly the film least known to American audiences, but this Cinderella tale of an eleven-year-old boy who pursues his dream of being a dancer, despite the stifling atmosphere of his North Country mining town and his father's implacability, had a transcendent theatrical imagination and enough heart to melt the iciest of critics; it was full of sentiment, but bracingly unsentimental. The musical was such a celebration of the power of dance and used its choreography (by Peter Darling) so imaginatively and as such an extension of character that Jerome Robbins would have done cartwheels. (Actually, if Robbins's father had been a miner in County Durham, rather than a corset manufacturer from New Jersey, *Billy Elliot* could well have been Robbins's own musical biography.) Elton John turned in a score (with lyrics and book by Lee Hall, who had written the original screenplay) that was fully in service to the show's narrative and, although the script was full of references to trade unionism in the Margaret Thatcher era, the show's basic local-boy-makes-good story vaulted over its gritty local roots. (An early plan to reset the show in the coal-mining belt of Pennsylvania was wisely abandoned.) *Billy Elliot* won the Tony

Trent Kowalik, one of three rotating performers, as Billy Elliot and Stephen Hanna, as a vision of his older self in Billy Elliot *(2009).*

Award for Best Musical, as well as nine other Tonys, including a rare joint award for the three young men who rotated in performances of the title role, and gave new hope to any pre-adolescents who wanted to grow up to be ballet dancers.

As the millennium jetéd along, it also became increasingly less likely that any aspiring Billy Elliot was going to get beaten up during recess. Among the younger generation, the Broadway musical became, if not totally hip, certainly pretty cool for the first time in four decades. The Disney Channel's original movie *High School Musical* (2006) went through the gymnasium roof, as did its two sequels (the soundtrack was the bestselling album of the year). *Glee*, the popular 2009 Fox network show about musically gifted high school geeks, not only tapped Broadway alums for its cast—Matthew Morrison (*Hairspray*, *South Pacific*) and Lea Michele (*Spring Awakening*)—but features guest performers with 42nd Street cred, such as Victor Garber and Kristin Chenoweth, who conferred her Broadway benediction on the show by singing "Maybe This Time." ("Working with Kristin is like what I would imagine a priest would go through working with Jesus," confessed one of the young cast members, Chris Colfer, whose own rendition of "Defying Gravity" from the program became a hugely popular iTunes download.)

Older audiences could enjoy reconstituted Broadway with Gwen Stefani sampling Bock and Harnick tunes, Beyoncé sampling Bob Fosse moves, Ethel Merman's voice on a commercial for Gap khakis, or Susan Boyle, storming the ramparts of popular culture by singing "I Dreamed a Dream" from *Les Misérables* on YouTube. *American Idol* invited the Broadway tune book into the prime-time mainstream by devoting entire competition evenings to songs from the Great White Way, and Broadway returned the favor by inviting former *American Idol* contestants to play the leads in such diverse shows as *Spamalot*, *The Color Purple*, and *Rock of Ages*. While the appearance of such vocal pyrotechnics undoubtedly sold thousands of tickets, there were some who decried the pop-diva sound infiltrating the Broadway soundscape. "Good, well-trained voices that can carry a tune and turn up the volume come cheap," wrote the chief theater critic of the *New York Times*, Ben Brantley. "Floating on a stream of exquisite sound is easy. Finding in that sound all the kinks and bumps and curls that make a person fascinating, exasperating and unique is what transforms a Broadway musical from a cookie-cutter diversion into ecstatic art."

If television widened Broadway's cultural appeal (and created a new batch of recognizable celebrities), the Internet broadened its ability to sell tickets and promote its brand. Every musical that opens on Broadway today has its own Web site, many of which become active online before the show even goes into rehearsal. The show sites provide direct contact between the production and the consumer—even something as revolutionary in its day as Tele-charge has become a relic. During the first decade of the twenty-first century, Internet ticket-purchasing activity grew 471 percent—it's now by far the most popular method used to buy seats. Now, when purchasing tickets, you can not only see where your seats are, you can practically see what the show looks like from your seats.

Join the club: **LEFT**: Glee *brings Broadway vets Lea Michele and Matthew Morrison (center) to primetime television,* **BOTTOM**: *along with guests such as Kristin Chenoweth.*

Show sites utilize new media such as Facebook, Twitter, and YouTube to build ongoing viral communities that connect the buying public with the musical while it's on the road, on Broadway, and on tour. (The creative team of the musical *Next to Normal* created both a complementary "script" to the show and a new song that was tweeted to Twitter users; the Twitter page, N2NBroadway, has developed a million followers worldwide.) In the old days, you'd purchase the original cast album to treasure after you'd seen the show; today, young fans from Sheboygan or Allentown can see clips from the show online (and even bootlegs of entire shows, if they're clever) before even buying their plane tickets to New York—one can essentially procure one's memories in advance on the Internet. When Alan Jay Lerner previewed his shows out of town a half-century earlier, he used to dread the appearance of what he called "the dear shits"—the so-called friends and acquaintances who'd travel to Boston, New Haven, or Philadelphia simply so they could report the bad news once they got back to town. Now, the inevitable Broadway chat rooms carry on the same tradition, spreading the word further and faster than Lerner could have imagined in his wildest nightmares.

But the Internet has also helped producers, publicists, and marketing gurus carve up a potential audience more efficiently by using social networking and the rapid response rate of cyberspace to create what the film industry calls "niche marketing." Decades ago, it required a lot of elbow grease (and thousands of postage stamps) to target a "target audience," but Broadway has finally harnessed the tools of the new age of media relations. Perhaps it's happening not a moment too soon—the traditional Broadway audience has for years gradually been transforming into something else, something more like a cable television audience. In the fall of 2009, theater journalist Howard Kissel lamented what he felt was the irretrievable dissolution of the Broadway audience that had been the backbone of the industry for decades:

> It also went way beyond the Hudson. In the decades after the war Broadway was a significant factor in middle class life all across the country. . . . The tourists who come to New York now, I'm afraid, are not really an audience. . . . Seeing a Broadway show is one of the things they're supposed to do while they're here, like visiting the Statue of Liberty or riding the subway.

Kissel is probably correct in that there is no longer a large Broadway audience that sees everything, but rather sub-sections of the public who eagerly seek out whatever they find attractive. If your family likes holidays, they can enjoy *Irving Berlin's White Christmas*; if your family is bi-polar, they can enjoy *Next to Normal*; if your family is simply creepy and kooky, they can enjoy *The Addams Family*. The audience for the American musical in 2010 may be less homogeneous and composed of increasingly diverse groups of people who attend fewer shows—but perhaps they feel greater enthusiasm and devotion for the shows they do attend.

A decade after the millennium, you can enjoy a first-rate tour of a Broadway musical in Melbourne, or thrill to a scaled-down ninety-minute version of *Phantom* in a brand-new theater in Las Vegas, or replay clips endlessly from a show in previews on your laptop while lounging in a hammock on a beach in St. Maarten. Amazing, really, that the kind of artistry that generates billion of dollars in every corner of the globe still originates from the same tiny geographical area—only a dozen city blocks—where it has made a happy home for more than a century.

Finale

It's an eternal question: what's the future of Broadway? The only safe prediction is that whatever it will be, it will be unpredictable. But a recent film, *WALL-E*, produced by Pixar in 2008, gave a tantalizing glimpse of the Broadway of the future.

Set roughly seven centuries from now, in a post-apocalyptic version of Manhattan, overrun with garbage and refuse and devoid of plant or animal life, *WALL-E* nonetheless provides a hero for its audience, an eponymous robot who continues his diurnal rounds of sweeping up, compacting, and depositing trash, long after anyone is around to care. As he tootles along in his, well, robotic manner, WALL-E keeps his spirits up by continually playing an ancient video cassette through a machine mounted inside his chest. We hear its music as the picture begins, zooming through the swirling cosmos:

> Out there
> There's a world outside of Yonkers
> Way out there beyond this hick town, Barnaby,
> There's a slick town, Barnaby . . . .

It's the voice of Michael Crawford, singing Jerry Herman's "Put on Your Sunday Clothes" from the 1969 film of *Hello, Dolly!* It's the ultimate anthem of Broadway optimism—you can leave your pedestrian life and transform yourself by visiting a magical place. The song continues on the tinny VCR tape:

> Out there
> Full of shine and full of sparkle
> Close your eyes and see it glisten, Barnaby . . .
> Listen, Barnaby . . .

Cornelius (that's the character) is singing about New York City; the lullaby of old Broadway lingers on, its strains still seducing us from the distant future.

Putting on your Sunday clothes, twenty-eighth century style: Wall-E meets Doll-E.

CAMERON MACKINTOSH ON PRODUCING

Interview for Broadway: The American Musical *(excerpt)*

WHEN I STARTED, an eight-year-old dreaming about becoming a producer, I thought one day I might have a show in London and—who knows—it would be an absolute miracle if I had a show on Broadway. I think you can have a huge hit in London and you can have great successes around the world, but in the musical theater that hit needs to also be a hit on Broadway.

My first trip to Broadway was in 1976. I'd saved up my Apex fare and landed and I saw *Chicago*, with Chita Rivera and Gwen Verdon. And I remember seeing that performance and having heard in the business that it was okay, but it wasn't a really big hit first time around. But I thought, If this is not a Broadway hit, what is? And it made me really want to go back to England and try and beef up what we did.

I remember keenly from when I was going to the theater in my teens that the hit you saw and loved in the first year, by the third year, if it was still running, was a pretty tired, pale copy of what people had raved about. I believe the longer my shows run the more effort I need to put into making sure that the audience expectation is surpassed. And I think that has helped the longevity, as well as the fact that they're cracking good shows.

I think that extraordinary sequence of British shows, starting with *Cats* and then *Les Miz*, *Phantom*, followed by *Saigon*, completely rebuilt the road. And when I sent my tours out on the road, I made absolutely sure that they were what the audience read about in the *New York Times;* the scenery wasn't left in the loading bay, it was on the stage; and people have seen that and that's why I think the shows go on and on and on.

I think the major thing that's got to happen in our industry is that we have to reinvent ourselves. My shows in particular helped Broadway become this huge financial machine. Before Andrew [Lloyd Webber] and I had these kind of worldwide successes, companies like Disney weren't interested in coming into the theater, Disney thought the theater was small beer, but then suddenly people said, "These shows made how much?" And a whole lot of people tried to turn the theater into an industry. The fact is that just as it's about to be exterminated the theater has always been saved by mad individuals believing in something and coming from left field and creating the next new thing, usually on a shoestring, and that is always going to happen. Andrew and I broke the rules when we started our shows, and history proves to us that every twenty or thirty years you have to reinvent the rules. You don't throw out everything; you need to put yourself back into Mickey and Judy putting on a show in the barn, because in the end the public will always come to see the great hit—they always will, they'll come in the middle of a hurricane—but our business depends on the good show and keeping it running.

As far as I'm concerned, the thing that defines a great musical is that the treatment of the story and the characters is original and that the music belongs on the stage, and sweeps the audience on a great emotional journey, whether it's to laugh or to cry. That's what defines a great musical. As far as the writing of the show—I don't know how many other producers work—but for me once I've been inspired by the authors' take on a subject I don't think about who's going to direct it or design it, I work with them to get the structure of it right; I become the midwife. It can take months, it can take years, and it's only when I feel I have a really good, strong draft that then I bring in the creative team and I want them to then pull it apart again. I found that my talent is to actually take the authors through that. I have a good sense of structure and I become their first audience. All the way through I interfere with everybody's job. I'm there with the orchestrator, I'm there with the choreographer, I'm there with the singers, I slip notes to the actors, they want to kill me.

To see where I stand compared with other producers, you'll have to come back in fifty years' time and ask someone else. When people say to me, "Oh well, you'll be remembered after you've done this and that," I say, "I doubt it." Personally, I don't care, because I think what gets remembered are the writers. The thing that I am very happy about is that I know several of the shows that I have been very instrumental in bringing to the stage are going to be performed in fifty or a hundred years' time. And if you asked anybody, unless they're an absolute buff, what do you remember about *Show Boat*, they'd remember Jerome Kern and Oscar Hammerstein, if they remember anything, and the clever ones might remember that P.G. Wodehouse wrote "Bill." But if you asked who produced it, they'd look at you glumly, but of course it was Ziegfeld. And I think it's right that it's only the writers and their work that live forever. Who remembers who produced Shakespeare's plays? And he's had the best run of all of us.

MEL BROOKS ON MUSICAL COMEDY

Interview for Broadway: The American Musical *(excerpt)*

IN 1935, MY UNCLE JOE BROOKMAN drove a Parmalee cab. It was a big Checker cab, and in the front there was a place with straps, where you could put your luggage, on a big kind of running board. In the back, there were folding seats, and there was room for about four people. When a Parmalee cab came down South 3rd Street and Hooper, where I lived in Williamsburg, and there was no driver and it appeared to be driving by itself, we knew it was Uncle Joe, because Joe was about four foot three and had to sit on many telephone books. Remember the telephone was just invented, there was nobody in the book, so you needed many telephone books to get high enough to get to the wheel, and he could just about see over the wheel, but we couldn't see his head.

So there was Joe, and Joe told me one day that he knew the doorman at a hotel who he did a favor for. I think it had something to do with delivering hooch somewhere. In '35 there was no more Prohibition, but they didn't know that on Broadway. So anyway, Joe was given two tickets to Cole Porter's new show, *Anything Goes,* and I was about nine or nine and a half, and he said, "How would you like to see a Broadway show?" And I said, "Well, what is it? What's a Broadway show?" He says, "Well, people sing and dance on the stage and—you know." I said, "Oh, it's like a movie?" I only knew movies, I didn't know what Broadway was. He said, "No, it's better. Melvin, it's thrilling. I'm going to take you to see your first Broadway show." My Uncle Joe.

So he puts me in his cab on South 3rd and Hooper. He says, "Lie down in the back, because I got the flag up. If they see a person in the back with the flag up, we're both arrested—it's illegal." So he leaves the flag up. I'm on the bottom. I can only see from the bottom of the cab. When I began to see girders, I knew we were crossing the Williamsburg Bridge, so I thought, that's good. And then I saw a glimpse of the Chrysler Building, I knew we were going uptown, things were good, and finally we arrive, I think it was the Alvin Theatre on 52nd Street. Then you could park. In 1935, you could park on the street. There's no signs, there's no nothing. We were probably the only car on the block. We go in, they tear the tickets, we turn left, we go up some stairs, we go around, we go up some more stairs, we go around, we go up

some more stairs—I'm beginning to find it hard to breathe. We are in the top of the Alvin, the last row of the Alvin Theatre. The orchestra starts to play. We sit down.

The lights hit a maroon curtain, a rich velvety maroon curtain, and they play an overture, one song after another. "Anything Goes" itself. And then "You're the top, you're the Coliseum. You're the top, you're the Louvre Museum." Just one song after another. And then "All through the night . . ." All these Russian Jewish melodies that came from Cole Porter. It was amazing. I loved it. And then the curtain opened and there was William Gaxton and there was Ethel Merman. And they had no mikes. I was sitting in the last row of the balcony with Uncle Joe, and Ethel Merman started to sing, and I had to hold my ears—she had a big voice. It was the most thrilling experience of my life. And I said to Joe, yelling from the back of the last row, "I'm gonna do that one day, Uncle Joe. I'm gonna do that. I love that. I've never seen anything like that." And he said, "Okay, kid, you can do it." And that's one of the songs in *The Producers,* "You Can Do It." And I did do it. It took me maybe sixty years to get there, but I did it. That day infected me with the virus of the theater, which has never left my blood.

A musical not only transports you, but stays in your brain because of the songs. The musical blows the dust off your soul, like no other phenomenon in the history of show business. There is nothing like the Broadway musical. It's the greatest thing that ever happened—that ever happened to me, anyway.

We send our films everywhere, but they send us films, and their films are as good as our films. We have John Ford, they have Fellini. Checkmate. What don't they have that we have? Ah. We have the Broadway musical comedy. They don't know what a musical comedy is. Not even in England. They know what musicals are, only recently. But we here in America started way back in the twenties, and then on to the great years of *Oklahoma!* and the great Frank Loesser musicals, not to mention Larry Hart, in *Pal Joey.* Look at the musicals. Look at the musical comedies we have exported. They say happiness. They say hope. They say esprit de corps. They say we're tough. They say we can survive. They say we're sharp. We're hip. We're America. It's the Broadway musical that is the unique artistic event that distinguishes us from every other country in the world. Nobody can make a musical comedy like Americans. Ask George M. Cohan, the Yankee Doodle Dandy, he'll tell you. And so I'm very proud to be part of it. Even in a small way.

EXIT MUSIC

Unique among all other popular entertainments, the Broadway musical enjoys the exalted status of being greater than the sum of its parts. Broadway is a street, a contractual classification, an industry, a tradition, and a state of mind. It is, at once, each of those things and all of those things.

A Hollywood movie can be screened in a thousand different venues; conversely, Teatro alla Scala, Milan's legendary opera house, has a mystique all its own, but it does not encompass the history of opera. A musical, however, can be large or small, a classic or a flop—it doesn't matter—but it must be baptized by the halo of neon lights that garland a relatively small patch of midtown Manhattan in order to be called a Broadway musical. Its artistic identity is ineluctably intertwined with the urban district where it burst forth upon the world.

Broadway the street may stand still, but its furiously racing denizens never will, nor will the adventures of the Broadway musical. A sensible person would have doomed the Broadway industry to extinction decades ago, but it is clever enough to adapt and adopt. Broadway holds a particularly neat trick up its sleeve: not its energy, nor even its talent, but a state of what Stephen Sondheim once called "perpetual anticipation." Because the show is a live event, anything, as writer and director Arthur Laurents reminds us, can happen. And anything can happen to the form, even things we can't yet imagine. The generation of theatergoers who reveled in the antics of Bert Lahr and Ethel Merman raised the generation who were inspired by the communal narrative of *Fiddler on the Roof;* they, in turn, have passed the torch to a generation who can sing all three hours of *Les Misérables* by heart. It is impossible to predict what kind of musical the heirs to this current generation will inherit.

The unique experience of the Broadway musical begins when you exit the subway or get out of your taxi and step out onto the gaudiest, sportiest, naughtiest entertainment district in the world. The expectation grows as you pick up your pasteboard tickets, grab your program, and take your red plush-velvet seat; the intensity builds at the downbeat of the orchestra, and you revel in the performances, fall in love with the leading lady or leading man, thrill to the first act closer, endure the rest room lines during the intermission, cheer the finale, stand to reward the players with your applause; and the experience only gets richer as you argue about the show over drinks or dinner, replay the tunes over and over in your head, purchase the original cast album, and regale your grandchildren over an unforgettable evening in your life. This active engagement in the experience of the Broadway musical is its most irreplaceable and enduring tradition, and because of this tradition, as a Jewish dairyman in a tiny Russian village once told us, it has kept its balance for many years.

And *that* deserves an encore.

BROADWAY: A SELECTED CHRONOLOGY

The following is a selected list of musicals that opened on Broadway over the last century, season by season, in chronological order of their openings. For the purposes of this list, a season is defined as June to May, which is the current definition of a season. Because of this delineation, from 1949 to 1972, occasionally more than one Tony winner falls in the same season. The year the show was awarded the Tony appears in parentheses. Each Tony-winning new musical is marked in *red*. The Pulitzer Prize winners are marked [PP].

The list excludes concerts on Broadway, the frequent brief revivals during Broadway's early days, productions at City Center in the 1940s and '50s, and the countless number of Gilbert and Sullivan productions (with one exception).

Minor shows by major artists are included, as well as major shows by minor artists; minor shows by minor artists rarely make the list.

1903–1904
Whoop-dee-doo
Babes in Toyland
Lew Dockstader's Minstrels
The Wizard of Oz

1904–1905
Mr. Wix of Wickham
Higgledy-piggledy
Little Johnny Jones
It Happened in Nordland

1905–1906
The Earl and the Girl
Twiddle-Twaddle
George Washington, Jr.
The Red Mill
Forty-five Minutes from Broadway

1906–1907
The Rich Mr. Hoggenheimer

1907–1908
The Follies of 1907
The Shoo-Fly Regiment
The Merry Widow
Bandanna Land

1908–1909
The Follies of 1908
Little Nemo

1909–1910
The Follies of 1909
The Chocolate Soldier
Mr. Lode of Koal
The Jolly Bachelors

1910–1911
The Follies of 1910
Madame Sherry
Naughty Marietta
La Belle Paree

1911–1912
The Ziegfeld Follies of 1911
The Little Millionaire
The Quaker Girl

1912–1913
The Passing Show of 1912
Hanky Panky
The Ziegfeld Follies of 1912
Roly Poly
The Firefly

1913–1914
The Ziegfeld Follies of 1913
The Passing Show of 1913
Sweethearts

1914–1915
The Ziegfeld Follies of 1914
The Passing Show of 1914
The Girl from Utah
Chin Chin
Watch Your Step

1915–1916
The Passing Show of 1915
The Ziegfeld Follies of 1915
Very Good Eddie
Stop! Look! Listen!
The Cohan Revue of 1916
Robinson Crusoe, Jr.
See America First

1916–1917
The Ziegfeld Follies of 1916
The Passing Show of 1916
Oh Boy
The Passing Show of 1917

1917–1918
The Ziegfeld Follies of 1917
Leave It to Jane
Jack O'Lantern [PP]
Chu Chin Chow
Miss 1917
Oh Lady! Lady!!
Sinbad

1918–1919
The Ziegfeld Follies of 1918
The Passing Show of 1918
Yip! Yip! Yaphank
The Royal Vagabond
The Fortune Teller
La, La, Lucille
George White's Scandals
A Lonely Romeo

1919–1920
The Ziegfeld Follies of 1919
Ziegfeld Midnight Frolic
Hitchy-Koo of 1919
The Passing Show of 1919
Irene
George White's Scandals

1920–1921
Ziegfeld Follies of 1920
The Midnight Rounders of 1920
Poor Little Ritz Girl
Tickle Me

Mary
Sally
The Passing Show of 1921
Shuffle Along

1921–1922
Ziegfeld Follies of 1921
George White's Scandals
Music Box Revue
Bombo

1922–1923
The Ziegfeld Follies of 1922
George White Scandals
The Gingham Girl
Sally, Irene and Mary
The Passing Show of 1922
Music Box Revue
The '49ers

1923–1924
The Passing Show of 1923
Helen of Troy, New York
Earl Carroll Vanities
Poppy
Music Box Revue
The Ziegfeld Follies of 1923
Runnin' Wild
Kid Boots
Andre Charlot's Revue of 1924
Wildflower
Sitting Pretty
I'll Say She Is

1924–1925
The Ziegfeld Follies of 1924
George White Scandals
Rose-Marie

The Passing Show of 1924
Earl Carroll Vanities
Lady, Be Good!
Music Box Revue
The Student Prince
Tell Me More
Garrick Gaieties

1925–1926

George White Scandals
Earl Carroll Vanities
No, No, Nanette
Dearest Enemy
The Vagabond King
Sunny
The Cocoanuts
Tip-Toes
The Girl Friend
Garrick Gaieties

1926–1927

George White Scandals
Earl Carroll Vanities
Oh, Kay!
The Desert Song
Peggy-Ann
Betsy
Rio Rita
Hit the Deck

1927–1928

The Ziegfeld Follies of 1927
Good News!
Manhattan Mary
The Five O'Clock Girl
A Connecticut Yankee
Funny Face
Golden Dawn
Show Boat
Rosalie
The Three Musketeers
Present Arms
Blackbirds of 1928

1928–1929

George White Scandals
Earl Carroll Vanities
The New Moon
Chee-Chee
Paris
Animal Crackers
Hold Everything
This Year of Grace
Whoopee!
Follow Thru
Spring Is Here
The Little Show

1929–1930

Hot Chocolates
Show Girl
Sweet Adeline
George White's Scandals
Great Day
Heads Up
Fifty Million Frenchmen
Wake Up and Dream
Strike Up the Band
Simple Simon
Flying High
Garrick Gaieties

1930–1931

Earl Carroll Vanities
Girl Crazy
Garrick Gaieties
Lew Leslie's Blackbirds
The New Yorkers
America's Sweetheart
The Wonder Bar
The Band Wagon

1931–1932

The Ziegfeld Follies of 1931
Earl Carroll Vanities
George White Scandals
Of Thee I Sing
Face the Music
Show Boat (revival)

1932–1933

Flying Colors
Earl Carroll Vanities
Americana
Music in the Air
Gay Divorce
Pardon My English
Threepenny Opera

1933–1934

As Thousands Cheer
Let 'Em Eat Cake
Blackbirds of 1933
Ziegfeld Follies of 1934

1934–1935

Life Begins at 8:40
The Great Waltz
Africana
Revenge with Music
At Home Abroad
Porgy and Bess
Jubilee
Jumbo
George White Scandals

Ziegfeld Follies of 1936
On Your Toes
New Faces of 1936

1936–1937

White House Inn
Red, Hot, and Blue
Johnny Johnson
The Show Is On
Babes in Arms

1937–1938

I'd Rather Be Right
Pins and Needles
Hooray for What!
The Cradle Will Rock
I Married an Angel

1938–1939

You Never Know
Hellzapoppin'
Sing Out the News
Knickerbocker Holiday
Leave It to Me!
The Boys from Syracuse
Stars in Your Eyes

1939–1940

Yokel Boy
George White Scandals
Too Many Girls
Very Warm for May
Swingin' the Dream
Du Barry Was a Lady
Earl Carroll Vanities
Higher and Higher
Louisiana Purchase

1940–1941

Cabin in the Sky
Panama Hattie
Pal Joey
Lady in the Dark
Hold on to Your Hats

1941–1942

Best Foot Forward
Let's Face It
Banjo Eyes
Porgy and Bess (revival)
By Jupiter

1942–1943

This Is the Army
Something for the Boys
Oklahoma!
The Ziegfeld Follies of 1943

One Touch of Venus
A Connecticut Yankee (revival)
Carmen Jones
Mexican Hayride

1944–1945

Bloomer Girl
The Seven Lively Arts
On the Town
Up in Central Park
The Firebrand of Florence
Carousel
Hollywood Pinafore

1945–1946

The Day Before Spring
Billion Dollar Baby
Show Boat (revival)
St. Louis Woman
Call Me Mister
Annie Get Your Gun

1946–1947

Park Avenue
Beggar's Holiday
Street Scene
Finian's Rainbow
Brigadoon

1947–1948

High Button Shoes
Allegro
Make Mine Mahattan
Inside U.S.A.

1948–1949

Magdalena
Love Life
Where's Charley?
Kiss Me, Kate (1949)
South Pacific (1950)

1949–1950

Miss Liberty
Lost in the Stars
Regina
Gentlemen Prefer Blondes

1950–1951

Call Me Madam
Guys and Dolls (1951)
Out of This World
The King and I (1952)
A Tree Grows in Brooklyn
Flahooley

1951–1952

Two on the Aisle
Top Banana
Paint Your Wagon
Pal Joey (revival)
Of Thee I Sing (revival)

1952–1953

Wish You Were Here
Two's Company
Hazel Flagg
Wonderful Town
Can-Can
Me and Juliet

1953–1954

Carnival in Flanders
Kismet (1954)
The Girl in Pink Tights
By the Beautiful Sea
The Golden Apple
The Pajama Game (1955)

1954–1955

The Boy Friend
Peter Pan
Fanny
House of Flowers
Plain and Fancy
Silk Stockings
Damn Yankees

1955–1956

Pipe Dream
My Fair Lady
Mr. Wonderful
The Most Happy Fella

1956–1957

New Faces of 1956
L'il Abner
Bells Are Ringing
Candide
Happy Hunting
The Ziegfeld Follies of 1957
New Girl in Town

1957–1958

West Side Story
Jamaica
The Music Man
The Body Beautiful
Oh, Captain!
Say Darling

1958–1959

Goldilocks

Flower Drum Song
Redhead
Juno
First Impressions
Destry Rides Again
Gypsy

1959–1960

Take Me Along
The Sound of Music
  (cowinner with)
Fiorello! (1960) [PP]
Once Upon a Mattress
Saratoga
Greenwillow
Bye Bye Birdie (1961)

1960–1961

Tenderloin
The Unsinkable Molly Brown
Camelot
Wildcat
Do Re Mi
Carnival!

1961–1962

Sail Away
Milk and Honey
How to Succeed in
  Business Without
  Really Trying (1962) [PP]
Kwamina
Kean
The Gay Life
Subways Are for Sleeping
A Family Affair
No Strings
All American
I Can Get It for You Wholesale
A Funny Thing Happened on the
  Way to the Forum (1963)

1962–1963

Stop the World—I Want to
  Get Off
Mr. President
Little Me
Oliver!
Tovarich
She Loves Me

1963–1964

110 in the Shade
The Girl Who Came to Supper
Hello, Dolly!
Foxy
What Makes Sammy Run?

Funny Girl
Anyone Can Whistle
High Spirits
Fade-Out, Fade-In

1964–1965

Fiddler on the Roof
Golden Boy
Ben Franklin in Paris
Bajour
Baker Street
Do I Hear a Waltz?
Half a Sixpence
Flora, the Red Menace
The Roar of the Greasepaint

1965–1966

On a Clear Day You Can
  See Forever
Skyscraper
Man of La Mancha
Sweet Charity
"It's a Bird . . . It's a Plane . . .
  It's Superman!"
Mame

1966–1967

Annie Get Your Gun (revival)
The Apple Tree
Cabaret (1967)
I Do! I Do!
Sherry!
Hallelujah, Baby! (1968)

1967–1968

Henry, Sweet Henry
How Now, Dow Jones
The Happy Time
Darling of the Day
George M!
Hair

1968–1969

Her First Roman
Zorbà
Promises, Promises
Dear World
1776

1969–1970

Jimmy
Coco
Purlie
Minnie's Boys
Applause (1970)
Company (1971)

1970–1971

The Rothschilds
Two by Two
The Me Nobody Knows
No, No, Nanette (revival)
Follies
70, Girls, 70

1971–1972

You're a Good Man, Charlie Brown
No Place to Be Somebody
Jesus Christ Superstar
On the Town (revival)
Two Gentlemen of Verona (1972)
Grease
A Funny Thing Happened on the
  Way to the Forum (revival)
Sugar
Don't Bother Me, I Can't Cope
Dude
Pippin
Via Galactica
A Little Night Music (1973)
Irene (revival)
Seesaw
Cyrano

1973–1974

The Desert Song (revival)
Raisin
Gigi
The Pajama Game (revival)
Lorelei
Over Here!
Candide (revival)
The Magic Show

1974–1975

Gypsy (revival)
Mack & Mabel
Where's Charley? (revival)
Good News (revival)
The Wiz
Shenandoah
Goodtime Charley

1975–1976

Chicago
A Chorus Line [PP]
The Robber Bridegroom
Treemonisha
Hello, Dolly! (revival)
Very Good Eddie (revival)
Pacific Overtures
Rockabye Hamlet
Bubbling Brown Sugar
My Fair Lady (revival)

Rex
1600 Pennsylvania Avenue

1976–1977

Godspell
Pal Joey (revival)
Guys and Dolls (revival)
Music Is
Your Arms Too Short to Box
 with God
Fiddler on the Roof (revival)
I Love My Wife
Side by Side by Sondheim
Annie
The King and I (revival)
Happy End

1977–1978

Beatlemania
Man of La Mancha (revival)
Hair (revival)
The Act
On the Twentieth Century
Timbuktu
Hello, Dolly! (revival)
Dancin'
Ain't Misbehavin'
Runaways
Working

1978–1979

The Best Little Whorehouse in
 Texas
Stop the World—I Want to
 Get Off (revival)
Eubie!
Ballroom
A Broadway Musical
The Grand Tour
They're Playing Our Song
Whoopee! (revival)
Sweeney Todd
Carmelina
I Remember Mama

1979–1980

Got Tu Go Disco
Peter Pan (revival)
Evita
Sugar Babies
The Most Happy Fella (revival)
Oklahoma! (revival)
West Side Story (revival)
Barnum
A Day in Hollywood/
 A Night in the Ukraine

1980–1981

42nd Street
Brigadoon (revival)
Tintypes
Pirates of Penzance
Sophisticated Ladies
Bring Back Birdie
Woman of the Year
Copperfield
Can-Can (revival)

1981–1982

Marlowe
Camelot (revival)
Merrily We Roll Along
Dreamgirls
Little Me (revival)
Pump Boys and Dinettes
Little Johnny Jones (revival)
Nine

1982–1983

Seven Brides for Seven Brothers
A Doll's Life
Cats
Merlin
On Your Toes (revival)
Show Boat (revival)
My One and Only
Dance a Little Closer

1983–1984

Mame (revival)
La Cage aux Folles
Zorbà (revival)
Doonesbury
Baby
The Tap Dance Kid
The Rink
Oliver! (revival)
Sunday in the Park with
 George [PP]
The Wiz (revival)

1984–1985

The Three Musketeers (revival)
The King and I (revival)
Harrigan 'n' Hart
Leader of the Pack
Take Me Along (revival)
Grind
Big River

1985–1986

Singin' in the Rain
Song and Dance
The Mystery of

Edwin Drood
Big Deal
Sweet Charity (revival)

1986–1987

Me and My Girl
Rags
Smile
Les Misérables
Starlight Express

1987–1988

Dreamgirls (revival)
Roza
Anything Goes (revival)
Cabaret (revival)
Into the Woods
Teddy and Alice
The Phantom of the Opera
The Gospel at Colonus
Chess
Carrie

1988–1989

Ain't Misbehavin' (revival)
Legs Diamond
Black and Blue
Jerome Robbins' Broadway

1989–1990

Shenandoah (revival)
Sweeney Todd (revival)
Meet Me in St. Louis
3 Penny Opera
Grand Hotel
Gypsy (revival)
City of Angels
Aspects of Love

1990–1991

Once on This Island
Oh, Kay! (revival)
Buddy
Fiddler on the Roof (revival)
Shogun, the Musical
Peter Pan (revival)
Miss Saigon
The Secret Garden
The Will Rogers Follies

1991–1992

Peter Pan (revival)
Nick & Nora
The Most Happy Fella (revival)
Crazy for You
Five Guys Named Moe
Guys and Dolls (revival)

Man of La Mancha (revival)
Jelly's Last Jam
Falsettos

1992–1993

Anna Karenina
My Favorite Year
The Goodbye Girl
The Who's Tommy
Blood Brothers
Kiss of the Spider Woman

1993–1994

She Loves Me (revival)
Camelot (revival)
Joseph and the Amazing
 Technicolor
 Dreamcoat
Cyrano—The Musical
My Fair Lady (revival)
The Red Shoes
Damn Yankees (revival)
Carousel (revival)
Beauty and the Beast
Passion
Grease (revival)

1994–1995

Show Boat (revival)
Sunset Boulevard
Smokey Joe's Café
How to Succeed . . . (revival)

1995–1996

Company (revival)
Hello, Dolly! (revival)
Swinging on a Star
Victor/ Victoria
State Fair
The King and I (revival)
A Funny Thing . . . Forum
 (revival)
Bring in 'Da Noise, Bring in
 'Da Funk
Rent [PP]

1996–1997

Chicago (revival)
Juan Darien
Once Upon a Mattress (revival)
Play On!
Annie (revival)
Dream
Titanic
Steel Pier
The Life
Jekyll and Hyde

1997–1998

Forever Tango
1776 (revival)
Side Show
The Triumph of Love
The Scarlet Pimpernel
The Lion King
Ragtime
The Capeman
The Sound of Music (revival)
Cabaret (revival)
High Society

1998–1999

Footlose
Little Me (revival)
On the Town (revival)
Peter Pan (revival)
Parade
Fosse
You're a Good Man, Charlie Brown (revival)
Annie Get Your Gun (revival)
The Gershwins' Fascinating Rhythm
It Ain't Nothin' but the Blues

1999–2000

Saturday Night Fever
Kiss Me, Kate (revival)
Marie Christine
Swing!
James Joyce's The Dead
Aida
Contact
The Wild Party
Jesus Christ Superstar (revival)
The Music Man (revival)

2000–2001

The Full Monty
The Rocky Horror Show
Seussical
Jane Eyre
A Class Act
Follies (revival)
Bells Are Ringing (revival)
The Producers
The Adventures of Tom Sawyer
42nd Street (revival)

2001–2002

Urinetown
Mamma Mia!
By Jeeves
One Mo' Time
Sweet Smell of Success

Oklahoma! (revival)
Thoroughly Modern Millie
Into the Woods (revival)

2002–2003

Hairspray
The Boys from Syracuse (revival)
Flower Drum Song (revival)
Amour
Movin' Out
Man of La Mancha (revival)
La Bohème
Dance of the Vampires
Urban Cowboy
Nine (revival)
Gypsy (revival)

2003–2004

Big River (revival)
Avenue Q
Little Shop of Horrors
The Boy from Oz
Wicked
Taboo
Wonderful Town (revival)
Never Gonna Dance
Fiddler on the Roof (revival)
Assassins
Bombay Dreams
Caroline, or Change

2004–2005

The Frogs
Dracula, the Musical
Pacific Overtures (revival)
La Cage aux Folles (revival)
Little Women
Good Vibrations
Dirty Rotten Scoundrels
Spamalot
All Shook Up
The Light in the Piazza
Chitty Chitty Bang Bang
The 25th Annual Putnam County Spelling Bee
Sweet Charity (revival)

2005–2006

Lennon
Sweeney Todd (revival)
Jersey Boys
The Woman in White
The Color Purple
Chita Rivera: The Dancer's Life
The Pajama Game (revival)
Ring of Fire

The Threepenny Opera (revival)
Lestat
The Wedding Singer
Hot Feet
The Drowsy Chaperone
Tarzan

2006–2007

Martin Short: Fame Becomes Me
A Chorus Line (revival)
The Times They Are A-Changin'
Grey Gardens
Dr. Seuss' How the Grinch Stole Christmas
Les Misérables (revival)
Mary Poppins
Company (revival)
High Fidelity
Spring Awakening
The Apple Tree (revival)
Curtains
The Pirate Queen
Legally Blonde
LoveMusik
110 in the Shade (revival)

2007–2008

Xanadu
Grease (revival)
Young Frankenstein
The Little Mermaid
Sunday in the Park with George (revival)
Passing Strange
In the Heights
Gypsy (revival)
South Pacific (revival)
A Catered Affair
Cry-Baby

2008–2009

A Tale of Two Cities
13
Billy Elliot: The Musical
Irving Berlin's White Christmas
Shrek The Musical
Pal Joey (revival)
Guys and Dolls (revival)
West Side Story (revival)
Hair (revival)
Rock of Ages
Next to Normal
9 to 5

2009–2010
(as of February 2010)

Bye Bye Birdie (revival)
Memphis
Finian's Rainbow (revival)
Ragtime (revival)
Fela!
A Little Night Music (revival)
Come Fly Away
The Addams Family
Million Dollar Quartet
Sondheim on Sondheim
American Idiot
Promises, Promises (revival)
La Cage aux Folles (revival)

SELECTED BIBLIOGRAPHY

If they asked us, we could write a book, to pluralize Larry Hart's words, but we are deeply indebted to the scholars, historians, and enthusiasts who came before. Below is a selected list of titles used for both this volume and the PBS series. With the exception of the occasional quoted introduction, librettos and cast albums for the dozens of shows referred to in the book do not appear here, as there are too many to list. *Broadway: The American Musical* prides itself on being a cultural history, so there are also many nonmusical books listed; they were equally helpful and entertaining, and we urge the reader to seek them out.

Some volumes are so seminal they were not only inspiring, they obviated extensive discussion in the text: Mary C. Henderson's exemplary history of the New Amsterdam Theatre; Ted Chapin's sine qua non of production histories on the birth of Sondheim's *Follies;* William Goldman's *The Season,* which remains one of the finest books about Broadway, thirty-five years after its publication; and, in particular, Robert Kimball's extraordinary volumes of collected lyrics by America's best songwriters. Each of these volumes is cited separately, not only because the information is so helpful and meticulously edited, but because they are just so much damned fun to read.

BOOKS

Abbott, George. *Mister Abbott.* New York: Random House, 1963.

Alessandrini, Gerard. *Forbidden Broadway: Behind the Mylar Curtain.* New York: Applause Books, 2009.

Alexander, Michael. *Jazz Age Jews.* Princeton: Princeton University Press, 2001.

Alpert, Hollis. *The Life and Times of Porgy and Bess: The Story of an American Classic.* Alfred A. Knopf, 1990.

Alpert, Hollis, and Museum of the City of New York. *Broadway: 125 Years of Musical Theatre.* New York: Arcade Publishing, 1991.

Altman, Richard, and Mervyn Kaufman. *The Making of a Musical: Fiddler on the Roof.* New York: Crown Publishers, 1971.

Altschuler, Glenn, C. *All Shook Up: How Rock 'n' Roll Changed America.* New York: Oxford University Press, 2003

Arntz, James, and Thomas S. Wilson. *Julie Andrews.* Chicago: Contemporary Books, 1995.

Asinof, Eliot. *1919: America's Loss of Innocence.* New York: Donald I. Fine, 1990.

Atkinson, Brooks. *Broadway.* New York: Macmillan Company, 1970.

Aylesworth, Thomas G. *Broadway to Hollywood.* New York: Gallery Books, 1985.

Bach, Stephen. *Dazzler: The Life and Times of Moss Hart.* New York: Alfred A. Knopf, 2001.

Baral, Robert. *Revue: A Nostalgic Reprise of the Great Broadway Period.* New York: Fleet Publishing Corporation, 1962.

Barrett, Mary Ellin. *Irving Berlin, a Daughter's Memoir.* New York: Simon and Schuster, 1994.

Barrios, Richard. *A Song in the Dark: The Birth of the Musical Film.* New York: Oxford University Press, 1995.

Bergreen, Laurence. *As Thousands Cheer: The Life of Irving Berlin.* New York: Viking Press, 1990.

Berlin, Irving, Robert Kimball, and Linda Emmet. *The Complete Lyrics of Irving Berlin.* New York: Alfred A. Knopf, 2001.

Bordman, Gerald. *American Musical Revue: From the Passing Show to Sugar Babies.* New York: Oxford University Press, 1985.

Brooks, Mel, and Tom Meehan. *The Producers: How We Did It.* New York: Hyperion/Miramax Books, 2001.

Brown, Jared. *Zero Mostel.* New York: Atheneum, 1989.

Burke, Billie. *With a Feather in My Nose.* New York: Appleton-Century-Crofts, 1949.

Burns, Ric, and James Saunders. *New York: An Illustrated History.* New York: Alfred A. Knopf/Random House, 1999.

Burton, Jack. *Blue Book of Tin Pan Alley.* Watkins Glen, New York: Century House, 1950.

Cantor, Eddie. *My Life Is in Your Hands and Take My Life: The Autobiographies of Eddie Cantor.* New York: Cooper Square Press, 2000.

Carter, Randolph. *Ziegfeld: The Time of His Life.* London: Bernard Press, 1988.

Chach, Maryann, and Staff of Shubert Archive. *The Shuberts Present 100 Years of American Theatre.* New York: Harry N. Abrams/Shubert Organization, 2001.

Chapin, Theodore S. *Everything Was Possible: The Birth of the Musical Follies.* New York: Alfred A. Knopf, 2003.

Charnin, Martin. *Annie: A Theatre Memoir.* New York: E.P. Dutton, 1977.

Charters, Ann. *Nobody: The Story of Bert Williams.* New York: Macmillan Company, 1970.

Churchill, Allen. *The Theatrical 20s.* New York: McGraw-Hill, 1975.

Clum, John M. *Something for the Boys: Musical Theater and Gay Culture.* New

York: St. Martin's Press, 1999.

Cohan, George M. *Twenty Years on Broadway.* Westport, Connecticut: Greenwood Press, 1953 (1925).

Cote, David. *Jersey Boys: The Story of Frankie Valli and the Four Seasons.* New York: Broadway/ Melcher Media, 2007.

———. *Wicked: The Grimmerie, a Behind-The-Scenes Look at the Hit Broadway Musical.* New York: Hyperion Books, 2005.

Coveney, Michael. *Cats on a Chandelier: The Andrew Lloyd Webber Story.* London: Random House, Hutchinson, 1999.

Curtis, James. *W.C. Fields: A Biography.* New York: Alfred A. Knopf, 2003.

Davis, Lee. *Bolton & Wodehouse & Kern.* New York: James H. Heineman, 1993.

De Mille, Agnes. *Speak to Me, Dance with Me.* Boston: Little, Brown and Company, 1973.

Dietz, Howard. *Dancing in the Dark: Words by Howard Dietz.* New York: Quadrangle/ The New York Times Book Co., 1974.

Douglas, Ann. *Terrible Honesty: Mongrel Manhattan in the 1920s.* New York: The Noonday Press, Farrar, Straus and Giroux, 1995.

Douglas, Susan J. *Listening In: Radio and the American Imagination from Amos 'n' Andy and Edward R. Murrow to Wolfman Jack and Howard Stern.* New York: Times Books, Random House, 1999.

Dunlap, David W. *On Broadway: A Journey Uptown Over Time.* New York: Rizzoli International Publications, 1990.

Dunn, Donald H. *The Making of No, No, Nanette.* Secaucus, New Jersey: Citadel Press, 1972.

Eells, George. *The Life That Late He Led: A Biography of Cole Porter.* New York: G.P. Putnam's Sons, 1967.

Eisner, Michael, and Tony Schwartz. *Work in Progress.* New York: Random House, 1998.

Eliot, Marc. *Down 42nd Street: Sex, Money, Culture, and Politics at the Crossroads of the World.* New York: Warner Books, 2001.

Engel, Lehman. *Their Words Are Music: The Great Theatre Lyricists and Their Lyrics.* New York: Crown Publishers, 1975.

Ewen, David. *The Life and Death of Tin Pan Alley.* New York: Funk and Wagnalls/Reader's Digest Books, 1964.

The New Complete Book of the American Musical Theatre. New York: Holt, Rinehart and Winston, 1958, revised 1971.

Ferber, Edna. *Show Boat.* Garden City, New York: Doubleday, Page & Co., 1926.

Feuer, Cy, and Ken Gross. *I Got the Show Right Here.* New York: Simon and Schuster, 2002.

Fields, Armond, and L. Marc Fields. *From the Bowery to Broadway: Lew Fields and the Roots of American Popular Theater.* New York: Oxford University Press, 1993.

Fordin, Hugh. *Getting to Know Him: A Biography of Oscar Hammerstein II.* New York: Random House, 1977.

Friedwald, Will. *Stardust Melodies: A Biography of Twelve of America's Most Popular Songs.* New York: Pantheon Books, 2002.

Frommer, Myrna Katz, and Harvey Frommer. *It Happened on Broadway: An Oral History of the Great White Way.* New York: Harcourt Brace, 1998.

Furia, Philip. *Irving Berlin: A Life in Song.* New York: Schirmer Books, 1998.

———. *The Poets of Tin Pan Alley: A History of America's Great Lyricists.* New York: Oxford University Press, 1990.

Gabler, Neal. *Winchell: Gossip, Power and the Culture of Celebrity.* New York: Alfred A. Knopf, 1994.

Gershwin, Ira. *Lyrics on Several Occasions.* New York: Viking Press, 1973.

Gershwin, Ira, and Robert Kimball. *The Complete Lyrics of Ira Gershwin.* New York: Alfred A. Knopf, 1993.

Golden, Eve. *Anna Held and the Birth of Ziegfeld's Broadway.* Lexington: University Press of Kentucky, 2000.

Goldman, Herbert G. *Fanny Brice: The Original Funny Girl.* New York: Oxford University Press, 1992.

Goldman, William. *The Season; A Candid Look at Broadway.* New York: Harcourt, Brace and World, Limelight Editions, 1969.

Gottfried, Martin. *All His Jazz: The Life and Death of Bob Fosse.* New York: Bantam Books, 1990.

———. *Balancing Act: Authorized Biography of Angela Lansbury.* Boston: Little, Brown and Company, 1999.

Gottlieb, Robert, and Robert Kimball. *Reading Lyrics.* New York: Pantheon Books, 2000.

Green, Abel, and Joe Laurie Jr. *Show Biz, from Vaude to Video.* New York: Henry Holt, 1951.

Green, Stanley. *The Great Clowns of Broadway.* New York: Oxford University Press, 1984.

———. *Ring Bells! Sing Songs! Broadway Musicals of the 1930s.* New York: Arlington House, 1971.

———, ed. *Rodgers and Hammerstein Fact Book: A Record of Their Works Together and Other Collaborators.* New York: Lynn Farnol Group, 1980.

Groce, Nancy. *New York: Songs of the City.* New York: Watson-Guptill Publications, 1999.

Grossman, Barbara W. *Funny Woman: The Life and Times of Fanny Brice.* Bloomington: Indiana University Press, 1991.

Hamm, Charles. *Irving Berlin: Songs from the Melting Pot: The Formative Years, 1907–1914.* New York: Oxford University Press, 1997.

———. *Yesterdays: Popular Song in America.* New York: Norton, 1979.

Hammerstein, Oscar II. *Lyrics.* New York: Hal Leonard Books, 1985.

Hammerstein, Oscar and Amy Asch. *The Complete Lyrics of Oscar Hammerstein II.* New York: Alfred A. Knopf, 2008.

Hanan, Stephen Mo. *A Cat's Diary: How the Broadway Production of Cats Was Born.* Hanover, New Hampshire: Smith & Kraus, 2001.

Hart, Dorothy. *Thou Swell, Thou Witty: The Life and Lyrics of Lorenz Hart.* New York: Harper and Row, 1976.

Hart, Lorenz, and Robert Kimball. *The Complete Lyrics of Lorenz Hart.* New York: Alfred A. Knopf, 1986.

Haygood, Will. *In Black and White: The Life of Sammy Davis, Jr.* New York: Alfred A. Knopf, 2003.

Hemming, Roy. *The Melody Lingers On:*

The Great Songwriters and Their Movie Musicals. New York: Newmarket Press, 1986.

Henderson, Amy, and Dwight Blocker Bowers. *Red Hot & Blue: A Smithsonian Salute to the American Musical.* Washington: Smithsonian Institution Press, 1996.

Henderson, Mary C. *The City and the Theater: The History of New York Playhouses—A 235-Year Journey from Bowling Green to Times Square.* Clifton, New Jersey: James T. White & Company, 1973.

———. *The New Amsterdam: The Biography of a Broadway Theatre.* New York: A Roundtable Press Book, Hyperion, 1997.

Herman, Jerry, with Marilyn Stasio. *Showtune: A Memoir.* New York: Donald I. Fine Books, 1996.

Hirsch, Foster. *Harold Prince and the American Musical Theatre.* New York: Cambridge University Press, 1989.

Hirschfeld, Albert. *The American Theatre As Seen by Hirschfeld.* New York: George Braziller, 1961.

———. *Hirschfeld: On Line.* New York: Applause, 1999.

Horowitz, Mark Eden. *Sondheim on Music: Minor Details and Major Decisions.* Lanham, Maryland: Scarecrow Press, 2003.

Houseman, John. *Run-Through: A Memoir.* New York: Simon and Schuster, 1972.

Jablonski, Edward, and Lawrence D. Stewart. *The Gershwin Years.* Garden City, New York: Doubleday, 1958.

Jackson, Arthur. *The Best Musicals: From Show Boat to A Chorus Line: Broadway, Off-Broadway, London.* London: Webb & Bower, Mitchell Beazley, 1977.

Jackson, Kenneth T., ed. *The Encyclopedia of New York.* New Haven, Connecticut: Yale University Press, 1995.

James, Alan. *Gilbert & Sullivan.* New York: Omnibus Press, 1989.

Kahn, E.J. Jr. *The Merry Partners: The Age and Stage of Harrigan and Hart.* New York: Random House, 1955.

Kander, John, Fred Ebb, and Greg Lawrence. *Colored Lights.* New York: Faber and Faber, 2003.

Kander, John, Fred Ebb, and Joe Masteroff.

Cabaret: The Illustrated Book and Lyrics. New York: Newmarket Press, 1999.

Kasha, Al, and Joel Hirschhorn. *Notes on Broadway: Conversations with the Great Songwriters.* New York: Fireside, 1985.

Kimball, Robert, and Brendan Gill. *Cole.* New York: Holt, Rinehart and Winston, 1971.

Kreuger, Miles. *Show Boat: The Story of a Classic American Musical.* New York: Oxford University Press, 1977.

Laas, William. *Crossroads of the World: The Story of Times Square.* New York: Popular Library Editions, 1965.

Lahr, John. *Notes on a Cowardly Lion: The Biography of Bert Lahr.* New York: Limelight Editions, 1984.

Larson, Jonathan, Evelyn McDonnell, and Katherine Silberger. *Rent.* New York: Rob Weisbach Books, 1997.

Lassell, Michael. *Elton John and Tim Rice's Aida: The Making of a Broadway Musical.* New York: Disney Editions, 2000.

Laurents, Arthur. *Original Story By: A Memoir of Broadway and Hollywood.* New York: Alfred A. Knopf, 2000.

Lawrence, Greg. *Dance with Demons: The Life of Jerome Robbins.* New York: G.P. Putnam & Sons, 2001.

Lerner, Alan Jay. *The Musical Theatre: A Celebration.* New York: McGraw-Hill, 1986.

———. *The Street Where I Live.* New York: W.W. Norton and Company, 1978.

Lillie, Beatrice, with James Brough. *Every Other Inch a Lady.* Garden City, New York: Doubleday and Co., 1972.

Lingeman, Richard. *Don't You Know There's a War On? The American Home Front 1941–1945.* New York: G.P. Putnam and Sons, 1970.

Lloyd Webber, Andrew, and Tim Rice. *Evita: The Legend of Eva Perón.* New York: Avon Books, 1978.

Loesser, Frank, Robert Kimball, and Steve Nelson. *The Complete Lyrics of Frank Loesser.* New York: Alfred A. Knopf, 2003.

Long, Robert Emmet. *Broadway, the Golden Years: Jerome Robbins and the Great Choreographer-Directors: 1940*

to the Present. New York: Continuum, 2001.

McBrien, William. *Cole Porter: A Biography.* New York: Random House, 1998.

McCabe, John. *George M. Cohan: The Man Who Owned Broadway.* Garden City, New York: Doubleday and Company, 1973.

McDonnell, Evelyn, with Katherine Silberger. *Rent, by Jonathan Larson.* New York: William Morrow and Company, 1997.

Mandelbaum, Ken. *A Chorus Line and the Musicals of Michael Bennett.* New York: St. Martin's Press, 1989.

———. *Not Since Carrie: 40 Years of Broadway Musical Flops.* New York: St. Martin's Press, 1991.

Maslon, Laurence. *The South Pacific Companion.* New York: Simon and Schuster, 2007.

Mercer, Johnny, collected and edited by Bob Bach and Ginger Mercer. *Our Huckleberry Friend: The Life, Times and Lyrics of Johnny Mercer.* Secaucus, New Jersey: Citadel Press, Lyle Stuart, 1982.

Mercer, Johnny, Robert Kimball, Barry Day, and Miles Kreuger. *The Complete Lyrics of Johnny Mercer.* New York: Alfred A. Knopf, 2009.

Merman, Ethel, and George Eells. *Merman: An Autobiography.* New York: Simon and Schuster, 1978.

Mordden, Ethan. *Broadway Babies: The People Who Made the American Musical.* New York: Oxford University Press, 1983.

———. *One More Kiss: The Broadway Musical in the 1970s.* New York: Palgrave/St. Martin's Press, 2003.

———. *Open a New Window: The Broadway Musical in the 1960s.* New York: Palgrave/St. Martin's Press, 2001.

———. *Rodgers and Hammerstein.* New York: Abradale, Harry N. Abrams, 1992.

Morley, Sheridan, and Ruth Leon. *Hey, Mr. Producer! The Musical World of Cameron Mackintosh.* New York: Back Stage Books, 1998.

Morris, James R., J.R. Taylor, and Dwight Block Bowers. *American Popular Song.* New York: CBS Special Products/Smithsonian Institute, 1984.

Morrison, William. *Broadway Theatres: History and Architecture*. Minneola, New York: Dover Publications, 1999.

New York Times. *The Century in Times Square*. New York: New York Times, Bishop Books, 1999.

Nolan, Frederick. *Lorenz Hart: A Poet on Broadway*. New York: Oxford University Press, 1994.

Odets, Clifford, William Gibson, Charles Strouse, and Lee Adams. *Golden Boy*. New York: Bantam/Atheneum, 1965.

Oliver, Donald, and various, ed. *The Greatest Revue Sketches*. New York: Avon Books, 1982.

Pleasants, Henry. *The Great American Popular Singers*. New York: Simon and Schuster, 1974.

Porter, Cole, and Robert Kimball. *The Complete Lyrics of Cole Porter*. New York: Alfred A. Knopf, 1983.

Prince, Hal. *Contradictions: Notes on Twenty-Six Years in the Theatre*. New York: Dodd, Mead & Company, 1974.

Raymond, Jack. *Show Music on Record: From the 1890s to the 1980s*. New York: F. Ungar, 1982.

Rich, Frank. *Hot Seat: Theatre Criticism for the New York Times, 1980–1993*. New York: Random House, 1998.

Rich, Frank, and Lisa Aronson. *The Theatre Art of Boris Aronson*. New York: Alfred A. Knopf, 1987.

Rodgers, Richard. *Musical Stages: An Autobiography*. New York: Random House, 1975.

Rose, Brian. *Televising the Performing Arts*. Westport, Connecticut: Greenwood Press, 1992.

Rosenberg, Deena. *Fascinating Rhythm: The Collaboration of George and Ira Gershwin*. New York: Plume, Penguin, 1993.

Rosenthal, Elizabeth J. *His Song: The Musical World of Elton John*. New York: Billboard Books, 2001.

Rowland, Mabel. *Bert Williams: Son of Laughter, A Symposium of Tribute to the Man and His Work by His Friends and Associates*. New York: Negro Universities Press, 1969.

Sagalyn, Lynne B. *Times Square Roulette: Remaking the City Icon*. Cambridge, Massachusetts: MIT Press, 2001.

Sanders, Ronald. *The Days Grow Short: The Life and Music of Kurt Weill*. Los Angeles: Silman-James Press, 1980.

Sante, Luc. *Low Life*. New York: Vintage, Random House, 1991.

Sater, Steven and Duncan Sheik, *Spring Awakening*. New York: Theatre Communications Group, 2007.

Schwarz, Daniel R. *Broadway Boogie Woogie: Damon Runyon and the Making of New York City Culture*. New York: Palgrave/Macmillan, 2003.

Secrest, Meryle. *Somewhere for Me: A Biography of Richard Rodgers*. New York: Alfred A. Knopf, Random House, 2001.

———. *Stephen Sondheim: A Life*. New York: Alfred A. Knopf, 1998.

Seldes, Gilbert. *The 7 Lively Arts*. New York: Sagamore Press, 1957.

Shaw, Arnold. *The Jazz Age: Popular Music in the 1920s*. New York: Oxford University Press, 1987.

———. *Let's Dance: Popular Music in the 1930s*. New York: Oxford University Press, 1998.

Sheward, David. *It's a Hit! The Back Stage Book of Longest-Running Broadway Shows, 1884 to the Present*. New York: Watson-Guptill Publications, 1994.

Spada, James. *Barbra Streisand: Her Life*. New York: Crown, 1995.

Steyn, Mark. *Broadway Babies Say Goodnight: Musicals Then and Now*. New York: Routledge, 1999.

Stone, Peter, and Sherman Edwards. *1776*. New York: Viking Press, 1970.

Suriano, Gregory R. *Gershwin in His Time: A Biographical Scrapbook, 1919–1937*. New York: Gramercy Books, 1998.

Taper, Bernard. *Balanchine*. New York: Collier Press, 1974.

Taylor, William R., ed. *Inventing Times Square*. Baltimore: Johns Hopkins University Press, 1991.

Taymor, Julie, with Alexis Greene. *The Lion King: Pride Rock on Broadway*. New York: Hyperion, 1997.

Trager, James. *The New York Chronology: The Ultimate Compendium of Events, People and Anecdotes from the Dutch to the Present*. New York: HarperResource, 2003.

Traubner, Richard. *Operetta: A Theatrical History*. New York: Oxford University Press, 1983.

Van Hoogstraten, Nicholas. *Lost Broadway Theatres* (updated and expanded edition). New York: Princeton Architectural Press, 1997.

Viagas, Robert. *I'm the Greatest Star*. New York: Applause Books, 2009.

Walker, Stanley. *The Night Club Era*. Baltimore: Johns Hopkins University Press, 1999 (1933).

Walsh, Michael. *Andrew Lloyd Webber: His Life and Works: A Critical Biography*. New York: Harry N. Abrams, 1989.

Ward, Geoffrey C., and Ken Burns. *Jazz: A History of America's Music*. New York: Alfred A. Knopf, 2000.

Waters, Ethel. *His Eye Is on the Sparrow*. New York: Da Capo Press, 1950, 1992.

Wilder, Alec. *American Popular Song*. New York: Oxford University Press, 1972.

Wilk, Max. *OK! The Story of Oklahoma!* New York: Grove Press, 1993.

———. *They're Playing Our Song* (expanded). New York: Da Capo Press, 1991.

Wilmeth, Don B., Christopher Bigsby, and various editors. *The Cambridge History of American Theatre Vol. III*. New York: Cambridge University Press, 2000.

Windeler, Robert. *Julie Andrews: A Life on Stage and Screen*. Secaucus, New Jersey: Carol Publishing Group, 1997.

Woll, Allen. *Black Musical Theatre: From Coontown to Dream Girls*. New York: Da Capo Press, 1991.

Zadan, Craig. *Sondheim and Company, 2nd Edition*. New York: Da Capo Press, 1994.

Ziegfeld, Richard, Paulette and Patricia Ziegfeld Stephenson. *The Ziegfeld Touch: The Life and Times of Florenz Ziegfeld, Jr*. New York: Harry N. Abrams, 1993.

TELEVISION SHOWS

AMERICAN MASTERS
"Danny Kaye: A Legacy of Laughter" (1996)
"Gene Kelly: An American Life" (2002)
"George Gershwin Remembered" (1987)
"Leonard Bernstein: Reaching for the Note" (1998)
"Richard Rodgers: The Sweetest Sounds" (2001)
"You're the Top: The Cole Porter Story" (1990)

GREAT PERFORMANCES
"Bernstein Conducts *West Side Story*" (1985)
"Best of Broadway" (1985)
"*Black and Blue*" (1993)
"*Cats*" (1998)
"Dance in America: Agnes: The Indomitable De Mille" (1987)
"Dance in America: Bob Fosse: Steam Heat" (1990)
"*Follies* in Concert" (1986)
"From Broadway—*Fosse*" (2002)
"The Gershwins' *Crazy for You*" (1999)
"The Gershwins' *Porgy and Bess*" (1993)
"*Hey, Mr. Producer!* The Musical World of Cameron Mackintosh" (1998)
"Jammin': Jelly Roll Morton on Broadway" (1992)
"*Les Misérables* in Concert" (1996)
"The Music of Kander and Ebb: Razzle Dazzle" (1997)
"*Porgy and Bess*—An American Voice" (1998)
"Recording *The Producers*" (2001)
"Rodgers & Hammerstein's *Oklahoma!*" (2003)
"*Show Boat*" (1989)
"*Sweeney Todd*" (1985)
"Sylvia Fine Kaye's Musical Comedy Tonight III" (1985)
"*Candide* in Concert" (2004)
"*South Pacific* in Concert from Carnegie Hall" (2006)
"*Company*" (2008)
"*Chess* in Concert" (2009)
"*In the Heights:* Chasing Broadway Dreams" (2009)
"*Passing Strange*" (2010)

AMERICAN PLAYHOUSE
"*Into the Woods*" (1991)

LIVE FROM LINCOLN CENTER
"*A Little Night Music*" (1990)

PBS NATIONAL FUND-RAISING SPECIALS
"Irving Berlin's America" (1986)
"Lerner and Loewe: Broadway's Last Romantics" (1988)
"Rodgers and Hammerstein: The Sound of American Music" (1985)
"The Songs of Johnny Mercer" (1997)

AVAILABLE FOR VIEWING AT THE MUSEUM OF TELEVISION AND RADIO IN NEW YORK
Ain't Misbehavin', NBC, 6/21/82
Annie Get Your Gun, NBC, 11/27/57
Applause, CBS, 3/15/73
Babes in Toyland, NBC, 12/18/54
Bloomer Girl, NBC, 5/28/56
Brigadoon, ABC, 10/15/66
A Connecticut Yankee, NBC, 3/12/55
Dearest Enemy, NBC, 11/26/55
Desert Song, NBC, 5/7/55
Eubie!, Showtime, January 1981
High Button Shoes, NBC, 11/24/56
Kiss Me, Kate, NBC, 11/20/58
Lady in the Dark, NBC, 9/25/54
Of Thee I Sing, CBS, 10/24/72
Once Upon a Mattress, CBS, 6/3/64
One Touch of Venus, NBC, 8/27/55
Panama Hattie, CBS, 11/10/54
Purlie, Showtime, 10/12/81
Roberta, NBC, 9/19/58
Rodgers and Hammerstein General Foods Special, 3/28/54
Sophisticated Ladies, 11/5/82
Toast of the Town (*The Ed Sullivan Show*)
Wonderful Town, CBS, 11/30/58
You're a Good Man, Charlie Brown, CBS, 2/9/73

INTERVIEWS

The following people were interviewed for the documentary series *Broadway: The American Musical* between December 1996 and March 2004:

Richard Adler, Mary Ellin Barrett, Dwight Blocker Bowers, Mel Brooks, Carol Channing, Ted Chapin, Kristen Chenoweth, Jerome Chodorov, Wayne Cilento, Betty Comden, Nancy Coyne, Hume Cronyn, Graciela Daniele, André de Shields, Stanley Donen, Ann Douglas, Fred Ebb, Michael Eisner, Cy Feuer, Harvey Fierstein, Philip Furia, Brendan Gill, Frances Gershwin Godowsky, William Goldman, Adolph Green, Michael Greif, Joel Grey, Marvin Hamlisch, Andrew Hammerstein, Stephen Mo Hanan, Ernie Harburg, Sheldon Harnick, Kitty Carlisle Hart, June Havoc, Jerry Herman, Al Hirschfeld, Margo Jefferson, John Kander, Michael Kidd, Robert Kimball, Miles Krueger, John Lahr, Rocco Landesman, Nathan Lane, James Lapine, Arthur Laurents, Baayork Lee, Andrew Lloyd Webber, Jo Sullivan Loesser, Galt MacDermot, Donna McKechnie, Cameron Mackintosh, Joe Mantello, Walter Matthau, Idina Menzel, Jerry Mitchell, Patricia Morison, James Nederlander Sr., Steve Nelson, Jim Nicola, Trevor Nunn, Dana O'Connell, Jerry Orbach, Marc Platt, Harold Prince, John Raitt, Tim Rice, Frank Rich, Chita Rivera, Tim Robbins, Mary Rodgers, Vincent Sardi Jr., Gerald Schoenfeld, Jonathan Schwartz, Stephen Schwartz, Jonathan Sheffer, Rob Snyder, Stephen Sondheim, Patricia Ziegfeld Stephenson, David Stone, Peter Stone, Susan Stroman, Julie Taymor, Michael Tilson-Thomas, Doris Eaton Travis, Tommy Tune, Ben Vereen, Mel Watkins, Onna White, Max Wilk, Iva Withers, George Wolfe.

MAPS OF THE THEATER DISTRICT
1928 AND 2010

These two maps provide a contrasting history of the Broadway houses in the Theater District. The first, from 1928, shows the number of Broadway theaters at its height, after the building boom of the '20s and before the Depression, when economics forced many theaters owners (including the Shubert Brothers, who owned forty-three theaters in 1928) into bankruptcy. Even by 1928, however, a number of legitimate theaters were being turned into far more profitable movie theaters. The second map shows the district as of January 1, 2010. More than the names have changed, but the Shubert Organization is still the primary theater owner, followed by the Nederlander Organization and Jujamcyn Theatres.

Only a handful of the contemporary Broadway theaters are actually *on* Broadway. A "Broadway" theater is a contractual classification for a theater that can seat between 499 and 1,499 (or more), provide for a "first-class" production (which means it will employ the major theatrical unions), and reside within the west 40s and 50s (although the Vivian Beaumont at Lincoln Center on West 65th Street is also considered a Broadway theater and its productions are eligible for the Tony Awards—go figure).

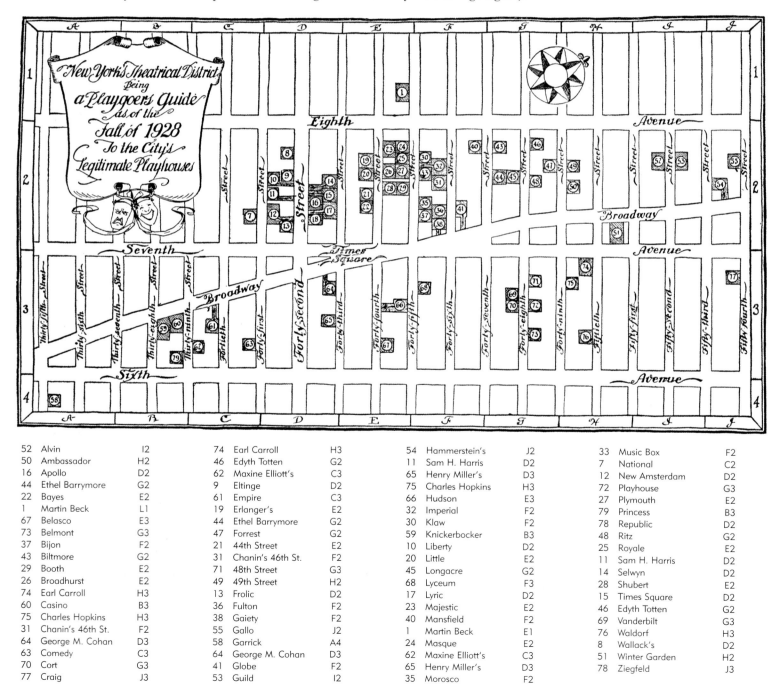

52	Alvin	I2	74	Earl Carroll	H3	54	Hammerstein's	J2	33	Music Box	F2
50	Ambassador	H2	46	Edyth Totten	G2	11	Sam H. Harris	D2	7	National	C2
16	Apollo	D2	62	Maxine Elliott's	C3	65	Henry Miller's	D3	12	New Amsterdam	D2
44	Ethel Barrymore	G2	9	Eltinge	D2	75	Charles Hopkins	H3	72	Playhouse	G3
22	Bayes	E2	61	Empire	C3	66	Hudson	E3	27	Plymouth	E2
1	Martin Beck	L1	19	Erlanger's	E2	32	Imperial	F2	79	Princess	B3
67	Belasco	E3	44	Ethel Barrymore	G2	30	Klaw	F2	78	Republic	D2
73	Belmont	G3	47	Forrest	G2	59	Knickerbocker	B3	48	Ritz	G2
37	Bijon	F2	21	44th Street	E2	10	Liberty	D2	25	Royale	E2
43	Biltmore	G2	31	Chanin's 46th St.	F2	20	Little	E2	11	Sam H. Harris	D2
29	Booth	E2	71	48th Street	G3	45	Longacre	G2	14	Selwyn	D2
26	Broadhurst	E2	49	49th Street	H2	68	Lyceum	F3	28	Shubert	E2
74	Earl Carroll	H3	13	Frolic	D2	17	Lyric	D2	15	Times Square	D2
60	Casino	B3	36	Fulton	F2	23	Majestic	E2	46	Edyth Totten	G2
75	Charles Hopkins	H3	38	Gaiety	F2	40	Mansfield	F2	69	Vanderbilt	G3
31	Chanin's 46th St.	F2	55	Gallo	J2	1	Martin Beck	E1	76	Waldorf	H3
64	George M. Cohan	D3	58	Garrick	A4	24	Masque	E2	8	Wallack's	D2
63	Comedy	C3	64	George M. Cohan	D3	62	Maxine Elliott's	C3	51	Winter Garden	H2
70	Cort	G3	41	Globe	F2	65	Henry Miller's	D3	78	Ziegfeld	J3
77	Craig	J3	53	Guild	I2	35	Morosco	F2			

Astute observers will notice that one theatrical landmark falls through the cracks between the two maps: the Mark Hellinger Theatre, which stood on the north side of 51st Street between Broadway and Eighth Avenue. Built in 1930 as a movie palace called the Hollywood Theatre, it began offering stage shows in the mid-thirties. It housed more than a decade of flops until 1948, when it was dubbed the Mark Hellinger after a Broadway raconteur, and limped along for another decade until a little trifle called *My Fair Lady* took up residence there for six years, beginning in 1956. (Another Alan Jay Lerner show, *Coco*, played there in 1969; its star, Katharine Hepburn, charmed construction workers across 51st Street into a six-minute work stoppage every Wednesday matinee day during her big number in Act Two.) In 1991, the Hellinger was sold and became the Times Square Church, which it remains as of 2010.

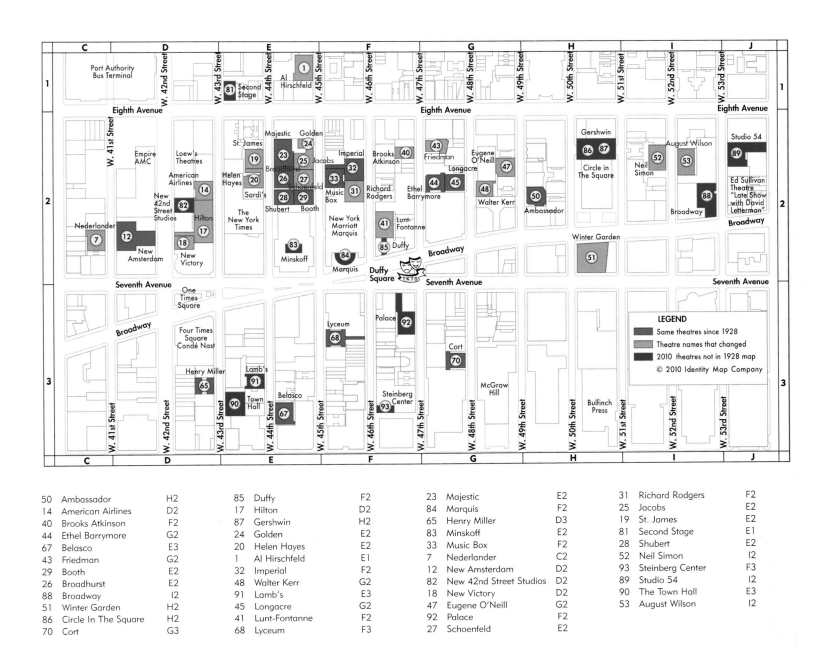

50	Ambassador	H2		85	Duffy	F2		23	Majestic	E2		31	Richard Rodgers	F2
14	American Airlines	D2		17	Hilton	D2		84	Marquis	F2		25	Jacobs	E2
40	Brooks Atkinson	F2		87	Gershwin	H2		65	Henry Miller	D3		19	St. James	E2
44	Ethel Barrymore	G2		24	Golden	E2		83	Minskoff	E2		81	Second Stage	E1
67	Belasco	E3		20	Helen Hayes	E2		33	Music Box	F2		28	Shubert	E2
43	Friedman	G2		1	Al Hirschfeld	E1		7	Nederlander	C2		52	Neil Simon	I2
29	Booth	E2		32	Imperial	F2		12	New Amsterdam	D2		93	Steinberg Center	F3
26	Broadhurst	E2		48	Walter Kerr	G2		82	New 42nd Street Studios	D2		89	Studio 54	I2
88	Broadway	I2		91	Lamb's	E3		18	New Victory	D2		90	The Town Hall	E3
51	Winter Garden	H2		45	Longacre	G2		47	Eugene O'Neill	G2		53	August Wilson	I2
86	Circle In The Square	H2		41	Lunt-Fontanne	F2		92	Palace	F2				
70	Cort	G3		68	Lyceum	F3		27	Schoenfeld	E2				

PHOTO, LYRIC, AND TEXT CREDITS

PHOTO CREDITS

AP/ Wide World: 131, 273, 405 top, 406, 433 bottom; **Lisa Aronson:** 294, 330; **Art Resource, National Portrait Gallery, Smithsonian:** 37; **Brown Brothers:** 188–89; **Corbis Images Inc.:** 7, 18, 26, 38, 40 left, 41 left, 44, 54, 56–57, 58, 60–61, 76 top, 100, 122–23, 128, 135, 175 top, 278, 307, 336, 345, 352, 361 top, 365, 420; **Culver Pictures Inc.:** i, vi, 2, 6 all, 8, 9 top, 15 all, 16 top, 17, 19 all, 20, 21 all, 22 all, 25, 27, 28, 34, 35, 36, 46, 48 bottom, 49 bottom, 55, 70, 71, 73, 81, 83 bottom right, 84, 85, 99, 115, 118, 124, 134, 137 top right, 140 top, 146–47, 149, 152 bottom, 153 top, 159 right, 183 bottom, 190, 203, 205 top, 210, 216, 217 top, 219, 220, 225, 243, 245, 255 top; **Disney:** 425 top (rendering by Julie Taymor), 427 top (photo by Tony Russell); **Frank Driggs:** 39, 40 right, 68; **Margo Feiden Gallery:** 265, 438 bottom, 439; **Jules Fisher, Estate of Jo Mielziner:** 241 bottom; **Ira & Leonore Gershwin Trusts:** 92, 150 top; **Philip Greenberg:** 423, 498; **Nils Hanson:** 53 all; **Yip Harburg Foundation:** 142, 143 bottom; **Lorenz Hart Jr.:** 165; **The John Hay Library, Brown University:** 67 inset; **Michael Holmes:** 361 bottom; **Hulton Archive/Getty Images:** 5, 12; **Michael Kantor:** 29 left, 47 bottom left, 48 top, 49 top, 69 center, 83 bottom left; **Kheel Center for Labor Management Documentation and Archives, Cornell University:** 169, 170; **Robert Kimball:** 86, 88; **Joe Kohen:** 372; **Paul Kolnik:** 429, 431, 432 all, 433 top, 462-63, 443; **Jonathan Larson Performing Arts Foundation:** 407 top (photo by Anthony Rapp), bottom; **Michael Lavine:** 77 all, 78 top, 105 top, 171 bottom, 196, 295, 388 top; **Library of Congress:** 66, 69 left, right, 172, 224 right; **The Maryland Historical Society, Baltimore, Maryland:** 87 top; **Norris McNamara:** 312; **Museum of the City of New York:** 9 bottom, 13, 14, 16 bottom, 33, 45, 47 top, bottom right, 76 bottom, 79 bottom, 83 top, 87 bottom, 97 all, 98 bottom, 113 top (photo by Arie deZanger), 120, 121, 148, 150 bottom, 152 top, 154 left, 162, 178–79, 204, 214–15, 226, 229, 274–75, 276–77, 284, 285 top, 291 (photo by Milton Greene), 292 top (gift of Harold Friedlander), 297 top, 297 bottom (drawing by Tom Crabtree), 298–99, 314 (The Mary Bryant Collection), 332 top, 333 top, 340–41, 355 all, 360 top (photo by Martha Swope), 363 (photo by Van Williams); **Joan Marcus:** iv-v, 399, 401, 402, 403, 406, 413, 418, 419, 425 bottom, 441, 445, 446, 448, 450, 451, 453, 454, 455; **Laurence Maslon:** 41, 43, 79 top, 164 top center, 246; **Laurence Maslon and Michael Kantor:** 426, 463 top; **National Archives:** 183 top; **New York Daily News:** 260; **New York Times:** 390 (photo by Michael Le Poer Trench); **Photofest:** xi, 29 right, 30, 31 all, 64, 75, 91, 95, 96, 98 bottom, 108 top left, 126–27, 130, 133, 137 bottom, 138, 139 all, 140 bottom, 144, 151, 153 bottom, 154–55, 158, 159 left, 160 all, 161, 167, 173 top, 174, 177, 193 right, 194–95, 198, 199, 202, 209, 217 bottom, 218, 222, 223, 224 left, 227, 228 all, 231, 232 left, 233, 234, 237, 238–39, 244, 249, 251, 252, 254, 261 right, 283, 286, 287 all, 288, 289, 292 bottom, 293, 296 all, 300, 301 top, 302–3, 304–5, 306–7, 308, 309, 310 all, 311 all, 313, 315 top, 319 bottom, 322–23, 326, 327, 328 left, 329, 334, 335 right, 337 all, 347, 353 top, 360 bottom, 370–71, 374, 375 top, 381, 382, 383

bottom, 391 bottom, 392 second from top, 393, 394–95, 401, 405, 408 bottom, 410, 411, 412, 414, 415, 416, 417, 421, 427 bottom, 428, 440, 444, 445, 459, 461, 465; **Cole Porter Music and Literary Trust:** 136, 137, 156 top; **The Harry Ransom Humanities Research Center, University of Texas at Austin:** 24 left, 197, 201, 235 top, 270, 271 all, 321; **Rodgers & Hammerstein Organization:** 10–11, 50 right, 51 (photo by Louis Harson), 62–63 (detail), 78 bottom, 106, 107 all, 108 top right and bottom, 111, 112, 114, 163 all, 164 top left and right, 180, 181 top, 185, 186–87, 192, 235 bottom, 272, 290, 301 bottom; **Billy Rose Theatre Collection, New York Public Library for the Performing Arts, Astor, Lenox and Tilden Foundations:** 23, 32, 42, 50 left, 52, 72, 80 all, 82, 89, 101, 102 all, 103, 104, 105 bottom, 109, 110, 113 bottom, 116–17, 141, 143 top, 145, 154–55, 156 bottom, 157, 166, 168, 171 top, 173 bottom, 180 bottom, 181, 182, 200, 205 bottom, 206, 208, 211, 212, 213 all, 230, 232 right, 242, 247, 248, 250, 253, 255 bottom, 256 all, 258, 259, 262, 266–67, 270 bottom, 281, 282, 285 bottom, 318 all, 322, 335 left, 352–53, 358, 380 all, 384 (photo by Martha Swope), 392 second from bottom and bottom; **Carol Rosegg:** 458; **Shubert Archive:** 67, 409; **Kenneth van Sickle:** 420, 422; **Marty Sohl:** x; **Martha Swope:** 263, 319 top, 331, 332 bottom, 333 bottom, 338, 339, 342, 343, 344, 348, 349, 350, 351 all, 354, 356, 357, 359, 362, 364, 366–67, 368–69, 376, 378–79, 385, 386, 387, 388 bottom, 389, 396, 397, 398, 416, 466–67; **Nigel Teare:** 383 top; **Theater Development Fund:** 431; **Time Life Pictures/Getty Images:** iv and 193 left (photos by Andreas Feininger), 236 (photo by W. Eugene Smith), 257 (photo by Leonard McCombe), 268–69 (photo by Hank Walker), 315 bottom and 316–17 (photos by Mark Kauffman), 320 (photo by John Dominis), 324 (photo by Ralph Morse), 325 (photo by Henry Grossman), 375 bottom (photo by Robin Platzer/Twin Images); **Michael Le Poer Trench:** 391 top; **Triton Gallery:** 328 right; **Joseph Urban Collection, Rare Book and Manuscript Library, Columbia University:** 24 right, 119; **Virginia Museum of Fine Arts, Richmond. The Council Graphics Art Fund (photo: Ron Jennings) / Estate of Joe Mielziner:** 241 top; **Kurt Weill Foundation for Music:** 175 bottom, 176; **Greg Weiner:** 436–37.

LYRIC CREDITS

"Adios Hermanos" by Paul Simon (BMI), coauthor of lyrics: Derek Walcott (BMI). Copyright © 1997 Paul Simon Music. All rights reserved. Used by permission.

"Another Hundred People" by Stephen Sondheim. © 1970 Range Road Music Inc., Jerry Leiber Music, Mike Stoller Music, and Rilting Music Inc. All rights administered by Herald Square Music Inc. Copyright renewed. Used by permission. All rights reserved.

"Any Old Place with You" by Richard Rodgers and Lorenz Hart. © 1919 (Renewed) by Warner Bros. Inc. Rights for Extended Renewal Term in U.S. controlled by The Estate of Lorenz Hart (administered by WB Music Corp.) and The Family Trust U/W Richard Rodgers and The Family Trust U/W Dorothy R. Rodgers (administered by Williamson Music). All rights reserved.

Used by permission. Warner Bros. Publications U.S. Inc., Miami, FL 33014.

"Bill" by Jerome Kern and Oscar Hammerstein II and Sir Wodehouse. © 1927 Universal-Polygram Internation Publishing Inc. All rights reserved. Used by permission.

"Broadway Baby" by Stephen Sondheim. © 1971 Range Road Music Inc., Jerry Leiber Music, Mike Stoller Music Inc. and Burthen Music Company Inc. All rights administered by Herald Square Music Inc. Copyright renewed. Used by permission. All rights reserved.

"Brother, Can You Spare a Dime?" by E.Y. "Yip" Harburg; music by Jay Gorney. Published by Glocca Morra Music (ASCAP) and Gorney Music (ASCAP). Administered by Next Decade Entertainment Inc. All rights reserved. Used by permission.

"Brush Up Your Shakespeare" by Cole Porter. © 1949 Cole Porter © Renewed, Assigned to John F. Wharton, Trustee of the Cole Porter Musical and Literary Property Trusts Publications and Allied Rights for the World assigned to Chappell & Co. All rights reserved. Used by permission. Warner Bros. Publications U.S. Inc., Miami, FL 33014.

"Come Rain or Come Shine" by Johnny Mercer and Harold Arlen. © 1946 (Renewed) The Johnny Mercer Foundation and S.A. Music Co. All Rights o/b/o The Johnny Foundation administered by WB Music Corp. All rights reserved. Used by permission. Warner Bros. Publications U.S. Inc., Miami, FL 33014.

"Den of Iniquity" by Lorenz Hart and Richard Rodgers. © 1941, 1950, 1962 (Copyrights Renewed) Chappell & Co. Rights for Extended Renewal Term in U.S. controlled by the Estate of Lorenz Hart (administered by WB Music Corp.) and The Family Trust U/W Richard Rodgers and The Family Trust U/W Dorothy F. Rodgers (administered by Williamson Music). All rights reserved. Used by permission. Warner Bros. Publications U.S. Inc., Miami, FL 33014.

"Don't Forget 127th Street" by Lee Adams; music by Charles Strouse. © 1964 (Renewed) Charles Strouse. Worldwide publishing by Charles Strouse Music, Helene Blue Musique Ltd. administrator, www.CharlesStrouse.com. All rights reserved. Used by permission.

"Dueling Pianos" (unpublished) Music and lyrics by Stephen Sondheim. All rights reserved. Used by permission of Stephen Sondheim.

"Fascinating Rhythm" by George Gershwin and Ira Gershwin. © 1924 (Renewed) WB Music Corp. All rights reserved. Used by permission. Warner Bros. Publications U.S. Inc., Miami, FL 33014.

"I Am What I Am" by Jerry Herman. © 1983 Jerry Herman. All Rights Controlled by Jerryco Music Co. Exclusive Agent: Edwin H. Morris & Company, A Division of MPL Music Publishing Inc. All rights reserved. Used by permission.

"I Wanna Be a Producer" by Mel Brooks. Copyright © 2000 Mel Brooks Music (BMI). All rights reserved. Used by permission.

TEXT CREDITS

FILM CREDITS

A FILM BY
Michael Kantor
DIRECTED AND PRODUCED BY
Michael Kantor
WRITTEN BY
Marc Fields
Michael Kantor
Laurence Maslon
JoAnn Young
COPRODUCERS
Jeff Dupre
Sally Rosenthal
EDITED BY
Kris Liem
Adam Zucker
Nancy Novack
HOSTED BY
Julie Andrews
CINEMATOGRAPHY
Buddy Squires
Mead Hunt
ASSOCIATE PRODUCERS
Lynn Badia
Lucia Touchstone-Haring
PRODUCTION COORDINATOR
Kristen Sullivan
PRODUCTION ASSOCIATE
Meredith McGuire
PRODUCTION ASSISTANTS
Katie Robbins, Georgina Javor
ASSISTANT EDITORS
Christy Denes, Syndi Pilar,
Jay Cornelius, Kate Schmitz,
Michael Weingrad
**MUSIC SUPERVISOR, ARRANGER,
AND PRODUCER**
Matthias Gohl
**INCIDENTAL MUSIC
PERFORMED BY**
The Eos Orchestra,
Jonathan Sheffer, Conductor
SOLO PIANO
David Loud, Isaac Ben Ayala
VOICES
Nancy Anderson, John Cullum,
Chris Ferry, Jonathan Freeman,
Leland Gantt, Joe Holt, Michael
C. Hall, John Herrera, Gene Jones,
Jane Krakowski, Audra
McDonald, John McMartin,
Jonathan Marc Sherman,
Stephen Spinella, Mary Testa,
Andrew Weems, Jeffrey Wright,
Chip Zien
ADDITIONAL CINEMATOGRAPHY
Ulli Bonnekamp, Jeff Dupre,
Tom Hurwitz, Steve Kazmierski,
Amy Rice

ASSISTANT CAMERA
Anthony Rossi, Kipjaz Savoie,
Anthony Savini, Jason Summers,
Craig Braden, Steve Nealey
SOUND RECORDING
Mark Roy, Mark Mandler,
Roger Phenix, John Zecca,
Joe Hettinger, Brenda Ray,
Bob Silverthorne, Jerry Stein
CONSULTING PRODUCERS
Allison Ross Hanna, Megan Donis
FREELANCE RESEARCH
Norman Cohen
SENIOR ADVISER
Laurence Maslon
BOARD OF ADVISERS
Dwight Blocker Bowers,
Ann Douglas, Michael Frisch,
Philip Furia, Amy Henderson,
Mary Henderson, Robert Kimball,
Jane Klain, David Leopold,
Steven Nelson, Jack Raymond,
Deane Root, Max Wilk, Allen Woll
INTERNS
Isaiah Camp, Kieran Cusack,
Ana Tinsly, Michael Weinstein,
Zeynep Zilelioglu, Sarah Zoogman
**REENACTMENTS
CINEMATOGRAPHY**
Mills Clark, Bernard McWilliams
GAFFER
Paul Daley
ASSISTANT CAMERA
Storn Peterson
GRIP
Gus Arvanitopoulos
CHOREOGRAPHER
Sergio Trujillo
LIGHTING CONSULTANT
Michael Lincoln
SET DESIGN
Charley Beal
PROPS
Erika Forster
COSTUME DESIGN
Wallace G. Lane III
HAIR AND WIG DESIGN
Bobby H. Grayson
WARDROBE SUPERVISOR
Diana Collins
MAKEUP
Toy Van Lierop, Gloria Grant
TECHNICAL DEPARTMENT
Rich DiMinno, Ed Puntin,
Jimmy Chen, Jen McMahon,
Paul Copeland, Peter Specce,
Jim Walen

REENACTMENT PERFORMERS
Timothy Breese, Richard Costas,
Paul Daley, Teri DiGianfelice,
Byron Easley, Chris Ferry,
Nina Goldman, Jack Haken,
Amy Hall, Michelle Kittrell,
Bernard McWilliams, Kenna Morris,
Michelle Pampena, Ipsita Paul,
Lacy Darryl Phillips, Stacie Precia,
Ed Puntin, Karina Ringeisen,
Kara Sandberg, Jennifer Savelli,
Kristen Sullivan, Michael Weinstein
REENACTMENT LOCATION
Tarrytown Music Hall
AFTER-EFFECTS DESIGN
Chris Kairalla, Lauren Wang
VOICEOVER RECORDING
A&J/Full House Recording,
Lou Verrico
SUPERVISING SOUND EDITOR
Deborah Wallach
DIALOGUE EDITOR
Branka Mrkic
MUSIC EDITORS
Dan Evans Farkas, Jamie Lowry
RERECORDING MIXER
Ed Campbell, Tonic
NEGATIVE MATCHING
Noelle Penraat
COLOR
DuArt Film Labs
**SPIRIT DATA CINE FILM
TRANSFER**
John J. Dowdell III
ARCHIVAL FILM TRANSFERS
DuArt
ONLINE EDITOR
David Noling
POST-PRODUCTION SUPERVISORS
Sean Riordan, Jeff Dockendorf
TITLE DESIGN
B.T. Whitehill
MUSIC SERVICES
John Adams
DIRECTOR, SPECIAL PROJECTS
Jan Gura
BUSINESS AFFAIRS
Arlen Appelbaum
PROJECT MANAGEMENT
Merle Kailas
PRODUCTION MANAGER
Jane Buckwalter
**DIRECTOR OF CULTURE & ARTS
DOCUMENTARIES**
Margaret Smilow
SUPERVISING PRODUCER
Bill O'Donnell

***BROADWAY: THE AMERICAN
MUSICAL* WAS CONCEIVED
BY AND DEVELOPED IN
ASSOCIATION WITH**
Martin Starger

EXECUTIVE PRODUCERS
David Horn
Jac Venza

**FOR GHOST LIGHT FILMS
LEGAL SERVICES**
Jim Kendrick; Brown, Raysman,
Millstein, Felder & Steiner
ACCOUNTING
Lawrence Brown
**BOOKKEEPING/COMPUTER
SERVICES**
Robert Spinner

A six-part series for public television, *Broadway: The American Musical* is a production of Ghost Light Films and Thirteen/WNET New York in association with Carlton International, NHK and BBC. For more information on the series, visit www.pbs.org or www.thirteen.org.

FUNDING FOR THE *BROADWAY: THE AMERICAN MUSICAL* SERIES WAS PROVIDED BY:

The Corporation for Public
Broadcasting (CPB)
The Public Broadcasting Service (PBS)
The National Endowment for the
Humanities
Dorothy and Lewis Cullman
The Shubert Organization
The LuEsther T. Mertz Charitable
Trust
The National Endowment for the Arts
Judith B. Resnick
Ira and Leonore Gershwin
Philanthropic Fund
The Cornelius V. Starr Fund for Arts
Programming
Vivian Milstein
Rosalind P. Walter
The Harold and Mimi Steinberg
Charitable Trust
The Max and Victoria Dreyfus
Foundation Inc.
Mary and Marvin Davidson
Allen & Company
The DuBose and Dorothy Heyward
Memorial Fund
Karen A. and Kevin W. Kennedy
Foundation
Mary Rodgers and Henry Guettel

For more information on *Broadway: The American Musical*, visit PBS online at pbs.org/broadway.

ACKNOWLEDGMENTS

The Series

If musical theater is the most collaborative art form of all, creating a historical documentary series for public television must rank a close second. In the thirteen years it has taken to see this project from conception to completion, a cast of thousands has contributed, but none more than my collaborator on this companion volume, Laurence Maslon. In his writing for both the book and the film series, Larry has been the "Oscar Hammerstein II" of our venture, always determined to find a simple, poetic, resonant way to tell this remarkable story.

Broadway: The American Musical, in both film and book form, owes an initial debt of gratitude to Stephen Ives, who coaxed me from the stage world of make-believe into the the equally fantastic arena of American history, and taught me most everything I know about documentary filmmaking. The project was first championed by Diane Von Furstenberg and Barry Diller, both of whom supported the work in a variety of important ways. In particular, Mr. Diller's seed money enabled me to start production in December of 1996 with an interview with Al Hirschfeld, and Barry's inspired suggestion that I work with Martin Starger also had a profound impact on the project's development. Marty Starger has had music theater in his bones since he first saw *Oklahoma!* from the balcony of the St. James Theatre, and *Broadway* benefited greatly from his input.

Without initial grants from both the Corporation for Public Broadcasting and the National Endowment for the Arts, the project would have remained a pipe dream. Thanks to their generous support, Lucia Touchstone Haring and I were able to shoot a variety of interviews, conduct research, and formulate development plans. (After two years of much-appreciated effort, Lucia wisely chose to graduate from Associate Producer to Re-Producer.) Cinematographers Buddy Squires and Mead Hunt worked at a cut rate to get the show off the ground, and writers Marc Fields and JoAnn Young laid a solid foundation for what was then an eight-part series.

When Karen Miles called with the great news that major funding from the National Endowment of the Humanities was secured, *Broadway* became a reality. The team at Thirteen/WNET, led by the passionate Vice-President for National Programming Tammy Robinson, voiced confidence in our work daily over the past three years. The sensitive input of Executive Producers Jac Venza and David Horn, the legal wisdom of Arlen Appelbaum, the musical know-how of John Adams, the omniscient problem solving of Bill O'Donnell, the grant-writing prowess of Jaime Greenberg, the cheerful efficiency of Brian Lonergan, and the prudent fiscal oversight of Jane Buckwalter and Merle Kailas is evidenced throughout the film series. Without Jan Gura, fund-raiser supreme, for whom this project was her "third child," there would be no series and no companion book.

The *Broadway* series was blessed with a devoted team of collegial consultants, including Max Wilk, Dwight Blocker Bowers, Mary Henderson, Philip Furia, Richard Barrios, Amy Henderson, Michael Frisch, Allen Woll, Steve Nelson, David Leopold, Ann Douglas, Jack Raymond, and Deane Root. Never too busy to meet a deadline and offer cogent suggestions, these teachers and writers improved our work immeasurably with every script meeting.

The "troupers" who created the film series will no doubt continue to distinguish themselves in all their future endeavors. Supervising Editor Kris Liem brought grace, beauty, and wit to everything she touched; Adam Zucker brought his invaluable experience as a writer/producer/director to bear on each moment of his episodes; and Nancy Novack edited with both balletic fluidity and tap-dancing panache. Christy Denes artfully shaped the film after hours, and Syndi Pilar made sure that we didn't lose the series in the bottom of the ninth inning.

There is no way to properly thank coproducers Jeff Dupre and Sally Rosenthal for their weekends of work spent on West 33rd Street instead of on Fire Island or Truro—their ribald wisecracks enlivened many a day amidst the overstuffed cubicles. Lynn Badia, Kristen Sullivan, Meredith McGuire, Allison Hanna, Georgina Javor, and many more poured their hearts into this project, all for little more than a song, and music director Teese Gohl called in many a marker to bring top-notch orchestrations to our recording sessions with Jonathan Sheffer's magnificent Eos Orchestra.

The business of this particular kind of show business was never a challenge for accountant Larry "Leo Bloom" Brown, and Jim Kendrick's sage counsel made the impossible possible. Special thanks must be accorded to Ted Chapin of the Rodgers and Hammerstein Organization, Mike Strunsky of the Ira and Leonore Gershwin Philanthropic Fund, Gerald Schoenfeld of the Shubert Organization, and our resident "angel" Judy Resnick, all of whom were instrumental in the realization of our project.

Finally, every frame of the Broadway film series and every word in this companion book owe their existence to one person above all, Kathy Landau. A Broadway baby who day and night has scrambled for a living, brother, has she spared a dime to keep my love alive for this project. "Something's coming, something good, if I can wait" was her motto, and after a decade, now *Broadway: The American Musical* can sing her praises.

—MICHAEL KANTOR

The Book

2004 EDITION

I want to first of all thank the staff of the Broadway Film Project for their patience and assistance during the process of writing this book. In addition to preparing and disseminating more than sixty original interviews, the staff has always been supportive and helpful to me, even when the book's needs kept them from finishing important work on the series.

As far as the staff for the book itself is concerned, Norman Cohen leapt into the breach at a moment's notice for a crash course on musicals and was invaluable in finding (and coordinating) the treasure trove of photographs and illustrations contained herein. Diana Bertolini was a relentless researcher and an eager and courteous assistant in the project's early days; I hope one day, in the words of her idol, she'll try to teach the things I taught her.

Various friends and colleagues have lent perceptive and much-needed critiques and comments on the manuscript: Amy Asch, Steven Blier, Fritz Brun, Theodore S. Chapin of the Rodgers and Hammerstein Organization, George Furth, Mark Eden Horowitz of the Library of Congress, Jane Klain of the Museum of Television and Radio, Thomas Lindblade, Bill O'Donnell of Thirteen, Anne Kaufman Schneider, and Don B. Wilmeth. Herb Scher from the Lincoln Center Library of the Performing Arts was very helpful in providing information about the library's 2003 exhibit on original cast recordings, as were the librarians of the Billy Rose Theatre Collection, especially Jeremy Megraw, photograph librarian. Likewise, Marguerite Lavin of the Museum of the City of New York was particularly attentive to our many needs. The staff at Culver Pictures was of great assistance, and two major photographers of the Broadway stage, Martha Swope and Joan Marcus, were helpful above and beyond the call of duty (and their work is so terrific). Michael Lavine kindly opened up his extensive sheet music collection for our use. Robert Kimball, the dean of us all and a mentor's mentor, gave me supportive and inspiring advice—and sublime it was, too. And, especially, for his ongoing geniality and generosity, gentlemen of the Congress, I say "yea" Bert Fink, also of R&H.

My colleagues at the Tisch School of the Arts at New York University were particularly generous in allowing me the time and indulgence I needed to write the manuscript: Associate Dean Randy Martin, Victor Pappas, Sarah Schlesinger, Kevin Kuhlke, and Zelda Fichandler, who I hope likes this book as much as the one she and I did together.

The grand folks at the Andrew Wylie Agency deserve our thanks, especially Andrew Wylie for his wise counsel in steering us into the arms of the dynamic Jill Cohen and her team at Bulfinch Press and Lisa Halliday for her elegant diplomacy and refined taste; she's Pepsodent.

Designer Beth Tondreau and Studio Manager Suzanne Dell'Orto of BTD handled our repeated demands and vacillations with considerable grace, artistry, and humor. At Bulfinch Press, production manager Denise LaCongo supervised the million and one details that make up this handsome book. And our editor, Karyn Gerhard, approached this project with such energy and enthusiasm that she can only be thanked in musical comedy terms: she combined the loyalty of Julie Jordan, the ebullience of Harold Hill, the patience of King Arthur, the tenacity of Dolly Levi, the faith of Maria Von Trapp, the acuity of Henry Higgins, the optimism of Annie Warbucks, and the laugh of Nellie Lovett.

Genevieve Elam, who is so nice to come home to, gave me every reason in the world to find the best in my work and in myself.

Finally, Michael Kantor not only proved to be a masterful filmmaker and writer, but, as befits a project about musicals, a superb collaborator. His devotion to this project, his kindness toward his colleagues, and his faith in me were exemplary. For me, our work together was the perfect blendship; I have no doubt that our friendship will still be "jake."

2010 EDITION

Our appreciation and gratitude to John Cerullo at Applause Books for taking the "impossible dream" project of bringing *Broadway: The American Musical* to a new and larger audience in paperback form and doing so with grace and care. Marybeth Keating and her production staff—especially designer Damien Castaneda and indexer Michael Pastore—were equally professional in assembling the thousands of details, large and small, of the new version, and a tip of the hat to Karyn Gerhard, the book's original editor, for her advice and support. Jeff Posternak at the Wylie Agency worked his wizardry to put everything together, for which we are grateful.

Joan Marcus was extremely helpful and generous with supplying the striking new images captured by her peripatetic lens over the last half-decade; Ron and Howard Mandelbaum at Photofest were, once again, great friends and supporters on this project.

Tom D'Ambrosio and David Stone shared some important clarifications on *Wicked* for this edition, as did Jeffrey Seller on our section on Jonathan Larson. Many thanks also to Heath Schwartz of Boneau/Bryan-Brown, Tia James, Rob Shapiro, and that Broadway babe, Jennifer Ashley Tepper. Stephen Sondheim graciously sent us a letter a week after the original publication, suggesting further clarifications and emendations; we're thrilled to be able to incorporate his notes in this edition.

Continued thanks are also owed to the *Great Performances* team at WNET.org, most notably Executive Producer David Horn and Series Producer Bill O'Donnell.

And much gratitude, finally, to the incomparable Julie Andrews for her touching and incisive foreword (and to Steve Sauer, for his help in coordinating our efforts). We're not certain that Julie had even signed up to host and narrate the 2004 PBS series when the original edition went to press, so it's a privilege to be able to thank her for her invaluable contributions to and support of *Broadway: The American Musical* in all its iterations. It was particularly nice to have her back with us on the paperback version—with apologies to Mssrs. Lerner and Loewe, we've grown accustomed to her face.

—LAURENCE MASLON

INDEX

Page numbers in *italics* refer to illustrations.

REMEMBER YOUR
FIRST TIME...
Why haven't I ever seen a baby pigeon?
THINKING SPECTACULAR?
mattress
1-800-Mattress
WEB WALL
SPECTACOLOR
THE BIGGEST SHOW ON BROADWAY!
THE
LION
COX
CHRISTY
CARLSON
ROMANO
TIMES
SQUARE
ALLIANCE
TIMES SQUARE
INFORMATION CENTER
GEORGE
M
COHAN
1878-1942
Give my Regards to Broadway